T0211498

Lecture Notes in Computer Science 10273

Commenced Publication in 1973
Founding and Former Series Editors:
Gerhard Goos, Juris Hartmanis, and Jan van Leeuwen

More information about this series at http://www.springer.com/series/7409

Sakae Yamamoto (Ed.)

Human Interface and the Management of Information

Information, Knowledge and Interaction Design

19th International Conference, HCI International 2017
Vancouver, BC, Canada, July 9–14, 2017
Proceedings, Part I

Springer

Editor
Sakae Yamamoto
Tokyo University of Science
Tokyo
Japan

ISSN 0302-9743   ISSN 1611-3349 (electronic)
Lecture Notes in Computer Science
ISBN 978-3-319-58520-8   ISBN 978-3-319-58521-5 (eBook)
DOI 10.1007/978-3-319-58521-5

Library of Congress Control Number: 2017939720

LNCS Sublibrary: SL3 – Information Systems and Applications, incl. Internet/Web, and HCI

Printed on acid-free paper

This Springer imprint is published by Springer Nature
The registered company is Springer International Publishing AG
The registered company address is: Gewerbestrasse 11, 6330 Cham, Switzerland

Foreword

The 19th International Conference on Human–Computer Interaction, HCI International 2017, was held in Vancouver, Canada, during July 9–14, 2017. The event incorporated the 15 conferences/thematic areas listed on the following page.

A total of 4,340 individuals from academia, research institutes, industry, and governmental agencies from 70 countries submitted contributions, and 1,228 papers have been included in the proceedings. These papers address the latest research and development efforts and highlight the human aspects of design and use of computing systems. The papers thoroughly cover the entire field of human–computer interaction, addressing major advances in knowledge and effective use of computers in a variety of application areas. The volumes constituting the full set of the conference proceedings are listed on the following pages.

I would like to thank the program board chairs and the members of the program boards of all thematic areas and affiliated conferences for their contribution to the highest scientific quality and the overall success of the HCI International 2017 conference.

This conference would not have been possible without the continuous and unwavering support and advice of the founder, Conference General Chair Emeritus and Conference Scientific Advisor Prof. Gavriel Salvendy. For his outstanding efforts, I would like to express my appreciation to the communications chair and editor of *HCI International News*, Dr. Abbas Moallem.

April 2017   Constantine Stephanidis

HCI International 2017 Thematic Areas and Affiliated Conferences

Thematic areas:

- Human–Computer Interaction (HCI 2017)
- Human Interface and the Management of Information (HIMI 2017)

Affiliated conferences:

- 17th International Conference on Engineering Psychology and Cognitive Ergonomics (EPCE 2017)
- 11th International Conference on Universal Access in Human–Computer Interaction (UAHCI 2017)
- 9th International Conference on Virtual, Augmented and Mixed Reality (VAMR 2017)
- 9th International Conference on Cross-Cultural Design (CCD 2017)
- 9th International Conference on Social Computing and Social Media (SCSM 2017)
- 11th International Conference on Augmented Cognition (AC 2017)
- 8th International Conference on Digital Human Modeling and Applications in Health, Safety, Ergonomics and Risk Management (DHM 2017)
- 6th International Conference on Design, User Experience and Usability (DUXU 2017)
- 5th International Conference on Distributed, Ambient and Pervasive Interactions (DAPI 2017)
- 5th International Conference on Human Aspects of Information Security, Privacy and Trust (HAS 2017)
- 4th International Conference on HCI in Business, Government and Organizations (HCIBGO 2017)
- 4th International Conference on Learning and Collaboration Technologies (LCT 2017)
- Third International Conference on Human Aspects of IT for the Aged Population (ITAP 2017)

Conference Proceedings Volumes Full List

1. LNCS 10271, Human–Computer Interaction: User Interface Design, Development and Multimodality (Part I), edited by Masaaki Kurosu
2. LNCS 10272 Human–Computer Interaction: Interaction Contexts (Part II), edited by Masaaki Kurosu
3. LNCS 10273, Human Interface and the Management of Information: Information, Knowledge and Interaction Design (Part I), edited by Sakae Yamamoto
4. LNCS 10274, Human Interface and the Management of Information: Supporting Learning, Decision-Making and Collaboration (Part II), edited by Sakae Yamamoto
5. LNAI 10275, Engineering Psychology and Cognitive Ergonomics: Performance, Emotion and Situation Awareness (Part I), edited by Don Harris
6. LNAI 10276, Engineering Psychology and Cognitive Ergonomics: Cognition and Design (Part II), edited by Don Harris
7. LNCS 10277, Universal Access in Human–Computer Interaction: Design and Development Approaches and Methods (Part I), edited by Margherita Antona and Constantine Stephanidis
8. LNCS 10278, Universal Access in Human–Computer Interaction: Designing Novel Interactions (Part II), edited by Margherita Antona and Constantine Stephanidis
9. LNCS 10279, Universal Access in Human–Computer Interaction: Human and Technological Environments (Part III), edited by Margherita Antona and Constantine Stephanidis
10. LNCS 10280, Virtual, Augmented and Mixed Reality, edited by Stephanie Lackey and Jessie Y.C. Chen
11. LNCS 10281, Cross-Cultural Design, edited by Pei-Luen Patrick Rau
12. LNCS 10282, Social Computing and Social Media: Human Behavior (Part I), edited by Gabriele Meiselwitz
13. LNCS 10283, Social Computing and Social Media: Applications and Analytics (Part II), edited by Gabriele Meiselwitz
14. LNAI 10284, Augmented Cognition: Neurocognition and Machine Learning (Part I), edited by Dylan D. Schmorrow and Cali M. Fidopiastis
15. LNAI 10285, Augmented Cognition: Enhancing Cognition and Behavior in Complex Human Environments (Part II), edited by Dylan D. Schmorrow and Cali M. Fidopiastis
16. LNCS 10286, Digital Human Modeling and Applications in Health, Safety, Ergonomics and Risk Management: Ergonomics and Design (Part I), edited by Vincent G. Duffy
17. LNCS 10287, Digital Human Modeling and Applications in Health, Safety, Ergonomics and Risk Management: Health and Safety (Part II), edited by Vincent G. Duffy
18. LNCS 10288, Design, User Experience, and Usability: Theory, Methodology and Management (Part I), edited by Aaron Marcus and Wentao Wang

Human Interface and the Management of Information

Program Board Chair(s): **Sakae Yamamoto, Japan**

- Takako Akakura, Japan
- Yumi Asahi, Japan
- Linda R. Elliott, USA
- Shin'ichi Fukuzumi, Japan
- Michitaka Hirose, Japan
- Yasushi Ikei, Japan
- Yen-Yu Kang, Taiwan
- Keiko Kasamatsu, Japan
- Daiji Kobayashi, Japan
- Kentaro Kotani, Japan
- Hiroyuki Miki, Japan
- Hirohiko Mori, Japan
- Shogo Nishida, Japan
- Robert Proctor, USA
- Ryosuke Saga, Japan
- Katsunori Shimohara, Japan
- Jiro Tanaka, Japan
- Takahito Tomoto, Japan
- Kim-Phuong Vu, USA
- Tomio Watanabe, Japan

The full list with the Program Board Chairs and the members of the Program Boards of all thematic areas and affiliated conferences is available online at:

http://www.hci.international/board-members-2017.php

HCI International 2018

The 20th International Conference on Human–Computer Interaction, HCI International 2018, will be held jointly with the affiliated conferences in Las Vegas, NV, USA, at Caesars Palace, July 15–20, 2018. It will cover a broad spectrum of themes related to human–computer interaction, including theoretical issues, methods, tools, processes, and case studies in HCI design, as well as novel interaction techniques, interfaces, and applications. The proceedings will be published by Springer. More information is available on the conference website: http://2018.hci.international/.

General Chair
Prof. Constantine Stephanidis
University of Crete and ICS-FORTH
Heraklion, Crete, Greece
E-mail: general_chair@hcii2018.org

http://2018.hci.international/

Contents – Part I

Information and Interaction Design

Knowledge and Service Management

Multimodal and Embodied Interaction

Contents – Part II

Recommender and Decision Support Systems

Intelligent Systems

Supporting Collaboration and User Communities

Case Studies

Visualization Methods and Tools

Extending an Association Map to Handle Large Data Sets

Tamara Babaian[✉], Wendy Lucas, Alina Chircu, and Noreen Power

Bentley University, Waltham, MA 02452, USA
{tbabaian,wlucas,achircu,npower}@bentley.edu

Abstract. This paper presents the Association Map-Large (AM-L), an interactive visualization of entity associations. AM-L is an extension of a previously reported AM interface that has been enhanced with search and interaction features for supporting larger data sets. We report on a user study with thirty two participants, which assesses user performance and experience with AM-L versus a tabular representation of the same data in the context of an enterprise system. Participants with varying levels of experience were given both simple and complicated tasks to complete with each system. Results indicate greater enjoyment and lower levels of mental effort when using AM-L, as well as less time spent on average when performing tasks. Accuracy results in terms of correctness indicate a learning curve, with overall performance worse with AM-L on the first two simple questions and first complex question, but then as well or better on subsequent questions. Given that the AM-L interface is unlike any with which the users had prior experience, it is not surprising that some exposure to the interface, such as training, would be helpful prior to use. Suggestions from the participants will inform future enhancements to the interface, which will be validated with further studies.

Keywords: Interactive visualization · ERP · Usability · User experience

1   Introduction

Interactive data visualizations are becoming more and more common in the news media but have not yet entered the mainstream of decision support systems in the workplace. In the context of enterprise information systems, tables remain the prevalent format for reporting and aiding in decision making processes. Studies show that users perceive visualizations as useful ways to reduce the complexities associated with enterprise information systems [1], yet investigating what kinds of visualizations would work well in practice is an open research area.

In our previous work, we presented an interactive visualization called the Association Map (AM) [2], which was designed to assist enterprise system users in exploring associative relationships between two or three entities. Such exploration occurs in a wide variety of contexts, such as when looking for doctors who treated a patient for a particular problem, or picking an alternative vendor for a material that is used in one or more plants. The AM visualization enables users to easily find connections from a single entity (e.g., view all doctors seen by a specific patient and all health issues for that patient). It also supports searching for connections between two or three specified entities and then

© Springer International Publishing AG 2017
S. Yamamoto (Ed.): HIMI 2017, Part I, LNCS 10273, pp. 3–21, 2017.
DOI: 10.1007/978-3-319-58521-5_1

highlighting all connections that are found. The results of a side-by-side evaluation of the AM interface with two table-based interfaces presenting similar association data are reported in [3]. In terms of task completion time and accuracy, user performance with the AM interface was superior to that achieved by the same users utilizing a standard SAP report. In another comparison, in which a customized version of an SAP report was used that showed the data in a simplified, three-column format, the results did not show any significant difference in user performance. Both of these comparisons, however, revealed the users' overwhelming preference for the AM.

The version of the AM used in the studies described above was designed for small data sets, limiting its use in practice. Given the users' performance and enthusiastic responses regarding their experience with the AM visualization [3] and the acknowledged difficulties in working with enterprise systems (see [4, 5] for example), it is valuable to further develop, fine tune and evaluate visual interactive interfaces for performing enterprise system tasks.

In this paper, we will present a new version of the AM designed to enable exploration of large data sets. The original AM interface required that all data items be displayed in sufficiently large font for the user to see while fitting on a single screen. The new version provides a way to work with large data sets by employing zooming to highlight selected items, while still keeping the visualization to one screen. To facilitate easy observation of the selected items, the selected items from the middle column are also moved to the center of that column (as shown in Fig. 5). Finally, a partial match search feature was added to facilitate searching. Displaying the same set of data in a tabular format would require multiple pages and the use of a scrolling mechanism in order to locate the needed records.

We have conducted a pilot evaluation involving 32 subjects performing tasks with varying levels of complexity using the new version of the AM, called the Association Map-Large (AM-L), versus a simplified, three-column table from SAP. The pilot revealed that, while the users were much more satisfied with AM-L compared to the table format, there was a learning curve associated with this unfamiliar interface. Initially, performance in terms of the correctness of responses with AM-L lagged behind the correctness of responses with the table when performing the first two simple tasks and the first complex task. After completing those initial tasks, however, user performance with AM-L matched or exceeded performance with the SAP table on both simple and complex tasks.

The rest of this paper is organized as follows: after presenting related work and the previous version of AM in Sect. 2, we describe the functionality of AM-L in Sect. 3. Section 4 outlines the user study setup for evaluating AM-L and comparing it to a tabular SAP interface. This is followed by a presentation of the findings from the study in Sect. 5. We then discuss lessons learned and directions for further fine-tuning of the interface in Sect. 6, followed by our conclusions in Sect. 7.

2 Related Work

In the introduction, we have already commented on the studies in enterprise system usability that provided the impetus to our work in developing novel interactive visualizations for common workplace tasks. While interactive visualizations have recently made their way into many online media outlets, there are only a few examples of developed systems employing such visual interfaces (e.g. [6–8]). Research on the efficacy of visual representations and techniques in the context of specific applications is scarce. Dilla and Raschke [9] present a review of existing data visualization applications for financial fraud investigation and detection and outline a research agenda for investigating the key factors in the effectiveness of such visualizations. Our work presented here is, generally-speaking, a step in that direction: although we do not situate the visualization in the context of any particular application, we aim to understand what representations and features contribute to effective use of a visualization for problem solving that is traditionally supported by a variety of tabular representations.

Visualization evaluation is different from HCI usability evaluation, because visualizations are often credited for enabling discoveries and insights into data - notions that are not captured by usability. The issue is further complicated given that these benefits are often achieved after long-term use and exploration and thus are difficult to establish via a simple user study or even an expert evalutaion. The challenges in evaluating visualizations gave rise to a special workshop (BELIV) dedicated to this topic. Saket, Endert, and Stasko [10] present a review of a number of recently introduced visualization evaluations that focus on memorability, engagement, enjoyment and fun. In the work we present here, in which we seek to create visualizations in service of specific user tasks, we combine the traditional metrics of effectiveness with an evaluation of enjoyment [11].

2.1 Background

The previous version of the AM interface, called AM-N, consists of a circular display in which three types of entities are arranged in sorted order as labeled circles on the left and right sides of the diagram and as rectangles along the vertical center (see Figs. 1, 2 and 3). The items of each entity type are shown in different colors. Connections between the items indicate the presence of a relationship. Interactive features of the diagram include:

- A search interface, consisting of three fields for searching on the left, the right, or the center entity item, respectively.
- A point-and-click interface for each item. Clicking on a circle reveals connections between that item and the two other entities in a ternary relationship. Clicking on a rectangle reveals binary relationships between the item in the center and items on the left and on the right.

Thus, the AM interface can be used to explore relationships between items.

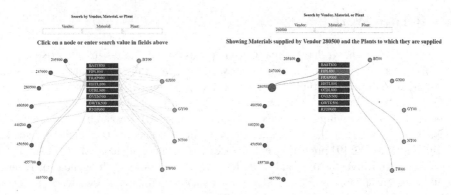

Fig. 1. AM-N interface showing all associations (from [3])

Fig. 2. AM-N interface showing associations for the selected Vendor on the left (from [3]).

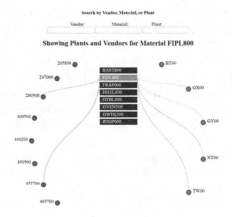

Fig. 3. AM-N interface showing associations for the selected Material in the middle (from [3]).

For example, consider an AM depicting associations between Vendors, Materials and Plants, as shown in Figs. 1, 2 and 3. The various states shown in these figures present the following information:

1. When no item is selected, all connections between items are shown in grey (Fig. 1).
2. Selecting a specific Vendor reveals the connections between that Vendor, the Materials it supplies, and the Plants that are being supplied with those Materials by that Vendor. All items and connections are displayed in the same color to indicate this ternary relationship (Fig. 2).
3. Selecting a specific Plant is similar to selecting a Vendor, though a different color is used.
4. Selecting a specific Material reveals connections between that Material, the Vendors that supply it, and the Plants that use it (Fig. 3).
5. Specifying two of three entity keywords in the search interface will result in highlighting the items and connections in the ternary relationship matching the search terms. For instance, a search for Vendor A and Material B will highlight connections

between Vendor A, Material B (if, indeed, A supplies B), and those Plants that receive B from A. Other Materials supplied by A and other Vendors supplying B will not be highlighted by this search.

6. Similarly, a search specifying all three entity keywords results in the highlighting of the connection between the matching entities of three different types, if that connection exists in the data.

3 AM-L

Following the encouraging results of our initial exploratory user study of the AM [3], we have developed a new version of the interface, AM-L, to improve the search capabilities and accommodate the need for working with a larger set of entity instances. Compared to the version of the AM interface outlined in Sect. 2.1, AM-L introduces several features motivated by the need to extend AM's applicability to handling larger data sets. In this version, we have modified the presentation and interaction features for the entity displayed in the center (corresponding to Materials in the instance of the AM-L presented here). To handle the situation where the set of materials is so large that the items cannot be represented using a font of a readable size, we added the following three features:

- When a mouse points to the material, the rectangle representing the material is highlighted in a different color and enlarged; furthermore, the highlighted material's label is shown in large font, to the left of the material box (Fig. 4).
- A partial search feature has been added to aid locating an item in a large set. When a user enters a search keyword in any of the search boxes on top of the page, all items of the specified type are highlighted in yellow. A partial search on the center column (Material) highlights the matching items in yellow and also enlarges and moves those items into the center of the diagram (Fig. 5).
- Any time the items in the central column are involved in a selection result, they are enlarged and moved to the center, as shown in Figs. 5 and 6.

To improve the readability of the diagram and better reflect the semantics of the data in the visual features, we made the following changes to the way the diagram reacts to selection:

- For the items displayed as circles, the selected circle is enlarged and the item label is highlighted in boldface font. Figure 7 demonstrates the selection of a Vendor.
- When an item is selected from the central column (Material), we use different colors for the connections between the selected Material and Plants versus the connections from the Material to the Vendors to emphasize that the connection lines visualize two different binary relationships in which the selected Material is involved, and not a ternary relationship (Fig. 6).

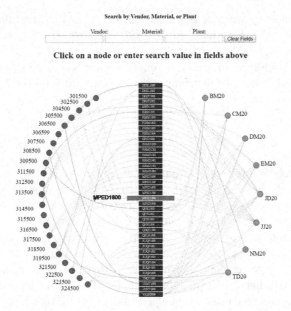

Fig. 4. AM-L interface with user pointing at an item in the central column highlights the item and shows an enlarged label on the left

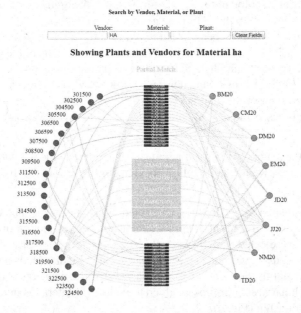

Fig. 5. AM-L interface showing results of a partial search for the central column. Materials matching the specified keyword 'HA' are highlighted, and shown in large in the center (Color figure online)

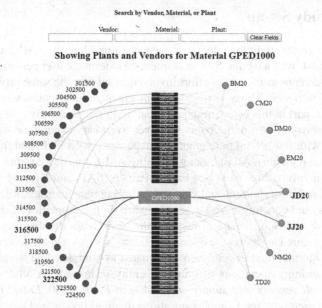

Fig. 6. AM-L interface showing results of selection of the central item (Material). The connections to items on left and on right sides are displayed in different colors.

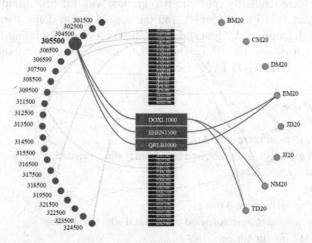

Fig. 7. AM-L interface showing results of selection of a left-side item

4   User Study Set-up

We conducted a user study to collect user feedback regarding the AM-L interface and to compare AM-L with a tabular SAP user interface in terms of user performance, satisfaction, and perceptions of mental effort involved in solving the same problems using the different interfaces. Thirty two students in graduate-level courses in a business university took part in this evaluation; participating in the user study was part of their required coursework. Two participants had over five years experience with SAP, 26 were novices with fewer than two months of experience with SAP, and the other four used it less than 6 months. All of them were using AM-L for the first time.

The study involved three parts (see Fig. 8). Parts A (SAP) and B (using AM-L) each consisted of watching a short tutorial video of the appropriate interface, followed by ten task questions, and concluded with a questionnaire on the properties of the interface. After each task question, we asked respondents to evaluate the degree of perceived mental effort required to answer the question. The first six task questions were internally designated as simple; the last four were designated as complex The simple questions required examining associations of only one entity instance with other entities, for example: *List all vendors that supply material(s) to Plant SD00. Enter 'none' if you don't find any such vendors.* Complex questions required review and analysis of associations of two or more entity instances to come up with the answer, for example, *Plants AL00 and SD00 order the same materials. List all vendors that supply a material to one of these two plants, but not to the other. Enter 'none' if you don't find such vendors.* We recorded the participants' answers and the time it took to answer each question. Questions in Parts A and B were identical in terms of structure but had data with different labels.

Participants were randomly split into two groups, with the first group performing Part A before Part B (15 participants), and the second group doing Part B first (17 participants). Both groups (SAP-first and AM-L-first) concluded by filling-out the Post-completion Questionnaire (Part C), which asked users about their experience and perceptions with SAP and AM-L interfaces.

AM-L vs SAP User Study
Part A - SAP

- SAP ME1P tutorial (approx. 3 min.)
- 10 task questions, each followed by a mental effort evaluation
- Post-SAP questionnaire

Part B - AM-L

- AM-L tutorial (approx. 3 min.)
- 10 task questions, each followed by a mental effort evaluation
- Post-AM-L questionnaire

Part C - Post-completion Questionnaire

Fig. 8. Components of the user study

5 Analysis of the Results

In this section we present our analysis of user performance, self-reported mental effort, perceived interface complexity, as well as satisfaction and enjoyment from using the interface (Sect. 5.1). The Post-completion Questionnaire included open-response answers regarding user preferences and improvement suggestions for AM-L, summarized in Sect. 5.2.

5.1 Quantitative Findings

We analyzed user performance using the common metrics of accuracy and time on task. The users answered six simple questions, referred to as s1 through s6, and four complex questions, labeled c1 through c4. We describe the accuracy of their answers first.

Accuracy. Figures 9, 10 and 11 depict the average percentage of correct answers per each question in the SAP-first group, AM-L-first group and overall. Table 1 presents the ranges of accuracy values for each question within each group and for each interface. The accuracy results depicted in Figs. 9, 10 and 11 suggest there might be a learning curve associated with using the AM-L visualization: notice that in both groups, the percentage of people that produced correct answers with AM-L rapidly increases from the first simple question (s1) to the third simple question (s3), thereby surpassing the accuracy with the SAP interface. The accuracy drops however at the first complex question (c1), and then picks up again and is slightly above the corresponding SAP numbers overall, with the exceptions of s1, s2, and c1 (Fig. 11).

The average percentage of correctly answered questions overall was 78% for SAP versus 76% for AM-L. If we consider per-question accuracy (see Fig. 11) and conjecture that the low accuracy results on questions s1, s2 and c1 are due to a learning curve associated with the use of a completely new interface, then the higher-or-comparable average accuracy with AM-L over SAP on all other questions is encouraging, as low initial accuracy may be overcome with training.

Table 1. Ranges of accuracy of responses per question in each group for each interface

Accuracy (% correct answers per question) ranges		
	SAP	AM-L
SAP-first	30%–100% (Avg 79%)	10%–100% (Avg 75%)
AM-L-first	40%–90% (Avg 76%)	50%–100% (Avg 77%)

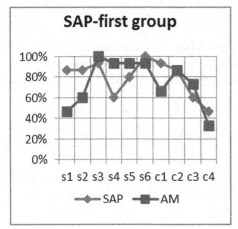

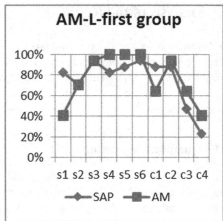

Fig. 9. Percentage correct answers in the SAP-first group

Fig. 10. Percentage of correct answers in the AM-L-first group

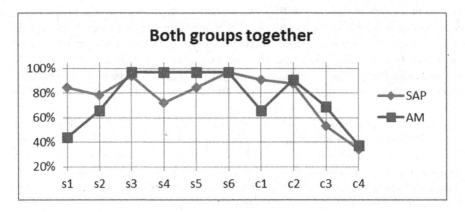

Fig. 11. Overall percentage of correct answers

Time-on-Task. Time-on-task measures are presented in Figs. 12, 13 and 14. The average time to complete the task is greater for the SAP interface for all questions except question c2 in the SAP-first group of participants. Notably, the steep jump in AM-L time on question c2 (Fig. 13, AM-L-first group) is due to one participant, who spent over forty five minutes on a task that took other users in this group less than two minutes on average. There is a similar outlier in the SAP-first group (Fig. 12) that explains the jump in the SAP time on question c4: one user took over 20 min, while others spent less than four minutes on average.

Overall, the average total time to complete all 10 questions was higher when SAP was used. When considering performance within each group (SAP-first or AM-L-first) on both interfaces, given that the structure of questions is the same, it is reasonable to expect that the time spent with the second interface will be reduced, since the general strategy for answering the question has already been developed while solving, essentially, an identical task using the other interface first. This explains the relatively closer times between the two interfaces in Fig. 13 compared to Fig. 12. Overall, users are faster with the AM-L interface, and the time difference between AM-L and SAP is greater when the participants have already solved the problem using SAP. In terms of the average total time per participant, in the SAP-first group, participants spent 27 min using SAP and 14 min using the AM-L interface. In the AM-first group the averages are 20 and 18 min, respectively.

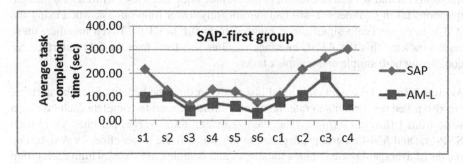

Fig. 12. Average task completion time per question in SAP-first group

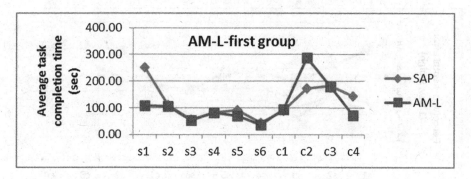

Fig. 13. Average task completion time per question in AM-L-first group

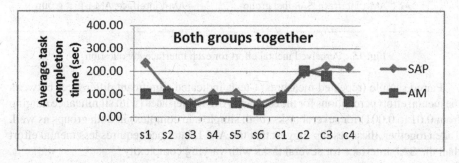

Fig. 14. Overall average task completion time per question.

Paired sample (repeated measures) t-tests indicated several significant differences between the time-on-task metrics for questions completed with the SAP versus the AM-L interfaces. In the SAP-first group, most simple questions (s1, s4, s5, and s6), most complex questions (c2, c3, c4), as well as all simple questions taken together (s1–s6), all complex questions taken together (c1–c4), and all questions taken together (s1–s6 and c1–c4) had significantly lower time-on-task when using the AM-L interface (with significance ranging from 0.1 to 0.01). In the AM-L first group, one third of the simple questions (s1 and s6) and one fourth of the complex questions (c4), as well as all simple questions taken together (s1–s6) had significantly lower time-on-task when using the AM-L interface (with significance ranging from 0.1 to 0.01). Taken together, these results indicate that the AM-L interface requires less time than the SAP interface for completing both simple and complex tasks.

Mental Effort. To obtain additional insights regarding the benefits of each interface, we also asked respondents to rate the mental effort required to complete each task on a scale from 1 (low) to 9 (high). The average mental effort values per question in both SAP-first and AM-first groups, depicted in Fig. 15, indicate lower effort for AM-L. The ranges of average reported values for simple and complex questions within each group and with each interface are presented in Table 2.

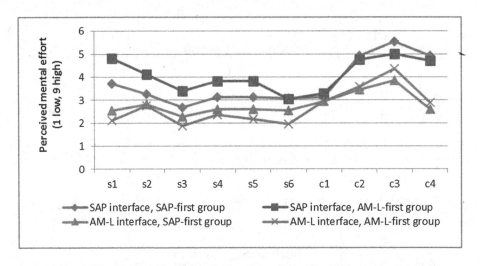

Fig. 15. Perceived mental effort for each interface, by question

Paired sample (repeated measures) t-tests indicated significant differences between the mental effort perceptions for the SAP and AM-L interfaces (with significance ranging from 0.01 to 0.001) for several tasks (both simple and complex) in both groups as well. Taken together, these results suggest that the AM-L interface requires less mental effort than the SAP interface for several tasks with varying complexity.

Table 2. Ranges of average mental effort values per simple (s1–s6) and complex (c1–c4) questions within each group for each interface.

Self-reported mental effort ranges				
	SAP		AM-L	
	s1–s6	c1–c4	s1–s6	c1–c4
SAP-first	2.67–3.73	3.13–5.53	2.27–2.80	2.60–3.87
AM-L-first	3.06–4.82	3.29–5	1.88–2.76	2.88–4.35

Search and Sort. We further analyzed user perceptions of the interface features by asking participants to rate the usefulness of the sorting and search capabilities provided by each interface on a scale from 1 to 7, or indicate that they were not aware of the specific capability. Questionnaire responses show users rating the search features in both SAP and AM-L interfaces highly (see Table 3). According to the SAP logs, none of the students used the sorting feature, which was demonstrated in the tutorial, while the majority (28 out of 32) used the search feature. Search is essential to operating with AM-L; the items for each entity are always presented in a sorted order.

Table 3. Average value of usefulness of search and sort features assigned by users who reported being aware of the feature.

Search and Sort usefulness values (1 lowest - 7 highest)				
	SAP		AM-L	
	Search	Sort	Search	Sort
SAP-first 15 users	5.8 (2 unaware)	1.3 (7 unaware)	6.4 (1 unaware)	5.4 (1 unaware)
AM-L-first 17 users	5.8 (1 unaware)	2.6 (2 unaware)	5.9 (1 unaware)	5.1 (1 unaware)

Percieved Interface Complexity and Enjoyment. Last, but not least, we analyzed the user perceptions of each interface using perceived interface complexity and perceived enjoyment metrics adapted from previous research studies (see Fig. 16 for question details and Fig. 17 for metrics summary).

As shown in Fig. 17, the average perception of complexity, measured on a 7-point scale, for SAP's tabular interface is more than one point higher than that of AM-L, regardless of which interface is used first. The average enjoyment score for AM-L is more than one point higher in both groups, and more than two points higher for users who experienced SAP first. Tables 4 and 5 show the ranges of reported measures of complexity and enjoyment within each group and for each interface.

Perceived Interface Complexity
(answers on a 7-point Likert scale ranging from 1 strongly disagree to 7 strongly agree)
PIC_1: The interface was complex.
PIC_2: The interface was crowded.
PIC_3: The interface was interactive. *(reverse coded)*
PIC_4: The interface displays lots of information.

Perceived Enjoyment
PE_1: Using the interface was: 1 Unexciting .... 7 Exciting
PE_2: Using the interface was: 1 Dull... 7 Neat
PE_3: Using the interface was: 1 Not Fun .... 7 Fun
PE_4: Using the interface was: 1 Unappealing .... 7 Appealing
PE_5: Using the interface was: 1 Boring .... 7 Interesting

Fig. 16. Questions on perceived interface complexity (adapted from [12]) and perceived enjoyment (adapted from [11]) regarding the AM-L and SAP interfaces

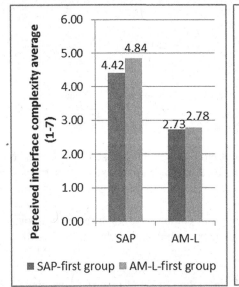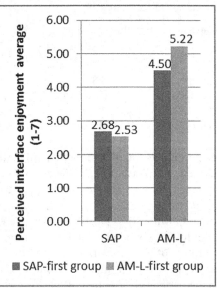

Fig. 17. Perceived interface complexity and enjoyment averages for each interface and in each group.

Table 4. Ranges of average reported interface complexity values on a 7-point scale (lower means less complex) per each group for each interface.

Perceived interface complexity (1-lowest - 7 highest)		
	SAP	AM-L
SAP-first	4.27–4.47 (Avg 4.42)	1.80–3.53 (Avg 2.73)
AM-L first	4.27–5.12 (Avg 4.84)	2.00–3.71 (Avg 2.78)

Table 5. Ranges of average reported values of enjoyment of interface on a 7-point scale (lower means less enjoyable) per each group for each interface.

Interface enjoyment (1-lowest - 7 highest)		
	SAP	AM-L
SAP-first	2.40–2.87 (Avg 2.68)	4.13–4.80 (Avg 4.50)
AM-L first	2.29–2.65 (Avg 2.53)	4.82–5.59 (Avg 5.22)

A paired sample (repeated measures) t-test indicated a significant difference between the composite interface complexity (the average of all four questions) for SAP and AM-L in both groups (at 0.001 significance level). A similar test for enjoyment also indicated a significant difference between the composite enjoyment (the average of all five questions) for SAP and AM-L (at 0.01 significance level in the SAP-first group and 0.001 significance level in the AM-L-first group). Therefore, users clearly perceive AM-L as being less complex and more enjoyable than SAP.

5.2 Qualitative Findings

The final portion of the evaluation asked participants to answer the five questions shown in Fig. 18. Question 2 was the only one that was not open-ended, with possible answers of AM-L, SAP, or Undecided. In those cases where it was relevant, we distinguish between the responses provided by the 17 participants who used the AM-L interface first and the 15 who used the SAP interface first in performing the required tasks.

---

1. How would you compare the Association Map to the way of finding the same information in SAP?

2. Assuming you have access to both the Association Map and the SAP interface, which one do you intend to use next time you have to perform similar tasks?

3. Please explain your answer to the above question regarding which interface you intend to use.

4. Do you have any suggestions for improving the Association Map?

5. Do you have any suggestions for improving the SAP interface?

Fig. 18. Open-ended questions on AM-L and SAP interfaces

Question 1. All of the participants who used the AM-L interface first and 12 of the 15 participants who used SAP first found AM-L to be superior to SAP for finding the same information. The most commonly used word was "easier," as is evident from the word cloud of responses shown in Fig. 19. This term was always used in reference to the AM-L interface. Participants also found AM-L to be more intuitive and user friendly. Of the three who did not find AM-L to outperform SAP, one commented it was "Difficult, unexiting [*sic*];" another preferred the visual aspect of AM-L but found it to be limited in functionality for defining the search criteria; and the third found AM-L to be more intuitive but still lacking in an easy way to extract results.

Fig. 19. Word cloud derived from responses to Question 1

Question 2. When asked which interface the participant would use for performing tasks similar to those in the study, assuming access to both AM-L and SAP, most participants chose AM-L. The responses to this question are shown in Table 6.

Table 6. Intention to use – number of users preferring each designated interface over another.

Intention to use			
	SAP	AM-L	Undecided
SAP-first	1	12	2
AM-L first	0	16	1
Total	1	28	3

Question 3. The reasons for the interface choices in question 2 were very similar to the answers given to question 1 in comparing the interfaces. The primary reason behind the intent to use AM-L over SAP was related to it being easier to use: it was easier to search, sort, learn, and view relationships. Several participants also noted that the visual interface required less typing, was quicker to use, and was aesthetically appealing. The one participant who preferred SAP stated that was due to being "a little familiar with it." The participant who used AM-L first and was undecided thought SAP might be faster for navigating certain functions but would give a slight edge to AM-L. The other two undecideds, both of whom used SAP first, felt that AM-L would be better for simpler tasks involving less data, but SAP could provide more information/better output for complex tasks.

Question 4. All but three of the participants (one of whom used AM-L first and two who used SAP first) had suggestions for improving AM-L. The most commonly requested improvement was to support searches on multiple values for each parameter. Several participants also offered suggestions for improving the clarity of the display, particularly for large datasets. These included more color coding, with the meaning for each color clearly identified; enlarging and displaying in bold the data related to a selection, not just the selected value; providing zoom functionality; using straight rather than curved lines for connectors; improving the alignment of data identifiers with the circles representing them; and having higher order sorting capabilities so that users could limit the scope of what is shown (such as by product family or category). Some participants would also like better support for copy and paste, with one noting that it is hard to copy from the middle column since the display is refreshed when a material is clicked on. Other suggestions that would lessen the need for a pad and pencil would be having the ability to drag and drop to a scratch pad or to export results from a search.

Question 5. Twenty-two participants offered suggestions or areas for improving SAP, seven expressed overall dissatisfaction with the interface, and three simply responded "no." The two most frequently cited areas for improvement were related to searching and sorting. The ability to search on multiple fields and for multiple values per field was a common suggestion. Several participants also suggested improving the visibility and ease of use of the sort functionality; some participants stated that their interface looked different from that in the tutorial, and they were unable to figure out how to sort the data. Another common complaint was that SAP is not intuitive. Suggestions for improvements in that area included getting rid of transaction codes; having icons on buttons that convey meaning; displaying relationships in visual rather than tabular formats; and using colors to differentiate the data.

6 Discussion

The user study revealed a number of interesting findings concerning the use of AM-L versus SAP. One such finding is that the correctness of user responses increased with a bit of practice. For the six simple questions, users did worse with AM-L than with SAP on the first two questions but then did better with AM-L on the remaining four. For the four complex questions, it was only in answering the first one that users fared worse with AM-L. Evidence of a learning curve is not surprising, in that AM-L is likely very different in appearance from other interfaces with which the participants might have prior experience. This issue could be mitigated with time and/or training.

In terms of task completion time, users answered questions more quickly with AM-L. The timing data also hints at a learning curve with SAP, as the time to complete the simple questions fell sharply after answering the first one. The difference in completion time between AM-L and SAP was larger for those who used SAP first. It is likely that lessons learned from using SAP carried over to the use of AM-L.

Overall, mental effort was rated lower when using AM-L, with the highest ratings on mental effort typically from users of SAP who had used AM-L first. AM-L highlights relationships between entities in ways that SAP does not. After becoming accustomed to seeing those relationships represented visually, it stands to reason that having to work through similar relationships presented in a tabular format would present more of a mental challenge. This is particularly true in the absence of a sorting feature, which can be very useful in working out relationships; in this study, none of the participants used SAP's sorting feature because they were either unaware of it or could not find it.

Participants also perceived AM-L to be less complex and more enjoyable to use than SAP. Their responses to open-ended questions about the interfaces provided additional evidence of the clear preference by the majority of participants for AM-L. Equally encouraging was that 24 of 28 of them would choose to use AM-L over SAP if given access to it for performing tasks similar to those in the study.

Most of the improvements suggested for AM-L focused on extending the search functionality, followed by improving the clarity of the display. By contrast, participants often viewed SAP as outdated technology with inadequate support features, particularly in the areas of searching and sorting. Their recommended improvements typically revealed a clear preference for interactive visualizations over tabular data formats for use in performing data-intensive tasks.

Limitations. Given the small sample size in our study, we can only conjecture at this time that the results are generally representative. In addition, the tasks and data used in the study, which were generated by an expert, may not be indicative of actual data and tasks performed in the workplace. Our study participants were students rather than real-life users. Lastly, the longer-term usefulness and effects of our approach has not yet been evaluated.

7   Conclusions

In this study, we evaluated user performance and experience in completing data exploration tasks using an interactive, visual interface (AM-L) versus a tabular data representation. While SAP was used for the latter, we believe our findings are generalizable for any table-based interface used for examining associative relationships between data entities. The participants overwhelmingly preferred AM-L, finding it less complex and more enjoyable to use. The lower mental effort ratings for AM-L may translate into a greater willingness to adopt and use the interface, which was also indicated in answers to a question concerning future use.

User performance was promising, with users faring as well or better with AM-L versus tabular data in terms of time. For correctness, user performance was worse with AM-L on the first two simple questions and the first complex question but then improved to being at or above the level of correctness achieved with SAP. It is expected that minimal training with the interface would help alleviate what appears to be a learning curve issue; this will be investigated in future studies. Our results also corroborate earlier reports that users find visualizations to be helpful in reducing the complexity of problem solving within the enterprise system context.

Outcomes from this study have confirmed the value in continuing with this work. Suggestions and observations from study participants will lead to further improvements in the AM-L interface, to be followed by experimentation for determining the optimal composition of features and interactions.

Acknowledgements. We are thankful to Yuge Xiao, who helped develop the AM-L prototype.

References

1. Lambeck, C., Fohrholz, C., Leyh, C., Müller, R.: (Re-) evaluating user interface aspects in ERP systems - an empirical user study. In: Proceedings of the 47th Hawaiian International Conference on System Sciences (2014)
2. Babaian, T., Lucas, W., Li, M.: Modernizing exploration and navigation in enterprise systems with interactive visualizations. In: Yamamoto, S. (ed.) HIMI 2015. LNCS, vol. 9172, pp. 23–33. Springer, Cham (2015). doi:10.1007/978-3-319-20612-7_3
3. Babaian, T., Lucas, W., Chircu, A., Power, N.: Interactive Visualizations for Workspace Tasks. LNBIP. Springer (2017, forthcoming)
4. Topi, H., Babaian, T., Lucas, W.: Informal notes on technology use as a mechanism for knowledge representation and transfer. In: Proceedings of The Sixth European Conference on Organizational Knowledge, Learning, and Capabilities (OKLC-2005) (2005)
5. Iansiti, M.: ERP End-User Productivity: A Field Study of SAP and Microsoft. Key-stone Strategy, LLC (2007)
6. Chang, R., et al.: Scalable and interactive visual analysis of financial wire transactions for fraud detection. Inf. Vis. 7(1), 63–76 (2008)
7. Liu, Z., Stasko, J., Sullivan, T.: SellTrend: inter-attribute visual analysis of temporal transaction data. IEEE Trans. Vis. Comput. Graph. 15(6), 1025–1032 (2009)
8. Sedlmair, M., Isenberg, P., Baur, D., Butz, A.: Information visualization evaluation in large companies: challenges, experiences and recommendations. Inf. Vis. 10(3), 248–266 (2011)
9. Dilla, W.N., Raschke, R.L.: Data visualization for fraud detection: practice implications and a call for future research. Int. J. Account. Inf. Syst. 16, 1–22 (2015)
10. Saket, B., Endert, A., Stasko, J.: Beyond usability and performance: a review of user experience-focused evaluations in visualization, pp. 133–142 (2016)
11. Xu, J.D., Benbasat, I., Cenfetelli, R.T.: The nature and consequences of trade-off transparency in the context of recommendation agents. MIS Q. 38(2), 379–406 (2014)
12. Wang, Q., Yang, S., Liu, M., Cao, Z., Ma, Q.: An eye-tracking study of website complexity from cognitive load perspective. Decis. Support Syst. 62, 1–10 (2014)

Identifying Root Cause and Derived Effects in Causal Relationships

Juhee Bae[(✉)], Tove Helldin, and Maria Riveiro

School of Informatics, University of Skövde, Skövde, Sweden
{juhee.bae,tove.helldin,maria.riveiro}@his.se

Abstract. This paper focuses on identifying factors that influence the process of finding a root cause and a derived effect in causal node-link graphs with associated strength and significance depictions. We discuss in detail the factors that seem to be involved in identifying a global cause and effect based on the analysis of the results of an online user study with 44 participants, who used both sequential and non-sequential graph layouts. In summary, the results show that participants show geodesic-path tendencies when selecting causes and derived effects, and that context matters, i.e., participant's own beliefs, experiences and knowledge might influence graph interpretation.

Keywords: Cause and effect · Strength and significance · Graph visualization · User study

1 Introduction

A very common way to visualize causal relationships is using graphs, in particular, node-link diagrams. However, not much has been done to evaluate the best ways of depicting causality and the associated strength and direction in graph visualizations [1], neither do we know very much in general about how people read graphs [2,3]. Bae et al. [4] provided a set of guidelines to draw graphs representing causal relations with associated direction, strength, and significance. They highlighted that brightness exhibits higher accuracy and understandability in user ratings when it is used to depict trustworthiness. Moreover, Bae et al. [5] showed that sequential graph layout does not play a crucial role when analyzing causal relationships.

Following the results presented in [4,5], we analyze in this paper the factors that help people to identify a root cause or a derived effect given a causal graph, and we compare the results obtained between groups using different sequential layouts.

In a complex biological pathway study [6], researchers acknowledged that topological ordering of closely related nodes helped to understand causality in biological pathways. Inspired by this work, we use the obesity influence map [7] to investigate the effectiveness and importance of sequencing the cause and effect relationship with influence values. The obesity influence map links 108 obesity-driving-factors to depict a web of causal relationships which was reviewed by over

© Springer International Publishing AG 2017
S. Yamamoto (Ed.): HIMI 2017, Part I, LNCS 10273, pp. 22–34, 2017.
DOI: 10.1007/978-3-319-58521-5_2

300 experts in various disciplines. However, we take only a part of the whole map to fit the causal graph in our study.

The paper is structured as follows: Sect. 2 presents previous work regarding causality visualization, recommendations for graph depiction and relevant studies on graph reading. Section 3 outlines the study background and motivation, followed by Sects. 4 and 5 with the study design and results. General discussion and limitations are listed in Sect. 6, and conclusions in Sect. 7.

2   Related Work

A commonly used visual representation for correlation and causal relations among variables is node-link diagrams [1,8,9]. It depicts a collection of elements (vertices or nodes) and a set of relations between them (edges). Edges often indicate a weight (such as the strength and significance), as well as the direction of a relationship between the nodes.

Guo et al. [1] evaluated user perception of undirected edges which encoded two variables at the same time: strength and certainty (i.e., causality was omitted from their study). Different combinations of visual variables (such as hue, width, fuzziness, etc.) were assessed for different tasks, and a list of design recommendations was suggested based on their results. These include, for example, the usage of brightness, fuzziness and grain to depict correlations, but also that the effects of the combinations of the different visual variables need to be carefully investigated together with the task to be conducted.

In spite of the increasing use of graphs in everyday life, little is known about how people read graphs [2,3], especially in causal relationships with several attributes. A series of experiments presented in [3,10] tried to understand how people read graphs through eye tracking. To a larger extent, the results of these studies focused on how people deal with edge crossings, however, there are some interesting implications for our experiments. First, the authors showed that people have geodesic-path tendency (people tend to follow links first that lead toward the target node), and second, in performing path search tasks, when eyes encounter a node that has more than one link, links that go towards the target node are more likely to be searched first.

Another result related to graph reading that deserves our attention is *localization*. Waldmann et al. [11] proposed a minimal rational model that was sufficient to judge participants' causal model. Participants perceived a causal relationship between a pair of variables locally without considering other dependencies. In another study on locality, Fernback and Sloman [12] found that people have difficulties in inferring chains, especially with additional links in between. The results showed that participants inferred a causal link individually (local) and ignored the rest of the relationships (global). Bramley et al. [13] claim that people maintain only a single hypothesis about the global causal model, rather than a distribution over all possibilities. In [12], the authors asked participants to make judgments following observations of several pre-selected interventions in causal learning. They found that participants were particularly bad at inferring

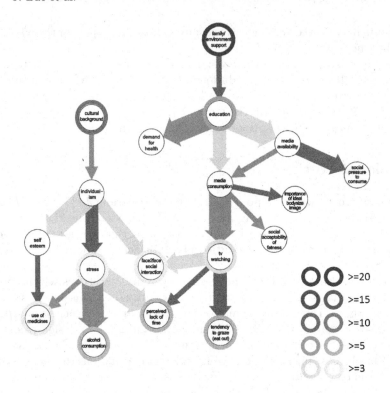

Fig. 1. Sequential layout. Darker red and darker green marked objects indicate more selections from participants for cause and effect objects–nodes, respectively. (Color figure online)

chains, often inferring spurious additional links from the root to the sink node. Fernbach and Sloman [12] proposed that this was a consequence of participants inferring causal relationships through local rather than global computations.

3   Study Background and Motivation

In this paper, we applied visual cues to represent direction, strength, and trustworthiness (significance) associated with edges from a recent study [4]. Given a casual diagram with direction, strength and significance values, we investigate the reasons why people consider a certain object to be a root cause and a derived effect in the causal graph. We aim to explore which potential factors – including context – influence people to decide which node is a root cause or a derived effect in causal relationships.

4   Study Design

Using the obesity map as our dataset, we utilize sequential and non-sequential graph layouts in our user study. We showed the sequential layout using graphviz

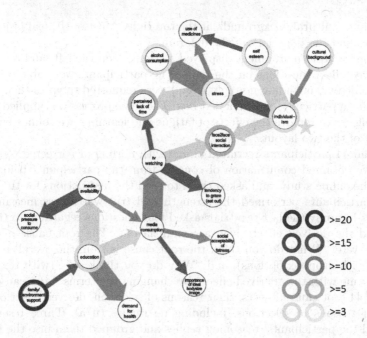

Fig. 2. Non-sequential layout. Darker red and darker green marked objects indicate more selections from participants for cause and effect objects–nodes, respectively. (Color figure online)

dot [14] and showed the non-sequential layout using Fruchterman and Reingold's algorithm [15]. Three researchers from the research group at our university investigated the obesity influence map and agreed upon which objects to put into our stimuli since some labels were difficult to understand at a glance. Our stimuli consisted of 18 objects and 20 edges. The edges depicted different strength and trustworthiness levels of the causal relationships, based on the approaches by Guo [1] and Bae [4], using width for strength and brightness for trustworthiness. The edges were depicted in three levels of strength (width 78, 48, 18 px for high, middle, and low) and trustworthiness (brightness controlled as from a previous study [1] with hue 240 in HSB model for low, middle, and high). The strength-trustworthiness combinations used for the 20 edges consisted of three of each H-L, H-M, M-H, M-L, and four of each L-H and L-Ms (H: high, M: medium, L: low). In order to show all combinations, we added two additional objects to the stimuli – "family/environment support" (we may use "family support" instead in the tables) as a cause of "education", and "cultural background" as a cause of "individualism".

Figures 1 and 2 (without the colored circle marks) illustrate the stimuli we used. We explain the colored circle marks in the results Sect. 5.3. Figure 1 displays the sequential layout with objects "family/environment support" and "cultural background" located at the top and 9 leaves at the bottom. Figure 2 shows a force-directed layout where "family/environment support" is located at the left bottom, but "cultural background" at the top right. Most of the leaf objects are located around the boundary of the diagram.

Our online test environment displayed a stimulus on the left, and root cause and derived effect questions on the right. The participants were able to choose from 19 objects – including no reply –, and were requested to write their reason for selecting a particular node in a text box. The same process was applied for the derived effect. To remove the effects of fatigue and learning, we counterbalanced the order of the two layouts.

We had 44 participants recruited online with normal or corrected-to-normal vision. We obtained confirmation of consent from the participants before they started the online study, and asked them to read the instructions for the experiment. Participants performed the strength and trustworthiness measurement tasks first but only the last two trials asked four questions regarding to the root cause and the derived effect given a certain layout. The root cause questions we asked were, "What do you think the root cause is from the overall relationships?" (with dropbox options), and "Why do you think so?" (with text box), and the same with the "derived effect" by changing the terms "root cause". We collected 44 root cause objects, their reasons of selection, derived effect objects, and their reasons of selections, including no replies (n/a). Three researchers examined the participants' reasoning replies and grouped them into the best-fit category (Fig. 5). The mapping between the categories and the individual's reasoning descriptions are described in Table 1 for the root cause and in Table 2 for the derived effect.

Table 1. Descriptions of root cause reasons and defined categories.

Category	Description of selection reason on the root cause
Starting point	"It's the beginning of the diagram"
	"It's shown at the very first root at the top"
	"All the arrows start here"
Global influence	"It influences most of other factors"
	"It has the indirect connections to most other state"
	"It causes the greatest number of effects"
Personal comments	"Family support is important"
	"Cultural background molds individuals"
	"Basic problem"
Higher strength/trustworthiness	"It has high strength and trustworthiness to other elements"
	"The trustworthiness is higher"
	"Stronger influence"

Table 2. Descriptions of derived effect reasons and defined categories.

Category	Description of selection reason on the derived effect
Personal comments	"Health is important"
	"Stress is a derived effect in life"
	"Managing face to face is very important"
Higher strength/trustworthiness	"It has the strongest connections"
	"The arrow is the thickest to this outcome"
	"Has the strongest and most trustworthy indirect relationship from family"
Many degrees	"It has the most influencing factors impacting on it directly and indirectly"
	"Most entities link back to or are caused from it"
	"Interacts with most entities in/out"
Local ending point	"It's the last and lowest effect listed"
	"This is the final arrow in that group"
	"End result of all diagrams"

5 Results

Figures 3 and 4 display the participants' selections on cause objects and effect objects by descending total number of selections. Almost half of the participants selected "family/environment support" and "cultural background" as causes. Many opted not to respond to the derived effect question, but second and third chosen were "perceived lack of time" and "tendency to graze (eat out)". We provide detailed information regarding dominant objects selected in one of our later sections.

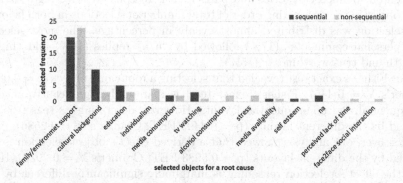

Fig. 3. Root cause objects selected by the participants (in descending order of total selections).

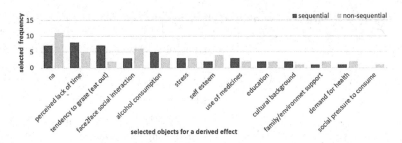

Fig. 4. Derived effect objects selected by the participants (in descending order of total selections).

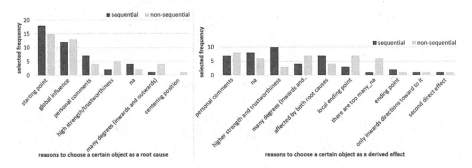

Fig. 5. Reasons of why participants chose a certain object as a cause or an effect (by descending total number of selections). Root cause reasons on the left and derived effect reasons on the right.

Table 1 shows the mapping between our defined categories and participants' reasons for selecting a cause object in descending order of total number of selections in both sequential and non-sequential layouts. Most participants described their reason of the cause selection as a "starting point" (38%) followed by "global influence" (28%) and "personal comments" (13%). Table 2 shows the mapping between our defined categories and participants' reasons for selecting a derived effect object in the descending order of total number of selections in both layouts. The selection was distributed almost evenly in percentage. The most selected was "personal comments" (17%) followed by "n/a" replies (16%) and "higher strength and trustworthiness" (15%).

Our Fisher's exact test revealed that selecting a root cause object (p = 0.0827, Cramer's V = 0.4457, Fisher's exact test) is marginally significantly affected by sequential and non-sequential layouts. However, describing its reason is not affected by the different layouts (p = 0.4499 FET, Cramer's V = 0.2586).

Moreover, our analysis showed that a derived effect's object selection is not affected by the different layouts (p = 0.5983 FET, Cramer's V = 0.2926). However, the effect's selection reasoning is marginally significantly different by the different sequential layouts (p = 0.0899 FET, Cramer's V = 0.3671). "Higher strength and trustworthiness" was selected more as an effect decision reason in the sequential layout while "there are too many to choose" was selected more in the non-sequential layout.

5.1 Pairs of Root Cause Objects and Perceived Reasons

Table 3(a) describes the root cause object and its perceived reason by descending total number of selections. We find that "family/environment support" is selected 20 times in total because it is a starting point. It is also selected 18 times more because participants perceived it to have a global influence. We find that there are certain nodes chosen as a cause object in the sequential layout while others in the non-sequential diagram. For example, "individualism" was never chosen in the sequential, but was chosen four times in the non-sequential diagram (special mark at "individualism" in Fig. 2). The top four responses from the participants regarding selecting a certain root cause object and its perceived reason indicated a non-significant difference from the different layouts (p = 0.4571 FET, Cramer's V = 0.2342).

5.2 Pairs of Derived Effect Objects and Perceived Reasons

In contrast to the cause object-reasoning pairs, the top four derived effect object-reasoning pairs were significantly affected by sequential and non-sequential layouts (p = 0.0279 FET, Cramer's V = 0.5593, Table 3(b)). "Perceived lack of time" and "tendency to graze" were selected as derived effects more times in the sequential layout due to "affected by both roots" and "higher strength/trustworthiness", respectively. Many chose "n/a" due to "there are too many to choose" which is six times more in the non-sequential than in the sequential diagram.

Table 3. Reason-cause and reason-effect pairs by descending total number of selections (displays four top ranking pairs).

Reason - cause object pairs (a)	Seq.	Non-Seq.
Starting point - family support	11	9
Global influence - family support	8	10
Starting point - cultural bkgd	6	2
Global influence - education	3	1
Reason - effect object pairs (b)	Seq.	Non-Seq.
n/a - n/a	5	5
Affected by both roots - perceived lack of time	5	2
Too many to decide - n/a	1	6
High strength/significance - tendency to graze	4	0

5.3 Dominant Selections

The colored circles in Figs. 1 and 2 show the dominance of participants' selections for both cause (red circles) and effect (green circles) objects.

In the sequential layout (Fig. 1), three objects positioned at top such as "family/environment support" (20 selections), "cultural background" (10 selections), and "education" (5 selections) were chosen in total 40% as a root cause. Although we did not perform a statistical analysis on each node's position, it is likely that participants selected root causes more from the top locations and derived effect objects more from the bottom of the diagram.

In contrast, the non-sequential layout (Fig. 2) shows that "family/environment support" is still dominantly selected disregarding of its position, but "cultural background" and "education" are lesser selected compared to the sequential layout. The star mark on "individualism" stands for an odd selection which was only selected as a root cause in the non-sequential layout, never in the sequential layout. In fact, it seemed that participants had a harder time to decide a cause or effect object in the non-sequential layout. More than 25% refused to respond to the cause and effect object selection task in the non-sequential layout (only 2% in the sequential layout).

5.4 Pairs of Cause Object-Effect Object and Cause Reason-Effect Reason

We investigated whether certain pairs of cause-effect objects or cause-effect reasons were selected depending on the different layouts. Table 4 shows these pairs in descending order of the total number of selections. From Table 4(a), we see that many chose "family/environment support" as a root cause but the effects are scattered to "perceived lack of time", "n/a", and "tendency to graze". However, we did not find evidence that the cause-effect object pairs are significantly different based on the two layouts ($p = 0.2241$ by FET, Cramer's $V = 0.4676$). Likewise, the difference of cause-effect reasons between different sequential layouts was not significant ($p = 0.1349$ by FET, Cramer's $V = 0.481$).

5.5 Other Factors

As we examined participants' replies, we found that there are other factors that need further investigation. For instance, the size of a graph (number of objects - nodes and edges), the number of connections on each object (a degree of a node), the context of the causal relationship, the importance of each object given the content, the strength and significance information in the causal relationship, and the position of the object (top, bottom, left, right) may affect the understanding and selection of root causes and derived effects in causal diagrams.

Although the frequency of selecting many-degree objects compared to few-degree objects was not significantly different in our experiment (for both cause and effect cases), we need to explore further if the number of degrees is a factor

Table 4. Cause-effect object pairs and cause-effect reason pairs by descending total number of selections (displays 8 top ranking pairs).

Cause object-effect object pairs (a)	Seq.	Non-Seq.
Family support - perceived lack of time	6	3
Family support - n/a	2	5
Family support - tendency to graze	5	2
Family support - face2face	1	5
Family support - alcohol consumption	3	3
Cultural bkgd. - use of med	3	0
Education - n/a	2	1
Tv watching - face2face	2	1
Cause reason-effect reason pairs (b)	Seq.	Non-Seq.
Global influence - many degrees	4	4
Starting point - local ending point	3	5
Personal comments - personal comments	5	2
Global influence - affected by both roots	3	4
Starting point - n/a	3	2
Starting point - high strength/significance	5	0
Starting point - personal comments	1	3
n/a - n/a	4	0

that affects viewers' decision. The number of sources and sinks may also influence selecting a root cause or a derived effect.

Looking at contextual information, we found that several participants used their own experiences and background knowledge when interpreting the causal relations of the obesity factors (marked in personal comments in Tables 1 and 2). Some examples of the comments given are "family support is important", "cultural background molds individuals", "media consumption is a basic problem", and "individualism is human's psychology".

According to the participants' responses, combinations of the factors described above may influence the results as well; this needs to be explored in future experimental studies.

We additionally examined whether being a root or a leaf node matters. However, the statistical results suggest that sequential layouts do not influence the selection of a cause object because it was a root node, $\chi^2(1,N=88)=0.7857$, $p=0.3754$. Likewise, there was no evidence that participants selected an effect object because it was a leaf node in a specific sequential layout, $\chi^2(1,N=88)=1.65$, $p=0.199$.

6   Discussion

Numerical outcomes of our investigations exhibit a marginal significant difference in cause object selection and effect reason selection between sequence and non-sequence layouts. In addition, there is a significant difference in the top four effect reason-effect object pairs for these groups. Clearly, we need to investigate this further, using, e.g. eye tracking sensors, with additional participants.

As illustrated by the sequential layout (Fig. 1), "family/environment support" and "cultural background" were selected over 50% of the time as a root cause, thus, it was likely that participants selected root causes more from the top locations and derived effect objects more from the bottom of the diagram. This result seems to match results discussed in the related-work section, since they show geodesic-path tendencies, as discussed as well in [3, 10].

The results also show that participant's own beliefs, experiences and knowledge might influence graph interpretation. Looking at the reasons given by the participants for selecting root causes and derived effects, several used the information shown in the graph to match their own beliefs and experience, i.e. they confirmed their own hypothesis, e.g. "family support is important", "cultural background molds individuals", etc.

Two interesting aspects were found from analyzing the personal comments: the weight or importance of each object (factor or node) and the fact that context matters. In fact, participants tend to measure the importance of each object and think how it affects or relates to their individual life. This brings up the issue of visualizing the importance weight of each object in a causal relationship, which can be subjective and controversial. It would be interesting to see how people perceive the obesity map with the importance of each obesity factor. Statistically measuring the strength and trustworthiness of causal relationships is still an on-going research topic. Since the obesity map selected did not provide the strength/trustworthiness of the relationships between the obesity factors, we had to manually make up combinations of strength and trustworthiness in our examples.

In some occasions, it has been a challenge to analyze and categorize the reasons regarding the cause and effects selected by the participants, since some did not fit well in the categories defined. In such occasions, we decided to classify them as "personal comments". Furthermore, we discovered that a lot of participants refused to reply what an effect is when there were too many options. There were a larger number of categories for the derived effect reasons compared with the root cause reasons (Fig. 5). Finally, since we carried out an online experiment, we did not further confirm whether participants' reasoning regarding the categorizations made hold.

7   Conclusion and Future Work

In this paper, we investigated factors that influence the process of finding a root cause and a derived effect in causal node-link graphs with associated strength and significance depictions. For doing so, we carried out an online study with 44 participants that read sequential and non-sequential node-link graphs. The results indicate that participants show geodesic-path tendencies when selecting causes and derived effects, and that context matters, i.e., participant's own beliefs, experiences and knowledge influence graph interpretation.

These results complement our previous findings presented in [4,5], which provided a set of guidelines for drawing graphs representing causal relations with associated direction, strength, and significance, and studied the role of sequence in graph reading.

In future work, we plan to perform similar studies in other domains and with other data sets, involving expert analysts as well.

Acknowledgements. This research has been conducted within the "A Big Data Analytics Framework for a Smart Society (BIDAF 2014/32)" and "New Opportunities through Visual Analytics for Big Data" (NOVA 2014/294) projects, both supported by the Swedish Knowledge Foundation.

References

1. Guo, H., Huang, J., Laidlaw, D.: Representing uncertainty in graph edges: an evaluation of paired visual variables. IEEE Trans. Vis. Comput. Graph. **21**(10), 1173–1186 (2015)
2. Huang, W., Eades, P.: How people read graphs. In: Proceedings of the 2005 Asia-Pacific Symposium on Information Visualisation, vol. 45, pp. 51–58. Australian Computer Society, Inc. (2005)
3. Huang, W., Eades, P., Hong, S.H.: A graph reading behavior: geodesic-path tendency. In: 2009 IEEE Pacific Visualization Symposium, pp. 137–144. IEEE (2009)
4. Bae, J., Ventocilla, E., Riveiro, M., Helldin, T., Falkman, G.: Evaluating multi-attributes on cause and effect relationship visualization (accepted). In: The 8th International Conference on Information Visualization Theory and Applications (IVAPP) (2017)
5. Bae, J., Helldin, T., Riveiro, M.: Understanding indirect causal relationships in node-link graphs (under review). In: 19th EG/VGTC Conference on Visualization, EuroVis, Barcelona (2017)
6. Dang, T.N., Murray, P., Aurisano, J., Forbes, A.G.: ReactionFlow: an interactive visualization tool for causality analysis in biological pathways. BMC Proc. **9**, 1–18 (2015). BioMed Central
7. Foresight: obesity system influence diagram (2007). https://www.gov.uk/government/uploads/system/uploads/attachment_data/file/296290/obesity-map-full-hi-res.pdf. Accessed 3 Mar 2017
8. Holten, D., van Wijk, J.: A user study on visualizing directed edges in graphs. In: Proceedings of the SIGCHI Conference on Human Factors in Computing Systems, pp. 2299–2308 (2009)
9. Holten, D., Isenberg, P., Van Wijk, J., Fekete, J.: An extended evaluation of the readability of tapered, animated, and textured directed-edge representations in node-link graphs. In: 2011 IEEE Pacific Visualization Symposium, pp. 195–202 (2011)

10. Huang, W.: Using eye tracking to investigate graph layout effects. In: 6th International Asia-Pacific Symposium on Visualization APVIS 2007, pp. 97–100. IEEE (2007)
11. Waldmann, M.R., Cheng, P.W., Hagmayer, Y., Blaisdell, A.P.: Causal learning in rats and humans: a minimal rational model. In: Chater, N., Oaksford, M. (eds.) The Probabilistic Mind: Prospects for Bayesian Cognitive Science, pp. 453–484. Oxford University Press, Oxford (2008)
12. Fernbach, P.M., Sloman, S.A.: Causal learning with local computations. J. Exp. Psychol. Learn. Mem. Cogn. **35**(3), 678 (2009)
13. Bramley, N.R., Lagnado, D.A., Speekenbrink, M.: Conservative forgetful scholars: how people learn causal structure through sequences of interventions. J. Exp. Psychol. Learn. Mem. Cogn. **41**(3), 708 (2015)
14. Gansner, E.R., North, S.C.: An open graph visualization system and its applications to software engineering. Softw. Pract. Exper. **30**(11), 1203–1233 (2000)
15. Fruchterman, T.M., Reingold, E.M.: Graph drawing by force-directed placement. Softw. Pract. Exper. **21**(11), 1129–1164 (1991)

Data Visualization for Network Access Rules of Critical Infrastructure

An-Byeong Chae[1]([⊠]), Jeong-Han Yun[2], Sin-Kyu Kim[2],
Kang-In Seo[3], and Sung-Woo Kim[1]

[1] Interaction Design, Graduate School of Techno Design,
Kookmin University, Seoul, Korea
monkeyactive@gmail.com, caerang@kookmin.ac.kr
[2] National Security Research Institute, Daejeon, Korea
{dolgam, skkim}@nsr.re.kr
[3] Interdisciplinary Program of Information Security,
Chonnam National University, Gwangju, Korea
knuei2014@gmail.com

Abstract. Control systems widely used in the national infrastructures are mainly aimed at regular performances of the specified tasks. Therefore, whitelisting security solutions or program that define all usable assets and approachable relationships between rules are widely applied to. The working procedure of the whitelisting control system can be described not just by simple accessing abilities, but various rules such as communication period, frequency, sequence of communication objects, concurrency and inclusion relation etc. As a whitelisting has recently developed more complicatedly, it is believed that the research of the information visualizing which helps the users recognize priority information and the research of the UI which let users manage those information more efficiently are necessary. We have set an extended form of whitelisting that is required for control system security, and it is also based on general requirements in that field. Basing on the analysis of relevant tools and interviews with security experts, we propose a visualize method to manage whitelist information more easily and effectively.

Keywords: Data visualization · Network access rules · Traffic log

1 Introduction

Most infrastructures such as power plant, dam, water sewage systems, and traffic control system have received accepted developed IT technologies, which are currently configured with a lot of network servers, PCs, and controllers. Since cyber-attacks are mainly caused by at the level of massive terrorist groups or nations, not by an individual who is looking for fun, lots of researches have been done to strengthen the cyber security for those infrastructures.

The background of the security starts from understanding exact assets and applying specific access control rules for each asset. The main purpose of the control systems is for regular execution of defined jobs. So, recent security studies are more about the defining of the accessible relationship of the rules among available assets.

© Springer International Publishing AG 2017
S. Yamamoto (Ed.): HIMI 2017, Part I, LNCS 10273, pp. 35–54, 2017.
DOI: 10.1007/978-3-319-58521-5_3

In order to visualize regular job executions of control systems by using whitelisting of access control rules (ARs), not just the fact that an actual access itself is made or not is checked, but also many rules are applied including communication cycle and frequency per access-allowed relationship, order, concurrency and inclusion relation between communication targets. As whitelisting becomes more complicated to use, it is now necessary that more studies which let the users enable to distinguish what is more important or not among information through the emphasized expression and primary location of the information.

This study aims to allow the users to easily manage expanded whitelist-based access rules, and suggests UX improvement plans that visualize communication status (traffic log) for easier understanding based on it.

2 Background

We have developed a network switch, called F.Switch which makes existing whitelist-based access rules be applied, and F.Manager by which many F.Switches can be managed comprehensively. The baseline in this study is the whitelist managing system in F.Manager we developed. This paper briefly introduces F.Manager.

Figure 1 is an overall conceptual diagram of how F.Manager manages the F.Switches installed in the control system network and manages the control system internal network security control.

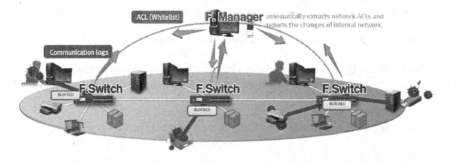

Fig. 1. A complete conceptual diagram of F.Manager and F.Switch

A network switch that can monitor all the traffic of the internal network without installing a SW agent in the control system and can apply a whitelist-based access list (AR List) remotely is called F.Switch, An integrated management system for efficiently managing and utilizing such F.Switches is called F.Manager.

F.Switch can log source (IP, MAC, port) – protocol – Destination (IP, MAC, port) information of all packets generated by the unit time set by the user. Unlike sampling-based monitoring (Ex. Netflow), F.Switch monitors all traffic passing through F.Switch and then solves many problems of control system security by blocking traffic and breaking alarms that violate the AR List. In addition, the security practitioner had to control and manage all the installed F.Switches of the control system all at once. So we designed F.Manager, an integrated management system that can manage multiple F. Switches installed in the control system network in one place.

3 Related Equipment Analysis

3.1 Comparative Analysis of Domestic and International Security Program Related to AR List

In the existing network access control list, visualization features of security-related programs in Korea and abroad were grasped to obtain information needed for extended access rules. Total 15 programs were analyzed and each programs were compared to identify the common elements of the visualization and their advantages and disadvantages (Table 1).

Table 1. Comparative analysis of domestic and foreign security program equipment.

Category	Name	Equipment features	Screen example
Korea	VIPM PLUS [1]	– Network Integrated Security Solution – Customizable information for user's intent – Icon + text form	
	Juniper Firewall/VPN [2]	– Integrated solution for secure network environment – Intuitively express information structure – Category names are difficult to understand.	
	SECUI-NGX [3]	– Providing external and internal network services and protecting services – Iconic representation is effective – Name Expression Intuitive	
	SubGATEplus [4]	– Effective handling of internal and external network threats – Use a variety of visual expressions – Many icons can cause confusion	

(continued)

Table 1. (*continued*)

Category	Name	Equipment features	Screen example
	SecuwayGate [5]	– Intrusion Prevention System – Use a lot of visual representation (icon) – Consistency of the menu is low	
	Genian NAC [6]	– User and terminal control accessing the network – Information structure Intuitively expressed – Difficult to recognize icon and visual representation	
	SNIPER AMS [7]	– Ensure safety through network management based on whitelist policy – It is difficult for the user to recognize because of the unusual sorting method	
	SNIPER IPS [8]	– High Performance Intrusion Prevention System – Priority for critical information is not appropriate	
Foreign	Algosec [9]	– Security management system focusing on blocking malicious traffic – Intuitively identifiable for Source and Destination elements – Use Easy Names	

(*continued*)

Table 1. (*continued*)

Category	Name	Equipment features	Screen example
	Firewall Builder5 [10]	– A standard firewall system that supports multiplatform and is easy to create and modify policies – Icon Visualization Excellent – Use a lot of visual representation (icon)	
	Solarwinds (Firewall Security Manager) [11]	– Role of firewall security management and network configuration management – This system only used text without icons – Priority for critical information is not appropriate	
	Tufin [12]	– Network Integrated Security Solution – This system only used text without icons – Category names are difficult to understand.	
	Paloalto [13]	– New concept security platform that recognizes and controls applications and users – Excellent grouping of relevant information	
	ProSecure [14]	– Next Generation Firewall System for Modern Business – The system uses a button function to provide a visual representation	
	Cisco RV Router [15]	– Implement a new dimension of basic connectivity to the user experience – This system only used text without icons	

3.2   Traffic Log Related Data Visualization Program

Traffic logs should be set to monitor entire of the characteristics of traffic at a glance. For this purpose, various data visualization programs were investigated. Total 40 programs were analyzed and the visualization data that can be used in connection with this task were referred to (Table 2).

Table 2. Data visualization resources

Characteristics of data	References
Change over time [18–23]	
Appropriate for expressing mutual relationship [24–28]	
Express size and quantity [23, 29–31]	
Changes in specific elements [32–36]	

4   Requirements for Creating Data Visualizations

With F.Manager, field administrators can easily manage the extended whitelist- based access rules. Therefore, UX should be improved its factors to visualize the communication history (traffic log) efficiently in general condition, especially required for in case an accident happens.

The required factors are gathered through consultations between several field managers and researchers. And relevant information regarding the access control list and the communication status is collected from them. Based on these requirements, we build the data visualizing system.

4.1 Requirements for AR List

Basically, the information provided in the AR List needs to be the key one for smooth management of the field manager, and the information expressed in the AR List should be configured in accordance with the priority.

For this purpose, we analyzed the information that is commonly used through analysis of domestic and foreign security program equipment. We also summarized the specific information that should be included in the AR considering the characteristics of F.Manager with the result of the interview with the field manager, field network analysis (Table 3).

Table 3. The kind of information required for the AR List

AR configuration information	Description of function
Source	IP, Name
Service	Src Port, Protocol, Transmission direction, Dst Port
Action	Allow, Allow time zone, Temporary time allowed, Inactive
Comment	User-written sentence
Flag	None/Red/Yellow/Green/Blue (User settings)
F.Switch List	F.Switches to which the AR applies
Features in AR	– Time period (seconds, minutes) – Prohibit concurrent sessions/Allow concurrent sessions (2, 3, many)
Associated ARs	– ARs that should generate corresponding traffic sequentially – At the same time, ARs to which the traffic should occur – At the same time, ARs that should not generate such traffic – ARs representing a single 'large service'

4.2 Traffic Log Requirements

There are several elements such as period, frequency and concurrent session, of which they are characteristics of the AR, and they need to be represented in the traffic log. Also, there are sequential, simultaneous, inclusion expression in the relation between ARs as well as an indication of traffic volume. Based on these factors, we investigated graphs which can be used for each characteristic and visualization methods that can efficiently express information and error perceptions. Particularly, the requirements for traffic log visualization are summarized.

Table 4. Characteristics required for traffic logs

Category	Element	Requirements	Visualization material
Features in AR	Period [19, 23, 29 and 35]	– Period representation over time – The communication with error is given the highest priority	
	Frequency [34, 36]	– The frequency of the normally occurring communication and the frequency of the communication with the change are distinguished and expressed – The communication with error is given the highest priority	
	Concurrent sessions	– The distinction between concurrently occurring ARs and isolated ARs (Allow concurrent sessions: 2, 3, any) – The communication with error is given the highest priority – A concise expression that does not interfere with the flow of the timeline	
Associated ARs	Sequential [24, 26 and 27] Simultaneous Inclusive	– A distinction between a related AR and a sole AR – A concise expression that does not interfere with the flow of the timeline – The ARs that have a relationship are expressed in groups.	

(*continued*)

Table 4. (*continued*)

Category	Element	Requirements	Visualization material
Traffic volume [23, 29 and 31]		– Express the amount of traffic without interrupting the flow of the timeline – Need size change for easy recognition of traffic volume change	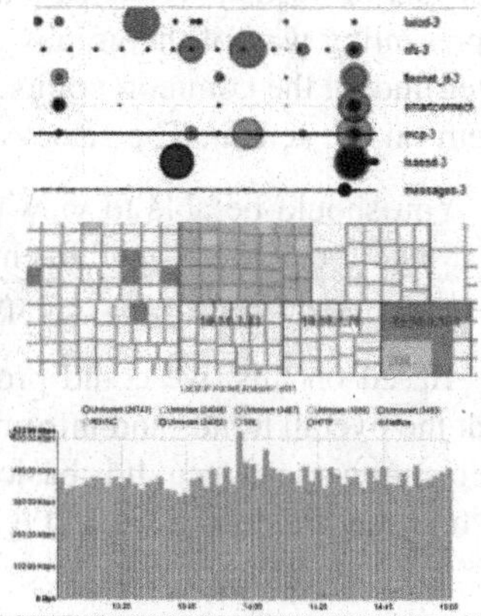

5   Making and Evaluating the 1st Improvement Plan

5.1   Prototype

We focused on data visualization features of their data presentation methods from the existing security programs, including 15 security related programs and 40 data visualization ones. Based on the analysis results, a prototype was created for the list of control system communication status and the traffic log. This prototype will play a big role in producing the final product after the verification of the expert interview and evaluation.

In this document, we propose two prototypes based on extended AR List and communication status (traffic log). Firstly, the AR List was derived the improvement keywords from the issues obtained by comparing and analyzing F.Manager and 15 security related programs. The keywords that we have focused on here are 'information priority', 'grouping' and 'intuitive expression' (Fig. 2).

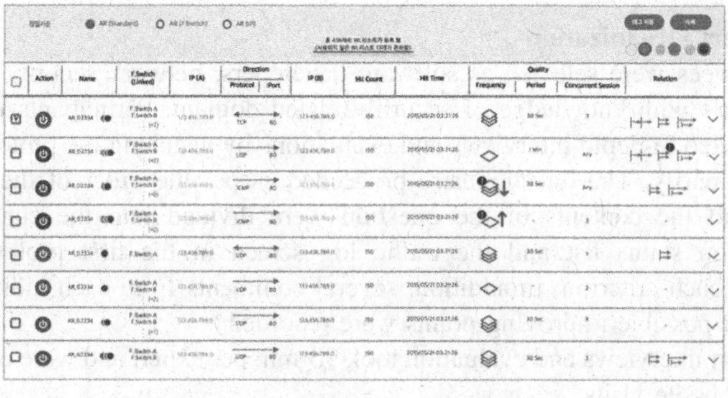

Fig. 2.   1st prototype (AR List)

Secondly, the elements which need to be represented in the traffic log and the graphs in line with the characteristic of each element needed to be verified. Through the analysis of 40 data visualization programs, we were able to find out the information representing way of the graphs. We were also able to set a guideline of our prototype after finding the common points among the elements which is required for representing them on the screen. The selected items are as follows.

1. You should be able to view the entire log as time passes.
2. Make a quick error judgment.
3. You should use intuitive expressions that help you recognize information.

Based on this, we could produce two prototypes. Prototype A has the advantage that the overall trends and information of ARs can be grasped by constructing the entire element on one screen. It is basically concentrating on some specific elements, it is easy to find the problematic AR (Figs. 3 and 4).

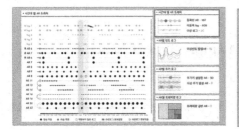 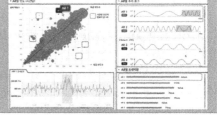

Fig. 3. Traffic Log 1st prototype (A Type)   **Fig. 4.** Traffic Log 1st prototype (B Type)

5.2   Expert Interview and Evaluation

In order to verify the importance and priority of the elements of the information display in the control system communication status list and the traffic log, an in-depth interview with the experts having experience with the security related domain was conducted in addition to the heuristics and the data visualization Likert scale evaluation.

5.2.1   Expert Organization

The interviewees were selected as software developers, network security researchers and UI experts with knowledge of security related domain. Participants in the interviews conducted in-depth interviews and evaluations by watching the prototype screen produced primarily. The questionnaire proceeded as per the order of the processing sequence, and the contents of the question were divided into the control system communication status list and the traffic log screen in the first prototype screen according to each criterion. In addition, several comments from each individual were collected and possible improving points were recorded.

The expert interviews and evaluation took 90 min per expert and were conducted in the form of on-site visits.

5.2.2   Expert in-Depth Interview

The interviews conducted for six experts, and firstly made them recognize the purpose of F.Manager's functions and tasks. The Think-Aloud method was used to investigate the impression of the primary prototype created through its own analysis.

The interview process is divided into AR List and traffic log. In the case of AR List, we verified the suitability of composition of visualization screen based on 'information priority', 'grouping', 'intuitive expression about language and time'. In the case of traffic logs, interviews were conducted on the basis of the selection of the production direction and the characteristics of the preferred screens, and A and B in the two prototypes were examined.

5.2.3   Expert Evaluation

After the in-depth interview, the expert evaluation was conducted to obtain quantified data on the results of the experts' tests. For the AR List, Jacob Nelson's heuristics evaluation was reorganized into 5 different attributes [16], and the traffic log was evaluated by using the Data visualization Likert scale of Hyo-Jeong Kwon [17].

Tables 5 and 6 below are the question list used in the evaluation process.

Table 5. Jacob Nelson, Heuristics Assessment

Property	Question
A. Strive for consistency and standards	Q1. Is the overall screen configuration consistent?
	Q2. Are the details elements (individual elements, icons) of the AR information consistent?
B. Match between system and the real world	Q1. Is it intuitive to understand the information provided?
	Q2. Is it easy to recognize information using visualization that fits the characteristics of the information?
	Q3. Are the comparisons between the provided information (AR) supported directly or indirectly?
C. User Control and freedom	Q1. Is it possible to find the information you want easily and quickly?
	Q2. Is it possible to change the state of the AR information as needed?
D. Design dialog to yield closure	Q1. Does it clearly separate the beginning and end of information access?
	Q2. Does category grouping interfere with viewing information?
E. Visibility of system status & informative feed-forward & back	Q1. Is the visual representation of the current state of the AR? (on/off, Error…)
	Q2. Could the user be aware of the problem himself or herself through a given information screen?

As a result of the evaluation, we were able to identify areas that need an improvement, they were generally rated high, though. The results of Jacob Nelson's heuristics-based AR List showed a high score for consistency of the overall screen configuration and visual representation of the current state and a low score for intuitive cognition received (Fig. 5).

Table 6. Hyo-Jeong Kwon, Data visualization Likert scale evaluation

Property		Question
Functional attribute	Functionality	[Information order/placement] Q1. Can you easily identify the characteristics between ARs? (Sequential, simultaneous, inclusive)
		Q2. Has the characteristics in the AR been adequately reflected? (Period, frequency, concurrent session)
		Q3. Are the information represented by a graph suitable for the characteristics of the AR log?
		Q4. Can the icon on the information screen predict the detail function?
	Familiarity	Q1. Is it possible to intuitively understand the information provided through the expressions commonly used in the nature of information?
		Q2. Is it easy to recognize information using visualization that fits the characteristics of the information?
Cognitive attribute	Understanding	[Explore Information] Q1. Is it possible to easily find the necessary information through the provided visualization information?
		[Interpret information] Q2. Is it easy to grasp the current state of the AR with a graph alone?
	Immersion	Q1. Are there any unnecessary expressions for identifying important elements?
Sensory attribute	Esthetic	Q1. Is visual information visually perceptible to the entire screen?
		Q2. Is it properly structured in size and color to aid in information awareness?
	Satisfaction	Q1. Is there a willingness to continuously check the information through this screen?
		Q2. Do you think it is user-centric?

The traffic log evaluation results using the data visualization Likert scale of Hyo-Jeong Kwon [17] were evaluated differently in both prototype A and B. Prototype A received high marks in the immersive sense of cognitive attributes because it represented only relevant information without unnecessary elements. Also, they received the same high score in satisfaction of sensory attributes. However, the score of the functional elements of the graph using the AR log is low.

In Prototype B, although it received a high score in the esthetic part of the sensory attribute, unlike the prototype A, the expression of unnecessary information was found and received a low score in the immersion feeling part of the cognitive attribute (Figs. 6 and 7).

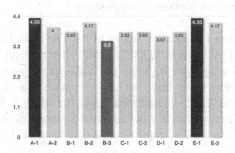

Fig. 5. Jacob Nelson, results of heuristics

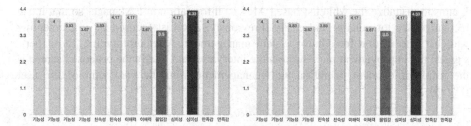

Fig. 6. Hyo-Jeong Kwon, information visualization Likert scale evaluation result (A Type)

Fig. 7. Hyo-Jeong Kwon, Information visualization Likert scale evaluation result (B Type)

5.2.4   Expert Interview Analysis Result

Through the expert interviews and evaluations, we were able to obtain the necessary insight in the final visualization of data visualization. The results of analysis by AR List and traffic log are as follows.

Firstly, the AR List was able to find total 57 issues. The contents of the issue were information expression, grouping of information, category order and information sorting. We have identified common factors in these issues and derived final improvements.

1. Visual configuration for fast error-detection.
2. How to express to the characteristics of information.
3. Priority-aware category arrays.

Secondly, total 40 issues in prototype A and 37 issues in prototype B were found in the traffic log. The final improvements were derived by combining the features and common issues of different prototypes A and B.

1. Structural Improvement for Integrated Information Verification.
2. Re-selection of a visualization method suitable for information property.
3. Added functions for seamless information search.

6 Data Visualizations Screen Suggestion

In this document, the data visualization screen of AR List and traffic log are shown in the paragraphs below. The screen includes case study, first prototype production, expert interview and evaluation analysis focusing on F.Manager's whitelist based communication status factor which are from the prior research. Based on the results, we propose a whitelist-based AR communication status list which is the main function of F.Manager, a security network switch management software of the National Security Research Institute and a method of improving the data visualized UX of the traffic log.

6.1 AR List Final Screen Suggestion

It aims to visualize the whitelist-based AR List information in F.Manager so that it can recognize it a lot quickly and easily. Previously, AR List focused on implementing whitelist information for control system management. After prototyping, the experts suggest the improvement plan through the interview, and finally the proposed screen is the result of efficient operation and management from the viewpoint of the user (Fig. 8).

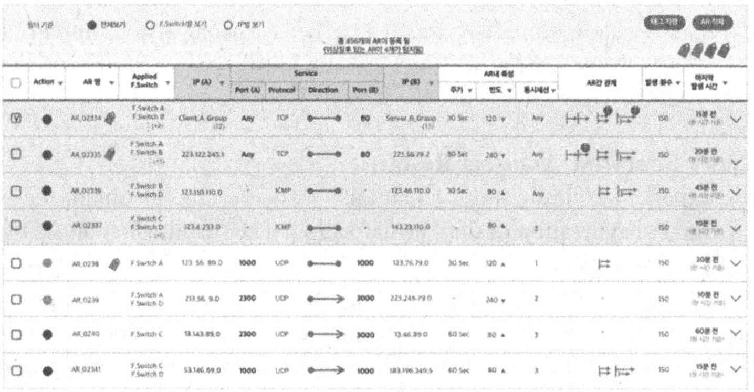

Fig. 8. AR List final screen

6.1.1 Visual Configuration for Fast Error Detection

The problematic AR in the AR List is provided at the top of the list, and it is expressed in the background by applying a red color so that it is easy to recognize the abnormality. In addition, a warning icon '!' is displayed in the area where the error occurred in regard to the detailed problem (Fig. 9).

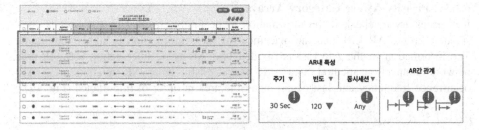

Fig. 9. AR List error occurrence screen (Color figure online)

6.1.2 How to Express to the Characteristics of Information

The name of the information about the provided information should be easily identifiable, and the visual representation of the function that may confuse the user should be limited. In Fig. 10, the indication of the IP forwarder and the receiver are not specified as 'Server' or 'Client' due to the protocol-related change in the protocol. Instead, it uses a different color in the output area to represent the role.

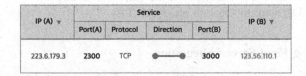

Fig. 10. IP and network connection method area in AR List

In Fig. 11, the tag function is used to enable smooth communication among users. Intuitive recognition is also possible by using different colors according to the level of importance. In addition to the color, several icon shapes are also commonly used.

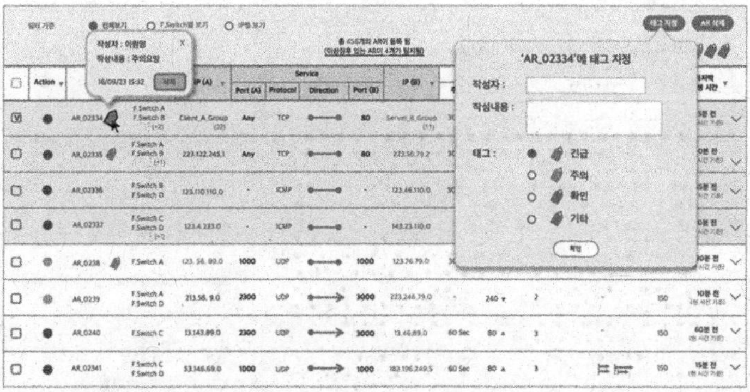

Fig. 11. AR List tag function

6.1.3   Priority-Aware Category Arrays

It is necessary to check if the information to be firstly checked by the user is conspicuous in the AR List, and the placement of such information is highly important. The information in the AR List is divided into AR basic information area, IP and network connection method area, AR characteristic area, AR relation area, AR occurrence frequency and last occurrence time area in order of importance (Fig. 12).

Fig. 12. AR List information providing area

- AR basic information: AR state(on/off), Name, Applied F.Switch
- IP and network connection method: IP(A) – Service – IP(B)
- AR characteristic: Period, Frequency, Concurrent session
- AR relation: Display information about sequential, concurrent, and inclusive relationships
- AR occurrence frequency and last occurrence time: Cumulative number of occurrences and the last occurrence time in the current time display
- Learn more: Detailed information about AR List

6.2   Traffic Log Final Screen Suggestion

It is aimed to visualize the logs of actual traffic of ARs so that they can be quickly recognized by expressing them in a suitable form for information characteristics. After making the first prototype, UX Direction was derived through an expert interview. The final result reflects the overall log flow and detailed frequency, period, and traffic volume of individual ARs at a glance. In Fig. 13, the number of communication

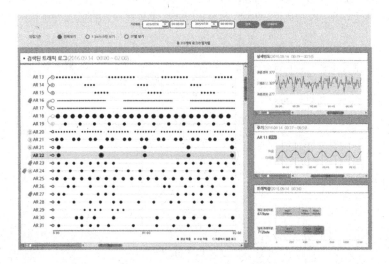

Fig. 13. Traffic log full screen (Color figure online)

operations in the X axis (time) and the Y axis (AR List) is expressed in dot form, the size, interval, and the repetition are displayed according to the characteristics. In addition, the part where the abnormality occurs is marked with red.

6.2.1 Structural Improvement for Integrated Information Verification

In order to comprehensively understand the overall log flow and detailed AR information, the features of A and B in the first prototype were collected. In A type, the overall tendency and information can be grasped. In B type, it is easy to grasp the problematic AR List, and it has an advantage in showing individual characteristics.

6.2.2 Re-selection of a Visualization Method Suitable for Information Property

The visualization method is changed to a commonly used visualization one so that detailed information can be grasped at a glance. In the case of frequency, the numerical value of the average frequency reference deviation was made into a line graph in a certain period. In the case of the period, the repetitive communication status are represented by the characteristics such as sequential, simultaneous, inclusion according to the relationship between the ARs. In the case of traffic volume, the actual traffic volume of the currently selected AR against the average traffic volume is shown in the form of a bar graph. The error expression of each characteristic makes red indication in the region of anomalies, enabling intuitive interpretation (Figs. 14, 15 and 16).

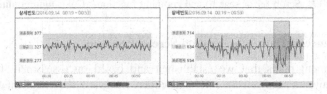

Fig. 14. Frequency graph (Color figure online)

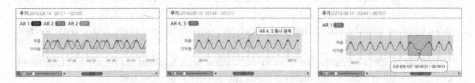

Fig. 15. Period graph (Color figure online)

Fig. 16. Traffic volume graph (Color figure online)

6.2.3   Added Functions for Seamless Information Search

Throughout the error detection and zooming function, the user can easily find the AR errors on full screen. In the case of the AR in which the error occurred, a red area is displayed on the scroll, so that the error position can be intuitively detected. In addition, the selected errors are provided for each characteristic in the frequency, period, and traffic volume areas on the right side of the screen (Fig. 17).

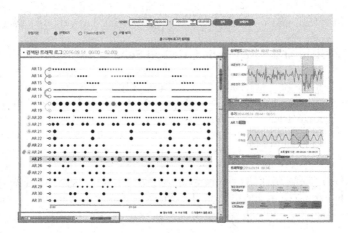

Fig. 17. Scroll (error search) and zooming functions (Color figure online)

6.3   Excellence of Data Visualization Screen Proposal

UX improvement plans that we established and based on assessment for existing products, requirements from the site, and expert interview are excellent for the following reasons.

1. Methods of data expression and prioritization were complemented. Therefore, it is possible to check whitelist data consistently by control system operators, not security experts.
2. It is easy to clearly recognize ARs that are identified as errors (ARs that are not followed at the site).
3. Utilize appropriate graphs for data visualization which based on important factors in communication status monitoring from the security perspective.

The improvement plans make it possible to rapidly search ARs that have necessary data for security work and to understand the entire communication status as well as individual AR's characteristics at a glance.

7   Conclusion

Our study allows to effectively manage the control networks by establishing guidelines for the visualization of traffic log data and whitelist-based AR communication status list. Suggested plans may serve as references that will contribute to more effective work management by users of security programs such as network firewall and network access control solutions. Site tests for various systems are planned in order to move towards easier and more efficient solutions.

References

1. Handreamnet: VIPM Plus Administrator's Guide v1.0 (2014)
2. Zungwon Engineering & Systems: Juniper Firewall/VPN (2008)
3. Secui: SECUI NGX (2011)
4. Handreamnet: SubGATE Plus 100&200 (2005)
5. Future Systems: SecuwayGate GateAdin Pro (2015)
6. Geni Networks: Genian NAC Suite (2013)
7. National Security Research Institute. AMS (2012)
8. Wins: SNIPER IPS v8.0 (2012)
9. Algosec: Algosec (2012–2015)
10. NetCitadel: Firewall Builder5 (2011)
11. Solarwinds: Firewall Security Manager (2012)
12. Tufin: Tufin (2016)
13. Palo Alto Networks: Paloalto PAN-OS (2014)
14. ProSecure Unified Threat Management (UTM) Appliance. http://www.downloads.netgear.com/files/GDC/UTM9S/UTM9S%20Firewall%20Quick%20Start%20Guide.pdf
15. CISCO: Cisco Small Business RV0xx Series Routers (2012)
16. Nelson, J., Robert, L.M.: Usability Inspection Methods. Wiley, New York (1994)
17. Kwon, H.-J.: Elements for Evaluating the Usability of the Web-Based Infographic Design (2013)
18. So-In, C.: A Survey of Network Traffic Monitoring and Analysis Tools. https://www.cse.wustl.edu/~jain/cse567-06/ftp/net_traffic_monitors3/
19. TNV. http://tnv.sourceforge.net/
20. Sankey Diagrams. http://jasonheppler.org/projects/csu-workshop/network-literacy.html
21. Ondas armonicas. http://acer.forestales.upm.es/basicas/udfisica/asignaturas/fisica/ondas/armonicas.html
22. Visualizing the Ebb and Flow of Jobs. https://www.datainnovation.org/2015/02/visualizing-the-ebb-and-flow-of-jobs/
23. Network Monitoring tools. http://www.gregconti.com/publications/insecure_conti.pdf
24. Email thread visualization. http://infosthetics.com/archives/2006/06/email_thread_visualization.html
25. Data visualization. https://mjalexandre.wordpress.com/2015/10/06/critical-design-process-the-design-industries/
26. Adobe After Effects tools. https://www.smashingmagazine.com/2015/06/fitting-after-effects-into-a-ux-workflow/
27. Adobe After Effects. https://forums.creativecow.net/thread/2/1037619

28. NetGrok's Network Graph Visualization. https://www.researchgate.net/figure/216017179_ fig2_Fig-2-NetGrok%27s-Network-Graph-Visualization
29. The Multi Router Traffic Grapher. http://oss.oetiker.ch/mrtg/
30. Visualization Techniques for Assessing Textual Topic Models. http://vis.stanford.edu/ papers/termite
31. Netmon. http://www.netmon.com/category/how-to-tutorial-network-monitor/
32. HINTON DIAGRAM. https://cs.brown.edu/people/daeil/research.html
33. Correlation Matrix. http://www.sthda.com/english/wiki/visualize-correlation-matrix-using- correlogram
34. Node Quilts. https://eagereyes.org/techniques/graphs-hairball
35. PWM graph. http://www.nlvocables.com/blog/?p=188
36. Timeline visualization. http://itblog.emc.com/2014/12/12/smart-data-visualization-helping- decision-makers-get-the-picture/

Visualization of Climate Data from User Perspective: Evaluating User Experience in Graphical User Interfaces and Immersive Interfaces

Vinícius Fagundes[1(✉)], Raul Fernandes[1], Carlos Santos[2], and Tatiana Tavares[1,3]

[1] Graduate Program in Informatics (PPGI), Federal University of Paraíba, João Pessoa, PB, Brazil
viniciuscfagundes@gmail.com, raulfelipe2@gmail.com,
tatiana@inf.ufpel.edu.br
[2] Graduate Program in Meteorology (PPGM), Federal University of Campina Grande,
Campina Grande, PB, Brazil
carlostorm@gmail.com
[3] Graduate Program in Computer Science (PPGC), Federal University of Pelotas (UFPel),
Pelotas, RS, Brazil

Abstract. Data visualization is an important factor in several areas of study, once understanding information is essential for any scientific advance. In meteorology field, for example, an efficient representation of the complex information approached is fundamental to produce any relevant results. According to this, there are several climatic visualization techniques that are used to represent varied phenomena. In order to investigate the most commonly used techniques in the field, this paper presents a systematic review that addresses representation methods and interaction devices within this context. Finally, this process has identified an approach gap within these techniques that motivated the accomplishment of an experience evaluation involving users that are familiar with such forms of visualization in climatic information.

Keywords: Climate data · GUI · Immersive interface · Systematic review · User experience

1 Introduction

The field of Human-Computer Interaction (HCI) is related to the functionality, design and evaluation of computer systems. It aims to provide an effective and enjoyable user experience for individuals. Human factors are therefore extremely important for the development and production of effective and efficient computational systems [1, 2].

Currently, computer systems are increasingly dedicated to providing users with more sophisticated sensory experiences. Therefore, user interfaces are increasingly approaching ubiquity within our reality and our physical world. This fact is tangibly observable due to the proximity of physical elements, as the sensations of everyday life, such as playing, talking and listening, Ishii et al. [4].

According with Tavares [3] new formats and technologies bring new possibilities. The design of effective user interfaces is a challenge and also a great opportunity to

S. Yamamoto (Ed.): HIMI 2017, Part I, LNCS 10273, pp. 55–70, 2017.
DOI: 10.1007/978-3-319-58521-5_4

promote multidisciplinary and innovative solutions what stimulate the participation of several skills integrated in a creative team.

In this scenario, this paper presents results from user experience tests using climate data visualization. For do that, we evaluate user experiences through graphical user interfaces and immersive interfaces. 3D glasses and Google Cardboard [5] were used for improve immersive experiences for users. The aim of this work is to use a complex data type (climate data) and observe which kind of visualization techniques can improve the user experience in data visualization. This comparison also consider the natural evolution of user interfaces in general. The evolution of the user interfaces brought news ways to visualize and interact with computer based applications in several areas such as data climate visualization.

GUIs are typically based in screens and users can interact with them through remote controls such as a mouse, a keyboard, or a touchscreen. The main functions of a GUI includes the visualization of digital information. In fact the current user interfaces technologies enable us to go further than graphical user interfaces or pixels on bit-mapped displays. Immersive environments, natural interaction user interfaces and interactive surfaces are example of approaches to supporting collaborative design and simulation to support a variety of spatial applications.

Such as the visualization of climate data which is a subject very discussed in the literature [3, 6–8] since it approaches several characteristics that go from the capture of the raw data of satellite, going through a filtration process and the visualization techniques in order to present data to users.

In order to identify visualization techniques used to represent climate data, this work also presents results from a systematic literature review where we considered the research questions: "What are the visualization techniques commonly used in climate data systems?" and "Which are the interaction devices commonly used in climate data systems?". For do that, we used Parsifal tool [9], which is an online tool designed to support researchers to perform systematic literature reviews. The next step was to realize the user experience tests performed with volunteers seeking to understand, in their perspective, how this experience affects them in each type of representation considering tangible and immersive interfaces. To capture user experience a survey using Attrack-Diff [10] was carried out based on two premises:

- plain visualization through native data presentation;

- immersive visualization, in which the user visualizes such climate data through VR-Glasses.

Therefore, our experiences demonstrated the feasibility of establishing relations between climate data visualization using different visualization techniques and devices. When considering user perspective, the visualization techniques can be the critical element in the way users understand information. Climate data professionals must recognise that the use of visualization technologies associated with immersive interfaces may require some specific efforts as the use of interaction devices and different modes of interaction. But, these efforts can improve the user experience and make the difference.

2 Visualization of Climate Data

According to Nascimento and Ferreira [11], the process of visualization is related to the transformation of something abstract data into images which can be visualized by human beings. A trend in visualization area is to help people to understand particular subjects, which, without a visualization tool will require more human effort to be understood. In this context, one of the challenges in the study of visualization techniques is to promote new ways to visualize data representations related to several areas of knowledge, such as archeology, hydrology, geology, agriculture, geography, among others.

According to Johansson et al. [12] visualization is a powerful persuasive tool that can provide intuitive and complex understanding of a given data, once visualization methods aims to communicate information clearly and efficiently. Kehrer [13] goes further, dividing the visualization objectives into three large use cases: (A) Visual Scan, which deals with the investigation of unknown data characteristics in order to propose hypotheses; (B) Visual analysis, representing the analysis of the data aspects to confirm or reject those hypotheses; (C) Presentation, which seeks to disseminate the results to the interested public.

According with Nocke et al. [6] visualization is a key technology for analyzing and presenting climate simulations and observations as well as related social and ecological data. Furthermore, mediating research results to decision makers and to the general public in an easily-understandable way is of growing importance. Also for Santos et al. [14] studies aiming the investigation of changes in extreme climate events are important due to the potentially high social, economic and ecological impact of such events.

In the dataset used in this work, the visual scan and visual analysis stages are essential to produce relevant results, since the information is generated on the basis of satellite images, and its presentation varies according to the studied climate phenomena. For this purpose, several visualization techniques were designed to represent climate data. As an example, there is the Color Mapping technique illustrated in Fig. 1, which separates

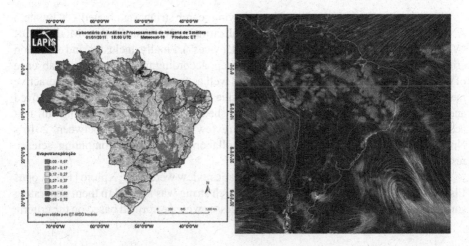

Fig. 1. Color mapping (left) and streamlines (right) representations (Source: [15])

through different colors on a map the regions or intensity levels related to some phenomena, such as temperature, atmospheric pressure, precipitation, etc. In turn, the Streamlines technique also shown in Fig. 1 uses directional flow lines in areas of a map to represent the orientation taken by some phenomena such as mass movements, hurricane formation, etc.

So, in the current work we aim to investigate the relation between visualization techniques to climate data representation. As we discussed there are a lot of visualization techniques but which one is more indicated to the content represented by climate data. In the next section results from a systematic review are discussed exploring this scenario.

3   A Systematic Review of Visualization Techniques Used in Climate Data Representation

According to Kitchenham [16], a mapping study serves to identify, evaluate and interpret all available studies that are relevant to a research question. This kind of study makes possible to identify if some area has any primary studies enough to develop a systematic review or even if some area has any gaps in a specific approach that may be explored. In this work, a systematic review was developed in order to investigate the usage of visualization techniques and interactive devices related to climate data.

To assist in the planning, refinement and analysis steps of the systematic review we used Parsifal [9] tool, which is an online tool designed to support researchers to perform systematic literature reviews. Parsifal provides a way to document the whole process reminding what steps are most important during the review.

The starting point of our review was defining a protocol with all guidelines used throughout the process. In order to reflect the goals of the current study, the following research questions were elaborated:

- "What are the visualization techniques commonly used in climate data systems?"
- "Which are the interaction devices commonly used in climate data systems?".

Based on those raised questions, the following search string was created: ("Climate") AND ("Data" OR ""Events") AND ("Visualization" OR "Visualization Models" OR "Visualization Techniques" OR "Interaction Devices"). Finally, inclusion and exclusion criteria were defined for the last refinement step, according to the presence or absence of techniques for visualizing climatic data, as well as the usage or not of any interactive methods or devices related to these data. Besides that, duplicated works were removed and at last only English written works, published since 2000 and providing full text access were considered. This systematic review was developed between 2016's November and 2017's January, with the collaboration of three computing science researchers.

The search engines chosen for this systematic review were IEEE Xplore [17], Scopus Elsevier [18] and ScienceDirect [19]. The search string was applied to them generating some primary results. Then, two filtering processes were performed based on the criteria

defined in the protocol, the first one considering only the abstracts filtered some intermediate results used for the second one, which the full text of those were considered.
The result of these refinement steps can be seen in Table 1.

Table 1. Refinement stages of the systematic review

	Primary results	Intermediate results	Final criteria results
IEEE Xplore	186	55	24
Scopus	392	52	24
ScienceDirect	47	16	10
Total	625	123	58

After the quantitative selection the analysis proceeds, now considering only the
remaining 58 works after applying all the criteria as seen in Table 1. At this stage of the
review, the focus becomes on the content of the papers based on the research questions
proposed in the protocol. In this sense, all the visualization techniques related to climate
data covered in these works were cataloged, as well as the interactive methods and
devices also related in this approach.

There were a total of 10 cataloged visualization techniques for climate data: (A)
Color Mapping, which separates regions or intensity levels of some phenomena through
different colors; (B) Glyphs, which uses icons in specific places to represent some value
or event; (C) Graphics, which represent values related to two or more variables through
a curve in a cartesian plane; (D) Height Mapping, which illustrates values through 3D
elevations on the surface of a region; (E) Histograms, which shows the distribution of
numerical data in relation to some event; (F) Isolines, which uses contours on the surface
of a region to delimit different levels of some phenomena; (G) Isosurfaces, which makes
an analogous representation of Isolines for a 3D projection; (H) Scatterplot, which
present data through collections of points arranged on a cartesian plane or even on maps;
(I) Streamlines, which uses directional flow lines on a map to represent the orientation

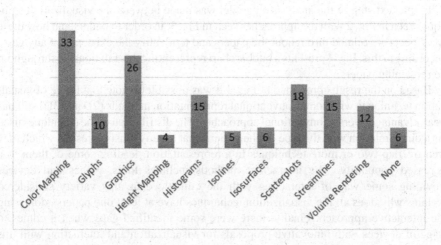

Fig. 2. Number of papers per visualization technique.

of some phenomena; (J) Volume Rendering, which illustrates a map with values of some phenomena through a 3D scalar field. The graphic shown in Fig. 2 illustrates the number of papers that address each of the techniques described.

Regarding the second research question, there were more methods of visualization and interaction among the works than properly devices, therefore it became relevant to also catalog these methods instead of only the devices eventually approached. They were cataloged: (A) 2D Representation, all conventional ways of data presentation and climatic visualization techniques; (B) 3D Representation, all conventional ways of three-dimensional representations of data and visualization techniques; (C) Interactive, encompassing methods, tools and devices that enable any interaction alternative for the user; (D) Augmented Reality, where virtual representation is generated by devices under real environment; (E) Virtual Reality, where the representation also uses devices, but for projection in a virtual environment. The graph shown in Fig. 3 shows the number of papers that includes those representation approaches.

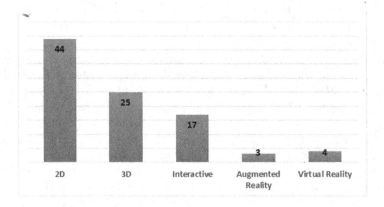

Fig. 3. Number of papers per representation approach

In the next step of the analysis a parallel was made between the visualization techniques seen in Fig. 2 with the approaches seen in Fig. 3, in order to understand how these two aspects are related throughout the papers and to identify the existence of any gaps. According to this, Fig. 4 presents a bubble chart representing this relationship throughout the remaining papers.

Based on the results presented at Fig. 4 it was possible to note that usage of visualization techniques with some conventional representation methods (2D and 3D) still has great advantage over unconventional approaches. The distribution of the techniques used has a direct relation with the type of phenomena that a study must represent, which may even overlap two or more techniques in a representation, leading some of them to a increased popularity. The interactive methods includes tools, games and devices providing some way of interacting with the climatic data, this variety considered explains why does all the visualization techniques have at least one papers addressing one interactive approach. Finally, there were some identified gaps when it comes to usage of devices with innovative proposals for visualization and interaction with this type of information. The were almost no papers with Augmented Reality (AR) and

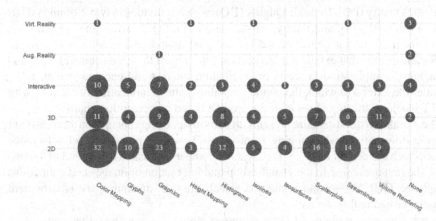

Fig. 4. Relation between visualization techniques and representation approaches

Virtual Reality (VR) approaches related to climate visualization found, despite the immersion capability proposed on both. The low exploitation of these alternatives in this context was one of the factors that motivated the evaluation developed in this work, in order to explore the potential of immersive means in the visualization of climatic data.

4   Materials and Methods

In order to explore immersive possibilities in the visualization of climatic data field, this study presents results from user tests considering the method of user experience (UX). ISO 9241-210 [20] defines user experience as "perceptions and reactions of a person which results from the predictable usage of a product". According to this definition, user experience includes all emotions, beliefs, preferences, perceptions, physical and psychological responses, users behaviors and achievements that happened before, during and after use.

According to DNX [21], a good user experience happens when nice, positive and satisfactory sensations occur using a system capable of getting users' fidelity. Such experience may be able to reflect the actual user impressions when participating in an experiment, which makes evaluations of these experiences an interesting alternative to absorb positive and negative opinions for a given product or system.

Based on concepts presented in previous sections, the main proposal of this work was to evaluate the user's experience submitted to different forms of representation of climate data, presented in a graphical interface and in an immersive interface. These climate data were presented to users from a conventional perspective, through interactive images and animations and then from an alternative perspective, through videos in an immersive virtual environment. At the end, two forms were applied, each referring to one of these experiences provided.

In order to perform the user experience evaluation, the AttrakDiff [10] tool was used, which methods of analysis can identify the qualities of a proposal from the perspective of the users. The form referring to this analysis is divided into three dimensions:

Pragmatic Quality (PQ), Hedonic Quality (HQ), which is divided in two, Stimulus (HQ-S) and Identity (HQ-I), and finally, Attraction (ATT). PQ describes the application's quality and indicates the degree of success and goals that users can achieve in using it. HQ-S indicates to what extend the application can support the needs of developing and advancing the application in terms of originality, interest and encouragement. HQ-I describes the extend to which the application allows the identification of the user with it. ATT indicates the global value of the product based on perception quality.

The AttrakDiff questionnaire presents 28 pairs of opposing concepts on a seven-point semantic differential scale, ranging from −3 to 3, with 7 possible levels of choice between each concept of the pair. Thus, each volunteer was asked to respond to the two forms, the first according to the visualization and interaction of images and animations through the GUI, the second related to visualization in an immersive environment through a virtual reality device.

It was initially explained to the volunteer about the research, that consists of presenting climate data in two different ways. The first one deals with visualization through native data presentation, in which the user visualizes the images and interacts with animations. After that, the immersive part in virtual reality of the experiment was started, in which the user uses VR glasses to visualize data in a 360° view, being able to visualize different regions of the world when moving the head in different directions.

4.1 Experimentation with Graphical User Interface (GUI)

The representation of climate data through images and animations consists of the conventional model, since it is the most common way to analyze this type of information. Within this perspective, the data are usually arranged on a screen with representations of some visualization techniques according to the phenomenon studied.

In the experiment carried out, the users were invited to visualize in a computer some images with climatic visualization techniques representing some common meteorological phenomena. Then the users were presented the tool proposed by earth [22], through which some techniques are represented by animations, in addition to enabling interaction with the environment.

Some of the images used in the research are seen in Fig. 5 and present some techniques used to represent phenomena: (A) Color Mapping and Isolines, representing sea level pressure; (B) Streamlines, representing wind flow; (C) Color Mapping, representing rainfall concentration; (D) Color Mapping, representing position and density of clouds.

After this, the animations were presented through the earth [22] tool, representing the climate event chosen by the user in one of the types of projection available at the menu. In Fig. 6, two distinct moments of this stage can be seen: (A) Color Mapping and Streamlines, representing temperature and wind flow at 850 feet in ortho projection; (B) Color Mapping and Streamlines, representing relative air humidity and wind flow at 1000 feet in equirectangular projection.

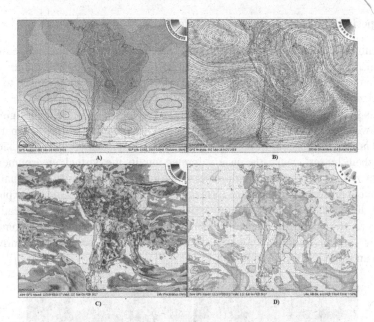

Fig. 5. Different phenomena and visualization techniques

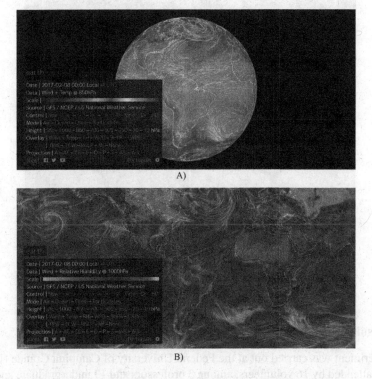

Fig. 6. Samples of animations shown by the tool (Source: [21])

4.2   Experimentation with Immersive Interfaces

Unconventional means of visualizing climate information involve alternative methods of visualization, such as augmented reality and virtual reality. The representation of the data in this perspective requires some device referring to the method chosen to design the visualization technique studied.

At this stage of the experiment, users were asked to use a virtual reality glasses to view the weather information in an immersive environment. To do this, a smartphone was used next to the glasses, which consists of a mask that isolates the user's vision and, through their lenses, cause the user's immersion in the virtual environment. All processing is done through the smartphone, which generates a stereoscopic visualization of the content presented, in this case 360° videos on YouTube, allowing the exploration of a three-dimensional scenario through the user's interaction by moving the head. Three videos were presented in sequence, showing different meteorological phenomena, as seen in Fig. 7, representing (A) direction and intensity of air masses, (B) cloud movement and (C) atmospheric CO_2 distribution:

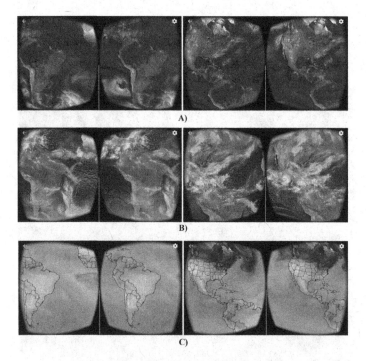

Fig. 7.   Samples of videos (Sources: [23–25])

4.3   Results

The experiment was carried out at the Federal University of Campina Grande (UFCG) and was attended by 16 volunteers, among 3 professors and 13 undergraduate and graduate students, who have contact with this type of climatic data. The choice of this audience familiar with the content contributes to a better evaluation to avoid negative impressions due to possible difficulties in understanding the information (Fig. 8).

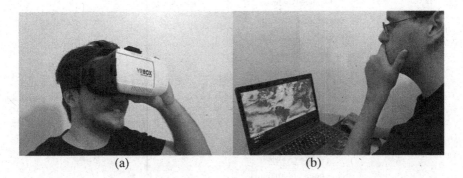

(a)   (b)

Fig. 8. Users tests. In (a) with VR-Glasses and in (b) with screen visualization.

After considering the quantitative data about users, the next step was to analyze the responses of the proposed questionnaires based on the AttrakDiff tool, where the same concepts were proposed according to the experience on the screen and, later, with the experience in the VR glasses.

4.4 Result Analysis

When dealing with the dimensions of the AttrakDiff, it is interesting to analyze each one individually, by addressing specific characteristics, as well as to identify differences between the visualization modes, as can be visualized in Fig. 9, where the orange color represents the experience on the screen and blue, the immersive experience with VR glasses.

In Pragmatic Quality (PQ), in spite of few differences, it is perceived that the viewing in the VR glasses was considered more "human" than "technical", while on the screen it seemed something more "clearly structured" than "confusing." This occur probably due to immersion being something less common, and more interactive, which showed less technicality to users.

In terms of Identity (HQ-I), it was observed that the on-screen visualization was considered more "isolating" and more "connective" in the VR glasses, besides the second perspective seemed to be more "stylish" and "premium" than the first, referring to the human side of the natural interaction.

On Stimulus (HQ-S), the biggest discrepancies occurred in "conventional - inventive" and "cautious - bold", where the use of glasses for this context seemed something innovative/creative to users. This impression must have been triggered by the first contact of users with such an approach in climate information.

In Attraction (ATT), a detachable difference did not occur "unpleasant - pleasant" where experience in wearing glasses brought better impressions to users. Again depicting an innovation in using this device.

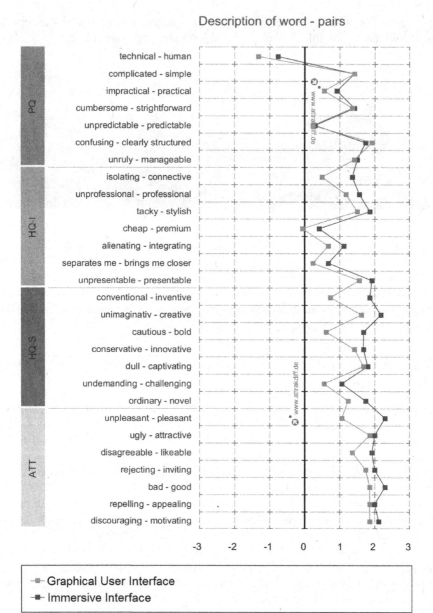

Fig. 9. Word pair of concepts by AttrakDiff

Figure 10 shows the mean of the results of Fig. 9. It is essential to emphasize that the fact that the average of the immersive interface experiment has been higher than the graphical interface does not indicate that it is superior to the other, since the research tries to represent different forms of representation of climatic data. Consequently, this average above traditional visualization indicates a promising area for future studies, since using climatic data with a virtual reality immersion device has obtained good results in all dimensions, indicating good usability, being stimulating, attractive and the user is able to identify himself with the device.

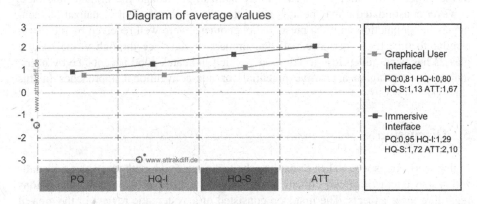

Fig. 10. Average of the questionnaire by AttrakDiff

Finally, the graph presented in Fig. 11 has the horizontal axis related to the Pragmatic Quality (PQ) dimension and vertical axis related to the Hedonic Quality (HQ) dimension. The central representation of the graph indicates neutral impressions in the experiment; on the other hand, as the resulting values move away from the center towards the upper right, the greater the indication of good acceptance by the users. Another important factor is the confidence rectangle, the larger this rectangle, the less confidence will be in the region in which it is located. Consequently, a small rectangle presents a smaller

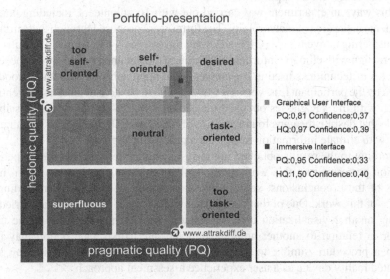

Fig. 11. Pragmatic quality vs hedonic quality by AttrakDiff

value and more concrete results, because it represents a more unanimous opinion in the evaluation done by the users.

Analyzing the presented graph, it is observed that both experiments are located closer to the upper right extremity. As for the visualization through the graphic interface, however consolidated it may be, it is noted that the combination of visualization techniques in conjunction with the presented phenomena were well received by the users. Similar to this, the experience with the immersive interface through virtual reality glasses has been quite close to "desired", which indicates good acceptance by users, indicating once again a positive potential for non-conventional approaches in this context.

5 Discussion

In this work, steps were taken to explore the techniques and methods used for visualization and interaction with climatic data, as well as to investigate user impressions regarding these aspects. The first step consisted of a systematic review in the area in order to identify the presence of these two approaches in this context. As a result of this mapping, it was possible to catalog the main visualization techniques used for this type of information, as well as the forms of representation commonly present in the area. Finally, the relationship between these two aspects was analyzed to understand what parallel could be traced among the cataloged materials. Through this analysis it was possible to conclude that the conventional means are more present than the non conventional ones in the representation of the techniques, which generates gaps in the approach of innovative alternatives in this approach. This impression contributed to a user experience assessment including traditional and alternative forms of visualization and interaction with climatic information in order to understand if the users' impressions justified the gaps identified in this approach.

In this way, an experiment was carried out with 16 volunteers, including teachers and students in the area of meteorology. The forms were proposed through the AttrakDiff tool, considering conventional (GUI) and non-conventional (VR) forms of visualization and interaction with climatic information. Through the obtained results, it was observed that the set of techniques used in the conventional approach was well understood and accepted by the participants, as well as it was possible to observe that the unconventional approach with the VR glasses obtained plausible results. With this, it was possible to conclude that despite the gaps found, the use of innovative alternatives to visualize and interact with climate information represents a promising approach.

According to the results obtained in the systematic review and the user experience evaluation performed by this work, and also based on the conclusions drawn in the analysis of these conclusions, some impressions could be considered regarding the sequence of this work. One of them is to extend the scope of the evaluation carried out, including another visualization method besides virtual reality to analyze the user's behavior in relation to another non-conventional alternative. One option may be to perform a procedure similar to the one presented in this paper considering some augmented reality device as a user experience assessment approach.

Another interesting direction for the sequence of the work would be to take advantage of the positive reaction of the users in the VR experience and to propose some means of interacting with climatic information within that perspective. In this way the immersion could be explored with a focus on helping to understand the data.

Acknowledgments. We would like to thank the volunteers and all the collaborators from the PRO-ALERTAS project for their participation in the survey who supported our work in this way and helped us get results of better quality. We are also grateful to the Coordination for the Improvement of Higher Education Personnel (CAPES) and the Brazil's Council for Scientific and Technological Development (CNPq).

References

1. Karray, F., Alemzadeh, M., Saleh, J.A., Arab, M.N.: Human-computer interaction: Overview on state of the art. Int. J. Smart Sens. Intell. Syst. **1**(1), 1–23 (2008)
2. Harper, R., Rodden, T., Rogers, T., Sellen, A.: Being Human: Human-Computer Interaction in the Year 2020. Microsoft Research Ltd., England (2008)
3. Tavares, T.A., Barbosa, H.A.: A step beyond visualization: Applying user interface techniques to improve satellite data interaction. In: Yamamoto, S. (ed.) HCI 2014. LNCS, vol. 8521, pp. 98–107. Springer, Cham (2014). doi:10.1007/978-3-319-07731-4_10
4. Ishii, H., Lakatos, D., Bonanni, L., Labrune, J.: Radical atoms: Beyond tangible bits, toward transformable materials. Magazine Interactions **19**(1), 38–51 (2012). doi:10.1145/2065327.2065337
5. Google Cardboard Homepage. http://vr.google.com/cardboard/
6. Nocke, T., Sterzel, T., Böttinger, M., Wrobel, M.: Visualization of climate and climate change data: An overview. In: Digital Earth Summit on Geoinformatics, pp. 226–232 (2008)
7. Ladstädter, F., Steiner, A.K., Lackner, B.C., Pirscher, B., Kirchengast, G., Kehrer, J., Doleisch, H.: Exploration of climate data using interactive visualization*. J. Atmos. Oceanic Technol. **27**(4), 667–679 (2010). doi:10.1175/2009JTECHA1374.1
8. Tominski, C., Donges, J. F., Nocke, T.: Information visualization in climate research. In: 2011 15th International Conference on Information Visualisation, pp. 298–305. IEEE (2011) doi:10.1109/IV.2011.12
9. Parsifal Homepage: http://parsif.al/
10. AtrackDiff Homapage: http://attrakdiff.de/
11. Do Nascimento, H.A., Ferreira, C.B.: Visualização de Informações–uma abordagem prática. In: XXV Congresso da Sociedade Brasileira de Computação, XXIV JAI. UNISINOS, S. Leopoldo–RS (2005)
12. Johansson, J., Neset, T.S.S., Linnér, B.O.: Evaluating climate visualization: An information visualization approach. In: 2010 14th International Conference Information Visualisation (IV), pp. 156–161. IEEE, July 2010. doi:10.1109/IV.2010.32
13. Kehrer, J.: Interactive visual analysis of multi-faceted scientific data (Doctoral dissertation, Ph.D. dissertation, Dept. of Informatics, Univ. of Bergen, Norway) (2011)
14. Santos, C.A.C., de Brito, I.B., dos Santos, E.G., Rao, T.V.R., da Silva, V.P.R.: Temporal variability of extreme temperature indices in Utah during the past few decades. Rev. Bras. de Meteorologia **28**(4), 364–372 (2013). doi:10.1590/S0102-77862013000400002
15. LAPIS: Laboratótio de Análise e Processamento de Imagens de Satélites. Accessed 04 Jan 2017. http://www.lapismet.com/

16. Kitchenham, B., Budgen, D., Brereton, P.: Using mapping studies as the basis for further research – A participant-observer case study. Inf. Softw. Technol. **53**(6), 638–651 (2011). doi: 10.1016/j.infsof.2010.12.011

17. IEEE Xplore Digital Library. http://ieeexplore.ieee.org.ez15.periodicos.capes.gov.br/Xplore/guesthome.jsp?reload=true. Accessed 16 Nov 2016

18. Scopus: Document Search. https://www-scopus-com.ez15.periodicos.capes.gov.br/. Accessed 16 Nov 2016

19. ScienceDirect: Explore Scientific, technical, and medical research on ScienceDirect. http://www-sciencedirect-com.ez15.periodicos.capes.gov.br/. Accessed 16 Nov 2016

20. ISO FDIS 9241-210: Ergonomia da interação sistema humano - Parte 210: Projeto centrado no ser humano para sistemas interativos. International Organization for Standardization (ISO). jithin dev (2011)

21. DNX: Usabilidad y Experiencia de Usuario. Microsoft España: Guía Práctica de Usabilidad Web (2005)

22. Earth: https://earth.nullschool.net/. Accessed 14 Jan 2017

23. Surface Winds 360 VR Data Visualization. https://www.youtube.com/watch?v=5F42 V045SFg&list=PLOuOWmPx1jjQM-8aJaRs6MNMyBipLjPln&index=1. Accessed 18 Jan 2017

24. Cloud cover 360 VR Data Visualization. https://www.youtube.com/watch?v=57LEN1iba-Q&list=PLOuOWmPx1jjQM-8aJaRs6MNMyBipLjPln&index=2. Accessed 18 Jan 2017

25. CO_2 360 VR Data Visualization. https://www.youtube.com/watch?v=tTQmGcaaEEE&list=PLOuOWmPx1jjQM-8aJaRs6MNMyBipLjPln&index=3. Accessed 18 Jan 2017

Management of Inconsistencies in Domain-Spanning Models – An Interactive Visualization Approach

Stefan Feldmann[1(✉)], Florian Hauer[2], Dorothea Pantförder[1],
Frieder Pankratz[3], Gudrun Klinker[3], and Birgit Vogel-Heuser[1]

[1] Institute of Automation and Information Systems,
Technical University of Munich, Munich, Germany
stefan.feldmann@tum.de
[2] Chair of Software Engineering, Technical University of Munich, Munich, Germany
[3] Chair for Computer Aided Medical Procedures & Augmented Reality,
Technical University of Munich, Munich, Germany

Abstract. The complexity of automated production systems increases steadily – especially due to the rising customer demand to manufacture individualized goods. To stay competitive, companies in this domain need to adapt their engineering to deliver machines and plants with higher quality in shorter time. Hence, to reduce design errors and identify problems already in early engineering stages, it is essential to ensure that the disparate engineering models – e.g., from mechanical, electrical and software engineering – are free from inconsistencies. This paper presents a concept for inter-model inconsistency management. In particular, the proposed concept provides an interactive visualization approach that captures the dependencies between the different engineering models explicitly and visualizes them to the involved stakeholders. By that, the location of and cause for inconsistencies can be identified more easily; dependencies between the different engineering disciplines can be visualized in a comprehensive manner.

Keywords: Model-based systems engineering · Automated production systems · Inconsistency management · Semantic web technologies

1 Introduction

Engineering in the automated production systems domain (aPS) is an interdisciplinary process and incorporates a multitude of heterogeneous, domain-specific models [9] – e.g., requirements models, engineering models as well as analysis models. Although these disparate models consider different aspects of the system under investigation, they are not completely disjoint [3]. Consequently, overlaps – that is, information being introduced redundantly – are present in between the different models [21] and, hence, inconsistencies are likely to occur [10]. Such inconsistencies reflect a state of conflict between the involved

© Springer International Publishing AG 2017
S. Yamamoto (Ed.): HIMI 2017, Part I, LNCS 10273, pp. 71–87, 2017.
DOI: 10.1007/978-3-319-58521-5_5

models that results from conflicting information [21] being introduced in the different, domain-specific views. Furthermore, inconsistencies do not necessarily lead to engineering errors, but may rather also indicate aspects that need to be further elaborated by the involved stakeholders [21]. Hence, to ensure a high quality engineering process, it is essential to continuously check for and handle these inconsistencies.

Especially within large-scale mechatronic systems, complex dependencies exist between the different models. The reasons for these complex dependencies are manifold: For one, the enormous system complexity that results, e.g., from the increasing customer demand for lower costs and better quality, is one essential reason for complexity. In addition, the variety of stakeholders from different domains and with individual mental models that are involved in the engineering of aPS is an essential factor that leads to numerous dependencies in between different engineering models. Hence, inconsistencies cannot be regarded individually – rather, they must also be regarded from an overview of the entire system. Especially as the various models also differ in the used modelling language and level of detail [9], system designers must be able to switch between different levels of detail to maintain this overview. Hence, this paper aims at extending our existing inconsistency management framework [7] by an interactive, configurable visualization approach that envisions three central objectives:

- an extensible framework based on a *standardized representational formalism* using Semantic Web Technologies – namely, the Resource Description Framework (RDF) [25] and the SPARQL Protocol and RDF Query Language (SPARQL) [23,24],
- an interactive, *graph-based visualization* capturing model *entities* and *dependencies*, and
- a *rule-based configuration* to configure and adapt the visualization regarding different levels of abstraction.

By means of such an interactive inconsistency management approach, we envision the basis for an adaptable and extensible framework that can be applied easily to a variety of applications. The remainder of this paper is structured as follows: From a comparison of the related research works (Sect. 2), we derive the requirements that must be solved by an interactive and configurable visualization approach for the purpose of inconsistency management (Sect. 3). Based on these requirements, we introduce our concept in Sect. 4. In Sect. 5, we show how our concept can be applied to a typical scenario in the aPS domain at the hand of a prototypical software implementation. The results obtained from our research as well as an outlook on further research potential are given in Sect. 6.

2   Related Work

Within this section, our inconsistency management approach is compared to the related work. In particular, we discuss related research in the field of model-based (systems) engineering (see Sect. 2.1), followed by inconsistency management approaches (see Sect. 2.2) and different visualization approaches that aim at visualizing the interconnections between heterogeneous engineering models (see Sect. 2.3). Finally, our findings are summarized in Sect. 2.4.

2.1   Model-Based (Systems) Engineering

Model-based engineering approaches are especially important to the software engineering domain [18], as they allow for problem and solution abstraction. A variety of description formalisms are available to the software engineering domain, e.g., modelling languages such as the Unified Modelling Language (UML). Such modelling languages are more and more applied in the aPS engineering domain. Especially model-based systems engineering (MBSE) is part of a trend from document-centric to model-centric approaches [12] and entails the specification of many other types of models like the Systems Modelling Language (SysML), which enables engineers to focus on an overarching system's perspective. However, the different disciplines involved in the development process of aPS use their domain specific models [6], e.g., CAD drawings in mechanical engineering or contact planes in electrical engineering. Especially due to semantic overlaps [21] that arise among these disparate models, inconsistencies are likely to occur and, hence, it is complex to handle this complexity and heterogeneity of the distinct model types [3]. Even standardized export formats such as the Extensible Markup Language (XML), which try to detach the abstract information from the model implementation and try to make the models tool independent, are not sufficient, as the tools and models are loosely coupled [15] and implementations differ, leading to compatibility issues [7].

2.2   Inconsistency Management Approaches

For the purpose of being able to address inconsistencies within the engineering process of aPS, the specification, diagnosis and handling of inconsistencies are essential steps [17]. In previous works [6], we identified three distinct approaches for inconsistency management – namely proof theory-based, rule-based and synchronization-based inconsistency management approaches. Our main findings indicate that, due to their flexibility, rule-based inconsistency management approaches are beneficial, as rules can be easily extended, adapted and configured according to company-, project- or stakeholder-specific needs.

Besides the means to specify, diagnose and handle inconsistencies, the incorporation of dependencies between the models – that is: model links – is another important requirement for inconsistency management. In the literature, a multitude of approaches, e.g. for model weaving [13] and model-merging [14], can be found. However, none of the approaches provides the appropriate means to interactively support stakeholders in verifying such links.

2.3   Visualization of Heterogeneous Models

Potentially, thousands of inconsistencies can be found in engineering models, so that a solely textual representation of diagnosed inconsistencies is not sufficient to adequately support the stakeholders. Additionally, in many cases, stakeholders in the aPS domain must be supported in better understanding the dependencies that lead to an inconsistency.

In information visualization, especially in graph visualization, many approaches are dealing with the representation of large amounts of information and their relationship and dependencies among each other. These approaches provide techniques and principles, not only to visualize the information, but also to navigate and modify it. *Focus and Context* [16] is one of the main principles to support the users in the recognition of relations and dependencies and in decisions making. It allows the user to focus on a special area of interest in a very detailed view, without losing the context of the information. The *Visual Information Seeking Mantra* [19] provides an approach of "overview first, zoom and filter, then details-on-demand" to get detailed information from a given visualization. Hence, visualization can be also an essential part of inconsistency management [7]. A first visualization approach is given in [2], where the requirement is stated that such an visualization approach has to be interactive and has to offer the possibility to change how information is visualized. It is noted in [2] that there is currently no such visual analytic tool available to system engineers. Although the approach is promising and provides first insights into visualization of model information, inter-model dependencies and inconsistencies, it does not provide the means of visualizing any input model type, since information is read in directly from the models. It is argued that by use of an abstraction mechanism, together with a hierarchy and filtering mechanism for complexity reduction, is flexible and extensible enough to visualize any kind of graph-structured information. An approach that aims at better describing the dependencies between engineering models is presented in [8]. Therein, templates are used to describe the relationships between models – however, visualization in the context of inconsistency management is not addressed by that approach.

2.4   Summary

As can be seen from the related work, a multitude of research works can be found in and around the field of inconsistency management in the aPS domain. However, to the best knowledge of the authors, there exists currently no approach that combines the distinct fields – namely model-based systems engineering, inconsistency management and visualisation – to a holistic approach that aids stakeholders in specifying, diagnosing and handling inter-model inconsistencies in a comprehensive and interactive manner.

3   Requirements

As a basis to develop an interactive visualization approach for the purpose of inconsistency management, a variety of requirements need to be fulfilled. These requirements mostly stem from a review of the related research, extended by our experiences gained throughout developing our inconsistency management framework as described in [7].

Requirement 1: Extensible and adaptable approach

Although a multitude of inconsistency management frameworks has been presented in the related literature [6], it is essential that such an approach is tailored to the specific application domain – i.e., the aPS domain. However, as the concrete model types to be investigated and the inconsistencies to be managed highly depend on the specific set-up – e.g., the respective company and its guidelines or the specific project – we argue that an inconsistency management approach must be *extensible and adaptable for company- and/or project-specific purposes*. Such an extensibility and adaptability can, e.g., be achieved by relying on standards and by providing reference implementations that are comprehensive to the respective domain experts. Besides, it is essential that, by means of configuration, tailoring to the specific set-up is enabled.

Requirement 2: Interactive approach

Inherently, inconsistency management is an interactive process. Mostly, critical inconsistencies stem from overlaps between engineering models – that is, from a set of distinct models being in conflict due to similar or redundant, but non-consistent information. If such an inter-model inconsistency is diagnosed automatically, stakeholders must decide, which handling action should be taken – e.g., to ignore, tolerate or resolve the inconsistency [17]. Whereas in some cases, inconsistency resolution proposals can be generated automatically, this is certainly not the normal case. Rather, stakeholders must negotiate with respective stakeholders from other disciplines to identify the cause for an inconsistency and to evaluate handling alternatives. In addition, if a respective handling action is performed, stakeholders must be supported in evaluating whether an appropriate result was achieved by the chosen handling alternative. Consequently, an *interactive inconsistency management approach* is essential for engineering in the aPS domain.

Requirement 3: Visual representation of dependencies

Especially in industrial settings, complexity is an essential issue to be addressed by inconsistency management. This complexity is the consequence of three essential reasons: First, this complexity results from the systems' complexity – models that are created during engineering of aPS often consist of thousands of entities. Second, the multitude of stakeholders from different domains with their individual mental models that are involved during engineering causes the introduction of a vast number of dependencies in between these domain. Third, and resulting from the first two reasons, the number of inconsistencies that are likely to occur is enormous. As a consequence, in order to address this enormous complexity, it is essential that stakeholders are supported visually. Therefore, we believe that a *visual representation of dependencies* between the different engineering models is a key requirement for engineering projects in the aPS domain.

Requirement 4: Comprehensive support in finding inconsistencies

Given an extensible (cf. Requirement 1) and interactive inconsistency management approach (cf. Requirement 2) as well as a visual representation of model
dependencies (cf. Requirement 3), the basis for an interactive inconsistency management approach in the aPS domain is laid. However, in order to support the
management – that is, the diagnosis and handling – of inconsistencies, it is
essential that stakeholders are supported in *finding relevant inconsistencies* in
the heterogeneous engineering model landscape. Thus, it is essential that the
interactive visualization approach is able to support engineers in determining,
which parts of the entire model landscape is interesting to them.

4   Concept

Based on the previously introduced requirements (cf. Sect. 3), this section introduces our conceptual interactive inconsistency management framework (see
Fig. 1). The *model management* part of the inconsistency management framework (cf. Sect. 4.1) is responsible for transforming models into a knowledge base.
Inconsistency *diagnosis and handling rules* are applied to diagnose and handle
inconsistencies (cf. Sect. 4.2). *Visualization rules* define and configure the interactive *visualization*, which is displayed to the user as a directed graph. This
rule-based concept for configuring the visualization to company-, project- or
stakeholder-specific needs is discussed in Sect. 4.3. By means of these rules, different levels of abstraction can be incorporated and displayed to support users
in finding the critical model aspects.

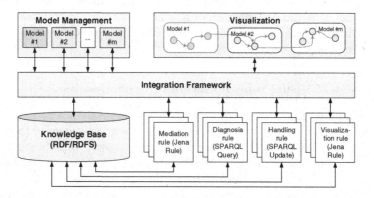

Fig. 1. Overview of the inconsistency management framework based on [7]

4.1   RDF(S) as Representational Formalism

As a basis for inconsistency management, it is essential to ensure a common representational formalism for all involved engineering models [7]. Within our inconsistency management framework, we, hence, make use of the Resource Description Framework (RDF). RDF is a highly flexible "framework for representing information in the Web" [25]. Knowledge is represented in form of RDF graphs, which are sets of triples, consisting of a *subject – predicate – object* statement. Especially as engineering models are, basically, a collection of such predicated statements (e.g., *sensor – is a – component*), such graphs are appropriate for capturing the knowledge modelled in the distinct engineering models. Hence, by means of RDF, a common representational formalism for the different engineering models is provided. More details on how RDF is applied for inconsistency management can be found in [7].

4.2   SPARQL for Diagnosing and Handling Inconsistencies

Given that such a common, representational formalism is available, respective concepts for diagnosing and handling inconsistencies can be put in place. In particular, we make use of the SPARQL Protocol and RDF Query Language (SPARQL). SPARQL defines a set of specifications that contain, among others, the set-based SPARQL Query Language [23] for querying against RDF graphs (i.e., for diagnosing inconsistencies) as well as the SPARQL Update Language [24] for manipulating RDF graphs (i.e., for handling inconsistencies). Especially as inconsistencies can mainly be regarded as patterns to be matched against the engineering models, we define each inconsistency type as a SPARQL pattern by means of a SPARQL query. Each pattern match found in the RDF graph is then a diagnosed inconsistency that is represented to the respective user. Analogously, any resolution rule that can be used to resolve the inconsistent pattern is represented through a SPARQL update action, which replaces the inconsistent pattern by a consistent one. More details on how SPARQL is applied for inconsistency management can be found in [7].

4.3   Rule-Based Interactive Graph Visualization to Support the Different Stakeholders in Diagnosing and Handling Inconsistencies

Although a multitude of different inconsistency diagnosis and handling rules can be specified by our inconsistency management framework, it is essential that stakeholders are supported in identifying the inconsistent parts of their models and in selecting the appropriate handling action to be taken. Especially as we use a graph-based representational formalism for the distinct engineering models, it is obvious that we use graph visualization technique for the respective stakeholders. Additionally, for an optimal stakeholder support, we envision a flexible visualization of the model and inconsistency information as well as the inter-model dependencies. In order to provide maximum flexibility and the possibility to visualize any model type, the visualization framework makes use of rules. By means of these rules, stakeholders can configure their specific visualizations on different levels of abstraction, thereby aggregating information and easing comprehensibility.

Additionally to providing the means to define and execute visualization rules, two essential concepts are necessary for visualization to the respective stakeholders: a *clustered graph structure* to allow for aggregating information and, hence, easing comprehensibility as well as a mechanism for finding the appropriate *hierarchical clusters* for visualization. These concepts are presented in the following.

Clustered Graph Structure. Given that all modelled information is present in RDF, the respective graph can be visualized. However, as especially industry models can contain thousands of entities, mechanisms to enhance comprehensibility are mandatory. Consequently, some sort of information filtering, aggregation and/or abstraction is required for our visualization approach. For various problems from the information visualization domain, the so-called *Overview and Detail* [4,19] paradigm is used. Following that, a top-level view is created (see Fig. 2(a)), consisting of a single vertex for each model instance (M#1 to M#6). If there is at least one link between an entity from one model instance and another entity from a distinct model instance, an edge in that top-level graph exists between the corresponding vertices. For the detailed view (see Fig. 2(b)), one or more model instances and, with that, their graph representations are

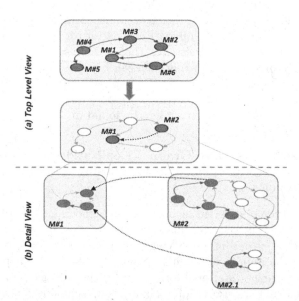

Fig. 2. Concept of an overview and detail visualization approach for an interactive inconsistency management framework

chosen from the top-level view and visualized in the detailed view. The vertices of each model instance are layouted inside a respective cluster, which get layouted on cluster level, similarly to the top-level graph. However, edges between clusters have vertices as endpoints inside those clusters. The clustering mechanism emerged as the best way of keeping the information of each model instance together, separated from other model instances. The graph of the detail view is layouted in two phases to suit the two level hierarchy, embodied by the clusters and their contained graphs. First, the coordinates of the clusters are computed. Second, for each cluster, the respective nodes are layouted. By that, a clustered graph structure is visualized to the stakeholder. Depending on what kind of level of detail is chosen, different hierarchy levels can be used to display the necessary information to the stakeholder.

Hierarchy Levels. By means of the clustered graph structure, different levels of detail can be displayed to the stakeholder. However, it is essential that stakeholders are supported in choosing for different levels of detail depending on their specific tasks. Therefore, an approach for finding and filtering according to different hierarchy levels is required. These hierarchy levels describe the different levels of aggregation and composition of the entities in the models.

In order to find these hierarchy levels, an algorithm was developed (see Fig. 3). As first step, the metamodel is analysed for aggregations and compositions for which hierarchical statements can be made. Solely from these and their related endpoints, a graph is created. For further steps, a hierarchy level has to be chosen, either by the user based on his specific task or by some heuristic, e.g. maximum path length of 2. Then, like for the metamodel, a graph is built for each model instance of the respective metamodel. All visited vertices up to there are contained in hierarchy levels up to the chosen depths. From this result in

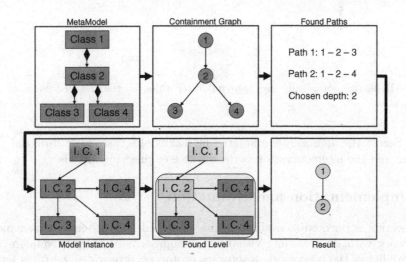

Fig. 3. Overview on the algorithmic steps for determining hierarchy levels

addition to the paths, a rule set is generated, which itself forms the visualized graph from the knowledge in the triple store.

Filtering. Independent from the used hierarchy level, filtering may be performed on the visualized information to reduce the complexity of the visualization. Based on the specific task of the user, only special, desired entities, relations and links may be chosen to be visualized. To achieve this, the configuration rules, which infer the necessary information for the visualization, are adapted by the user (see Fig. 4).

For the task of inconsistency management, the top level view represents the whole map of models, where each vertex represents a single model and each edge represents the links, respectively the information flows between the models. If there is an inconsistency between two models (M#1 and M#2), the edge between the representative vertices is marked. In Fig. 2(a) this is visualized by a dotted edge. The user is now able to select the vertices/models he wants to see on a detailed level. In this level, the graph representation of the chosen model instance and the inconsistencies between the single elements of the models are shown (see Fig. 2(b)).

Vertices and edges can have different colours to give additional information to the user (e.g. red for errors, orange for warnings or yellow for information). To reduce complexity the user is able to hide all vertices and edges, which are not involved in the inconsistency management task.

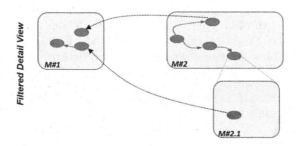

Fig. 4. Reducing complexity by applying filter rules in the detailed view of the visualization

In Sect. 5 the approach is evaluated by means of a case study from the aPS domain and the interconnection between three engineering models.

5   Implementation and Evaluation

This section is devoted to evaluating the presented inconsistency management framework with its according visualization approach. In order to validate the applicability of the framework, a software prototype is provided, which is introduced in Sect. 5.1. Subsequently, an inconsistency management case study is provided as an excerpt from [6] (see Sect. 5.2). Accordingly, the approach to diagnose and handle inconsistencies by means of RDF and SPARQL is discussed at the hand of this case study (see Sect. 5.3) and it is shown how the visualization approach supports stakeholders throughout this process (see Sect. 5.4).

It has to be noted that, within this publication, we do not aim at a full usability evaluation of our software prototype, but rather at a principle evaluation that shows the feasibility of our presented approach. A full evaluation together with experts from the aPS domain is subject to future work.

5.1 Software Prototype

As a basis to evaluate the proposed framework, a software prototype was implemented. Therein, the inconsistency management framework is designed as a Java-based Eclipse plugin. The Eclipse Modeling Framework (EMF) [5] is therein used as the main component, as it allows to specify metamodels and create model instances as well as to automatically generate texts from the models. The Apache Jena Framework, especially the included RDF triple store Fuseki [1], was used for RDF handling. The transformation between the EMF and RDF was implemented by means of the EMF Triple API [11]. Moreover, the visualization framework is implemented in C♯ as a Windows Presentation Foundation (WPF) application. The dotNetRDF API [22] serves as the RDF backend and access to the triple store on the Fuseki server. For the visualization and the graph drawing purposes, the WPF-based GraphX API [20] is used.

5.2 Inconsistency Management Case Study

A second basis for the purpose of evaluating the feasibility of our approach is an appropriate inconsistency management case study. We use an excerpt of a case study from the aPS domain, which was initially presented in [6].

Within our case study (see Fig. 5), three distinct model types are used: A *planning model*, which is used to evaluate different alternatives to realize the required engineering solution, a *SysML model*, which is intended to describe the logical system architecture, as well as a *MATLAB/Simulink model* to predict, whether the respective system architecture is capable of fulfilling the demanded properties. Although these three model types only represent a small excerpt of typical models in the aPS domain, we argue that they are representative for a multitude of potential engineering models.

As visualized in Fig. 5, the involved engineering models are overlapping, i.e., there exist links in between these different models. In particular, three link groups are specified within our case study, one for every combination of two model instances from the three models in the case study: Between the planning and the SysML models, so-called *refines* links are introduced to denote that modules in the planning model are refined by blocks in the SysML model. Accordingly, *equivalentTo* links are established to denote, e.g., that requirements in both planning and SysML models are equivalent to each other. In order to denote that the output of the MATLAB/Simulink is used to verify, whether certain properties in the planning model are fulfilled, *satisfies* links are introduced. We use these different link types in order to explicitly capture the dependencies between the different engineering models.

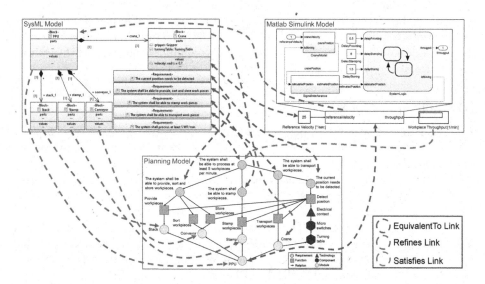

Fig. 5. Exemplary inconsistency management case study, excerpt from [6]

5.3   Evaluation of the Inconsistency Management Framework

In order to illustrate the feasibility of the presented concept for the purpose of diagnosing and handling inconsistencies, disparate types of inconsistencies were defined by means of the SPARQL query and update languages. Due to spatial restrictions, only an excerpt of these different inconsistency types can be illustrated in the following. In particular, we focus on a naming inconsistency in the following, which demands that, for each entity within our engineering models, an appropriate name in *UpperCamelCase* style is specified.

As can be seen from Fig. 6, an inconsistency diagnosis rule is specified by means of the SPARQL Query Language to check, whether all entities are named in *UpperCamelCase* style (Fig. 6a). Therein, the rule body includes three essential parts: First, the pattern identifies all named entities (`?x base:name ?xName`). Second, the entity's name `xName` is compared with a pre-defined regular expression that identifies, whether the name meets the *UpperCamelCase* style or not – the result of the comparison is bound to the variable `isInconsistent`, which denotes, whether an inconsistency occurs (`true`) or not (`false`). Third and finally, the original property is retrieved, which shall later be replaced by a custom name. An according inconsistency handling rule is specified by means of the SPARQL Update Language (Fig. 6b). Within the rule, placeholders are used to replace the name `xName` with the new name `customName`[1].

---

[1] For simplicity reasons, the new name is not checked for (in-)consistency.

Properties	
Property	Value
Name	Naming convention for all entities
Severity	Warning
Message Pattern	Entity x is not correctly named (name was $xName$, but should be named in UpperCamelCase style).
Rule Body	

```
prefix rdfs: <http://www.w3.org/2000/01/rdf-schema#>
prefix base: <http://example.org/base#>
SELECT * WHERE {
  ?x base:name ?xName .
  BIND (!regex(?xName, "^([A-Z]{1}[a-z]+)+$.")
    AS ?isInconsistent) .
  ?x ?oldname ?xName .
  ?oldname rdfs:label "origin" .
} ORDER BY DESC(?isInconsistent)
```

Properties	
Property	Value
Name	Replace name by custom name
Type	Solution
Message Pattern	Replace name of entity x (name was $xName$) by custom name.
Rule Body	

```
prefix rdfs: .<http://www.w3.org/2000/01/rdf-schema#>
prefix base: <http://example.org/base#>
DELETE {
  $x$ $oldName$ $xName$ .
}
INSERT {
  $x$ $oldName$ $customName$ .
}
WHERE { }
```

(a) Inconsistency diagnosis rule   (b) Inconsistency handling rule

Fig. 6. Inconsistency diagnosis and handling rules for resolving naming inconsistency

Additionally to the presented inconsistency diagnosis and handling rules, further rules can be introduced, e.g., to ensure that only the allowed entity types are linked to each other. Especially due to the expressiveness of RDF and SPARQL, we expect that a multitude of inconsistency types can be specified, diagnosed and handled through our approach.

5.4 Evaluation of the Visualization Approach

Although we argue that a multitude of different types of inconsistencies can be diagnosed and handled by our inconsistency management framework, there are certainly many cases in which a visualization is essential to supplement the process of inconsistency management. In these cases, stakeholders need to be supported for a better understanding of the relationships and dependencies. Consequently, using a pre-defined configuration of the visualization, both the hierarchy and the filtering concept are applied to the engineering models in the case study.

In particular, three distinct views are generated for the engineering models of the case study (see Fig. 7): one for a top-level overview on the model links (see Fig. 7a), one for a detail-level overview on the model links (see Fig. 7b) and one filtered view that only contains the linked model entities (see Fig. 7c). By means of switching between the different views, we argue that stakeholders get appropriate support in identifying the location and cause for specific inconsistency types.

Within the top-level visualization (see Fig. 7a), all three engineering model instances are represented through a single node. Edges between the distinct model nodes represent the aggregated links between the models. Accordingly, the user can interact with the visualization by selecting one or more models or links and, hence, the detailed graphs show the respective clusters. These clusters are connected by inter-model links, according to the chosen hierarchy and filter.

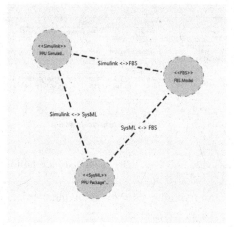

(a) Top-level visualization

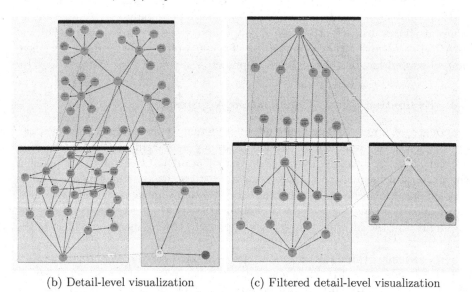

(b) Detail-level visualization   (c) Filtered detail-level visualization

Fig. 7. Visualization for the engineering models of the case study

Hierarchy Visualization. For each model, different hierarchy levels are chosen. For instance, for the MATLAB/Simulink model instance, it can be seen that all inner blocks of the simulated subsystem are not affecting the inconsistency management process. As a result, the rules are created in such a way that the whole simulated subsystem is contracted to a single node – only the input and output values of the simulation block are illustrated as their are interesting for inconsistency management. In contrast, the planning model instance is not abstracted and not contracted, because many entities on the most detailed abstraction level are directly affected by links to entities from other models.

For the third model, the SysML model, an abstraction level in between is chosen, as some of the entities within the model are interesting for the inconsistency management process. By means of color-coded inconsistencies (e.g., red for an error, orange for a warning and green for no error), stakeholders can be informed on the respective inconsistency status of their models.

Filtering. Additional to or instead of solely visualizing all elements of a certain hierarchy level, filtering may be applied. While the visualization result from above (cf. Fig. 7b) shows the structure of the model entities, the filtering provides the functionality to reduce the number of entities to a desired minimum. For instance, the entities of the same hierarchy level as above may be filtered for those, which could possibly be start or end point of a link (see Fig. 7c). Therein, only the requirements and modules for the planning model as well as the requirements and blocks of the same hierarchy level in SysML are visualized, while the MATLAB/Simulink model stays the same. Even though in Fig. 7c, many entities and their respective nodes are filtered out, the relationships among the remaining entities still gives an impression about the overall structure, e.g. the hierarchical requirement and module structure in the planning model instance as well as the structure of the physical parts in the SysML model instance are still contained. Despite the smaller amount of objects, which need to be grasped in the visualization, the amount of individually visualized inconsistencies is the same as without filtering.

6   Conclusion

This article introduces an interactive inconsistency management approach for engineering in the automated production systems (aPS) domain, which makes use of Semantic Web Technologies and combines the (semi-automatic) diagnosis and handling of inconsistencies with an interactive visualization approach. This interactive visualization approach allows stakeholders to pre-define views, which visualize the different engineering models on disparate, pre-defined levels of detail. The feasibility of the presented approach was illustrated at the hand of a lab-scale case study.

By means of the presented approach, we argue that a multitude of benefits can be achieved: For one, the visualization approach extends the already existing inconsistency management framework by comprehensive means to specify, diagnose and handle inconsistencies. Especially as views can be configured by means of pre-defined rules, any application of the framework is, basically, possible. Hence, stakeholders in the aPS domain are supported in identifying possibly erroneous parts in their engineering solution. The visualization of inter-model dependencies also supports the expansion of the stakeholders' individual mental models and leads to a common understanding of interfaces between and overlaps of the different models. This may also prevent inconsistencies in the future.

However, still a lot of research effort needs to be done. One essential step to be performed in future research works is an appropriate usability evaluation together with experts from the aPS domain. Using the experts' feedback, appropriate visualization views (and, consequently, rules) can be identified and defined. Further on, in order to apply the presented concept, knowledge and expertise in the Semantic Web Technologies domain is required as, e.g., inconsistency diagnosis and handling rules as well as visualization rules must be configured. We argue that, through appropriate abstraction mechanisms (e.g., modelling techniques), such rules can be automatically generated from pre-defined models. This will especially increase transparency of the approach and, hence, make the concept more attractive for industrial engineering applications.

References

1. Apache Jena: Fuseki: serving RDF data over HTTP (2016). https://jena.apache.org/documentation/serving_data/
2. Basole, R.C., Qamar, A., Park, H., Paredis, C.J.J., McGinnis, L.F.: Visual analytics for early-phase complex engineered system design support. IEEE Comput. Graph. Appl. **35**(2), 41–51 (2015)
3. Broy, M., Feilkas, M., Herrmannsdoerfer, M., Merenda, S., Ratiu, D.: Seamless model-based development: From isolated tools to integrated model engineering environments. Proc. IEEE **98**(4), 526–545 (2010)
4. Cockburn, A., Karlson, A., Bederson, B.B.: A review of overview+detail, zooming, and focus+context interfaces. ACM Comput. Surv. **41**(1), 2 (2009)
5. Eclipse Foundation: Eclipse Modeling Framework (2016). http://www.eclipse.org/modeling/emf/
6. Feldmann, S., Herzig, S.J.I., Kernschmidt, K., Wolfenstetter, T., Kammerl, D., Qamar, A., Lindemann, U., Krcmar, H., Paredis, C.J.J., Vogel-Heuser, B.: A comparison of inconsistency management approaches using a mechatronic manufacturing system design case study. In: IEEE International Conference on Automation Science and Engineering, Gothenburg, Sweden, pp. 158–165 (2015)
7. Feldmann, S., Herzig, S.J.I., Kernschmidt, K., Wolfenstetter, T., Kammerl, D., Qamar, A., Lindemann, U., Krcmar, H., Paredis, C.J.J., Vogel-Heuser, B.: Towards effective management of inconsistencies in model-based engineering of automated production systems. In: 15th IFAC Symposium on Information Control Problems in Manufacturing, Ottawa, Canada, pp. 916–923 (2015)
8. Friedl, M., Weingartner, L., Hehenberger, P., Scheidl, R.: Model dependency maps for transparent concurrent engineering processes. In: Proceedings of the 14th Mechatronics Forum International Conference, Mechatronics 2014, pp. 614–621 (2014)
9. Gausemeier, J., Giese, H., Schäfer, W., Axenath, B., Frank, U., Henkler, S., Pook, S., Tichy, M.: Towards the design of self-optimizing mechatronic systems: Consistency between domain-spanning and domain-specific models. In: ASME International Design Engineering Technical Conferences & Computers and Information in Engineering Conference, pp. 1141–1148 (2007)
10. Herzig, S., Qamar, A., Reichwein, A., Paredis, C.: A conceptual framework for consistency management in model-based systems engineering. In: ASME International Design Engineering Technical Conferences & Computers and Information in Engineering Conference, Washington, DC, USA, pp. 1329–1339 (2011)
11. Hillairet, G.: EMF Triple (2016). https://github.com/ghillairet/emftriple

12. International Council on Systems Engineering: Systems engineering vision 2020. Technical Report INCOSE-TP-2004-004-02 (2007). http://oldsite.incose.org/ProductsPubs/pdf/SEVision2020_20071003_v2_%03.pdf

13. Jossic, A., Fabro, M.D.D., Lerat, J., Bézivin, J., Jouault, F.: Model integration with model weaving: A case study in system architecture. In: 1st IEEE International Conference on Systems Engineering and Modeling, pp. 79–84 (2007)

14. Kolovos, D.S., Paige, R.F., Polack, F.A.C.: Merging models with the epsilon merging language (EML). In: Nierstrasz, O., Whittle, J., Harel, D., Reggio, G. (eds.) MODELS 2006. LNCS, vol. 4199, pp. 215–229. Springer, Heidelberg (2006). doi:10.1007/11880240_16

15. Kovalenko, O., Serral, E., Sabou, M., Ekaputra, F.J., Winkler, D., Biffl, S.: Automating cross-disciplinary defect detection in multi-disciplinary engineering environments. In: Janowicz, K., Schlobach, S., Lambrix, P., Hyvönen, E. (eds.) EKAW 2014. LNCS (LNAI), vol. 8876, pp. 238–249. Springer, Cham (2014). doi:10.1007/978-3-319-13704-9_19

16. Leung, Y.K., Apperley, M.D.: A review and taxonomy of distortion-oriented presentation techniques. ACM Trans. Comput. Hum. Interact. 1(2), 126–160 (1994)

17. Nuseibeh, B., Easterbrook, S., Russo, A.: Leveraging inconsistency in software development. IEEE Comput. 33(4), 24–29 (2000)

18. Schmidt, D.C.: Guest editor's introduction: Model-driven engineering. IEEE Comput. 39(2), 25–31 (2006)

19. Shneiderman, B.: The eyes have it: A task by data type taxonomy for information visualizations. In: IEEE Symposium on Visual Languages (1996)

20. Smirnov, A.: GraphX (2016). https://github.com/panthernet/GraphX

21. Spanoudakis, G., Zisman, A.: Inconsistency management in software engineering: Survey and open research issues. In: Handbook of Software Engineering & Knowledge Engineering: Fundamentals, vol. 1, pp. 329–380. World Scientific Publishing Co Pte. Ltd., Singapore (2001)

22. Vesse, R., Zettlemoyer, R., Ahmed, K., Moore, G., Pluskiewicz, T.: dotNetRDF (2016). http://dotnetrdf.org/

23. World Wide Web Consortium: SPARQL Protocol and RDF Query Language (SPARQL) 1.1 Query Language (2013). https://www.w3.org/TR/sparql11-query/

24. World Wide Web Consortium: SPARQL Protocol and RDF Query Language (SPARQL) 1.1 Update (2013). https://www.w3.org/TR/sparql11-update/

25. World Wide Web Consortium: Resource Description Framework (RDF) 1.1 Concepts and Abstract Syntax (2014). https://www.w3.org/TR/rdf11-concepts/

Development Environment of Embeddable Information-Visualization Methods

Takao Ito[1]([✉]) and Kazuo Misue[2]

[1] Department of Computer Science, University of Tsukuba,
Tennodai, Tsukuba, Ibaraki 305-8573, Japan
ito@vislab.cs.tsukuba.ac.jp
[2] Faculty of Engineering, Information and Systems,
University of Tsukuba, Tennodai, Tsukuba, Ibaraki 305-8573, Japan
misue@cs.tsukuba.ac.jp

Abstract. The development of information-visualization systems requires the design of visualization methods based on data and purposes. Visual tools are desirable solutions supporting the development of visualization programs. However, the applicability of the tools is limited. Therefore, we allowed the developers to embed visualization methods into visualization programs easily to increase the application field. We designed a visualization execution environment that includes the following features: (1) Independence of data formats and Graphics APIs used in target programs, (2) Embeddability of visualization methods into visualization programs, and (3) Low-cost implementation of interface functions. We showed that our execution environment had practical performance through two experiments. Then, using use cases, we showed that our environment could be used in the low-cost development of visualization systems. The design of our execution environment reinforced the practicability of visual tools that support the development of visualization programs.

Keywords: Visualization · Implementation

1 Introduction

Information visualization is used in various applications, such as searching, monitoring, and analyzing data. The demand to use information visualization increases according to the increase in data size. To utilize information visualization effectively, developers have to design appropriate visualization methods for target systems.

The number of appropriate visualization methods for a certain purpose or data is limited. Then, the effectiveness of a visualization method is difficult to determine before visualization results are observed, which requires implementation of visualization methods. Therefore, developers are required to have many trial-and-error attempts involving repeated implementation of these methods. As a countermeasure, visualization systems are often developed according to

© Springer International Publishing AG 2017
S. Yamamoto (Ed.): HIMI 2017, Part I, LNCS 10273, pp. 88–102, 2017.
DOI: 10.1007/978-3-319-58521-5_6

the following processes: developers implement many visualization methods on a prototype environment, and appropriate methods are implemented into a target program. However, we believe that the implementation costs would prevent the utilization of visualization.

This study aims to reduce the implementation costs of visualization methods to promote their utilization. We developed a visual tool to support implementation of visualization methods, because use of visual tools is one of good solutions to reduce the implementation costs [1,2]. We supported prototyping by building a development environment called Iv Studio (Fig. 1) with a data flow visual language (DVL) for information visualization [3]. However, we need to enhance the following for improving the practical applicability of Iv Studio.

(i) Embeddability of visualization methods into programs that require visualization features.
(ii) Extensibility of the DVL parts.

We assumed that visualization features are added to existing programs. To enable the addition of visualization features to existing programs, (i) is important. Then, various visualization methods are required in practical use, which makes (ii) also important. Our objective is to enable developers to embed easily the developed methods by Iv Studio into their programs even if parts of the DVL are extended.

We consider various data formats, description languages, and Graphics APIs because developers are assumed to add visualization features to existing programs. Developing runtime libraries that support all environments is ideal, but it is not realistic. Thus, we designed an embeddable visualization execution environment that includes the following features:

1. Independence of data formats and Graphics APIs used in target programs.
2. Executing visualization methods on the embeddable virtual machine of the script language.
3. Exporting developed visualization methods as source codes.
4. Low-cost implementation of interface functions.

This study provides an implementation guide for development environments of visualization methods not only for Iv Studio but also for other environments.

2   Target Environments

Visualization programs require features that include loading data and showing images. Additionally, receiving inputs from viewers is necessary to support interactive visualization. We aim to execute visualization methods developed by Iv Studio in the following environments:

– Programming language
  • C, Java, JavaScript, C#

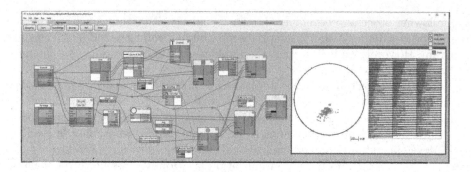

Fig. 1. Screen shot of Iv Studio.

- Data format
  - CSV, Spreadsheet, SQL, Original formats, on memory, etc.
- Graphics API
  - GDI, Processing, Java2D, Canvas, OpenGL, DirectX, etc.
- GUI system (GUI toolkit)
  - WIN32 API, Cocoa, X, Swing, Qt, etc.

3   Design of the Execution Environment

We want to support various environments considering Graphics APIs and GUI Systems. Developing runtime libraries that support all environments is ideal, but it is not realistic. Therefore, we designed an execution environment according to the following procedure:

1. Separating dependent parts from independent parts.
2. Choosing an execution environment of independent parts and adding an export feature to Iv Studio.
3. Designing interface functions between dependent and independent parts such that the implementation costs are reduced.

3.1   Separating Dependent Parts from Independent Parts

We investigated the support range of execution environments by considering the dependent/independent parts of visualization execution systems. Data formats, Graphics APIs, and GUI systems were considered. Visualization systems are formed similar to the information visualization reference model [4]. Therefore, based on the model, we considered parts that depend on Data formats, Graphics APIs, and GUI systems (Fig. 2).

Raw Data are just Data format; therefore, Data Transformations depend on Data formats. Rendering is the process of showing Views on displays, which is dependent on Graphics APIs. Considering interactive visualization, the process of receiving inputs from viewers depends on the GUI systems. Conversely, Visual

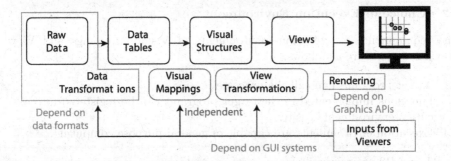

Fig. 2. Separation of dependent parts from independent parts.

Mappings and View Transformations are independent from the target programs because they are pure logical operations.

Based on the above consideration, we decided that Data Transformations, Rendering, and the process of receiving inputs from viewers are executed by the target programs. Then, Visual Mappings and View Transformations are executed by our designed execution environments. Figure 3 illustrates the execution image, which is realized as follows.

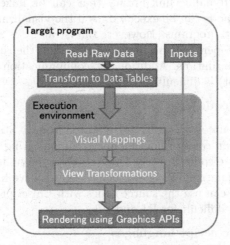

Fig. 3. Execution image of visualization.

- Choosing an execution environment.
- Developing a feature to export visualization methods to the execution environment.
- Designing interface functions that receive Data Tables and inputs from viewers and send graphics parameters to Rendering.

3.2   Choice of Execution Environment

The requirements of execution environments of Visual Mappings and View Transformations are as follows:

R1. Target programs can call the processes easily.
R2. Functions implemented in the target programs can be registered into execution environments easily.
R3. Execution environments are capable of general-purpose computing.

R1 and R2 are requirements for easy embedding of execution environments into target programs. R3 is a requirement for extensibility of the parts of the DVL. In this study, we aimed to extend the parts of the DVL by general-purpose programming languages, which would require general-purpose computing.

We considered three strategies to satisfy these requirements as follows.

[Use of virtual machines]

In this strategy, a runtime executed on JavaVM or .NET Frameworks is provided, and data and graphics parameters are communicated to target programs by sockets or interprocess communication. By exporting visualization methods from Iv Studio as a dynamic link library that can be linked to the runtime, the visualization methods can be executed, as if the visualization methods were embedded into target programs. However, this strategy is not enough to R1 and R2 because developers have to implement booting the runtime process and communicating to the runtime. Additionally, communication to web pages (the program in JavaScript) is difficult to implement.

[Exporting source codes in C]

In this strategy, source codes in C are exported from Iv Studio. This strategy reduces implementation costs of booting and communicating. Programs written in C can use the source codes directly. Programs written in Java or C# can use the source codes with native interfaces, such as Java Native Interface. Programs written in JavaScript can use the source codes with Emscripten[1]. However, this strategy also remains difficult for R1 and R2.

[Use of embeddable script languages]

In this strategy, embeddable script languages of which execution environments are provided as software libraries are used. Visualization methods can be used from various programs by exporting source codes in a script language from Iv Studio and executing the source codes. Embeddable script languages are well designed to communicate to target programs; therefore, calling and registering functions are easier than the strategy of exporting source codes in C.

---

[1] http://emscripten.org.

Based on the above consideration, we adopted the use of embeddable script languages. There are some embeddable script languages, such as Lua[2], Squirrel[3], AngelScript[4], and Xtal[5]. We adopted Lua because of its implementations in C, Java, .NET, and JavaScript. Accordingly, Lua was also adopted to the description language of the parts of the DVL.

3.3 Exporting Feature from Iv Studio

We developed a feature that exports source codes in Lua from Iv Studio to execute visualization methods on LuaVM, which is the execution environment of Lua. The processes of the parts of the DVL were described in Lua, and we enabled Iv Studio to generate source codes to call the processes according to a dataflow diagram. Then, we enabled Iv Studio to export a visualization method as a single Lua script file by integrating generated codes and codes of the parts of the DVL. Figure 4 illustrates the procedure of exporting source codes.

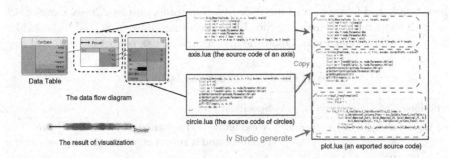

Fig. 4. Procedure in exporting source codes.

Iv Studio exports only source codes for Visual Mappings. For other processes, such as View Transformations and receiving inputs from viewers, a support library in Lua was provided.

Developers can execute visualization methods developed by Iv Studio on target programs by linking Lua libraries to the programs and executing exported script files and the support library. Additionally, in our environment, even if target programs are running, developers can update the visualization methods, which is highly advantageous in the development of visualization programs because it is assumed that fixing visualization methods is a repetitive process.

3.4 Design of Interface Functions

For easy embedding, the implementation costs of interface functions between target programs and LuaVM must be reduced. Therefore, we reduced the number

---

[2] https://www.lua.org/.
[3] http://squirrel-lang.org/.
[4] http://www.angelcode.com/angelscript/.
[5] https://code.google.com/archive/p/xtal-language/.

of essential functions requiring implementation. Additionally, we have shortened
the implementation of the functions.

The functions were designed as low-level commands to reduce the number of
functions. The implementation costs of each function were also reduced because
we designed the functions such that they could be implemented using only the
commands of most programming languages and Graphics APIs. Additionally,
the use of arrays for arguments and return values was avoided because sending
or receiving arrays required complex descriptions.

Table 1 shows the specifications of the functions to send Data Tables to
LuaVM. The functions are called from LuaVM. Practically, the functions
for reading files or HTTP connections are provided, such as ivs_OpenFile,
ivs_ReadLine, and ivs_Close. In Table 1, names that express their operations are
shown for explanation. Sending Data Tables to LuaVM is executed by implementing the functions in programming languages used in target programs and
registering them to LuaVM. The implementation of the functions is simple. For
example, in C, developers can implement reading CSV or TSV files by calling
fopen, fread, and fclose in ivs_OpenFile, ivs_ReadLine, and ivs_Close. Developers
can implement not only reading files but also connections to SQL databases, by
executing SQL queries in ivs_OpenFile and returning one record in ivs_ReadLine.

Table 1. Functions for sending Data Tables.

Functions	Specification
obj OpenTable(filename, format)	A file name and a format (CSV or TSV) are received, and a reference object is returned
string ReadRecord(obj)	A string that expresses one record in the format of CSV or TSV is returned
void CloseTable(obj)	A table expressed by an argument is closed

Table 2 shows the specifications of the essential draw functions that developers must implement and register. The upper four functions are for setting colors
or font sizes. The lower five functions are for drawing or painting figures. There
is a design choice where the upper four functions are integrated into the lower
five functions. A function to draw lines is DrawPath only. Therefore, if Draw-
Path receives the thickness and the color of lines, SetPenColor and SetPenWidth
are not necessary. However, to reduce the implementation costs of the optional
draw functions, which are described below, we chose a design where functions
for setting parameters are separated from the functions for drawing.

We provided the optional draw functions that developers do not always need
to implement and register. Table 3 shows the specifications of these functions.
The optional draw functions are higher-level functions than the functions in
Table 2, but they can be also implemented by using only the commands of most

Table 2. Essential draw functions.

Functions	Specification
void SetPenColor(r, g, b, a)	The color of lines is set
void SetPenWidth(w)	The thickness of lines is set
void SetBrushColor(r, g, b, a)	The color of filling is set
void SetFont(size)	The font size is set
void BeginPath(x, y)	A path is began
void MoveTo(x, y)	A point is added to a path
void DrawPath(isClose)	A polygon or lines are drawn with a path
void FillPath()	A polygon is filled with a path
void DrawText(x, y, text, angle, rx, ry)	A string is drawn on a specified position

Graphics APIs. If the optional draw functions are not registered, the support library executes them by breaking their operations down to the essential draw functions. However, this execution will cause deterioration in execution performance. Therefore, we provided choices that allow developers to select priority either implementation costs or execution performance.

Table 3. Optional draw functions.

Functions	Specification
void DrawLine(x1, y1, x2, y2)	A straight line is drawn
void DrawRect(x, y, w, h)	A rectangle is drawn
void FillRect(x, y, w, h)	A rectangle is filled
void DrawEllipse(x, y, w, h)	A ellipse is drawn
void FillEllipse(x, y, w, h)	A ellipse is filled
void DrawWedge(x, y, iRad, oRad, startAngle, sweepAngle)	A wedge is drawn
void FillWedge(x, y, iRad, oRad, startAngle, sweepAngle)	A wedge is filled

Table 4 shows the functions for interactive visualization. Developers call the functions from target programs. All functions receive the position of a pointer, the operation amount of the mouse wheel, and the information of down buttons. Then, they return True if some operations are done in the functions. Developers can execute interactive visualization in a target program by calling it when input events occur. This design of the functions can be used in touch panel systems.

Table 4. Functions of receiving inputs from viewers.

Function	Timing of calling
boolean OnMouseDown(x, y, wheel, button)	When a mouse down event occurs
boolean OnMouseMove(x, y, wheel, button)	When a pointer moved event occurs
boolean OnMouseUp(x, y, wheel, button)	When a mouse up event occurs
boolean OnMouseWheel(x, y, wheel, button)	When a mouse wheel control event occur

4   Performance Evaluation

Visualization is executed on LuaVM in our environment. Although Lua has relatively higher performance among script languages, the performance is lower than native codes. To confirm whether our environment has enough performance to treat visualization, we conducted evaluations of the execution performance.

First, we evaluated the performance of about four visualizations shown in Fig. 5. Figure 5(a) is a bar chart, Fig. 5(b) is a bar chart of sorted data, Fig. 5(c) is a scatter plot, and Fig. 5(d) is a node-link diagram using a force-directed algorithm [5]. The size of data is shown in Table 5. We evaluated the performance on C(C++) and JavaScript. On C(C++), LuaJIT[6] was used. LuaJIT is a library that has Just-In-Time Compiler for Lua. On JavaScript, lua.vm.js[7], a library that is made by compiling an original Lua library with Emscripten, was used. JavaScript was run on Electron 1.4.1[8]. A PC with Windows 10 and Intel Core i7-6700K was used. We measured the execution time of Visual Mappings exported from Iv Studio.

Table 5 shows the results of the first evaluation. The time unit used is millisecond, and each result is an average of 100 executions. Note that (d) shows the time of executing a single iteration in the layout algorithm.

If visualization is executed in more than 30 fps (frames per second), we can conclude that the environment has enough performance for interactive visualization. However, this evaluation does not include the time for rendering. The execution of Rendering often takes longer time than Visual Mappings empirically. Considering this finding, we concluded that our environment had enough performance when the measured time is less than 10 ms.

As a result, on C(C++), all visualizations were executed in less than 3 ms. Our environment fast treated (d), which visualized large data. We believe that this is the effect of the optimization of JIT compiler in LuaJIT. On JavaScript, (a), (b), and (c) were executed with enough performance, while (d) took a long time. We need to optimize the exported source codes from Iv Studio.

---

[6] http://luajit.org/.

[7] https://daurnimator.github.io/lua.vm.js/lua.vm.js.html.

[8] http://electron.atom.io/.

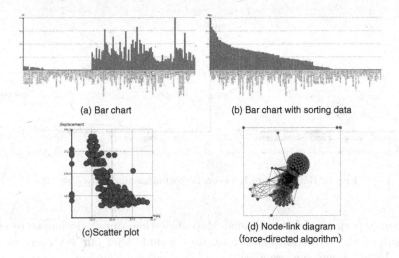

(a) Bar chart

(b) Bar chart with sorting data

(c)Scatter plot

(d) Node-link diagram
(force-directed algorithm)

Fig. 5. Visualization used in the first evaluation.

Table 5. Performance evaluation (time unit: millisecond).

Visualization	Size of data	C(LuaJIT)	JavaScript(lua.vm.js)
Fig. 5(a)	123 records	0.87	5.19
Fig. 5(b)	123 records	0.83	5.52
Fig. 5(c)	406 records	1.43	8.53
Fig. 5(d)	123 nodes 4094 edges	2.96	70.13

Second, we conducted an evaluation on the number of records that could be treated by our environment. We measured the execution time of the visualization of two-dimensional data with scatter plots. LuaJIT and lua.vm.js were also used. The size of data records increased by 500 from 500 to 50000, and we measured an average time of 100 executions in each the number of records.

Figure 6 illustrates the results of the second evaluation. In this figure, the X-axis illustrates the number of records, and Y-axis illustrates the average time of 100 executions. Figure 6(a) and (b) shows the same data, but their scales are different for explanation. On lua.vm.js, our environment crashed because of lack of memory, and we could not measure the performance. Therefore, only the results until 22500 records are shown.

For the result of LuaJIT, suppose that in interactive visualization, we focus on the number of records that visualized about 10 ms. The time taken to visualize 9000 records was 10.11 ms. Suppose that in static visualization, our environment can be used for visualizing large data because 50000 records were visualized with 53.50 ms. Recent information visualization treats more than a million records and several tens of dimensions of Raw Data. This visualization often reduces the data size by using filtering, dimension reduction, or clustering. However, the

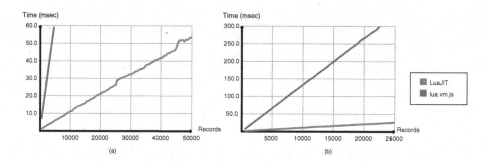

Fig. 6. Relationship between performance and data size.

reduction is performed before Visual Mappings, then our environment receives the result of the reduction. Therefore, we conclude that our environment has practical and enough performance.

For the result of lua.vm.js, suppose that in interactive visualization, the visualization of 1000 records took 12.99 ms. If interactive visualization is used on web pages, it is difficult to visualize more than 1000 records. However, the commonly used scenes of visualization on web pages are presentations. In this visualization, small size data, for example, several tens of records are often visualized. We conclude that our environment has enough performance for commonly used scenes on web pages. Suppose other implementations exist in static visualization. For example, to avoid JavaScript on clients, an SVG of a visualization result is generated on a server. Our environment has high flexibility for implementations; therefore, we conclude that executing large data in JavaScript is not needed always.

5   Use Cases

In this section, two systems are shown using Iv Studio and our environment. Although each system was developed by the first author, it had been developed before the addition of visualization features. Therefore, the use cases shown in this section are examples that have visualization features added to existing systems.

5.1   The Web Site

The first use case is a management web page of digital contents managed by the first author. The first author was motivated to add a feature to observe the overview of the downloads and time trends. Then, using Iv Studio, a feature visualizing the overview of trends was added (Fig. 7).

First, a feature that exported lists of downloads and contents as CSV from SQL database was added into a program on the server side. Next, a visualization of the CSV was developed by Iv Studio. In the visualization, a ChronoView [6]

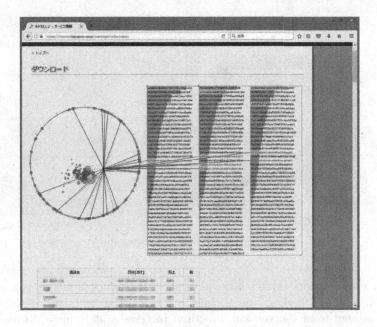

Fig. 7. A web page added a visualization feature. (Color figure online)

was shown in the left side to show the overview of the download time, and a matrix to show contents' names and bars representing the number of downloads was shown on the right side. Then, when marks were selected by viewers, the ChronoView and the matrix were connected by blue lines, and blue circles on the circumference of the ChronoView and marks of the ChronoView were also connected by gray lines. After the development of the visualization, source codes in Lua were exported. Finally, the codes were executed on the web page.

The first author had knowledge on JavaScript and Canvas, but no development experience with them. Therefore, we conclude that implementing this visualization on web pages using only JavaScript took more time than using Iv Studio.

5.2 Test Program of the Developing Device

The second use case is a test program for a pose capture device developed by the first author. The device is a doll equipped with multiple 3D accelerometers and 3D magnetic sensors. The program reads acceleration and magnetism data from the device, computes poses, and renders a posed 3D character model. While in development, errors of computing poses from magnetism were found. To analyze the errors, a visualization feature was added (Fig. 8).

This program was written in C++, and it was built on the original GUI toolkit with the original Graphics APIs. By implementing the draw functions with the GUI toolkit, the visualization feature was added in about 30 min.

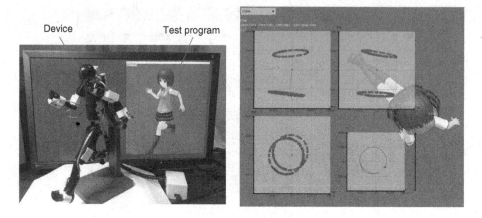

Fig. 8. Device and the test program.

In the visualization, three scatter plots show the values of magnetism on the X-Y, Y-Z, and X-Z planes, and a chart at the bottom right shows values of magnetism seen from the vertical direction. In these scatter plots, the vertical directions obtained from 3D accelerometers are also shown by orange lines. After the design of the visualization, the source codes in Lua were exported. Then, the codes were executed in the test program. To compare a result of the visualization with a pose, the visualization was semi-transparently shown overlapping the 3D character model. The semi-transparent display was realized by drawing the result of the visualization with the same Graphics APIs as the target program.

While developing the visualization, the transparency and color of the charts were tuned frequently as the results of the visualization were confirmed on the test program. Our environment allows the developer to tune the parameters while executing the program, resulting in efficient tuning of the parameters.

6   Related Work

Textual programing languages are widely used to develop programs not only for visualization. There are some toolkits to support the development of visualization programs with textual programing languages, such as Prefuse [7], Protovis [8], and D3 [9]. Alternatively, some researchers provided design patterns [10,11] to support building visualization programs. The methodology to build visualization system and data structure for visualization was proposed.

There are other information-visualization development tools, e.g. FLINA [12], Snap-Together Visualization [13], Lyra [1], iVis Designer [2], and GeoVISTA Studio [14]. Visualization methods developed with some of these tools can be used from external programs. For example, visualization methods developed with Lyra or iVis Designer can be used on web pages. GeoVISTA Studio can export Java components.

The major difference from the above research is that we focus on execution environments for embedding visualization methods into existing programs. Toolkits can be used only if they support the environments of the target programs. In other words, the use scene of toolkits is limited. The design patterns show us important guides. However, there is a difference that we focused on more practical problem, for example, the choice of execution environments considering programing languages and Graphics APIs. Although some existing visual tools provide execution environments for external programs, they have not achieved the level defined in Sect. 2, such as independence from Graphics APIs and GUI systems.

7 Conclusion

In this study, we designed an execution environment that could be embedded into various program environments easily. Then, the use scenes of visual tools were expanded. We separated the independent parts from visualization systems, adopted the embeddable script language to execution environments of independent parts, and designed interface functions such that implementation costs of embedding were reduced. Then, an exporting feature of source codes in the embeddable script language was added to Iv Studio, which is a visual tool for information visualization. We showed that our environment had enough performance for practical use. Additionally, using use cases, our environment could be used in the development of visualization systems with low costs.

The design of the execution environment is an implementation guide for visual tools for visualization development. Visual tools are one of good solutions to support the development of visualization systems. We conclude that the design reinforces the practicability of the visual tools for development of visualization.

References

1. Satyanarayan, A., Heer, J.: Lyra: an interactive visualization design environment. Comput. Graph. Forum (Proc. EuroVis) **33**(3), 351–360 (2014)
2. Ren, D., Hollerer, T., Yuan, X.: iVisDesigner: expressive interactive design of information visualizations. IEEE Trans. Visual Comput. Graphics **20**(12), 2092–2101 (2014)
3. Ito, T., Misue, K.: A development environment using a visual dataow language for multidimensional data visualization methods. IPSJ J. **57**(7), 1638–1651 (2016). (in Japanese)
4. Card, S.K., Mackinlay, J.D., Shneiderman, B. (eds.): Readings in Information Visualization: Using Vision to Think. Morgan Kaufmann Publishers Inc., San Francisco (1999)
5. Eades, P.: A heuristic for graph drawing. In: Congressus Numerantium, vol. 42, pp. 149–160 (1984)
6. Shiroi, S., Misue, K., Tanaka, J.: ChronoView: visualization technique for many temporal data. In: Proceedings of the 2012 16th International Conference on Information Visualisation, IV 2012, pp. 112–117 (2012)

7. Heer, J., Card, S.K., Landay, J.A.: Prefuse: a toolkit for interactive information visualization. In: Proceedings of the SIGCHI Conference on Human Factors in Computing Systems, CHI 2005, pp. 421–430 (2005)
8. Bostock, M., Heer, J.: Protovis: a graphical toolkit for visualization. IEEE Trans. Visual Comput. Graphics 15(6), 1121–1128 (2009)
9. Bostock, M., Ogievetsky, V., Heer, J.: D3 Data-driven documents. IEEE Trans. Visual Comput. Graphics 17(12), 2301–2309 (2011)
10. Heer, J., Agrawala, M.: Software design patterns for information visualization. IEEE Trans. Visual Comput. Graphics 12(5), 853–860 (2006)
11. Giereth, M., Ertl, T.: Design patterns for rapid visualization prototyping. In: Proceedings of the 2008 12th International Conference Information Visualisation, IV 2008, pp. 569–574 (2008)
12. Claessen, J.H.T., van Wijk, J.J.: Flexible linked axes for multivariate data visualization. IEEE Trans. Visual Comput. Graphics 17(12), 2310–2316 (2011)
13. North, C., Shneiderman, B.: Snap-together visualization: a user interface for coordinating visualizations via relational schemata. In: Proceedings of the Working Conference on Advanced Visual Interfaces, AVI 2000, pp. 128–135 (2000)
14. Takatsuka, M., Gahegan, M.: GeoVISTA studio: a codeless visual programming environment for geoscientific data analysis and visualization. Comput. Geosci. 28, 1131–1144 (2002)

Analysis of Location Information Gathered Through Residents' Smartphones Toward Visualization of Communication in Local Community

Koya Kimura[1]([✉]), Yurika Shiozu[2], Ivan Tanev[1], and Katsunori Shimohara[1]

[1] Graduate School of Science and Engineering, Doshisha University, Kyoto, Japan
{kimura2013,itanev,kshimoha}@sil.doshisha.ac.jp
[2] Faculty of Economics, Aichi University, Nagoya, Japan
yshiozu@vega.aichi-u.ac.jp

Abstract. This research aims to achieve the resident-centered community design by utilizing information and communication technology (ICT), and to create a trigger to regain rich relationship within a community by visualizing media spots which is defined as places where residents communicate much more than the other areas. In order to improve the media spot estimation method proposed by the previous research, we extracted and analyzed location information under various conditions. As a result, we could confirm that a portion of the highest density of location information corresponds to a resident's home place, and found that a home place can be accurately derived irrespective of the scattering in accuracy. Also, the analysis on how the distribution of location information varies depending on time zone suggests that it is necessary to use location information which is minutely divided in time or aggregated every day of the week.

1 Introduction

The structure of local communities in Japan has needed to change after the Tohoku Earthquake. Japan is the first country to have a super-aging society, first noted in 2007. According to the latest Annual Health, Labor and Welfare Report, on the other hand, the connections has been weak among members of the communities, but the number of people who want to help in the community has increased [2]. That is, local communities need to be vitalized for the regaining relationships.

This type of social situation has prompted the development of several approaches from the computer science field. For example, the Strategy Proposal of 2012, the Japan Science and Technology Agency includes the person-watching system for the elderly and smart city system are examples of these approaches [3]. Despite the need for these approaches in many communities, most communities cannot use them casually.

© Springer International Publishing AG 2017
S. Yamamoto (Ed.): HIMI 2017, Part I, LNCS 10273, pp. 103–111, 2017.
DOI: 10.1007/978-3-319-58521-5_7

The research on "constructing" the system has been successful, but that on its "usage" is in the developing stage. Moreover, the introduction of the system does not always guarantee local activation, which always depends on the locals who will notice their problems and act to solve them. If residents can be aware of their invisible relationship that they are usually unconscious, and if they understand its importance, they could vitalize their community through sustaining and promoting it? That is the concept of resident-centered vitalization of local communities.

This research aims to achieve the resident-centered community design by utilizing information and communication technology (ICT). We defined "media spots" as places where residents communicate much more than the other areas. As a place for creating and strengthening relationships, we visualize media spot and create an opportunity to regain relationship within the community. In this research, we have been considering a method of estimating media spots using location information acquired by smartphones. In this paper, in order to improve the media spot estimation method of the previous research [1], we extracted and analyzed location information under various conditions.

2   Resident-Centered Vitalization of the Local Community

Ushino's research (1982) on local resident-based regional development has explained the importance of such concept and proposed a system called "Kande System" [4]. Ushino has said that after the industrialization and urbanization in the 1950s, the village communities in the rural areas are divided by the agricultural policy and then re-integrated in the 1970s to create a new regional system. The importance of local resident-based regional development has already been a significant research topic since the 1980s.

Meanwhile, Yoshizumi's case study (2013) has analyzed the way for locals to develop regions sustainably and suggested the "Eco Card System" [5]. In this system, the locals are given a stamp card called "Eco Card" that promotes environmental activities, thereby creating a setup for the locals to be involved in the region. This system highlights the importance of visualizing or making the locals notice the problems for them to manage local resident-based regional development.

According to the introduction of ICT technology, it is temporarily possible to solve challenges of a local community. However, to vitalize a local community continuously, residents should solve challenges of a local community positively. To solve challenges of a local community themselves, residents needs to be conscious of them. "Resident-centered" means that "residents solve challenges of a local community themselves." In this research, we are aiming to establish a methodology that enables them by visualization.

3   Experiment Method

3.1   Overview of Field Experiment

We acquired residents' activity data with smartphones lent to them in the Makishima area in Uji City, Kyoto, Japan, in cooperation with members of the non-profit corporation Makishima Kizuna-no-Kai. Activity data means "location information," "send and receive emails," "telephones reception and transmission" and "passing-each-other data from Bluetooth [6]." In this paper, we analyzed "location information" to improve the media spot estimation method.

3.2   Experimental Area and Cooperators' Attribute

This field experiment has been conducted in the Makishima area in Uji City, Kyoto, Japan.

Uji City is located in the south of Kyoto on the south side of Kyoto City. The population of Uji City as of April 1, 2016, is about 190,000 and 15,000 (about 8%) of them live in Makishima area. Uji City has attracted lots of attention as a residential area near Kyoto, Osaka, and Kobe since the early 1960's. As a result, residential land was developed in Uji City and the population remarkably increased. Makshima area is one of the development areas in Uji City, and there is a densely-populated area such as a housing complex. Blocks of the development area in the early 1960's are aging, but population of the whole Makishima area is slightly increasing.

The experimental cooperators live in Makishima area. They are members of the non-profit corporation Makishima Kizuna-no-Kai. Table 1 shows the attributes of the experimental cooperators. A lot of experimental cooperators are over 65 years old. The reason is that people who retired at mandatory age mainly join the regional development.

Table 1. Attributes of field experiment

Area	Makishima, Uji, Kyoto, Japan
Cooperators	20 to 50
Age	30 to 70yo

Table 2 shows the periods of the field experiment. We instructed the experimental cooperators to use the lent smartphone at all times for the duration of the experiment. The location information was acquired every minute, except for the following situations:

- From the perspective of informed consent, we instructed that the experimental cooperators can switch off the smartphone when he/she does not want to inform his/her location information.

Table 2. Periods of field experiment

1st. period	Nov. 11, 2013 to Dec. 10, 2013
2nd. period	Feb. 11, 2015 to Mar. 27, 2015
3rd. period	Jul. 11, 2015 to Jan. 11, 2016

- The smartphone has run out of battery/the experiment cooperator forgets to carry the smartphone.
- The smartphone cannot transmit location information as it is out of range.
- The timing when the Android finishes to acquire location information is not determined exactly.

3.3 Experimental Installation

Table 3 shows the specification of smartphones that are used in the field experiment.

Smartphones used in the first period (the right side of Fig. 1) were discredited mostly due to sluggish actions and small screen. Accordingly, we lent them stylus pens for the improvement of usability. This way partly resolves that discredit.

Following the suggestion of the first period, smartphones using the second and third period (the left side of Fig. 1) was chosen as quick action and big screen. Some of the experimental cooperators have his/her smartphone due to the spread of smartphones compared to the first period. That discredit is significantly resolved by these external factors also.

Fig. 1. Smartphones

Table 3. Specification of smartphones

	First period	Second and third period
Manufacture	Fujitsu	ASUS
Model number	ARROWS Kiss F-03E	ZenFone 5 A500KL
OS	Android 4.0.4	Android 4.4.2
Network career	NTT docomo	IIJ Mobile (MVNO of NTT docomo)
CPU	Qualcomm snapdragon S4 MSM8960	Qualcomm sapdragon 400 MSM8926
Clock frequency	1.5 GHz	1.2 GHz
Core	Dual Core	Quad Core
RAM	1 GB	2 GB
Location information	GPS	GPS and GLONASS
Bluetooth	4	4
Sensor	G-Sensor	G-Sensor/E-Compass/Proximity light/hall sensor

3.4 Inspection Method

We used KDE, a nonparametric technique to estimate probability density function. It is not necessary to set a boundary. The estimated kernel probability density function is expressed as follows.

$$\widehat{f}_h(x) = \frac{1}{Nh} \sum_{i=1}^{N} K\left(\frac{x - x_i}{h}\right) \tag{1}$$

$K(x)$ is a kernel function and h is a bandwidth. We used (2) Gaussian kernel for a kernel function.

$$K(x) = \frac{1}{\sqrt{2\pi}} e^{-\frac{1}{2}x^2} \tag{2}$$

In addition, we applied Scott's Rule expressed in (3) to the bandwidth.

$$h = \frac{1.06\sigma}{n^{0.2}} \tag{3}$$

$$\sigma = min\left\{ S.D., \frac{q(0.75) - q(0.25)}{1.34} \right\} \tag{4}$$

where n is the number of dimensions, $S.D.$ is standard deviation, and $q(0.75) - q(0.25)$ is four-quantiles acquired by subtracting first four-quantiles from third four-quantiles.

3.5 Estimation Method of Media Spot

The two-dimensional (2D) location information (the point showing a position) consisted of latitude and longitude that recorded a person's action at a specific time. The point that showed many positions at the spot where the person stayed in will be plotted, and then density would become higher. The part that is high in density appears as the maximum value. Subsequently, we derived the probability density function of this location information using KDE and then estimated the place where each person was usually found by counting the number of maximum value locations. The inspection of the hypothesis followed. A media spot was defined as the place where communication is active in an area. "Active communication" refers to the place where many residents gather in an area.

In the previous research, the media spot estimation method entailed the following steps:

- Find the local maximums using KDE from each person's location information.
- The local maximums show places who was usually found as it shows density of location information.
- Delete location information around the global maximums, which are expected main activity places such as the home and workplace.
- Collect the dataset with deleted information on the home and workplace.
- Apply KDE to the collected dataset and then find the local maximums as media spots.

In this paper, we analyzed the following points toward improving media spot estimation algorithm.

- Does a portion of the highest density of position information match the home?
- How the distribution of location information changes with the time zone?

We also used Numpy and Scipy, which are libraries for high-level scientific calculations of Python for the inspection.

4 Results of the Analysis and Discussion

First of all, we verified whether a portion of the highest density of location information and the home place match. As a result of the verification, a portion of the highest density of location information matched the home place. We used the Google Maps API when converting your home address to latitude and longitude, but the phenomenon that latitude and longitude got out of position when a specific address was entered. This phenomenon proceeded from Japanese address notation.

Table 4 shows a descriptive statistics value of accuracy for each experimental cooperator. From this table, the scattering in the accuracy of location information could be found, but irrespective of this scattering, a portion of the high density of location information matched the home place. In other words, it can

Table 4. A descriptive statistics value of accuracy (sampling data)

User id	1	2	3
The total number of location information having accuracy	118693	142574	54907
Mean	478.58	78.56	30.85
Standard deviation	631.41	213.01	13.06
Minimum	3.9	3.9	3.9
25 percentiles	25	36	20
50 percentiles	33	37.5	29
75 percentiles	1170	40.5	42
Maximum	1994	4747	248

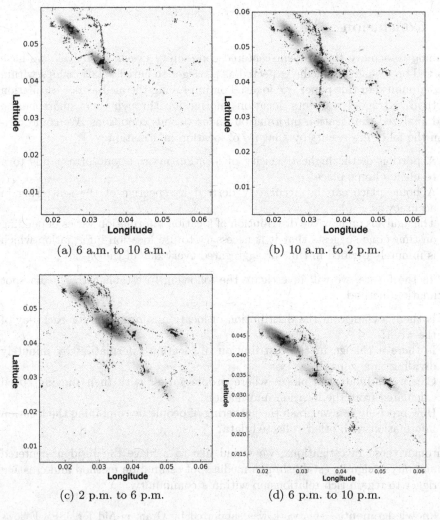

(a) 6 a.m. to 10 a.m.

(b) 10 a.m. to 2 p.m.

(c) 2 p.m. to 6 p.m.

(d) 6 p.m. to 10 p.m.

Fig. 2. The change in the distribution of location information in the time zone of an experimental cooperator

be said that it is more accurate than using APIs to derive the home place by the kernel density estimation method using location information.

Next, we verified how the distribution of location information varied depending on the time zone. Distribution of location information was drawn separately in 4 time zones (6 a.m. to 10 a.m., 10 a.m. to 2 p.m., 2 p.m. to 6 p.m., 6 p.m. to 10 p.m.) Fig. 2 shows the change in the distribution of location information in the time zone of an experimental cooperator. A green triangle indicates a home place, and a red circle indicates a portion of the highest density of position information. From this figure, the position of the density shifted only during the day (from home to workplace), and no notable change in the distribution was observed. This result suggests that it is necessary to analyze by using location information which minutely divides time or aggregates every day of the week.

5   Conclusion

Aiming to achieve the resident-centered community design with ICT, we have worked on visualizing media expected as a trigger to enrich relationships within a community. In this paper, we focused on improving the media spot estimation method, extracted residents' location information through their smartphones, and analyzed the location information under various conditions. We could confirm the following results by analysis of location information.

- A portion of the highest density of location information corresponds to a resident's home place.
- A home place can be accurately derived irrespective of the scattering in accuracy.
- The analysis on how the distribution of location information varies depending on time zone suggests that it is necessary to use location information which is minutely divided in time or aggregated every day of the week.

In the future, we will investigate the following to establish the media spot estimation method.

- Is there a change in the distribution of location information for each day of the week?
- Is there a change in the distribution of location information by minutely dividing time zones?
- Can we estimate the places where people gather with their moving speed calculated from the location information?
- How precisely can we grasp the gathering of people by combining the location information with other collected data?

Through these investigations, we would like to achieve the resident-centered community design by establishing a media spot estimation method and creating a trigger to regain rich relationship within a community.

Acknowledgements. This work was supported by Grant-in-Aid for JSPS Fellows Grant Number 16J03602.

References

1. Kimura, K., Shiozu, Y., Tanev, I., Shimohara, K.: A leader and media spot estimation method using location information. In: Yamamoto, S. (ed.) HIMI 2016. LNCS, vol. 9735, pp. 550–559. Springer, Cham (2016). doi:10.1007/978-3-319-40397-7_53
2. Ministry of Health, Labour and Welfare: Annual Health, Labour and Welfare Report 2013-2014 (2014)
3. Japan Science and Technology Agency: Research and development on fundamental technologies of cyber physical systems and their social implementation. A case study on promoting aged people to social activities, CDS-FY2012-SP-05 (2013)
4. Ushino, T.: Comprehensive district plan by inhabitants and "Kande" system. J. Rural Plann. Assoc. 1(3), 19–29 (1982)
5. Yoshizumi, M.: A study on actively community-based environmental town planning toward sustainable communities: a case study on the eco-community program in Nishinomiya, Hyogo, Japan. J. City Plann. Inst. Japan 48(3), 831–836 (2013) .
6. Kimura, K., Shiozu, Y., Tanev, I., Shimohara, K.: Visualization of relationship between residents using passing-each-other data toward resident-centered vitalization of local community. In: Proceedings of the Second International Conference on Electronics and Software Science (ICESS), pp. 122–127 (2016)

Making Social Media Activity Analytics Intelligible for Oneself and for Others: A "Boundary Object" Approach to Dashboard Design

François Lambotte[✉]

Université Catholique de Louvain, Mons, Belgium
Francois.lambotte@uclouvain.be

Abstract. Created in 2013, our laboratory works on the intelligibility of the activity of social media for others (e.a community animators) and for oneself (e.a member of the community) in a professional context. To bridge the gap between existing measures of activity, visualization of data and intelligibility of activity, we have set up a multidisciplinary team at the crossroads of these various players and knowledge. The goals of this team are to develop intelligible measures of the activity grouped together in a dashboard and to evaluate their contribution to the community's dynamics. Inspired by the work of Star and Griesemer [16] on boundary objects and standardized methods, this paper aims to explain how we create, adapt and negotiate the current development of our dashboard's prototype - conceived as a boundary object - sufficiently "robust" to achieve common objectives and "plastic enough" to meet the diverse interests of the different actors involved in the project.

Keywords: Intelligibility · Boundary object · Dashboard · Social media · Analytics

1 Introduction

Created in 2013, our lab focuses on **social media use in professional context**. What we consider as professional use of social media includes corporate social networking, knowledge sharing, social TV broadcasting, crowdsourcing platforms and to a certain extent corporate and professional usage of massive social media (Facebook, Twitter, etc.). In this applied-research project, we work specifically on **the intelligibility of social media activity** for community animators (others) and community members (oneself). There are different reasons that push us in this research direction.

The growing use of social media in professional context is generating an exponential amount of data. As Cardon and Marshall [8] research on corporate social networking illustrates: "*social networking will become the primary communication tool for teams. Based on our survey results combined with results from industry surveys (i.e., AON Consulting, 2009; Azua, 2010; Bughin et al., 2009; Kiett, 2011), we believe that adoption of enterprise SNPs is in the beginning of the early majority stage according to Rogers' (1962) model of innovation adoption.*" Although it is necessary to understand the

© Springer International Publishing AG 2017
S. Yamamoto (Ed.): HIMI 2017, Part I, LNCS 10273, pp. 112–123, 2017.
DOI: 10.1007/978-3-319-58521-5_8

activity to assess the added value of the use of social media in the professional context, there is very little or no research on the subject.

1. As pointed out by Cardon [7] and Bowker [6], these data are highly desired by several industrial actors who would dream of predicting users' behavior (especially as consumers) to create value. By contrast, we seek to empower and educate users by helping them understand their role, place and common interests in the community to which they belong, and assume that this can influence future development of the use of these platforms.

2. Even if studies show a professionalization of their practices, this research also highlights that community managers remain ill-equipped to develop pro-active governance tactics (e.g. editorial policy based on communities of interests, identification of key actors in the community) [20]. Surprisingly, outside the consumer goods realm, the analytics developed about the use of social media in professional context are rather simplistic (i.e., descriptive statistics) [11]. So how can we evaluate the added value of social media use in professional context if we cannot make sense of the activity?

Scientific advances in the understanding of these phenomena depend, in our opinion, on several correlated issues:

1. The first issue is access to data. It is possible to work on these issues through interviews or observations of uses and practices but very quickly the analysis reaches its limits if this access does not include access to the data and metadata produced by the participants. Yet, once the access is obtained, it is still necessary to be able to apprehend the mass of data, their structuring to then choose appropriate analytical treatments etc.

2. More, a quick look at existing research from different fields such as applied mathematics [2, 12] or to studies of natural language processing [13] highlights that several algorithms and statistics can help us to deepen our understanding of social media activity. Yet, researchers in those fields also admit that the intelligibility to the average mortal of «how, what and for what» behind the measure does not appear on their research agenda. The issue is therefore not the absence of relevant measures but their intelligibility for the average user.

3. Finally, data visualization and information visualization research addresses these issues, but these works and results often remain confined to scientific communities [14].

To bridge the gap between existing scientific measures of social media activity, their visualization and their intelligibility by community members and animators, we have created a multidisciplinary team at the crossroads of these different actors and knowledge:

1. Scientists and the measures they develop in the studies of natural language processing, applied mathematics and statistics,

2. Scientists and the principles emerging from the field of data and information visualization,

3. Users and their working environment.

The objectives of the team are to develop a dashboard prototype gathering several "intelligible" measures directed to and to assess their added value to community animators and members.

The challenges of the design process of this dashboard (from the selection of measures, the selection of visualizations to its intelligibility to users) will be the central topic of my paper. Inspired by Star and Griesemer's work [16] on boundary objects and standardized method, the present communication aims to explain how we are creating, adapting and negotiating the current development of our dashboard prototype – conceived as a boundary object – "robust enough" to reach common goals and "plastic enough" to suit diverse interests of the stakeholders involved in the project. Just as Griesemer emphasizes in his tributes to Leigh Star work [10], I will also explain how we develop our research and development protocol to preserve the emerging and fragile status of boundary object of the dashboard.

To understand the emergence of the dashboard as a boundary object, we detail, in the next section, the ecosystem of the project. Then we recount the first stages of the project.

2   The Ecosystem of the Project

2.1   Scholars in Organizational Communication

Researchers in this field are at the initiative of the project. Two researchers (one being the author) have, as explained above, identified an opportunity to position themselves in their field of research on issues related to the use of social media in a professional context. The place of technology in professional and organizational practices is an important dimension of their work. Through the development of these projects, these researchers are seeking access to organizations, professionals and data that will enable them to improve their understanding of online collaborative practices, of the intelligibility of online activity and its impact on members' behaviors and practices. However, based on the existing literature and exchanges with several colleagues, these researchers found that advances in their own research depended heavily on the involvement of scientists from other research domains.

Beyond research itself, communication researchers are also maneuvering in the setting up of research projects and the raising of funds. As a result, they are responsible for the administrative management of projects and are accountable to funders. They are also the guarantor of the achievement of the objectives included in the various projects funded.

2.2   Human-Computer Interaction Scholars

These researchers also in communication sciences work on users' media literacy. The intelligibility of data through visualizations and dashboard design are research objects enabling studies focusing on media literacy. These scientists bring a methodological know-how in the development of experimental protocols favoring the participation of the users in the choices of the visualizations and the design of the dashboard. Moreover, these researchers benefit, through this project, from an access to a state-of-the-art infrastructure (a usability lab) to increase the scientific quality of the experimental protocols and the results generated. Finally, working also on the impact of the social and working environments on the appropriation of technological tools, access to users *in situ* through industrial partners provides an additional reason to get involved in the project.

2.3   Scholars in Applied-Mathematics

They provide the technical and scientific tools (e.g., recommendation algorithms, clustering algorithms, etc.) needed to process data and measure online activity. Access to quality data that are both valid, reliable and representative of the population at the heart of the phenomenon is the first challenge for these researchers. Issues of visualizing the processed data or the measures produced and their intelligibility outside the scientific community are not a research priority; even if they recognize the barrier that this can create in the diffusion of the knowledge produced. Very sought after, these researchers are very selective in their research partnerships.

2.4   Scholars in Natural Language Processing

These researchers, initially trained in linguistics, also have a training in computer science which enables them to develop algorithms optimizing the search for information in large-scale thematic documentary corpuses. Their expertise in the processing and analysis of textual corpuses is very complementary to the analysis based on activity logs. Indeed, they allow the analysis of the activity regarding the contents exchanged, shared and modified, making it possible to consider the organizational and/or sectoral context in the analysis. The challenge, as well as researchers in applied mathematics, for these researchers is access to textual data. The additional difficulty is the confidentiality and sensitivity of the textual data. Activity logs are easily anonymized without affecting the analysis. This is much more complex regarding textual data.

The laboratory grouping these researchers is responsible for developing automatic language processing tools for its internal "clients" (researchers from other disciplines working on textual and oral corpus) and its external clients. The creation of interfaces facilitating access to tools and the intelligibility of the measures developed is an increasingly important topic for this laboratory.

2.5   Scholars Experts in Consumer Behavior Analysis

Digital marketing researchers specialize in behavioral analysis of digital content's consumers. The interest of these researchers in the project lies in the analysis of the impact of visual stimuli on consumer behavior. Access to an equipped usability laboratory will also enable these researchers to develop high-quality experimental protocols. Access to industrial partners through the project is also a point of convergence. The added value of this research in digital marketing is also to allow the project bearers to achieve the objectives of economic valorization justifying the funding.

2.6 Funding Institutions

Currently the donors are the regional public authorities of two regions. The main fund obtained is a ERDF (European Regional Development Fund) financed by the European Commission but granted by the Walloon Region. These research budgets aim essentially to stimulate the socio-economic development of the region on strategic axes defined by the political authorities of the region in agreement with the European Commission. The primary objective is not the production of scientific knowledge but the production of value for the socio-economic actors of the region. Thus, the project is not evaluated according to the number of doctoral theses defended or published scientific articles but rather according to indicators or deliverables with added value for the region (e.g., patent, spin-off, or any technological bricks creating economic value, etc.). Funding institutions enforce many legal and regulatory constraints on the use of funds, the fulfillment of tasks and the achievement of objectives.

2.7 Industrial Partners

The industrial partners work in collaboration with the research actors either by explaining the needs and stakes of the industry or by giving access to resources (e.g. information, data, research field). The industrial partners have a rhythm of work and needs that are not compatible with those of research. The fact that the project benefits from public funds also leads to caution in relations with industrial partners to prevent relationships from producing benefits considered as state aid for partners.

2.8 Final Users of the Dashboard

The end users of the dashboard are the online community managers. Their interest is to be better equipped to make sense of the activity of their community and then to act on it more pertinently (even if the pertinence of an action is debatable). We solicited them in the first phase of *intéressement* of Callon and Latour [1] to access their data. In exchange, they have access to the prototype of dashboard to analyze their communities. The challenge is to find a balance between solicitations (sometimes considered too time-consuming) and the development of tools that best meet their needs.

3 Our Iterative Research and Development Protocol: The Story so Far…

From the beginning of the project, we have worked with a partner whose core business is the development and the sale of instances of its online social knowledge sharing platform. Sold to companies of varying sizes, this system aims to support the activities of archiving, monitoring and collaboration between the employees of the organization using this service. Activity measures made available to community coordinators are poorly developed. However, they navigate blindly and lack objective benchmarks to more effectively engage their communities. It is also necessary to think about ways to

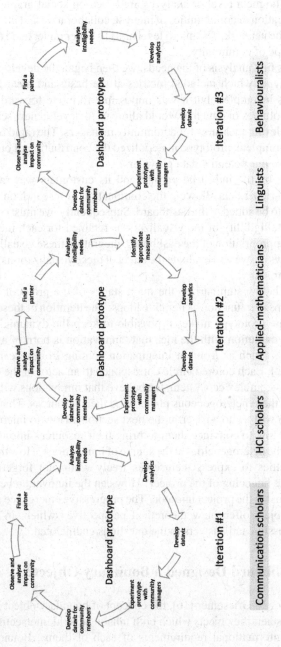

Fig. 1. Iterative research protocol

make activity intelligible to the members of the community itself. Thus, we have identified three possible levels of analysis: the basic level where activity measures are very descriptive (e.g., numbers of likes or publications per month, activity growth rate on the platform, etc.). The meta level of analyzes are based on social graphs algorithms and allow the identification of communities of interest, collaborative and information sharing practices across the network. The micro level aims to better understand the typical users' profiles in this type of community.

Thanks to this first analysis of the needs, we then began the development of the first dashboard prototype, which included metrics at the basic and meta levels. We were aware that it was incomplete but it was impossible to move forward without having access to larger volumes of data that would allow us to develop new scientifically valid and potentially relevant measures for community managers. The rapid realization of this first, although incomplete, prototype materialized the contribution of our research to the companies that are our potential data providers.

The reception by the industrial partner and its customers was rather positive. It allowed access to richer data allowing the continuation of research on the relevance of certain measures to be added to the dashboard. Subsequently, we must continue the work by the tests of intelligibility of the visualizations retained for each measure. Next, we will analyze the appropriation of the dashboard integrating these visualizations. Finally, if the project allows us, we will evaluate the effect of these visualizations on the dynamics of the online community.

The diagram below summarizes the main stages of the protocol implemented. It includes eight steps that function as iterative loops. The iteration of these stages between the versions of the prototype makes it possible to keep the dynamic centered on the prototype and its evolution with the idea that "innovation is born of a market demand (*Demand* pull), as much as from an imagination coming from research (*Technology push*)" [22, p. 262]. Each colored circle corresponds to an actor of the ecosystem.

In view of this complex ecosystem, we believe that innovations will be produced at the crossroads of these heterogeneous players and their resources. This leads to several questions that we will try to answer in the next sections. How to interest these heterogeneous actors? How to convince them to bring their resources into the' project while avoiding stifling the heterogeneities at the source of innovations? How then can we allow these heterogeneities to express themselves freely while not forgetting the finality constrained by the financing of the project? How can the innovation be beneficial to all partners and not just to the project initiator? The progressive emergence of the dashboard as a boundary object offers new theoretical perspectives which, in our view, open avenues for discussion and answers to the questions enumerated.

4   Is the Dashboard Designed a Boundary Object?

According to Star and Griesemer [16], the concept of boundary object is an "analytical concept of those scientific objects which both inhabit several intersecting social worlds *and* satisfy the informational requirements of each of them…Boundary objects are objects which are both plastic enough to adapt to local needs and the constraints of the several parties employing them, yet robust enough to maintain a common identity across sites. They are weakly structured in common use, and become strongly structured in individual-site use. These objects may be abstract or concrete. They have different meanings in different social worlds but their structure is common enough to more than one world to make them recognizable, a means of translation. The creation and management of boundary objects is a key process in developing and maintaining coherence across social worlds" (p. 393).

As Boland [3, p. 232] argues: "By naming boundary object, Star named a place in which actors with heterogeneous knowledge succeed in cooperating to do the work of science without having any prior agreement on the nature of the objects, actions, measures, or goals that they working on..." Key to Boland's reflection about Leigh Star's contribution is that boundary objects help different groups to work together without consensus [18] on the symbolic meaning of the boundary object: "when presented with a boundary object in an inquiry dialogue, we are not led to believe we know what each person involved will name it or how they will make it meaningful, but with a named symbol, we believe we do".

The prototype of the dashboard can be considered at this stage as a boundary object in the sense that it is simultaneously concrete and abstract, specific and general, standardized and customized:

1. Its purpose is clear for all actors, namely to offer intelligible measures of activities for members of online communities.
2. For the industrial partners this purpose is sufficient. Moreover, even if the dashboard is far from being finalized, the regular discussions around the project and the measures envisaged allow them to feed their own reflections on the needs of their customers. For example, we helped them validate the descriptive measures and their potential visualizations without waiting for the dashboard to be completed.
3. For others, such as researchers in applied mathematics or automatic language processing, this purpose is not binding and allows them to have access to data that would otherwise be impossible to access. These data, themselves, allow them to progress in their research on issues that can in return feed the dashboard with new measures of activity. For example, categorizing users according to their activity patterns is debated within the scientific community [9]. The data collected allow us to deepen this question and to validate or invalidate existing typologies. These typologies can then be exploited in the dashboard.

The dashboard being progressively constructed corresponds in our opinion to the type of boundary object named "repositories" by Leigh Star [17]. "Repositories are ordered piles of objects (visual representations of measures) that are indexed in a standardized fashion (following norms of visualization and interface design). Repositories are built to deal with problems of heterogeneity caused by differences in unit of analysis." [19, p. 253]. Thus, the dashboard in this vaguer design allows everyone to add a brick that he wishes to develop and/or consolidate. Its modularity, both in its development and in its use, enables the various actors in the ecosystem to tailor the object "to local use within a social world and therefore to make it useful for work that is not interdisciplinary" [18, p. 605]. This construction takes place at the border between several actors.

It makes it possible to redraw the boundaries between the actors of the project and allows them to work and share information [18].

4.1   From the Notion of Boundary Object to that of Intermediate Object or How to Maintain the Status of Boundary Object for the Dashboard?

Objects do not necessarily remain boundary objects. This status is not stable over time (Star 2010). It is the dynamic of "tacking" (Star 2010) between the two forms of the object, namely specific and general, which allows each of the actors to continue their cooperation without consensus. Verchère and Anjembe [21] point out that it is difficult to engineer and maintain such objects which "in reality take diversified forms and are part of complex trajectories". Take note that the protocol described above as well as the prototype seen as a boundary object that emerges from it have not been preconceived as such. It was through a meeting with Geoff Bowker that we made the connection between the interdisciplinary stakes experienced within the project and the notion of boundary object.

In their 1999 book, Bowker and Star invite us to pay attention to the power of membership to a community of practices (i.e. those of linguists, management mathematicians, community leaders). The ambiguous or unclear status, on one side, and the specific meanings that the boundary object takes in function of these memberships, on the other, is not envisaged as something temporary but rather as durable arrangements among communities of practices. Consequently, they warn us of the potential slippage of the boundary object towards another status where one symbolic meaning (Boland 2015) would take precedence over others.

Based on this warning, Verchère and Anjembe [21] analyze an interdisciplinary project whose objectives and ecosystem are very similar to our project. Their analysis highlights several factors or dynamics that have been obstacles to the emergence and maintenance of boundary objects and which fairly illustrate Bowker's and Star's warning. To synthesize, they identified three types of organizational and communication practices that could lead to shifts: sub-project organization, strengthening the sense of membership to a community of practice within the project, and the sequencing of project's phases. Organizing by subcategory or sub-project by discipline (e.g., communication, linguistics, mathematics) would increase the sense of membership to a community of practice and reduce the interest in working with other communities. The sequencing of the deliverables over time between the actors can potentially create time lags between the different deliverables and decrease their complementarities. These two dynamics have the effect of reinforcing the boundaries and of transforming the status of the boundary object towards an object called intermediate.

"The intermediate objects represent those who conceived them. It expresses their intentions, their habits of work or thought, their relationships and their interactions, their perspectives and the compromises they have established" [23]. Both boundary and intermediate objects intervene in the temporal and social division between the actors [23, p. 56]. However, as pointed out by Peters and his colleagues [15], intermediate objects, as opposed to boundary objects, "reflect the translation of a main actor (the innovator) who

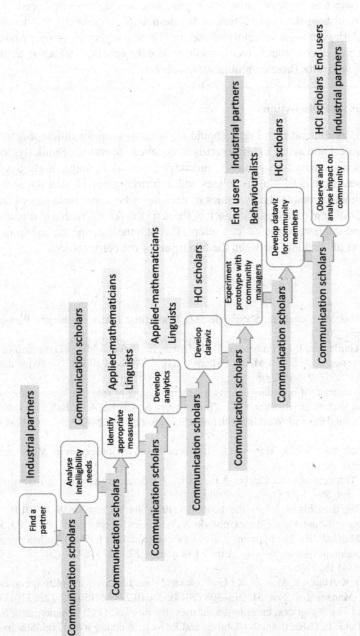

Fig. 2. Sequenced research and development protocol

seeks to enroll other actors and stabilize the process around the object, which becomes the witness of the process of connection between the various actors" (p. 67).

Adapting our initial schema (see Fig. 2), these dynamics would cause a fragmentation of the boundary object in favor of the technological bricks which in sequenced and staggered way would feed the construction of the dashboard. Ultimately, this would recreate the boundaries between the actors whose contribution within the project would be limited to a precise stage of the protocol, would reduce the benefit of all actors to the benefit of a single innovator (here communication scholars).

4.2 Implications and Discussion

Multiple iterations as illustrated in Fig. 1 should allow us to keep the different actors involved in the project and avoid a shift towards a sequenced operation. Similarly, the creation of places and times for systematic meetings (co-working days, study days) between researchers from different disciplines and industrial partners, in a open and flexible format, should promote the dynamics of exchanges between the actors of the ecosystem. More, bilateral meetings with each of the actors make it possible to monitor the specificities and interests of the various actors. Through these elements, one stimulates the movement of "tacking" between the two forms of the border object.

References

1. Akrich, M., Callon, M., Latour, B.: Sociologie de la Traduction: Textes Fondateurs. Presses des MINES, Paris (2006)
2. Blondel, V.D., Guillaume, J.-L., Lambiotte, R., Lefebvre, E.: Fast unfolding of communities in large networks. J. Stat. Mech. Theor. Exp. **2008**, P10008 (2008). doi: 10.1088/1742-5468/2008/10/P10008
3. Boland, D.: The concept of boundary objects and the reshaping of research in management and organization studies. In: Bowker, G.C., Timmermans, S., Clarke, A.E., Balka, E. (eds.) Boundary Objects and Beyond: Working with Leigh Star, pp. 229–238. MIT Press, Cambridge (2016)
4. Bowker, G.C., Star, S.L.: Sorting Things Out: Classification and Its Consequences. MIT Press, Cambridge (1999)
5. Bowker, G.C., Timmermans, S., Clarke, A.E., Balka, E.: Boundary Objects and Beyond: Working with Leigh Star. MIT Press, Cambridge (2015)
6. Bowker, G.C.: Big data, big questionsl the theory/data thing. Int. J. Commun. **8**, 5 (2014)
7. Cardon, D.: A quoi rêvent les algorithmes: nos vies à l'heure des big data. Seuil, Paris (2015)
8. Cardon, P.W., Marshall, B.: The hype and reality of social media use for work collaboration and team communication. Int. J. Bus. Commun. **52**, 273–293 (2015). doi: 10.1177/2329488414525446
9. Füller, J., Hutter, K., Hautz, J., Matzler, K.: User roles and contributions in innovation-contest communities. J. Manage. Inf. Syst. **31**, 273–308 (2014). doi:10.2753/MIS0742-1222310111
10. Griesemer, J.R.: Sharing spaces, crossing boundaries. In: Bowker, G.C., Timmermans, S., Clarke, A.E., Balka, E. (eds.) Boundary Objects and Beyond: Working with Leigh Star, pp. 201–216. MIT Press, Cambridge (2016)
11. Grignon, T.: L'expertise communicationnelle au prisme de ses instruments L'exemple de Google Analytics. Les cahiers du Resiproc **3**, 23–99 (2015)

12. Jacomy, M., Venturini, T., Heymann, S., Bastian, M.: ForceAtlas2, a continuous graph layout algorithm for handy network visualization designed for the Gephi software. PLoS ONE **9**, e98679 (2014)

13. Jurafsky, D., Martin, J.H.: Speech and Language Processing, 2nd edn. Prentice Hall, Upper Saddle River (2008)

14. Keim, D., Andrienko, G., Fekete, J.-D., Görg, C., Kohlhammer, J., Melançon, G.: Visual analytics: definition, process, and challenges. In: Kerren, A., Stasko, John T., Fekete, J.-D., North, C. (eds.) Information Visualization. LNCS, vol. 4950, pp. 154–175. Springer, Heidelberg (2008). doi:10.1007/978-3-540-70956-5_7

15. Peters, S., Faulx, D., Hansez, I.: Le rôle des objets-frontière dans le découpage temporel et social d'une innovation de service. Revue d'anthropologie des connaissances **4**(1), 65–86 (2010)

16. Star, S.L., Griesemer, J.R.: Institutional ecology, translations' and boundary objects: amateurs and professionals in Berkeley's museum of vertebrate zoology, 1907-39. Soc. Stud. Sci. **19**, 387–420 (1989). doi:10.1177/030631289019003001

17. Star, S.L.: The structure of ill-structured solutions: boundary objects and heterogeneous distributed problem solving. In: Huhns, M. (ed.) Distributed Artificial Intelligence, vol. 2, pp. 37–54. Morgan Kaufmann Publishers Inc., San Francisco (1989)

18. Star, S.L.: This is not a boundary object: reflections on the origin of a concept. Sci. Technol. Hum. Values **35**, 601–617 (2010). doi:10.1177/0162243910377624

19. Star, S.L.: The structure of ill-structured solutions: boundary objects and heterogeneous distributed problem solving. In: Bowker, G.C., Timmermans, S., Clarke, A.E., Balka, E. (eds.) Boundary Objects and Beyond: Working with Leigh Star, pp. 243–259. MIT Press, Cambridge (2016)

20. van Osch, W., Steinfield, C.W., Balogh, A.B.: Enterprise social media: challenges and opportunities for organizational communication and collaboration. In: 48th Hawaii International Conference on System Sciences, 5–8 Jan 2015 (2015)

21. Verchère, C., Anjembe, E.: De la difficulté de fabriquer des objets-frontières. Revue d'anthropologie des connaissances **4**(1), 36–64 (2010)

22. Vinck, D., Laureillard, P.: Coordination par les objets dans les processus de conception. In: Centre de Sociologie de l'Innovation E des M de P (ed) Représenter, Attribuer, Coordonner, Paris, France, pp. 289–295 (1996)

23. Vinck, D.: De l'objet intermédiaire à l'objet-frontière. Revue d'anthropologie des connaissances **3**(1), 51–72 (2009)

Sorting Visual Complexity and Intelligibility of Information Visualization Forms

Mingran Li$^{(\boxtimes)}$, Wenjie Wu, Yingjie Victor Chen, Yafeng Niu, and Chengqi Xue

Department of Computer Graphics Technology,
Purdue University, West Lafayette, USA
li1940@purdue.edu

Abstract. Faced with the challenge of information explosion, almost everyone have been exposed to some kind of information visualization in varies of forms. Understanding how people read, understand, interpret and distinguish various forms of visualizations helps designers and developers think about how to improve the designs from the perspectives of users. This paper applied a mixed research method of quantitative and qualitative to explore how the designs of visualization forms evolved, and whether those kinds of graphs and charts are easy for users to understand, and how much information the users can get from the visualization. By testing if users are able to easily and accurately reach the information and providing the scales of simple to complex, and easy to hard, we see that basic visualizations like bar, pie, bubble, line, and scatter charts have been distributed in areas which are relatively simple in design and easy to read. Nonetheless, visualizations like the tree, parallel coordinate, sunburst, heat map, box plot and Sankey graphs have been concentrated in the regions of relatively complex in design, and are difficult to understand. In addition, the visualizations, including stacked bar, word cloud, box plot, and theme river that frequently appeared in the middle region of the grid, embodied the transitions of visualization design from simple to complex, and easy to hard.

Keywords: Visual Literacy · Visual complexity · Intelligibility · Readability · Sorting · Visualization distributions

1 Introduction

In the era of information explosion, it is inevitable that everyone will be exposed to some kinds of data visualizations, even if they are non-professionals in the field of information visualization (InfoVis) or fields related to information science. In the research on InfoVis, designers try to present information by utilizing different kinds visual forms of charts, graphs, and diagrams, providing readers quick interpretation, visible outliers, and insightful explorations [1]. Information visualization is both science and art. It has solid scientific foundation especially in human perception and cognition, such as preattentive visual processing, Gestalt

© Springer International Publishing AG 2017
S. Yamamoto (Ed.): HIMI 2017, Part I, LNCS 10273, pp. 124–135, 2017.
DOI: 10.1007/978-3-319-58521-5_9

laws of perception, and color perception theories. Preattentive processing refers to an initial organization of the visual field based on cognitive operations believed to be rapid, automatic, and spatially parallel [2, 3]. Preattentive processing has been well utilized in visualization designs, to enable intuitive high-speed target detection, boundary identification, and region detection [3]. Gestalt principles were developed to help describe and explain the rules of the organization of relative complex visual fields [4, 5]. Color perception is additional main research direction in the visualization field. Color selection in data visualization is not merely an aesthetic choice, it is a crucial tool to convey quantitative information [6]. Information visualization is also a design. The same data can be represented in different forms with different colors. How to properly select the right form, right layout, and right colors to convey the underlying information accurately, and create better understandings for users are always challenging and as ongoing research topics for many researchers.

Visual Literacy (VL) is the ability for a human to interpret and make sense from information presented in visual forms. By applying the concept of Visual Literacy, researchers put forward the visual design and composition principles, including clear indication of the nature of the relationship, accurate representations of the quantities, comprehensible comparisons of quantities, obvious hierarchy of values, etc. [7], to evaluate and explore whether the designs achieve the goals. Those principles are of fundamental importance for the production of effective visual instructional material [8].

By referring the past research, we brought forward a new method in this paper that sorting the information visualization forms by visual complexity and intelligibility. In other words, participants would conduct visualization distributions that help with researchers to study what kinds of graphs are easy for users to comprehend and interpret, how accurately the users are able to obtain the information, and how the designs of visualization charts evolved. It is beneficial for users to realize how the understandings they have for each kind of visualization by applying the standards of simple to complex, and easy to hard. Furthermore, the finding of threshold of chart evolution would help designers and developers think about how to improve the designs from the perspectives of user-centered [9]. Reading information visualization as one of the 21st century important skills, inspires designers to study harder on how to match tools with users of different age and knowledge background, tasks and real problems.

We used both quantitative and qualitative research methods to distinguish the readability and intelligibility of each type of chart. There a large amount of results have been collected from total 20 participants' tasks and interviews. By readability, we mean to test if users can obtain the information that's delivered from the charts accurately and easily, which was the important step for our team to verify whether the readers fully understand the graphs. By providing them with scales of simple to complex, and easy to hard, users were able to independently create a clear distribution based on their judgments of the complexity of the charts, and corresponding simplicity of reading, that is the readability and intelligibility in their minds. Through integrating gathered data, we could explore the reasons why charts found themselves on either side of the complexity threshold, indicate how the complexity threshold looks like in the evolution of graphs, as well as what the common features the threshold has.

The current result shows that visualizations like bar, pie, bubble, line, and scatter charts have been distributed in areas which are relatively simple in design and easy to read. However, visualizations like the tree, parallel coordinate, sunburst, heat map, box plot and Sankey graphs have been concentrated in the regions of relatively complex in design, and are difficult to understand. In addition, the built distributions from most of the participants showed the charts like stacked bar, word cloud, box plot, and theme river were transitions that made users' readings and understandings changed from easy to difficult, and simple to complex.

In the rest of this paper, we present a brief overview of previous research, summarizing the key reasons why sense making problems of familiar and unfamiliar visualizations had important research significance for non-professional areas and readers, and highlighting the institutions of current literature on visual literacy technologies. We then present our study, the procedures of data collection and analysis, and the primary research results from interviewing and observing participants, concluding with a discussion of the implications of such experiment as a research base for the subsequent study of the sense-making problems of familiar and unfamiliar interactive visualizations.

2   Previous Research

Much of the previous research focused on exploring sense-making problem with data through the process of visualization. Past researchers used a variety of methods to investigate and assess the visualization literacy, including the visualizations that people are familiar or unfamiliar with [10,11]. According to Catherine's studies, the challenges of visualization included: how to match tools with users, tasks and real problems, how to improve user testing, including looking categorically at the same data from different perspectives, answering questions participants didn't know they had, factoring in the chances of discovery and the benefits of awareness, and addressing universal usability [12], which were not only for adults, but also for younger groups, i.e. secondary school students [13]. Therefore, Visual Literacy was defined as a significant ability within the scope of 21st century skills [13–15].

Visual Literacy (VL) was first proposed in 1969 by John Debes, which was mentioned by Avgerinou and Ericson in the article of a review of the concept of Visual Literacy [8,16]. In that article, the authors also defined the concepts of Visual Literacy by referring to other researchers' statements, such as "Visual Literacy is the ability to understand (read) and use (write) images and to think and learn in terms of images, i.e., to think visually" [8,17], "Visual Literacy refers to a group of vision-competencies a human-being can develop by seeing, and at the same time having and integrating other sensory experiences. The development of these competencies is fundamental to normal human learning.

When developed, they enable a visually literate person to discriminate and interpret the visible actions, objects, symbols, natural or man-made, that he encounters in his environment" [8,16], and Sinatra's proposition about Visual Literacy should be considered as a prerequisite indispensable to human thinking [8,18].

To be more specific, an early 2016 article investigated how people make sense of unfamiliar visualizations by applying a grounded model of NOVIS [19]. Sukwon put forward NOVIS model consisting of five cognitive activities, including encountering visualization, constructing a frame, exploring visualization, questioning the frame, and floundering on visualization. It emphasizes how the users complete these five activities based on parallel coordinate, chord diagram, and tree map, and observes how participants express their feelings and opinions about impressions. In 2014 and 2015, Boy and Borner used different research methods to investigate and assess the issue of visualization literacy, respectively. Boy focused on building a set of visualization literacy tests for line graphs, bar charts, and scatter plots [20]. He developed the method based on Item Response Theory (IRT) and conducted six specific tasks to get the scores from participants. The authors obtained the most accurate characteristic values for each item according to finding the best variant of the model. Borner found that people were more familiar with basic charts, maps, and graphs, but very few were familiar with network by conducting experiments with 20 information visualizations and 273 science museum visitors [21].

With reference to these previous studies, our team wants to improve upon existing research by conducting a study which involves a more varied range of visualization charts, and demonstrates whether the information the users get is correct on the basis of understanding.

3 Research Questions

Although numerous studies helped us with analyzing and exploring how people read and understand visualization charts, our team not only wants to improve upon existing research by conducting a study which incorporates a more diverse range of visualizations but also indicate the complexity threshold in the evolution of charts, by which we mean the phase of chart development beyond which each chart category only serves to confuse users. In addition, our study explored reasons why charts found themselves on either side of the complexity threshold. Faced with this problem, we tried to produce a useful and understandable visual evaluation study to explore questions such as

- How much information do people obtain accurately, including topics, values, and relationships, etc.?
- How does the visualization distribute based on readability and complexity in users' minds?
- How the complexity threshold in the evolution of charts is indicated? What regular pattern brings out?

And, to help users fully understand the levels of their cognition of each type of chart through dragging and constructing the charts' distributions in the scale grid. The expectation of our research is to get specific experimental results such as

- Based on each chart, how many people (percentage) can/cannot make sense of the chart?
- If he/she can make sense some charts, he/she will go with the specific tasks that we have designed. But not all the answers are correct.
- If he/she can make sense some charts, he/she will go with the specific tasks that we have designed. And, all the answers are correct.
- On the basis of the judgements of visual complexity and intelligibility, how will the participants create charts' distributions?

4 Mixed Research Method of Quantitative and Qualitative

4.1 Participants

Our team focused on collecting 20 participants to take part in the study, and each participant would be asked to provide diverse demographic background, including age, gender, education, and profession. All of our participants had a basic computer operation capability. The majority of our participants are students who came from Purdue University (West Lafayette, IN), representing 10 different majors, and their educational levels scattered from Freshmen to Graduated. Participants in groups also involved several professors who came from the programs of Computer Graphics Technology, and Art & Design at Purdue University.

Using Autodesk Sketch Pro as a fundamental tool, the participants created the distributions with forms by pulling and dragging each graph. Before that sorting, the participants would be asked to make all the visualizations classified that depended on their readings and understandings of each chart. The participants would work up to 2 hours to complete the experiments.

4.2 Data Collection

4.2.1 Experimental Questions

Each participant was provided 54 static visualizations (forms/charts/graphs) as the experimental elements (Fig. 1), and all the gathered visualizations were with full labels in order to help with readings and understandings. Figure 1 shows partial image resources. Name or title of each image file didn't affect the process of the experiment. Based on reading each visualization, the participants were asked to decide whether they could make sense of it within 3 min, and if they could understand, they would be required to answer several particular questions in order to verify whether they got the information accurately. The bullets and the mind map (Fig. 2) below showed the specific experimental process.

Visualization Name	Visualization	Visualization Name	Visualization
03_Line_Chart_3		23_3D_Pie_Chart	
04_Bar_Chart		24_Donut_Chart	
05_Multi-Set_Bar_Chart_1		25_Multiple_Donut_Chart	
06_Multi-Set_Bar_Chart_2		26_Sunbrust_Diagram	
07_Variant_Bar_Chart		27_Arc_Diagram	
08_Radial_Bar_Chart		28_Scatter_Plot	
09_Radial_Column_Chart		29_Multiple_Scatter_Plot	
10_Spiral_Plot		30_Bubble_Chart	
11_3D_Bar_Chart		31_Bubble_Map	
12_Stacked_to_Grouped_Bar_Chart		32_Heat_Map	
13_Normalized_Stacked_Bar_Chart		33_Choropleth_Map	
14_Marimekko_Chart		34_Area_Chart	
15_Nightingale_Rose_Chart		35_Flow_Chart_1	
16_Span_Chart		36_Flow_Chart_2	
17_Diverging_Stacked_Bar_Chart		37_Flow_Chart_3	
18_Bullet_Graph		38_Parallel_Sets	
19_Waterfall_Chart		39_Sankey_Diagram	
20_Box_Whisker_Plot		40_Bidirectional_Hierarchical_Sankey_ Diagram	

Fig. 1. Visualization forms

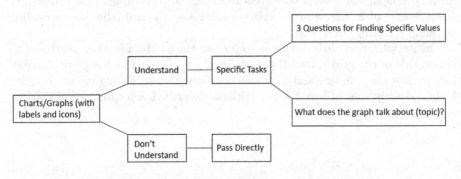

Fig. 2. A mind map shows the experimental process

1. Do you think you understand this visualization? If no, skip to next visualization. If yes, continue.
2. Tell us the meaning of this visualization. The participants will verbally explain their interpretations of the visualization. Specifically, what does the graph talk about (topic/Q1)? Under the premise of answering the questions accurately, participants can sum up the theme easily and neutrally.
3. If the visualization encodes some special information, we will ask two or three specific questions related to the visualization, for example:
   - What is the relation between A & B (Q2)?
   - What is the trend of X in recent Y years (Q3)?
   - What is the meaning of the peak value, and why there (Q4)?

We recorded the answers and interactions from each participant, and filled in the following table (Fig. 3). Researchers would help the participants to mark understand or not-understand with Y or N at first, then note the accuracy with correct, incorrect, or partially correct, which was for the Q1 and Q4. In addition, the descriptions of participants about topics were transcribed for researchers to verify if the users fully made sense of the main idea.

Visualization No.	Understand or Not (Y/N)	If Understand									
		Q.1.			Q.2.		Q.3.		Q.4.		
		Correct	Incorrect	Partially Correct	Correct	Incorrect	Correct	Incorrect	Correct	Incorrect	Partially Correct

Fig. 3. Table for collecting participants' answers

4.2.2   Visualization Sorting

We were asking the participants to rank these visualizations by visual complexity and intelligibility in their minds. By applying Autodesk Sketch Pro, we conducted a blank grid for them to build their own visualization distributions. Those 54 visualizations provided above would be pulled and dragged into the grid area, even if there might be overlap. The grid had been set up by two axises, which specifically presented the levels from simple to complex (the complexity of the charts) of X axis, and the degrees from easy to hard (the ease of reading and understanding) of Y axis.

The initialization of the task was to present the 54 visualizations scattered on the left side of the grid. Then, the participants were asked to complete distributions by how they understand each visualization (Fig. 4). Moreover, we recorded the text descriptions of how the participants described, interpreted and thought

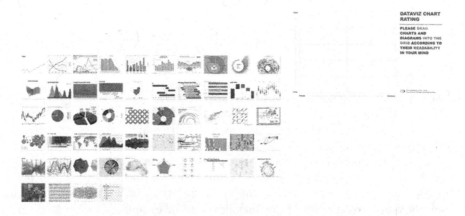

Fig. 4. Participants created visualization distributions by dragging and pulling forms into grid

about each visualization, and the reasons they dragged and took out the visualization to a particular location.

We processed the data analysis for two aspects: one was to verify the correctness of participants' answers, and another one was to transcribe and convert their verbal descriptions that could be used for data analysis. For example, we translated participants' narrations into text files, and presented them with quotes.

"This kind of basic bar chart is easy to understand for me. But if it is added up, the stacked bar chart feels more difficult. One more problem is it's hard for me to actually compare the height of the bar to the corresponding values on the left (Y axis)."

5   Findings

Over 400 hours of data were collected from the 20 users. The interviews with participants, and observations of their actions, revealed some prevailing patterns of visualization distribution and chart evolution threshold. Below we present a discussion of three themes that emerged in our exploration of visualization sorting and distribution studies.

5.1   Answer Accuracy

We used a total of 1080 answer tables in the statistical analysis to record answers of participants, and applied accuracy rate. Figure 5 showed the answers of numerical problems and the interpretations of topics from visualization No. 41. The users who had never been trained to read the relatively complex visualizations of parallel coordinates, could not interpret the meaning of such intensive lines in a short period of time. Moreover participants found the exploration of relationships between each line, and the nodes on each line, difficult to understand.

Visualization No.	Understand or Not (Y/N)	If Understand											
		Q.1.			Q.2.		Q.3.		Q.4.				
		Correct	Incorrect	Partially Correct	Correct	Incorrect	Correct	Incorrect	Correct	Incorrect	Partially Correct
41	N										
				✓	✓		✓				✓

Fig. 5. Answer records - visualization No.41

By contrast, the No. 22 visualization obtained a better result in user response. Pie charts are common in daily life; individuals are trained to read, explain, and interpret proportions and distributions of the chart when they were young. Combined with the simple graphic design and years of accumulated knowledge, most of the participants were able to identify the topic issue and verify the correct answers successfully (Fig. 6).

Visualization No.	Understand or Not (Y/N)	If Understand									
		Q.1.			Q.2.		Q.3.		Q.4.		
22	Y	Correct	Incorrect	Partially Correct	Correct	Incorrect	Correct	Incorrect	Correct	Incorrect	Partially Correct
		✓			✓		✓		✓		

Fig. 6. Answer records - visualization No.22

5.2   Visualization Distribution

We know from literature that Visual Literacy (VL) as defined by past research is the capability to read, understand, interpret, and make meaning from information presented in the form of images. Our research applied a method by asking users to construct a distribution of visualizations to study and present users' abilities in respect of VL. We have provided users a tool, Autodesk Sketch Pro, to construct their own visualization periodically according to their readability and intelligibility in their minds. After an analysis of completed research we understand how human perception, cognition, and particular mental models work on readings, and understandings, of the visualization. As we can see (Fig. 7) most of bar, pie, bubble, line, and scatter charts have been distributed in the areas that were easy to read because of relatively simple design. However, the majority of the graphs, including the tree, parallel coordinate, sunburst, heat map, box plot and Sankey have concentrated in regions of relative complexity in design and are more difficult to understand.

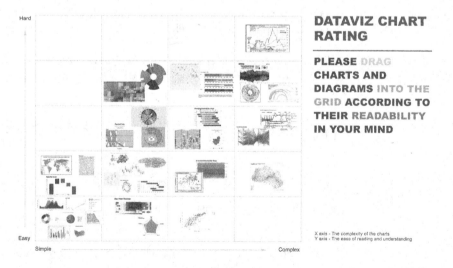

Fig. 7. Visualization distribution

5.3   Chart Evolution

Through integrating gathered data, we could indicate how the threshold looks like in the evolution of graphs, as well as what the common features the threshold has. The builded distributions from most of the participants showed the charts, such as stacked bar, word cloud, box plot, and theme river were regarded as the transitions that made users' readings and understandings changed from easy to difficult, and simple to complex. Figure 8, which congregated the ideas from a majority of participants, gave out an obvious comparison, and a relative expression of evolutionary thresholds.

The reason why most of users put these visualizations in the transitional zone, and treated them as thresholds was those visualizations expressed the kind of the same ideas by more innovative ways. There was a greater difference between these designs and basic knowledge in their brains. Several relevant quotes from the participants:

"Why I put the word cloud in the middle area because this is my first time to see it. I know the visualization wants to express a topic that relates to the words, or texts. But it's a new form so that I can not make an interpretation."

"I have an idea about how to read the line graphs. But this visualization, which is called 'theme river' seems be composed with thousands of lines. Then, I don't know how to read that."

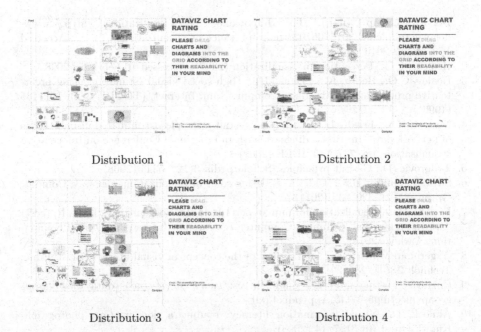

Fig. 8. Visualization distributions with thresholds

6   Conclusion and Future Work

In this research, we investigated how the visualization design evolved, which specifically measured how the participants sorted the visualizations and built the distributions, and how they thought about the threshold issues based on their readings and understandings. The findings showed that visualizations like bar, pie, bubble, line, and scatter charts have been distributed in areas which are relatively simple in design and easy to read. Contrastively, visualizations like the tree, parallel coordinate, sunburst, heat map, box plot and Sankey graphs have been concentrated in the regions of relatively complex in design, and are difficult to interpret.

There were many past literatures also mentioned interaction plays a very important role in creating a good design of a visualization chart. Designers have always focused on how to better use interactive methods to help users read and understand charts. Based on this, we will consider a more sophisticated way that involves interactive charts in the studies in the subsequent stage. In addition, we will explore in depth the process participants undergo to obtain accurate information, which specifically means how do they judge the topics, values, and relationships through reading and interpreting the visual elements.

References

1. Denovo Group. (n.d.). The Importance of Visualizations. http://www.denovogroup.com/2016/06/02/the-importance-of-visualizations/. Accessed 15 October 2016
2. Healey, C. G.: Perception in visualization (2007). Accessed 10 February 2008
3. Healey, C.G., Booth, K.S., Enns, J.T.: High-speed visual estimation using preattentive processing. ACM Trans. Comput. Hum. Interact. (TOCHI) **3**(2), 107–135 (1996)
4. Nesbitt, K.V., Friedrich, C.: Applying gestalt principles to animated visualizations of network data. In: Proceedings of Sixth International Conference on Information Visualisation, pp. 737–743. IEEE (2002)
5. Todorovic, D.: Gestalt principles. Scholarpedia **3**(12), 5345 (2008)
6. Silva, S., Santos, B.S., Madeira, J.: Using color in visualization: a survey. Comput. Graph. **35**(2), 320–333 (2011)
7. Few, S.: Data visualization for human perception. In: Soegaard, M., Dam, R. (eds.) The Encyclopedia of Human-Computer Interaction. Interaction Design Foundation, Aarhus (2013)
8. Avgerinou, M., Ericson, J.: A review of the concept of visual literacy. Br. J. Educ. Technol. **28**(4), 280–291 (1997)
9. Cognitive testing interview guide. https://www.cdc.gov/nchs/data/washington_group/meeting5/WG5_Appendix4.pdf
10. Abilock, D.: Visual information literacy: reading a documentary photograph. Knowl. Quest **36**(3), 7–14 (2008)
11. Carpenter, P.A., Shah, P.: A model of the perceptual and conceptual processes in graph comprehension. J. Exp. Psychol. Appl. **4**(2), 75 (1998)

12. Plaisant, C.: The challenge of information visualization evaluation. In: Proceedings of the Working Conference on Advanced Visual Interfaces, pp. 109–116. ACM, May 2004

13. Kibar, P.N., Akkoyunlu, B.: Searching for visual literacy: secondary school students are creating infographics. In: Kurbanoğlu, S., Boustany, J., Špiranec, S., Grassian, E., Mizrachi, D., Roy, L. (eds.) ECIL 2015. CCIS, vol. 552, pp. 241–251. Springer, Cham (2015). doi:10.1007/978-3-319-28197-1_25

14. Nuhoğlu Kibar, P., Akkoyunlu, B.: A new approach to equip students with visual literacy skills: use of infographics in education. In: Kurbanoğlu, S., Špiranec, S., Grassian, E., Mizrachi, D., Catts, R. (eds.) ECIL 2014. CCIS, vol. 492, pp. 456–465. Springer, Cham (2014). doi:10.1007/978-3-319-14136-7_48

15. https://github.com/INRIA/Visualization-Literacy-101

16. Fransecky, R.B., Debes, J.L.: Visual Literacy: A Way to Learn–A Way to Teach. Association for Educational Communications and Technology, Washington, D.C. (1972)

17. Hortin, J.A.: Visual Literacy and Visual Thinking (1980)

18. Sinatra, R.: Visual Literacy Connections to Thinking, Reading and Writing. Charles C. Thomas, Springfield (1986). 2600 South First St., PO Box 4709, IL 62708–4709

19. Lee, S., Kim, S.H., Hung, Y.H., Lam, H., Kang, Y.A., Yi, J.S.: How do people make sense of unfamiliar visualizations? A grounded model of novice's information visualization sensemaking. IEEE Trans. Vis. Comput. Graph. 22(1), 499–508 (2016)

20. Boy, J., Rensink, R.A., Bertini, E., Fekete, J.D.: A principled way of assessing visualization literacy. IEEE Trans. Vis. Comput. Graph. 20(12), 1963–1972 (2014)

21. Brner, K., Maltese, A., Balliet, R.N., Heimlich, J.: Investigating aspects of data visualization literacy using 20 information visualizations and 273 science museum visitors. Inf. Vis. 15, 198–213 (2015)

Visual and IR-Based Target Detection from Unmanned Aerial Vehicle

Patrik Lif[(✉)], Fredrik Näsström, Gustav Tolt, Johan Hedström, and Jonas Allvar

Swedish Defence Research Agency, Linköping, Sweden
{patrik.lif,fredrik.nasstrom,gustav.tolt,johan.hedstrom,
jonas.allvar}@foi.se

Abstract. In many situations it is important to detect and identify people and vehicles. In this study the purpose was to investigate subject's performance to detect and estimate number of stationary people on the ground. The unmanned aerial vehicle used visual- and infrared sensor, wide and narrow field of view, and ground speed 8 m/s and 12 m/s. Participants watched synthetic video sequences captured from an unmanned aerial vehicle. The results from this study demonstrated that the ability to detect people was affected by type of sensor and field of view. It took significantly longer time to detect targets with the infrared sensor than with the visual sensor, and it took significantly longer time with wider field of view than with narrow field of view. The ability to assess number of targets was affected by type of sensor and speed, the infrared sensor causing more problems than the visual sensor. Also, performance decreased at higher speed.

Keywords: Target detection · Visual sensor · IR sensor · UAV · Human factors

1 Introduction

The information explosion that comes from gathering information with new and better sensors is positive since users can access more information. At the same time it is a challenge to select the vital information in a specific situation. Data overload may be a serious problem, and it is necessary to have an understanding of the whole system. How to help human cognition using a medium (i.e. computer) is fundamental to ensure good user performance in the current situation. To build an effective system in a military setting a number of factors must be taken into account. From an ecological approach [1] and representation design [2] there is a cognitive triad between *domain or environment*, *interface* and *users*. There is a reciprocal coupling between the user and the environment which often is mediated by a user interface. The components of the triad are the cognitive demands from the domain or environment, user resources and limitations, and the interface. The interface effectiveness is determined by the mapping between the environment and interface (correspondence) and the mapping between the user and interface (coherence). To develop an effective and user friendly system all these three parts must be taken into account.

In many applications part of the information that reaches the user has been acquired with some type of sensor system, involving one or several sensors and signal processing,

S. Yamamoto (Ed.): HIMI 2017, Part I, LNCS 10273, pp. 136–144, 2017.
DOI: 10.1007/978-3-319-58521-5_10

acting as a filter between the environment and the interface. In order to be able to under-stand the complete picture and study sensor-related aspects the model has to be extended.

In our research we aim for an understanding of the whole picture and therefore also sensor type are included since this is an important part of the system we work with (Fig. 1).

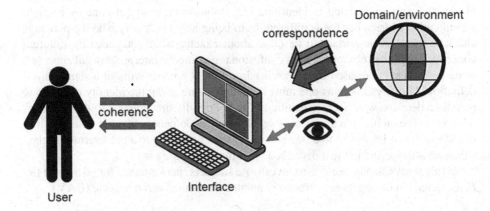

Fig. 1. The relation between user, interface, environment and sensor.

Even though the whole system must always be taken into account, the research presented here focuses on the ability and limitations of the users to extract the correct information about the environment based on data from sensors observing it. The purpose of this study was to investigate and compare performance of manual visual and IR-based detection of static targets seen from a simulated unmanned aerial vehicle (UAV).

It is not always certain what seeing an object means. One way to analyze observers' ability to perform visual tasks is to use the Johnson criteria [3, 4], often used by scientists who study the capability of sensors, e.g., infrared systems. A differentiation is made on *detection* (i.e. whether there is something of potential interest), *orientation* (which sometimes are excluded), *recognition* (e.g. the difference between a human and car) and *identification* (e.g. whether it is a friend or foe). The Johnson criteria proposes in detail how many pixels (originally line-pairs) an object needs to contain to make the classification possible. According to Johnson criteria, the detection distance is calculated based on how many pixels an object must contain. In order to detect static objects it requires 2×2 pixels, orientation 8×2.8 pixels, 8×8 pixels for recognition and identification required 12.8×12.8 pixels [5]. These figures should not be interpreted as guidelines but rather as values under the best possible conditions. It is not entirely clear in various descriptions but the described values probably mean that the task can be solved in 50% of the cases, which in most cases is unacceptably low. There is also a variety of factors that must be considered, including the contrast between objects and background, atmos-pheric disturbances, the number of objects in the picture, light, contextual clues, color and type of optics. Moreover, performance is affected by the type of task, the experience of the participants and their level of training for the specific task, motivation, and the relative importance between quick decisions and correct results [3]. There are several methods that can be regarded as further development of Johnson criteria, e.g. TOD (Triangle Orientation Discrimination), TTP (Targeting Task Performance) and TRM (Thermal Range Model). For further description of these methods see Näsström et al. [6], Wittenstein [7], and Vollmerhausen and Jacobs [8].

In order to assess and evaluate a system, experiments with users should be conducted. Theoretically calculated values could be of some value to get an indication of what objects that can be detected or identified (e.g. Johnson criteria) but is never enough. Identification of friend or foe is different from being able to identify who the person is and it is therefore important to be clear about exactly what you mean by different concepts. There is an obvious risk for confusion regarding the interpretation of concepts, since the concepts are used by researcher in different context without a standardized definition. In many situations one must be absolute sure about the identity of a person to make a decision whether to use military force. Friendly fire, where a soldier accidentally opens fire on his own troops, is a well-known phenomenon. In other cases, such as intelligence, is it important to describe what is seen according to a predetermined classification scheme and not just described what they think they see.

In this study the purpose was to investigate subjects' performance for visual and IR-based detection of targets seen from a simulated unmanned aerial vehicle (UAV).

2   Method

Participants watched synthetic video sequences captured from an UAV. All video sequences were generated by a sensor simulation system. The task was to detect and count stationary humans (referred to as targets in this paper). The participants also estimated how confident they were in their answers on a scale from 0 to 100%. A within-group design with *two visualizations* (visual and IR) × *two field of view* × *two UAV speeds* (12 m/s and 8 m/s) was used. The field of view (FOV)) used were 2.3 × 1.7° and 1.4 × 1.1°.

2.1   Subjects

Eight subjects (four women and four men) participated in the experiment. All had adequate vision with or without correction.

2.2   Apparatus

The video sequences were presented on a 21.5 inch full HD widescreen display with a resolution of 1920 × 1080 pixels. A PC with Windows 7, Intel® Core™ 2 Duo processor with 3 GHz and 4 GB of RAM memory was used. The software Matlab [9] was used on a separate computer to register response time when the participants clicked with the left mouse button. The response tool was designed so participants could always look at the screen where the stimuli material (video sequences) were presented.

2.3 Stimuli

A total of eight videos (640 × 480 pixels) were generated during a clear sunny day with shadows from targets on the ground to depict sensor information from a visual and IR sensor (Fig. 2). The overall mission was similar to a real UAV flying along a predefined path (Fig. 3) with humans (targets) standing on the ground.

Fig. 2. Still images from the visual sensor (left) and the IR sensor (right).

Fig. 3. Location of subjects on the ground at eighteen areas with different position for each of the four scenarios.

According to the mission, four scenarios were generated with the visual- and IR-sensor respectively. Each scenario had eighteen areas with different target positions. The same areas and positions were used for the visual- and IR scenarios. A total of eight videos were generated according to the aforementioned design. The visual and IR scenarios were presented in a balanced order between subjects', and within each sensor the four scenarios were presented in a randomized order.

2.4 Procedure

After welcoming the participants individually and briefing them about the experiment purpose and procedure they received written information and had the opportunity to ask questions to the experiment leader. Then an introduction was given to make sure that the participants were familiar with the situation and test material. They were introduced with both visual and IR image visualizations and received about ten minutes training. The participants watched the videos and answered by first pressing the left mouse button whereby the response time (RT) was recorded, then continued looking at the video and verbally answered how many targets they spotted and how confident they were (Fig. 4). The participants were instructed to always focus on the screen with the stimuli. Because the task was mentally demanding it was divided into eight separate videos with the possibility to rest before continuing with the next one.

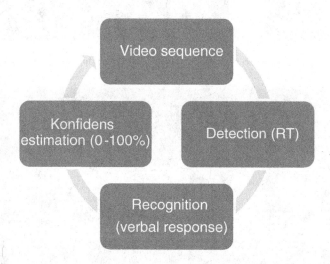

Fig. 4. Process for answering with video sequence, detection, recognition and confidence estimation.

3 Results

The results include statistical analysis of time to detect targets and estimation of number of targets with confidence estimations. The data were analyzed with a three-way ANOVA [10] with type of visualization (visual and IR), speed (12 m/s and 8 m/s), and field of view (1.4 × 1.1°). Tukey HSD were used for post hoc testing [11].

3.1 Detection

The ability to detect targets were measured by response time (RT) and analysis was performed by ANOVA repeated measures. The results showed a main effect for type of sensor $F(1, 7) = 33.62$, $p < .001$, where the response time of the visual sensor was shorter than for the IR sensor (Fig. 5).

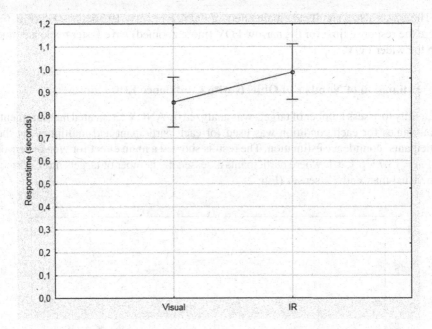

Fig. 5. Mean and standard error of mean for response time for visual and IR sensor.

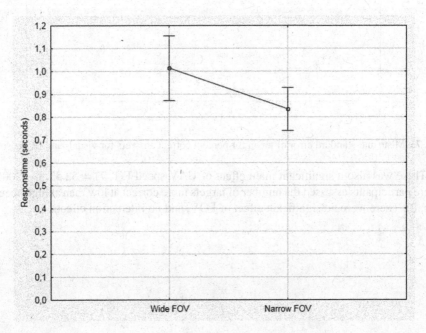

Fig. 6. Mean and standard error of mean for response time for wide and narrow FOV.

There was also a significant main effect of FOV, F (1, 7) = 19.36, p < .005 (Fig. 6), where the response time for the narrow FOV (more zoomed) gave faster response time than the wider FOV.

3.2   Estimation of Number of Objects with Confidence Estimation

The ability to assess number of targets was analyzed by ANOVA repeated measurement. Mean values for each condition was used for each participant and multiplied by the participants' confidence estimation. The results showed a main effect for type of sensor F(1, 7) = 13.73, p < .01, where participants assessed the number of targets more correct with visual than with IR sensor (Fig. 7).

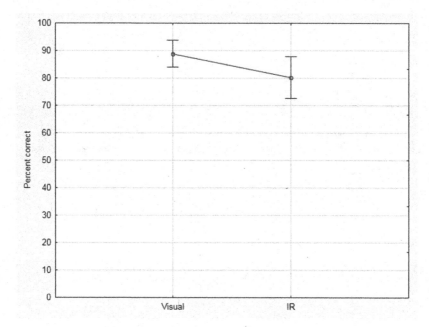

Fig. 7. Mean and standard error of mean for percent correct answers for visual- and IR-sensor.

There was also a significant main effect of UAV speed F(1, 7) = 52.53, p < .001, where participants assessed the number of targets more correct at low than at high speed (Fig. 8). There were no significant effect of FOV, and no interaction effects.

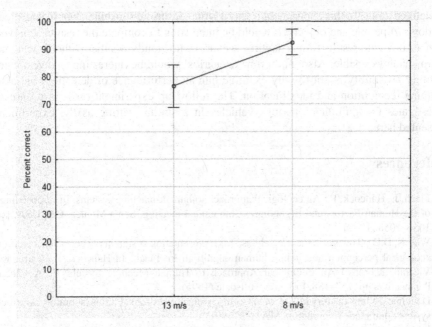

Fig. 8. Mean and standard error of mean for percent correct answers for 13 m/s and 8 m/s.

4   Discussion and Summary

The results from this study demonstrated that the ability to detect targets was affected by type of sensor and FOV. It took significantly longer time to detect targets with the IR sensor than with the visual sensor and it took significantly longer time with wider FOV than narrow FOV. The ability to assess the number targets was affected by type of sensor and speed, IR sensor causing more problems than the visual sensor. The ability to assess the number of targets was overall very high, at 8 m/s (93–99%) and relatively high at 12 m/s (79–91%).

This study also shows a method that can be used to investigate the users' performance related to detection of ground targets from an UAV. The task was to detect and count number of humans on the ground and make confidence estimations. The task can be modified to identify different type of targets, e.g. to investigate possible differences between target types or classify objects as friend or foe.

One limitation of this study is that although the visual and IR sensor data are realistic, no scientific verification has been made to confirm the similarity between the used stimuli material and real data from sensors. However, one researcher compared the simulated videos with real sensor information and confirmed that the material looked similar. In the future, this procedure need to be improved with objective measures.

This experiment was the first experiment in a series of planned experiments, where different platform speeds and field of view angles were studied. Another possibility for further studies is to use other missions, e.g. manually control the UGV instead of using predefined paths. In this experiment it was daytime in strong sunshine, which gave clear shadows of people and objects. It would be interesting to compare the results achieved in this study with results from a daytime scenario with cloudy weather without clear and sharp shadows visible. Also, night time scenarios' would be interesting to investigate. Another possibility is not to only examine human performance of detection, but also examine recognition and identification. The follow-up experiment (now in progress) investigates recognition of various vehicles in a similar setting as the experiment presented here.

References

1. Flach, J., Hancock, P.: An ecological approach to human-machine systems. In: Proceedings of the Human Factors and Ergonomics 36th annual meeting, Santa Monica, CA, USA, pp. 1056–1058 (1992)
2. Woods, D.D.: Towards a theoretical base for representation design in the computer medium: ecological perception and aiding human cognition. In: Flach, J., Hancock, P., Caird, K., Vicente, K. (eds.) An Ecological Approach to Human Machine Systems I: A Global Perspective, pp. 157–188. Erlbaum, Hillsdale (1995)
3. Donohue, J.: Introductory review of target discrimination criteria. Philips laboratory Air force system command, Wilmington, MA, US (1991)
4. Johnson, J.: Analysis of image forming systems. Technical report, U.S. Army Engineer Research and Development Laboratories, Fort Belvoir, Virginia, US (1958)
5. Kopeika, S.: Contrast-limited resolution and target acquisition. In: A System Engineering Approach to Imaging, vol. PM38. SPIE (1998)
6. Näsström, F., Bergström, D., Bissmarck, F., Grahn, P., Gustafsson, D., Karlholm, J.: Prestandamått för sensorsystem (FOI-R–4139–SE). Linköping: Sensor och TK-system (2015). (In swedish)
7. Wittenstein, W.: Thermal range model TRM3. Paper presented at the SPIE Conference in Infrared Technology and Application XXIV, San Diego (1998)
8. Vollmerhausen, R., Jacobs, E.: The targeting task performance (TTP) metric. Technical report AMSEL-NV-TR-230, Modeling and Simulation Division, Fort Belvoir, VA (2004)
9. MATLAB (2017). https://se.mathworks.com/products/matlab.html
10. Hays, W.L.: Statistics. Harcourt Brace College Publishers, Fort Worth (1994)
11. Greene, J., D'Oliveira, M.: Learning to Use Statistical Tests in Psychology. Open University Press, Milton Keynes (1982)

The Fuzzification of an Information Architecture for Information Integration

Rico A. R. Picone[1,2]([✉]), Jotham Lentz[1,2], and Bryan Powell[2]

[1] Department of Mechanical Engineering, Saint Martin's University, Lacey, USA
rpicone@stmartin.edu
[2] Dialectica, LLC, Olympia, USA

Abstract. We present a new information architecture based on one recently introduced to structure categorized but otherwise unstructured information. The new architecture is based on fuzzy set theory subset operations that define graph theory nodes. Two types of graph edges are defined such that a user interface based on this architecture can logically minimize the number of visible navigable edges and atoms of information. This minimization is understood to be one of the primary advantages of the architecture for human-computer interaction due to its mitigation of information overload. The advantages of hierarchical, organic, and sequential information architectures are fused by the new architecture and the dialectical method is also integrated—all of which are intended to enhance human-computer interaction. The new architecture can easily incorporate quantitative information, which can be converted into a fuzzy set theory representation with fuzzy clustering and other techniques. Moreover, traditionally qualitative information such as narrative, audio, and video, although naturally represented with crisp sets, can be represented with fuzzy sets. Therefore, the new architecture can fuse traditionally disparate types of information.

1 Introduction

Memory is recategorization. This identity is supported by recent neuroscience, psychology, and artificial intelligence research [4,14,16], and even if the provocative identity is not strictly true, it provides insight into memory; as Rosenfield puts it:

> We can recognize paintings of Picasso as well as adept imitations of Picasso. When we recognize a painting we have never seen as a Picasso or as an imitation, we are doing more than recalling earlier impressions. We are categorizing: Picasso and fakes. Our recognition of paintings or of people is the recognition of a category, not of a specific item. People are never exactly what they were moments before, and objects are never seen in exactly the same way.[1] [16]

---

[1] Quoted from Pfeifer [14, pp. 311–312].

© Springer International Publishing AG 2017
S. Yamamoto (Ed.): HIMI 2017, Part I, LNCS 10273, pp. 145–157, 2017.
DOI: 10.1007/978-3-319-58521-5_11

Memory plays a central role in intelligence; furthermore, the computer's relative stability of memory is one of its most promising features for the enhancement of intelligence, be it artificial or human. For these reasons, computers have long used forms of categorization to store and present information: the two most striking architectures are the venerable hierarchy and the organic tag-based systems. The authors have previously presented an information architecture—the *dialectical architecture*—with a structure explicitly designed to incorporate the advantages of each of these [15]. In the present work, we fuzzify this architecture in order to include information best categorized in each category to a certain degree—that is, fuzzily categorized information. This type of information is especially important in applications such as robotics in which sensor information is quantitative. Well-established techniques such as fuzzy clustering [6,13] and direct assignment of membership functions can assign each atom of information fuzzy categories (sets). The architecture is developed as a method for human-computer interaction to enhance human intelligence through integrating disparate types of information—narrative, audio, video, and now quantitative data—into a single representation fundamentally based on categorization. We believe beginning with human intelligence enhancement (a worthy application) may provide insight into artificial intelligence development as well.

The fuzzy dialectical architecture, like the "crisp" dialectical architecture, unites three information "planes." The first is the *structure* plane, which is built from fuzzy set operations that define relations among nodes defined by category (set) intersections. The second is the *flow* plane, which allows information to be distributed through the structure in a sequential fashion. Flows can represent many types of information: narrative, audio, video, and data streams. The third and final plane is the *dialectic* plane, which provides a mechanism for flows to evolve within the framework of thesis–antithesis–synthesis. Together, these three planes comprise the fuzzy dialectical architecture, as will be described in detail in Sect. 2, which especially focuses on the fuzzification of the dialectical architecture. In Sect. 3, algorithmic considerations are explored. The human interface and a specific instantiation are described in Sect. 4.

2   Fuzzifying the Dialectical Architecture

The dialectical information architecture was introduced as a way of enhancing human intelligence by a synthesis of structure, flow, and dialectic. These teleological foundations remain intact and the methodology has been developed to include an additional type of information, that which is quantitative. The primary tool for this is fuzzy set theory, with which quantitative information can be interpreted qualitatively in the form of categories. The original or "crisp" architecture defined its structure from crisp set theoretic relations from unstructured categorized information; in this section, the structure of the fuzzy architecture will be defined from fuzzy set theoretic relations from unstructured (fuzzily) categorized information.

Consider a collection of data, each member of which we call an *atom*. Each atom is associated to a certain degree with a collection of *categories* which are represented as fuzzy sets. Crisp set operations union ∪ and intersection ∩ are analogous the fuzzy set operations union and intersection [17, 25]. We exploit this analog to define the fuzzy dialectical architecture in a way similar to the definition of the crisp dialectical architecture, which made much use of the crisp set operations.

The fuzzy structure is, as its crisp analog, a *directed graph* of nodes and edges [2, 21]. Other than the "universal" *union node*, which contains all atoms, every node in the graph represents the fuzzy intersection of a collection of categories (fuzzy sets). Just as an atom can belong to a given category with membership value in the interval $[0, 1]$, with zero meaning "no" membership and unity meaning "full" membership, so an atom can belong to a given node to a certain degree (membership value). This degree is computed from the fuzzy intersection operation, which returns the minimum membership value for a given atom shared between two nodes; i.e. let the element x in the universe X have membership $\mu_A(x)$ in fuzzy set A, where μ_A is the membership function for set A, let x have membership $\mu_B(x)$ in fuzzy set B with membership function μ_B, and let ∧ be the operator that takes the minimum of its two arguments—then the membership of x in the fuzzy intersection $A \cap B$ is [17]

$$\mu_{A \cap B}(x) = \mu_A(x) \wedge \mu_B(x). \tag{1}$$

Directed edges connect the nodes to generate a natural hierarchy. All edges are defined by *has a priori subcategory* relations or s-relations; for instance, the node $A \cap B$ is an *a priori* subcategory (fuzzy subset) of fuzzy sets A and B. This generates a natural hierarchy with graph *levels* defined by the number of categories that intersect to define the node; e.g. node $A \cap B$ has level two.

Two types of s-relation are defined: the suggestively named (1) *has visible a priori subcategory* or vs-relation and (2) *has hidden a priori subcategory* or hs-relation. The definition of the hs-relation first requires the concept of a *metacategory*. A "minimal" metacategory for a given node is a collection of subcategories that contain as a subset all atoms associated with the node. A node's vs-relations are those that have tails connected to the node and heads connected to subcategory nodes contained in a minimal metacategory. By minimal, we mean containing the minimum number of subcategories to fully contain all atoms. An hs-relation is defined as any s-relation that is not a vs-relation.[2]

Finally, atoms themselves can be either "visible" or "hidden," names suggestive of how the user interface in later sections will be defined. An atom is visible at a given node if and only if it has nonzero membership in all categories intersected to define the node and zero membership in all others. This definition requires that an atom be visible in one and only one node in the structure.

---

[2] These definitions have strong parallels in [15], where more mathematically oriented definitions are presented. We favor a narrative approach here. The interested reader may find the explicit mathematical definitions of the previous work elucidating.

2.1   Visibility and Hiddenness

The names given to the two types of atoms and s-relations—"visible" and "hidden"—are a crucial aspect of the structure's advantage for intelligence amplification in human-computer interaction. In a user interface (one instantiation to be discussed in Sect. 4), these signifiers will be taken literally: at a given node, hidden atoms and hidden s-relations (edges) will not be presented to the user. The definition of each guarantees that a hidden atom will be visible if one navigates via visible s-relations to a lower level. The primary advantage of this from a usability standpoint is that the user is not inundated with as much information, one of the key aspects of a hierarchy, while remaining in a logically categorized structure—the other key aspect of a hierarchy.

2.2   Structure as Estimation

Let us consider what type of structure this graph has. It is constructed from a collection of fuzzily categorized atoms (in the case of quantitative information, these atoms are data points with membership values in each category). For a given variable, say temperature, the subset relationships are pre-defined by the membership function of the data; e.g. "luke-warm" will be a subset of "warm." However, the inter-variable relationships are typically not so; for instance, "cold" might be a subset of "high-pressure." The structure defined here can be understood as an estimation process for these relationships, one of several applications to be discussed in later sections.

2.3   Organic Hierarchy

The term *organic hierarchy* was introduced when defining the crisp dialectical architecture [15], and it still applies to the fuzzy architecture. It is "organic" in the sense that it evolves with each new atom's introduction to the structure. Unlike a traditional static hierarchy that requires insertion into the structure at a specific node, an organic hierarchy evolves with the information, and a user need not explicitly define the hierarchy, which is implicit in the user's categorization of each atom.

2.4   Invariance of Path

Another aspect of the crisp architecture that ports almost directly to the fuzzy architecture is that of the invariance of path—that is, the fact that navigation of the structure is invariant to the order in which one navigates. Let us represent each navigation along a vs-relation as the "selection" of the additional category for the intersection that defines the edge's head node. Let each selection add that category to the path, similar to a traditional file system path (e.g. /A/B/C). For the dialectical architecture, the order of the selection is inconsequential; for instance, /A/B/C, /B/A/C, and /C/A/B all point to the same node, due to the invariance of the fuzzy intersection operation.

2.5   Fuzzy Flows

The concept of a *flow* was introduced in the context of the crisp dialectical architecture [15]. It's definition—a flow is a series of atoms—applies directly to the fuzzy dialectical architecture, but unique implications emerge. Previously, flows have been used to represent the sequential aspect of several types of information, such as narrative, audio, and video. In a fuzzy dialectical architecture representing quantitative information, each data point is an atom and a data stream is a flow. Thus each atom should not be presented to a user as an isolated data point at each node, but should be displayed in a plot (more on plotting in Sect. 4) with a trace representative of a flow. This yields an additional method of navigation, as well. A flow may intersect a node and continue on another node; the user should be able to "follow the flow" to the other node in addition to navigating the categorical structure directly, via edges.

2.6   Fuzzy Dialectic

The Fichtean *dialectic* is the evolution of understanding. It is often represented as a position taken, a thesis; an alternative position taken, an antithesis (not necessarily in conflict with the thesis); and a sublation of the two to form a synthesis [9].[3] Fichte goes so far as to claim that every act of thinking is a synthesis [10], and so it is natural for an information architecture designed to enhance human thinking to express this model.

The crisp dialectical architecture includes a special type of flow to express the dialectic called the *thesis flow*, which also applies to the fuzzy dialectical architecture (and it is this aspect that is its namesake). A thesis flow is defined for each node and can be considered to be a user's description of the intersection of the categories defining the node. When another flow intersects a thesis flow, it is considered an antithesis flow to the thesis. A user would then be prompted to resolve these to form a newly informed thesis. But flow intersections are in fact not limited to thesis flows, so each intersecting flow is an antithesis to a given flow. This dialectical manner can have many instantiations; for instance, consider a thesis flow for the node $A \cap B$ (the relationship between A and B). Perhaps a user has written a document comprising this thesis flow, and then brings in a new quantitative data set such that the flow it defines intersects $A \cap B$. The thesis flow would then require the sublation of the thesis and the antithesis (data). In this way, when newly connected information is introduced to the information system, those flows that are affected can be immediately identified.

3   Algorithmic Instantiation of the Structure

A naïve approach to writing an algorithm to instantiate the fuzzy dialectical architecture would yield exponential computation time. In this section,

---

[3] See Ref. [9] for a discussion of the similarities and differences between the Fichtean and Hegelian dialectics.

we discuss some salient ideas to consider when instantiating the architecture. A highly efficient algorithm for the structure remains an open problem, but progress has been made.

A key insight is that the entire structure need *not* be recomputed when a new atom is inserted or removed. This allows us to incrementally build a structure, which should, of course, be invariant to the order in which atoms are inserted. This is especially important for real-time applications such as robotics.

What requires recomputation when an atom is inserted? Only the relations originating at those nodes that are constructed by categories in associated with the new node need be recomputed. That is, (typically) most of the structure is untouched by the insertion of a new atom. Furthermore, the visibility or hiddenness of an atom never needs to be computed because an atom is visible in only one node, that which is defined by the intersection of all categories associated with it.

Moreover, any node that is *new* to the structure requires no structural computation, since all its relations must be vs-relations because no relation can possibly contain more than the others, since only one atom (the new one) is at the "bottom" of those paths. This allows extremely quick insertions for new categories and combinations of categories.

The unavoidably most computationally intensive aspect of the computation is the re-computation of metacategories for those nodes affected by the insertion of a new node. It is important to note that once a minimal metacategory has been found at a given level, no more levels are required.

It is also of note that memory resources can become an issue if the structure is maintained in memory (especially if metacategories are stored). It is advisable to use a graph database to persist and access the structure.

4   Human Interfacing for the Fuzzy Architecture

As with any information architecture, the fuzzy dialectical architecture may have innumerable instantiations. In this section, we describe general guidelines for these instantiations and present a specific example in Sect. 4.1.

The user should be able to browse nodes like a traditional hierarchy.
The nodes represent the intersection of categories, as they typically do in a hierarchy or in tag-based browsing. The hierarchy has a long and illustrious history of value to human thinking [5]. Although the structure is, in fact, a graph, it will be natural to most users to experience it as a hierarchy. The "hierarchy" the user interacts with will be *organic* in the sense that it may change when new information is added to the system. All the spatial metaphors so valuable to hierarchies will be applicable, like "up" and "down," "in" and "out." At each node, the visible edges should be represented as single categories—the category that would be intersected with the current node to yield the lower node.

The user should be presented only visible edges.

"Information overload" has been identified as a significant challenge to our information age [19,24]. One of the primary advantages of the dialectical architecture is that it minimizes the amount of information a user is presented at each node, much like a traditional hierarchy, which "tucks" the information that is further-categorized into lower levels. This means "hidden" atoms and edges should not be presented, explicitly (although exceptions can be made, of course). In some instances, hidden atoms, as defined above, might also be hidden from the user's view; however, caution is advisable here, since in some instances, the interface might call for their visibility.

The user should be able to browse "up" to any parent node.

The property of the architecture that the path order is invariant can be exploited to allow browsing the structure in a manner analogous to the hierarchical "up-one-level," but with multiple possibilities. The user can traverse "up" to any parent node, of which there may be several, unlike in the hierarchy, which allows each node to have only a single parent. This can be visualized by allowing the user to de-select any selected category along the path, and not merely the last-selected.

The user should be able to browse by following edges or flows.

Following edges is the *structural* method of navigating and is isomorphic to browsing traditional hierarchies. The dialectical architecture adds the ability to browse along *flows* as well. A flow can intersect a node for one or more consecutive atoms, then move to another node. For instance, an article may be discussing the intersection of several topics, then drill deeper into it with an additional categorization, which would lead it to a child node. This could be navigated by "going with the flow," such that the user continues to see the series of atoms that comprise the flow.

The user should be able to synthesize newly intersecting flows.

The dialectical aspect of the architecture requires the thesis–antithesis–synthesis structure of information development. An information attempting to enhance human thinking should certainly capture the development of that thinking, which this feature accomplishes. A flow can be "intersected" when another flow is coincident with a node the flow traverses, and this intersection may provide a new perspective to the original flow (antithesis). A user should be able to synthesize the two perspectives such that their information system remains well-curated.

The user should be able to view quantitative data in graphs.

With the inclusion of quantitative information, the fuzzy dialectical architecture should have a user interface that presents quantitative information in a concomitant manner, typically a graph. A data point (atom) that is visible at a given node may belong to a multivariate data set and belongs to the node with some membership value in the range $[0, 1]$. A two-dimensional graph of given data set intersecting a node is often the best option; the user's ability to change which variables are plotted on the abscissa and ordinate axes is important. Data series should be connected and multiple series on the same graph should appear with different line properties or colors.[4]

The user should be presented the membership of an atom in a node.

The fuzziness of the architecture yields an interesting aspect of the information: the degree to which each atom belongs to a given node. For quantitative information, the membership value of each point in the node should be presented; we suggest opacity of the data point. For other types of information, several techniques are possible, including sorting, iconic differentiation, color, and opacity.

We now turn to an example instantiation for demonstration purposes.

4.1   A Demonstration

An exemplar set of data was generated for demonstrative purposes as if from sensors on a balloon deployed to measure atmospheric data at various altitudes. Each data point consists of four quantities: altitude, air temperature, air pressure, and air density. The Committee on Extension to the Standard Atmosphere (COESA) [1] has defined a mathematical model used here to synthesize sensor data. The data points were categorized using fuzzy set theory, parsed with an algorithm that computes the fuzzy dialectical structure, and presented to the user. This data set was chosen for demonstration purposes because changes in air properties with altitude are well-understood.

Simulated sensor data was generated in Python [18] using Scikit Aero [8]. An objective of this project is to analyze continuous streams of sensor data coming from scientific robots, so Python was chosen for compatibility with the robotics simulation environment MORSE [3]. Scikit Aero has the COESA standard atmosphere model. In order to simulate sensor variability, the generated data was randomized with a standard distribution appropriate to the type of data, the results of which are displayed in Fig. 1.

The fuzzy architecture presents data based on relationships between categories. Quantitative information such as sensor data require preprocessing in order to be actionable by the algorithm. Fuzzy set theory was utilized to categorize the data. Three categories were defined for each variable by assigning membership functions. For simplicity all modifier categories are titled high, medium, and low for each variable. Assigning the original data membership in each category resulted in each measurement having 16 separate values (four variables plus membership values in 12 categories). All category membership functions are triangularly shaped and evenly divided across the data. The Python package Scikit Fuzzy [7] was employed to generate the membership functions and to

---

[4] We suggest a designer to make liberal use of the advice given by Tufte [22] for the visual display of quantitative information.

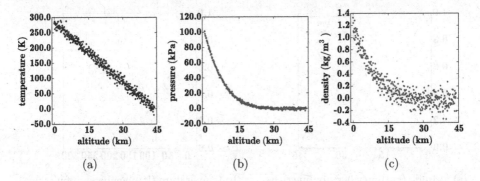

Fig. 1. Simulated sensor data. Atmospheric data was generated from the COESA standard atmosphere model from 0 up to 44 km. Normal distributions simulating sensor variability applied to altitude, temperature, pressure and density variables with standard deviations 25 m, 10 K, 1 kPa, 0.1 kg/m^3.

assign a fuzzy membership value to each category for each data point.[5] Fuzzy membership functions are visualized in Fig. 2.

User Interface. Although not demonstrative of every aspect of the fuzzy dialectical architecture, the user interface we new describe follows the guidelines described at the beginning of this Sect. 4 to present the atmospheric data described above. We first consider the data presented at the node defined by the intersection of two categories: high-temperature and mid-pressure. Atoms having a strong association with both of these categories should be most strongly visible. A screen-capture of the information presented at this node are displayed in Fig. 3a. The opacity of each data point is representative of its membership in the node. In this instantiation, all graphs present the altitude on the abscissa and the other variables on the ordinate.[6] This node from which we begin our description is displayed in the upper-right corner in green: two categories have been selected (t_hi intersect p_md) and can be deselected by clicking the "x." This node has available to it the edge traversals described by the categories in purple. Figure 3b shows what the user is displayed when browsing the node t_hi intersect p_md intersect rho_hi. Note how the display has changed such that only the data most strongly associated with these three nodes is displayed. Finally, Fig. 3c shows the result of an "up" traversal performed by deselecting the p_md category.

---

[5] While these categories are adequate for this demonstration, the Scikit Fuzzy package offers the flexibility to tune membership functions to more accurately align with user selected categories. A user would have the ability to quickly and intuitively define categories based on data type and origin.

[6] In future instantiations, the authors envision allowing the user to select which variable is plotted on each axis.

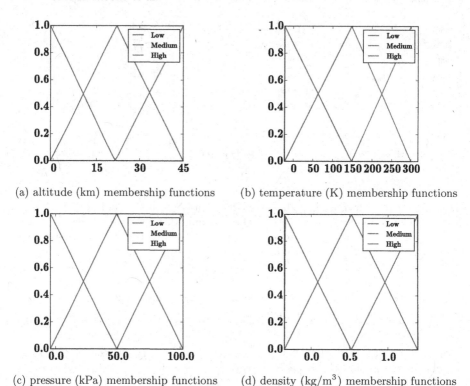

(a) altitude (km) membership functions   (b) temperature (K) membership functions

(c) pressure (kPa) membership functions   (d) density (kg/m^3) membership functions

Fig. 2. Fuzzy membership functions. Three fuzzy categories for each variable are evenly distributed across the range of values for that variable.

Implementation Considerations. To review, sensor data can be processed by a fuzzy categorization engine, written to a database, read by the fuzzy dialectical algorithm, and displayed by a user interface, as shown in Fig. 4. In this instantiation, simulated measurements and their corresponding membership values were written to a PostgreSQL database [20] for later retrieval by the fuzzy dialectical algorithm. The use of the database separates categorization from analysis and presentation. This modular hierarchy of simulation, categorization, storage, and retrieval was chosen because it enhances the resiliency and flexibility of the system. Each module can be run on a different physical system at a different geographical location depending on the requirements of the individual implementation. Once continuous streams of data are categorized and stored, they are no longer time-sensitive, and can be batch-processed by the fuzzy architecture algorithm.

The fuzzy dialectical algorithm was written in Ruby [23, v 2.4.0] and powers the user interface, which was built using the Pakyow [12, v 0.11] web application framework, which features graphs generated by c3.js [11, v 0.4.11]. Future implementations will include flow visualization and traversal disparate data types (this instantiation shows only quantitative information, but this is incidental and not an inherent limitation).

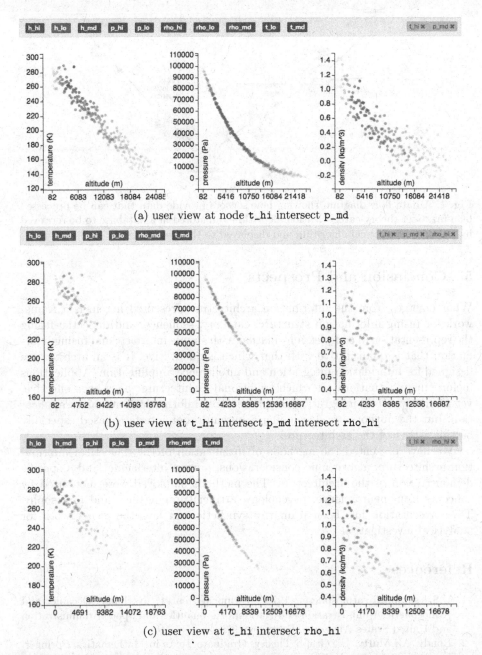

(a) user view at node t_hi intersect p_md

(b) user view at t_hi intersect p_md intersect rho_hi

(c) user view at t_hi intersect rho_hi

Fig. 3. The user interface for the demonstration of the fuzzy dialectical architecture. In Fig. 3a, the user begins at node t_hi intersect p_md. In Fig. 3b, the user has traversed "down" to node t_hi intersect p_md intersect rho_hi. In Fig. 3c, the user has traversed "up" to node t_hi intersect rho_hi. Opacity is a function of the data point's membership in the node.

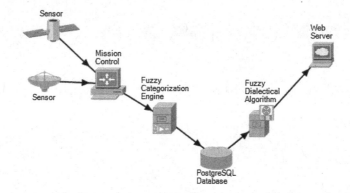

Fig. 4. A data flow diagram showing how sensors provide data that can be processed by a fuzzy-set theory categorization algorithm and stored in a database to be retrieved by the fuzzy dialectical algorithm and displayed to the user.

5   Conclusion and Prospects

What emerges from the information architecture presented herein is a framework for fusing information structure, category, sequence, and dialectic; fusing the representation of complex information with simple interface; and fusing information that is quantitative with that which is qualitative. It is an architecture designed for information integration and intelligence amplification. Applications include many situations for which traditional architectures have been effective, yet restrictive. The integration of quantitative information has many application, but the authors are developing a human-robot interface based especially on this aspect of the architecture.

We have presented the methods of fuzzification of the dialectical information architecture, algorithmic considerations, human interfacing, and a specific demonstration of the architecture. The methods employed were motivated by concepts from neuroscience, psychology, artificial intelligence, and philosophy. This presentation has been primarily synthetic and lays the groundwork for analytical investigation.

References

1. U.S. standard atmosphere, 1976. Technical report, National Oceanic and Atmospheric Administration and National Aeronautics and Space Administration and United States Air Force, February 1976
2. Bondy, A., Murty, U.: Graph Theory. Graduate Texts in Mathematics. Springer, London (2011)
3. Echeverria, G., Lemaignan, S., Degroote, A., Lacroix, S., Karg, M., Koch, P., Lesire, C., Stinckwich, S.: Simulating complex robotic scenarios with MORSE. In: Noda, I., Ando, N., Brugali, D., Kuffner, J.J. (eds.) SIMPAR 2012. LNCS (LNAI), vol. 7628, pp. 197–208. Springer, Heidelberg (2012). doi:10.1007/978-3-642-34327-8_20

4. Edelman, G.M.: Neural Darwinism: The Theory of Neuronal Group Selection. Basic Books, New York (1987)
5. Garrett, J.: Elements of User Experience, The: User-Centered Design for the Web and Beyond. Voices That Matter. Pearson Education, Boston (2010)
6. Jain, A.K., Murty, M.N., Flynn, P.J.: Data clustering: a review. ACM Comput. Surv. **31**(3), 264–323 (1999). http://doi.acm.org/10.1145/331499.331504
7. Warner, J.: Scikit-fuzzy: A fuzzy logic toolbox for scipy. http://pythonhosted.org/scikit-fuzzy/
8. Cano, J.L.: Scikit-aero: Aeronautical engineering calculations in python. https://github.com/AeroPython/scikit-aero
9. Kaufmann, W.: Hegel: A Reinterpretation. A Doubleday Anchor Book. Doubleday, Garden City (1966)
10. Kroeger, A.E.: The difference between the dialectic method of hegel and the synthetic method of kant and fichte. J. Specul. Philos. **6**(2), 184–187 (1872). http://www.jstor.org/stable/25665792
11. Tanaka, M.: C3.js: D3-based reusable chart library. http://c3js.org
12. Metabahn: Pakyow: A realtime web framework for Ruby. https://www.pakyow.org
13. de Oliveira, J., Pedrycz, W.: Advances in Fuzzy Clustering and its Applications. Wiley (2007). https://books.google.com/books?id=Pn0e1xm4YBgC
14. Pfeifer, R., Bongard, J.: How the Body Shapes the Way We Think: A New View of Intelligence. MIT Press (2006). https://books.google.com/books?id=EHPMv9MfgWwC
15. Picone, R.A.R., Powell, B.: A new information architecture: a synthesis of structure, flow, and dialectic. In: Yamamoto, S. (ed.) HIMI 2015. LNCS, vol. 9172, pp. 320–331. Springer, Cham (2015). doi:10.1007/978-3-319-20612-7_31
16. Rosenfield, I.: The Invention of Memory: A New View of the Brain. Basic Books (1988). https://books.google.com/books?id=5e_aAAAAMAAJ
17. Ross, T.: Fuzzy Logic with Engineering Applications, 3rd edn. Wiley, New York (2011)
18. Rossum, G.: Python reference manual. Technical report, Amsterdam, The Netherlands (1995)
19. Strother, J.B., Ulijn, J.M., Fazal, Z.: Information Overload: An International Challenge for Professional Engineers and Technical Communicators. Wiley-IEEE Press (2012). No. ISBN 9781118360491. http://ieeexplore.ieee.org/servlet/opac?bknumber=6354045
20. The PostgreSQL Global Development Group: Postgresql. https://www.postgresql.org/docs/9.6/static/index.html
21. Trudeau, R.: Introduction to Graph Theory. Dover Books on Mathematics. Dover Publications, New York (2013)
22. Tufte, E.: The Visual Display of Quantitative Information. Graphics Press (2001). https://books.google.com/books?id=GTd5oQEACAAJ
23. Matsumoto, Y.: Ruby. https://ruby-lang.org
24. Zeldes, N., Sward, D., Louchheim, S.: Infomania: Why we can't afford to ignore it any longer. First Monday **12**(8), August 2007. http://firstmonday.org/ojs/index.php/fm/article/view/1973/1848
25. Zimmermann, H.: Fuzzy Set Theory–and Its Applications. Springer, Netherlands (2001)

Information and Interaction Design

Programming of a Visualization for a Robot Teach Pendant

Sebastian Galen[1], Dirk Liedtke[2], and Daniel Schilberg[1(✉)]

[1] Bochum University of Applied Sciences, Bochum, Germany
daniel.schilberg@hs-bochum.de
[2] Miele AG, Munich, Germany

Abstract. The intention of this paper is to develop and implement a user interface for the teach pendant of the new generation of robot controllers by Stäubli. The user interface is realized on the basis of an already existing visualization in the production of Miele in Bielefeld. In order to guarantee a structured development, the method of software-reengineering is used. In the first two steps it is necessary to analyze the tasks and functions of the existing software and to model the current state and the actual technical implementations. The requirements for the redesign of the software have to be compiled next. With the help of this requirements it is possible to develop a new user interface which includes the future layout and utilization [1, pp. 385–387]. The finished software helps to introduce the new technology into familiar operational procedures without any training of the employees.

Keywords: Robotics · User interface

1 Introduction

In the age of globalization and irresistible technical progress it is indispensable to constantly improve the production and automation processes to be able to place new, innovative and competitive products in the market at a reasonable price. In order to automate the production processes, the application of robots plays a more and more important role. The control of a robot can also be used to control other devices within the robot cells via industry bus systems. Industrial computers with touch panels are often used to guarantee the service and the supervision of devices and the robot. These computers allow, e.g. the settings, the visualization of sensors or the starting of processes. In order to steadily improve safety and handling of the robots, controls have been developed whose teach pendants are able to take over the real programming tasks of the robots as well as over the just explained service and supervision of the external devices. As a consequence of individually provided visualizations indicated on this extended teach pendants, industrial computers with touch panel are no longer necessary.

At this, the always returning job of introducing the new processes and functions to the employees as simple as possible plays an important role. This will only be possible if, in spite of new devices and controls, the usual work flow can be retained and changes can be reduced to a necessary minimum. If the operating surfaces of new machines are

S. Yamamoto (Ed.): HIMI 2017, Part I, LNCS 10273, pp. 161–169, 2017.
DOI: 10.1007/978-3-319-58521-5_12

adaptable, optics and functionalities should be as close to the visualization known by the employee as possible in order to minimize the training effort and to maximize the acceptance. Hence, the operating surface of the new teach pendant should orientate itself very strongly towards those of the industrial computer with touch panel.

This paper deals with the development and conversion of the visualization of the teach pendant of the new robot control by means of a practical example in the production of Miele in Bielefeld where robots of the company Stäubli are used.

1.1 Objective of the Paper

In this paper, the basics of the necessary computer languages for the surface programming HTML and JavaScript are explained first. Afterwards, the requirements for the development of the visualization possibilities of the operating surfaces of touch panels are developed and adapted for the special use of Miele. The aim of this conversion is to program an adaptably applicable and very intuitively served visualization which relieves the later user who has to adapt himself from an old to a new operating surface. Besides, the enlargement and the adaptation of the operating surface should be very simple to move by additional functions for the programmer.

The visualization is realized with HTML. JavaScript is used for the control of the HTML visualization and VAL3 for the linking with the robot computer language.

1.2 Approach

In order to guarantee a structured development, the method of software reengineering is used. An already existing software is adapted to a new system in the form of a so-called "1:1* separation". This means that the structure of the software is redesigned, but it has still the same functionalities. The software reengineering method includes two

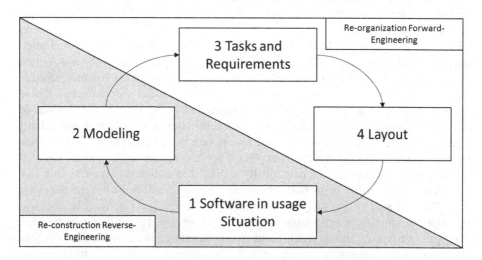

Fig. 1. Re-engineering method [1, pp. 385–387]

phases, the reverse engineering and the forward engineering, which are again subdivided into two steps.

During the first step (Fig. 1) the tasks and functions of the already existing software product are analyzed in order to model the current status and the present technical conversion is modeled (step 2). In the next step the requirements for the redesign of the software are listed regarding the point of view of the later user and the programmer. Finally, a new software concept can be developed by means of these requirements (step 4) [1, pp. 385–387].

2   Essentials

2.1   HTML

HTML means "Hypertext Markup Language" and is a standard markup language to create documents for web pages. The HTML code is interpreted by the browser and forms the basic construction of a website. The source code is built up with so-called "Tags" which are responsible for the representation and arrangement of the elements. These are embedded in so-called "Markups" [2]. In the following the basic structure of a HTML web page is shown:

```
<HTML>
<HEAD>
<TITLE>title of the website </TITLE>
</HEAD>
<BODY>
main part of the website
  </BODY>
</HTML>
```

2.2   JavaScript

JavaScript is a computer language which is used and translated in all current web browsers. In contrast to the high-level languages, like C or Java, JavaScript is evaluated line by line and does not have to be compiled. Web pages written with HTML are very static, without any functions or events. JavaScript is used to make these websites dynamic. With JavaScript it is possible to change and control the appearance and the contents of websites, the web browser and document contents. A so-called "event handling" can be used to detect the operator's actions, e.g. mouse click on a button. Different functions and events can be effected according to the detected action [3, 4].

2.3   VAL3

There is a huge number of computer languages for robots which differ within the manu-facturers. The probably mostly used languages are VAL3 of the company Stäubli and KRL of the company KUKA. Both are very similar to the high-level languages, like C,

BASIC and Java. Loops and statements, main programs and subroutines as well as the declaration of variables form the basis of the program. In addition, special extensions have been implemented for programming of movements of the robot and input and output instructions.

3   Requirement Analysis

3.1   Analysis of the Current State

As already described in the introduction, the robot control is able to control all external devices connected via bus systems, e.g. inputs and outputs or conveyor belts. In order to monitor and request these devices clearly, an additional industrial computer with an operating surface is required. The industrial computer is connected with the robot control and is able to communicate with all devices in the system.

The operating surface looks the same on every industrial computer, there are just little differences when it comes to the complexity of the robot cell. In spite of the separately running visualization on the industrial computer, the robot still has a teach pendant with which his movements can be programmed and controlled. As the robot control is connected to the local network, the programmer has access to the operating surface on the industrial computer (Fig. 2).

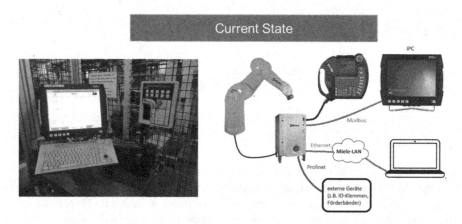

Fig. 2. Current state

One of the disadvantages of this set-up is the high costs for acquisition and installation because the integration of an industrial computer with touch panel is necessary in every robot cell. The maintenance of the software is very complex because the implementation of enlargements and new functions requires a solid knowledge of the computer language C# and the robot computer language VAL3. A change of visualization requires an immediate configuration and implementation of the programming environment of the Stäubli Robotics Suite. Combining the control and the functions of the robot and of the periphery just in the teach pendant would not have these disadvantages.

The new robot control of the company Stäubli allows exactly this (Fig. 3). It has a teach pendant on which not just the robot movements can be programmed and controlled, but also self-programmed visualizations can be shown. The programmer has no longer problems with the integration in the Stäubli Robotics Suite and the development of enlargements and functions because the visualization can be developed directly in the Robotics Suite. Therefore, an example program which contains the JavaScripts with the necessary functions is provided by Stäubli. Nevertheless, the programmer is free to create the surface and the development of other own functions. The surface is realized with the programming language HTML which is controlled with the functions of the JavaScripts and connected with the robot programming language VAL3.

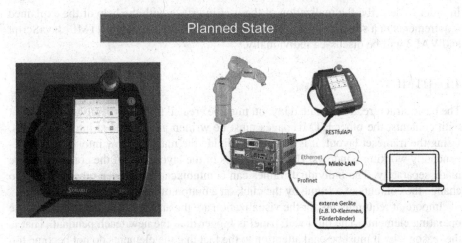

Fig. 3. Planned state

3.2   Requirements for the Visualization

With the help of the new set-up described in the current state analysis arise different requirements for the new surface to be developed. This should also guarantee that the work routines remain unchanged for the operator.

1. Look and Feel:
   - Optics very similar to the old operating surface:
     - Menu structure
     - Arrangement and size of the operating elements
   - Same function of the buttons
   - Feedback after activity of an element
2. Modular site:
   - Inputs and outputs are indicated
   - Construction always similar, functions and labels different
3. VAL3 standards
   - Later changes of the program maybe just necessary in VAL3
   - Keep programming standard in VAL3

- Maintain program structure in VAL3
4. XML databank
    - A XML databank has to be used and integrated in the new visualization. In this
      databank the names of the single menu dots and sensors as well as the inscriptions
      of the possible switch states are built. By the use of this databank, updates or
      extensions of the software must not be customized in the source code, but only
      the accompanying entry in the XML file.

4   Realization

In order to describe the realization of the user interface with the help of the explained
requirements in a structured way, the three programming languages HTML, JavaScript
and VAL3 will be discussed individually.

4.1   HTML

The basic structure, the so-called layout, must be created first. In order to fill this layout
with contents, the other HTML pages must be written and uploaded into the frames.
Using the frameset layout, it is possible to divide the main window into various independently working windows. Hereby, updates of the layout and of the contents can be
made separately. The individual frames can communicate with each other in order to
change the contents of a frame by the click on a button of another frame [5].

Important requirements for the visualization are the arrangement and the size of the
operating elements. The old touch panel is bigger than the new teach pendant. That is
the reason why it must be paid attention to the fact that the elements do not become too
small and are still comfortable for the operator when it comes to the handling. However,
this problem only appears if several columns with operating elements are needed. For
the solution of this problem a button has to be added which leads to a page on which
other columns with operating elements can be displayed.

Any functions of the operating elements in the menu bar and on the main page have
to stay the same. This allows an easier familiarization for the user with the new software.
Every single function must be analyzed in detail with the help of the experts' know-how
of the old system. In addition, after a button is pressed by the operator, the background
color of it has to be changed as soon as the desired function is executed. This feedback
must be initiated from the robot control. That is why the background color should not
be overwrote by an already firmly defined color in HTML or in the Stylesheet (Fig. 4).

There are also several different menu dots which open a page on which different
inputs and outputs can be indicated. The indicated modular page is always the same,
merely the inscriptions and of course the functions of the buttons change. The inscription
is performed by the import of a XML databank. In order to differ between the functions
of the buttons depending on the selected menu dot, the VAL3 program has to call the
suitable subroutine. In this subroutine the inputs and outputs can be selected and a feedback can be sent to the teach pendant.

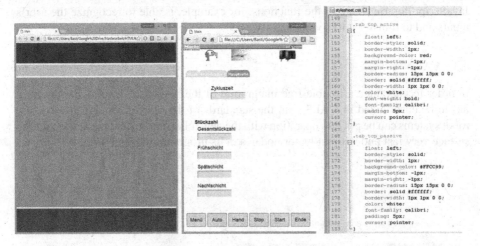

Fig. 4. Style and menu setup

4.2   JavaScript

In order to make the described HTML pages dynamic, different JavaScript functions have to be written. These functions are necessary e.g. to open pages, to control the navigation bar, to import the XML databank or to establish the link between the robot control and the visualization. Every HTML document has its own JavaScript which is read by loading the actual page. The functions of the scripts are now available to the document and can be activated. The JavaScript can access and change the operating elements of the HTML document with the help of an assigned ID or a certain tag.

The import of the XML databank and automatic marking of the operating elements are important requirements for the visualization. Therefore, a function was created which reads the XML file by means of a XMLHttpRequest and marks the operating elements (Fig. 5).

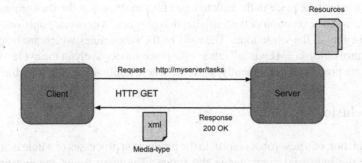

Fig. 5. Communication setup

In order to allow the communication between the operating elements on the HTML surface and the robot control, the company Stäubli has provided the already mentioned

JavaScript libraries. One of the functions, for example, is able to recognize the user's inputs and to transfer it to a variable in VAL3.

4.3   VAL3

In order to guarantee a trouble-free integration of the new visualization, the program has to be customized in VAL3 with the standards of the old software. Thus, existing robot systems can be put into operation with the new robot control and the new operating surface very fast and without major updates in its programming (Fig. 6).

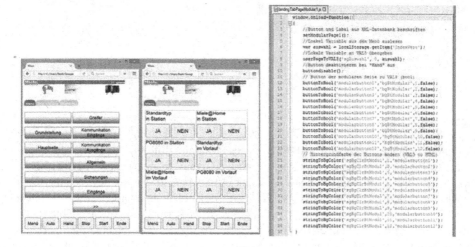

Fig. 6. Menu structure detachment

First the function "start()" is executed automatically after the start of the application. The HTML surface is loaded on the teach pendant with the command "User-Page("main")". Then the task for the control of the user interface is called. The initialization processes take place in the task to unset all variables, e.g. the background colors of the buttons. The execution of this initialization program is necessary only once before the cycle begins in the while loop. The calls of the subroutines which are responsible for the control of the HTML visualization take place successively in the cycle. All these programs are processed permanently, until the whole application is quit by the user.

5   Conclusion

The introduction of a new robot control to the production processes of Miele is supposed to replace the industrial computer in the future. The control and monitoring of the external devices is now possible via the new teach pendant. Therefore, it is necessary to develop a new user interface which guarantees the service of the connected devices with all functions used before. The main purpose of the present work is to make the conversion from the old to the new operating software for the user as easy as possible.

Therefore, the software reengineering process was applied. In the course of that process the old software product was analyzed and the requirements for the new software were defined. With the help of that a fully operational user interface corresponding to the requirements with the explained programming languages has been created. On the basis if this work and the new developments of Stäubli, the efficiency in the automation areas of the production of Miele can be increased in the future (Fig. 7).

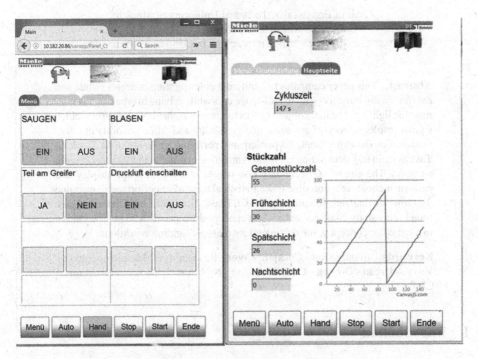

Fig. 7. Menu 1:1* detachment

References

1. Henning, K., Gramatke, A., Schilberg, D.: Informatik im Maschinenbau, Aachen (2008)
2. IT Wissen, HTML (2016). http://www.itwissen.info/definition/lexikon/hypertext-markup-language-HTML.html. Accessed 24 May 2016
3. Feuerstack, T.: JavaScript in 2 Tagen, Hagen (2004)
4. IT Wissen, JavaScript (2016). http://www.itwissen.info/definition/lexikon/JavaScript-Java Script.html. Accessed 25 May 2016
5. Daum, M.: LOS!Web (2004). http://los.webdaum.de/inhalt/inhalt_schule/seite_teilen.html#tab. Accessed 11 July 2016

A Comparison of Two Cockpit Color Concepts Under Mesopic Lighting Using a CRT Task

Martin Götze[(✉)], Antonia S. Conti, and Klaus Bengler

Chair of Ergonomics, Technical University of Munich,
Boltzmannstraße 15, 85747 Garching, Germany
{martin.goetze,antonia.conti,bengler}@tum.de

Abstract. This paper compares two different color lighting concepts (white and red) for the instrument cluster in mid-range cars while driving in urban areas under mesopic lighting. The main objective was to assess whether both concepts yielded similar results in terms of attention, interpretability and differentiability of information. For the experiment, 30 participants performed a Continuous Tracking Task as main task demanding continuous attention in order to model a real driving situation. The aim of the secondary task was to observe a cockpit display and perform a choice reaction time task. Statistical tests were performed to examine the error rates and reaction times for the CRT task. No significant differences were found. This study confirms that a white concept shows no disadvantages relative to a red color concept while driving under mesopic lighting conditions.

Keywords: Illumination · Cockpit · Color · Readability · Mesopic · Scotopic · Vision · Urban · Driving · Car · Occlusion · Night-time · Choice reaction time · CRT

1   Introduction

1.1   Motivation

Driving is a process inducing high visual and cognitive load. Consequently, the driver experiences high workload on visual perception, cognitive information processing as well as manual responses (Recarte and Nunes 2003). In order to perform well, additional effort is needed to deal with the task load. This exceptional effort is even more crucial while driving at night time or twilight in urban areas as the driver needs to continually readapt and adjust to the items on the road and inside the car. Driver attention depending on the frequency and duration of glances away from the road scene (Jahn et al. 2005). The aim of developing such systems must to create more efficient in-vehicle displays that draw even less attention away from the primary driving task, decreasing driver workload and providing a safer driving experience as a consequence.

The National Highway Traffic Safety Administration Report gives a good overview of which consequences a lack of concentration might bring (Neale et al. 2005). The report states that driver inattention is associated with 78% of traffic collisions and 65% of near collisions. One of the reasons is assumed as "driving related inattention to the

© Springer International Publishing AG 2017
S. Yamamoto (Ed.): HIMI 2017, Part I, LNCS 10273, pp. 170–183, 2017.
DOI: 10.1007/978-3-319-58521-5_13

forward roadway and non-specific eye glances". Designing in-vehicle interfaces and cockpit displays that do not distract is advantageous.

1.2   Mesopic Vision in Urban Areas

Driving at night time is more risky than driving during the day. Although only 25% of the overall traffic takes place during hours of darkness, the number of accidents is equal compared to the day time traffic (Rumar 2002). In the dark hours, road lighting and in-vehicle lights play an important role in visual performance during night driving. One major goal when designing in-vehicle information systems is decrease distraction associated with the device. The information displayed on an instrument cluster should be acquired quickly and safely without distracting too much from the primary driving task. Studies on visual performance while driving show that stimuli presented under different lighting levels are interpreted differently. Specifically, the error rate and reaction time increases with a decreasing luminance level. (Alferdinck 2006).

For some brands, the first in-vehicle color concept for the instrument cluster to be used for night-time driving were developed based on the light and luminance used in sea or underground vehicles, such as submarines. In such environments, persons were completely deprived of external light sources and operated in the scotopic visual range (Boyce 2006). The color chosen for those instrument cluster concepts was red as to not disrupt dark adaptation (Purkinje effect). At this lower levels the color red (700 nm) is not affected, because the sensitivity of the human eye shifts toward the blue end of the color spectrum as can be seen in Fig. 1. If the dark adapted eye senses only light of wavelength at the right end of the spectrum like red, then the rods of the eye won't

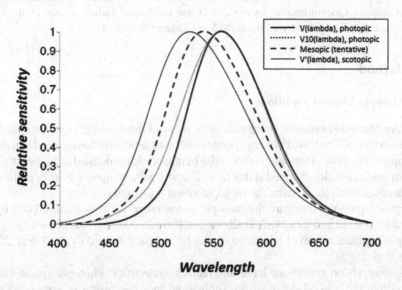

Fig. 1. The CIE spectral luminous efficiency functions for photopic vision, V(k) and V10(k), and scotopic vision V'(k) compared with an example of a tentative spectral mesopic function for a typical mesopic light level (based on Alferdinck 2006, p. 265)

become saturated and stay adapted to the dark, because they are not sensitive to long-wavelengths.

Ordinarily, driving in rural areas at night time is classified as scotopic. However, an urban setting at night or twilight consists of many signals, signs, other vehicles and external street lamps that serve as light sources in addition to instrument cluster lights (Stockman and Sharpe 2006; Viikari 2008). Furthermore, other internal light sources such as navigation or entertainment systems also contribute to the overall lighting. These multiple light sources can activate mesopic vision in the driver. Since previous studies have shown that urban driving does not operate under scotopic vision, the possibility of a new instrument cluster lighting concept, other than red, becomes available.

In this study, our main objective was to compare task performance between two interior color concepts (old and new) in terms of interpretability and differentiability, attention, readability under mesoscopic lighting conditions. Specific to these terms, we defined the following research questions:

- **Interpretability and differentiability.** How accurately can the information be read from each display? How efficiently can targets be recognized and identified?
- **Attention.** How quickly can the information be read from the display?
- **Readability.** Can the information presented in each cockpit be seen with the same efficacy? What is the detection threshold for information presented on the display?

In this paper, only the terms specified in the first two points are addressed. Both subjective (e.g., questionnaire-based; already published in (Götze et al. 2013) and objective (e.g., performance-based) data was collected in this experiment. The participants performed two separate experiments evaluating the aforementioned criteria. In this paper, only the first experiment is presented. The subjective data using a modified Post-Study Usability Questionnaire (Lewis 2002) was published earlier (Götze et al. 2013) and, the second experiment was published in Götze et al. (2014).

2 Method

2.1 Mesopic Vision Conditions

The aforementioned mesopic vision condition is one of the three light levels defined for the human vision. The visual system operates over a wide range of luminance from about 10–6 up to 106 cd/m^2. Photopic vision is the luminance level defined as higher than 3–10 cd/m^2 and is usually obtained at day time. Starting with twilight or even at night with streetlamps, moonlight or stars, the mesopic vision condition is active.

Depending on the literature the mesopic vision range is defined from 0.001 up to 3-10 cd/m^2 (Boyce and Rea 1987; Dacheux and Raviola 2000). It is acknowledged that the upper luminance limit of this range cannot be precisely defined (Viikari et al. 2005; Plainis et al. 2005).

All three vision conditions have different characteristics: Photopic vision allows color vision and a good detail of discrimination, mesopic vision is associated with diminished color vision and less detail discrimination while scotopic vision is associated with no color vision and poor detail discrimination (Boyce 2006).

2.2 Instrument Cluster and Colors Used

In this study two different cockpit color concepts of an instrument cluster were compared in order to determine if a new color concept (e.g., white) is not worse than the currently used red color concept as can be found in many mid-range cars. Figure 2 shows the design of the concept as well as the size.

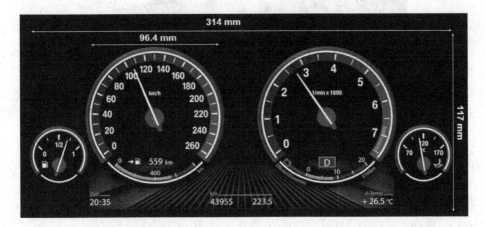

Fig. 2. The cockpit concept used in this study with its measurements

The whole cockpit width including two small (fuel and water temperature) and two large rings (speedometer and tachometer) is 314 mm with a height of 117 mm. The diameter of the large rings was 96.4 mm each. All measurements were equal to the actual size of those in instrument clusters used in current vehicles.

The baseline color red had the wavelength of 603.2 nm. The luminance level of the cockpit was tailored for mesopic vision conditions and set to 7.8 cd/m^2 while the white display had 11.0 cd/m^2.

2.3 Framework Conditions of the Study

The study took place in an experimental room under mesopic lighting conditions in a range from 0.01 cd/m^2 up to a maximum of 1 cd/m^2 to maintain visual function within a mesopic range.

The experiment included two separate experiments, each consisting of two experimental parts assessing the white and the red color concept. Both experiments and experimental parts were fully randomized among all participants. The second part was described and published earlier as mentioned before (Götze et al. 2014). For this experiment a setting resembling a real vehicle was established. The participants sat in a car seat and had to perform two task simultaneously (see Fig. 3).

Participants had to perform two tasks. The main task presented on the larger upper screen was a driving-like continuous tracking task (CTT) demanding continuous attention and control in order to model a real driving situation and to ensure the participants were not constantly observing the cockpit display where the secondary task was shown.

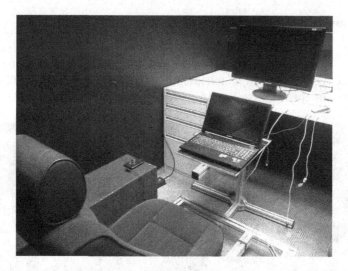

Fig. 3. Experimental setting of the first experiment. Participants sat in the car seat and performed two tasks simultaneously. On the lower screen a discrimination task was presented and on the upper screen, subjects observed a continuous tracking task.

The aim of this secondary task was to observe the cockpit display shown on the smaller screen (Fig. 3) and perform a choice reaction time (CRT) task.

The CTT screen used was a Samsung 24' computer screen (contrast 20000:1, reaction time 5 ms). The distance between the CTT screen and the cockpit screen was 60 cm. The cockpit screen had a presentation angle of 24' and was placed on a 66 cm table in a distance of 70 cm from the participant's eyes. All distances and presentation angles matched a real car setup.

In order to respond to the CTT, a joystick was placed on an arm rest to the right of the participants. In addition, a keypad to the left was used to respond to the CRT task.

2.4   Continuous Tracking Task (CTT)

A CTT is a visual-manual task, which requires continuous control activity of the participant (Eichinger, 2011). The task in this type of CTT was to control the position of a vertically and horizontally moving cross-hair toward a central point using a joystick. The movement of this target cross can be described as a first order instability. With no influence of the participant on the cross-hair movements, the cross-hair divergently approaches the display edges. In order to bring the target back to the center of the screen, participants have to make a corrective joystick input.

2.5   Discriminating Warning and Information Signals

The aim of the discrimination task was to observe the cockpit display and respond to small arrows in different colors (green, yellow, and red) presented in the upper part of the cockpit (Fig. 4). The chosen colors corresponded to regular colors in a car used for warnings (yellow), danger (red) and informative signals (green). The wavelength of the specific colors presented was as following: red 609.4 nm, yellow 578.8 nm and green 554.4 nm.

Fig. 4. Cockpit display with a left arrow shown in the upper mid. Participants had to respond to this arrow in time using the keypad.

Participants had to respond to the direction of the presented arrows using the keypad. Only left and right arrows were used. In addition, three different positions of the arrows were shown to prevent guessing of the participants. In summary, a total of 12 different options per cockpit color could appear (2 directions [left/right] * 3 colors [red/yellow/green] * 3 positions [left/mid/right]).

The following performance errors were possible: Miss (participant did not respond in time), erroneous response (participant responded with the incorrect direction) and false alarm (participant responded with no arrow shown). If the participant discriminated and indicated the correct direction within the permitted timeframe, the response was a hit.

One experimental block (with either red or white display concept) contained of 108 trials and lasted 10 min. To decrease the predictability of the arrows even more, three inter-stimulus intervals were used: 3000, 5000 and 7000 ms. The signal presentation time was 1000 ms (as per Jahn et al. 2005; Merat and Jamson 2008). The task was to be as fast and as accurate as possible.

2.6 Procedure

After each volunteer's arrival at the laboratory, information about the study was provided. All had to perform a visual acuity test using the Landolt C as well as a color vision test to check for visual impairments. Participants then completed a demographic questionnaire before initiating a dark adaptation period, which lasted at least 20 min (Lamb and Pugh 2004). Participants then started to perform the main experimental tasks. Before each experimental part, a training (54 trials) was carried out in order to counteract learning effects. After each part, participants answered the Post-Study Usability Questionnaire adapted to our study (Götze et al. 2013).

After the first experimental part, which contained two blocks (2 × 108 trials) of a particular display color concept, a five-minute block performing only the CTT without a discrimination task was performed. This established a baseline level of the CTT performance.

2.7 Data Acquisition

The cockpit display presentations of both experiments were prepared and executed with E-Prime 2.0 (Psychology Software Tools, Inc.). The data of the CRT experiment was acquired for both tasks separately (CRT task and CTT) using two computers. The results and performance time of the CTT was saved in a MySQL database. The reaction times and error rates of the CRT task were recorded with E-Prime. Questionnaires after each experimental part were performed orally by the supervisor since the mesopic vision of the participants did not allow otherwise.

2.8 Participants

Thirty healthy male volunteers participated in this study. The sample was limited to only male participants due to findings indicating possible gender effects on visual task performance (see Der and Deary 2006). All volunteers were aged between 24 and 54 years, with a mean age of 43 years. None of the participants reported to suffer from any visual or motoric impairments. The visual acuity and color vision tests were also successfully completed by all participants. The driving experience varied between 15 and 36 years with an average of 25 years. The driving distance per year ranged from 8000 to 70000 km with a mean of 25000 km.

3 Results

Statistical power of the analysis is assessed by two types of errors, α-error and β-error. In this study, in order to increase the power of the analysis, the α-error was established on the level of $\alpha = 25\%$, simultaneously decreasing the β-error to $\beta = 75\%$ (Bortz 2005).

3.1 CTT Performance

The Continuous Tracking Task was performed simultaneous to the CRT task in order resemble a real driving, multitask situation. The performance of the CTT was assessed as a standard error of the regression (RMSE) for each participant. Additionally, the mean global performance level and the global standard deviation (SD) of all participants were calculated. Participants with a result lower than mean $\pm$ 2.0 SD in at least two blocks were excluded as they did not fulfill the criterion of carrying out both tasks simultaneously. Three participants were excluded in this step (Table 1).

Table 1. Mean RMSE and SD of the CTT in particular experimental blocks are presented. Twenty-seven of 30 participants performed the CTT in the range of M ± 2 SD of the global performance of all participants.

	Baseline	White 1	White 2	Red 1	Red 2
Mean	35.62	42.38	42.87	41.15	42.33
SD	5.860	7.304	6.539	4.949	7.921

3.2   CRT Task – Error Rate

The error rate for each participant was calculated in order to examine the difference in global accuracy between the white and red cockpit color concept. The global accuracy is defined as the number of correct responses. The total number of trials was 432 (two blocks of each color with 108 trials) (Table 2).

Table 2. Error rate with SD and global accuracy of the CRT task. Twenty-seven of 30 participants performed the participants.

	White	Red
Mean	0.0174	0.0167
SD	0.0113	0.0114
Accuracy	98.26%	98.33%

A paired-samples two tailed t-test was used to examine differences in error rates between the two lighting concepts. There was no significant difference in global error

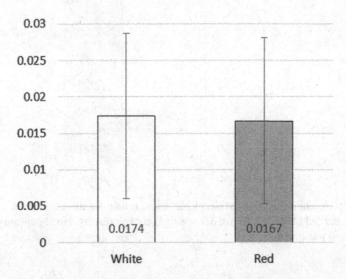

Fig. 5. Choice reaction time task. Mean global error rate for the white ($M = 0.0174$, $SD = 0.0113$) and red ($M = 0.0167$, $SD = 0.0114$) cockpit display. No significant difference between the two color concepts was found.

rate between the white ($M = 0.0174$, $SD = 0.0113$) and red ($M = 0.0167$, $SD = 0.0114$) display found, $t(26) = 0.5273$, $p = 0.6024$, see Fig. 5.

3.3   CRT Task – Reaction Time

For the reaction time analysis only hits were used. Furthermore, trials shorter than 200 ms and higher than 1500 ms were excluded as outlines. Additionally, for each participant the mean reaction time was calculated and trials in a range $M \pm 2.5$ SDs were excluded (287 trials) (Baayen and Milin 2010) (Table 3).

Table 3. Reaction times of the CRT task. Only hits were used. Trials shorter 200 ms and higher 1500 ms were excluded.

	White	Red
Mean	716.50 ms	717.10 ms
SD	89.26	84.55

The mean global reaction time for the two lighting color concepts across all participants was calculated. A paired-sampled t-test was executed to examine any difference in global reaction time between the two colors. There was no significant difference found between white ($M = 716.50$ ms, $SD = 89.26$) and red ($M = 717.10$ ms, $SD = 84.55$) cockpit display, $t(26) = 0.077$, $p = 0.939$, see Fig. 6.

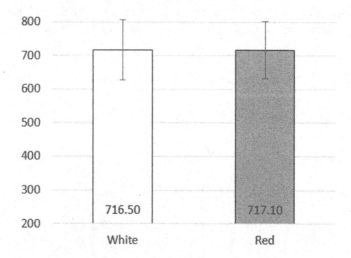

Fig. 6. Choice reaction time task. Mean global reaction time for the white ($M = 716.50$ ms, $SD = 89.26$) and red ($M = 717.10$ ms, $SD = 84.55$) cockpit display. No significant difference between the two was found.

3.4   CRT Task – Reaction Time for Different Arrow Colors

To examine the effect of color concept on reaction time to the three different arrow colors (red, yellow, green), a two-way repeated measures ANOVA was performed for the two cockpit color concepts. Additionally, paired-samples t-tests were performed to examine any difference between the arrow colors in particular.

The arrow color had a significant effect on the reaction time (independent of the lighting color concept): $F(2,52) = 46.166$, $p < 0.001$ (Table 4).

Table 4. Reaction times of the CRT task for a specific arrow color. Only hits were taken into account. Trials shorter 200 ms and higher 1500 ms were excluded.

	Green	Red	Yellow
Mean	720.20 ms	731.400 ms	701.70 ms
SD	88.01	88.37	85.72

Participants responded to yellow arrows ($M = 701.70$ ms, $SD = 85.72$) significantly faster than to both other colors green ($M = 720.20$ ms, $SD = 8801$) and red ($M = 731.40$ ms, $SD = 88.37$), $t_{green}(53) = 5.8302$, $p < .001$, $t_{red}(53) = 8.7454$, $p < .001$, see Fig. 7. Furthermore, green arrows were recognized and responded to significantly faster than red ones, $t(53) = 3.4190$, $p < 0.001$.

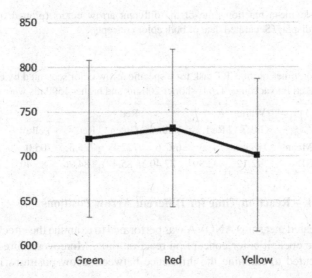

Fig. 7. CRT task. mean reaction time of the different arrow colors presented on the display. Merged data of both color concepts.

A significant interaction between the cockpit color and the arrow colors was found, $F(2,52) = 5.469$, $p = 0.007$, see Fig. 8. No significant difference was found between the green arrows presented on the white ($M = 718.4$ ms, $SD = 92.12$) and red ($M = 722.10$, $SD = 85.43$) color concept, $t(26) = 0.3994$, $p = 0.6929$. There was a significant difference found between the red arrows presented on the white ($M = 737.3$ ms, $SD = 92.89$) and

180   M. Götze et al.

red ($M = 725.5$, $SD = 84.96$) display, $t(26) = 1.6085$, $p = 0.1198$. No significant difference was found between the yellow arrows presented on white ($M = 697.6$ ms,
$SD = 87.40$) and red ($M = 705.8$ ms, $SD = 85.40$), $t(26) = 0.9287$, $p = 0.3616$, see
Table 5.

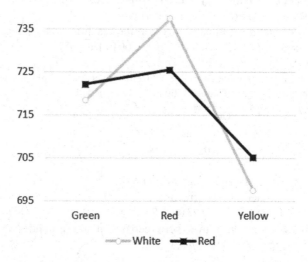

Fig. 8. CRT task. mean reaction time of the different arrow colors (plotted on the x-axis)
presented on the display. Separated data of both color concepts.

Table 5. Reaction times of the CRT task for a specific arrow color separated by color concept.
Only hits were taken into account. Trials shorter 200 ms and higher 1500 ms were excluded.

	White			Red		
	Green	Red	Yellow	Green	Red	Yellow
Mean	718.4	737.3	697.6	722.1	725.5	705.0
SD	92.12	92.89	87.40	85.43	84.96	85.40

3.5 CRT Task – Reaction Time for Different Arrow Positions

A two-way repeated measures ANOVA was performed to examine the effect of an arrow
position and the cockpit color concept on reaction time. Moreover, paired-samples t-
tests were executed to examine the difference between arrow positions in particular
(Table 6).

Table 6. Reaction times of the CRT task for a specific arrow position separated by color concept.
Only hits were taken into account. Trials shorter 200 ms and higher 1500 ms were excluded.

	White			Red		
	Left	Center	Right	Left	Center	Right
Mean	719.5	708.0	725.8	719.2	710.4	723.8
SD	91.87	91.90	88.45	89.20	88.81	79.00

The arrow position had a significant effect on the mean reaction time $F(2,52) = 8.201$, $p = 0.001$. There was no significant interaction found between the lighting color concept and the arrow position $F(2,52) = 0.250$, $p = 0.780$, see Fig. 9.

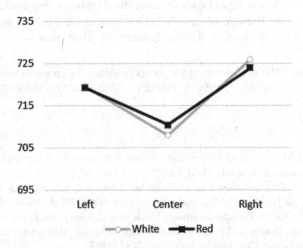

Fig. 9. CRT task. mean reaction time of the different arrow colors (plotted on the x-axis) presented on the display. Separated data of both color concepts, white (gray line) and red (black line).

4   Discussion

The main aim of the current study was to compare two colored cockpit concepts (white and red) in terms of interpretability, differentiability and attention under mesopic conditions (relevant for driving in urban areas at night or twilight). A Choice Reaction Time task was used to facilitate a comparison between the accuracy and speed of recognizing a specific signal in the cockpit display while doing a driving-like task. The aim was to investigate whether the two color concepts yielded the same results for the accuracy and reaction time using different signal colors (red, yellow, and green) and positions (left, center, and right) with a CRT task. No significant difference for the accuracy was found. Furthermore, no significant difference for the reaction time depending on the position and direction was found. For the colors, no significant difference between the cockpit concepts were found for yellow and green; exclusively the red color showed a significantly faster reaction time with the red color display compared to the white one. Taking these results into account as well as the results of the previously published parts of this study, no difference between the two concepts can be established. The interpretability, differentiability, readability and attention of and towards information under mesopic vision, based on the performance and data recorded in this study, is independent of the lighting color concept. Possible future directions may involve investigating possible effects that may occur when drivers' vision has not yet adapted to the environment and or is interrupted in some way.

5 Conclusion

Summing up, the study shows that a white color lighting concept for in-vehicle cockpits, as tested, has neither objective and nor subjective disadvantages over a red color concept under mesopic vision. These results can help in-vehicle display designers or car manufactures with new possibilities for lighting concepts in urban areas

Acknowledgments. The authors would like to acknowledge the cooperation with the BMW Group on this project. We appreciate the opportunity to have carried out this study.

References

Alferdinck, J.W.A.M.: Target detection and driving behaviour measurements in a driving simulator at mesopic light levels. Ophtalmic Physiol. Opt. **26**, 264–280 (2006)

Baayen, R.H., Milin, P.: Analyzing reaction times. Int. J. Psychol. Res. **3**(2), 12–28 (2010)

Bortz, J.: Statistik für Human- und Sozialwissenschaftler: Mit 242 Tabellen (6., vollst. überarb. und aktualisierte Aufl.). Springer-Lehrbuch. Heidelberg: Springer Medizin (2005)

Boyce, P.R, Rea, M.: Plateau and escarpment: the shape of visual performance. In: Proceedings 21st Annual Session of CIE, Venice, Italy, pp. 82–85 (1987)

Boyce, P.R.: Illumination. In: Salvendy, G. (ed.) Handbook of Human Factors and Ergonomics, pp. 643–669. Wiley, Hoboken (2006)

Dacheux, R.F., Raviola, E.: Functional anatomy of the neural retina. In: Albert, D.M., Jacobiec, F.A., Azar, D.T., Gragoudas, E.S. (eds.) Principles and Practice of Ophthalmology, 2nd edn., pp. 1601–1624 W.B. Saunders Company, Philadelphia (2000)

Der, G., Deary, I.J.: Age and sex differences in reaction time in adulthood: results from the United Kingdom Health and Lifestyle Survey. Psychol. Aging **21**, 62–73 (2006)

Eichinger, A.: Bewertung von Benutzerschnittstellen für Cockpits hochagiler Flugzeuge. Dissertation. Universität Regensburg. Fakultät II Psychologie, Pädagogik und Sportwissenschaft (2011)

Götze, M., Conti, Antonia S., Keinath, A., Said, T., Bengler, K.: Evaluation of a new cockpit color concept under mesopic lighting for urban driving. In: Marcus, A. (ed.) DUXU 2013. LNCS, vol. 8015, pp. 359–366. Springer, Heidelberg (2013). doi:10.1007/978-3-642-39253-5_39

Götze, M., Conti, A.S., Keinath, A., Said, T., Bengler, K.: The assessment of a new cockpit colour concept using the Occlusion Method. In: de Waard, D., Brookhuis, K., Wiczorek, R., di Nocera, F., Brouwer, R., Barham, P., Weikert, C., Kluge, A., Gerbino, W., Toffetti, A., (eds.) Proceedings of the Human Factors and Ergonomics Society Europe Chapter 2013 Annual Conference (2014). ISSN: 2333–4959 (online)

Jahn, G., Oehme, A., Krems, J.F., Gelau, C.: Peripheral detection as a workload measure in driving: Effects of traffic complexity and route guidance system use in a driving study. Transp. Res. Part F **8**, 255–275 (2005)

Lamb, T.D., Pugh, E.N.: Dark adaptation and the retinoid cycle of vision. Prog. Retinal Eye Res. **23**, 307–380 (2004)

Lewis, J.R.: Psychometric evaluation of the PSSUQ using data from five years of usability studies. Int. J. Hum. Comput. Interact. **14**(3-4), 463–488 (2002). Lawrence Erlbaum Associates, Inc.

Merat, N., Jamson, A.H.: The effect of stimulus modality on signal detection: implications for assessing the safety of in-vehicle technology. Hum. Factors **50**(1), 145–158 (2008)

Neale, V.L., Dingus, T.A., Klauer, S.G., Sudweeks, J., Goodman, M.: An Overview of the 100-Car Naturalistic Driving Study and Findings. National Highway Traffic Safety Administration, United States (2005)

Plainis, S., Murray, I.J., Charman, W.N.: The role of retinal adaptation in night driving. Optom. Vis. Sci. **82**, 682–688 (2005)

Recarte, M.A., Nunes, L.M.: Mental workload while driving: effects on visual search, discrimination, and decision making. J. Exp. Psychol. App. **9**, 119–137 (2003)

Rumar, K.: Night driving accident in an international perspective. In: Charlet, M. (ed.) Proceedings in the First International Congress "Vehicle and Infrastructure Safety Improvement in Adverse Conditions and Night Driving", VISION, Rouen, Suresnes, France (2002)

Stockman, A., Sharpe, L.T.: Into the twilight zone: the complexities of mesopic vision and luminous efficiency. Oph. Phys. Optics. **26**, 225–239 (2006)

Viikari, M., Eloholma, M., Halonen, L.: 80 years of V(λ) use: a review. Light Eng. **13**, 24–36 (2005)

Viikari, M.: Modeling spectral sensitivity at low light levels based on mesopic visual performance. OPTH **2**(1), 173–185 (2008)

The Emotional Superiority of Effecter Affordances

Zhaohui Huang[✉], Ziliang Jing, and Xu Liu

Department of Industrial Design, Huazhong University of Science and Technology, Wuhan, China
huangzhaohui@hust.edu.cn

Abstract. Affordance has been well discuss in HCI field since Gibson created this concept. Based on Kaptelinin and Nardi's notion of instrumental affordance, we explore the influence of emotional attributes of effecter affordance on user experience, according to the data of experiment, we argue that (1) the effecter affordances have emotional attributes (e.g. Positive, negative, neutral) that can be pick up by user and impact user experiences. (2) Positive effecter affordance can provide emotional superiority to user experience. We propose several design guidelines according the result of experiment, we hope these principles can help designer avoid mistake and back those good designs up.

Keywords: Affordances · Effecter affordances · Emotional experience · User experience · Design

1 Introduction

The concept of affordances was created by Gibson. He argue that animal can naturally pick up the "action possibilities" latent in the environment. Then his student Don Norman introduce this term into HCI scope. With the development of this concept, Kaptelinin and Nardi improved Gibson's original idea; they think there are two aspects affordances of an instrument: handling affordances and effecter affordances. Then Grünbaum and Simonsen found several interactive design guidelines and they think effecter affordances need not be directly perceivable to the user.

The aim of this paper is to explore more in this filed, we believed that the effecter affordances have Emotional Attributes (e.g. Positive, negative, neutral); we believe that it can be pick up by user and impact user experiences.

2 Related Works

The concept of Affordances were created by Gibson, J. J. in his 1977 article "The Theory of Affordances" and explored it more fully in his book The Ecological Approach to Visual Perception in 1979 [1, 2]. Gibson use this term to explain the correspondence between physical properties of nature and animals. He propose the idea that affordances of an object can be directly pick up by animals. Yet most objects have multiple usages, choose which one is depend on the subject's psychological state.

© Springer International Publishing AG 2017
S. Yamamoto (Ed.): HIMI 2017, Part I, LNCS 10273, pp. 184–193, 2017.
DOI: 10.1007/978-3-319-58521-5_14

Norman applied the term "affordances" to HCI and industrial design disciplines. He argue that affordances result from the mental interpretation of things, it was based on our past knowledge, experience, and applied to our perception of things about us [3]. Then he realize that the term has been widely used and misused, so he clarify that he would like to replacing all instances of the word "affordances" with the phrase "perceived affordances." He separates "real" affordances (the physical properties of the world) from 'perceived' affordances (subjective representations in the mind), and is more concerned with the perceptual properties of affordances rather than the actual properties of the objects themselves [4]. He propose that the most important thing is let people understand the product or service, give them sign of what it is for, and what the alternative actions are [5].

Gaver introduce Gibson's affordances into HCI field with a different way then Norman dose [6]. He state that affordances can be group in space (nested affordances). An affordance can be nest into a father affordances, and contain a sublevel affordances. For instance, the affordances of pulling the handle is nest within an affordance of opening the door. He also propose that affordances are independent of perception. They exist whether the perceiver cares about them or not, whether they perceived or not. Distinguishing affordances from perceptual information about them is useful in understanding ease of use.

Kaptelinin and Nardi argue that the concept of affordances has a number of fundamental inherent limitations and cannot be directly extended to HCI field. They create technology affordances to serve the needs of HCI research and practice [7]. When people interact with an instrument through technology, they consider the technology as a mediational means. The affordances provided by an instrument comprise two aspects: handling affordances, possibilities for interacting with the technology; effecter affordances, possibilities for employing the technology to make an effect on an object.

Grünbaum and Simonsen work based on instrumental affordances, they investigate what it means to break an affordance, and propose several design principles, they argue that there is largely unexplored design space for designing, and redesigning objects with broken affordances [8].

From above we know that there is a great deal of debate of affordance. But the most important things is when we talk about affordances in HCI field, we should ignore the affordances of screens, and focus on the affordances of interface, or we can use Gaver's theory to explain: the affordance of interface is nested into a father affordance. Grünbaum and Simonsen argue that effecter affordances need not be directly perceivable to the user in their paper "the affordances of broken affordances". But this point make me confused, there are many examples in our life indicate that effecter affordances need be perceivable to user, for instant, the bottom use warning color (e.g. red, yellow) if the consequence of press is important. The reason why it design in this way is to indicate the user that they should think twice before they press the bottom or highlight the important bottom to the user.

3   The Problem of Effecter Affordances

Here is another example that proved effecter affordances can influence user's action. When I work as an intern in one of biggest internet company in China, Baidu, I have an interesting finding while I follow up on a project.

Three are three different version of login page shown in Fig. 1. (The interface in Fig. 1 has been revised, but the thing is same) The color and the sentence both influence the conversion rate (The conversion rate here is the proportion of visitors that success-fully login with Facebook account and all of the visitors that arrive this login page). The conversion rate rise about 3.8% after the bottom's color change into standard Facebook blue (B), and it rise another 4.2% after the sentence has been add above the login bottom (C), the sentence tell user that their privacy will never leak form this app. 4.2% is really a huge number when your app have hundreds of millions of users.

Fig. 1. Three different version of login page

Effecter affordances can activate the low-level mental reflection of user; people might fell unsafety about their privacy through the perceptual information like color, sentence or any other elements in this interface (A). It is because the elements in this page bring positive effecter affordances to user, make they feel more safety when login with Facebook account and lead to the conversion rate raised.

The aim of this paper is to improve Grünbaum and Simonsen's work, we argue that the emotional attributes of effecter affordances have correspondence with user experience, positive effecter affordances can improve user experience, and vice versa.

This example also inspire us that the intensity of handling affordance may influence people's action too. The intensity here is the degree of similarity between object's usage and user's mental interpretation. For instance, two objects (a, b) that both can afford the possible of sit down, A has an appropriate height to sit, but B's height is too short to sit. The possibility that people choose to sit on A is higher than B. Therefore, we said the intensity of handling affordance of A is higher than B. We believe this theory can apply to interface design. We believe that there is largely unexplored research space, but in this paper we focus on effecter affordance and user experience.

4   Experiment – The Impact of Emotional Attributes of Affordance to User Experience

The aim of this experiment is find out the correlation between emotional attributes of effecter affordances and user experience. We invite five senior UI designers and five design researchers extract elements from interface. The effecter affordance of those elements must be easy to identify and highly associated with emotion. We got five elements that are color, graphic, disturb elements, font and dynamic effect.

Independent variable are the emotional attributes of effecter affordance of those elements (positive, negative and neutral). Dependent variable are user experience, we use "reliability", "satisfaction", "happiness" as emotional experience factors, "usefulness" and "ease of use" as practical experience factors, we stress that the above five factors can be replaced by more refined principles of design. For example, Norman argue that emotional experience contain hedonics, aesthetics and fun/pleasure [9]; Rober Rubinof's four elements of user experience: Branding, usability, functionality and content. [10] Control variable are operate instrument (iOS 10.1.1), environment, handling affordance (the process of all tasks and touchable area remain invariant), and brand effect (A good brand can delivery reliable feeling to participants).

We use mobile payment flow as experiment material, because:

User can easily distinguish the emotional attributes of result in payment scene. (E.g., this payment page makes me feel safety/unsafety);

After years of development, the basic environment of China's Mobile Payment had been formed. Mobile payment became one of indispensable tool in people's life. The data from BigData-Research shown [11], there are 1.8 billion active users of Alipay in 2016 July.

Therefore, we choose payment flow of Alipay as prototype; we define the form of five elements respectively in different kinds of emotional attributes, shown in Table 1. Then we design experiment task according to Table 1 (Fig. 2)

Table 1. The form of elements respectively in different kinds of emotional attributes.

Elements	Effecter affordance					
	Positive		Negative		Neutral (comparative group)	
Color	1	Blue	2	Red	11	White
Graphic	3	Shield	4	Bug		N/A
Distrub elements	5	Natural utilization	6	Abrupt utilization		N/A
Font	7	Order, layering, Same font	8	Disorder, without layering, different font		Same font
Dynamic effect	9	Smooth, Detail	10	Abrupt		System

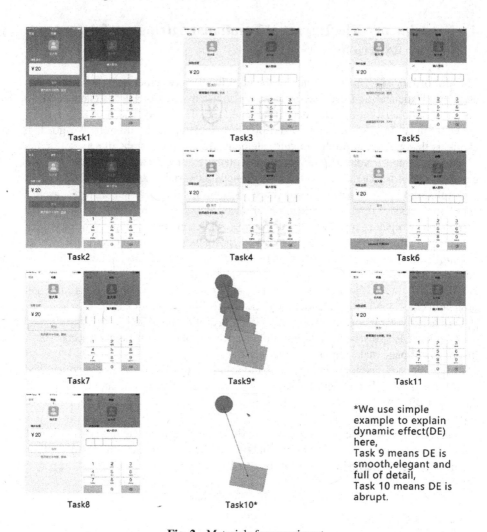

Fig. 2. Materials for experiment

In task 5 and 6, Natural utilization means the disturb elements (e.g. advertisement) use same visual style as interface dose; Abrupt utilization means the disturb elements use different visual style as interface dose. In task 9, the effect is smooth, elegant and full of detail, but in task 10 there basically has no dynamic effect, the elements abruptly emerge when page change.

Participants are 15 college students aged 18~29, 7 male and 8 female, 5 major in industrial design, 10 major in mechanical engineering, all subjects are familiar operator of iOS, and frequently use mobile payment to pay.

Subjects were asking to transfer 20 yuan through mobile payment interface, the trading password which is easy enough to remember has been told to the participants before experiment, all participants were asking to finish each task through their instinct, subjects need to filled out questionnaire as follow after each task has been finished.

The interface and flow in this task:

- It is reliable and makes me feel safety (reliability)
- Makes me feel satisfied (satisfaction)
- It is funny to use (happiness)
- Do help me reach my goal (usefulness)
- It is easy to operate (ease of use)

The questions asks participants choose the closest answer on a 5-point scale (1 = strongly disagree, 5 = strongly agree). The question of questionnaire respectively represent the five factor of user experience. We use SPSS analyze the data of questionnaire.

The data illustrated that:

1. All positive groups (1 3 5 7 9) shows higher user experience than negative groups (2 4 6 8 10); There is significant difference between positive and negative groups on user experience, positive effecter affordance can provide emotional superiority to user experience (Fig. 3).

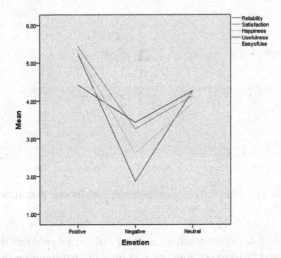

Fig. 3. Relationship between emotional attributes of effecter affordance and dependent variables

2. Color: positive group provide much more "reliability" than comparative group, the negative group comes out completely opposite situation. (Figure 4) Both negative and positive group provide more "satisfaction" and "happiness" than comparative group (Figs. 4 and 5), but show no difference with comparative group on "usefulness" and "ease of use" (Figs. 5 and 6).

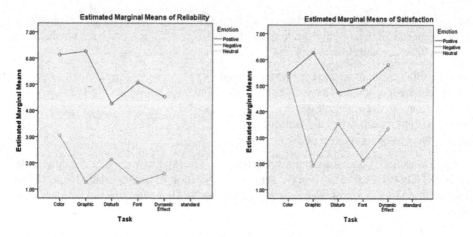

Fig. 4. The estimated marginal means of reliability and satisfaction

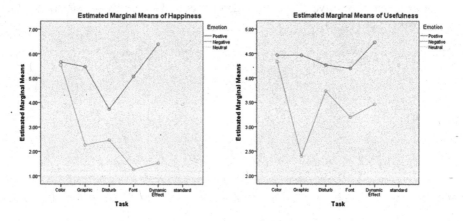

Fig. 5. The estimated marginal means of happiness and usefulness

Result: Positive EA (effecter affordance) of color can enhance the "reliability", "satisfaction" and "happiness", negative color can also improve the "satisfaction" and "happiness", but it will provide a much lower "reliability", both positive and negative color show no significant impact on "usefulness" and "ease of use".

3. Graphic: positive group show much more "reliability", "satisfaction" and "happiness" than comparative group (Figs. 4 and 5), and provide the highest "reliability" and "satisfaction" among all user experience factors (Fig. 4). Positive groups and comparative group appear to be no difference in the "usefulness" and "ease of us" (Figs. 5 and 6). All user experience factor of negative group show lower score than comparative group.

Result: Positive EA of graphic can enhance the "reliability", "satisfaction" and "happiness" of interface, especially on "reliability" and "satisfaction", but it cannot enhance "usefulness" and "ease of us"; Negative graphic will lower all user experience factors.

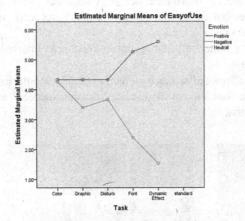

Fig. 6. The estimated marginal means of ease of use

4. Disturb elements: positive group (natural utilization) only show slightly higher on "satisfaction" than comparative group, negative group (abrupt utilization) provide "reliability" and "happiness" far below those of comparative group.

   Result: natural utilize disturb elements (Positive EA) only slightly enhance the satisfaction of interface, but abrupt utilize disturb elements (Negative EA) will strongly lower the "reliability" and "happiness".

5. Font: Positive group provide higher "reliability", "satisfaction", "happiness", "ease of use" than comparative group, All user experience factor of negative group show lower score than comparative group.

   Result: positive EA of Font can enhance all user experience factors except "usefulness"; Negative EA of Font will lower all user experience factors.

6. Dynamic effect: Positive group provide no less of "reliability" than comparative group, but show higher on the rest of user experience factors. All user experience factor of negative group show lower score than comparative group.

   Result: positive EA of Dynamic effect can enhance "satisfaction", "happiness", "usefulness" and "ease of use", especially on "satisfaction" and "happiness". Negative EA of dynamic effect will lower all user experience factors.

5 Goal-Oriented User Study

To investigate mental activity of user while the feedback and effecter affordance of interface was broken. We conducted a small user study concerned with accomplishing four task, participants were asking to talk aloud about their thinking and feeling when finishing the task (Fig. 7).

- Task A: Positive effecter affordance, intact feedback: interface provide positive effecter affordance
- Task B: Positive effecter affordance, defective feedback: interface provide positive effecter affordance, but the result display 'transfer succeed' instead of "transfer failed" and vice versa.
- Task C: Negative effecter affordance, intact feedback: interface provide negative effecter affordance
- Task D: Negative effecter affordance, defective feedback: interface provide negative effecter affordance, but the result display 'transfer succeed' instead of "transfer failed" and vice versa.

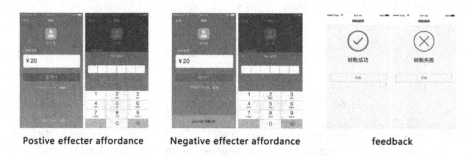

Postive effecter affordance   Negative effecter affordance   feedback

Fig. 7. Materials for user study

According to the records of user's feeling, we found that:

1. Task A: all subjects feel satisfaction and reliable about this interface.
2. Task B: despite the interface provide positive effecter affordance, several participants still worried about their goal have been reach or not. In this situation, people will feel disappoint, and blame themselves or external factors.
3. Task C: many subjects worried about their goal have been reach or not because their feel unsafety about interface. In this situation, Users will experience a bad emotional experience
4. Task D: most of subjects feel unreliable about interface, and they blame the unreliable of interface instead of themselves.

6   Conclusion

The experiment research, explore the influence of emotional attributes of effecter affordance on user experience, the result of experiment give rise to several design guidelines:

1. Use positive color and graphic, the effecter affordance of positive color and graphic can significantly affect the emotional experience (reliability, satisfaction, happiness), but cannot enhance the practical experience (usefulness, ease of use).

2. Avoid adding disturb elements to interface, if cannot avoid, adding through a natural way will be better. Abrupt adding disturb elements will sharply lower reliability and happiness of interface.
3. Avoid using disorder and different font, the negative effecter affordance of disorder font will bring negative emotional experience, and significantly lower the practical experience.
4. Make dynamic effect smoothly and naturally, avoid abrupt dynamic effect. Fluent dynamic effect can significantly improve the practical experience and happiness of interface.

Positive effecter affordance will working especially in those interface that have an obviously positive or negative result. For example, mobile payment, login, permission of location or other function of mobile. Make sure that provide a positive effecter affordance to user, it is important to those Apps that still in early stage of competition, because competitor's brand effect has not been established, positive effecter affordance will provide emotional superiority in early stage of competition for your App.

References

1. Gibson, J.J.: The theory of affordances. In: Shaw, R.E., Bransford, J. (eds.) Perceiving, Acting, and Knowing. Lawrence Erlbaum Associates, Hillsdale (1977)
2. Gibson, J.J.: The Ecological Approach to Visual Perception. Houghton Mifflin, Boston (1979)
3. Norman, D.A.: The Psychology of Everyday Things. Basic Books, New York (1988)
4. Norman, D.A.: Affordance, conventions, and design (2004)
5. Norman, D.A.: The way I see it: Signifiers, not affordances. Interactions 15(6), 18–19 (2008)
6. Gaver, W.W.: Technology affordances. In: Proceedings of CHI 1991, pp. 79–84 (1991)
7. Kaptelinin, V., Nardi, B.: Affordances in HCI: Toward a mediated action perspective. In: Proceedings of CHI 2012, pp. 967–976 (2012)
8. Grünbaum, M.G., Simonsen, J.G.: The affordances of broken affordances. In: Abascal, J., Barbosa, S., Fetter, M., Gross, T., Palanque, P., Winckler, M. (eds.) INTERACT 2015. LNCS, vol. 9298, pp. 185–202. Springer, Cham (2015). doi:10.1007/978-3-319-22698-9_13
9. Rubinoff, R.: How to quantify the user experience [OL], 17 February 2009
10. Norman, D.A.: Emotional Design: Why We Love (or Hate) Everyday Things. Basic Books, New York (2004)
11. http://www.bigdata-research.cn/content/201606/299.html

Research on the Design Method of Extracting Optimal Kansei Vocabulary

Xinhui Kang[(✉)], Minggang Yang, Yixiang Wu, and Haozhou Yuan

School of Art, Design and Media,
East China University of Science and Technology,
No. 130 Meilong Road, Xuhui District, Shanghai 200237, China
2634175918@qq.com

Abstract. In the relevant researches on Kansei Engineering, the Kansei Vocabulary extraction has a vital significance. In previous time, the Kansei words are selected by experts' focus interviews or customers' giving marks. Such kind of method is easy, but it is difficult to explore the customers' inner feeling, which seems to be so hasty. In this research, a method of selecting optimal Kansei Vocabulary is proposed to assist the designers establish the high correlation degree's emotion cognition of customers. The factor analysis is used to classify the Kansei semantic style. Using the Fuzzy Analytic Hierarchy Process to make comparisons of each two specific Kansei words can get the final weight order. Through this method in the minicar's case study, the modern factors' "concise", "smooth" words are defined as the words which can most arouse the customers' emotional resonance. The research proves that the design method of extracting the optimal Kansei Vocabulary is the most effective one. Meanwhile, it can be applied into the modeling design of other industrial products.

Keywords: Kansei engineering · Minicar · Fuzzy analytic hierarchy process · Kansei vocabulary · Semantic attributes (SA)

1 Introduction

In this research, the author classifies the relevant Kansei words of the screening minicars by utilizing the fuzzy analytic hierarchy process to make comparisons of each two quality dimension and sub-criteria. According to the comparison result of 8 relevant experts with high involvement, the relative weight of each evaluation criterion can be got, thus establishing the Kansei Semantic priority in the Kansei Engineering's research. It can provide some references for the later modeling factors' selection.

The research framework is as follows: this chapter is the introduction; chapter two is the literature review on the factorial analysis, the analytic hierarchy process, and the fuzzy analytic hierarchy process; Chapter three is the theoretical background; in chapter four, the author takes minicar as the case study to verify the research methods; the last chapter is the summary of the whole paper.

© Springer International Publishing AG 2017
S. Yamamoto (Ed.): HIMI 2017, Part I, LNCS 10273, pp. 194–207, 2017.
DOI: 10.1007/978-3-319-58521-5_15

2   Literature Review

2.1   Kansei Engineering

Kansei is the personal subjective impression which gets from certain illusion, environments or situations. Human body's all senses organs are utilized in Kansei, including the vision, hearing, sense of touch, gustation and cognition [1]. Kansei Engineering is a technology which oriented by the customers and it commit itself to the new product's development process. It is based on ergonomics and computer science, which can transform the customer's psychological needs or emotion into the products' design factors. Kansei Engineering includes six types, which are Category Identification, Kansei Engineering System, Hybrid Kansei Engineering System, Kansei Engineering Modeling, Virtual Kansei Engineering, Collaborative Kansei Engineering Designing [2, 3]. In the Kansei Engineering method, expanding semantic attributes (SA) and products attributes' space is of great importance (Fig. 1) [4], especially the establishment of the semantic attributes (SA) is the first step of the Kansei design's success. In the previous researches, the final Kansei words are mostly got from the focused interviews or customers' scoring, thus getting highest score. Such kind of method is so easy to take. The purpose of this research is to adopt the factor analysis and combine with the fuzzy analytic hierarchy process to determine the method of optimal Kansei Vocabulary, thus assisting the designers more accurately to get to know the customers' inner heart and improving the Kansei meaning's accurate rate.

2.2   Factor Analysis

Factor analysis employs the thought of reducing dimensions; under the precondition of losing little information, many indexes can be transformed into several comprehensive

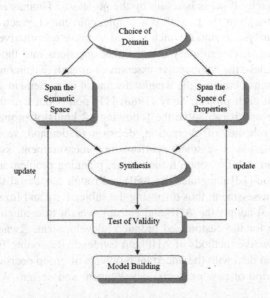

Fig. 1. Kansei engineering process (Sources: Schütte, 2002)

indexes. By making researches about the interior dependency relations of many indexes' correlation matrix, the author finds out all the variables' a few common factors and takes each target variable to indicate common factors' linear relation, thus representing the correlation between original variable and factors. The purpose of factor analysis is to seek the variables' basic structure, simplify the observation system and reduce the variables' dimensions, thus using a few variables to explain the complex problems in the research [5]. In the related fields of design, the main purpose of factor analysis is to find out many Kansei words and then carry out the grouping, thus getting the potential products' semantics which represents the maximum factors variables. Consequently, the evaluation criterion of the products style can be established, which is used for the following study. Yu-Ming Chang [6] through factor analysis extraction, three types of factors affecting consumer emotional perfection toward car steering wheels were identified: esthetic factors, operational strength factors and modernity factors. Chih-Fang Huang [7] by applying factor analysis extraction, 14 pairs of adjectives about China's melody intention are extracted, thus getting three intention factors. Qianru Qiu [8] in the design of name card, the factor analysis is applied to identify the five semantic groups and the extractive factors which uses the orthogonal rotation method, thus effectively distinguishing the original variables. Achmad Shergian [9] adopting the factor analysis is to divide the originality alarm clock's 8 Kansei adjectives into two main factors, thus meeting the demand of Kansei Engineering's utilization of mapping process to establish the correlation between Kansei intention and physical design elements. Simon Schütte [10] adopts the factor analysis to process the candy products' ordered correlation Kansei words in the AVI scale and get the 4 principle factors: attraction, lifestyle, familiarity and snacks.

2.3   Analytic Hierarchy Process

The Analytic Hierarchy Process is set up by the professor, Thomas L. Saaty of U.S.'s University of Pittsburgh in 1971. AHP is a simple, convenient, practical, multi-criteria decision-making analysis method, which is used to make quantitative analysis for the qualitative problems. It can simplify the complex questions into the systematic level elements and then make the comparative assessment of each two among the importance of level elements, thus obtaining the weighted value of each element and arranging the priority ordering of each project. Satty (1980) [11] points out that the application of AHP is quite wide and it can solve the following 12 kinds of problems: decision of priority ordering, schemes of alternation, decision of demand, resource allocation, scheme assessment, risk assessment, performance measurement, systematic design, guarantee of system stability, optimization issue, planning problem and conflict resolution. Guo-Niu Zhu [12] integrates the AHP and rough number at the early stage of designing concept assessment, thus disposing the subjectivity and fuzziness of experts' decisions. Li Li [13] adopts the AHP and entropy weight to evaluate the consumer's satisfaction degree for the customized products' development. Kwai-Sang Chin [14] integrates the innovative methods of AHP and Evidence Reasoning(ER), thus helping the manufacturers to deal with the uncertain problems of group decision-making in the early screening period of new products' development and design. Wang [15] applies the AHP to evaluate human's sensitivity to the colored light. Comparing the results of AHP and constant stimulus method indicates that AHP is a kind of effective method to evaluate the difference threshold values. Through the experience of telecommunication department's experts and the literature reviews, Gülfem Işıklar [16] applies the AHP to evaluate the mobile phones' options about users' preference order, thus establishing the relative weight of evaluation criteria.

However, The AHP is also easily affected by the extreme value; the establishment of hierarchical relation easily tends to be subjectivity. The interviewees probably can't get to know the problems which involved in all the hierarchies. Therefore, in accordance with this problem, this research applies the fuzzy theory with the combination of AHP to evaluate the experts group's opinions.

2.4 Fuzzy Analytic Hierarchy Process

The AHP cannot overcome the decision-making quality fuzziness issue. So in order to solve the differences between interviewees' subjection perception, evaluation and the group decision-making as well as solve the fuzziness issue, Laarhove and Pedrycz [17] lead the concept of fuzzy theory into the AHP, thus developing the FAHP.

The application of fuzzy theory and AHP's combination can effectively solve the problem of imprecise decision-making of experts. It utilizes the triangular fuzzy function to compare the original obtained values of each two and transform them into fuzzy number and membership function, and then take the triangular fuzzy function into comparative matrix. The fuzzy weighted value of each hierarchy can be worked out by the fuzzy operation and finally the experts' group opinions can be integrated, thus getting the final fuzzy weight. Selcuk Cebi and others [18] apply the FAHP to make sure the importance degree of car instrument panel's function demand. Jaemin Cho [19] applies the FAHP to distinguish the success factors in the early period of new products' commercialization process and analyze the elements which need to be given priority. H. Shidpour and others [20] applies the FAHP to evaluate the related important criterion and also establish the products' optimum structural design plan, assembling process and component suppliers. Ren Bin and others [21] applies the FAHP and multi-level matching algorithm, realizing the transition from the customers' demand model to the products' structure model and establishing the bridge between customer demand and products structure. Therefore, the feasibility design of demand-driven quick response is established. Mahdi Sabaghi and others [22] apply the FAHP and make combination with Shannon's entropy formula to set up the user interface's relative importance in the hierarchical structure's each element, thus promoting the continuity evaluation of different manufactured goods and process.

3 Theoretical Background

3.1 Fuzzy Sets, Triangular Fuzzy Numbers and Linguistic Terms

In 1965, the Fuzzy Set Theory was proposed in the journal of *Information and Control* by the professor L. A, Zadeh of University of California, Berkeley. Through 50-year

expansion and evolution, the Fuzzy Sets Theory's theoretical framework and application technology become increasingly mature. One outstanding advantage of Fuzzy
Set Theory is that it can preferably describe and imitate human's thinking mode and
summarize and reflect human's feelings and experience, thus carrying out the fuzzy
measurement, fuzzy recognition, fuzzy deduction, fuzzy control and fuzzy decision for
the complex things and systems [23]. Triangular fuzzy membership function (as the
Fig. 2) is used to describe certain fuzzy set's membership function of the whole domain
X, which is to show the element X is the member of this fuzzy set's membership
degree. And a, b, c are the parameters of real-value; x is the input variables. The most
common triangle membership function is introduced as follows:

$$\mu_{\tilde{A}}(x) = \begin{cases} 0 & , if\ x \leq a \\ x-a/b-a & , if\ a \leq x \leq b \\ c-x/c-b & , if\ b \leq x \leq c \\ 0 & , if\ c \leq x \end{cases} \tag{1}$$

Linguistic term is proposed by Zadeh (1975), which uses the linguistic value to
replace the definite value and takes the natural language to express the relation between
the two criterions. It is beneficial for the experimental subjects to truly evaluate the
objects. This research adopts 9 point linguistic values (Table 1) to distinguish the different degrees of emphasis. Its correspondent membership functions are from 0 to 1. If it
is more important, its membership is closer to 1; if not, its membership is closer to 0.

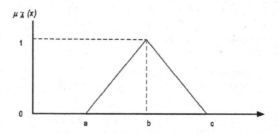

Fig. 2. Triangle membership function

Table 1. Semantic variables used in FAHP

Semantic value	Fuzzy number
Equally important	$\tilde{1} = (1,1,2)$
Slightly important	$\tilde{3} = (2,3,4)$
important	$\tilde{5} = (4,5,6)$
Very important	$\tilde{7} = (6,7,8)$
Extremely important	$\tilde{9} = (8,9,9)$
Intermediate value inserted between two continuous dimensions	$\tilde{2} = (1,2,3);\ \tilde{4} = (3,4,5);\ \tilde{6} = (5,6,7);$ $\tilde{8} = (7,8,9)$

3.2   Fuzzy Analytical Hierarchy Process and the Procedure

In combination with AHP, the fuzzy theory can transform the definite value into fuzzy number and membership function. The method of utilizing the triangle fuzzy number to take it into the comparative matrix can transform all the people's opinions into the fuzzy positive reciprocal matrix, thus solving the inaccuracy problem and developing the FAHP. This method is precise but the calculation is excessively complex [24].

This research establishes the semantic attribute's hierarchy framework in accordance with the obtained Kansei Vocabulary grouping after the factors analysis, thus calculating the related weight. The FAHP operation procedure is as follow:

After the paired comparison matrix, it will generate a matrix $i \times j$, matrix $\tilde{A} = [\tilde{a}_{ij}]$, and n is the number of the evaluation criterion.

$$
A = [\tilde{a}_{ij}] = \begin{bmatrix} \tilde{a}_{11} & \tilde{a}_{12} & \cdots & \tilde{a}_{1j} \\ \tilde{a}_{21} & \tilde{a}_{22} & \cdots & \tilde{a}_{2j} \\ \vdots & \vdots & \vdots & \vdots \\ \tilde{a}_{i1} & \tilde{a}_{i2} & \cdots & \tilde{a}_{ij} \end{bmatrix}
$$

Applying the geometric mean technology which proposed by Buckley (1985) can get each criterion's fuzzy geometric mean and fuzzy weight:

$$
\tilde{r}_i = \left(\prod_{j=1}^{n} a_{ij} \right)^{1/n} = (\tilde{a}_{i1} \otimes \tilde{a}_{i2} \otimes \cdots \otimes \tilde{a}_{in})^{1/n}, \tag{2}
$$

$$
\tilde{W}_i = \tilde{r}_i \otimes (\tilde{r}_1 \otimes \tilde{r}_2 \otimes \cdots \otimes \tilde{r}_n)^{-1}. \tag{3}
$$

$$
W = [\tilde{w}_a]_{1 \times n} = [\tilde{w}_1 \quad \tilde{w}_2 \quad \cdots \quad \tilde{w}_n], \text{ then } W^T \begin{bmatrix} \tilde{w}_1 \\ \tilde{w}_2 \\ \vdots \\ \tilde{w}_n \end{bmatrix}.
$$

$$S = A \otimes W^T \begin{bmatrix} \tilde{a}_{11} & \tilde{a}_{12} & \cdots & \tilde{a}_{1j} \\ \tilde{a}_{21} & \tilde{a}_{22} & \cdots & \tilde{a}_{2j} \\ \vdots & \vdots & \vdots & \vdots \\ \tilde{a}_{i1} & \tilde{a}_{i2} & \vdots & \tilde{a}_{ij} \end{bmatrix} \otimes \begin{bmatrix} \tilde{w}_1 \\ \tilde{w}_2 \\ \vdots \\ \tilde{w}_i \end{bmatrix}$$

$$= \begin{bmatrix} \tilde{a}_{11} \otimes \tilde{w}_1 \oplus \tilde{a}_{12} \otimes \tilde{w}_2 \oplus \cdots \tilde{a}_{1j} \otimes \tilde{w}_n \\ \tilde{a}_{21} \otimes \tilde{w}_1 \oplus \tilde{a}_{22} \otimes \tilde{w}_2 \oplus \cdots \tilde{a}_{2j} \otimes \tilde{w}_n \\ \vdots \\ \tilde{a}_{i1} \otimes \tilde{w}_1 \oplus \tilde{a}_{i2} \otimes \tilde{w}_2 \oplus \cdots \tilde{a}_{ij} \otimes \tilde{w}_n \end{bmatrix}$$

$$= \begin{bmatrix} \tilde{s}_1 \\ \tilde{s}_2 \\ \vdots \\ \tilde{s}_i \end{bmatrix}$$

$$\lambda_{\max} = \frac{1}{n} \left(\frac{\tilde{s}_1}{w_1} + \frac{\tilde{s}_2}{w_2} + \cdots \frac{\tilde{s}_i}{w_i} \right) \tag{4}$$

$\tilde{w}_i$ is the relative importance of No.i evaluation criterion; $\tilde{a}_{ij}$ is the relative importance of No. i evaluation criterion corresponding to No.j evaluation criterion $\lambda_{\max}$ is the maximum eigenvalue of the matrix function.

Calculate CI and CR at the same time and then carry out the consistency check.

$$CI = \frac{\lambda_{\max} - n}{n - 1} \tag{5}$$

Table 2. RI value

n	1	2	3	4	5	6	7	8	9	10	11
RI	0.00	0.00	0.58	0.90	1.12	1.24	1.32	1.41	1.45	1.49	1.51

$CR = CI/RI$, RI's value is showed in Table 2 (Satty 1980)

If $CR \leq 0.1$, the paired comparison data $\tilde{A}$ is reasonable and consistent and the output result of relative weight is W_i; if $CR > 0.1$, the paired comparison data $\tilde{A}$ is inconsistent, which needs to be repeated the paired comparison experiment.

4   Case Study

In the Kansei Engineering's research method, the primary step is to extract specific products' Kansei intention. Therefore, selecting the products' semantic factors which can satisfy the customers' requirement seems to be extremely important, which also has the direct bearing on the mapping products' form element. In this research, the author takes the minicar as the experimental subject and makes research that the procedure can be divided into two stages: the first stage uses the factors analysis to group the 18 Kansei adjectives into 4 main factors; the second stage is to adopt the FAHP to work out the relative weight of customers' evaluation Kansei meaning. Such a systematic procedure can help the designers and relevant manufactures to make sure the customers' real emotional appeals.

4.1 Stage One: Extract Product Image

Semantic Screening. Expanding products' semantic attributes and property space are two important constituent parts for elaborating the products field. This research has widely made survey on minicar's relevant journals, magazines, networks, thus getting 50 Image-word. In order to avoid the Kansei meaning so similar that the experimental process is complex, 5 graduate students with industrial design major make up a focus group and make comparison of the 50 adjectives. Finally they extract 18 relevant adjectives which have the high correlation with the minicar's perceptual cognition level (concise, free, leisure, smooth, lively, romantic, transparent, curvilinear, enthusiastic, strong, practical, rounded, vigorous, feminine, eye-catching, harmonious, luxurious, and wild).

30 experimental subjects who have the design background uses the Likert scale to mark the 18 screened products' Kansei meaning. If people think that this Kansei meaning really accords with people's minicar emotion in their heart, they can mark 5 points; if the coincidence degree is at an average level, people can mark 1 point. Finally the formed 18×30 matrix date will be imported into the SPSS software and then carry out the factors analysis. Then the author uses the maximum variance method to rotate each factor, and then get the following rotation composition matrix (Table 3)

Result. In the explanatory total variance result, four main factors are got by taking the initial eigenvalue which is greater than 1 as the criteria: the factor 1 is the modern factor, including concise, leisure, and smooth, harmonious, lively; factor 2 is the attractive factor, including practical, rounded, romantic, and transparent, curvilinear and enthusiastic; factor 3 is the elegant factor, including vigorous, feminine, free, and eye-catching; factor 4 is the dynamic factor, including luxurious, wild and strong. The factor analysis result shows that the 18 Kansei adjectives variables' four factors accounts for 73.746% of the total variables.

4.2 Stage Two: Weight of Measuring Criterion

Hierarchy Framework. The core of FAHP is to set up the hierarchy framework. This research is divided into three hierarchies: objective hierarchy, criterion hierarchy and sub-criteria hierarchy. The objective hierarchy is defined as the minicar's kansei semantic choice; the criterion hierarchy is defined as modern factor, attractive factor, elegant factor and dynamic factor. The sub-criteria hierarchy is defined as 18 Kansei adjectives (Fig. 3).

Table 3. Factor analysis results for the 18 image-words

Image-word	Factor 1 modern-style	Factor 2 attractive-style	Factor 3 elegant-style	Factor 4 dynamic-style
Concise	0.820	0.260	0.223	0.275
Leisure	0.737	0.275	0.487	−0.108
Smooth	0.664	0.425	0.231	0.304
Harmonious	0.922	0.075	0.120	0.077
Lively	0.759	0.339	0.350	0.086
Practical	0.209	0.595	0.560	−0.142
Rounded	0.432	0.745	−0.105	−0.075
Romantic	0.344	0.664	0.154	0.288
Transparent	0.264	0.710	0.051	0.280
Curvilinear	0.039	0.772	0.273	0.304
Enthusiastic	0.162	0.816	0.128	0.223
Vigorous	0.524	0.442	0.536	0.291
Feminine	0.273	−0.058	0.725	−0.002
Free	0.490	0.259	0.644	0.124
Eye-catching	0.208	0.323	0.537	0.421
Luxurious	−0.048	0.315	−0.021	0.597
Wild	0.231	0.016	0.198	0.844
Strong	0.222	0.387	−0.405	0.568
Total	8.636	2.211	1.294	1.133
Variance(%)	47.977	12.285	7.189	6.295
Cumulative(%)	47.977	60.262	67.450	73.746

Evaluation value after calculating and integrating the group's opinions. After getting each expert's paired comparison value, the expert's fuzzy positive reciprocal matrix is set up. Then the matrix's original accurate value a_{ij} is transformed into $\tilde{a}_{ij} = (a_{ijl}, a_{ij}, a_{iju})$ in accordance with the semantic value. Each expert's relative importance evaluation value for No.i and No.j items is a_{ij}. The triangle fuzzy number will transform a_{ij} into three numbers, a_{ijl}, a_{ij} and a_{iju}; the a_{ijl} represents the experts evaluation minimum value of item i to j's comparative judgment. a_{iju} represents the experts evaluation's maximum value. The following takes the first expert evaluation's attractive factor, subset P1 as an example:

$$
P1 = \begin{bmatrix}
1 & (7,8,9) & (8,9,9) & (1,2,3) & (1,1,2) & (4,5,6) \\
(0.111,0.125,0.1429) & 1 & (0.333,0.5,1) & (0.2,0.25,0.333) & (0.125,0.1429,0.1667) & (0.2,0.25,0.333) \\
(0.111,0.111,0.125) & (1,2,3) & 1 & (0.333,0.5,1) & (0.111,0.125,0.1429) & (3,4,5) \\
(0.333,0.5,1) & (3,4,5) & (1,2,3) & 1 & (0.2,0.25,0.333) & (4,5,6) \\
(0.5,1,1) & (6,7,8) & (7,8,9) & (3,4,5) & 1 & (6,7,8) \\
(0.1667,0.2,0.25) & (3,4,5) & (0.2,0.25,0.333) & (0.1667,0.2,0.25) & (0.125,0.1429,0.1667) & 1
\end{bmatrix}
$$

In order to get each criterion's fuzzy weight, the formula (2) should be used to get each line's geometric mean. The following is the value of calculating $\tilde{Z}_i$:

Level 1
Goal

Level 2
Criteria

Level 3
Sub-criteria

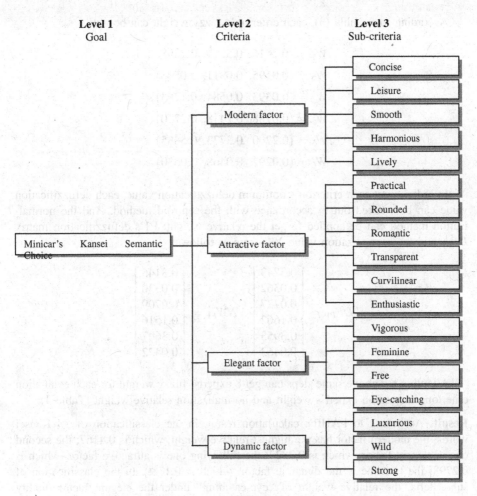

Fig. 3. The hierarchy framework of minicar's Kansei semantic choice

$$\tilde{Z}_1 = (2.4644, \ 2.9938, \ 4.4246)$$
$$\tilde{Z}_2 = (0.2387, \ 0.2806, \ 0.4175)$$
$$\tilde{Z}_3 = (0.4807, \ 0.6177, \ 0.9012)$$
$$\tilde{Z}_4 = (0.9635, \ 1.3077, \ 1.9786)$$
$$\tilde{Z}_5 = (2.6889, \ 3.4085, \ 4.2339)$$
$$\tilde{Z}_6 = (0.3574, \ 0.4228, \ 0.4533)$$

According to formula (3), each criterion's fuzzy weight can be got:

$$\tilde{W}_1 = (0.2016, \ 0.3314, \ 0.5898)$$
$$\tilde{W}_2 = (0.0195, \ 0.0311, \ 0.0580)$$
$$\tilde{W}_3 = (0.0393, \ 0.0684, \ 0.1253)$$
$$\tilde{W}_4 = (0.0788, \ 0.1448, \ 0.2750)$$
$$\tilde{W}_5 = (0.2200, \ 0.3773, \ 0.5885)$$
$$\tilde{W}_6 = (0.0292, \ 0.0468, \ 0.0630)$$

In order to get each criterion's optimum defuzzification value, each defuzzification value can be worked out in accordance with the centroid method. And the normalization method can be applied to get the relative weight; P1's defuzzification matrix DF_{P1} and the normalization value NW_{P1} are as follows:

$$DF_{P1} = \begin{bmatrix} 0.3743 \\ 0.0362 \\ 0.0777 \\ 0.1662 \\ 0.3953 \\ 0.0463 \end{bmatrix} \quad NW_{P1} = \begin{bmatrix} 0.3145 \\ 0.0330 \\ 0.0709 \\ 0.1516 \\ 0.3607 \\ 0.0422 \end{bmatrix}$$

Adopting the above same steps can get 8 experts' fuzzy weight for each evaluation criterion, integration expert's weight and normalization relative weight (Table 4).

Result. According to FAHP's calculation result, in the classification of 18 Kansei words, the modern factor has the highest relative weight, which is 0.4167; the second one is elegant factor, which is 0.2824; the following one is attractive factor, which is 0.2798; the last one is the dynamic factor, which is 0.1789. In the classification of sub-criteria, the relative weight of "eye-catching" under the elegant factor quality dimension is 0.1171. It is the most important emotion among the customers' all Kansei words, which indicates that the customer has a favorable impression on the eye-catching car's appearance molding when they purchase the minicar. The designers should attach great importance to the cognition of eye-catching car's appearance molding in the automobile form design. The second one is the Kansei meaning of modern factor's smooth, which indicates that the customers have a high expectation for the concise auto-body modeling. In the modern factor, the "smooth" automobile language which ranks third is also welcomed by the customers. In the attractive factor, curvilinear minicar's appearance has the highest relative weight. In dynamic factor, the luxurious Kansei words get the highest mark. To sum up, in order to satisfy the wide customers' emotional needs, the relevant manufacturers and products designers should choose to design the concise and smooth minicars. They should make the modeling creativity with a certain objective after determining the perceptual cognition (Table 5).

Table 4. 8 experts' weight value for each evaluation criterion

Modern factor	P1	P2	P3	P4	P5	P6	P7	P8	Normalized weight
Concise	0.2955	0.0923	0.5227	0.2034	0.5518	0.2432	0.0344	0.3031	0.2613
Leisure	0.1116	0.0394	0.0600	0.2015	0.0565	0.1117	0.0874	0.1603	0.1122
Smooth	0.3773	0.1795	0.1899	0.1372	0.1133	0.1050	0.2506	0.3933	0.2400
Harmonious	0.0545	0.5425	0.1926	0.0391	0.0810	0.4394	0.4247	0.0773	0.1853
Lively	0.1611	0.1456	0.1926	0.4188	0.1975	0.1007	0.2030	0.0660	0.2012
Attractive factor	**P1**	**P2**	**P3**	**P4**	**P5**	**P6**	**P7**	**P8**	**Normalized weight**
Practical	0.3145	0.1342	0.2448	0.1081	0.3514	0.2034	0.0641	0.0277	0.1647
Rounded	0.0330	0.0584	0.0649	0.0774	0.0179	0.0842	0.1759	0.1057	0.0753
Romantic	0.0709	0.0827	0.2006	0.4481	0.1815	0.1176	0.1204	0.1409	0.1709
Transparent	0.1516	0.2758	0.1584	0.0420	0.0683	0.275	0.0633	0.3615	0.1612
Curvilinear	0.3607	0.4121	0.2821	0.1517	0.3226	0.1791	0.3999	0.2519	0.3302
Enthusiastic	0.0422	0.0367	0.0493	0.1728	0.0583	0.1421	0.1763	0.1123	0.0976
Elegant factor	**P1**	**P2**	**P3**	**P4**	**P5**	**P6**	**P7**	**P8**	**Normalized weight**
Vigorous	0.1974	0.1177	0.2106	0.1525	0.1728	0.2425	0.0713	0.0831	0.1683
Feminine	0.0376	0.4594	0.1139	0.1104	0.0386	0.1169	0.0591	0.1521	0.1150
Free	0.2623	0.0700	0.5284	0.1937	0.2022	0.5132	0.4116	0.2488	0.3022
Eye-catching	0.5027	0.3529	0.1471	0.5433	0.5864	0.1274	0.4580	0.5160	0.4145
Dynamic factor	**P1**	**P2**	**P3**	**P4**	**P5**	**P6**	**P7**	**P8**	**Normalized weight**
Luxurious	0.1237	0.7682	0.3726	0.2405	0.7562	0.4034	0.4519	0.5004	0.4935
Wild	0.1100	0.1080	0.3137	0.6948	0.1157	0.4934	0.4926	0.4390	0.3429
Strong	0.7662	0.1238	0.3137	0.0647	0.1281	0.1032	0.0555	0.0606	0.1636

Table 5. Relative weight analysis table of minicar's each quality factors

Quality dimension	Weight	Sub-criteria	Weight	Relative weight	Order
Modern factor	0.4167	concise	0.2613	0.1089	2
		Leisure	0.1122	0.0468	12
		Smooth	0.2400	0.1000	3
		Harmonious	0.1853	0.0772	8
		Lively	0.2012	0.0838	7
Attractive factor	0.2798	Practical	0.1647	0.0461	13
		Rounded	0.0753	0.0211	18
		Romantic	0.1709	0.0478	10
		Transparent	0.1612	0.0451	14
		Curvilinear	0.3302	0.0924	4
		Enthusiastic	0.0976	0.0273	17
Elegant factor	0.2824	Vigorous	0.1683	0.0475	11
		Feminine	0.1150	0.0325	15
		Free	0.3022	0.0853	6
		Eye-catching	0.4145	0.1171	1
Dynamic factor	0.1789	Luxurious	0.4935	0.0883	5
		Wild	0.3429	0.0617	9
		Strong	0.1636	0.0293	16

5 Conclusion

In the research of Kansei Engineering, it is very important to extract customers' emotional needs in the specific products. Kansei image is directly related to the modeling factors' choice. In this paper, the author proposes a kind method which combines the factors analysis and fuzzy analytic hierarchy process to extract the products' high correlation meaning, thus leading a direction for the designers' modeling creativity. The minicar is taken as the object in this paper, finding that the modern factors of "concise" and "smooth" are most easily to attract the customer's inner heart, thus causing the customers' emotional resonance. Meanwhile, the research method can be applied into other industrial products' design.

References

1. Nagamachi, M.: Workshop 2 on kansei engineering. In: Proceedings of International Conference on Affective Human Factors Design, Singapore (2001)
2. Nagamachi, M.: Kansei Engineering: A New ergonomic consumer-oriented technology for product development. Int. J. Industr. Ergon. **15**(1), 3–11 (1995)
3. Nagamachi, M.: Kansei Engineering as a powerful consumer-oriented technology for product development. Appl. Ergon. **33**(3), 289–294 (2002)

4. Schutte, S.T.W.: Designing feeling into products—integrating Kansei Engineering Methodology in product development. Institute of Technology, Linkoping, LiU-Tek-Lic 2002:19 (2002)
5. Dilong, X.: Experimental Course of SPSS Application. Hunan University Press, Changsha (1), p. 227 (2007)
6. Chang, Y.-M., Chen, C.-W.: Kansei assessment of the constituent elements and the overall interrelations in car steering wheel design. Int. J. Ind. Ergon. **56**, 97–105 (2016)
7. Huang, C.-F., Lian, Y.-S., Nien, W.-P., Chieng, W.-H.: Analyzing the perception of Chinese melodic imagery and its application to automated composition. Multimedia Tools Appl. **75** (13), 7631–7654 (2016)
8. Qiu, Q., Omura, K.: Developing a document creating system for affective design: A case study in card design. Kansei Engineering International (2015)
9. Shergian, A., Immawan, T.: Design of innovative alarm clock made from bamboo with kansei engineering approach. Agric. Agric. Sci. Procedia **3**, 184–188 (2015)
10. Schütte, S.: Evaluation of the affective coherence of the exterior and interior of chocolate snacks. Food Qual. Prefer. **29**(1), 16–24 (2013)
11. Saaty, T.: The Analytic Hierarchy Process. McGraw-Hill, New York (1980)
12. Zhu, G.-N., Hu, J., Qi, J., Gu, C.-C., Peng, Y.-H.: An integrated AHP and VIKOR for design concept evaluation based on rough number. Adv. Eng. Inform. **29**(3), 408–418 (2015)
13. Li, L., Liu, F., Li, C.: Customer satisfaction evaluation method for customized product development using entropy weight and analytic hierarchy process. Comput. Industr. Eng. **77**, 80–87 (2014)
14. Chin, K.-S., Xu, D., Yang, J.-B., Lam, J.P.-K.: Group-based ER-AHP system for product project screening. Expert Syst. Appl. **35**(4), 1909–1929 (2008)
15. Wang, M.-J.J., Lee, Y.-J.: Applying the AHP approach to evaluate human sensitivity to chromatic light. Behav. Inf. Technol. **16**(6), 348–358 (1997)
16. Işıklar, G., Büyüközkan, G.: Using a multi-criteria decision making approach to evaluate mobile phone alternatives. Comput. Stand. Interfaces **29**(2), 265–274 (2007)
17. Laarhoven, P., Pedrycz, W.A.: Fuzzy extension of saaty's priority theory. Fuzzy Sets Syst. **11**(1–3), 229–241 (1983)
18. Cebi, S., Kahraman, C.: Indicator design for passenger car using fuzzy axiomatic design principles. Expert Syst. Appl. **37**(9), 6470–6481 (2010)
19. Cho, J., Lee, J.: Development of a new technology product evaluation model for assessing commercialization opportunities using Delphi method and fuzzy AHP approach. Expert Syst. Appl. **40**(13), 5314–5330 (2013)
20. Shidpour, H., Shahrokhi, M., Bernard, A.: A multi-objective programming approach, integrated into the TOPSIS method, in order to optimize product design; in three-dimensional concurrent engineering. Comput. Ind. Eng. **64**(4), 875–885 (2013)
21. Ren, B., Qiu, L., Zhang, S., Tan, J., Cheng, J.: Configurable product design considering the transition of multi-hierarchical models. Chin. J. Mech. Eng. **26**(2), 217–224 (2013)
22. Sabaghi, M., Mascle, C., Baptiste, P., Rostamzadeh, R.: Sustainability assessment using fuzzy-inference technique (SAFT): A methodology toward green products. Expert Syst. Appl. **56**, 69–79 (2016)
23. Baoqing, H.: Fuzzy Theory Basis. Wuhan University Press, Wuhan (2005)
24. Buckley, J.: Fuzzy hierarchical analysis. Fuzzy Sets Syst. **17**(3), 233–247 (1985)

Points of Interest Density Based Zooming Interface for Map Exploration on Smart Glass

Doyeon Kim[1], Daeil Seo[1(✉)], Byounghyun Yoo[1,2], and Heedong Ko[1,2]

[1] Center for Imaging Media Research, Korea Institute of Science and Technology,
Seoul, Republic of Korea
`ehdus0219@imrc.kist.re.kr`, {`xdesktop,ko`}`@kist.re.kr`,
`yoo@byoo.net`
[2] Department of HCI and Robotics, University of Science and Technology,
Daejeon, Republic of Korea

Abstract. Smart glass devices have become popular in our daily lives, and many people have applied its advantages to their application fields. In particular, smart glass has the advantage of receiving desired information by maintaining their context of the real world without dispersing their attention. Smart glass is also widely used to obtain information about points of interest with map interfaces. However, smart glass has an insufficient user interface with which to interact with its map applications via the smart glass. This problem restricts the map's ability to provide specific functions and makes users feel constrained compared to hand-held devices. In this paper, we focus on a map exploration method for smart glass to solve the limitations of map interaction via the smart glass. We propose an interaction design with zooming interface based on region's point of interest density. This approach is intended for a region search without any other interaction tools. Users search and browse their regions of interest with the smart glass by using the proposed method.

Keywords: Point of interest · Wearable user interface · Wearable user interaction · Smart glass · Region-based navigation

1 Introduction

The advent of mobile computing technology has popularized the use of smart glass devices in our daily lives. Wearable applications for smart glass devices allow people to obtain information through optical see-through display in front of their eyes. This characteristic helps people obtain information by maintaining their context of the real world. Thus, many wearable device applications have been released and have received attention in recent years.

One of the most common application areas for smart glass is map services; people use the map services to browse their surroundings and obtain geometric information including points of interest (POIs). For example, Google Maps service [1] helps people find geometric information such as location of POIs, route information, and detailed information about POIs. These map services provide a keyword search with a speech

© Springer International Publishing AG 2017
S. Yamamoto (Ed.): HIMI 2017, Part I, LNCS 10273, pp. 208–216, 2017.
DOI: 10.1007/978-3-319-58521-5_16

recognition technique to obtain the desired information about POIs by speaking the name of POIs into the microphone integrated in the smart glass device. However, it is difficult to obtain information about regions of interest (ROIs), because current map service applications for smart glass do not provide zooming and panning capabilities. Because of this limitation, users cannot identify their interesting information in ROIs. For example, a user visits New York City for the first time and searches the central park with a keyword search. The map service changes the center of the map to the central park to show a search result. However, the user is not able to browse the surroundings around the central park, because the map service does not provide panning and zooming user interfaces for nearby locations.

In this paper, we propose a POI density based zooming interface for map exploration on smart glass that enables users to zoom and pan their map to examine a desired region. The proposed method is designed with both a keyword search and region-based search. We have implemented the keyword search with speech recognition technique to identify keywords and move the map to the appropriate place. In addition, we provide region search with a POI density based zooming algorithm according to the number of POIs in a region.

This section has introduced and provided the motivation for the work; the rest of this paper is structured as follows. The state of the art and the problem statement are given in Sect. 2. We explain our proposed approach in Sect. 3 and describe architecture and prototype implementation in Sect. 4. We then conclude the paper and consider future works in Sect. 5.

2   Related Work

2.1   User Interface on Smart Glass

User interface designs for smart glass devices have been researched for a long time, ever since Sutherland [2] proposed the first head-mounted display (HMD). In recent years, many smart glass devices have been released in the commercial market, such as Google Glass [3] and Vuzix M100 [4]. These devices have unfamiliar user interfaces [5], and thus researchers have studied how to improve user experiences of smart glass devices [6].

Kerr et al. [7] introduced a hand gesture interface with a colored marker glove to interact with users and their systems. Similarly, Caggianese et al. [8] proposed a hand gestural interface with a depth camera to detect and track a user's hands in the physical space. The study also adopted a Windows, Icons, Menus, and Pointers (WIMP)-style user interface for their proposed system. However, interfaces with hand tracking require additional devices to detect a user's hand. In addition, users with the interfaces have to remember gestures and pay attention to their interactions. Baldauf et al. [9] proposed an vision based eye gaze tracking method that uses computer vision algorithm and mobile sensors to guide geo-referenced digital information. The eye gaze interface has an advantage that easily obtains geo-referenced information around users, but it is difficult to explore a remote site.

In another work, Mayer et al. [10] proposed an approach for controlling smart things recognized by the camera in smart glass devices, controlled via a smart watch, and described with a smartphone. The method provides easy interaction method by applying third party remote controllers as interaction tools. However, the method requires additional devices and only uses smart glass device to identify physical objects.

Previous studies applied third party devices and complicated interfaces to interact with smart glass devices. In addition, the works are not appropriate for exploring a map. To solve the existing limitations, we use the user interface of smart glass devices without any additional devices, and design user interface for map exploration.

2.2 Map Interaction Methods

In traditional handheld and desktop environments, interaction devices such as a two-dimensional multi-touch interface, mouse, keyboard, or trackball are used to communicate with applications.

In handheld devices, map services use a two-dimensional multi-touch interface to zoom or pan a map, and provide a virtual keyboard that enables to search interesting places and areas (e.g., Google Maps [11] and Foursquare [12]). As a representative example, the Google Maps service for handheld device uses a multi-touch interface to zoom a map. A user pinches with his/her thumb and another finger or taps with two fingers to zoom out the map. To zoom in the map, the user spreads two fingers or double taps on the touch pad of the device. The service also provides a keyword search using a keyboard interface.

Users use a mouse wheel and a keyboard as interaction tools to interact with map services in desktop environments. The Google Maps for desktop employs a wheel mouse and a keyboard. The user scrolls the mouse wheel for zooming, or presses the plus or minus keys on the keyboard to zoom in or out. The WIMP interface supports a keyword search and a region search. The WIMP interface enables map services to provide better ease of use for their interactions.

In contrast with handheld and desktop devices, numerous smart glass devices only provide a touch interface, and lack of interactions becomes a limitation. For example, commercial smart glass devices such as Google Glass and Vuzix M100 do not support mouse, keyboard, or multi-touch interfaces. Map services for smart glass have gradually increased to enable smart glass users to search for places, and the map service providers have studied interaction methods to control the map. Map2Glass [13] provides map services to explore interesting places, and the service receives a keyword with keyboard on the smartphone. However, users do not maintain their real-world context because they have to pay attention to the smartphone whenever they search for places. Altwaijry et al. [14] suggested an approach that recognizes landmarks with a computer vision algorithm and provides a guide to the recognized landmarks using the smart glass device. The approach delivers guide information when a user looks at the landmark. However, it is difficult to obtain information at distance, because the approach only works for landmarks that are visible from the user's perspective. Google provides the Google Maps service for Google Glass [1], which searches for places with voice command input. Google Glass users search their desired place by speaking a keyword. However, it is not possible to zoom regions. We split the current region to sub-regions for zooming in an attempt to solve this problem and the smart glass user chooses a ROI by selecting sub-regions.

3   Methodology

The proposed approach in this paper is defined in two ways: The one is a region search with a POI density based zooming interface that is used to divide a given region into sub-regions according to their number of POI groups. The other one is a keyword search using a voice user interface (VUI). In this section, we introduce our proposed map exploration method and interaction design to enable users to explore a map using smart glass. We apply a POI density based region division method for zooming the map and speech recognition technique for panning the map.

3.1   Map Exploration with POI Density

We design our approach to reduce user interactions and maximize the smart glass usability. Because the resolution of the smart glass display is too small to give much information, we cluster POIs into distance based groups to give abstracted information. Figure 1 depicts the comparison between POIs with and without clustering. POIs as shown in Fig. 1(a) occlude the map and other POIs, because there are too many POIs such as historical sites, transportations, and accommodations in the given region boundary. Consequently, a user is unable to find the desired place quickly, thus confusing the user. Therefore, we cluster POIs into groups to clearly see map and each group. The POI clustering method provides an abstraction layer of POI information. Figure 1(b) shows our POI clustering result, which is clustered by distance among POIs. Each POI group has a different color and number; the color represents the density degree of a POI group and the number in the circle icon is the number of POIs in the POI group. For example, the red circle icon shown in the middle of Fig. 1(b) represents the range from 100 to 1000 POIs, and the exact number is 293. The POI groups are recalculated whenever the map change zoom level or boundary.

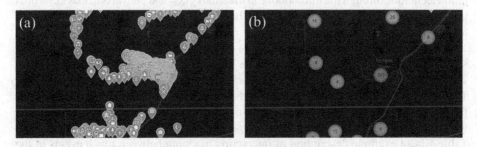

Fig. 1. Comparison between (a) without clustering and (b) with clustering

Figure 2(a) describes the concept of our approach for zooming with smart glass. The user explores a map by zooming with our proposed approach. In our approach, the current ROI is divided into four sub-regions according to the POI density. The regions are used for selecting the next interesting region, and the user selects a sub-region by moving ROI. The selected sub-region is expressed as the orange rectangular box, as shown in Fig. 2(a), and the box is used for zooming the map.

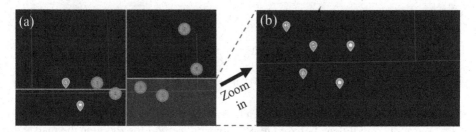

Fig. 2. POI density based zooming interface for smart glass device: (a) an interesting region at the bottom right is selected and (b) the region is zoomed in.

We apply a POI density based zoom interface that divides the region into sub-regions according to the number of POI groups. In other words, each sub-region has an equal number of POI groups. By this approach, a user can find the desired POI more quickly rather than sub-regions divided by the equal region size. For example, the user does not want to explore a region that has no POI such as the top left region as shown in Fig. 2(a). As an aside, POIs are sometimes crowded in a specific region and the user examines the region. The selected interesting region is zoomed in as shown in Fig. 2(b) and the region is divided again as shown in Fig. 2(a). The process is repeated until the user stops the zooming in action because the user finds their desired POI.

3.2 Interaction Design on Smart Glass

In this paper, we apply a VUI in the smart glass to provide a keyword search interface. The keyword search enables a user to find a named POI such as the Eiffel Tower, Disneyland, or Central Park. The advantage of VUI is natural and intuitive for smart glass applications [5]. The proposed system detects a user's speech with a voice recognition technique through the microphone in the smart glass and converts to text keywords using the speech-to-text (STT) technique. The text keywords are sent to the map service to pan the place of interesting on the map.

In addition, the system allows a user to zoom in and out on the map for a region search interface when the user examines an ROI or the area around interesting places. The region search helps the user obtain geometric information or POIs within the ROI. The system provides a touch interface in the smart glass to interact with the map for providing a region search. It minimizes the modification of traditional map interactions with the smart glass and provides a user-friendly interface for smart glass users. Table 1 is an example description of interaction mapping between touch events in the Google Glass and actions on the map with the proposed approach.

Table 1. Mapping of map interactions on the smart glass

Gesture	Action on map
Swipe left	To left region of interesting
Swipe right	To right region of interesting
Tab	Zoom into a selected area

Gesture	Action on map
Long press	Zoom into the center of the current region
Two tab	Zoom out the map

4 System Design

4.1 System Architecture

The proposed approach employs a touch interface and voice command in smart glass device. With the interfaces, the user searches desired for POIs and retrieves the related information about the POI and the region surrounding it. The retrieved POIs appear as several POI groups when there are too many POIs to display on a map.

The proposed system performs the method proposed in this paper in three-parts, as shown in Fig. 3: the smart glass, the POI server, and the map service provider. The map service provider supplies geometric information such as the shapes of buildings and roads. The POI server provides information about POIs in ROI. The smart glass device is connected to the map services provider and the POI server. When a user inputs commands, the smart glass perceives the user's input, and shows geometric information and POIs via the smart glass display.

The input handler receives the user inputs via the microphone and the touch pad of the smart glass. The STT engine converts the user's voice commands to text keywords

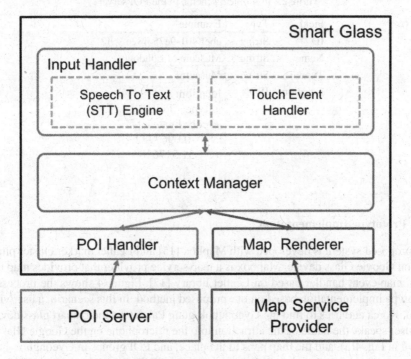

Fig. 3. System architecture

for the keyword search. The touch event handler perceives the user's touch actions for the touchpad on the smart glass. These inputs are sent to the context manager. The context manager manages the user's context. The context of the system is its current zoom level, the position of the ROIs, and the previously selected interesting region. The context is changed depending on the user's commands when user's input is detected. The context manager sends the context to the map handler and POI handler. The map renderer is connected to the map service provider to obtain map tiles, renders the map tiles on the map, and shows POIs in the ROI on the smart glass display. Whenever the map is panned or zoomed, the POI handler requests information of the POIs in the current ROI. Once the POI handler obtains POIs from the POI server, the POI server sends the result to the map renderer through the context manager and the map handler clusters obtained POIs by distance.

The POI server stores the digitalized POI contents, which are used to provide geo-referenced information about POIs to the user. The digitalized POI contents are in Java-Script Object Notation (JSON) format, and the POI schema is described in Table 2. The *ID* field identifies each POI, and it is composed of a unique string. The *name* field contains the representative name in the real world. The *type* field is the category of the POI such as museum, art gallery, or restaurant. The *type* field is used to display POIs on the map as different icons according to the characteristics of the POIs. The *location* field contains geo-location information, which is useful for locating POI icons on the exact location.

Table 2. POI object schema in the POI server

Field	Type	Example
ID	String	ebeff401-9c75-482e-99f2
Name	String	Museum of London
Type	String	Museum

Location	JSON	location: {
		    type: "Point",
		    coordinates: [
		      -0.0967782,
		      51.5176183
		    ]
		}

4.2 Prototype Implementation

The proposed system is developed with Mapbox [15] and Leaflet marker cluster plugin [16] on Google Glass device. Mapbox is a map service provider that provides map tiles and a map event handler based on Leaflet library [17]. Figure 4 shows the process of prototype implementation based on our proposed method. In this scenario, a user visits Seoul, Korea and tries to find the Gyeongbok-gung Palace via their smart glass device. The user speaks the name of the attraction into the microphone on the Google Glass as shown in Fig. 4(a), and the map pans to the place, and POI groups in Gyeongbok-gung Palace are shown as colored circle icons that represent POI groups, as shown in Fig. 4(b).

When a user examines a specific region, the user selects the desired region by moving the position of the orange-colored rectangular box, as displayed in Fig. 4(c) and (d) which shows the result of zooming interaction. After finishing sightseeing Gyeongbok-gung Palace, the user visits other places around his/her current location. When the user explores the wider area, the user zooms out the map to the desired zoom level, and the map is zoomed out to the previous ROI, as shown in Fig. 4(e). The user explores ROIs via the smart glass based on their interest level by repeating the process.

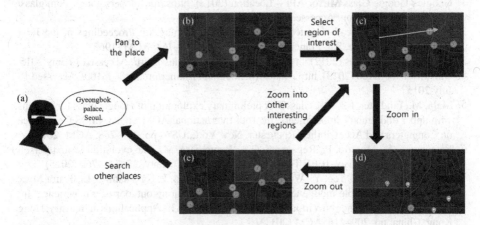

Fig. 4. Process overview of prototype implementation in our approach: (a) A user speaks the name of a POI. (b) The map pans to the location of the POI. (c) The user chooses a ROI. (d) The user zooms in the map to look closely at the interesting region, and (e) The user zooms out the map to browse the wider area.

5   Conclusion and Future Work

This paper presents the concept of our approach and prototype implementation to enhance the user experiences when the users explore a map via smart glass device. This approach use a region segment algorithm based on a POI density based zooming interface with the smart glass user interface to zoom in/out the map. We apply a speech recognition technique to interact with the map services to pan the map. The proposed approach allows users to search for POIs and navigate the map using the smart glass user interface without additional interaction devices or techniques. Therefore, we maintain the advantages and complement the disadvantages of smart glass. We expect that our proposed method will help people to feel at ease when obtaining geometric information using a smart glass device.

Regarding future work, we will conduct an evaluation to verify our approach's usefulness and effectiveness, which will help us improve its quality. Another future work is adding user-defined POIs to gather more POIs because it would be more useful to gather meaningful POIs for individual people. User-defined POIs also allow people to make private maps, and users can use private maps in their daily lives.

Acknowledgments. This work was supported in part by the National Research Council of Science & Technology (NST) grant by the Korea government (MSIP) (No. CMP-16-01-KIST) and the Korea Institute of Science and Technology (KIST) Institutional Program (Project No. 2E27190).

References

1. Google.: Google Glass Mirror API – Location (2013). https://developers.google.com/glass/develop/mirror/location. Accessed 18 Apr 2016
2. Sutherland, I.E.: A head-mounted three dimensional display. In: Proceedings of the Joint Computer Conference, San Francisco, California, pp. 757–764. ACM (1968)
3. Google.: Google Glass (2012). https://www.google.com/glass/start/. Accessed 17 July 2015
4. Vuzix.: Vuzix M100 (2013). http://www.vuzix.com/consumer/products_m100/. Accessed 17 July 2015
5. Malu, M., Findlater, L.: "OK Glass?" A preliminary exploration of Google glass for persons with upper body motor impairments. In: 16th International ACM SIGACCESS Conference on Computers and Accessibility, Rochester, New York, USA, pp. 267–268. ACM (2014)
6. Betancourt, A., Morerio, P., Regazzoni, C.S., Rauterberg, M.: The evolution of first person vision methods: a survey. IEEE Trans. Circ. Syst. Video Technol. **25**, 744–760 (2015)
7. Kerr, S.J., Rice, M.D., Teo, Y., Wan, M., Cheong, Y.L., Ng, J., Ng-Thamrin, L., Thura-Myo, T., Wren, D.: Wearable mobile augmented reality: evaluating outdoor user experience. In: International Conference on Virtual Reality Continuum and Its Applications in Industry, Hong Kong, China, pp. 209–216. ACM (2011)
8. Caggianese, G., Neroni, P., Gallo, L.: Natural interaction and wearable augmented reality for the enjoyment of the cultural heritage in outdoor conditions. In: De Paolis, L.T., Mongelli, A. (eds.) AVR 2014. LNCS, vol. 8853, pp. 267–282. Springer, Cham (2014). doi: 10.1007/978-3-319-13969-2_20
9. Baldauf, M., Fröhlich, P., Hutter, S.: KIBITZER: a wearable system for eye-gaze-based mobile urban exploration. In: ACM International Conference on Augmented Human, Matthias Baldauf, France, pp. 1–5. ACM (2010)
10. Mayer, S., Sörös, G.: User interface beaming – seamless interaction with smart things using personal wearable computers. In: 11th International Conference on Wearable and Implantable Body Sensor Networks Workshops, Zurich, pp. 46–49 (2014)
11. Google.: Google Maps (2005). https://maps.google.com/. Accessed 09 Feb 2017
12. NYC & SF.: Foursquare (2009). https://www.foursquare.com/. Accessed 16 July 2015
13. Zheng, L.: Map2Glass (2014). http://map2glass.com/. Accessed 31 Mar 2016
14. Altwaijry, H., Moghimi, M., Belongie, S.: Recognizing locations with Google Glass: a case study. In: IEEE Winter Conference on Applications of Computer Vision, pp. 167–174 (2014)
15. Mapbox.: Mapbox (2010). https://www.mapbox.com/. Accessed 09 Feb 2017
16. Agafonkin, V.: Marker Clustering plugin for Leaflet (2012). https://github.com/Leaflet/Leaflet.markercluster. Accessed 10 Feb 2017
17. Agafonkin, V.: Leaflet (2011). http://leafletjs.com/. Accessed 10 Feb 2017

How We Improve Sense of Beauty? Kansei Improvement Process and Its Support System

Tomoko Kojiri[✉] and Yoshihiro Adachi

Faculty of Engineering Science, Kansai University, 3-3-35, Ymate-cho, Suita, Osaka, Japan
kojiri@kanwai-u.ac.jp

Abstract. Some art works need Kansei, such as a sense of beauty, to create. Kansei is implicit so that it is difficult for improving our artistic ability to create the art works. The objective of our research is to propose a method for improving Kansei for creating art works. Firstly, we define process of improving Kansei. Then, methods for supporting each steps in the process are proposed. Kansei improvement support system which embeds proposed methods is also developed, whose target art works are designs created only by circles. According to the example use of the system, our Kansei improvement process and its support methods are proved to be effective in broaden Kansei.

Keywords: Kansei improvement process · Kansei improvement support system · Artistic ability

1 Background

Some art works need Kansei, such as a sense of beauty, to create. For instance, when we draw an image, we need to decide what to draw, where to locate them in a canvas, what color to use, and so on, according to our Kansei. Kansei is implicit so that it is difficult to improve our artistic ability to create art works. Some people take lessons. However, in the most case, the way to improve Kansei is not explained clearly even in the lessons. Instead, people obtain Kansei of teachers implicitly through the experience of imitating the teachers' art works, or being modified their art works by teachers. This way of acquiring Kansei makes some people difficult to improve their artistic ability. In addition, people cannot create better art works by themselves without teacher.

The objective of our research is to propose a method for improving the Kansei of creating art works. Several researchers developed systems that introduce Kansei to support creating art works [1, 2]. These researches tried to recommend some ideas to create art works according to the Kansei words input by users. Following the given ideas, users are able to create art works easily that fit for their Kansei. However, user's Kansei is not improved so that they are not able to create art works by themselves without the system. Mukai, et al. developed simulation environment in which users are able to practice artistic activity that needs Kansei, such as flower arrangement [3]. This research only provides environment for enjoying artistic activity without preparing real flowers. It does not support creating art works nor improving ability for creating them.

© Springer International Publishing AG 2017
S. Yamamoto (Ed.): HIMI 2017, Part I, LNCS 10273, pp. 217–225, 2017.
DOI: 10.1007/978-3-319-58521-5_17

Systems of CAI (Computer-Assisted Instruction) or CAL (Computer-Assisted Learning) supported people to acquire knowledge [4, 5]. Such systems usually store knowledge to teach as teaching materials. However, Kansei is implicit and correct or appropriate Kansei cannot be defined, and teaching materials are not able to be prepared. On the other hand, skill support systems focus on improving implicit knowledge, such as physical skill [6, 7]. Many of such systems point out differences between students' performance and teacher's performance. In these systems, users are able to understand the inappropriateness of their performances, but are difficult in obtaining the ability of how to perform like a teacher. In addition, in the context of the artistic activity, the performance corresponds to the art works and teacher's art works are not always prepared. Thus, people should improve Kansei without using art works of others. Some idea inducement support systems encourage users to derive new ideas by themselves [8, 9]. The aim of these systems is to make users derive new ideas, not to improve ability for deriving ideas.

Our research supports learners of improving Kansei. Kansei is a part of artistic ability of creating art works. Since creating art works is subjective activity and it is sometimes difficult to find teachers who have the same Kansei, our system does not introduce teacher's help. Instead, we focus on thinking process in creating art works and propose methods for improving the Kansei by themselves. Firstly, the process of improving Kansei while creating art works is defined. Then, methods for supporting each steps in the process are proposed. As an example of our proposal, the system for improving Kansei is developed, whose target art works are designs created only by circles. We believe that if people are able to improve Kansei by the developed system, the proposed process of improving Kansei is valid and the supporting methods are effective. We have executed the experiment using the developed system to evaluate them.

2   Approach

2.1   Process of Improving Kansei

The art works have several features. In the case of drawing image, features are colors to use, size of objects, the number of objects, and so on. In creating art works, people decide values of these features in the way they satisfy. Features to recognize and consider are different according to the people. For example, some people do not consider the space between objects in the image, while others are strict on it. Such differences lead to the quality of the art works.

In this research, the Kansei is defined as states of features that people prefer. The states have both quality and quantity aspects. In the case of designing clothes, if the designer likes to design pink silk dress with three buttons, his/her Kansei is represented as "material=silk, color=pink, the number of buttons=three". Since "prefer" is a subjective sense, it is difficult to define what is the improvement of Kansei. However, if the preferable states of features are increased or changed, we can think their Kansei has been changed. In this research, to improve Kansei is defined as to increase the number of states of features that people prefer.

Based on this definition, we have proposed Kansei improvement process as Fig. 1. In step 1, people discover features of art works. Without recognizing features, they are not able to find preferable states of the features. In step 2, people create several art works by changing states of the features. In this step, they know how art works changes according to the features. In addition, since people try to create art works that they satisfy, they may use their Kansei implicitly to consider the states of features that they prefer. In step 3, they find the states of features that they prefer by comparing art works that they have created in step 2. If they found new states of features, their Kansei has been improved.

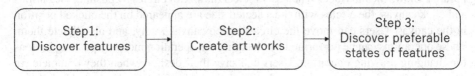

Fig. 1. Kansei improvement process

2.2 Support for Improving Kansei

Usually, Kansei is improved implicitly and people are not conscious of Kansei improvement process. Therefore, we believe that to follow Kansei improvement process shown in Fig. 1 helps people to improve their Kansei. However, the steps has several difficulties, so we propose support methods for performing each steps easily.

- **Method 1: for supporting step 1, to give hints for noticing new features that are not considered.** People are sometimes difficult for observing art works from different points of view. For such people, to give small hints for unknown features may trigger them of noticing new features. Hints do not need to indicate unknown features directly. Instead, the hints should push people feel to observe consider art works from different point of views.
- **Method 2: for supporting step 2, to provide simulation environment for creating art works.** In real world, there are several constraints so that it is sometimes difficult for creating art works freely. Let's consider designing houses as artistic activity. Building a house is expensive and takes a lot of time. Therefore, designers cannot build several houses in a short period even if they wish. In order to cope with such constraints in a real world, the simulation environment may help. People are able to create any art works by considering states of features freely without considering any constraints.
- **Method 3: for supporting step 3, to provide environment in which their art works are compared.** Art works that people prefer are created based on their Kansei. In most cases, Kansei is represented implicitly in their art works and may appear as common characteristics in their art works. Here, characteristics mean feature and its state. When their art works are displayed side by side in one environment, people may notice of the common characteristics and grasp them as their preferable states of features.

3   Case Study: Kansei for Designs Using Circles

In order to evaluate our Kansei improvement process and its support methods, we have developed the system as a case study. Target art works is designs that consist of circles of three different sizes, such as 25, 50, and 100 pixels. Some of the features of the art works are the number of circles, the area of circles in the canvas, positions of circles, the way of ordering circles, and so on.

Our system embeds functions correspond to the support methods described in Sect. 2.2. As for the method 2, drawing tool using circles of three sizes are prepared. Figure 2 shows the interface. When users select the size of circles by pushing the buttons and click canvas, the circles with the selected size are appeared on the clicked position in the canvas. Users can move the circles in the canvas freely, and also delete them. These operations can be performed by changing the operation mode by pushing buttons for changing drawing operation. Users can save their designs when they complete. In this tool, users cannot change the colors and sizes of circles freely. Instead, they can select sizes of circles by selecting one from three candidates and can put them at any locations. When the button for comparing designs is pushed, interface for comparing users' art works is appeared.

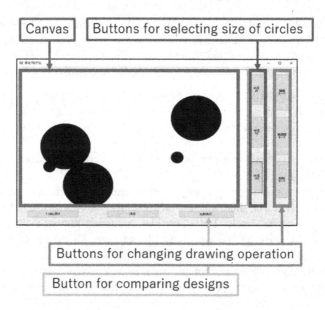

Fig. 2. Interface of drawing tool

The interface for comparing art works is shown as Fig. 3. By observing all art works that they have created, users may find common characteristics of their art works. When users find common characteristics and push the button for discovering features, the interface for inputting the characteristics is appeared.

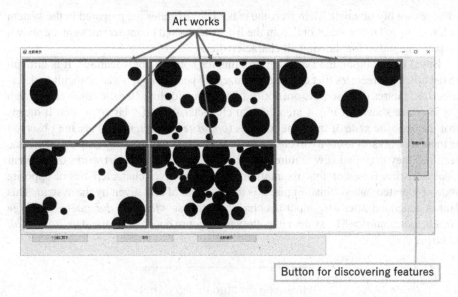

Fig. 3. Interface for comparing art works

Figure 4 is the interface for inputting the discovered characteristics. In order for the system to give hints, the system needs to know the characteristics that users recognize. Characteristics are represented by features and their values. Therefore, the interface has two input areas. One is for inputting feature and the other is for state. The representation of features are different among users, so text area is prepared for inputting features and users can describe features freely. On the other hand, states represent quality or quantity values of features and the ways of representing them are different according to the types of features. If the feature indicates the number of items, its states are large or small. If the feature shows the quality, its states are better or worse. If the feature indicates size,

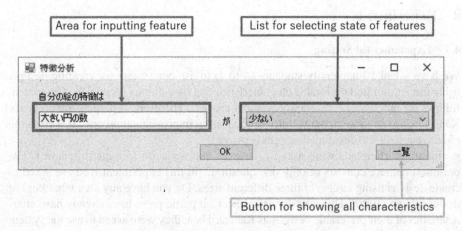

Fig. 4. Interface for inputting characteristics

its states are big or small. Therefore, the candidates of states are prepared in the system beforehand and users select one from the list. All inputted characteristics can be shown by pushing button for showing all characteristics.

Based on the input, the system gives hints for notifying new features. It is difficult to list up all the features that can be recognized by people, so it is also difficult to determine the features that users are not noticed. The inputted characteristics by users through the interface shown in Fig. 4 are common characteristics of their art works. It means that the opposite state of the same features (*opposite characteristics*) are not observed in their art works. If users try to create art works based on the opposite state of the same features, they may find new features and, hopefully, reach to the art works of different characteristics. Based on this assumption, our system gives characteristics of opposite state of inputted one as hints. Figure 5 is the example of hint given by the system. This hint is generated after user input his characteristics as *<feature: the number of large circles, state: small>* The system uses the same feature but changes the state from *small* to *large*.

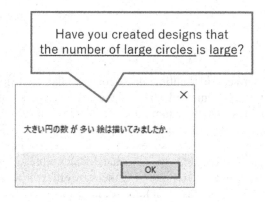

Fig. 5. Hint given by system

4 Experiment

4.1 Experimental Setting

We have asked 10 university students (*A* to *J*) to use our system for creating designs using circles and find preferable characteristics that they did not recognize. The system follows the process of Kansei improvement process. Therefore, if participants improve Kansei using our system, the validity of the Kansei improvement process as well as the effectiveness of the developed system is proved.

Firstly, participants were asked to answer questionnaire (pre-questionnaire). The pre-questionnaire consists of only one question: "In this experiment, you are asked to create designs using circles of three different sizes. Do you have any idea what kind of designs do you like?" This questionnaire checks if participants have already have characteristics of their preferable designs as Kansei. Then, they were asked to use the system for about 15 min. During the experiment, they were asked to write down characteristics of their preferable designs when they noticed and the timing in Kansei improvement process in which they noticed. After using the system, they were asked to answer questionnaire (post-questionnaire). The post-questionnaire consists two questions: 1) "Did the system help you for finding characteristics of designs that you prefer?" and 2) "Did the hints given by the system help you for creating designs of different characteristics?" For both questions, participants were asked to select one answer from "yes" or "no."

4.2 Result

The number of characteristics that participants recognized before they used the system, which was acquired from the pre-questionnaire, and the number of characteristics that they have noticed while using the system are shown in Table 1. All participants were able to find new characteristics of the designs that they prefer by using the system. Table 2 shows some of characteristics that noticed. Some participants described about the features that are manipulated directly by the participants through the interface, such as size of circles. Others focused on the features that are not indicated directly through the interface, such as areas of circles. Such characteristics may be noticed through the repetitive designing activity.

Table 1. The number of preferable characteristics that participants noticed

	A	B	C	D	E	F	G	H	I	J
Before using system	0	2	0	0	1	0	0	0	0	0
After using system	3	5	3	2	4	2	4	6	4	3

Table 2. Examples of characteristics that participants noticed

- I prefer circles with smaller sizes.
- I prefer designs with circles of different sizes.
- I prefer to divide the circle area and empty area clearly.
- I prefer to put circles in the corner.
- I prefer to order circles in the even interval.
- I prefer to order circles in line.

Table 3 shows the total number of designs that was created during the experiment and the number of designs that were drawn after hints were given in the step 1 in the Kansei improvement process. As the results of Tables 1 and 3, participants who have created more designs (B, E, G, H, I) recognized more characteristics than others. On the contrary, participants who did not created many designs could not list up many characteristics.

Table 3. The number of designs drawn by participants

	A	B	C	D	E	F	G	H	I	J
In whole experiment	5	9	4	4	9	5	8	7	7	4
After hints were given	2	2	1	0	0	2	5	4	1	0

Table 4 describes the number of characteristics that was noticed during each step. According to this result, participants could find more characteristics when they finish creating designs and comparing their designs. However, they could not find out characteristics when they considering new features. As shown in Table 3, some participants did not create any new designs after hints were given.

Table 4. The number of discovered features for each step

Step1: discovering features	Step2-1: during creating images	Step2-2: finish creating images	Figure 3: comparing their designs
4	7	10	15

Table 5 shows the post-questionnaire results. "y" means "yes" and "n" indicates "no." According to the result of the first question, all participants answered that system was effective in finding new characteristics of designs that they prefer. One participant commented that to compare created designs was very useful in finding common characteristics. Therefore, our system as well as Kansei improvement process were proved to be effective in improving Kansei. On the other hand, from the second question, not all participants thought the hints from the system were effective. The participant who answered "yes" said he could successfully discover new characteristics by creating designs according to the hints. However, the participants who answered "no" complained that he have already recognized the characteristics given as hints and he did not like it. Current our system only indicates the opposite state of inputted features and does not consider whether user already know the characteristics or not. The hint function should be updated so as to consider the preference of user more correctly.

Table 5. Post-questionnaire results

	A	B	C	D	E	F	G	H	I	J
Did the system help you for finding characteristics of designs that you prefer?	y	y	y	y	y	y	y	y	y	y
Did the hints given by the system help you for creating designs of different characteristics?	y	y	y	n	n	y	y	y	n	n

5   Conclusion

In this research, we have proposed the method for improving the Kansei of creating art works. Firstly, we have defined the process of improving Kansei. Then, the methods for supporting each steps in the process were proposed. In order to prove the effectiveness of the defined process and our support methods, we have developed the Kansei improvement support system for the creating designs that consists of only circles. According to the experimental use of the system, creating many art works and comparing created art works were effective in recognizing new characteristics of the art works that they prefer. However, hints for noticing new characteristics that were given by the system were not so useful.

As hint, current our system only gives the characteristics whose state is opposite to the inputted characteristics. These hints sometimes have already been recognized by some participants. During the experiment, some participants said that they wanted to see art works for others. Current our system was developed for improving Kansei by users themselves. However, if they could not find new characteristics, hints from others may help them. Therefore, as future work, we plan to embed functions for exchanging art works with others for finding new features.

This research realized Kansei improvement system for only art works of creating designs with circles of different sizes. We believe that our Kansei improvement process is applicable for other artistic activity as well. In order to prove it, we need to develop systems for other art works and evaluate if our Kansei improvement process and its support methods are effective for other artistic activities.

Acknowledgement. The work was supported in part by JSPS KAKENHI Grant-in-Aid for Scientific Research (B) (16H03089) and JSPS KAKENHI Grant-in-Aid for challenging Exploratory Research (16K12563)

References

1. Jindo, T., Hirasago, K.: Application studies to car interior of Kansei engineering. Int. J. Ind. Ergon. **19**, 105–114 (1997)
2. Jahanian, A., Liu, J., Lin, Q., Tretter, D., O' Brien-Strain, E., Lee, S.C., Lyons, N., Allebach, K.,: Recommendation system for automatic design of magazine covers. In: Proceedings of the 2013 International Conference on Intelligent User Interfaces, pp. 95–106 (2013)
3. Mukai, N., Takara, S., Kosugi, M.: A training system for the Japanese art of flower arrangement. In: Modelling and Simulation Society of Australia and New Zealand and International Association for Mathematics and Computers in Simulation, pp. 1671–1677 (2009)
4. Franzoni, A.L., Assar, S., Defude, B., Rojas, J.: Student learning styles adaptation method based on teaching strategies and electronic media. In: Proceedings of the Eighth IEEE International Conference on Advanced Learning Technologies, pp. 778–782 (2008)
5. Murray, T.: Authoring intelligent tutoring systems: an analysis of the state of the art. Int. J. Artif. Intell. Educ. **10**, 98–129 (1999)
6. Ota, S., Soga, M., Yamamoto, N., Taki, H.: Design and development of a learning support environment for apple peeling using data gloves. In: CwC Workshop in ECAI2012 (2012)
7. Toyooka, H., Matsuura, K., Gotoda, N.: A learning support system regarding motion trigger for repetitive motion having an operating instrument. In: Proceedings of 13th IADIS International Conference of CELDA, pp. 33–40 (2016)
8. Miura, M., Sugihara, T., Kunifuji, S.: GKJ: Group KJ method support system utilizing digital pens. IEICE Trans. Inf. Syst. **94**(3), 456–464 (2011)
9. Connolly, T., Jessup, L.M., Valacich, J.S.: Effects of anonymity and evaluative tone on idea generation in computer-mediated groups. Manage. Sci. **36**(6), 689–703 (1990)

Research on the Relationships Between Shape of Button and Operation Feeling

Hanhui Li[✉], Keiko Kasamatsu, Takeo Ainoya, and Ryuta Motegi

Tokyo Metropolitan University, 6-6 Asahigaoka, Hino-shi, Tokyo, Japan
huikino23@gmail.com

Abstract. This study through surveying on the user's operation process on the heater control by simulating driving environment and the evaluation of the operation feeling on the elements are related to the shape of button, ascertain users' mental model to the user interface of heater control and the influence between the shape elements of button the operation feeling, provide theoretical support for the design for automatic driving direction of the heater control user interface.

Keywords: Button · Form · Operation feeling · User interface

1 Introduction

With the development of technology, products become more and more electronic. There are many different user interfaces in the process of interaction between people and products are made up of various operating units. Before user start to operate the product, they would make an impression about the method of operation and operation flow in their mind in advance by observing the user interface on product. If this impression is consistent with the design of user interface, we can feel that the product is easy to operate. Like above, so that we can say the feeling of the operating units is an important element that could decide the product operability. Here, the appearance of operating units is composed of various factors that are related to the shape, so that we can think every change of those factors would have a great impact on the feeling of operation [1].

Figures 1, 2, 3, 4 and 5 are the results of the classification about the shape of the button that appears to be circular in the face (The following is called a circular button) of daily life.

By the above analysis of the shape of the circular button, it is found that the shape of the circular button is determined by the shape of the side and the top surface, Relative to the height of the plane where button is and the division between the plane and the button. The combination of different shapes of elements will bring a lot of changes in the feeling of operation.

In this study, we will take the button of car's heater control as the main research object.

With the advancing of science and technology and the development of the automatic driving, All operations related to driving a car are going to the direction of the

© Springer International Publishing AG 2017
S. Yamamoto (Ed.): HIMI 2017, Part I, LNCS 10273, pp. 226–234, 2017.
DOI: 10.1007/978-3-319-58521-5_18

technology control With this change, high-tech equipment that equipped in car are increase gradually.

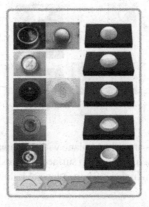

Fig. 1. The model's side that has an inclined plane with upward and inward, the gap between the button and the plane can be seen, and the top surface changes from raised to concave

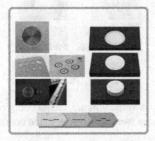

Fig. 2. The model's side that has a vertical plane, the gap between the button and the plane can be seen, and the top surface is flat, height ranges from lower than the plane to higher than the plane

Fig. 3. The model's side that has a vertical plane, the gap between the button and the plane can not be seen, and the top surface changes from the horizontal to convex, the button is higher than the plane

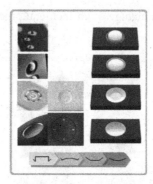

Fig. 4. The model's side that has an inclined plane with downward and inward, the gap between the button and the plane can be seen, and the top surface changes from the convex to the concave, the height changes gradually from higher than the plane to below the plane

Fig. 5. The model's side that has a vertical plane, the gap between the button and the plane can be seen, and the top surface changes from the convex to the concave, and the underside is higher than the plane

According to the result of investigation from JD Power (Fig. 6), compared with the result previous year, the installation rate whether voice recognition system or function of Bluetooth connectivity increased in 2015 year [2]. In order to realize the function of the additional high-tech equipment and the change to the direction of technology control, there has been great changes taken place in car's user interface. The points about "Is it easy to operate?" "Is it easy to understand Operation method" "How about the position" "Is it easy to press button?" and so on which are related to the feeling of operation about user interface became the important factors to improve customer's satisfaction.

Figure 7 is result of a survey which conducted by JD power in December 2015 for User's degree of dissatisfaction with vehicle equipment, the lower the score, the less dissatisfaction. According to the result, dissatisfaction can be divided into dissatisfaction of manufacturing and dissatisfaction of design, the score of is still the same as last year 1.7 points, but dissatisfaction of design by last year's 8.6 points rose to 9.6 points, is 5 times more than dissatisfaction of manufacturing. I think the problems that are related to the feeling of operation such as not easy to use and difficult to understand which caused by design become reasons for user dissatisfaction.

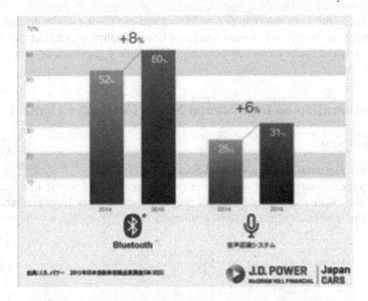

Fig. 6. The installation rate about voice recognition system and function of Bluetooth connectivity

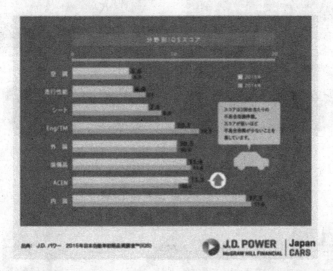

Fig. 7. The survey of user's degree of dissatisfaction with vehicle equipment

In this study, first, through experiment of operating buttons with different functions to achieve a certain goal based on the impression of operation which formed in the mind in advance before the actual operation in order to achieve a certain goal which can be realized by heater control to make the user's mental model more clearly.

Through the experiment to evaluate how the change of each factor which related to button's shape will bring the impact to the feeling of operation to clear the influence between the elements of the shape of the button and the feeling of the operation. And further, make the proposal of a new design of heater control's user interface that can improve the user experience in combination with people's unconscious action in daily life as the goal.

2 Consideration on User Mental Model for Heater Control

2.1 Experiment

2.1.1 Experimental Installation and Space Composition

For the experimental installation, HP personal computer and visual line measuring device (Tobii) were used. In addition, we prepared four kinds of Japanese cars' heater controls (Fig. 8) as user interface to be evaluated.

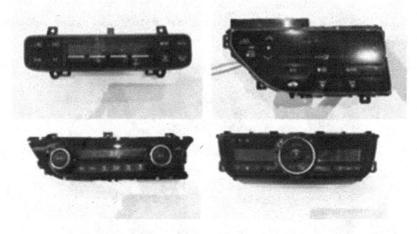

Fig. 8. Four kinds of Japanese cars' heater controls

Fig. 9. Experiment space

For the composition of the experiment space (Fig. 9), we used the 'Thrustmaster T500 RS Racing Wheel' as steering (foil), the SECT international company's play seat as car seat, and the other operation panel was made 1/1 model with corrugated cardboard.

2.1.2   Evaluation Method

First, imagined four scenes about when it is hot, cold, need to remove the fog of the glass and use the function of Auto (Fig. 10), and We evaluated the operation on these scenes. There are seven items in Evaluation items (ease of operation, ease of searching, ease of seeing in icons, understandability of icons, similarity with operation images, goodness of feedback, understandability of layout), we conducted seven grades by SD method. We also made a comment on the feeling of operation freely (Fig. 11) [3] Finally, we compared the four types in the questionnaire (Figure 12).

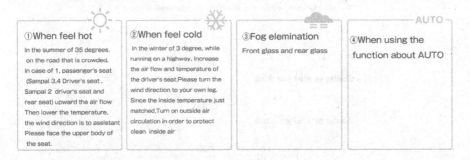

Fig. 10.   Four scenes assumed

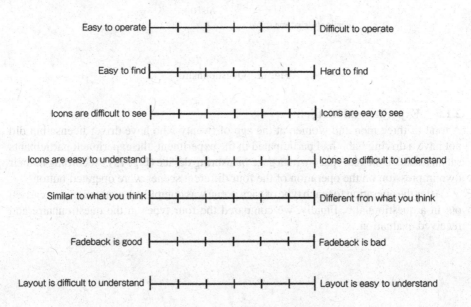

Fig. 11.   Evaluation item by SD method

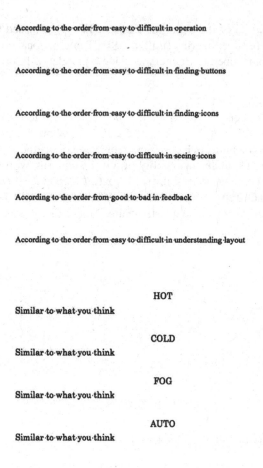

According to the order from easy to difficult in operation

According to the order from easy to difficult in finding buttons

According to the order from easy to difficult in finding icons

According to the order from easy to difficult in seeing icons

According to the order from good to bad in feedback

According to the order from easy to difficult in understanding layout

HOT

Similar to what you think

COLD

Similar to what you think

FOG

Similar to what you think

AUTO

Similar to what you think

Fig. 12. Questionnaire

2.1.3 Experimental Method

A total of three men and women at the age of twenty who have driver license but did not have a driving habit had participated in the experiment, the experiment participants sat on a seat on the real space with a gaze measuring device (Fig. 13). According to their own impression on the operation of the four different scenes were operated buttons.

After the operation for each type of each scene was completed, evaluation was carried out in a questionnaire. Finally, we compared the four types in the questionnaire and received evaluation.

Fig. 13. Experimental situation

3 The Influence that the Element of Buttons' Shape Brings to the Feeling of Operation

3.1 About Shape

We will discuss the concept of shape in this research. Shape refers to the appearance that the eye can see and state [4]. Not only the appearance but also the meaning of the state of things that can be recognized externally by touching with the hands or seeing with eyes. Therefore, the elements related to shape in this study include not only the appearance of the button of the heater control, but also the position on the operation panel and the inclination of the panel.

3.2 The Summary of Buttons' Shape and Operation Panel

Figure 14 shows the result of classification about the shape of the buttons in the heater control and the operation panel. From the photographs of various heater controls, after classifying the buttons with different shapes by function, we classified again by the operation method.

The three types of operation panels that have the base structure summarized from the photographs of many operation panels are shown on the right side of Fig. 8. By adding changes in inclination, bulging, dents and so on to these three types, it can become structures of others operation panel.

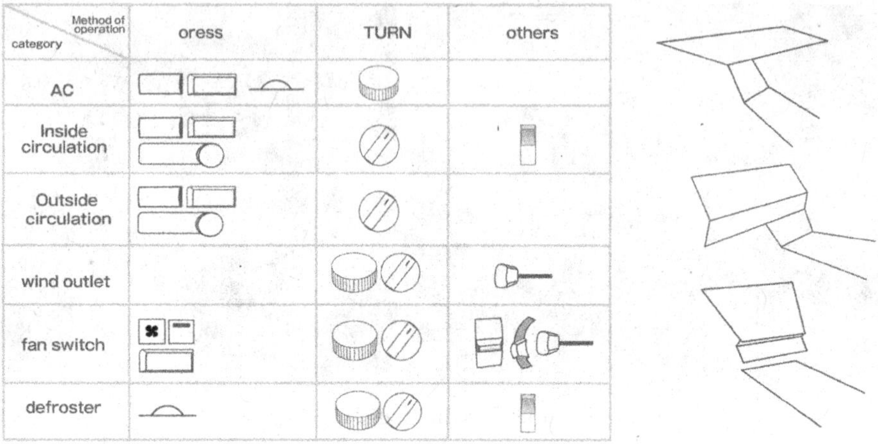

Fig. 14. result of classification about the shape of the buttons in the heater control and the operation panel

4   Future Works

In order to clarify the user's mental model for heater control, we will continue to do experiment and collect data. The part of the preliminary experiment that have done so far is just to verify the rationality of the experiment procedure, the assumed four scenes and evaluation items'. We are planning to conduct experiments on making the environment during driving from now on, using the LCD screen, connected to the play seat and the handle in the current experimental environment, operate the handle and pedal according to instructions issued on the screen. It is necessary to separate experiment participants according to the frequency of driving a car to analyze On the other hand, a model was made according to the appearance of buttons along with each kind of operation panel made of corrugated cardboard, It is necessary to clarify the influence that the shape element of the button bring to the feeling of operation by changing the position on the operation panel and the inclination of the panel.

References

1. Woo, J., Hosoya, S., Amida, K., Takatera, M., Shimizu, Y., Shirai, H.: Research on the relation between shape of the operating parts and the operation, studies on design. Bull. Jpn. Soc. Sci. Des. **51**(1), 55–62 (2004)
2. http://jdpower-japan.com/report/328/2
3. Kajihara, C., Munechika, M.: A method for improving usability based on the knowledge on high-performance touch panels. J. Jpn Ind. Manage. Assoc. **67**(3), 232–241 (2016)
4. http://www.weblio.jp/content/形状

A Study of Interaction Interface Design of Digital Contents on Hand-Held Intelligent Products

Ming-Chyuan Lin[1(✉)], Yi-Hsien Lin[1], Shuo-Fang Liu[2], and Ming-Hong Wang[2]

[1] Department of Creative Product Design and Management, Far East University, Tainan, Taiwan
minglin@mail.ncku.edu.tw, yisam0915@yahoo.com.tw
[2] Department of Industrial Design, National Cheng Kung University, Tainan, Taiwan
{liusf,p38031020}@mail.ncku.edu.tw

Abstract. Recently, Internet applications have been integrated in 3C hand-held intelligent products such as smart phones, vehicle navigation devices and driving recorders that help improve our living quality. Among these products, digital contents which displayed by a small screen plays an important role in displaying information. The research objective is to explore an optimum representation of character contents for hand-held intelligent products having a better viewing and operating interface. In this research, the character contents for study included typeface, size, distance between two words, distance between two lines and character and background color matching. The research first collected and analyzed existing character contents. Three Chinese and English typefaces were chosen. A threshold value was determined for each character attribute. Based on the defined character attributes, the research developed a user interface for experimental simulation. The experiment was implemented with 48 tested subjects and their experimental data were forwarded to the simulation process of back-propagation neural network for determining an optimum display of character characteristics. It is expected that the results will be helpful for developing better digital content interfaces for hand-held intelligent products.

Keywords: Hand-held intelligent product · Digital content · Character visual representation · Interface design · Back-propagation neural network

1 Introduction

The progress of Internet development has made our daily hand-held intelligent products become more functional. In general, these products such as smart phones, global positioning systems (GPS), driving recorders and smart watches have a specific screen with digital content information to allow users to operate the interface and view information, and even support functions for entertainment and leisure activity [1]. Among these products, the way of presentation on digital contents is usually a combination of pictures, characters, voices and dynamic image displays, such as electronic books, e-news and e-articles. Although the pictures can attract people more attention than characters, Tomioka [2] noted that only characters can communicate accurate information to people. Since characters in digital contents are most suitable for presenting abstract and objective

© Springer International Publishing AG 2017
S. Yamamoto (Ed.): HIMI 2017, Part I, LNCS 10273, pp. 235–247, 2017.
DOI: 10.1007/978-3-319-58521-5_19

information and transmitting accurate and subtle meaning of message, an appropriate presentation of characters absolutely plays an important role in displaying information and would be a valuable issue to research. Sanders and McCormick [3] stressed that the cognitions of visibility, readability and legibility are important criteria for character content design, especially on color matching between characters and the corresponding background. Preece et al. [4] suggested that a good design should optimize the user's interaction with a usable interactive product system in a way of easy to learn, effective to understand and enjoyable to use. Stone et al. [5] indicated that some factors such as typeface, type size, letter spacing, line spacing, line length and color will affect the legibility of text in current digital displays. Jung and Im, [6] recommended that character icons with suitable touch area and desirable hit rate be important guidelines for a smart phone user interface design. Crundall et al. [7] observed that larger text sizes will have high relatively short glances, whereas smaller text will lead to have long glances. In general, familiar typefaces such as Times New Roman and Arial will have a better cognition [5, 8]. Darroch et al. [9] also found that the aged people prefer character size to be 9 to 12 pts (points, 1 point = 0.35 mm). Based on the observation of interfaces of existing hand-held intelligent products, current character representation of digital contents is usually restricted in a specific scale of adjustment and some character colors associated with background colors do not show a high degree of visibility. Besides, most arrangements of characters in digital contents rely on the designer's subjective opinion, knowledge and experience and seldom consider users preferences. The above mentioned situations will make the character representation cannot achieve the most suitable viewing effect, especially for specific groups of users. To help users accurately read and conveniently operate the hand-held intelligent products in relatively a short time, the designer need to consider factors including characters and background color matching, sizes of characters, distances between characters, line distances and typefaces of characters. As such the objective of this research is to explore the optimum character representation of digital contents display model for specific size of hand-held intelligent products that can help users improve better viewing and operating display.

2   Development Procedures

The research will involve the above mentioned design factors in the optimum combination of parameters for a most suitable character content representation model. The proposed model is designed to be changeable and adjustable for specific size of displays. In this research, typefaces of characters include three types of Chinese and English, respectively. As to the units, the millimeter and point will be used in the measurement and experiment. Note that the position of characters will be placed in center of the display. The development of the research divides the process into three stages. They are (1) organization of experimental parameters and design of simulation display, (2) experimental interface design and implementation, and (3) back-propagation neural network for optimum character contents recommendation. In the first stage, the research collects and summarizes characteristics of character contents of current hand-held intelligent products, defines threshold values for character parameters, investigates and clusters the color matching between characters and backgrounds, and designs representation interfaces of experiments and outcomes. The second stage includes experimental design and interaction interface design, experimental programming, optimum character representation for experiment, and experimental data collection and analysis. As to the third stage, the research will apply back propagation neural network to data training and simulation, and then derive an optimum display of character contents representation. The research will use Microsoft Visual Basic 6.0 or higher version to plan the interaction interface experimental system for hand-held intelligent products.

3   Organization of Experimental Parameters and Design of Simulation Display

In the development procedure, the research will focus on determining the most suitable combination of character content characteristics for hand-held intelligent products. The identified character content characteristics are regarded as experimental parameters and will be used in defining and designing an adjustable user interface simulation mode for the research experiment.

3.1   Organization of Experimental Parameters

According to the research objective, the character content attributes to be involved in the research include: (1) character typeface, (2) character size, (3) distance between two words, (4) distance between two lines and (5) character and background color matching. To determine the threshold ranges of these character content attributes for the design of simulation display, the research collected and investigated relevant data from several brands of intelligent hand-held products on GPS navigations, driving recorders, MP4 and smart phones such as Garmin, Mio, HTC, Samsung and Apple iPhone. Based on the summarized data, the threshold ranges of the character content attributes can be defined. In this research, the character typefaces will consider three types of Chinese and English as illustrated in Fig. 1. Note that in Fig. 1, Chinese typefaces of Mingliu, Kaiw and SimHei and English typefaces of Times New Roman, Arial Unicode MS and Calibri are chosen respectively for further experiment. Based on the chosen typefaces associated with the data collection and investigation on existing intelligent hand-held products, the character sizes will be set at 5 to 26 points/pts. Note that 1 pt = 1/72 in. = 0.352 mm (mm). As such the typeface sizes will range from 1.76 mm to 9.15 mm. Figure 2 illustrates the conceptual representation of character sizes. The distance between two words will be set at 0.4 to 8 points/pts, or 0.14 mm to 2.82 mm. Figure 3 illustrates the conceptual representation of the distance "d" between two words. Similarly, the distance between two lines is set at 1 to 25 points/pts, or 0.35 mm to 8.8 mm. Figure 4 illustrates the conceptual representation of the distance "d" between two lines. As to the character and background color matching, the research used a color measurement function in software CorelDraw associated with a popular RGB (R: Red, G: Green, B: Blue) color system to help define colors for character contents as well as the corresponding backgrounds. The RGB color system is used in representing digital color images with scale values range from 0 to 255 for red, green and blue colors, respectively. In other words, any color can be defined by combining each specific scale value of red, green and blue colors. In this research, a total of 48 current color combinations of character and the corresponding background were collected from existing intelligent hand-held products. Figure 5 illustrates a sample of collected color combination of character and the corresponding background. Note that the numeric values in Fig. 5 denote R, G and B color scale values for a specific character and the corresponding background.

細明體   標楷體   正黑體

(a) Chinese Mingliu   (b) Chinese Kaiu   (c) Chinese SimHei

Times New Roman   Arial Unicode MS   Calibri

(d) Times New Roman   (e) Arial Unicode MS   (f) Calibri

Fig. 1. Three typefaces of Chinese and English characters

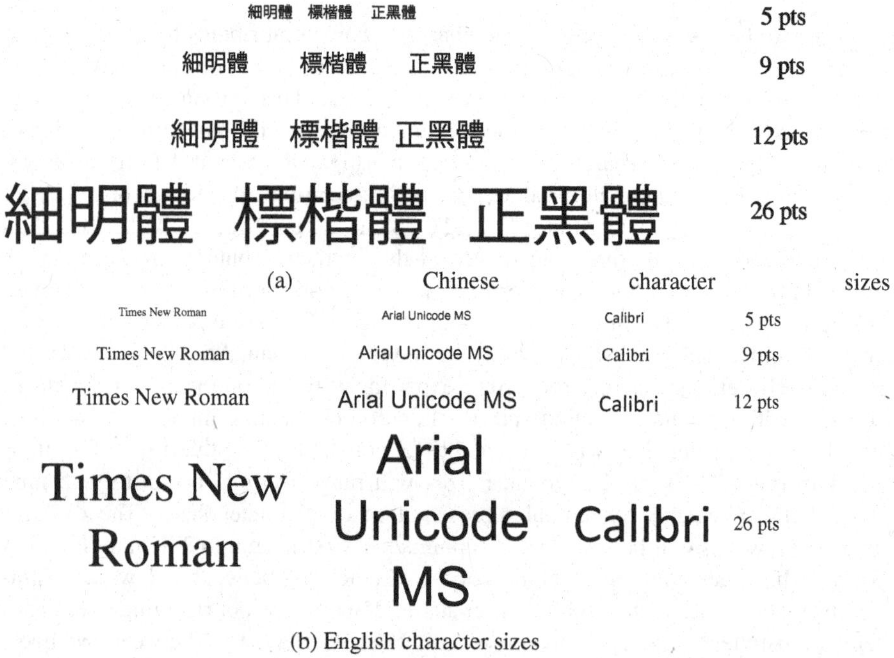

細明體 標楷體 正黑體	5 pts
細明體 標楷體 正黑體	9 pts
細明體 標楷體 正黑體	12 pts
細明體 標楷體 正黑體	26 pts

(a)   Chinese   character   sizes

Times New Roman	Arial Unicode MS	Calibri	5 pts
Times New Roman	Arial Unicode MS	Calibri	9 pts
Times New Roman	Arial Unicode MS	Calibri	12 pts
Times New Roman	Arial Unicode MS	Calibri	26 pts

(b) English character sizes

Fig. 2. Illustration of defined character sizes

Fig. 3. Illustration of defined distance between two words

Fig. 4. Illustration of defined distance between two lines

Sample No. 8	R	G	B
Character Color	8	4	3
Background Color	245	251	7
Color Combination Representation	中文字ABC		

Fig. 5. A collection of character and background color combination

A cognition evaluation questionnaire was designed with assistance of the Internet network MySurvey to help select better cognition of color combinations. The research remained 26 color combinations. To cluster the above 26 color combinations, the research designed a legibility 5-priceple-questionnaire regarding adjustable character content attributes of character typefaces, character sizes, distance between two words, distance between two lines, and character and background color matching for digital content preference measurements. The questionnaire evaluation criteria include personal preference, color combination feeling, viewing custom, color combination appropriation and reading comfort [10]. Again, the questionnaire was distributed to the Internet tested subjects for evaluation of the 26 color combinations. The questionnaire results were forwarded to the hierarchical clustering analysis to generalize some groups of represented digital contents [11]. Note that the statistical analysis software SPSS 17 was used and 10 groups of color combinations were determined. Table 1 illustrates representative color combinations for these 10 groups. The representative color combinations will be used in the design of simulation display.

Table 1. 10 Groups of character and background color combinations

Group	Color combination sample no.	Character color			Background color			Representative sample
		R	G	B	R	G	B	
1	41	121	251	6	252	6	130	中文字ABC
2	13	250	251	123	0	1	2	中文字ABC
3	6	244	254	251	6	3	127	中文字ABC
4	11	2	255	3	3	5	2	中文字ABC
5	2	5	129	247	133	6	3	中文字ABC
6	16	126	123	124	0	0	252	中文字ABC
7	14	251	122	120	0	0	122	中文字ABC
8	48	4	132	255	252	251	131	中文字ABC
9	8	245	251	7	8	4	3	中文字ABC
10	4	11	20	7	4	248	5	中文字ABC

3.2 Design of Simulation Display

After character content characteristics having been determined, the research considered a suitable scenario for the design of a simulation display.

Since driving navigation systems in hand-held intelligent products perform a dynamic representation and can display instantly different pictures, the research decided to choose a popular driving navigation system as a targeted scenario and design a representative display for further simulation and experiment. According to the collection of possible locations that character contents frequently show up in a driving navigation system, the research chose eight similar displays of current navigation systems and designed a questionnaire for a preference evaluation on these displays. It appears that a display illustrated in Fig. 6 is a most favorable one. Based on the display shown in Fig. 6, the research defined eight blocks in a display for presenting character contents. Figure 7 illustrates the conceptual framework for the design of a display in the character content cognition experimental process. According to the defined framework shown in Fig. 7, Fig. 8 presents a conceptual display. A selection menu display that will be used in the experimental simulation process is designed including choice of (1) character typeface, (2) character size, (3) distance between two words, (4) distance between two lines, (5) character and background color matching and (6) area selection

Figure 9 illustrates the designed selection menu display for experimental simulation. The designed selection menu Display was developed by Microsoft Visual Basic 6.0. As to the driving simulation display, the research used 60 GIF (Graphics Interchange Format) pictures and pooled to be an animated display that can run circularly with two pictures per second and about 30 s per cycle time. Note that during the adjustment period, the driving animation will not proceed until the tested subject satisfies the adjustment of each character content attributes.

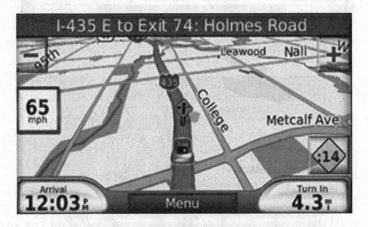

Fig. 6. Representative display for design of simulation

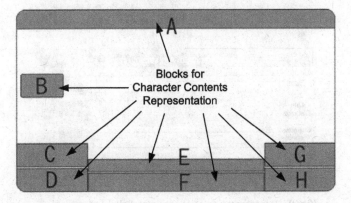

Fig. 7. Conceptual framework of character contents representation

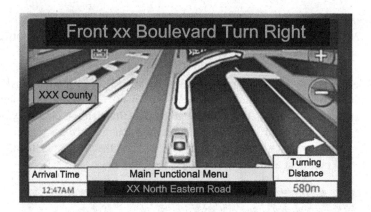

Fig. 8. Conceptual simulation display based on framework of Fig. 7

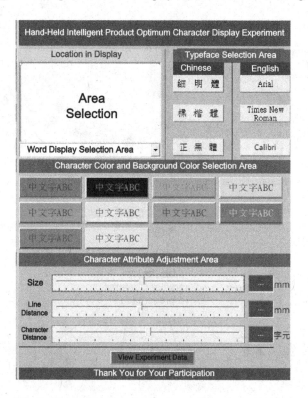

Fig. 9. Representation of experimental simulation display

4 Experimental Interface Design and Implementation

In the conduction of experimental design, the tested subject will first input about 15 questions, including (1) name, (2) sex, (3) age, (4) residence area, (5) education, (6) occupation, (7) monthly income, (8) academic background, (9) visual acuity, (10) type of vehicle used, (11) frequency of evening driving, (12) number of driving navigation devices or recorders used, (13) understand degree on driving navigation or recording systems, (14) expected budget for purchasing a driving navigation or recording system and (15) most favorable function. The tested subject who responds the above 15 questions at the first stage of questionnaire will request to get into the experimental system. During the experiment, the tested subject can adjust each character content attribute value based on his or her visual preference and cognition. All tested subjects should be able to easily adjust the character-blocks in the simulated display by the system of optimum experiment and re-adjust the character-blocks until the optimum display is determined. In the experimental environment, one laptop computer connects with a screen. The laptop computer displays a static map when the tested subject uses the screen to adjust character content attributes or displays an instantly updated map when he or she runs the simulation on the screen. Figure 10 illustrates representational displays for the laptop computer associated with the screen during the conduction of an experimental simulation. The environment scene is shown in Fig. 11. A total of 48 tested subjects including 25 male and 23 female college students are voluntarily invited to participate in this experiment. All tested subjects have at least some sort of experiences on using hand-held intelligent products especially the driving navigation system and corrected normal visual acuity. Each run of the experiment, the adjusted values of character content attributes will be stored in the tables of Microsoft Excel 2007. Table 2 illustrates experimental data of tested subject No. 1. Note that the values of charter size, line distance and word distance shown in Table 2 are denoted as 1 unit equals to 1 point (pt). The information of subjects' features and experimental data will be applied in the training-stage of neural network to generate an optimum display of character characteristics.

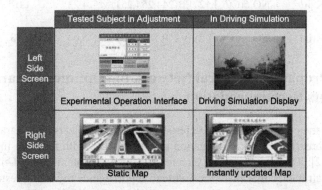

Fig. 10. Representation of displays in experimental simulation

Fig. 11. Experimental environment scene

Table 2. Example showing experimental data of tested subject No.1

Sample no.	Typeface	Character and background color matching	Character size	Line distance	Word distance
Block A					
1	Kaiu	NO.4(C(4,248,5),B(11,20,7)	11.99	0.71	1
Block B					
1	Kaiu	NO.11(C(3,5,2),B(2,255,3)	6.00	1.42	1
Block C					
1	Kaiu	NO.6(C(6,3,127),B(244,254,25)	4.59	0.71	1
Block D					
1	Arial	NO.6(C(6,3,127),B(244,254,251)	4.94	0.71	1
Block E					
1	Kaiu	NO.6(C(6,3,127),B(244,254,251)	4.59	1.07	1
Block F					
1	Kaiu	NO.6(C(6,3,127),B(244,254,251)	4.59	0.71	2
Block G					
1	Kaiu	NO.6(C(6,3,127),B(244,254,251)	4.23	1.07	1
Block I					
1	Arial	NO.13(C(0,1,2),B(250,251,123)	5.64	1.78	0

5   Back-Propagation Neural Network for Optimum Character Contents Recommendation

According to the collected data characteristics of tested subjects and character content attributes, a three-layer back-propagation neural network with multiple-input neurons is selected [12]. The neuron model selected for the experiments is a 14–10–5 type of network, which means that there are fourteen input signals regarding tested subjects' information in the input layer, ten actual outputs of neurons in the hidden layer, and five actual outputs of neuron regarding parameter attribute values of digital contents in the output layer [13, 14]. The fourteen input signals are: (1) sex, (2) age, (3) residence area, (4) education, (5) occupation, (6) monthly income, (7) academic background, (8) visual acuity, (9) type of vehicle used, (10) frequency of evening driving, (11) number of driving navigation devices or recorders used, (12) understand degree on driving navigation or recording systems, (13) expected budget for purchasing a driving navigation or recording system and (14) most favorable function. As to the five actual outputs, they are: (1) character typeface, (2) character size, (3) distance between two words, (4) distance between two lines, and (5) character and background color matching. Note that the concept of binary code transformation for genetic algorithms is incorporated with the neural network learning and simulation. The data of fourteen inputs regarding questionnaire results of tested subjects associated with outputs of eight blocks of five character attributes are normalized, respectively. To simplify the study, 48 tested subjects are divided into male and female groups. The computer software Matlab 7.0 is used for the analysis of back-propagation neural network training and simulation. In Matlab 7.0, the research defined transfer function, number of neurons and transfer function variable settings. As to the expected goal values, they are all defined as less than 0.05. Having finished the training and simulation process of back-propagation neural network, the research derives two optimum combinations of five parameters of character contents for respective male and female group of users. Figure 12 illustrates one optimum combination of character attributes for male group. It appears that most typefaces presented in Fig. 12 are in Chinese are primarily because the experiment was implemented by Chinese tested subjects.

Block	Typeface	Character and Background Color	Character Size	Line Distance	Character Distance
A	SimHei	NO.8	8.113	1.42	1
		Front XX Boulevard Turn Right			
B	Kaiu	NO.48	5.291	0.71	1
		XXX County			
C	SimHei	NO.4	5.291	0.71	0
		Arrival Time			
D	Arial	NO.6	5.64	1.42	0
		12:47AM			
E	SimHei	NO.4	5.29	0.71	1
		Main Functional Menu			
F	SimHei	NO.6	5.64	0.71	1
		XXX North Eastern Road			
G	SimHei	NO.4	5.64	1.065	1
		Turning Distance			
H	Calibri	NO.6	5.99	1.775	1
		580 m			

Fig. 12. An optimum representation of character contents for male group

6 Conclusions

Hand-held intelligent products have become part of our daily essentials. Many newly technologies as well as applications are introduced to be functions of hand-held intelligent products. These functions share more spaces than ever in a limited size of screen and will cause the users much burden on reading and cognition. The digital contents involve a combination of pictures, characters, and dynamic images. Although pictures or images can be more attracted than characters, only characters can communicate accurate information to people. Therefore, good presentation of character characteristics in digital contents can help enhance the user ability in legibility and cognition. The research proposed an integrated procedure to explore an optimum combination of character attributes including typefaces, character sizes, distance between two words, distance between lines and character and background color matching. The parameter attributes and values for the above mentioned character characteristics are identified and defined for designing an experimental simulation display. Some experienced voluntarily male and female college students are invited as tested subjects. The experimental data including their basic information and preferable settings of character attributes are then forwarded to the process of back-propagation neural network training and simulation. Two optimum combinations of character attribute values for male and female are obtained. It is noted that the outcomes of this research are all experiment-oriented so that the optimum character contents are highly objective results, which can be applied to the process of development in digital contents, and reduce the time in setting attributions of digital contents. However, more experiment data collection and validation are needed for further studies so that the final results can be more reliable and useful. It is expected that through the implementation of this research, the following results can be obtained: (1) a suitable interaction interface connection between digital contents and users, (2) an optimum structure of digital contents on operation performance, and (3) an appropriate mode of digital contents information display on hand-held intelligent products. In addition, this research will provide referencing information and research process with designers to help establish users' awareness on the digital content information interface and make human-computer interaction be more humanized and intelligent.

Acknowledgements. The authors are grateful to the National Science Council, Taiwan for supporting this research under the grant number MOST 105-2221-E-269-004.

References

1. Lin, M.-C., Chen, M.-S., Lin, C.-C., Chang, A.C.: The study of optimum cognition on character images for in-vehicle navigation systems. In: 4th International Conference on Applied Human Factors and Ergonomics 2012 (AHFE 2012), San Francisco, pp. 6796–6805 (2012)
2. Tomioka, K.: Study on legibility of characters for the elderly-effects of character display modes on legibility. J. Physiol. Anthropol. **26**(2), 159–164 (2006)
3. Sanders, M.S., McCormick, E.J.: Human Factors in Engineering and Design, 7th edn. McGraw-Hill Inc, New York (1993)

4. Preece, J., Rogers, Y., Sharp, H.: Interaction Design: Beyond Human-Computer Interaction. Wiley, New York (2002)
5. Stone, D., Jarrett, C., Woodroffe, M., Minocha, S.: User Interface Design and Evaluation. Morgan Kaufmann Publishers, San Francisco (2005)
6. Jung, E.S., Im, Y.: Touchable area: an empirical study on design approach considering perception size and touch input behavior. I. J. Ind. Ergon. **49**, 21–30 (2015)
7. Crundall, E., Large, D.R., Burnett, G.: A driving simulator study to explore the effects of text size on the visual demand of in-vehicle displays. Displays **43**, 23–29 (2016)
8. Kingery, D., Furuta, R.: Skimming electronic newspaper headlines: a study of typeface, point size, screen resolution, and monitor size. Inf. Process. Manage. **33**(4), 685–696 (1997)
9. Darroch, I., Goodman, J., Brewster, S., Gray, P.: The effect of age and font size on reading text on handheld computers. In: Costabile, M.F., Paternò, F. (eds.) INTERACT 2005. LNCS, vol. 3585, pp. 253–266. Springer, Heidelberg (2005). doi:10.1007/11555261_23
10. Solomon, M.R.: Consumer Behavior: Buying, Having, and Being, 6th edn. Pearson Prentice-Hall, New Jersey (2004)
11. Sharma, S.: Applied Multivariate Techniques. Wiley, New York (1996)
12. Lin, M.-C., Lin, Y.-H., Lin, C.-C., Lin, J.-Y.: A study on the interface design of a functional menu and icons for in-vehicle navigation systems. In: Yamamoto, S. (ed.) HCI 2014. LNCS, vol. 8522, pp. 261–272. Springer, Cham (2014). doi:10.1007/978-3-319-07863-2_26
13. Jung, J.-R., Yum, B.-J.: Artificial neural network based approach for dynamic parameter design. Expert Syst. Appl. **38**, 504–510 (2011)
14. Lin, M.-C., Lin, Y.-H., Lin, C.-C., Chen, M.-S., Hung, Y.-C.: An integrated neuro-genetic approach incorporating the Taguchi method for product design. J. Adv. Eng. Inf. **29**, 47–58 (2015)

UX Design of a Big Data Visualization Application Supporting Gesture-Based Interaction with a Large Display

Stavroula Ntoa[1], Chryssi Birliraki[1], Giannis Drossis[1],
George Margetis[1(✉)], Ilia Adami[1], and Constantine Stephanidis[1,2]

[1] Institute of Computer Science (ICS), Foundation for Research
and Technology – Hellas (FORTH), Heraklion, Greece
{stant,birlirak,drossis,gmarget,
iadami,cs}@ics.forth.gr
[2] Department of Computer Science, University of Crete, Heraklion, Greece

Abstract. The explosion of information has led to the proliferation of Big Data as an influential business and research domain. Data center infrastructure management is a sector largely affected by Big Data, however the visualization of, and interaction with, Big Data in the context of a data center room is a challenging endeavor. This paper presents the iterative design and development of a 3D Data Centre Visualization application featuring gesture-based interaction with a high resolution large screen display. As result of the design iterations three distinct system versions were developed, evolving the supported functionality, the User Interface and the interaction methods. The paper presents the evolution of the system, the results of an expert-based evaluation which was carried out during the development life-cycle, as well as the challenges faced and lessons learned regarding the User Experience design of a big data application deployed in a large display, supporting gestural interaction.

Keywords: Big data · Big data visualization · 3D data center · Data center infrastructure management · Gestural interaction · Natural interaction · Large screen display · User experience design · UX

1 Introduction

Information Technology has penetrated all aspects of life, leading to the era of born digital natives [1] who do not know life without smartphones, tablets or computers. This paradigm shift has led to an "explosion" of data and the proliferation of Big Data as part of every sector and function of the global economy [2]. Data center infrastructure management is a sector largely affected by Big Data, as it provides the means for supporting Big Data storage, retrieval and monitoring [3], while it uses Big Data itself.

Several challenges have been identified in the literature regarding Big Data, many of which refer to the visualization of data in order to be meaningful and useful for the targeted audiences [4, 5]. This paper presents the User Interface of a 3D Data Centre Visualization application [3] and the interaction techniques employed, identifies

© Springer International Publishing AG 2017
S. Yamamoto (Ed.): HIMI 2017, Part I, LNCS 10273, pp. 248–265, 2017.
DOI: 10.1007/978-3-319-58521-5_20

specific UI design and interaction challenges that were encountered and addressed during the iterative process that was followed, and ends up with design tips that pertain to gesture-based interaction with large screen displays for the manipulation of the 3D Data Centre.

The paper is structured as follows: Sect. 2 discusses related work in terms of big data visualization and gesture-based interaction with large screen displays. Section 3 provides an overview of the 3D Data Centre and describes how its UI and interaction design evolved during an iterative process. The lessons learned are summarized in Sect. 4, while Sect. 5 provides conclusions and future work directions.

2 Related Work

Data centers are routinely employed by large companies for storage, web search and large-scale computations; with the rise of cloud computing, service hosting in data centers has become a multibillion dollar business that plays a crucial role in the future Information Technology (IT) industry [6]. Although several solutions for data center management are available, it has been reported that there is a lack of efficient tools to assist operators in handling situations that cannot be addressed by autonomic control systems [7], a gap which can be bridged using appropriate visualization tools. On the other hand, in terms of visualization approaches, technologies are now mature to move beyond the desktop metaphor towards new multi-sensory modalities supporting novel interactions [8]. For instance, it is reported that using a larger display with more pixels increases the number of observations made by the users, and affords the acquisition of more complex and integrative insights [9]. The 3D Data Centre Visualization application presented in this paper takes advantage of novel interaction technologies with the aim to address users' needs in the context of a control room, and thus supports gesture-based interaction with a large display. Two main issues were explored during the iterative design of the application, namely data visualization and interaction techniques for the given context.

Data visualization can be characterized as a sense-making tool, assisting users to identify meaningful correlations and explore them to develop models and theories [10], and make good decisions [11]. A challenge for big data visualization is the large size and high dimension of Big Data, which can be tackled using not only aesthetics but also functionality to achieve intuitive and effective knowledge presentation [4]. There is currently an important amount of research and innovation in the field of visualization, i.e., techniques and technologies used for creating images, diagrams, or animations to communicate, understand, and improve the results of big data analyses, such as tag clouds, clustergrams, history flows, and spatial information flows [2]. A widely used Big Data visualization technique is OLAP [12], which allows users to analyze multidimensional data interactively from various perspectives. An important limitation of 2D visualizations such as the aforementioned ones is the increased clutter which is imposed, and which discards humans' visual system's natural ability to perceive and interpret 3D spaces [13]. A 3D visualization, on the other hand, allows designers the freedom of layering information in 3D to reduce clutter and potentially improve comprehension and performance [13]. Nevertheless, user interaction in 3D user interfaces is challenging due to the additional degrees of freedom, requiring complex manipulation controls and a rich interaction vocabulary [14].

Gestures are a powerful feature of human expression, which can be used in such 3D UIs, however an important challenge is that although gesture-based systems and natural interfaces in general are widely accepted and have great potential, gestures are unconstrained and are apt to be performed in an ambiguous manner [15]. Furthermore, gesture-based systems lack standardization, since a universal gesture vocabulary does not exist yet [16], so a good gesture vocabulary may only match one specific application and user group. A gesture vocabulary should be tailored for the specific application and context of use so as to contain gestures that are ergonomic, intuitive, easy to perform and remember, which are metaphorically and iconically appropriate for the addressed functionality [17]. The biggest problem with making gestures self-revealing is getting over the idea that gestures are somehow natural or intuitive, as it has been shown that users cannot and will not guess any custom gesture language [18]. This problem can be overcome if UI affordances are put on the screen to which users can react. Furthermore, research in gestural vocabularies has suggested that gestures triggering manipulation of objects should be dynamic iconic representations of the motion required for the manipulation, rather than static iconic hand poses, while gestures to trigger tasks that suggest the use of a tool should pantomime the actual action with imagined tool in hand and gestures in space to trigger manipulation of objects should be two-handed [19].

On the other hand, large high-resolution displays impose their own interaction challenges, since traditional desktop metaphors do not always scale well to large format displays, bringing forward the need for novel metaphors and interaction techniques. Usability issues and interaction challenges reported in the literature include reaching distant objects, pointing and selecting, managing space and layout and transitioning between interactions [20]. In terms of visualization, large screen displays facilitate scaling up the amount of information represented by hosting more data entities, offering greater data dimensionality, providing more data details, accommodating more data complexity and heterogeneity and providing more space for processing, sense making, and collaboration [21].

The 3D Data Centre Visualization application that is described in this paper discusses how some of the aforementioned challenges were faced in the domains of big data visualization and gesture-based interaction with a large screen display used for presenting 3D Big Data. The main requirements that have shaped the design and development of the application were to make the Big Data visualization useful and decision-enabling for data center operators, to support an easy to learn and use gestural vocabulary, and to employ the large screen display in an optimal way to achieve a powerful visualization and finally to facilitate user interaction with the large screen display.

3   Design of the 3D Data Centre Visualization Application

The development of the 3D Data Centre Visualization Application has followed an iterative approach, continuously evolving the supported functionality, the User Interface and the interaction methods. Three major application versions emerged during the evolution of the application, as it is described in summary in Table 1 and illustrated in Figs. 1 and 2. More specifically, the first version of the application aimed at providing a 3D visualization of a data center room, while the second version incorporated gesture-based interaction and an updated user interface which better exploited the screen real estate and provided a more contemporary look-and-feel. The second version of the application was assessed through heuristic evaluation [22] by three User Experience (UX) experts. Based on the results of the evaluation, the third version of the application was implemented, featuring UI improvements and new functionality to support users' spatial orientation in the visualized room.

Table 1. Evolution of the 3D Data Centre Visualization application in terms of supported functionality and interaction methods. For each version only the changes or newly introduced features are listed.

Functionality	
Version 1	• 3D Visualization of the racks, following the metaphor of a room • Orbit camera • Filter displayed results by server attribute, criticality level, timestamp • Change view by sparseness • Navigation controls for zoom in/out and move forward/backward/right/left • Anomalies detection and notification • Close-up view of a selected rack • Detailed information through charts for a specific unit of a rack
Version 2	• Navigation controls for translation and rotation of the camera • Play/pause of live data retrieval • Lock/unlock interaction with gestures • Data center room selection
Version 3	• Mini map • Reset room view • Units indexing in selected rack close-up view • Markers, value labels, and value for the currently visualized time on the chart in the full screen mode
Interaction	
Version 1	• Mouse movement: Raised pointer finger of one hand • Mouse click: Raised pointer finger of the one hand, closed fist which opens for the other hand
Version 2	• Mouse click: Raised pointer finger of the one hand, open fist which closes for the other hand (click in the air) • Gestures to move and rotate the camera forward/backward/left/right/up/down
Version 3	–

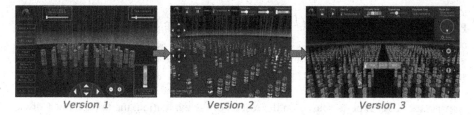

Fig. 1. Evolution of the UI of the data center room view across the three versions

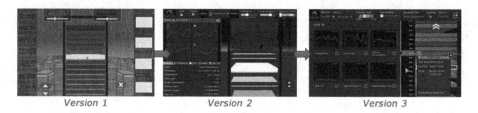

Fig. 2. Evolution of the UI of the selected rack close-up view across the three versions

3.1   Initial Design

The main screen of the 3D Data Centre Visualization application features a virtual representation of a data center room populated with 3D server racks, controls to navigate in the virtual world, and options to filter the displayed racks (Fig. 3a). Each rack is placed in the virtual room according to its physical location and may contain at most 40 units, each displayed as a slice with a specific color, annotating its current condition. The virtual environment that encloses the scene is spherical and the servers' grid is placed at the center, so that users can have a 360 degrees overview. Navigation in the scene is achieved through navigation controls for zooming in/out and moving forward, backward, right and left. On the left side, options are available for filtering the displayed units according to the following fundamental attributes of a server: temperature, CPU load, power consumption, network Bytes In/Out, and Disk I/O. For each of the aforementioned visualizations the criticality level filter facilitates the exclusion of

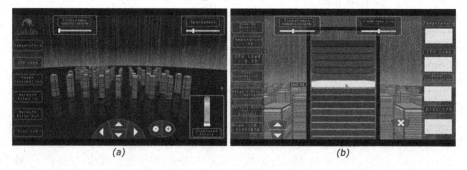

Fig. 3. Initial design approach: (a) Data center room (b) rack close-up view (Color figure online)

visualized elements according to their state, allowing for example the user to focus only on servers in critical state. Finally, users can define the desired level of visualization sparseness according to their needs and preferences.

In order to facilitate the efficient handling of critical situations, the system also provides a mechanism for the representation of anomaly detections regarding temperature or power consumption. When a problematic unit is detected, the color of the rack that contains this unit changes to red and a notification message pops-up above it, displaying a short description of the problem and the unit's number.

A close-up rack view (Fig. 3b) is provided upon selection of a rack, in order to facilitate further inspection of the rack's information at a per-server level, through viewing the current values of the server's attributes (e.g., temperature, CPU load, etc.) along with line charts. Any of these charts can be enlarged upon user request, in order to provide a more detailed view. The close-up view of a rack provides up-down navigation to the user for selecting a particular unit. When the user does so, the current values of the selected unit are illustrated on the left side of the screen, while history values are depicted as line charts on the right side.

Interaction with the system is achieved through applying a cursor metaphor (hand-mouse). In more details, through a hand tracking mechanism, the user's hand movements are mapped to mouse cursor movements. When the user moves their right hand in the space in front of them, the mouse moves accordingly in the scene. In order to select an interactive element, the user has to raise one hand and open the palm, pointing at the same time with their other hand at the component to select.

3.2   Re-design

The main goal of the redesign iteration was to improve the overall user experience through a better organization of the menu options and an update of the look and feel of the user interface, as well as through augmenting interaction with gestures beyond the hand mouse metaphor. Additionally, the following functionalities were added to the system in order to better address user needs: data center room selection, play/pause of live data retrieval, lock/unlock interaction with gestures.

Augmenting the interaction with gestures was considered necessary in order to achieve a more natural interaction moving beyond the mouse metaphor and to allow experienced users to speed-up their interaction. From a UX perspective, gestures were designed so as to be easily to remember following a natural mapping approach, applying the concept of image schemas and primary metaphors [23] and taking into account design guidelines for the development of gestural vocabularies [16–18]. More specifically, the gestural vocabulary includes the following (Fig. 4):

- Move Forward/Backward: Both hands are open and move forward/backwards.
- Move Up/Down: Both hands are open and move up/down.
- Move Right/Left: Both hand are open and move right/left (panning).
- Turn Left/Right: Both hands are open and one hand in a smaller depth than the other.

A fundamental observation that guided the redesign was that although the application was deployed in a large screen, the screen real estate that was eventually available for displaying the actual data was not adequate since the various options were

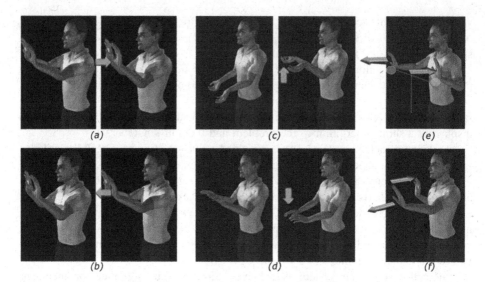

Fig. 4. Gestural Vocabulary: (a) move backward, (b) move forward, (c) move up, (d) move down, (e) rotate left and (f) rotate right

scattered all around the screen. As a result, an important change that was made was to reorganize the main menu at the top of the screen and the navigation controls at its left (Fig. 5). In more details, the new horizontal menu featured the following options:

- Lock/unlock button, to enable or disable the interaction with gestures, using an icon illustrating a closed/open lock.
- Play/pause button, to enable or disable retrieval of live data and update of the view and information regarding the racks and servers. The typical play/pause icons employed in media players were employed.

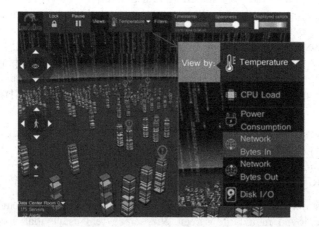

Fig. 5. Updated data center room design (version 2)

- View by drop-down menu, to change the visualization of racks and servers according to the fundamental server attributes. The drop-down menu replaced the six vertical buttons that were used in the first version. Furthermore, each option of the drop-down menu was accompanied by an icon to further enhance the understandability and intuitiveness of the UI.
- Options to filter the racks displayed, according to the selected timestamp, sparseness, or criticality level of the servers for the selected representation. By changing the "displayed colors" horizontal slider value the user can select the minimum criticality level of the displayed servers. Warmer colors indicate higher criticality, while cooler colors indicate servers in good status.

As already mentioned, the application was enhanced with gesture-based interaction, allowing users to navigate in the room through appropriate gestures. With the aim to support multimodality, navigation controls were added to provide equivalents for all the potential gestures. The updated navigation controls were placed on the left side of the screen. More specifically, the navigation controls were as follows:

- the first control moves the camera up, right, down, or left
- the second control moves the camera forward, backward and supports rotation (i.e., implements the metaphor of moving in the room), and
- the third control features two buttons, one to elevate and one to lower.

It should be noted that the controls were implemented following a joystick approach. Therefore, it is not required that a user carries out consecutive click actions to one of the four arrows of the button. Instead, a more "continuous" interaction is pursued as follows: once a user "clicks" on the control - by carrying out the select gesture - a knob appears, indicating the currently selected area of the control, which can be anywhere in the periphery of the circle. As long as a user keeps his one fist closed (therefore a "release" action is not carried out), they can move the knob by moving the pointer finger of their other hand and therefore alter the direction of the movement in a continuous manner. In addition, the joystick-like controls are sensitive in terms of speed, as their effect is increased when the knob is moved towards the radius of the circle and eliminated when approaching the center.

Below the navigation controls, an indication of the currently selected data center room is displayed, accompanied by a pop-up menu for selecting a different room. In addition, an evidence of the number of servers and issued alerts for the selected room is displayed.

In addition to the horizontal main menu and vertical navigation menu changes, the updated UI featured the following major redesigns:

- sans-serif fonts were employed to increase legibility
- a teal color has been consistently used to indicate the currently active menu option
- alerts were no longer indicated by moving white arrows, but by red location pins.

Finally, the information displayed for a rack when the user moves the hand pointer over it has undergone changes, with the aim to provide important information at a glance (Fig. 6). When no alerts have been issued for the rack, a teal pop-up indicates the visualized attribute via an appropriate icon (e.g., CPU load), rack number (e.g., L36), name of the server (e.g., Unit 32) and CPU load value of that unit (e.g., 86%). When at least an alert pertains to the specific rack, a red pop-up indicates the visualized attribute via an appropriate alert icon (e.g., temperature anomaly), the number of the temperature anomalies detected in the specific rack and the rack number. The exact details of the alert (e.g., duration, the cause and the status) are available once the user selects to view the rack more closely, or selects the alert to expand information. If more than one anomaly types have been detected for the units of a rack, all the corresponding icons are included in the location pin.

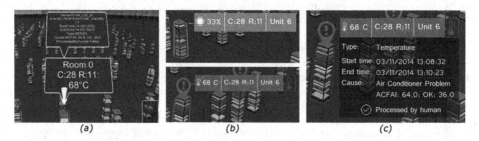

Fig. 6. Alerts redesign: (a) version 1 (b) different pop-ups for a rack without alerts and a rack with alerts (c) alert details (Color figure online)

Finally, the rack close-up view went through major redesign, so as to reduce visual clutter and facilitate focusing on the actual data. In more details, in the first version of the application, when a user selected a rack, the rack visualization was overlaid on top of the room, accompanied by four charts in the right side of the screen. The redesigned rack close-up view featured:

- the horizontal menu located consistently at the top of the screen. The time window filter option has replaced the sparseness option from the room view, allowing users to set the time frame used for the calculation of the visualization of the mean values illustrated by the graph representations (charts)
- a close-up view of the rack itself and the contained servers in the right side of the screen, allowing users to navigate upwards and downwards to the servers through the up and down arrows, or via gestures
- detailed information about the selected rack and the currently selected unit in the left side of the screen (Fig. 7), featuring: the rack and selected unit name; an exit button to return to the room view; four charts illustrating the server temperature, CPU load, power consumption and network and disk I/O for the selected timestamp; buttons for switching to specific chart view; and server overview including the room it is located in, the selected timestamp, and numerical values of all its attributes.

In summary, the first redesign attempted to eliminate any evident UI design errors and apply established UI design guidelines - such as minimalistic design, consistency, feedback, error prevention, recognition, etc. - to improve the usability of the application. However, the most important change that was pursued was to facilitate users in focusing

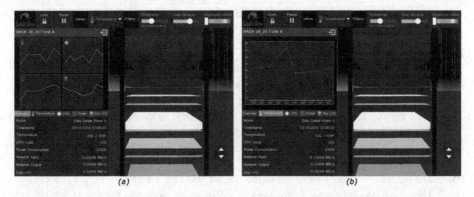

Fig. 7. Selected rack close-up view: (a) Overview of a selected unit (b) Temperature of a selected unit

on the data itself, to enhance the visualization with meaningful and useful information in order to assist end-users decision making, and to encourage natural interactions.

3.3 Heuristic Evaluation

The redesigned 3D Data Centre Visualization application was first evaluated by three UX experts, following the Heuristic evaluation method [22], according to which a small number of evaluators examine the interface and try to identify if it follows recognized usability principles. Each evaluator inspects the interface by carrying out as many iterations as needed with the aim to locate if it violates recognized usability principles, named heuristics [24] or other relevant to the system usability principles. Each evaluator reports the problems that were located, and explains which principle is violated by each problem [25]. Given that several problems may be identified by different evaluators, all the evaluation reports are consolidated into a single report, listing each usability problem only once. Then, the evaluators review the unified list of problems and provide a severity rating for each one ranging from 0 to 4 [25], with the aim to prioritize them.

For the heuristic evaluation of the 3D Data Centre Visualization application, each evaluator was initially introduced to the system, its purpose, functionality and the supported interaction methods. Then, the evaluator inspected the system through free exploration and reported the problems that were found. Given the novelty and the domain-specificity of the system, a facilitator was present during each session to assist evaluators - if required - regarding the interaction, or the terminology used. In total, 25 unique problems were identified and aggregated into one single report, which was reviewed by each evaluator with the aim to rate each problem regarding its severity. The final severity of each problem resulted from averaging the ratings of all three evaluators. Problems were sorted according to severity and classified into the following categories: room view, close-up view, interaction. All the problems that were identified during the heuristic evaluation are presented in Table 2, organized in categories and sorted according to their severity per category.

Table 2. Problems identified by the heuristic evaluation

Id	Description	Severity
Room view		
01	The moving background is distracting and creates a lot of "noise"	3.5
02	The initial view of the room should be zoomed out, so that all racks can be seen before starting to move in the room	3.2
03	Once the user has moved inside the room and "walked" inside the columns, they may lose completely the sense of spatial orientation	3.2
04	Users are allowed to move way beyond the map view, which can disorient them	3.2
05	The navigation buttons often get in the way of selecting a rack	3.2
06	The elevate/lower buttons do not work in a continuous mode like the other two navigation buttons. All similar buttons should behave consistently	3.2
07	A "safety" button for resetting the map view if the user is lost is required	2.8
08	The navigation buttons may be difficult to reach for right-handed persons. Right-handed users will use their right hand to point and may not think that they can switch hands to point the navigation buttons	2.7
09	The colours used for representing the criticality of the servers are too bright and result in a colour pollution effect, especially in combination with the moving background	2.3
10	Why is blue used as a criticality state colour? The usual and most widely accepted metaphor is a range from green (which means that everything is fine) to red (which indicates high criticality)	2.0
11	The label filters, in front of the three filter options may become confusing. Since each filtering option has already a title, this can be removed	2.0
12	Although users will be experts in the field, the word timestamp might cause confusion	1.3
13	Gestures lock/unlock might cause confusion as a terminology	1.3
Close-up view		
14	The alert icons on the left of the units sometimes appear in empty spaces	3.7
15	The alert icons on the left of the units may cause visual clutter and confusion, especially in the case of more than one alerts	3.7
16	The exit button (to return to the room view) is in the middle and between the selected unit title and the rack, which makes it hard to locate	3.7
17	The legends inside the graphs are unreadable	3.7
18	The hover colour of the racks is the same as the selected, so the user doesn't understand if the unit has been indeed correctly selected	3.3
19	There are 6 options on the top menu dropdown, whereas there are only 4 tabs in the left panel. That's because three views under the same label, but the icon that is shown is not indicative of that	3.2
20	It is not easily to identify which unit server has currently been selected in the rack	3.0
21	The size of the rack of units is disproportionately wide in relation to the left side panels which are more important to the user	3.0

(continued)

Table 2. (*continued*)

Id	Description	Severity
Interaction		
22	The cursor is moving erratically on the screen even when the user is holding his hands steady	3.7
23	In the close-up view, when units are on top of one another inside a rack, selecting the middle one is very difficult because the cursor jumps around	3.7
24	Interacting with the slider controls may impose physical strain to the user, as these controls are placed at the top of the screen	3.7
25	The cursor icon is visible at all times, even if the user is not carrying out a mouse emulation gesture (e.g., raising their index finger and moving their hand)	3.2

In summary, the evaluation highlighted that an important concern regarding the 3D visualization was the orientation of users in the simulated room, which should be assisted by the application. In addition, experts highlighted that physical strain might be imposed to users given that all interaction is feasible only through gestures, and especially since the interactive elements have been placed at the top of the screen. Finally, the experts agreed on the intuitiveness of the navigation gestures, however they suggested that additional tests with users should be carried out to assess their learnability.

3.4 Final Design

Following the heuristic evaluation results, the 3D Data Centre Visualization application went through some additional changes in order to improve its usability, both in the room view and the rack close-up view. In addition, the issues regarding the cursor movement (problems with id 22 and 23) were addressed, by increasing the mouse pointer smoothing factor and increasing each unit's interactive area. Finally, the cursor changed to be shown only while the user raises the pointer finger and not while applying hand gestures (problem 25).

An important problem that has been identified by the evaluators is that of the user's orientation in the room (problems 02, 03, 04, 07). To help users so as to better orient themselves and avoid confusions, the following changes were introduced:

- Initially users view the room zoomed out, so that they can build a mental model of it and orient themselves more easily
- Moving beyond the map view was disabled. As a result, users will not be able to move far away from the room and lose orientation
- A mini-map functionality has been added, as well as a "reset" button which resets the map view to its initial state. The mini-map represents the scene as a blue circle, given the spherical layout of the room's 3D representation. The user is represented as a white bullet inside the room, while the metaphor of holding a torch was used to indicate the user's movement direction.

In addition, the following changes were made to address other identified problems:

- The moving background was removed (problem 01)
- A less bright shade of criticality level colours was employed, while criticality was represented on a green-red scale (problems 09 and 10)
- The label "Timestamp" was replaced by the label "Visualized Time" (problem 12)
- The label "Filters" was removed (problem 11), which "earned" horizontal space, and allowed placing the selected room indication and room selection pop-up, in the top-right corner.

Finally, changes were accomplished to resolve the problems that were found regarding the navigation buttons:

- The navigation buttons were moved to the right, right below the mini-map (problems 05 and 08). As a result, all the components relevant to the user's navigation in the room – including the room title, the mini-map and reset view button, and the three navigation buttons – were grouped in one side of the screen
- The behaviour of the third set of buttons (elevate/lower) was adapted to work consistently with the other two buttons, in a continuous manner (problem 06).

The final representation of the selected room view features a horizontal top menu and a vertical navigation menu, placed at the right side of the screen, as shown in Fig. 8. Last, with the aim to address the interaction issue that was identified for the slider controls placed at the top of the screen (problem 24), once the user selects an option of the horizontal menu which involves handling a slider, a large vertical slider is displayed, facilitating interaction and handling. Furthermore, the "Visualized Time" control was replaced by a scrollable list containing the exact values which can be selected in an easier way, since the slider employed in the previous version induced difficulties and physical strain for selecting the preferred value.

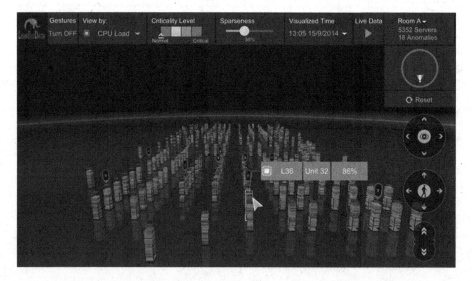

Fig. 8. Final design of the data center room view (Color figure online)

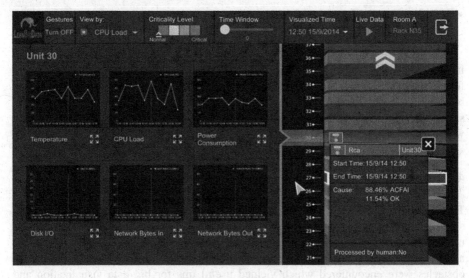

Fig. 9. Rack close-up view

Moreover, components of the close-up view have been rearranged in order to resolve the problems that were identified by the heuristic evaluation (Fig. 9). Namely, the following major changes were made:

- The close-up view of the rack servers was moved towards the right side of the screen, occupying less space (problem 21), while in order to better exploit the available space, the move up and down buttons were placed correspondingly overlaid on the topmost and bottom servers.
- Left to the close-up view, a list of legends indicating the unit number was placed, clearly marking each unit (problems 17 and 20).
- The selected rack color was changed to teal, as employed in the room view for highlighting the selected items (problem 20), while the hover color remained white (problem 18).
- The currently visualized rack title was placed below the room title, in teal, while right next to it the exit button was placed (problem 16). The selected room and rack names, as well as the exit button were made to occupy the same horizontal space as the current room indication and selection menu of the room view.
- The left side of the screen was expanded, featuring six charts presenting information for the selected rack, regarding the six server attributes visualized by the application (problems 17 and 19).
- On top of the charts, the selected unit server name in large teal font color was placed. Furthermore, the left side (with the charts) was divided by the right side (with the visualized rack) by a thick teal vertical line, which ends in an arrow pointing right towards the currently selected unit server (problem 20).
- The alert icons were placed inside the various units in the right side with the close-up view (problems 14 and 15). If a user places their finger over the alert icon, or selects the icon, a pop-up window is displayed presenting the details of the alert.

- All the textual information from the left side has been removed and the entire left space is occupied by six large charts, one for each server attribute (problem 19).

Furthermore, it should be noted that charts are selectable, allowing users to view information in more details if they wish to. The zoomed versions of the charts are further enhanced with specific value markers. However, given that the space occupied by the charts has expanded, users are expected to be able to get a good overview of the server status through the initial view and select to enlarge charts only for specific cases, were problems may have occurred.

4   Challenges Encountered and Lessons Learned

The iterative process of evaluating and redesigning the 3D Data Centre Visualization application principally aimed to meet the goal of creating a visualization that would be useful and decision-enabling for data center operators who would have to use the application in a large data center room in a large display. During this phase several obstacles were encountered which yielded useful tips for big data visualization and gesture-based interactions with large screen displays, which are discussed in this section.

Big Data need large visualization spaces - don't waist a bit of your screen's real estate with unnecessary UI elements. A key challenge that the first redesign addressed was the exploitation of the entire screen and the removal of visual clutter, in order to allow users to focus on the Big Data and not the interface. It was observed that the large screen had initially misled the design towards scattering interaction elements all around the screen, leaving less space for the actual visualization. The updated design aimed at a better information organization, using space more wisely, giving the focus to the Big Data itself.

Animations are bad – large screen, Big Data animations are even worse. An important concern for Big Data visualization is how to draw user's attention to a change that has been made or a point that they should look at in the data set. Although several approaches can be applied for accommodating this need, an alternative that should be definitely avoided is the use of animations. In such a large data set, there may be eventually many points that will satisfy the condition which determines that a user should be alerted, which will lead to a visualization with plenty of animations urging the user to pay attention to them, leading to user frustration. In the case of the 3D Data Centre, when the application was running and fed with real-time data, a multitude of moving arrows appeared above racks, indicating that one of the 40 units hosted in each rack had triggered an alert. This approach could in the end have the opposite effect and stress the user instead of assisting them to better prioritize their actions.

Strive for minimalistic and aesthetic design – the opposite can be quite disruptive in Big Data visualizations. In any UI design it is good to aim for aesthetic and minimalistic design. In a Big Data application however, it is imperative to choose colors with great consideration. The evaluation indicated that too many and too bright colors were used to represent units in a rack, resulting in a color pollution effect. Given the diversity of Big Data, it is highly possible that the visualization will employ a great number of colors. Therefore, colors should be selected with caution, avoiding very bright shades. Furthermore, this color diversity will leave only a few colors for the application UI elements, which should be again very carefully selected so as not to stand out too much and allow the user to focus on the data visualization. For example, in the 3D Data Centre, dark grey and white were used for the menu items, teal for highlighting the currently selected menu item, and a shade of red for displaying alerts and servers in critical state.

Users may become lost in the visualization – support orientation with tools and cues. A Big Data visualization by definition accommodates a large volume of data, therefore usually providing tools for zooming in specific data. As users navigate in the data, it is quite easy to lose orientation, as they would in the real world if cues were not provided by the environment itself. Therefore, as streets in a real world feature names and numbers, so the Big Data visualizations should provide a unique identification of the user's whereabouts. For instance, in the 3D Data Centre each rack is uniquely identified by a column and row number. When appropriate, additional tools may be employed to assist users' orientation, as the mini-map with the torch metaphor in the 3D Data Centre and the reset button. Such functionality that allows users to undo their movements and return to the initial view of the visualization can act as a safety net in situations where the user may be lost and frustrated.

Gesture-based interaction with a large screen may become strenuous, if frequently used options are placed in screen locations that require users to make coarse movements. A primary requirement for Big Data visualizations is to facilitate users' focusing on the data and not design a UI that will easily take their attention away, either due to animations and colors used or the placement of the controls. However, this requirement imposes one more challenge in the context of gesture-based interaction with a large screen display, since if objects are place too far away, users will encounter difficulties reaching them. This trade-off was addressed in the 3D Data Centre by placing the navigation controls, which are expected to be used more often, lower in the screen. Furthermore, it was noticed that the gesture-detection system recognizes a gesture in a relative manner, i.e., in relation to the users' hand posture when the gesture was initiated. Therefore, users are expected to be trained in avoiding the need for large abrupt movements by "re-calibrating" their hands closer to their torso. Given that the target users of the application are expected to soon become experts in the system, as they are daily users, this system feature is anticipated to become a powerful asset towards efficient and effective user interactions. Yet, the efficiency and learnability of the gestural vocabulary remains to be evaluated with real users.

5   Conclusions and Future Work

This paper has presented the evolution of the 3D Data Centre Visualization application, a Big Data visualization system deployed in a large screen display which can be handled remotely via gestures. Three major application versions were developed during the evolution of the application, and have been presented in the paper, each one addressing different needs. The first version of the application aimed at providing a 3D visualization of a data center room supporting all the fundamental functionality for navigating in the room and retrieving information. The second version was targeted towards incorporating gesture-based interaction and improving the UI so as to better exploit the real estate of the screen and enhance operators' decision making by allowing them to focus on the data. The third version of the application applied UI and interaction improvements based on the results of an expert-based evaluation that was carried out.

The iterative design and development process of the 3D Data Centre Visualization application was mainly guided by the requirement that the Big Data visualization should be a powerful tool for the intended users, fostering decision-making and facilitating their daily tasks, while user interaction with the technologies employed should not only be effective but also efficient. During this process, based on the difficulties that were met and the solutions that were explored, several useful conclusions for the design of Big Data visualization applications were reached, which have been discussed in details. Although the expert-based evaluation has substantially assisted the visualization and interaction design of the application, the need for a user-based evaluation is indisputable to further validate the design decisions and assess the gestural vocabulary that has been developed in the context of this work. Future activities will therefore include a user-based assessment of the 3D Data Centre Visualization application, as well as the exploration of positive impact of other novel technologies, such as augmented or immersive reality.

Acknowledgements. This research has been partially funded by the European Commission under project LeanBigData (FP7-619606).

References

1. Palfrey, J.G., Gasser, U.: Born Digital: Understanding the First Generation of Digital Natives. Basic Books, New York (2013)
2. Manyika, J., Chui, M., Brown, B., Bughin, J., Dobbs, R., Roxburgh, C., Byers, A.H.: Big Data: The Next Frontier for Innovation, Competition, and Productivity. McKinsey Global Institute (2011)
3. Drossis, G., Birliraki, C., Patsiouras, N., Margetis, G., Stephanidis, C.: 3D visualization of large scale data centres. In: Cardoso, J., Ferguson, D., Muñoz, V.M., Helfert, M. (eds.) Proceedings of the 6th International Conference on Cloud Computing and Services Science (CLOSER 2016), Rome, Italy, 23–25 April, vol. 1, pp. 388–395. SCITEPRESS, Portugal (2016)
4. Chen, C.P., Zhang, C.Y.: Data-intensive applications, challenges, techniques and technologies: a survey on big data. Inf. Sci. **275**, 14–47 (2014)
5. Fox, P., Hendler, J.: Changing the equation on scientific data visualization. Science **331** (6018), 5–8 (2011)
6. Bari, M.F., Boutaba, R., Esteves, R., Granville, L.Z., Podlesny, M., Rabbani, M.G., Zhang, Q., Zhani, M.F.: Data center network virtualization: a survey. IEEE Commun. Surv. Tutor. **15**(2), 9–28 (2013)
7. Fisher, D., Maltz, D.A., Greenberg, A., Wang, X., Warncke, H., Robertson, G., Czerwinski, M.: Using visualization to support network and application management in a data center. In: Internet Network Management Workshop (INM 2008), pp. 1–6. IEEE (2008)

8. Roberts, J.C., Ritsos, P.D., Badam, S.K., Brodbeck, D., Kennedy, J., Elmqvist, N.: Visualization beyond the desktop–the next big thing. IEEE Comput. Graph. Appl. **34**(6), 26–34 (2014)
9. Reda, K., Johnson, A.E., Papka, M.E., Leigh, J.: Effects of display size and resolution on user behavior and insight acquisition in visual exploration. In: Proceedings of the 33rd Annual ACM Conference on Human Factors in Computing Systems, pp. 2759–2768 (2015)
10. Bollier, D., Firestone, C.M.: The Promise and Peril of Big Data. Aspen Institute, Communications and Society Program, Washington, DC (2010)
11. Shah, S., Horne, A., Capellá, J.: Good data won't guarantee good decisions. Harvard Bus. Rev. **90**(4), 23–25 (2012)
12. Cuzzocrea, A., Mansmann, S.: OLAP visualization: models, issues, and techniques. In: Wang, J. (ed.) Encyclopedia of Data Warehousing and Mining, 2nd edn, pp. 1439–1446. IGI Global, Hershey (2009)
13. Reda, K., Febretti, A., Knoll, A., Aurisano, J., Leigh, J., Johnson, A., Papka, M.E., Hereld, M.: Visualizing large, heterogeneous data in hybrid-reality environments. IEEE Comput. Graph. Appl. **33**(4), 38–48 (2013)
14. Drossis, G., Margetis, G., Stephanidis, C.: Towards Big Data Interactive Visualization in Ambient Intelligence Environments. In: Streitz, N., Markopoulos, P. (eds.) DAPI 2016. LNCS, vol. 9749, pp. 58–68. Springer, Cham (2016). doi:10.1007/978-3-319-39862-4_6
15. Norman, D.: Natural user interfaces are not natural. Interactions **17**(3), 6–10 (2010)
16. Dong, H., Danesh, A., Figueroa, N., El Saddik, A.: An elicitation study on gesture preferences and memorability toward a practical hand-gesture vocabulary for smart televisions. IEEE Access **3**, 43–55 (2015)
17. Nielsen, M., Störring, M., Moeslund, Thomas B., Granum, E.: A procedure for developing intuitive and ergonomic gesture interfaces for HCI. In: Camurri, A., Volpe, G. (eds.) GW 2003. LNCS, vol. 2915, pp. 409–420. Springer, Heidelberg (2004). doi:10.1007/978-3-540-24598-8_38
18. Wigdor, D., Wixon, D.: Brave NUI World: Designing Natural User Interfaces for Touch and Gesture. Elsevier, Amsterdam (2011)
19. Grandhi, S.A., Joue, G., Mittelberg, I.: Understanding naturalness and intuitiveness in gesture production: insights for touchless gestural interfaces. In: Proceedings of the SIGCHI Conference on Human Factors in Computing Systems, pp. 821–824. ACM (2011)
20. Ni, T., Schmidt, G.S., Staadt, O.G., Livingston, M.A., Ball, R., May, R.: A survey of large high-resolution display technologies, techniques, and applications. In: Virtual Reality Conference, pp. 223–236. IEEE (2006)
21. Andrews, C., Endert, A., Yost, B., North, C.: Information visualization on large, high-resolution displays: Issues, challenges, and opportunities. Inf. Vis. **10**(4), 41–55 (2011)
22. Nielsen, J., Molich, R.: Heuristic evaluation of user interfaces. In: Proceedings of the SIGCHI Conference on Human Factors in Computing Systems, pp. 249–256. ACM (1990)
23. Hurtienne, J., Stößel, C., Sturm, C., Maus, A., Rötting, M., Langdon, P., Clarkson, J.: Physical gestures for abstract concepts: inclusive design with primary metaphors. Interact. Comput. **22**(6), 75–84 (2010)
24. Nielsen, J.: Enhancing the explanatory power of usability heuristics. In: Proceedings of the SIGCHI Conference on Human Factors in Computing Systems, pp. 152–158. ACM (1994)
25. Nielsen, J.: Heuristic Evaluation. In: Nielsen, J., Mack, R.L. (eds.) Usability Inspection Methods, pp. 25–62. Elsevier, Amsterdam (1994)

JoyKey: One-Handed Hardware Keyboard with 4 × 3 Grid Slide Keys

Ryosuke Takada[✉], Buntarou Shizuki, and Shin Takahashi

University of Tsukuba, Tsukuba, Japan
{rtakada,shizuki,shin}@iplab.cs.tsukuba.ac.jp

Abstract. In this paper, we show a one-handed hardware keyboard with 4 × 3 grid slide keys, called a JoyKey. It can be used for Japanese text entry based on the flick input method. We conducted a user study to compare the accuracy and input speed of the JoyKey and a software keyboard on a touch screen under two conditions (eyes-free and non-eyes-free). Results show that the software keyboard cannot be used under the eyes-free condition because users cannot feel tactile feedback on a touch screen. In contrast, using the JoyKey, users can enter text under both the conditions with relative ease.

Keywords: Text entry · KANA input · Flick input · Joystick · Multi input · Mouse · Game controller

1 Introduction

The flick input method, which originated from Apple Newton and was adopted into Apple iPhone, is now one of the de facto standard Japanese input methods in small mobile devices with touch screens. This method is designed for entering Japanese KANA letters as shown in Fig. 1. The keyboard consists of twelve keys aligned into a 4 × 3 grid: 10 consonant letter keys and punctuation key. A Japanese KANA letter is transcribed into one consonant and one vowel as shown in Table 1. There are ten consonants and five vowels in Japanese. With the flick input method, a user touches one of the consonant keys to enter a consonant. In response, a menu appears with five items corresponding to the five vowels. To enter a vowel, the user selects an item by simply releasing the finger or performing a flick gesture (upward, downward, rightward, or leftward).

In contrast, we developed a one-handed hardware flick text entry keyboard, called a "JoyKey" as shown in Fig. 2. It has twelve keys aligned into a 4 × 3 grid, each of which is composed of a joystick and a tact switch that can detect X and Y axis movements. Using JoyKey, the user can enter Japanese KANA letters in an eyes-free manner because each key provides a tactile feedback. In contrast to the one that Google Japan released on April 1st, 2016 [4], whose size is large (240 mm × 180 mm × 50 mm) and must be placed on a desk to be used, the user can use JoyKey with one hand due to its small size (59 mm × 85 mm × 24.5 mm).

© Springer International Publishing AG 2017
S. Yamamoto (Ed.): HIMI 2017, Part I, LNCS 10273, pp. 266–279, 2017.
DOI: 10.1007/978-3-319-58521-5_21

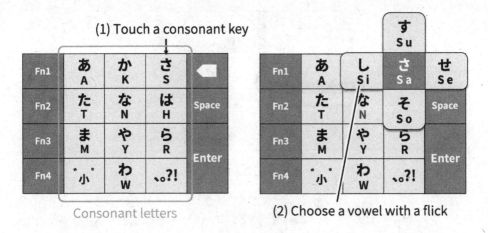

Fig. 1. Flick input

Table 1. Japanese syllabary ('S*' can be transcribed into the combination of consonant 'S' and symbol '*', and can be transcribed as 'G' in a phonetic alphabet. The same applies to other voiced letters and p-sound letters.)

Vowels	Consonants																		
	Basic letter											Voiced letter				P-sound	Small letter		
	A	K	S	T	N	H	M	Y	R	W	-	K*(G)	S*(Z)	T*(D)	H*(B)	H**(P)	A*	Y*	T**
a	あ	か	さ	た	な	は	ま	や	ら	わ		が	ざ	だ	ば	ぱ	ぁ	ゃ	
i	い	き	し	ち	に	ひ	み		り			ぎ	じ	ぢ	び	ぴ	ぃ		
u	う	く	す	つ	ぬ	ふ	む	ゆ	る			ぐ	ず	づ	ぶ	ぷ	ぅ	ゅ	っ
e	え	け	せ	て	ね	へ	め		れ			げ	ぜ	で	べ	ぺ	ぇ		
o	お	こ	そ	と	の	ほ	も	よ	ろ	を		ご	ぞ	ど	ぼ	ぽ	ぉ	ょ	
-											ん								
-											ー								

Moreover, JoyKey can be used as a keyboard, mouse, and video game controller as well, as shown in Fig. 3.

In addition, we conducted a user study in order to compare the accuracy and input speed of the software keyboard on a touch screen and JoyKey under two conditions (non-eyes-free and eyes-free). We will show the procedure and discussion of the user study in subsequent sections.

2   Related Work

JoyKey is based on the following previous works.

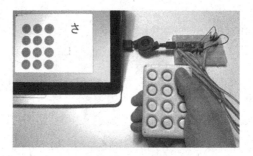

Fig. 2. JoyKey

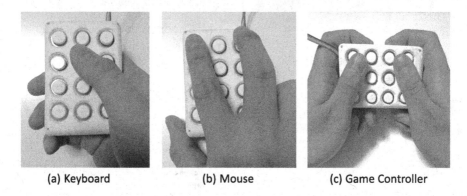

(a) Keyboard   (b) Mouse   (c) Game Controller

Fig. 3. Different uses of a JoyKey.

2.1 Japanese KANA Letters Entry

Since JoyKey is a Japanese KANA letter entry system based on flick input method, we will describe three conventional methods of entering Japanese KANA letters.

QWERTY. Japanese speakers use QWERTY keyboard to enter KANA letters when they use desktop and laptop computers. Japanese QWERTY keyboards have both KANA and Roman letters printed on key tops as shown in Fig. 4. Japanese speakers can enter KANA letters by KANA or Roman input modes. KANA input mode is used to directly input a KANA letter. The KANA letters are also arranged in a consistent way across different keyboards. For example, the 'Q', 'W', 'E', 'R', 'T', and 'Y' keys correspond to "た", "て", "い", "す", "か", and "ん", respectively. In Roman input mode, a number of Japanese input method editors allow Japanese text to be entered using Roman letters, which can then be converted to KANA, based on the Japanese syllabary as shown in Table 1. This method does not require the use of a Japanese keyboard with KANA letters.

Fig. 4. Japanese QWERTY keyboard

Multi-tap Entry. On Japanese cell phones with no touch screens, hardware keyboards are usually used. Figure 5 outlines a typical key layout for such keyboards. This key layout consists of 12 keys, including 10 consonant keys, that are arranged in a 4 × 3 grid. Users enter a KANA letter by pressing a consonant key one to five times (i.e., multi-tap) to enter a vowel. A special KANA letter can be input using the other two keys. For example, "ぎ", which is transcribed into 'Gi*' is entered by pressing the '2' key twice, and then pressing the '*' key once.

Pocket Bell Entry. In Japan, pagers called *pocket bells* were widely used as personal communication tools before mobile phones became popular. To enter a letter on this device, users used an input method called *pocket bell entry*. In this method, a letter is coded with two digits as shown in Table 2. Therefore, users can enter a KANA letter by pressing two numeric keys sequentially. For example, users input "し" by pressing the '3' key followed by the '2' key.

Fig. 5. Key layout for multi-tap entry

Table 2. Letter correspondence table for pocket bell entry

First input	Second input									
	1	2	3	4	5	6	7	8	9	0
1	あ	い	う	え	お	A	B	C	D	E
2	か	き	く	け	こ	F	G	H	I	J
3	さ	し	す	せ	そ	K	L	M	N	O
4	た	ち	つ	て	と	P	Q	R	S	T
5	な	に	ぬ	ね	の	U	V	W	X	Y
6	は	ひ	ふ	へ	ほ	Z	?	!	-	/
7	ま	み	む	め	も	¥	&			
8	や		ゆ		よ	*	#			
9	ら	り	る	れ	ろ	1	2	3	4	5
0	わ		を		ん	6	7	8	9	0

2.2 Multi Input on a Hardware Keyboard

There are many research projects of gestures on a keyboard to improve the input performance. FlickBoard [12] uses a silicon keyboard cover that contains a capacitive sensing grid for the detection of pointing and gestures. Keyboard Clawing [9] is an input technique that can detect keytop clawing gestures using acoustic sensing. Dietz et al. [1] proposed a technique to sense the force level on membrane keyboards. GestKeyboard [16] is a technique to detect gestures by using intervals between key presses on an ordinary unmodified keyboard. Type-Hover-Swipe in 96 Bytes [11] detects mid-air gestures on a keyboard using 64 photo reflectors. Surfboard [7] recognizes swipe left/right gestures by using a built-in microphone on the hardware keyboard.

2.3 Text Entry Using Joystick

Various text entry methods using joystick have been proposed in the past. Wobbrock et al. [14] proposed text entry using joystick based on EdgeWrite [15]. TwoStick [8] is an alphabet text input method using a game controller's two joysticks. It divides the input area into 3×3 zones, each of which has 3×3 grids. Each grid represents one letter, hence there are total 81 different letters that can be entered. The user can select a letter by first selecting a zone with one joystick and then selecting a grid within that zone with the other joystick. IToNe [2] is a Japanese text input method using a game controller's two joysticks. It uses one joystick to select a consonant, while the other to select a vowel. Wilson and Agrawala [13] used a game controller's two joysticks to select letters from two halves of a split software keyboard. Isokoski and Raisamo [6] reported a text entry rate using two joysticks and Quikwriting [10].

3   Implementation of JoyKey

JoyKey is a hardware keyboard based on flick input. It is designed to be used with one hand. JoyKey is connected to a PC via Arduino Leonardo board.

3.1   JoyKey

Joykey (81 mm × 59 mm × 24.5 mm) is a hardware keyboard that has 12 keys aligned into a 4 × 3 grid. Figure 6 shows the construction of a JoyKey. Each key is composed of a tact switch (Switronic Industrial Corp., 1273) and a joystick (Top-Up Industry Corp., JT8P-3.2T) that can detect X and Y axis movements. To detect simultaneous key presses and reduce wiring, each key has a microcontroller (Atmel, ATTiny85) connected to the joystick and a tact switch, and this microcontroller is assigned to a unique I^2C address. These microcontrollers are connected to Arduino Leonardo by I^2C. When a user presses or flicks the key, he/she can feel tactile feedback from the key's joystick and tact switch.

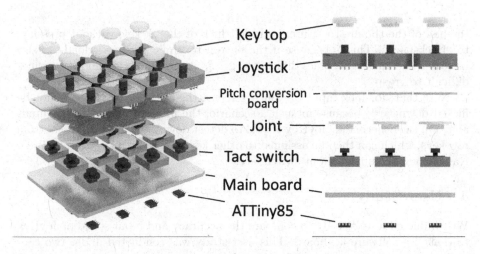

Fig. 6. Construction of a JoyKey

3.2   Key Layout

The user holds the JoyKey in one hand and types a letter with his/her thumb as shown in Fig. 3a. Figure 7 shows JoyKey's 4 × 3 keys, which correspond to the ten consonants, comma/period, and marks. Moreover, in JoyKey, there is no "Enter", "Space", "Next", or "Backspace" key, which differs from the keyboard for flick input method on touch screens. Instead, we assigned simultaneous pressing of these special letters such as pressing 'S' and '!' keys, using the pad and

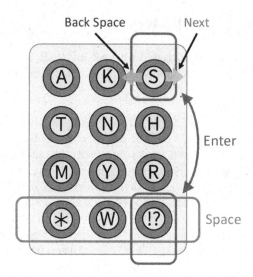

Fig. 7. Key layout of JoyKey

the ball of the thumb, to "Enter" and left flick of the 'S' key, without pressing, to "Backspace". This is because if the button to input keys are added, its size increases and thus it becomes difficult to grasp. its size increases and it becomes difficult to grasp.

Note that, for flick input on touch screens, the bottom row keys cannot be flicked downwards because in such a scenario, the finger would leave the input area. On the other hand, JoyKey is able to detect downward flicks on the bottom row keys, which can then be assigned to other key inputs, such as "Shift","Tab", Kana/Roman/Number input switch, etc.

4   User Study

We conducted a user study to compare the accuracy and input speed of JoyKey to that of a software keyboard. This user study was conducted under two conditions: non-eyes-free and eyes-free.

4.1   Participants

The participants were six university graduates in our laboratory (23–24 years old; male; right handed). They have been using smartphones from 24 to 106 months (M = 67.17). All participants were familiar with the flick input keyboard on smartphones. We instructed them to use flick input with their right hand.

4.2   Devices and Software

The main device is the JoyKey (81 mm × 59 mm × 24.5 mm) connected to a PC. As the software keyboard, we used Google Japanese input [3] on

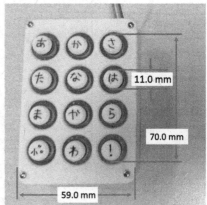

Fig. 8. Software keyboard size   **Fig. 9.** JoyKey size

Xperia Z5 Compact E5823 (Android OS 6.0.1; 4.6-inch screen with a resolution of 720 px × 1280 px; 127 mm × 65 mm × 8.9 mm). Flick input of the smartphone sends keyboard events to the PC via Wi-Fi using the Intel Remote Keyboard application [5]. Figures 8 and 9 show the input area sizes of the two keyboards.

For investigating the accuracy and time of text entry, we implemented a typing game as shown in Fig. 10. The typing game was implemented in Processing 3.1.1, and running on VAIO Z VJZ13A1 (OS: Windows 10 Pro 64 bit, CPU: Intel Core i7-5557U 3.10 GHz, memory: 16.0 GB). It randomly displays a KANA word and measures the time, number of backspaces, and error inputs until the user presses the enter key when he/she finishes. For the KANA words, some Japanese daily life words that consists of 3–7 letters were used, such as greetings, days of the weeks, months, family relationships, subjects of study, fruits, foods, drinks, animals, flowers, places, vehicles, and clothings.

4.3   Procedure and Task

The user study was conducted in a quiet office environment. First, the purpose of the user study was explained to the participants.

We divided the participants into two groups: one group performed the tasks with JoyKey first; the other group performed the tasks with the software keyboard first. Both the groups performed the tasks in the order of non-eyes-free condition to eyes-free condition.

Participants first practiced a keyboard until they got familiar with it. In each trial, the participants entered a word displayed in the typing game. One task consisted of 10 trials with five tasks in each session. We conducted one session for each keyboard as shown in Fig. 11. We also gave a break longer than a minute

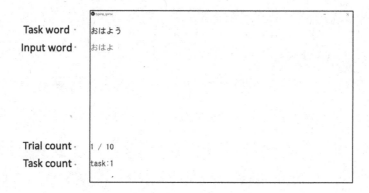

Task word ·   おはよう
Input word ·   おはよ

Trial count ·   1 / 10
Task count ·   task : 1

Fig. 10. Typing game

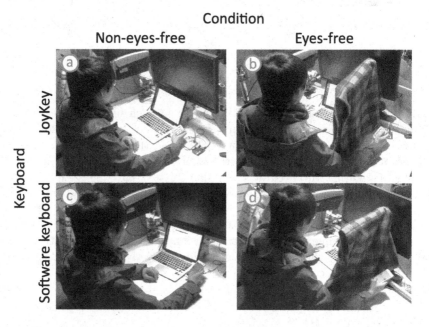

Fig. 11. Experimental setup for each condition (a: JoyKey and non-eyes-free condition, b: JoyKey and eyes-free condition, c: software keyboard and non-eyes-free condition, d: software keyboard and eyes-free condition).

to avoid fatigue between the sessions. If the participants felt tired, they could freely take a break between the tasks.

In summary, the user study design involved:

2 keyboards ×
2 conditions ×
5 tasks ×
10 trials
= 200 trials per participant.

After finishing the sessions, we asked them to answer the questionnaire with the following four questions with five-point Likert scales (1: easy – 5: difficult).

- Is it easy to operate JoyKey with non-eyes-free?
- Is it easy to operate JoyKey with eyes-free?
- Is it easy to operate software keyboard with non-eyes-free?
- Is it easy to operate software keyboard with eyes-free?

The user study took about one hour for each participant.

5   Result and Discussion

While the text entry speed is described in words per minute (wpm) for Roman letters, we use KANAs per minute (kpm) to describe a text entry speed of Japanese KANA letters. Figure 12 shows kpm under each condition (error bars show standard deviations). The mean text entry speed of JoyKey in kpm in the two conditions are 24.95 (SD = 2.23) and 25.67 (SD = 3.80), respectively; The mean text entry speed of the software keyboard in kpm are 55.52 (SD = 8.06) and 20.71 (SD = 5.69), respectively. Figure 13 shows backspace count per letter under each condition (error bars show standard deviations). The mean backspace count per letter of JoyKey under the two conditions are 0.269 (SD = 0.116) and 0.299 (SD = 0.121), respectively; the mean backspace count per letter of the software keyboard are 0.048 (SD = 0.036) and 1.208 (SD = 0.772), respectively.

Since Levene's test showed homogeneity of variances ($p = 0.092 > 0.05$) in the result of the text entry speed, we ran a two-way factorial ANOVA. As we observed a significant interaction effect between the kind of keyboard and two conditions ($p = 0.000 < 0.05$), we ran a Scheffe's test for posthoc analysis.

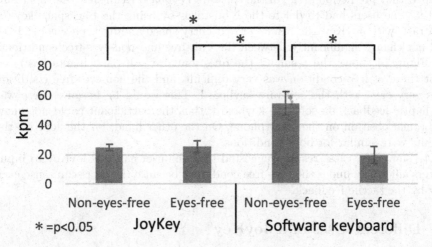

Fig. 12. Text entry speed in kpm under each condition (error bars show standard deviations)

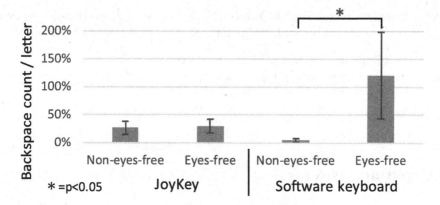

Fig. 13. Backspace count per letter under each condition (error bars show standard deviations)

The result shows a significant difference between the non-eyes-free condition with the software keyboard and the other conditions, especially between the two conditions with the software keyboard.

We ran a Kruskal-Wallis test to examine the result of backspace count per letter, since Levene's test showed heterogeneity of variances ($p = 0.019 < 0.05$) in the data. The result shows a significant difference between the two conditions with the software keyboard ($\chi^2 = 18.42$, df $= 3$, p $= 0.000$).

The above results revealed that the eyes-free condition is significantly worse than the non-eyes-free condition with the software keyboard. This means that the user cannot enter letters under the eyes-free condition correctly with the software keyboard. During the user study, we observed that the participants accidentally tapped the "prediction area" of the software keyboard frequently. As this result of this, the users had to delete those mistakes by using the Backspace key. In contrast, with JoyKey, the results of text entry speed and backspace count both did not change significantly between the eyes-free and non-eyes-free conditions.

Figure 14 shows the result of the questionnaire. All participants answered that the eyes-free condition was very difficult, and the non-eyes-free condition was very easy with the software keyboard. This would be because there was no haptic feedback on software keyboard; thus the participant could not know the touch position on the smartphone. On the other hand, for the JoyKey, the results were similar for both conditions.

In summary, these results suggested that the user can use JoyKey to input letters efficiently under the eyes-free condition, because the users can sense each key by the tactile feedback.

6   Different Uses of a JoyKey

Since JoyKey has twelve keys, each of which consists of a joystick and a tact switch, it can provide various input modes. Currently, JoyKey can be used in

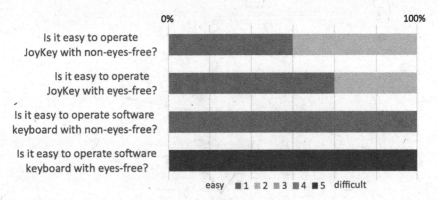

Fig. 14. Result of the questionnaire

three modes: flick input mode described above and the two modes described in this session. The user can switch between these three modes by pressing two keys simultaneously.

6.1 Mouse

In this mode, the user places his/her hand on the JoyKey as shown in Fig. 3b. The user can move the cursor using the joystick of the top-left key. Furthermore, the user can perform left/right clicks and scroll operations using the top row keys as shown in Fig. 15 (left picture). Typically, Ctrl + scroll is used for scaling. In JoyKey, the user can perform pinch in/out gestures for scaling using the two keys as shown in Fig. 15 (right picture).

6.2 Game Controller

In this mode, the user holds the JoyKey with both hands as shown in Fig. 3c. The user can input commands of a video game as shown in Fig. 16. Game creators can design a suitable key assignment for each game.

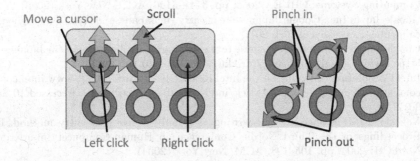

Fig. 15. Mouse mode

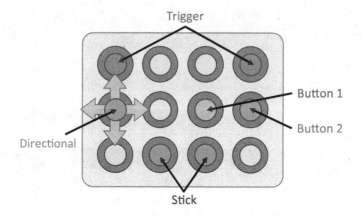

Fig. 16. Game controller mode (an example)

7 Conclusion

In this paper, we presented the JoyKey, which is a one-handed hardware keyboard for Japanese KANA input based on flick input method. We conducted a user study to compare the accuracy and input speed between JoyKey and software keyboard. Results show that the participants using the software keyboard cannot feel where they were touching and were unable to enter letters correctly under the eyes-free condition. In contrast, the participants could enter letters correctly under the eyes-free condition with the JoyKey because they could feel tactile feedback.

References

1. Dietz, P.H., Eidelson, B., Westhues, J., Bathiche, S.: A practical pressure sensitive computer keyboard. In: Proceedings of the 22nd Annual ACM Symposium on User Interface Software and Technology, UIST 2009, pp. 55–58. ACM, New York (2009)
2. Go, K., Konishi, H., Matsuura, Y.: IToNe: a Japanese text input method for a dual joystick game controller. In: CHI 2008 Extended Abstracts on Human Factors in Computing Systems, CHI EA 2008, pp. 3141–3146. ACM, New York (2008)
3. Google Japan Inc.: Google Japanese text entry (in Japanese). https://www.google.co.jp/ime/. Accessed 10 Feb 2017
4. Google Japan Inc.: Google Japanese text entry hardware flick version (in Japanese). https://www.google.co.jp/ime/furikku/. Accessed 10 Feb 2017
5. Intel Corpolation: Introducing the Intel Remote Keyboard. http://www.intel.com/content/www/us/en/compute-stick/intel-remote-keyboard.html. Accessed 10 Feb 2017
6. Isokoski, P., Raisamo, R.: Quikwriting as a multi-device text entry method. In: Proceedings of the Third Nordic Conference on Human-Computer Interaction, NordiCHI 2004, pp. 105–108. ACM, New York (2004)

7. Kato, J., Sakamoto, D., Igarashi, T.: Surfboard: keyboard with microphone as a low-cost interactive surface. In: Adjunct Proceedings of the 23rd Annual ACM Symposium on User Interface Software and Technology, UIST 2010, pp. 387–388. ACM, New York (2010)
8. Költringer, T., Isokoski, P., Grechenig, T.: TwoStick: writing with a game controller. In: Proceedings of Graphics Interface 2007, GI 2007, pp. 103–110. ACM, New York (2007)
9. Kurosawa, T., Shizuki, B., Tanaka, J.: Keyboard Clawing: input method by clawing key tops. In: Kurosu, M. (ed.) HCI 2013. LNCS, vol. 8007, pp. 272–280. Springer, Heidelberg (2013). doi:10.1007/978-3-642-39330-3_29
10. Perlin, K.: Quikwriting: continuous stylus-based text entry. In: Proceedings of the 11th Annual ACM Symposium on User Interface Software and Technology, UIST 1998, pp. 215–216. ACM, New York (1998)
11. Taylor, S., Keskin, C., Hilliges, O., Izadi, S., Helmes, J.: Type-Hover-Swipe in 96 Bytes: a motion sensing mechanical keyboard. In: Proceedings of the 32nd Annual ACM Conference on Human Factors in Computing Systems, CHI 2014, pp. 1695–1704. ACM, New York (2014)
12. Tung, Y.C., Cheng, T.Y., Yu, N.H., Wang, C., Chen, M.Y.: FlickBoard: enabling trackpad interaction with automatic mode switching on a capacitive-sensing keyboard. In: Proceedings of the 33rd Annual ACM Conference on Human Factors in Computing Systems, CHI 2015, pp. 1847–1850. ACM, New York (2015)
13. Wilson, A.D., Agrawala, M.: Text entry using a dual joystick game controller. In: Proceedings of the SIGCHI Conference on Human Factors in Computing Systems, CHI 2006, pp. 475–478. ACM, New York (2006)
14. Wobbrock, J.O., Myers, B.A., Aung, H.H.: Joystick text entry with date stamp, selection keyboard, and EdgeWrite. In: CHI 2004 Extended Abstracts on Human Factors in Computing Systems, CHI EA 2004, p. 1550. ACM, New York (2004)
15. Wobbrock, J.O., Myers, B.A., Kembel, J.A.: EdgeWrite: a stylus-based text entry method designed for high accuracy and stability of motion. In: Proceedings of the 16th Annual ACM Symposium on User Interface Software and Technology, UIST 2003, pp. 61–70. ACM, New York (2003)
16. Zhang, H., Li, Y.: GestKeyboard: enabling gesture-based interaction on ordinary physical keyboard. In: Proceedings of the 32nd Annual ACM Conference on Human Factors in Computing Systems, CHI 2014, pp. 1675–1684. ACM, New York (2014)

A Design Process of Simple-Shaped Communication Robot

Yuki Takei[1]($\boxtimes$), Naoyuki Takesue[1]($\boxtimes$), Keiko Kasamatsu[1], Takeo Ainoya[1],
Toru Irie[2], Kenichi Kimura[2], and Masaki Kanayama[2]

[1] Graduate School of Systems Design, Tokyo Metropolitan University,
6-6 Asahigaoka, Hino-shi, Tokyo 191-0065, Japan
otter.0720@gmail.com, ntakesue@tmu.ac.jp
[2] Design Strategy Division, Fujitsu Design Limited, 1812-10, Shimonumabe,
Nakahara-ku, Kawasaki-shi, Kanagawa 211-0011, Japan
http://www.sd.tmu.ac.jp/en/
http://www.fujitsu.com/jp/group/fdl/en/

Abstract. In recent years, many communication robots have been developed. To find the new direction of communication robots, a workshop was examined and the role of motion of communication robots was focused on. Based on the workshop, a robot called "hako" in the simple shape of a cube was fabricated as a platform of motion-based communication robot. In this paper, the flow of the workshop on communication robots and the development of a prototype robot are presented.

Keywords: Workshop · Communication robot · Prototype · Motion · Cube

1 Introduction

Currently, robots are being introduced in various places in daily life. Robots communicating with people have been developed and become available as products. In Japan, "Pepper" [1] developed by Softbank can be seen in various stores as an assistant. Communication robots are getting closer to us.

In the near future, it is expected that robots will become more familiar and communicate with people more often. It is also assumed that robots will play a role in facilitating conversation and business between people. Fujitsu names such kind of robot "Mediator" robot and has developed a prototype called "RoboPin" [2].

To find the new direction of communication robots which will be more important, the authors examined a workshop in points of views of "situation", "appearance" and "motion". In this paper, a part of the design process is presented such as brainstorming, development and evaluation of prototype. The prototype "hako" in the simple shape of a cube is developed. The detail of the hardware and software is described and some examples of realized motions are illustrated.

© Springer International Publishing AG 2017
S. Yamamoto (Ed.): HIMI 2017, Part I, LNCS 10273, pp. 280–289, 2017.
DOI: 10.1007/978-3-319-58521-5_22

2   Workshop and Brainstorming

To find the new direction of communication robots, a workshop and brainstorming were examined together with about 10 people.

In the communication between a person and a person, not only the contents of the conversation but also the expression and motion of the partner are important. In the communication between a person and a robot, it is expected that the motion of the robot influences human emotions. Conversely, a person will be able to grasp the intention of the robot from the motion without the verbal communication. Therefore, we consider "situation" where people and robots communicate and focused on "motion" assumed along the situation and scenario.

In the workshop, people were divided into two groups. The first group was thinking based on the expansion and contraction deformation robot [3]. The viewpoints were "what can be expressed by the motion of robot ?", "how does it apply to daily life ?", and "what can it do for ?". Following ideas were obtained.

1. Direction instructions for guiding people
2. Welcome a person
3. Lighting
4. Expression of feeling
5. Cuddling motions to people

The second group thought that the robot had a certain scenario. For example,

1. "the person speaks to the robot"
2. "the robot responses to the person"
3. "the robot hear a talk"
4. "the robot speaks to the person"

There were many appearance of robots such as human, animals, plants and geometric shapes. "PARO" [4] is the most famous therapy robot that looks like a seal. It selects an unfamiliar animal because people are concerned with the differences between a real animal and a robot if a robot looks like a familiar animal such as a cat or a dog. Therefore, the shapes of animals and plants were excluded as a robot shape.

Based on these facts, we decided to focus on "what can be expressed by motions of a simple shape robot".

3   Related Study

As a simple shape, we focused on a cube.

Expression by the motion is often found in the animation. For example, a literature of "The illusion of life" of Disney animation describes about the techniques [5]. Cento Lodigian expresses 12 principles by animation including motion and shape deformation of a cube [6].

In addition, "WALKING Cube" [7] and "Morphing Cube" [8] can be cited as actual objects of a cube. These interest us in not only motion and rotation of the cube but deformation of the cube itself.

These examples can be classified into two types: a pattern expressing with the motion and a pattern expressing with the deformation of the exterior shape. As a example of the latter, Aka [9] has studied the expansion and contraction deformation robot using shape deformation of Mandala (Flexi-Sphere) [3]. It can deform from a sphere to a cylinder, a disk, and a gourd shape.

In addition, in order to communicate more intimately, it is important for a person to perceive animacy from the robot. Researches on animacy perception can be found in

Yamaoka [10] proposed the three design guides of robots of interpersonal behavior from the viewpoint of developmental psychology as follows:

(1) The robot can react according to the motion of the partner without contact.
(2) It can be both a passive role and an active role in the interaction.
(3) It behaves to show the will and purpose

Nakayama [11] developed linear motion simple group robots in simple cube to realize animasy perception according to the design guides. It is confirmed that subjects talk to the robots.

Heider [12] showed that the motion of the object realized animacy perception even if the object is a geometric figure.

It is thought that animate motion is important even in the case of a geometric simple shape robot, Since the behavior depends on situations, various behaviors are required to perceive animacy. In this study, we investigate the motion of a cube shaped robot. We named the developed robot "hako", which means a box in Japanese.

4   Development of Prototype

4.1   Hardware Specification and Design

We considered the specification of the prototype "hako" under the condition that "its shape is simple" and "its exterior does not deform". As mentioned in the previous section, it was decided that the shape of robot is a cube as a simple shape. Cubes can have directionality such as front and left/right unlike spherical shapes. Also, by making it a non-rounded geometric shape and undeformable, the likeness of life due to the shape of the exterior can be eliminated, and we can pay attention to the motion. We also decided that the size of the cube was within 150 mm so as not to give a feeling of pressure.

The specification of the motion generation mechanism is considered. As an example of situations, we assume a situation where a person talks to a robot. The following motions can be considered as the perceiving reaction of the robot when it is spoken to by the parson.

– Roll (around roll axis)

- Raise the face (around pitch axis)
- Turn (around yaw axis)

The axes in these parentheses show the corresponding motion axes of the robot, respectively.

Next, the following motions can be considered as a reaction when the robot is given a message.

- Incline (around roll axis)
- Nod (around pitch axis)
- Look away (around yaw axis)
- Escape (X and Y axes translation)
- Bounce (Z axis translation)
- Rejoice (combined motion)

The mechanisms that realize these motions are required in the robot.

Based on these requirements, the configuration scheme of the developed prototype is shown in Figs. 1 and 2. The configuration can be roughly divided into three subsystems: control system, frame system and drive system.

Arduino Yún mini is used for the controller. It controls LEDs and actuators and communicates with external devices via Wi-Fi. As an option to express the robot emotion, full color LEDs are used. The exterior is made of acrylic plates whose color is semitransparent milky to make the light of the LEDs easier to diffuse.

In order to realize the above-mentioned "turning" motion around the yaw axis and "X-Y translational" motion, two wheels, which are driven by geared motors, are used. In addition, in order to realize motion about the roll and pitch

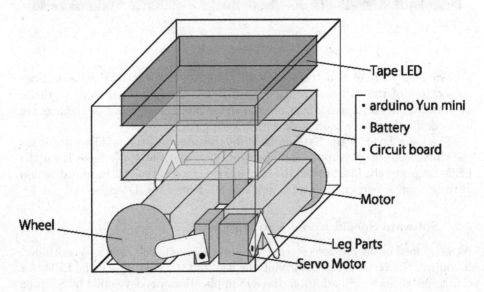

Fig. 1. Illustrated scheme of "hako"

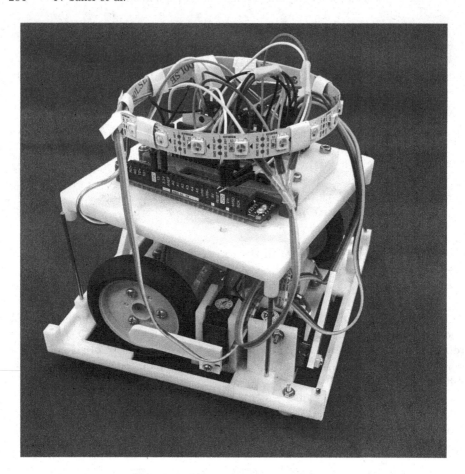

Fig. 2. Photo of inner "hako"

axes such as "incline" and "raise the face", four legs that extend downward from the bottom of the cube are provided and R/C servos are used to drive them. To translate in the Z axis direction, the shape and arrangement of the legs are devised. The legs were fabricated with a laser cutter.

The lower layer as the base frame is for the actuator, the middle layer is for the circuit, the power supply and the controller, and the upper layer is for the LEDs, respectively. In addition, the base was designed with CAD in consideration of the layout of parts and fixtures and was fabricated by 3D printer.

4.2   Software Specifications and Design

As mentioned in the previous section, Arduino Yún mini was used as a controller. It controls the R/C servos for driving the legs and the wheels, and the LEDs for expressing the color. In addition, the iOS application was developed by Swift as a UI to send commands to Arduino via Wi-Fi.

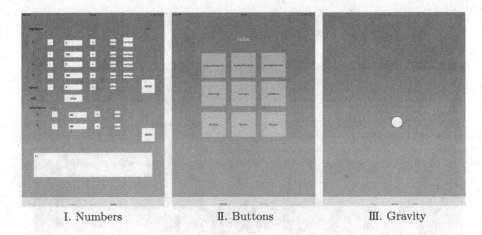

I. Numbers   II. Buttons   III. Gravity

Fig. 3. User interfaces of iOS application

In the prototype "hako", to create the motion, three types of UIs shown in Fig. 3 are prepared as below.

I. Number Interface The actuators in the robot are directly commanded according to the numerical parameters.

II. Button Interface The robot responds according to pushed button corresponding to a predetermined motion. The motion is coded in the Arduino on the robot.

III. Gravity Interface The robot moves so that it synchronizes to the inclination state by using the accelerometer of iPad. A ball is depicted in the iPad's screen to show the degree of inclination.

5   Motion of Prototype "hako"

As shown in the previous section, three types of interfaces were implemented on the iPad. In this paper, only the motion by the legs is presented as the preliminary tests.

5.1   Number Interface

In this interface, parameters of each actuator can be directly selected by inputting numerical values. Therefore, this interface is mainly used to determine the arbitrary posture of "hako". It is also used for checking the parameters.

5.2   Button Interface

This button interface performs predetermined motions. More complex motions can be performed than other interfaces. Six patterns of motions and LED colors are prepared as below.

(a) Button 1: Motion and Red LED

(b) Button 2: Motion and Green LED

Fig. 4. Motion by button interface (predetermined motions) (Color figure online)

1. Alternately slow roll motion (lighting in blue)
2. Alternately fast roll motion (blinking in red)
3. Pull out the legs in turn to rotate (lighting in green)
4. Stand up motion (lighting in light blue)
5. Nodding motion (blinking in blue)
6. Motion to put out all the legs slowly to the limit (lighting in blue)

As examples, photos corresponding to buttons 1 and 2 are shown in Figs. 4 (a) and (b), respectively.

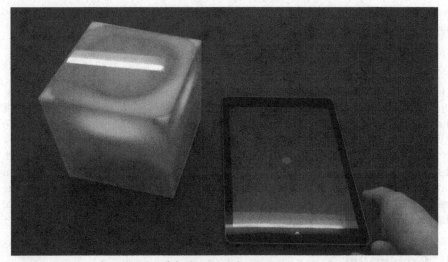

(a) Horizontal posture

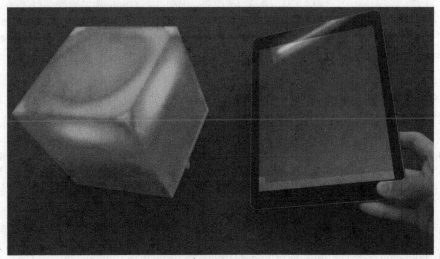

(b) Tilted posture

Fig. 5. Motion by gravity interface (inclination of iPad)

5.3 Gravity Interface

This interface uses the inclination information of the iPad. The ball in the iPad screen moves according to the inclined posture, and the command to the robot is decided according to the position of the ball. When there is a ball at the edge of the screen, the leg motor is fully rotated and "hako" is tilted the most. As an example, Fig. 5 (a) shows the horizontal posture and Fig. 5 (b) depicts the tilted posture of iPad and "hako".

This interface allows the most interactive motion at present. Because it cooperates with the inclination of iPad, a person could intuitively operate it. However, communication delay is one of problems. Real-time motion is important to realize interactive motion.

5.4 Discussion

Changes in the color of LEDs made it easier to express emotions and intentions. On the other hand, it was difficult to focus on motion. It was confirmed that the impression was influenced more by the color of the LED than assumed. To investigate the effect of the robot motion, LEDs may be a disturbance.

To generate the robot motion, in this paper, three types of UIs were prepared. However, it was not easy to create the motion patterns by hands. The motion pattern generated a robot-like motion. Even in the recent CG animation, the realistic motion is base on the motion of 3D tracked person. In order to solve the problem, the realization of motion generator is needed.

6 Conclusion

In this paper, we described the flow of the workshop on communication robots and the development of a prototype robot "hako". As future works, development of the motion generator of the robot and subjective evaluation of the robot motion are required.

References

1. Softbank: pepper. http://www.softbank.jp/en/robot/
2. Fujitsu: Robopin. http://journal.jp.fujitsu.com/en/2016/06/10/01/
3. Takei, Y., Takesue, N.: Design of wireframe expansion and contraction mechanism and its application to robot. In: Kubota, N., Kiguchi, K., Liu, H., Obo, T. (eds.) ICIRA 2016. LNCS (LNAI), vol. 9834, pp. 101–110. Springer, Cham (2016). doi:10.1007/978-3-319-43506-0_9
4. PARO Robotics: PARO. http://www.parorobots.com/
5. Thomas, F., Johnston, O.: The Illusion of Life: Disney Animation. Disney Editions (1981)
6. Lodigiani, C.: The Illusion of Life. http://the12principles.tumblr.com/
7. 1024architecture: WALKING Cube. http://www.1024architecture.net/en/2015/05/walking-cube/

8. Yamaoka, J.: Morphing Cube. http://www.junichiyamaoka.net/posts/1748995? categoryIds=406893
9. Aka, T., Takesue, N.: Development of flexi-sphere robot, In: Proceedings the 15th SICE System Integration Division Annual Conference, 2H1-2 (2014). (in Japanese)
10. Yamaoka, F., Kanda, T., Ishiguro, H., Hagita, N.: The design guide for "Lifelike" communication robots based on developmental psychology findings. J. Robot. Soc. Japan **25**(7), 1134–1144 (2007). (in Japanese)
11. Nakayama, M., Yamanaka, S.: Animacy perception by linear motion simple group robots. In: IPSJ Interaction 2016, pp. 323–236 (2016)
12. Heider, F., Simmel, M.: An experimental study of apparent behavior. Am. J. Psychol. **57**(2), 243–259 (1944)

Effectiveness Research of Safety Signs in Coal Mines Based on Eye Movement Experiment

Shui-cheng Tian[1,2(✉)], Lu Hui[1,2(✉)], and Hong-xia Li[1,2]

[1] College of Safety Science and Engineering,
Xi'an University of Science and Technology, Xi'an 710054, China
1255398120@qq.com, 779377800@qq.com, 406144519@qq.com
[2] Key Laboratory of Western Mines and Hazard Prevention,
Ministry of Education of China, Xi'an 710054, China

Abstract. Through the analysis of major fatal accidents occurred within 30 years from 1986 to 2016 in China's coal mines, it reflects that human errors accounting for up to 80% of the total accidents. The coal mines have set up a variety of safety signs that can alert miners to be careful with the insecurity in the workplace, and guide them to behave safely in accordance with legal standards. However, the human-induced accidents still occur. The problem is that although the safety signs have been adopted universally in the coal mines as a kind of management strategy, they are hard to play the safety signs' due role in the practical application. The low effectiveness of safety signs is one of the important reasons for the coal mines accidents. In order to settle the practical problems and improve the safety level of coal mines, this research is designed to study the effectiveness of safety signs in coal mines.

As a result of the previous researches, the author divided safety signs in coal mines' practical application into four stages by utilize 'communication-human' information processing model and determined the effective factors of safety signs in accordance with the transfer characteristics of each stage. Thus the author had already established the effective factors system of safety signs and determined the weight of factors that influence the safety signs' effectiveness by using the method of Analytic Hierarchy Process. The paper selected the setting positions of safety signs according to the importance ranking of safety signs' effectiveness factors.

In order to study the setting positions that affect the safety signs' effectiveness, the author carried out an experiment of eye movement. Through the use of an experimental plat of eye-movement Tobii Studio 4.3.2, whose hardware service is an eye tracker Tobii T60XL, a series of experiments were performed. The attention in visual feature of experiment participants can be gotten quantificationally from the angle of visual. In this experiment, in the light of the most common scenes in coal mines' daily producing activities, the belt transportation is selected as well as the mine opening, underground roadway and other four typical scenes as the visual stimulating materials, which used picture pattern to present. This experiment adopted 36 pictures totally to be the experimental materials that covered with four different scenes and safety signs set in different positions respectively, including 18 pictures on the ground of coal mines and 18 pictures under the ground of coal mines. The experiment began with the instructions and then participants conducted an experiment through clicking the buttons

S. Yamamoto (Ed.): HIMI 2017, Part I, LNCS 10273, pp. 290–300, 2017.
DOI: 10.1007/978-3-319-58521-5_23

on their own. The presentation time of each picture was 2 s and before playing the picture, it should have five unit-vectors with eye-movement calibration. The eye tracker could record and gather eye-movement data of different participants automatically, such as the time of first fixation, the first fixation duration, and the first fixation count and other eye-movement data. After collecting the eye-movement data, it was necessary to set up the safety signs in selected scenes to be the regions of interest (RIO). With the purpose of studying thoroughly, the paper divided the plane visual stimulating images into nine regions that could cover the whole pictures and numbered for each region. No. 1 to No. 9 showed different setting positions of safety signs in simulative scenes and selected the setting positions as the control factors. Then the author stacked the experimental data of each participant and exported orbit diagrams of fixation point of different setting positions' safety signs in the scenes of belt transportation, underground roadway and the mine opening. Finally, the experimental data was analyzed with the combination of the commercial software SPSS20.0, statistical methods and the theory of visual attention. It can be seen from the results of the homogeneity of variance that when safety signs set in the different positions, a significant test of the first fixation count in regions of interest is .000 < 0.05 and a significant test of the time of first fixation in regions of interest is .045 < 0.05, both reaching the significant level. The results indicate that there is significant difference among the eye-movement parameters of different setting positions. As for the safety signs on the ground of coal mines, the maximum number of the first fixation count is 0.850 and the minimum time of first fixation is 0.4015 s in the position of No. 5 and for the safety signs under the ground of coal mines, the maximum number of the first fixation count is 0.925 and the minimum time of first fixation is 0.508 s in the position of No. 2. Consequently, these results suggest that the position of No. 5 and No. 2 attract the most attention of participants. The position of No. 5 and No. 2 are proved to be the most effective setting position. The study can be helpful to the establishment and application of the safety signs in coal mines and ensure safety production.

Keywords: Coal mine · Safety signs · Effectiveness · Eye tracker · Experimental research

1 Introduction

The role of safety signs in coal mines is to prohibit, warn and indicate unsafe behavior of miners' in workplaces and surroundings, and it is a fast and effective way to avoid accidents, mitigate the consequences of accidents and transmit risk information.

The key study of safety signs is whether they can convey the information effectively [1], the research on safety signs can be carried out from five characteristics: familiarity, specificity, conciseness, clarity and semantic closeness [2]. In 2005, Jun Zhicai et al. [3] considered the cognitive psychology as a research point of view, used the perceptual theory to explained the phenomenon that the identification of safety signs existed differences and explained the uniqueness of safety signs with the theory of characteristics. In 2007, Du Penghong et al. [4] evaluated on the collected information by the analysis methods of information processing evaluation and pattern coding from the view of human mechanics. In 2011, Yuan Wei et al. [5] studied the influence of vehicle speed and signs height on the breadth of visual search, persistence and distribution of viewing angle by means of eye-tracking measuring time-of-flight and variance. In 2012, Hu YiCheng et al. [6] extracted the effective factors of safety signs using the expert scoring and analytic network process from the view of ergonomics, and established evaluation index system. In 2013, Ma Qingguo et al. [7] studied the risk level of safety signs using the target paradigm from the perspective of psychology. In 2014, Niu Guoqing et al. [8] proved the significance and feasibility of eye movement technology to introduce the identification of safety signs from statistics, with Eyelink II type eye tracking instrument. In 2014, Li Linna et al. [9] selected the college students and graduate students as the test objects and used two groups of elements including shape and color to design two experiments in order to determine a unified background color from the principles of color psychology. In 2016, Li Shibo [10] studied the different positions of coal miners' unsafe actions from the behavioral safety "2–4" model. On the basis of finding the appropriate unsafe actions, combined the characteristics of safety signs, combination of characteristics and the design standards of safety signs to design a safety sign. In 2016, Tian Shuicheng et al. [11] established the effective factors system of safety signs by adopting factor analysis. On the basis of determining the weight of the three levels of indicators, the importance degree of each influencing factor was studied theoretically.

To sum up, at present, the research on safety signs involves a lot of aspects such as definition, domain, characteristic factors and influencing factors of validity. However, in the actual use of the safety signs, there existed a plenty of problems such as lack of standardization, unreasonable locations and imperfect fixed measures. Therefore, the author set up the eye movement experiment platform and used the eye movement instrument to observe the experiment objects' attention frequency, time and the other parameters. And then analyzed data collected by the eye movement instrument through SPSS20.0, proposed a scheme that's beneficial to improve the validity of the safety signs.

2   The Experiment Platform Building

Eye movement experiment used the platform Tobii Studio 4.3.2 and the hardware device for the Tobii T60XL. This eye tracker can easily and accurately test the users' response to widescreen stimuli material. The Tobii T60XL is integrated in a high-definition 24-inch TFT widescreen display that allows subjects to move closer to the screen during testing. The Tobii T60XL automatically measures the gaze position of a subject within 17 ms (60 Hz) and accurately measures the response of the person when faced the displayed images (Fig. 1).

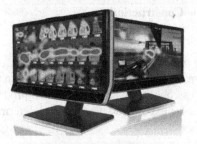

Fig. 1. Tobii T60XL

Other experimental equipment parameters such as Table 1:

Table 1. Experimental equipment parameter table

Hardware equipment	Configuration information
Assembly desktop computer	CPU frequency of 3.6, video memory 1G, memory 8G
Wireless mouse	Signal transmission distance 10 m
Table	A white table, in line with man-machine design
Chair	Two, in line with man-machine design
Lab environment	Good light, quiet, closed

3 Experiment Procedures

3.1 Experiment Purpose

Constructed a number of simulative scenes of coal mine and used eye tracker to record the whole process of eye movement. The eye tracker recorded and gathered eye-movement data automatically, and then analyzed the first fixation count, the time of first fixation and other eye-movement data of safety signs in different positions. And finally determined the effective location of the safety signs.

3.2 Selection of Experiment Objects

As a result of coal mines' special environment and experimental platform constraints, it's inconvenient to build the experimental platform in coal mine for real-time measurement. Therefore, in order to be as close as possible to the reality, the author selected 50 graduate students with the practical experience in coal mine as a test. As shown in Table 2:

Table 2. The table on the constitution of experimental subjects

Profession	Number of people
Safety engineering	30
Mining engineering	30
Total	60

3.3 Experimental Scene Construction

(1) Selective basis of eye-movement experimental images

This paper selected the most common scenes in coal mines' daily producing activities as the visual stimulating materials, which used picture pattern to present. To determine whether the selected scenes could truly reflect the actual production of coal mines, the author analyzed and asked for experts' advice and then determined the following principles:

(a) Can reflect the coal mine actual production and have the representative, versatility and universality;
(b) Key information areas can maintain a certain stability and can be divided into areas of interest for data analysis;
(c) Picture quality is clear and picture quality is in 1280 * 768 above.

(2) Scene building

The experimental scenes were divided into underground and ground, including the belt transportation, underground roadway and the mine opening, the gas extraction stations. The specific experimental scenes were shown in Figs. 2, 3, 4 and 5.

Fig. 2. The scene of coal mine belt transportation

Fig. 3. The scene of coal mine roadway

Fig. 4. The scene of coal mine opening

Fig. 5. The scene of gas extraction stations

(3) The selection of eye-movement parameters

Based on the literature [5–7, 9, 10], combined with the specific parameters of Tobii T60XL eye tracker, determined the main eye-movement parameters including time to first fixation and fixation count according to the actual situations of the coal mines.

3.4 Experimental Implementation

The first step: create and edit the experiment project

(1) Instruction

Instructional words can be used to provide instructions to the experimental subjects during the course of the experiment.

(2) Insert stimulative images

Before playing the stimulative images, it should have five unit-vectors with eye-movement calibration. The presentation time of each picture was 2 s and then started playing the stimulative images directly.

(3) Closing

The concluding remarks are used to indicate that the experiment is completed.

The second step: test the eye-movement data

This experience adopted 5-point calibration and required more than 70% of the calibration data and then accepted the calibration results. Experimental subjects were asked to sit in the relaxed state of mind and comfortable position before the experiment, keep the eye distance from the eye tracker screen 60 cm to 65 cm and put the fixation point in the middle of the eye tracker screen.

The third step: start the experiment

After completing the calibration, inform the experimental subjects to start the experiment, play experimental instructions, show the pre-experimental materials and the experiment proper started after subjects understanding the experimental content and requirements. During the experiment, keep the lighting and quiet of the experiment site and cannot be disturbed by external stimuli, the whole experimental process control in less than 5 min.

The fourth step: collect data

The eye tracker can automatically record and collect the eye-movement data during the experiment. Some subjects were unable to record the data or caused inaccurate data recording due to eye strain or other reasons. During the results analysis, the data was deleted.

4 Experimental Data Analysis

4.1 Experimental Data Processing

(1) Divide the scene

With the purpose of studying thoroughly, the paper divided the plane visual stimulating images into nine regions that could cover the whole pictures and numbered for each region. As shown in Fig. 6. No. 1 to No. 9 showed different setting positions of safety signs in simulative scenes. However, in the actual production of coal mine, No. 7 to No. 9 belonged to the visual blind area of the miners, generally not set the safety signs, so only considered the location No. 1 to No. 6 when studied the effective location of the safety signs.

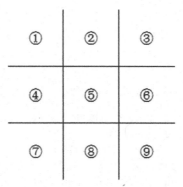

Fig. 6. The number of scene classification

(2) Create an AOI

This paper created a scene in the picture taking the coal mine roadway area for example, as shown in Fig. 7.

Fig. 7. The interest area figure of the scene of coal mine roadway

In the chosen scene, the region of interest was the safety sign, but the positions of the safety sign were different. And then studied the questions whether the subjects had the fixation points in the regions of interest and the time when the fixation point reached the regions of interest for the first time.

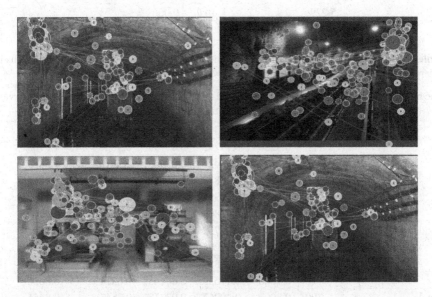

Fig. 8. The graph of fixation trajectory of prohibitive signs at different position in coal mine's underground and ground

4.2 Experimental Data Processing and Analysis

The Gaze Plot visualization interface in Tobii Studio 4.3.2 presents the order and position of fixation points on static stimuli. The size of the dot indicates the time of fixation, and the number in the dot indicates the order of the fixation. The experimental results of 50 experimental subjects were superimposed and finally got graphs of fixation trajectory of prohibitive signs at different position in coal mine's underground and ground. List four of the stimulus pictures as a note, the results shown in Fig. 8.

In order to clarify the validity of the setting position, the first fixation points of 50 subjects were analyzed by SPSS20.0.

(1) The first fixation count of prohibitive signs

The test of variance was performed on the number of first fixation points in the region of interest, as shown in Tables 3 and 4.

Table 3. Homogeneity of variance of first fixation count of prohibitive signs in coal mine underground

Levene statistics	df1	df2	Significance
16.546	5	294	0.000
5.229	2	147	0.006

Table 4. Variance analysis of descriptive statistics of first fixation count of prohibitive signs in underground

The number of position	N	Average	Standard deviation	Standard error	The 95% confidence interval	
					Lower limit	Upper limit
1	50	0.7400	0.44309	0.06266	0.6141	0.8659
2	50	0.9250	0.19795	0.02799	0.9600	1.0163
3	50	0.8100	0.39428	0.03943	0.7318	0.8882
4	50	0.8500	0.35887	0.03589	0.7788	0.9212
5	50	0.9600	0.19795	0.02799	0.9037	1.0163
6	50	0.8200	0.38809	0.05488	0.7097	0.9303
Total	300	0.8500	0.35752	0.01788	0.8149	0.8851
1	100	0.7700	0.42295	0.04230	0.6861	0.8539
2	100	0.8500	0.35887	0.03589	0.7788	0.9212
3	100	0.7800	0.41633	0.04163	0.6974	0.8626
Total	300	0.8000	0.40067	0.02313	0.7545	0.8455

A significant test of the first fixation count in underground regions of interest is .000 < 0.05 and in ground regions of interest is .006 < 0.05, both reaching the significant level. As for the prohibitive signs on the underground of coal mines, the maximum number of the first fixation count is 0.925; as for the prohibitive signs on the ground of coal mines, the maximum number of the first fixation count is 0.850. Consequently, these results suggest that the position of No. 5 and No. 2 attract the most attention of participants.

(2) The time to first fixation of prohibitive signs

The test of variance was performed on the time of first fixation in the region of interest, as shown in Tables 5 and 6.

Table 5. Homogeneity of variance of the time to first fixation of prohibitive signs in coal mine underground and ground

Levene statistics	df1	df2	Significance
1.699	5	294	0.134
2.759	5	144	0.045

Table 6. Variance analysis of descriptive statistics of the time to first fixation of prohibitive signs in coal mine ground

The number of position	N	Average	Standard deviation	Standard error	The 95% confidence interval	
					Lower limit	Upper limit
1	100	.4291	.41411	.04141	.3993	.5637
2	100	.4015	.46655	.04666	.3365	.5217
3	100	.5131	.47353	.04735	.4191	.6071
Total	300	.4746	.45199	.02610	.4232	.5259

A significant test of the time to first fixation in underground regions of interest is . 134 < 0.05 not reaching the significant level. This indicates that there is little difference in this indicator. A significant test of the time to first fixation in ground regions of interest is .045 < 0.05 reaching the significant level. As for the prohibitive signs on the ground of coal mines, the minimum time of first fixation is 0.4015 s in the position of No. 2 that attracts the most attention of participants.

4.3 Result Analysis

This experiment adopted 36 pictures totally to be the experimental materials that covered with four different scenes and safety signs set in different positions respectively, including 18 pictures on the ground of coal mines and 18 pictures under the ground of coal mines. Through eye-movement experiment analysis of fixation point trajectory figure and software SPSS20.0, it indicated the average number of the first fixation point of the position No. 5 and No. 2 are the largest and the variation are the smallest in the ground scene simulation experiment. As for the underground scene simulation experiment, it indicated the average number of the time to first fixation of the position No. 2 is the shortest and the variation is the smallest.

5   Conclusion

Safety signs are a timely and effective prompting and early warning of coal miners before or at the time of the occurrence of a hazard, which is very important for the prevention of accidents. Through the research on the effectiveness of the safety signs' position of ground and underground in coal mine, the following conclusions are obtained:

(1) Reasonable safety signs setting can alert people the dangerous situations in the workplace or the surrounding environment and guide people to take reasonable actions and reduce unsafe behaviors, which is an effective visual safety measure to avoid accidents and reduce casualties.
(2) Eye-movement experiments show that the locations of the different safety signs have different eye-movement indices, such as the number of the first fixation point and the time to first fixation, indicating that the safety signs in different positions have significant influence on the experimental subjects and it is meaningful to study the validity of the safety signs location.

(3) These results suggest that the position of No. 5 and No. 2 attract the most attention of participants and the position of No. 5 and No. 2 are proved to be the most effective setting position.

References

1. Duarte, M.E.C., Rebelo, F.: Comprehension of safety signs: internal and external variable influences, pp. 172–176. International Ergonomics Association Press (2005)
2. McDougall, S.J.P., Curry, M.B., De Bruijin, O.: Measuring symbol and icon characteristics: norms for concreteness, complexity, meaningfulness, familiarity, and semantic distance for 239 symbols. Behav. Res. Meth. Instrum. Comput. 31(3), 487–519 (1999)
3. Juan, Z., Cao, P., Wu, W.: Study on driver traffic signs comprehension based on cognitive psychology. China Saf. Sci. J. 15(8), 8–11 (2005)
4. Du, P.: Study on identification of Safety Signs. Capital University of Economics and Business, Beijing (2007)
5. Yuan, W., Fu, R., Ma, Y., et al.: Effects of vehicle speed and traffic sign text height on driver visual search patterns. J. Traffic Transp. Eng. 11(1), 119–126 (2011)
6. Hu, Y., Zhou, X., Wang, L.: Evaluating effectiveness of safety signs on building site. China Saf. Sci. J. 22(8), 37–42 (2012)
7. Ma, Q., Shang, Q., Jin, J.: The hazard level of warning signal words modulates attention effect. J. Psychol. Sci. 37(3), 704–709 (2013)
8. Niu, G., Cui, C., Zhang, K.: An eye movement study of auxiliary words effect to safety signs' recognition. J. Henan Polytech. Univ. 33(4), 410–415 (2014)
9. Li, L., Jiang, W., Zhang, Y.: Background shape and the background color of safety sign. China Public Secur. (Acad. Ed.) (1), 117–120 (2014). No.1 Sum. No.34
10. Li, S.: Research on the design and effect evaluation of coal mine safety sign. Beijing China University of Mining & Technology, Beijing (2016)
11. Tian, S., Chen, Y., Zou, Y., Li, G.: Analysis of factors influencing effectiveness of mine safety signs. China Saf. Sci. J. 26(2), 146–151 (2016)

Godzilla Meets 'F' Museum: Case Study of Hand-On Museum Event with Augmented Reality Technology

Ryoko Ueoka[1,2(✉)] and Kenta Iwasa[1,2]

[1] Faculty of Design, Kyushu University, 4-9-1 Shiobaru Minami ku, Fukuoka, Japan
r-ueoka@design.kyushu-u.ac.jp, kerop1no@gmail.com
[2] Graduate School of Design, Kyushu University, 4-9-1 Shiobaru Minami ku,
Fukuoka, Japan

Abstract. We planned and organized a museum exhibition and an experiential event with a related story, as a concrete example of an AR technology event. Specifically, an AR backyard tour "Godzilla meets 'F' museum" was conducted on August 2–6, 2016, as an event related to "Godzilla at the Museum: Creative Tracks of Daikaiju" exhibition in Fukuoka City Museum of Art, held from July 15 to August 31, 2016 [8]. In this paper, we describe the characteristics and implementation state of this event, using a questionnaire-based survey obtained from the event participants. From the results, we discuss the significance of holding AR technology-based art museum exhibitions and the novelty of related events.

Keywords: AR based museum backyard tour · AR contents · Actor act

1 Introduction

Museums do not only display various exhibits, they also have various undisclosed facilities in their backyard, such as building structures to keep, restore and preserve valuable artworks. Through backyard tours that introduce the facilities behind museum buildings, visitors can visit the normally inaccessible area and obtain understanding on the roles that art museums play, in addition to the individual artworks being displayed. In this paper, we describe the characteristics and implementation state of "Godzilla meets 'F' museum," an event that expanded the conventional backyard tour by utilizing the highly entertaining AR technology, held by Fukuoka City Art Museum. This event was a part of an exhibition that summarizes the trajectory of the Godzilla series, which can be said to be the masterpieces of Japanese special effects, held from July 15 to August 31, 2016, using a questionnaire-based survey obtained from the event participants. From the results, we discuss the possibility of application of AR technology in events that link museum exhibitions to museum backyard tours.

© Springer International Publishing AG 2017
S. Yamamoto (Ed.): HIMI 2017, Part I, LNCS 10273, pp. 301–312, 2017.
DOI: 10.1007/978-3-319-58521-5_24

2   Related Work

As a related work, we introduce several spatial mobile events and applications that utilize AR technology similar to this content, analyze common terms with examples, and propose the production of novel events that use AR technologies.

AR HOPE TOUR [2] will organize a demonstration experiment for disaster prevention, in which participants wearing smart glass (glasses-type wearable device) can experience AR images of areas affected by the Tohoku earthquake before and after the disaster, by actually moving round on their feet. Participants can view the state of the affected area at the time of the disaster, the height of the tsunami, and the surrounding changes from the time of the disaster to the present, superimposed on the actual place through the smart glass. The purpose of this tour is to show how the recovery and reconstruction of the disaster area proceeded, to show the reconstruction process that immersed the past and the present time of the disaster area by simulating the surroundings in AR images. This event will allow the participants to experience the damage caused by the earthquake in real space by experiencing the content where participants can feel walking around the actual disaster area on their own feet.

Next, as an example of existing popular contents such as animation and events that use AR technology, there is an AR digital stamp rally organized using the contents of Evangelion animation series [3]. As participants move through multiple check points, information on their positions are obtained from the GPS system in their smartphones and digital stamps are collected in the installed application. Unlike the traditional stamp rally, there is a function to receive a digital image of a specific character as a stamp-paid reward, giving the user a motivation to go around each stamp point. In addition, there are other AR-infused stamp rally events that are tied up with TV programs and movies, such as "Ultraman AR Stamp Rally" [6] and "Godzilla AR Stamp Rally" [7]. Furthermore, there is the Tomioka Silk Mill CG Video Guide Tour, which is a tour around the Tomioka Silkscreen, a historic tourist facility. Participants can experience CG images reproducing the conditions of silk screening in the Meiji era, displayed in smart glass [4].

In addition, there was the "AR Hyakki Yako," an AR technology-infused event, funded by a cloud funding system in June 2016 [5]. Centered on the "Hyakki Yako" legend, in which demons gather and march in Kyoto, the event used AR technology to fill a town with Hyakki Yako motifs and transformed a shopping street into a demon street. The content was a tour-type event in which participants superimpose the demons shown by 3DCG through a simple head-mounted display using smartphones while watching the real landscape of the shopping street.

In the AR application created for educational purpose, Itamiya et al. described a disaster-assumption immersion experience application using smartphone and simple paper-based goggles [1]. This is an application that superimposes a flood environment in 3DCG onto actual landscapes by using simple VR google-mounted smartphones. The flood CG is set based on a hazard map, and

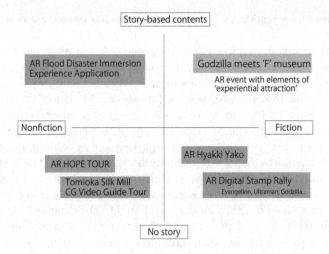

Fig. 1. Existing AR applications classification

it simulates how far water reaches the actual environment, which is aimed to emphasize the importance of evacuation at the time of a disaster.

Based on the above mobile collaborative AR applications, in this research, in order to examine what kind of new event production can be performed in the collaboration with the exhibition of fictional works on Godzilla movie series that was carried out in the museum, we classified the existing AR applications based on the viewpoint of whether there is a context in the content experience and whether the content subject is fiction or nonfiction as shown in Fig. 1.

The existing AR related events and research are arranged based on the following: in the lower right of the figure, there is no context in the order of experiencing the content and the content subject is fictional; in the upper left, there is a context in the order of experiencing the content and the content subject is non-fictional; and in the lower left there is no context in the order of experiencing the content and the content subject is non-fictional.

In the upper right corner of the figure was arranged for those with contexts in the order of experiencing the content and the content subject is fictional. However, there were no relevant events/projects in the existing examples that were examined. The event that the authors carried out involved having a group of people traveling through the museum with an order of places to visit, centered on a fictional subject of Godzilla. This event may be applied into the aforementioned upper left corner of the Fig. 1, suggesting that this is a novel AR content from the view point of context and the nature of subject. In planning this content, we thought of this as an AR event with elements of 'experiential attraction' that can be found in large theme park facilities.

Experience-type attractions found in large theme park facilities usually involve a group of participants that move as one of the characters or move on a mobile vehicle to simulate the world of the event. Participants can be immersed into the attraction's surroundings by being guided by real-life or animated guides.

Therefore, in this research, authors propose an AR-infused event in a context with an order of contents that incorporates elements of the above experience-type attraction and contains a nonfiction subject.

Through a concrete realization of a fantasy world theme via AR contents superimposed with real-world space rendering using a tablet terminal, and by actually moving through the art museum space, we created an event tailored to bridge a bridge between the story and participant by adding an actor to act as a guide for the participants to gradually be immersed into the fantasy world perspective. In the case of a system in which participants move around the art museum and watch AR contents at each point, or if the guide is not a real person but is shown in a video or other means, we thought that experiencing with many people was difficult due to a positional shift or time lag in receiving the content as each participant has his/her own individual terminal. Furthermore, in an AR experiential event, since a story moves along a certain space, an accompanying story facilitator that act as a guide is necessary. For that reason, we decided to appoint a real actor as a guide for the whole event and to move with the event onward. This enabled us to give a lot of information to the participants, such as real voice, facial expression, and gesture, rather than presenting a guide assistant in the form of a video, and improve the concentration and immersion level of the participants naturally into the world of the story.

3   Godzilla Meets 'F' Museum

3.1   Contents

We produced an AR content set at a museum backyard tour using motif from a Godzilla movie. The story outline is as follows.

> Participants of the museum backyard tour carrying an under-developed backyard tour support system (M-AR) encounter various events during the tour that caused a sign of Godzilla appearance, and head to the roof. After the backyard tour participants find Godzilla footprints on the roof, the tour is stopped and they and escape outside the museum. When they try to escape towards a park adjacent to the museum, from the reaction of the M-AR with a special Geiger counter that the developer brought, as they look to the direction of a pond, they saw a blue light that the blue Godzilla fires from behind, destroying a city at the end of the park. Looking back to the museum, they realize that the museum has been destroyed by Godzilla.

Based on this story, two actors play a role as a scientist and an assistant who develop the M-AR system Fig. 2, and the acting screenplay and backyard tour contents were created. In the backyard tour, we selected 8 places where it was easy to deploy the content related to Godzilla at the event part, in places that

Fig. 2. Two actors: scientist (left) and assistant (right)

cannot be seen through the back door from the permanent exhibition site of the museum. Also, as the participants were informed that the Fukuoka City Museum of Art will be closed for renewal for the 2 years following the exhibition, we devised to relate the content of the story to a real-world event by having a video that the museum will be renovated at the end of the content after being destroyed by Godzilla. The screen transition and the contents of the superposition system are shown in Fig. 3. The tablet iPad Air 2 combined with a cabinet made of MDF plywood, assuming a fictitious system called the Museum Archive Reader (M-AR) was used in the event. By displaying the reference image of the indoor-outdoor overlapping points on the tablet and superimposing it on the real image captured from the camera mounted on iPad Air 2, and when judging the feature point of the image and judging it as a recent point, we set up a mechanism in which a maximum of 30 s of motion picture is played at each point.

3.2   Event Description

"Godzilla meets 'F' museum" was held at Fukuoka City Art Museum three times a day for 5 days from August 2 to 6 (a total of 14 times due to bad weather). Participation was accepted at the reception on the day, with 5 groups each time (up to 4 people in each group) and preschool children had to be accompanied by parents as one of the participation criteria. The time required for the execution of the main part of the back yard tour was about 35 min, and a total of 45 min, which include a waiting time in the waiting room and the time needed to answer a questionnaire, etc., was used as the event time. Figure 4 shows the condition of the event participants.

3.3   Result

We conducted a questionnaire-based survey for visitors of "Godzilla meets 'F' museum". The survey items were designed to explore whether the respondents

Fig. 3. Screen transition and the contents of M-AR system

were able to immerse into a fantasy world perspective through AR production and experience-based attraction. Basically, for each group who used the M-AR system, one person was asked to become a respondent, and one person who participated as a chaperone was asked to be an additional respondent. The number of respondents was 107 out of 132 participants (Male 63 Female 43).

(1) Age Group. Figure 5 shows the distribution of age group of the participants. The youngest generation among the participants were younger than 10 years old (toddlers aged 3 and 4 years), and the oldest generation was in their 60s. Since elementary and junior high school students were in a summer vacation period, there were many families consisting of parents and children or groups of grandchildren and grandparents.

(2) Why did you participate in the backyard tour? Figure 6 shows the distribution of the reasons to participate the event. Most respondents answered "Because I heard about the event in advance". This was probably a result of an

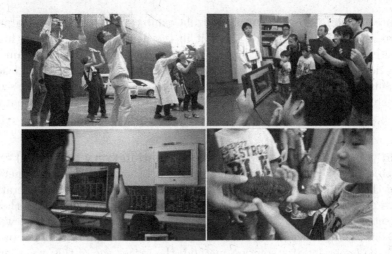

Fig. 4. Event participants

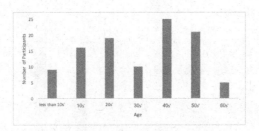

Fig. 5. Age group of participants.

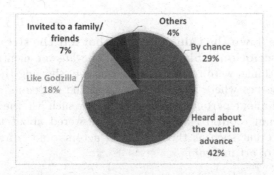

Fig. 6. Reasons participating the event.

announcement on the webpage of Godzilla exhibition. There were also people who answered "Because I read about it in the newspaper." The next highest was those who answered "By chance," they are considered to have obtained an information about this event on the day from the notice posted at the 1F lobby of the museum. For another reason, which is "Because I like Godzilla," it seemed that there are many participants who happened to know about this event after browsing the Godzilla exhibition.

(3) Did you enjoy the event? (5 state evaluation (very boring (1) - very enjoyable (5))). Figure 7 shows the responses of the participants whether they enjoyed the event. We were able to obtain good evaluation from all generations. Evaluations from younger participants such as children, teenagers, and those in the twenties, were higher than those from the older generation. There was an impression that this event was "Good for children." We think that because we applied the experiential attraction method, the target age of this event shifted toward the younger ones.

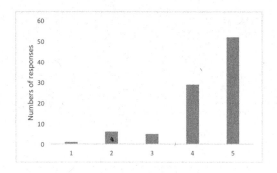

Fig. 7. Did you enjoy the event?

(4) Please write down the thing or event that left the strongest impression. (Free description). Sixty percent of the answer mentioned that the most impressive things were related to AR contents showing the "footsteps of Godzilla" and "scenes where Godzilla destroyed the museums". Twenty nine-percent answered about parts of the backyard tour such as "the museum backside" and "museum rooftop". Seven percent answered about the acting and directing of this event such as the "acting of actors" and "directing together with the renewal of art museum".

(5) Was M-AR operation difficult? (Yes/no). A part of Fig. 8 shows the result of difficulty of the system. This is an item about the usability of M-AR system. To summarize the contents of item (3) "What point was difficult?", there were two answers: "M-AR system superposition did not work well" and

"Tablet screen was hard to see due to sunshine". In particular, many participants experienced difficulties because the recognition of superposed image could not be performed well outdoors.

(6) In this event, we planned a backyard tour in the form of a dramatic make-over of the current Godzilla exhibition. Did you feel the relationship between the tour and the Godzilla exhibition? (Yes/no) A part of Fig. 8 shows the result. Participants in all age groups felt the relationship with the Godzilla exhibition. It seemed that we were able to convey Godzilla as the world perspective theme of the story through AR production.

(7) Do you think that the backyard tour became more fun by the actors' performance? (Yes/no). A part of Fig. 8 shows the result. We obtained high evaluation from all age groups. It seemed that we were able to increase the degree of immersion into the world perspective through the actors' performance, which is the main element in an experience-type attraction. Excerpt from the impression column, "The tour directing was good. The setting of a scientist and assistant, and the flow to the rooftop created a lot of tense moments." It seemed that the performance functioned well as a part of the directing.

(8) If you have an opportunity to join a similar backyard tours, would you like to participate in the future? (Yes/no). A part of Fig. 8 shows the result. We obtained high evaluation from all age groups.

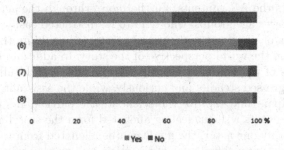

Fig. 8. Results of question (5) to (8)

(9) If this backyard tour was a paid event, how much would you consider paying for it? The satisfaction level of this event was measured by willingness to pay (WTP). We added a WTP item to the questionnaire at the middle of the event and we provided 4 options on how much a participant is willing to pay if this was a paid event (1. Less than 100 yen 2. 100–500 yen 3. 500–1,000 yen 4. 1,000 Yen or more). This question item was asked in the middle of the event, so the effective number of responses was 37 people. The results are shown in Fig. 9. The largest number of responses was in the range of 100 to 500 yen (18 people), followed by 500–1,000 yen (14 people), suggesting that the participants felt a certain level of satisfaction.

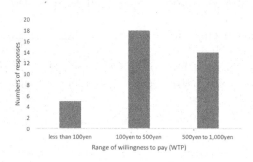

Fig. 9. Willingness to Pay

4 Discussion

In general, this event was well accepted by all participants. There was an impression that participants were able to obtain general perspective of the AR technology through this event, and to understand the characteristics and enjoyed the technology through the content. Particularly, AR production could be developed according to the story by the feature of this event, which was the acting technique that tailors the AR contents. Furthermore, through the actors' guidance, participants in lower age groups, who tend to be distracted easily, could concentrate on progress of the event without losing interest, enabling the participants to be immersed in the world perspective of the story. In addition, by setting two contrasting roles of the actors as a self-paced scientist and a gullible assistant, the scientist progressed steadily and curiously, while the assistant took the position as a participant and reprove the scientist, the participants could actively took part in the events without feeling alienated form the storyline.

If there was only one actor, the guide can be alienated from the participants and it would have been difficult for the participants to maintain the immersed feeling. It seemed that the story atmosphere was maintained through the interaction of the two actors, retaining the feeling of immersion in the story within the participants. While the real actors were responsible for the explanation and progress of the event, the AR contents played the role of presenting the theme of the world perspective with the theme of Godzilla and backyard tour to the participants. The AR content reference method of superimposing the reference images and viewing the images by combining the contents of the actors was also accepted by the participants as a natural action performed in the story rather than simply watching the information on the tablet.

For the challenge on the superimposition technology, especially in the case of overlaying outdoor environments, the matching accuracy with the reference image was likely to change due to the change in the illumination condition caused by the change in weather, causing superimposition did not go smoothly and there were opinions that it was difficult to operate the device. Challenges still remain for a widespread use as a general system.

5   Conclusion

In a story composition in line with the museum's exhibition, we expanded conventional backyard tour by including AR technology and proposed an example of a new backyard tour content by making it entertaining, and organized it at Fukuoka City Art Museum. By creating a narrative composition tailored to the backyard of an art museum exhibition, the relationship between the event and space became stronger. In addition, by including actors as guides, participants could acquire the ability to operate the tablets and other equipments in the event more naturally, and while moving through the real space and observing the museum backyard, each participant could feel deeply immersed into the fictional story. In the free description item in the questionnaire, although the event and Godzilla were regarded as fiction, there were several participants who thought that the M-AR system could be put into practical use, meaning that the function of the system itself was considered as genuine. All of the above indicated that the boundary between fiction and non-fiction will continually be obscured through the incorporation of contents that are related to the art museum context at a site where the event is held. From this event, we were able to gain insights that in order to create contents that take advantage of AR technology characteristics that adds location-dependent information, it is important to truly understand he meaning of the place where the content is used in the content production process.

Acknowledgments. We thank Sohei Osawa, Junichi Nakano, Takuji Narumi of the University of Tokyo and all the members of Hirose, Tanikawa and Narumi Laboratory of the University of Tokyo helping to make a M-AR system. We also thank Saburo Tsuda and Kazuhiko Ikeura for creating wonderful Trilobite sculptures, Kichiro Nakayama, an assistant director of the Fukuoka City Museum of Art and all the staffs to kindly assist us to realize the event and all the volunteers who helped the event.

References

1. Itamiya, T.: The virtual Tsunami disaster situation experience system using a Head-mounted display, Media and Communication for Disaster Risk Reduction. In: Showcasing Innovation, An initiative for the Third UN World Conference on Disaster Risk Reduction in Sendai, pp. 2–3 (2015)
2. AR HOPE TOUR in Sendai, AR HOPE TOUR in Tagajo. http://www.dmp.co.jp/ar-hope-tour
3. Evangellion AR Stamp rally (Japanese). http://www.hakone.or.jp/eva/

4. Tomioka Mill CG picture Guided Tour. http://www.tomioka-silk.jp.e.wv.hp.
   transer.com/tomioka-silk-mill/visit/group.html?_ga=1.124798410.1985905280.
   1488691668
5. AR Hyakki Yako Crowd Funding (Japanese). https://a-port.asahi.com/projects/
   youkai/
6. Ultraman AR Stamp Rally Event News Release 2016 (Japanese). http://m-78.jp/
   news/n-3847/
7. Godzilla AR Stamp Rally (Japanese). http://www.godzilla-tokusatsu.com/
   stamprally/
8. Godzilla at the museum: Creative Tracks of Daikaiju. http://www.fukuoka-art-
   museum.jp/godzilla/english/

Proposal for a Design Process Method Using VR and a Physical Model

Tetsuhito Yamauchi[✉], Takeo Ainoya, Keiko Kasamatsu, and Ryuta Motegi

Graduate School of System Design, Tokyo Metropolitan University, Hino, Tokyo, Japan
tystg1132@gmail.com, kasamatu@tmu.ac.jp

Abstract. Recently, studies on space evaluation using virtual reality (VR) are being performed for a wide range of subjects ranging from those for private houses through to cityscapes of entire towns, and their significance is becoming increasingly important. In addition, architects and interior designers are increasingly making use of simple VR kits to suggest new spaces to customers. However, such studies tend to be used for evaluation only upon personal sight of the virtual space, and joint ownership of the opinion with the designer is difficult to achieve, and there are occasions when there is a mismatch between the virtual reality and the actual reality. In this study, we conduct an experiment using the interior of a car space in which not only the impression of the space but also the operability of the space is evaluated by building a model having identical dimensions to those of the VR model so as to be able to gain an opinion of the sense of faithfulness the virtual space has to the actual (real) space. In addition, by means on an in-space experiment we receive feedback on differences in posture and confirm the usefulness of sense-of-touch feedback for each area of the vehicle's operation panel. We propose this combination of VR and a physical model as a new design inspection technique through which a designer can share consciousness with an evaluator by conducting a usability evaluation rather than being tied to the concept and practice of a subjective evaluation using a virtual space created by VR.

Keywords: Evaluation of sense of faithfulness · Sense-of-touch feedback · Joint ownership · Usability

1 Introduction

Evaluation techniques using virtual reality (VR) often only offer a visual impression for the evaluation of a proposal, and it is often difficult to perform a usability evaluation based solely upon a VR model. Research on design method using VR has been increasing in recent years. Murakami et al. [1] developed a wearable Augmented Reality (AR) system with haptic feedback as a research on constructing a significant interface in the work environment. They developed the system combining the wearable haptic feedback device and the markerless AR technology and evaluated the system from a different of the operability of virtual objects in the assembly task. As the result, they confirmed the significance on haptic feedback in the task using AR. Moreover, there is research focusing on sharing the consciousness of designers and evaluators in the virtual space.

© Springer International Publishing AG 2017
S. Yamamoto (Ed.): HIMI 2017, Part I, LNCS 10273, pp. 313–321, 2017.
DOI: 10.1007/978-3-319-58521-5_25

"Dollhouse VR" [2] is composed of two viewpoints "space layout interface" and "immersive interface". "Spatial layout interface" allows multiple designers to change the spatial layout of walls, furniture, etc. from the bird's-eye viewpoint by operating with the multi-touch panel. The "immersive feeling interface" allows the user to immerse in the VR space laid out using the head mounted display, and can experience the space layout from the first person viewpoint. With this VR interface, the evaluator can directly recognize the space laid out by the designer. In response to these researches, this research aims to study the usefulness of tactile feedback during design work in virtual space and real space, and to construct a design work environment system utilizing these. Therefore, we construct a simple actual size model and VR together and conduct experiments targeting the operability of the in-car environment.

In an experiment we conduct in this study, we divide the interior environment of car into three areas: armrest/console box, air conditioner operation panel, and navigation monitor and then build a full-scale mockup of the mechanisms. The basic design and feeling of faithfulness to the VR design are then evaluated using a positioning scale as the basis of a design inspection technique that could be used for designing spaces in which the designer can share consciousness with an evaluator regarding the versatility of the bodily sensation evaluation. In addition, we perform a separate experiment for evaluations of the panel using a tactile sensor to inspect the usefulness of sense-of-touch feedback for each area of the operation panel.

2   Spatial Composition

Figure 1 shows the virtual space modeling of the vehicle interior, while Fig. 2 shows the experimental space, which consists of a 1:1 scale model of an air-conditioner operation panel and a dummy seat made from corrugated cardboard (Sect International), the picture presentation on a Thrustmaster T500RS Racing Wheel (THRUSTMASTER), the driving seat using HMD (HTC VIVE) [3–5]. Unity was used for the placement of each part used in the construction of a virtual space modeling a sport utility vehicle for use in an evaluation of space in the vehicle.

Fig. 1. In-car model in virtual space

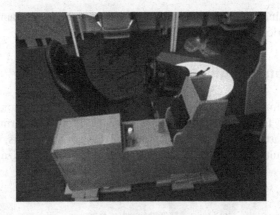

Fig. 2. In-car model in real space

3 Evaluation of Immersion in Interior Space

3.1 Evaluation Measurement Method

For the evaluation of the impression of the virtual space in VR, we adopted seven phases of subjectivity evaluations using the SD method and had you describe a part to feel other sense of incongruity freely.

3.2 Experimental Procedure for Evaluation of Immersion

The experiment participants were five men and women (A - E) in their 20s. We had each participant sit in the driving seat in the true space wearing a head-mounted display and

Fig. 3. Experimental setup

conducted the evaluation in interview form while having the participant operate the air-conditioner operation panel (Fig. 3).

4   Experimental Result of Evaluation of Immersion

About the evaluation of the positioning (Fig. 4) of each part "navigator, some panels of the air-conditioner feel it with a picture toward you." "I feel a real armrest to be in the depths." All the participants gave evaluations in excess of five points, while there was opinion, and a result to be relatively appropriate about a feeling of size was provided.

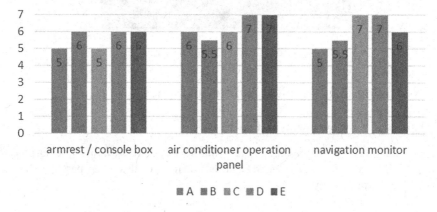

Fig. 4. Evaluation of positioning of each part

Figure 5 shows the evaluation of the size of each part. The virtual space model received a low evaluation in form (so that it is almost median 4 adequately) that we gave a high score for a model of the true space so as to be small so as to be big. It shows below the result. In this place "there is not the swelling of the armrest of the true space." "Some steps of the true space are uncomfortable." The evaluators felt that there was a sense of incongruity with respect to the size of the detail, part received a mean 4 for an armrest and the air-conditioner operation panel part which we made although there was it each, and a result to be almost appropriate about the scale was provided.

We evaluated the feeling of faithfulness of the virtual space as to whether it matched the true space after having evaluated positioning and size (Fig. 6). The scoring average was high, about 5.7, and the experiment participants felt the virtual space accurately reflected the real space—giving evaluations greater than five points.

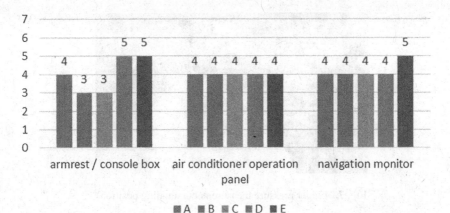

Fig. 5. Evaluation of size of each part

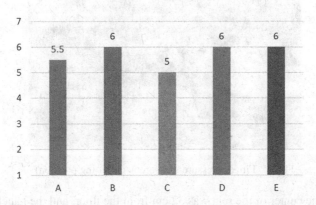

Fig. 6. Evaluation of immersive feeling of the virtual space

5   Preliminary Verification of Button Evaluation by Finger Pressure

The panels to be evaluated were presented in two types: a piano touch type; and a push button type. These panels were positioned on a desk and two kinds of operating methods were used: (1) manipulating in the standing position (Fig. 7); and (2) manipulating in the sitting position (Fig. 8). The sitting position used reflected the position of the seat in the vehicle.

Under these test conditions, the participants operated the two types of buttons to determine whether the inclination and height of the installation exerted an influence on finger pressure. Finger pressure was measured using Haplog (Kato Technical Center Company).

In the standing position evaluation, with the floor surface as a reference, the desk height was 71.5 cm, and the panels were arranged horizontally on top of the desk, and the participants operated the panels in this position. In the sitting position evaluation,

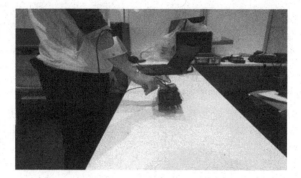

Fig. 7. Finger pressure measurement (standing position)

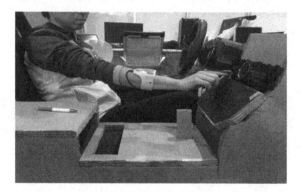

Fig. 8. Finger pressure measurement (sitting position)

the height of the center of the seat was 32 cm from the floor, and the panel was 69 cm from the floor, and the distance between the panels and the seat was about 70 cm. The panel was placed perpendicular to the cardboard model used in Sect. 2. Furthermore, the experiment participants were permitted to move the seat to a comfortable driving.

The participants were asked to make three evaluations for each of the two positions (standing and sitting).

6 Panel Evaluation Based on Required Finger Pressure

The results for the piano touch panel are shown in Figs. 9, 10 and 11, while the results for the push button panel are shown in Figs. 12, 13 and 14.

Although the reference value deviated in the standing position and the sitting position, it was found from the state of the amplitude that the finger pressure applied to the button was larger in the standing position than in the sitting position. In the sitting position, it is thought the buttons were operated using only the muscular strength of the arm and fingers, whereas in the standing position it is considered that bodyweight can be applied to the fingertip when pushing a button.

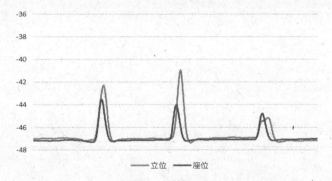

Fig. 9. Result for piano touch panel (participant A)

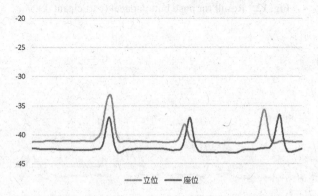

Fig. 10. Result for piano touch panel (participant B)

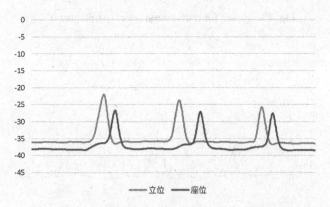

Fig. 11. Result for piano touch panel (participant C)

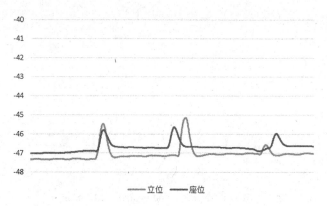

Fig. 12. Result for push button panel (participant A)

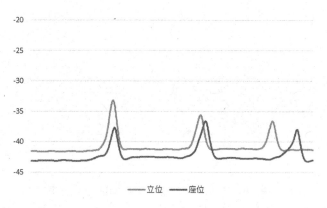

Fig. 13. Result for push button panel (participant B)

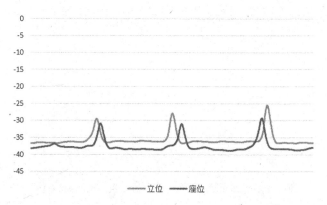

Fig. 14. Result for push button panel (participant C)

7   Conclusion and Future Works

Regarding the evaluation of the sense of immersion, we gained a high score in the evaluations of positioning and size, but the evaluation for the sense of immersion was 5 points. This is thought to be due to the fact that the real object was in a primitive shape and the difference in the texture of visual sense and tactile sense. However, a realistic feeling for placing the same environment in real space as in virtual space was obtained, and its significance could be evaluated in this experiment.

In the preliminary verification of the panel evaluation using the finger pressure measurement, a difference was seen in the finger pressure applied to each button in the standing posture and the sitting posture, so it is necessary to verify the inclination and sinking in further studies.

As a future work, we plan to consider the following items: The test participants' arms will be displayed in virtual space using motion capture; actual buttons will be placed in real space; and an evaluation of the feeling of presence, including the load placed upon the buttons, will be performed.

Our policy is to propose a design verification method that allows the evaluator and the designer to share consciousness.

References

1. Murakami, K., Kiyama, R., Imura, J., Narumi, T., Tanikawa, T., Hirose, M.: Wearable augmented reality system with haptic feedback, IEICE Techinical report, MVE2012-27, vol. 112(106), pp. 119–124 (2012)
2. Ibayashi, H., Sugiura, Y., Sakamoto, D., Miyata, N., Tada, M., Okuma, T., Kurata, T., Mochimaru, M., Igarashi, T.: Dollhouse VR: a multi-view, multi-user collaborative design workspace with VR technology. In: ACM SIGGRAPH ASIA 2015 Emerging Technologies (2015)
3. Automotive Engineering Society: Handbook of Automotive Technology Human Engineering, pp. 235–290 (2016)
4. Automotive Engineering Society: Ergonomics Technology for Automobiles, pp. 29–61 (1998)
5. Macey, S., Wardlle, G.: H Point, pp. 99–109 (2009)

Improve Neighborhood Map Design by Using Kano's Model

Bo Yuan[2], Chuan-yu Zou[1(✉)], and Yongquan Chen[1]

[1] Research Group of Way Guidance, China National Institute of Standardization,
Beijing 100191, China
zouchy@cnis.gov.cn
[2] Department of Visual Communication Academy of Arts and Design, Tsinghua Universiy,
Beijing 100084, China

Abstract. Objective: Based on the result of users' satisfaction survey of the neighborhood map, the classification of neighborhood information was studied.
The 15 information carried by neighborhood maps were extracted from relative stansards. And then Kano questionnaire were made to analysis the attribute of 15 neighborhood information. Methods: 317 volunteers participated in the user satisfaction survey and the Kano questionnaire survey. Results: There were 4 must-be information, 7 one-dimensional information, 1 attractive information and 3 indifferent information. Conclusion: Based on the above discussion, a new national standard (GB/T 20501.4) on neighborhood map design has been developed, and is be issued.

Keywords: Neighborhood map · Sign · Map · Kano model

1 Introduction

Wayfinding refers to the activities and processes of individuals navigating and finding their ways in an environment (Golledge [1]). A neighborhood map is a special kind of maps that navigates individuals in unfamiliar and/or complex outdoor spaces. Many neighborhood maps in use are designed as same as the standard handheld maps, where all places are treated with the same priority and the maps' orientation are always north upward. But the cognitive style of neighborhood maps is different in many ways.

Previous researches on maps mainly focused on the theory of cognitive science, geography, cartography, and graphic/information design (Allen [2]; Casakin et al. [3]; Zipf 2006). However, findings about the usability of information in maps are still little.

This paper studies the information usability of neighborhood maps by using Kano's model to improve the design of neighborhood maps in China and support the relevant national standard development.

2 Background: Neighborhood Maps in Beijing

Neighborhood maps in China, take Beijing as an example, are used to help users finding their locations in the city. In 2015, to collect basic information for the revision of

© Springer International Publishing AG 2017
S. Yamamoto (Ed.): HIMI 2017, Part I, LNCS 10273, pp. 322–330, 2017.
DOI: 10.1007/978-3-319-58521-5_26

GB/T 20501.4—2006 "Guidance system for public information——Design principles and requirements of elements——Part 4: Street guidance map", a field research on neighborhood maps was conducted at Olympic Forest Park (see Fig. 1) and Xueyuan Lu block, Haidian District, Beijing, China.

Fig. 1. Neighborhood map in Olympic Forest Park

Most neighborhood maps are alike, they cover a wide area, present various information and are designed in a colorful way. The advantages of those neighborhood maps are easy to find different kind of information. While the disadvantages are also clear. First, it's difficult to find information of public facilities among colorful surroundings. Second, compared with the covering area, the setting density is too low. In actual environment, users can not catch sight of neighborhood maps when needed (Fig. 2).

Many researchers studied the theory of wayfinding and maps. Casakin et al. [3] studied on spatial aspects of the physical environment, and use prototypical branching points and connecting road types to evaluate the cognitive effects in the schematization of maps. The study of Meilinger et al. [4] is concerned with the empirical investigation of different types of schematised maps. They conclude that providing unambiguous turning information (route knowledge) rather than survey knowledge is most crucial for wayfinding in unknown environments. Meilinger [5] investigated human wayfinding and knowledge acquisition in urban environments. The authors argue that both verbal directions and maps are memorized in a language-based format, which is mainly used

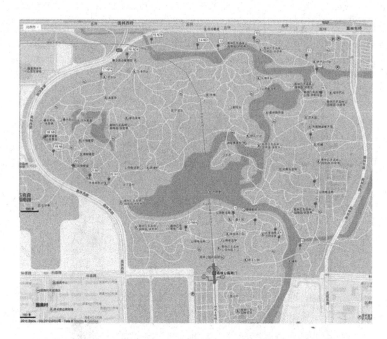

Fig. 2. Setting density of neighborhood maps in Olympic Forest Park

for wayfinding. Kueh [6] tried to apply a systemic approach to study human-map-space interactions that will benefit the design of a wayfinding map. He suggested that external systems such as maps and the actual environment affect an individual's latent and patent actions, while their behaviour affects the way they perceive the external systems. Li [7] combined route- and survey-based strategies in wayfinding and switched from the most familiar knowledge to a less familiar strategy. Previous researches on maps mainly focused on the theory of cognitive science, geography, cartography, and graphic/information design. However, findings about the usability of information in maps are still little.

3   Research Methods: Kano Model and Neighborhood Maps

This paper use the Kano model to find out what kind of information neighborhood maps present. In his model, Kano et al. [8] distinguish five types of product or service quality attributes according to their objective performance and the feeling of users. The five quality attributes are must-be, one-dimensional, attractive, indifferent and reverse attributes.

Since 1984, Kano model is widely used in the management of various fields, e.g. customer need analysis (Xu et al. [9]), commercial bank (Chen and Kuo [10]), stationery industry (Chen, Chang and Huang [11]), the Internet Protocol Television industry (Jan, Lu and Chou [12]), people management (Martensen and Gronholdt [13]), product development (Matzler and Hinterhuber [14]), and international airlines (Shahin and Zairi [15]). But, seldom studies use Kano model in the design of neighborhood maps.

In order to provide qualitative and quantitative suggestions for design neighborhood maps, this paper analyses the common neighborhood map information using Kano model, categories them into different information attributes, and then comes up with improvement design suggestions. It would help to improve the information communication effect of neighborhood maps, raise the efficiency of wayfinding, and create a convenient and comfortable urban environment by using standardized design techniques.

This paper aimed to improve the design of neighborhood maps in Beijing. Firstly, The user satisfaction was surveyed and analyzed by using questionnaires. Secondly, those information that scored highly unsatisfied were picked out. The neighborhood information carried by those neighborhood maps were analyzed and categorized by using Kano's model. Finally, based on the possible improve aspects analyzed and good practices around the world, a new design of neighborhood map was provided. The findings are also included in the standard revision.

3.1 User Satisfaction Survey

Based on the field investigation, this paper conducts user satisfaction survey on neighborhood maps. The primary objective of the survey was to provide national standard(GB/T 20501.4) revision with a means to identify users' concerns on neighborhood maps.

Respondents. This survey conducted from June to September 2015. A total of 319 questionnaires are collected, among which there are 317 valid questionnaires. The ratio of men to women was 59.9:40.1. Regarding the age distribution of the participants, those under the age of 18 was 1.58%, those between 19 and 44 accounted for 67.19%, those between 45 and 59 accounted for 23.66%, while those over the age of 60 accounted for 7.57%. Regarding the education level distribution, those under the education level of senior high school or technical secondary school was 34.07%, those with undergraduate education level was 51.1%, while those over the education level of Master degree was 14.83%.

Questionnaire preparation and analysis. The questionnaire included two parts, respondent self-report part, and Kano test part. In the respondent's self-report part, the following personal data was collected: age, sex, education level and annual income. 1 open question was also included in the test part. The open question collected respondents' ideas about existing problems and improvement suggestions.

The result of the survey was: extremely unsatisfied 9%, unsatisfied 19%, average 54%, satisfied 17%, extremely satisfied 1.0% (Fig. 3).

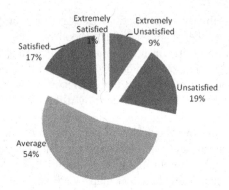

Fig. 3. Result of the survey on neighborhood maps

Above volunteers also participated in the Kano questionnaire survey. According to ISO standard ISO 28564-1:2010 and Chinese national standard GB/T 20501.4—2006, 15 neighborhood information were included in the questionnaire, they were: traffic transportation facilities (subway, overground, railway stations, bus stops), educational institution (primary school, middle school, university), hotels and shops, tourist attractions, public toilets, parking, scale, north indicator, orientation of map, 'You are here' identifier, walking circle, 2D or 3D buildings, legend, index, location in the city. Those information were mainly selected from on-site survey.

The questionnaire was formulated by questions in pair to which volunteers can answer in one of five different ways. By combining the two answers in the Kano evaluation table, the 15 information can be classified. The functional form of the question was to collect volunteers' attitude when one specific information provided in neighborhood maps; while the dysfunctional form of the question was to collect volunteers' attitude when one specific information not provided in neighborhood maps. A sample paired question for 'traffic transportation facilities' was given in Table 1. For the functional form and dysfunctional form of each information, there were 5 × 5 possible answers. And the combination of the questions in the evaluation table produces six different category A, O, M, I, R, Q (see Table 2) (Matzler and Hinterhuber [14]).

Table 1. Functional and dysfunctional questions for 'traffic transportation facilities'

If you can find the information of traffic transportation facilities in a neighborhood map, how do you feel?	• I like it that way • It must be that way • I am neutral • I can live with it that way • I dislike it that way
If you can not find the information of traffic transportation facilities in a neighborhood map, how do you feel?	• I like it that way • It must be that way • I am neutral • I can live with it that way • I dislike it that way

Table 2. Kano evaluation table

Riding information		Dysfunctional form of the question				
		1. I like it that way	2. It must be that way	3. I am neutral	4. I can live with it that way	5. I dislike it that way
Functional form of the question	1. I like it that way	Q	A	A	A	O
	2. It must be that way	R	I	I	I	M
	3. I am neutral	R	I	I	I	M
	4. I can live with it that way	R	I	I	I	M
	5. I dislike it that way	R	R	R	R	Q

4   Result Analysis

The questionnaire is evaluated using the Kano evaluation table in Table 2. Combine two paired answers to the functional and dysfunctional questions in the Table 2. And the attributes of 15 neighborhood information can be gained according to the frequency of answers (see Table 3). Thus, from Table 3, there were 4 must-be information, 7 one-dimensional information, 1 attractive information and 3 indifferent information. Furthermore, SI/DSI were calculated using the formula of Matzler and Hinterhuner (1998). A SI/DSI sensitivity matrix was drawn (see Fig. 4).

Table 3. of results

Information (frequency)	A	O	M	I	R	Q	Category	SI	DSI
1. Traffic transportation facilities	13.6	34.7	30.9	19.9	0.3	0.6	O	0.49	−0.66
2. Educational institution	13.2	23.0	17.7	44.2	1.3	0.6	O	0.37	−0.41
3. Hotels and shops	16.4	25.9	16.1	39.1	1.3	1.3	O	0.43	−0.43
4. Tourist attractions	14.8	27.1	18.0	37.9	0.6	1.6	O	0.43	−0.46
5. Public toilets	7.9	45.1	32.8	12.9	0.6	0.6	O	0.54	−0.79
6. Parking	9.1	27.4	27.8	34.4	0.6	0.6	M	0.37	−0.56
7. Scale	8.8	12.6	13.9	64.7	0.0	0.0	I	0.21	−0.26
8. North indicator	15.5	26.2	23.0	35.3	0.0	0.0	O	0.42	−0.49
9. Orientation of map	17.7	22.1	27.4	27.4	4.1	1.3	M	0.42	−0.52
10. 'You are here' identifier	15.1	30.9	24.9	28.1	0.6	0.3	O	0.46	−0.56
11. Walking circle	0.0	0.0	0.0	58.7	0.0	41.3	I	0.00	0.00
12. 2D or 3D buildings	24.0	14.5	11.7	48.9	0.6	0.3	A	0.39	−0.26
13. Index	16.4	20.8	21.1	40.7	0.0	0.9	M	0.38	−0.42
14. Legend	12.6	19.6	24.0	41.6	1.3	0.9	M	0.33	−0.45
15. Location in the city	15.5	19.6	18.9	44.5	0.9	0.6	I	0.36	−0.39

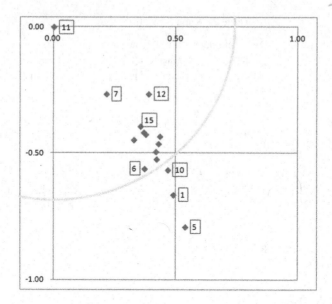

Fig. 4. SI/DSI sensitivity matrix

5 Discussion

The new neighborhood map design (see Fig. 5) provide all information according to its category: '2D or 3D buildings' (A) were used to present landmark buildings.

Fig. 5. Neighborhood map design in national standard

All O category information were provided in outstanding way. M category information were provided according its relevance with wayfinding.

6 Conclusion

If one has investigated and studied comprehensively into the need of wayfinding and the characteristics of neighborhood map, the Kano model can give an accurate judgment on map design: guarantee providing all Must-be information (e.g. Index, Legend, Orientation of map), improve actively the one-dimension information (e.g. North indicator, 'You are here' identifier), outstand those attractive information and SI > 0.5 information, that is, provide those information in outstanding way.

Based on the above discussion, a new national standard (GB/T 20501.4) on neighborhood map design has been developed, and is be issued.

Acknowledgement. This research was supported by China National Institute of Standardization through the "special funds for the basic R&D undertakings by welfare research institutions" (522014Y-3354, 522016Y-4487) and National Quality Infrastructure Program (2016YFF02 01700).

References

1. Golledge, R.G.: Human wayfinding and cognitive maps. In: Golledge, R.G. (ed.) Wayfinding Behavior: Cognitive Mapping and Other Spatial Processes, pp. 5–45. The Johns Hopkins University Press, Baltimore (1999)
2. Allen, G.L., Golledge, R.G.: Spatial abilities, cognitive maps, and wayfinding - bases for individual differences in spatial cognition and behavior. Przem. Chem. **9**, 46–80 (1999)
3. Casakin, H., Barkowsky, T., Klippel, A., et al.: Schematic maps as wayfinding aids. In: Freksa, C., Habel, C., Brauer, W., Wender, K.F. (eds.) Spatial Cognition II, Integrating Abstract Theories, Empirical Studies, Formal Methods, & Practical Applications. LNCS, vol. 1849, pp. 54–71. Springer, Heidelberg (2000)
4. Meilinger, T., Hölscher, C., Büchner, Simon J., Brösamle, M.: How much information do you need? schematic maps in wayfinding and self localisation. In: Barkowsky, T., Knauff, M., Ligozat, G., Montello, Daniel R. (eds.) Spatial Cognition 2006. LNCS, vol. 4387, pp. 381–400. Springer, Heidelberg (2007). doi:10.1007/978-3-540-75666-8_22
5. Meilinger, T., Knauff, M.: Ask for directions or use a map: a field experiment on spatial orientation and wayfinding in an urban environment. Spat. Sci. **53**(2), 13–23 (2008)
6. Kueh, C.K.T.: A sociocybernetic approach to wayfinding map studies: The systems of people-map-space interactions. Kybernetes **36**(9/10), 1406–1421 (2007)
7. Li, R.: Human wayfinding and navigation in a large-scale environment: cognitive map development and wayfinding strategies. Wayfinding Strategies (2007)
8. Kano, N., Seraku, N., Takahashi, F.: Attractive quality and must be quality. J. Japan. Soc. Qual. Control **14**(2), 39–48 (1984)
9. Xu, Q., Jiao, R.J., Yang, X., et al.: An analytical Kano model for customer need analysis. Des. Stud. **30**(1), 87–110 (2009)
10. Chen, L., Kuo, Y.: Understanding e-learning service quality of a commercial bank by using Kano's model. Total Qual. Manage. Bus. Excellence **22**(1), 99–116 (2011)

11. Chen, S., Chang, L., Huang, T.: Applying six-sigma methodology in the Kano quality model: an example of the stationery industry. Total Qual. Manage. Bus. Excellence **20**(2), 153–170 (2009)
12. Jan, P., Lu, H., Chou, T.: Measuring the perception discrepancy of the service quality between provider and customers in the internet protocol television industry. Total Qual. Manage. Bus. Excellence **23**(8), 981–995 (2012)
13. Martensen, A., Gronholdt, L.: Using employee satisfaction measurement to improve people management: an adaptation of Kano's quality types. Total Qual. Manage. **12**(7–8), 949–957 (2001)
14. Matzler, K., Hinterhuber, H.: How to make product development projects more successfulby integrating Kano's model of customer satisfaction into quality function deployment. Technovation **18**(1), 25–38 (1998)
15. Shahin, A., Zairi, M.: Kano model: a dynamic approach for classifying and prioritising requirements of airline travellers with three case studies on international airlines. Total Qual. Manage. Bus. Excellence **20**(9), 1003–1028 (2009)

Knowledge and Service Management

The User-Product Ontology: A New Approach to Define an Ontological Model to Manage Product Searching Based on User Needs

Francesca Gullà[✉], Lorenzo Cavalieri, Silvia Ceccacci, Alessandra Papetti, and Michele Germani

Department of Industrial Engineering and Mathematical Sciences, Università Politecnica delle Marche, Via Brecce Bianche, 12, 60131 Ancona, Italy
{f.gulla,lorenzo.cavalieri,s.ceccacci,a.papetti,
m.germani}@univpm.it

Abstract. Search engines play an important role in determining the success of e-commerce. Despite many efforts have been made to improve searching methods (SM) they remain mostly limited to semantic elaboration of keywords. This implies that the SM are not capable of supporting the research of products that best satisfy customers, according to their characteristics and background. To overcome this limitation, this paper introduces an approach able to define a new ontological model that formalizes the knowledge necessary to implement a search engine capable to guide the customer to search the desired product or service according to his/her characteristics and needs. To this purpose, three essential aspects have been considered: a User Ontology (UO), a Product Ontology (PO) and rules (or properties) to link the user and product ontologies. The described approach is applied, as an example, to the products class known as Smart Objects that are part of the Internet of Things (IoT) market.

Keywords: User Ontology · Product Ontology · Ontologies connection · User-centred design · Internet of Things

1 Introduction

Nowadays, e-commerce is becoming a very important business opportunity, with a high growth potential (i.e., by 2015 goods for a value of about $2,251 will be purchased on e-commerce) [1].

However, the e-commerce success is closely linked to the customer experience related to product purchasing process, starting from the product search. Accordingly, search engines play an important role in this context, as they represent a powerful and simple tool to facilitate the purchase of products and to help consumers to find what they want. Many efforts have been made to improve searching methods and processes based on the linkage of websites with keywords [2], so that search engine have actually reached a good level of efficacy. However, as they operate through the semantic processing of the keywords typed by the user and/or according to specific searching criteria set by user

© Springer International Publishing AG 2017
S. Yamamoto (Ed.): HIMI 2017, Part I, LNCS 10273, pp. 333–346, 2017.
DOI: 10.1007/978-3-319-58521-5_27

(e.g., search filter), they do not allow to find products that fall outside the user's knowledge sphere.

To improve search engine effectiveness, other techniques are used to track the user actions during the browsing with the aim to collect information in order to identify user profile. Among them, the most widespread is known as "profiling cookies". A cookie profiling, also called web profiling [3], is based on the use of persistent or permanent cookies to track the user's overall activity online. Information collected about users' preferences is used to enhance search engine, by proposing other contents (e.g., products, topics, etc.) related to that previously searched. However, the massive use of these techniques may be considered detrimental to privacy and can negatively affect the consumer experience on the web. Moreover, they do not allow the user to find products or services that s/he does not already know or that s/he has not ever searched for. Furthermore, the consumer often has simply a need and does not know which is the product or the service that can satisfy it.

A possible solution for this issue could be the introduction of a search engine able to guide the customer in searching the desired product or service according to his/her characteristics and needs. However, a management strategy of several knowledge domains is needed to achieve this objective.

In particular, three essential aspects should be considered:

(1) Define a User Ontology (UO) able to proper conceptualize the user characteristics and needs;
(2) Define a Product Ontology (PO) by analysing existing products in order to cluster them according to their features, functionalities and application context;
(3) Define link properties able to act as a bridge between the user and product ontologies.

This research work aims to provide a method able to support the achievement of these points. As it is almost impossible to define ontologies which are independent by context, the described method is applied, as an example way, to the products class known as Smart Objects that are part of the Internet of Things (IoT) market.

2   Research Background

The Web has become the most important global means of communication, changing the everyday life of people. However, the high number of Internet users and accessible Web pages makes difficult for users to find documents that are relevant for their needs [4, 5]. Starting from a set of keywords, web search engines help people to find the resources they are looking for [6]. Although they index much of the Web's content, they often fail to select the pages that a user wants or needs. To face this issue, the Semantic Web, which is an extension of the Web that use the standards of the World Wide Web Consortium (W3C), has been developed [7, 8]. It aims to identify the contextual meaning of terms and understand the searcher's intent behind the query to generate accurate and relevant results [9]. Considering its peculiarities, it has been adopted by several e-commerce web sites.

To ensure an efficient search activity, a well-structured knowledge, a consistent and flexible database, and a proper information management are necessary. The goal is to enable a more effective access to knowledge contained in heterogeneous information environments, such as the web.

However, in order to meet the demands of extremely high query volume, search engines tend to avoid the personalization of information access [10]. However, in real life, different users may have different preferences. It generates two important challenges: the identification of the user context and the organization of the information in such a way that matches the particular context.

Since the acquisition of user interests and preferences is an essential element in identifying the user context, it is a new challenge for the user modeling [11, 12]. It consists in the acquisition of the user's information (e.g., goals, needs, moods, preferences, intentions, etc.) by an explicit [13] or implicit [14] process and the interpretation of the user's actions, for a software system [15]. The collection of user information used for the service customization is the profiling process. In general, two are the main problems in the user modeling: firstly, understand what are the most significant user's characteristics that need to be taken into account in a software system; secondly investigate how to acquire the user information through a system [16]. The user modeling process can be described as a sequence of three steps taken during user interaction with the system [17]: (1) collecting data, in this phase the system collects all the information concerning the user; (2) inference, at this stage, the system processes the previously collected data and performs the user's profiling by classifying his interest features, preferences and objectives; (3) adaptation, this step is the actual procedure of the user model aimed to provide personalized experiences. As shown in [18] there are two types of user modeling approaches: behavioral-based and knowledge-based. The knowledge-based approach for modeling considers the level of user's knowledge identified through questionnaires presented to users [19]. The behavioral-based approach instead considers the user's behavior observed during the interaction with the system [18].

One of the first to introduce the concept of user model based on ontology was [20] who presented a generic architecture for Ontology-based User Modeling, called OntobUM. Some of the most common and used ontologies for modeling the user profile known in literature are the following. Gumo is OWL ontology that is based on UserML and allows to describe the important aspects of user dimensions such as objectives, interests, knowledge, preferences, emotional state, personality. Furthermore, it allows to represent information related to the context as the place and time, and even information about the emotional status and device preferences [21]. The FOAF ontology makes it understandable and actionable information to the machines more often present and widespread in the personal social network user such as name, interests, phone number etc., [22]. OPO is an ontology which aims to facilitate exchange and integration of information about the online presence of users in different types of web applications [23]. The CUMO ontology aims to represent the cultural background of a user and to make this information interchanged by different applications [24].

The definition of a user ontology supports the formalization of the knowledge about consumers' behaviors and expectations while they are browsing the web enabling certain kinds of automated reasoning. In the same way, to conceptualize the entities and the relative interrelationships of a specific domain of discourse allows organizing the information of the web in order to simplify the search activity. Focusing on the IoT domain, the large-scale deployments of devices and services, information flow and involved users foster the need of a common architecture, but make this challenge very arduous [25]. The extent of the theme has led to the definition of several ontologies, which have approached the topic from different points of view. They are collected in an online catalogue, Linked Open Vocabularies for Internet of Things (LOV4IoT) [26]. Such a dataset aims to supports the building Semantic Web of Things applications, the extraction of frequent terms used in existing ontologies and the reuse and combination of domain ontologies by different stakeholders [27]. In particular, the SAREF ontology [28] describes the Smart Appliances domain has been created to reduce their energy consumption. It aims to support their management on a system level to ensure interoperability. For this aim, the connection between SAREF and the oneM2 M architecture has been studied to facilitate the communication between the smart appliances and any remote application [29]. Komninos et al. tried to deal with the limited effectiveness of smart city applications and increase their problem-solving potential by proposing an overall ontology for the smart city [30]. To achieve a good expressiveness without increasing the complexity and processing time, Bermudez-Edo et al. created the IoT-Lite ontology that describes the key IoT concepts that allows interoperability and discovery of sensory data in heterogeneous IoT platforms [31].

Analyzing the most relevant ontologies, it emerges the lack of a model that describes the IoT domain from another perspective: the consumers. In particular, all data related to connected devices used in everyday life (e.g., household appliances, smartwatches, activity trackers, health monitoring devices, etc.) should be organized with the final aim to increase the users' awareness about new technologies. Moreover, a link between the user ontologies and the IoT ontologies should be investigated in order to increase the consumers' satisfaction in the search, benchmarking and purchase activity, while browsing the web. The present research work aims to face these challenges.

3   The Proposed Ontological Model

3.1   User Ontology (UO)

User ontology is constructed by using a hybrid perspective. It starts from the representation of the user characteristics through incomplete descriptions of interests and preferences, approach based on stereotypes. For each stereotype, characteristics and objectives are defined. Subsequently following a feature based approach the dynamic aspects linked to preference changes and interest are modelled [32]. By using a top-down approach, the user profile category is defined into the two associated subcategories: user goals and user characteristics.

User characteristics include three user information domains: demographic, technical and health-related (Fig. 1). Such information can be collected by the system during both the registration and search phase.

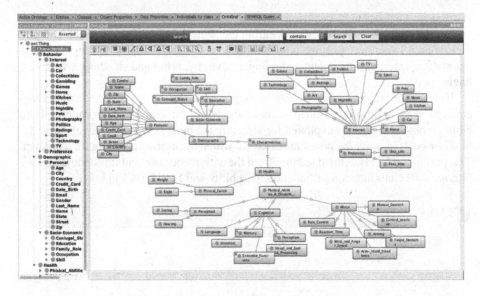

Fig. 1. Protégé view of the user characteristics

Demographic attributes concern the user's personal and socio-economic characteristics. The user's personal information include age, gender, name, address, etc. The socio-economic characteristics include five classes and it is important to determine the level of expertise possessed by the user in performing the activities/tasks that have to be considered as a prerequisite for the use of the product itself (e.g., swimming, using smartphone, etc.). The classes are: (1) education (e.g. master, degree, etc.), (2) occupation (e.g. student, engineer, office worker, etc.), (3) family role (e.g. father, mother, etc.), (4) skill (e.g. cognitive, management, relational, personal effectiveness, etc.) and (5) conjugal status.

The behavioral attributes refer to user's preferences and interest, which are important to determine the user favorites (e.g., "loves cats", "likes blue color" or "dislikes classical music") and user hobby or work-related interests (e.g., "interested in sports", "interested in cooking").

Health related attributes aim to define the spectrum of abilities of the individual, according to his/her health status (e.g., motor abilities, sensorial abilities, etc.). In particular, the health information includes two different classes Physical Factor (e.g. weight, eight, etc.,) and Physical Abilities & Disabilities which is divided into Cognitive, Perceptual and Motor abilities. In particular Cognitive Abilities includes: perception, recognition and interpretation of sensory stimuli (smell, touch, hearing, etc.); attention, ability to sustain concentration on a particular object, action, or thought, and ability to manage competing demands in our environment; memory, short-term/working memory (limited storage), and long-term memory (unlimited storage); language, skills allowing us to translate sounds into words and generate verbal output, visual and spatial processing, ability to process incoming visual stimuli, to understand spatial relationship between objects, and to visualize images and scenarios, executive functions, abilities that enable goal-oriented behavior, such as the ability to plan, and execute a goal. Perceptual Abilities include seeing, hearing etc. Finally, Motor Abilities according to Fleishman's Taxonomy [33] include: control precision, rate control, aiming, response orientation, reaction time, manual and finger dexterity, arm-hand steadiness, wrist and finger speed.

User profile models sourced from bibliography were also considered and derived concepts were appropriately adapted and included in the ontology. Information from bibliographic sources was exploited for selecting the basic set of upper level classes.

User goals identify the possible reason for which the user is searching for a product. This part of the UO is defined starting from the activity domain and it is codified by the International Classification of Function, Disability and Health (ICF) [34] (Fig. 2).

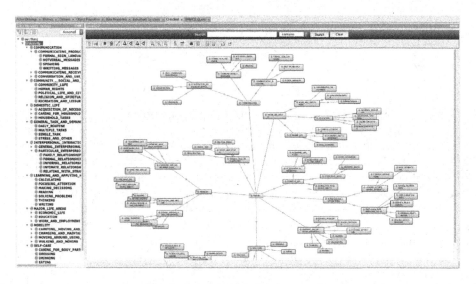

Fig. 2. Protégé view of the user goals

3.2 Product Ontology (PO)

Product Ontology is constructed with a bottom-up approach. In particular, it started with the analysis of the Smart Object (SO) characteristics (i.e., any everyday use object equipped with sensors, memory and communication capabilities [35]).

First of all, the information related to common standard data for various consumer products have been gathered (e.g., producer, price, warranty, certifications, etc.). Subsequently, a depth analysis to identify the specifics of the smart products has been carried out.

In order to accomplish the task for which it was designed, the SO performs one or more functions. They have been classified in the following four groups: actuating (i.e., ability to transmit data to actuators to control a system remotely); event (i.e., ability to manage a particular scenario as, for example, by notifying another device that a certain threshold value has been exceeded); meter (i.e., ability to monitor the value of a specific attribute by getting data from a meter) and sensing (i.e., ability to detect a specific event). In relation to these functions the parameters that can be controlled (i.e., status parameters such as on, off, open, close, etc.), measured (e.g., activity parameters such as steps, speed, sleep time, etc.; ambient parameters such as temperature, humidity, air quality, etc.; health parameters such as heart rate, blood pressure, SPO2, etc.) and detected (e.g., fall, gas leakage, intrusion, etc.) has been identified and classified.

According to its nature, each SO is able to communicate with other devices or SOs, enabling a set of specific functions. For this aim, the communication protocols (both wired and wireless), the compatible devices (smartphone, tablet, laptop, and desktop), the compatible Operating System (e.g., android, iOS, windows phone, etc.) and the applications have been mapped.

In addition to the main function, the SO can offer a set of more general functionalities grouped in eleven classes. They refer to the geolocation (e.g., GPS); the user management (e.g., multi-user, automatic user recognition, etc.); time and date (e.g., time of day, calendar, etc.); settings (e.g., wizard, customized thresholds, personalized scenarios, etc.); data management (e.g., export, share, etc.); the interaction with compatible devices (e.g., answer to phone call, read a message, play music, etc.); the interaction mode with user (e.g., gesture, touch, voice over, etc.); the power management (e.g., battery status indicator, power saving mode, etc.); the user training in relation to the main function of the object (e.g., goals to reach, rewards, personal assistant, etc.), notifications (e.g., alerts, alarm, message received, incoming call; etc.) and add-on (e.g., holter, plug and play, night mode, etc.). Different channels (e.g., audio, video, haptic) can be exploited by the SO to communicate information or give feedbacks to the user. For this aim, the class related to the interaction mode has been created.

Another important aspect concerns the technical specifications, which distinguish each SO: they include operating conditions (e.g., temperature range), languages, power requirements (e.g., source, autonomy, charge time, etc.), physical characteristics (e.g., dimensions, colour, material, etc.), the box content, the data management for-mats and warnings. Moreover, all the characteristics of the main components are considered such as the display resolution, the memory capacity, CPU frequency, sensors (e.g., accelerometer, gyroscope, altimeter, etc.), etc. Also the specifications related to the measured parameters are taken into account: accuracy, range, resolution, unit, etc.

The class of unit of measure collects the standard for measurement of a quantity that can be related both to parameters and specifications. Furthermore, through the use of clustering algorithms, SOs have been classified for categories and sub-categories (i.e., health, sport, home, etc.) to define their domain of action.

Finally, a set of services has been identified according to the main function of existing SOs in order to simply the matching with the users' needs. The main goals for which these products are designed refer to the possibility to control, improve, monitor, save or manage some aspects of people daily life in several contexts (e.g., office, home, outdoor, etc.).

In Fig. 3, a partial representation of Product Ontology is shown. Some classes had not been expanded for not affecting the readability.

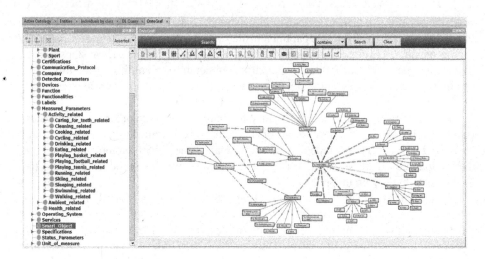

Fig. 3. Protégé view of product ontology

3.3 Definition of Rules to Enable Ontologies Connection

Once identified the User and Product Ontology, the identification of possible connections between UO and PO, that allows to define the relations between user profiles and products, has been defined.

In order to ensure that subcategories defined in UO link with the subcategories defined in PO, the definition of subcategories related to User Goals must be performed with a bottom-up approach, so that the specification of user goals is carried out basing on functions/services offered by the products.

The resulting User-Product Ontology allows to identify the knowledge domain necessary to identify correlations between User profile and available products.

To define the proper links between UO and PO several rules have been identified. Basically, the UO domains named User Goals (UG) and User Characteristics (UC) have been connected with three PO domains: the Product Service (PS), the Product Categories (PC) and the Product Specification (PSp) domains. In particular, the UG domain has been linked with PS and PC domains, while the UC domain has been linked with PF and PSp domains.

The linkage between various domains has been detected by using a two-step method. Firstly, a knowledge base has been identified by considering the evident logical correlations that exist "a priori" between the two ontologies. Then, to discover other not evident relationships and to assess the strength and utility of predictive relationships, proper training sets and test sets have been carried out. In this way, the knowledge base has been refined and enriched (Fig. 4).

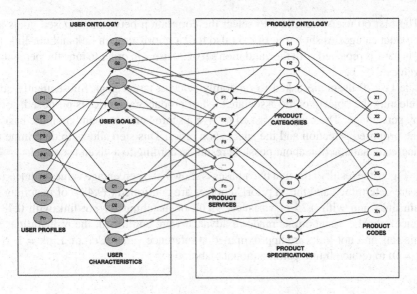

Fig. 4. The proposed ontological model

3.4   Example of Rules Defined to Connect the Two Ontologies

To define a-priori relationships, possible links between the considered domains are analysed, through the construction of four relationship matrices to correlate the four pairs of domains [i.e., UG-PS, UG-PC, UC-PS, UC-PSp]. In particular, the logical linkages that certainly exist (or do not) are defined and consequently a shortlist of uncertainly correlations is identified. Figure 5 shows part of the relationships defined in this way between the UG and the PC domains.

For example, the goal "Maintaining one's health" is linked "a priori" all health subcategories, while the goal "Ensuring one's physical comfort" is not linked "a priori" with any product category. At this point, a learning procedure has been performed to predict relationships in those uncertain cases, and to confirm the a-priori assumptions. A sample of 100 users (average age 34 years, 40% female, familiar with technology) has been involved to identify the probability associated to uncertain links. The sample size has been chosen according to literature [36] to guarantee a low degree of variance.

In particular, the sample is distributed as follow:

- A training set of 60 users to define the weight of linkages;
- A validation set of 20 users to tune the parameters and improve performance;
- A test set of 20 users to assess the performance of the presented linkage system, according to [37].

Once collected the data related to their characteristics (e.g., gender, age, etc.) and identified possible goals, according to the User Ontology architecture, the experimental protocol has been carried out as follows:

1. The first 60 users are asked to select the correlation between proposed goals and product categories shown in Fig. 5 (also for "a priori" certain link and not-link);
2. The task is repeated with the validation set of 20 users in order to tune the percentage values;
3. The last 20 users are asked to randomly select a target goal. Subsequently, after selecting the objective, the associated list of product categories is proposed, sorted by percentage. The users are asked to give a score between 1 and 5 on the basis of the proposed selection and the succession order. This step allows to determine the degree of satisfaction about possible results according to a given user goal.

In Fig. 6, the result of the first two phases is shown: the percentage values of uncertain links are determined and the "a priori" choices are confirmed (99,48% of matching for certain links and with 0,25 of variance, 99,67 of matching for not link with 0,78 of variance). As the assumptions made in advance were confirmed, the probabilities for certain link and not-links are approximated at reference value (Certain Link = 1, Not-Link = 0) to reduce future computational elaborations.

Not Link   ○ Uncertain Link   ● Link

Fig. 5. Example of relationship identified "a priori" between UG and PC domains.

USER GOALS	SPORT	Basket	Tennis	Skiing	Football	Cycling	Running	Swimming	HEALT	Blood Pressure Monitor	ECG	Fall Detector	Glucometer	Pill Reminder	Posture Monitor	Pulse Oximeter	Body Scale	Breathalyzer	Spirometer	Thermometer	Vital Signs Monitor	DAILY LH	Earphones	Smartwatch	Activity Tracker	Sleep Monitor
MOBILITY — Walking and moving (d4450-d469) — d 459 Walking — d 4500 Walking short distances	•						•		81%	64%	43%				69%	74%		53%		86%	•	79%	•	•		
d 4501 Walking long distances	•						•		89%	60%	49%				63%	79%		63%		84%	•	94%	•	•		
d 4502 Walking on different surfaces	•						•		58%	48%	49%				73%	76%		68%		93%	•	90%	•	•		
d 4503 Walking around obstacles	•						•		49%	49%	46%				64%	53%		61%		86%	•	88%	•	•		
d 455 Moving around — d 4550 Crawling	•								46%		30%				78%	43%		40%		55%	•	16%	•	•		
d 4551 Climbing	•								60%		53%				81%	83%		74%		84%		65%	•	•		
d 4552 Running	•	80%	71%		85%	•	•		•		69%				68%	84%		58%			•	•	95%	•	•	
d 4553 Jumping	•	•		78%		•	•		•		56%				71%	66%		44%			•	•	43%	•	•	
d 4554 Swimming	•						•	•	•		54%										•	•				
SELF CARE — d 550 Eating							•			73%	69%	•				•					•	•	68%	78%		
d 560 Drinking							•			41%	48%					•	•				•	•	56%	80%		
d 570 Looking after one's health — d 5700 Ensuring one's physical comfort	79%	69%	55%	40%	85%	41%	91%	36%	95%	89%	68%	43%	46%	33%	51%	40%	96%	28%	16%	98%	83%	98%	81%	96%	56%	
d 5701 Managing diet and fitness	93%	44%	50%	51%	69%	80%	93%	76%	•	75%	•		•	•		•	•	•	•	•	•	•	•	•		
d 5702 Maintaining one's health	•	69%	40%	31%	85%	36%	90%	35%	•	•	•	•	•	•	•	•	•	•	•	•	•	•	•	•		

☐ Not Link   ○ Uncertain Link   ● Link

Fig. 6. Example of relationship identified by training set between UG and PC domains

The last phase provided data shown in Fig. 7. The evaluation data are normalized to max score (5) to show up percentage values. In order to guarantee a high degree of accuracy a selective threshold is set to 80%: as the chart shows, twelve goals exceed it,

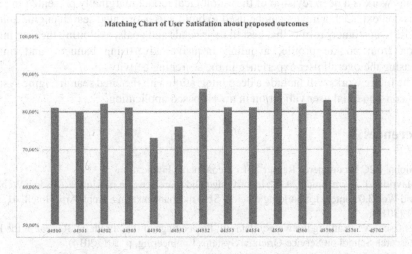

Fig. 7. Satisfaction of test users about result proposed according a given goal.

while two goals are critical. Crawling and Climbing fail to meet the requirements (respectively with 73% and 76%). Perhaps, such failure is particularly due to the activity that the goal includes: being uncommon activity they could lead to very different perceptions among similar users.

On the other hand, the goals that present the highest rate are in the field of Self Care (Managing diet and fitness with 87% and Maintaining one's health with 90%): these finding allows confirming the previous statement about the user perceptions about common and uncommon action domains.

4   Conclusion and Future Works

In this paper, an approach able to define a new ontological model in order to merge the knowledge of user and product domains is proposed. After a deep analysis of existing ontology models of these two domains, an overall model to connect user characteristics and goals and product features is developed. About the user model, a structured ontology is defined according to the major reference models available in literature. On the other hand, as a lack of a user-oriented product ontology was detected, a custom model is developed taking a cue from existing domain ontologies.

To test the goodness of this approach, an experimental evaluation is carried out with 100 users, splitting them in a training and validation set (80) and a test set (20). The evaluation shows two mean outcomes:

- The "a priori" assumptions are confirmed in the training step;
- The "weights" derived from the training session have shown a good accuracy, except for two critical goals.

The results show the need to improve the training phase in order to tune the weight parameters, resolve the observed issues and create a knowledge model able to keep a high degree of accuracy and reliability.

This work is a deep revision of the ontological model marginally presented in [38]: in this context, such a model can be used to build a user-oriented search engine able to propose to customers results that best fit their needs and goals, exploiting the user information from cookie profile, avoiding intrusive advertising banners, and finally increasing the overall user experience in the searching activity.

The future works will include a deep integration with the cited search engine system and a consequential user validation in a web-based application.

References

1. Global B2C E-commerce Report 2015, Ecommerce Foundation
2. Mavridis, T., Symeonidis, A.L.: Identifying valid search engine ranking factors in a Web 2.0 and Web 3.0 context for building efficient SEO mechanisms. Eng. Appl. Artif. Intell. **41**, 75–91 (2015)
3. Jentzsch, A.: Profiling the web of data. In: Proceedings of the 8th Ph. D. Retreat of the HPI Research School on Service-Oriented Systems Engineering, p. 101 (2014)

4. Jansen, B.J., Booth, D.L., Spink, A.: Determining the user intent of web search engine queries. In: Proceedings of the 16th International Conference on World Wide Web, pp. 1149–1150. ACM (2007)

5. Gauch, S., Chaffee, J., Pretschner, A.: Ontology-based personalized search and browsing. Web Intell. Agent Syst. Int. J. 1(3–4), 219–234 (2003)

6. Schwartz, C.: Web search engines. J. Am. Soc. Inf. Sci. 49(11), 973 (1998). (1986-1998)

7. Berners-Lee, T., Hendler, J., Lassila, O.: The semantic web. Sci. Am. 284(5), 28–37 (2001)

8. XML and Semantic Web W3C Standards Timeline (2012)

9. John, T.: What is Semantic Search?. Techulator Retrieved July 13 (2012)

10. Lawrence, S.: Context in web search. IEEE Data Eng. Bull. 23(3), 25–32 (2000)

11. Sieg, A., Mobasher, B., Burke, R.D.: Learning ontology-based user profiles: a semantic approach to personalized web search. IEEE Intell. Inf. Bull. 8(1), 7–18 (2007)

12. Razmerita, L., Lytras, Miltiadis D.: Ontology-based user modelling personalization: analyzing the requirements of a semantic learning portal. In: Lytras, Miltiadis D., Carroll, John M., Damiani, E., Tennyson, Robert D. (eds.) WSKS 2008. LNCS, vol. 5288, pp. 354–363. Springer, Heidelberg (2008). doi:10.1007/978-3-540-87781-3_39

13. Pannu, M., Anane, R., Odetayo, M., James, A.: Explicit user profiles in web search personalisation. In: 2011 15th International Conference on IEEE Computer Supported Cooperative Work in Design (CSCWD), pp. 416–421 (2011)

14. Shen, X., Tan, B., Zhai, C.: Implicit user modeling for personalized search. In: Proceedings of the 14th ACM International Conference on Information and Knowledge Management, pp. 824–831. ACM (2005)

15. Sosnovsky, S., Dicheva, D.: Ontological technologies for user modelling. Int. J. Metadata Semant. Ontol. 5(1), 32–71 (2010)

16. Rich, E.: User modeling via stereotypes. Cogn. Sci. 3(4), 329–354 (1979)

17. Brusilovsky, P.: Methods and techniques of adaptive hypermedia. User Model. User-Adap. Inter. 6(2–3), 87–129 (1996)

18. Scime, A. (ed.): Web Mining: applications and techniques. IGI Global (2005)

19. Kobsa, A.: User modeling in dialog systems: Potentials and hazards. AI Soc. 4(3), 214–231 (1990)

20. Razmerita, L.: User model and user modeling in knowledge management systems: an ontology-based approach. Paul Sabatier University, Toulouse (2003)

21. Heckmann, D., Schwartz, T., Brandherm, B., Schmitz, M., Wilamowitz-Moellendorff, M.: Gumo – the general user model ontology. In: Ardissono, L., Brna, P., Mitrovic, A. (eds.) UM 2005. LNCS, vol. 3538, pp. 428–432. Springer, Heidelberg (2005). doi:10.1007/11527886_58

22. Grzonkowski, S., Gzella, A., Kruk, S.R., Breslin, J.G., Woroniecki, T., Dobrzanski, J.: Sharing information across community portals wit FOAFRealm. Int. J. Web Based Communities 5(3), 351–370 (2009)

23. Stankovic, M.: (2010). http://online-presence.net/ontology.php

24. Reinecke, K., Reif, G., Bernstein, A.: Cultural user modeling with CUMO: an approach to overcome the personalization bootstrapping problem. In: Proceedings First International Workshop on Cultural Heritage on the Semantic Web at the 6th ISWC, pp. 83–90 (2007)

25. Hachem, S., Teixeira, T., Issarny, V.: Ontologies for the Internet of Things. In: ACM/IFIP/USENIX 12th International Middleware Conference. Springer (2011)

26. http://sensormeasurement.appspot.com/?p=ontologies#iot

27. Gyrard, A., Atemezing, G., Bonnet, C., Boudaoud, K., Serrano, M.: Reusing and unifying background knowledge for internet of things with LOV4IoT. In: 4th International Conference on Future Internet of Things and Cloud (FiCloud 2016) (2016)

28. http://ontology.tno.nl/saref/

29. ETSI: TS 103 264 - V1.1.1 - SmartM2 M; Smart Appliances; Reference Ontology and oneM2 M Mapping (2015)
30. Komninos, N., Bratsas, C., Kakderi, C., Tsarchopoulos, P.: Smart city ontologies: improving the effectiveness of smart city applications. J. Smart Cities 1, 31–46 (2015). doi:10.18063/JSC.2015.01.001
31. Bermudez-Edo, M., Elsaleh, T., Barnaghi, P., Taylor, K.: IoT-Lite: a lightweight semantic model for the internet of things. In: IEEE Conferences on Ubiquitous Intelligence & Computing (2016). doi:10.1109/UIC-ATC-ScalCom-CBDCom-IoP-SmartWorld.2016.0035
32. Brusilovsky, P., Millán, E.: User models for adaptive hypermedia and adaptive educational systems. In: Brusilovsky, P., Kobsa, A., Nejdl, W. (eds.) The Adaptive Web. LNCS, vol. 4321, pp. 3–53. Springer, Heidelberg (2007). doi:10.1007/978-3-540-72079-9_1
33. Fleishman, E.A., et al.: Taxonomic efforts in the description of leader behavior: a synthesis and functional interpretation. Leadersh. Quart. 2(4), 245–287 (1991)
34. WHO: International classification of functioning, disability and health., Geneva, Switzerland: World Health Organization (WHO) (2001)
35. Papetti, A., Iualé, M., Ceccacci, S., Bevilacqua, R., Germani, M., Mengoni, M.: Smart objects: an evaluation of the present state based on user needs. In: Streitz, N., Markopoulos, P. (eds.) DAPI 2014. LNCS, vol. 8530, pp. 359–368. Springer, Cham (2014). doi: 10.1007/978-3-319-07788-8_34
36. Kalayeh, H.M., Landgrebe, D.A.: Predicting the required number of training samples. In: IEEE Transactions on Pattern Analysis and Machine Intelligence, vol. PAMI-5, no. 6, pp. 664–667, November 1983
37. Ehsani, N., Fekete, B.M., Vörösmarty, C.J., Tessler, Z.D.: A neural network based general reservoir operation scheme. Stoch. Environ. Res. Risk Assess. 30(4), 1151–1166 (2016)
38. Cavalieri, L., Capitanelli, A., Ceccacci, S., Gullà, F., Papetti, A., Germani, M.: A new smart strategy for web searching of commercial products. In: ASME 2016 International Design Engineering Technical Conferences and Computers and Information in Engineering Conference. American Society of Mechanical Engineers (2016)

Understanding Parental Management of Information Regarding Their Children

Theresa Matthews[✉] and Jinjuan Heidi Feng[✉]

Department of Computer and Information Sciences, Towson University,
Towson, MD 21252, USA
tscott2@students.towson.edu, jfeng@towson.edu

Abstract. Parents and caregivers need to process large volumes of information regarding their children's education. Effective parental management of this information is critical for parents to actively participate in their child's educational development. However, existing educational information management tools are designed from the perspective of the educator or student, not the parent. The objectives of this research were to identify how parents currently manage their children's educational information and identify areas where challenges are perceived and/or realized for parents managing information regarding their children's education. Two surveys were designed and conducted to gather the data. The first survey was conducted to understand the types of information parents receive regarding their children, ascertain a high-level view of what is done with the data and if there were any perceived difficulties in managing any particular type of data. Based on the results of the first survey, another survey was conducted that focused primarily on parental management of their children's educational information. The results confirm that parents must manage a large volume of information regarding their children. The majority of issues related to this information management are associated with educational and medical information. Regarding educational information management, web-based software applications used by school districts allow parents to keep track of their students' academic progress for the school year, but do not effectively allow parents to compare progress across years, integrate educational information from other sources or organize information in ways that may better meet the needs of the parent. For these reasons parents find themselves interfacing with numerous data sources or tools to maintain a current understanding of their children's academic progress. Few tools are available and/or used by parents to manage the data. The results support the fact that parents need technological solutions to improve their management and use of educational information regarding their children.

Keywords: Parents · Education · Personal Information Management · PIM · Information organization · Questionnaire based survey

1 Introduction

The involvement of parents has been widely discussed as a major contributing factor in the development of children. Research evidence shows children whose parents are

© Springer International Publishing AG 2017
S. Yamamoto (Ed.): HIMI 2017, Part I, LNCS 10273, pp. 347–365, 2017.
DOI: 10.1007/978-3-319-58521-5_28

involved in their learning perform better in school, both academically and behaviorally (Patrikakou 2008). In Carpe Data, Van Kleek, et al. suggested that a "common goal for the release of [open data made available by the government] has been to provide end users with the ability to make more informed decisions pertaining to their health, wealth, and well-being" (Van Kleek et al. 2013). The motivation to provide information to parents regarding their children is similar. Because the importance of parent involvement in their children's development is recognized, parents are often overloaded with their children's medical, educational, social, extracurricular and financial information. The idea is that parents will use the provided information to make informed decisions regarding the health, education, finances, etc. of their children.

People can be overwhelmed by available information due to jargon, volume and other factors. This can degrade the quality of their decision making (Pratt et al. 2006). For this reason, it is not unusual for people to turn to technology for help with managing data. However, technical solutions to assist parents in the management of information regarding their children seem to be lacking. Existing educational information management tools are designed from the perspective of the educator or student, not the parent. Getting a better understanding of how parents receive and share information regarding their children as well as the purposes for which parents use the information can lead to the development of technology to assist them. This can lead to improved parental monitoring of the progress of their children, the ability for parents to more easily identify trends and anomalies in their children's development and improved effectiveness of communications with providers and educators. In the short term, a better understanding of the information usage patterns of parents may lead to the development of more structured experiments and research studies.

The objectives of this research were to identify how parents currently manage their children's educational information and identify areas where challenges are perceived and/or realized for parents managing information regarding their children's education. Literature review and online surveys were conducted to gather the data. The first survey was conducted to understand the types of information parents receive regarding their children, ascertain a high-level view of what is done with the data and if there were any perceived difficulties in managing any particular type of data. Based on the results of the first survey, another survey was conducted that focused primarily on parental management of their children's educational information.

2   Related Literature

Areas reviewed included Personal Information Management (PIM), data integration and existing applications and tools relevant to educational information. The topics of the reviewed literature can be categorized as PIM and data integration; parents accessing educational resources and student use of technology for organization and learning; and information management by teachers and administrators. The management of personal information, whether that of one's self or one's child, shares the same basic requirements. For this reason, literature pertaining to PIM was reviewed. The management of personal information, whether that of one's self or one's child, shares the same basic requirements. As described by Buttfield-Addison et al., PIM is concerned with the study of the process of information capture, organization and re-finding of information individuals deal with in daily life (Buttfield-Addison et al. 2012). Although tools and apps exist to facilitate communication between parents and teachers, no tools for parental management of information regarding their children's education were identified in this research. For this reason, tools used by teachers and other educators were reviewed with the motive that these could be used to model a solution for parents.

Common concepts resonated throughout the literature regarding the characteristics of personal information and basic requirements for PIM tools. Those concepts that are of particular interest are listed below.

- Personal information collections include content in various forms (documents, Web pages, mail, notes, calendars, address books, etc.) (Bruce et al. 2004)
- Personal information collections include structures for representing and organizing this information (folder hierarchies, piles, lists, etc.) (Bruce et al. 2004)
- Personal information collections include pointers to information (people, links, Favorites, etc.) (Bruce et al. 2004)
- Information management systems must seamlessly integrate and correlate information across a variety of media, sources and formats (Callan et al. 2007).
- PIMs ensure having the right information in the right place in the right format and of sufficient completeness and quality to meet a current need (Ma et al. 2007).

The method(s) by which information management tools should meet those functions were not so consistent. Some argued that the development of tools alone could not achieve the desired level of information management functionality, but the key is in standardization. Jones and Anderson proposed standardizing metadata using Extensible Markup Language (XML) (Jones and Anderson 2011, 2012). Karger and Jones discussed five approaches of data unification to meet the information management goal. The approaches are implementing a standard data type, unified presentation, implementing a unified namespace, grouping, metadata standardization, cross-reference and relations. These tie in with Jones and Anderson's recommendation regarding cross-reference and relations as means to support information management (Karger and Jones 2006).

Still other researchers proposed the use of digital libraries. Per Ma et al., digital libraries either have relatively stable collections or rigorous routines for adding new documents. The researchers proposed that personal digital libraries must handle changing collection and that storage locations may not be constant. Another difference between traditional digital libraries and personal digital libraries as described by Ma et al. is that traditional digital libraries have control over the data formats it contains, however there can be no limitation on the formats in personal repositories because in most cases the user does not have control over the formats in which data is provided (Ma et al. 2007). Tagging was also presented as an approach for information management (Kazai et al. 2010). Tagging and metadata standardization are similar, however many of the researchers who proposed tagging did not go as far to recommend standardizing the metadata using XML.

Pratt et al.'s research regarding personal health information management uncovered challenges related to integrating personal, professional and health-related information, using integrated information to make health decisions and sharing information while maintaining personal privacy (Pratt et al. 2006). These challenges are also applicable to parental management of information regarding their children. Parents have access to personal information, like family history and professional information given to them by providers, educators, etc. As mentioned previously, the desire is for parents to use the information they receive to make decisions regarding their children.

Another aspect of PIM is understanding the reasons why people choose to keep information and the methods by which people deem information useful. Oh and Belkin's research presents the forms of information people keep and their reasons for keeping it. Oh and Belkin found that some reasons for keeping personal information were to re-use the information in the future, as a reminder of tasks that need to be performed, to record or create personal archives and to share with others. Depending on the reason the data was kept, people kept the information in paper form, as an electronic file, email, bookmark (for web information) or photographs, either digital or printed (Oh and Belkin 2011). An excerpt from one of the tables from Oh and Belkin's paper is presented in Table 1.

Table 1. Reasons for keeping different forms of information (Oh and Belkin 2011)

	Paper	Electronic file	Email
To re-find/re-access information	•	•	•
To record memories/to create archive	•		•
To remind tasks	•	•	•
To share with others/to show to others	•		
To express and reinforce identities	•		
To preserve the original format	•		
To allay fears of loss		•	
To manage tasks/time/info/contacts/schedules			•
To make backups			•

Jones, Dumais and Bruce presented research that showed how users made decisions on what information to keep and what information to leave in place with respect to online data in particular. They provided insight into how users make their keeping and leaving decisions where "keeping" involves downloading or saving the information and "leaving" involves creating or saving a link to find the data in place at another time. The researchers were surprised to find that even when users used bookmarks or favorites, they were still more likely to use a search engine to find the information again instead of referring to the saved link (Jones et al. 2002).

As parents acquire information regarding the education of their children via different means, the ability to integrate data is critical to their management of such information. PIM can be accomplished through technical and non-technical means as discussed by Trullemans and Signer (2014). Their study looked at organization and re-finding strategies in physical and digital space. The study did not find any correlations or dependencies between respondents' digital organization and retrieval method and their physical organizational and retrieval methods. The lack of correlation between methods that work well in digital space versus physical space may have contributed to the transitional issues and should be considered. Other sources describe the challenges teachers and administrators face when attempting to transition from paper-based to technology-based solutions to manage information (Bishop 2002; Marcu et al. 2013; Piper et al. 2013; Turner 2010). Marcu et al.'s paper Why Do They Still Use Paper? Understanding Data Collection and Use in Autism Education summarizes a study on why many autism education programs still use paper to collect student data vice a technical solution. Reasons for why staff members use paper to collect data are data needs are complex and non-standard, immediate demands of the job make data collection challenging and existing technology is inadequate (Marcu et al. 2013).

As previously stated, the motivation for schools to provide additional information with increased frequency to parents is similar. Information is given under the assumption that it provides parents with the ability to make more informed decisions pertaining to the education of their children. Many schools have on online tools that parents can use to access their children's educational information.

The majority of the resources found discuss educational related information management needs of parents related to children with learning disabilities. However, many of the recommendations are applicable to children who do not require learning assistance. The educational information parents should manage as recommended by the Wrights and Crabtree includes provider information, Individualized Educational Programs (IEP), evaluations by the school system, medical records, progress reports and report cards, standardized test results, notes on your child's behavior or progress, correspondence with teachers, special education administrators and evaluators, documents relating to discipline and/or behavioral concerns and samples of schoolwork (Crabtree 1998; Patrikakou 2008). The Wrights also recommended documenting the following information about each file/record maintained: date, author, type and significance (Wright and Wright 2008). In a software tool this information may be recorded as metadata.

As identified by Van Kleek et al. as an issue, the wealth of available information cannot be used as intended to influence decisions or actions if the data cannot be accessed, organized, processed and re-accessed in ways that are meaningful to the user. Data integration is challenging because it involves combining data and/or "data systems that were developed for slightly (or vastly) different [...] needs (Van Kleek et al. 2013)." Regarding their children's education, parents must manage information from a variety of sources including, but not limited to, teachers, administrators, counselors, advocates and tutors. Each of these may have a different method for conveying the information to parents. Those methods may or may not align with each other or with the parent's preferred method(s) for receiving educational information about their children.

Prince George's (PG) County school system uses the electronic student information system, SchoolMAX. SchoolMAX allows authorized caretakers to log in from any computer with an Internet connection and view the child's student information, including current attendance records and assignment scores. PG's version of SchoolMAX allows parents or guardians to view a child's educational records for as long as they are a part of the PG County school system. Parents are able to look back at previous school years, view grades, tardiness, progress reports and report cards. ParentCONNECTxp is the electronic student information system used by Anne Arundel (AA) County Public schools. ParentCONNECTxp has pages for student information, assignments, report card grades, attendance and school information. Like SchoolMAX, it also allows parents to view information regarding each child enrolled in the school system using a single login. Teachers are usually required to update the information on the sites weekly, at a minimum. Reviewing information regarding their children's education via the school sites affords parents more insight into their children's academic progress than what they can glean from report cards and progress reports alone. This more frequent access to information could enable parents to influence change in derogatory behavior or address learning challenges and see the results of their involvement sooner. Unfortunately, as documented by Roshan et al., information that is updated or entered too frequently may not be reviewed by parents because they may be overwhelmed by the volume of available information or they simply do not have time to access the information in accordance with the frequency with which it is provided (Roshan et al. 2014).

According to Piper et al., in some educational communities there has been a shift "from measuring development through standardized tests to conducting observational reports that track development" (Piper et al. 2013). A similar style of reporting, or structuring of data, may be useful in helping parents not only manage information regarding their children's education, but also track development. Those reports are underpinned by documentation that may include "samples of a child's work at several different stages of completion: photographs showing work in progress; comments written by the teacher or other adults working with the children; transcriptions of children's discussions, comments, and explanations of intentions about the activity; and comments made by parents" (Piper et al. 2013). This information is documented in a portfolio. To build the portfolios teachers gather three types of information: written observations, photos and work samples. These types of information that are collected align with the types of information Ms. Dennis, one of the subject matter experts interviewed, recommends that parents retain regarding their children's education.

An information management app or website designed to assist parents in managing information of their children was not identified in the searches performed for this review. Therefore, it is believed that there is still an opportunity to make a contribution to the creation of such an app or website. The majority of the websites and/or tools found via tool reviews and Google searches can be categorized as one of the following:

- web-based software application used by school districts that allows parents to keep track of their students' academic progress
- web-based school management systems
- learning community management systems that schools use for school and class organization
- apps for teachers to send announcements and other notifications to parents
- apps to organize a group, of volunteers for example, or a particular purpose or event
- apps to manage to-do or checklists

Only one tool found, MyIEPmeeting, was specifically designed to assist parents in organizing and gathering information related to the education of their children. As the name implies, the tool was designed to help parents participate in the child's Individualized Education Program (IEP) process by documenting and organizing relevant information between IEP meetings in a way that it can be easily accessed during the meeting or reported to teachers and administrators. The tool allows parents to type notes, record audio and takes pictures. From the overview it could not be determined if the app ingests data from the school information management system (IMS) or sources other than manual data entry (Excent 2014; Swanson 2012).

Table 2 lists the tools identified by category. School information management and/or learning community management systems are listed in the "standard educational information management system (IMS)" category.

Table 2. Education information management tools/applications

Standard educational information management system	Google for Education (Teach.com 2015), Edmodo (Ponsford 2015; Teach.com 2015), SchoolMAX, Edline, Pupil Asset (Ponsford 2015)
Teachers publishing to parents	Buzzmob (Teach.com 2015), ClassMessenger (Teach.com 2015), Mailchimp (Teach.com 2015), ClassDoJo (Ponsford 2015), Remind/Remind101 (Klein 2013; Ponsford 2015; Teach.com 2015), Animoto (Klein 2013), Educreations (Klein 2013), What Did We Do Today (WDWDT) (Klein 2013), Aurasma (Klein 2013), Bambizo (Ponsford 2015)
Parent-driven information management	MyIEPmeeting (Excent 2014; Swanson 2012)
To-do/Checklist	IEP Checklist (Swanson 2012), IzzyTodo, SquareLeaf, Wipee List

3   Objectives

This study aims to identify the types of information parents manage regarding their children, needs and challenges of parents in managing information of their children and the purposes for which parents use the information they receive. Two web-based surveys were used to collect data from parents. The first survey, Study 1, was conducted to gather information regarding the types of information parents receive regarding their children, ascertain a high-level view of what is done with the data and if there were any perceived difficulties in managing any particular type of data. The results of the first survey led to a more focused second survey, Study 2, to gain insight regarding parental use of and challenges with information received concerning their children's education.

4   Research Methodology

Online surveys were conducted to gather data regarding how parents are currently managing their children's information, the types of information managed, sources of the information, the context and types of information shared and the sensitivity of the information. The surveys were also used to gather information regarding parents' perceived challenges with managing the information. Parents will be asked questions so that the areas where most challenges are perceived could be identified as areas for potential improvement. Pilot groups were identified to take the surveys initially and not only provide the data requested in the questionnaires, but also provide feedback on how the survey can be improved (i.e. identify questions that should be revised for clarity) and metrics for the time it takes to actually complete the survey. After the surveys were revised based on input from the pilot respondents, invitations to complete the survey were more widely distributed. Recipients of the invitation were encouraged to invite other parents to participate in the survey. The target audience was parents of children between less than 1 year and 18 years of age.

5   STUDY 1: Parental Information Management Methods and Challenges

The authors developed a 58-question web-based survey to collect feedback from parents on challenges with managing their children's educational, financial, medical, social, recreational, extracurricular and other information. The survey included a combination of multiple choice questions (with only one option to be checked), multiple choice questions (where respondents could check as many as they liked) and open ended questions. Survey participants were parents of children between 0 and 18 years of age. Ten parents were asked to participant as the pilot group for the survey. In addition to providing responses to the survey, these users were asked to provide feedback on the clarity of the survey questions so that, if necessary, the survey could be revised prior to its general release. During the trial period, the survey was only accessible by members of the pilot group, Baseline – Campus Labs personnel and persons conducting the study.

Parents were invited to participate in the survey via email. The message contained an embedded link to the survey; respondents were informed that they could access the survey by clicking on the link or pasting the URL in their web browser. In the invitation parents were encouraged to forward the survey link to other parents.

5.1   Demographics

Overall there were 45 responses to the survey invitation. Most survey respondents were between 31 and 50 years of age (75%). Of the remaining respondents, 11.36% were between 21 and 30 and 13.64% were age 51 or older. More than half (68.18%) of the respondents were female. The majority of the respondents (65.91%) had more than one child in their household under the age of 18. Figure 1 reflects the grade distribution of the children of the survey respondents.

5.2   Results

The responses to the survey confirmed that the five categories presented (educational, financial, medical, recreational/extracurricular and social) are important (Fig. 2).

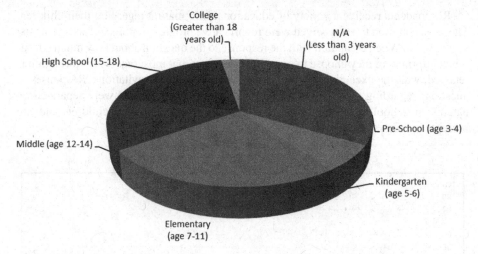

Fig. 1. Grade level distribution of the children of survey 1 respondents

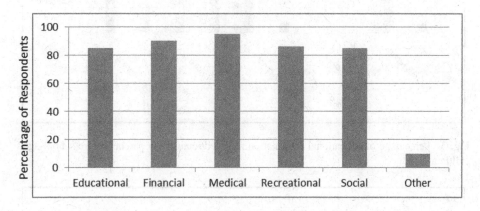

Fig. 2. Types of information parents manage regarding their children

Photographs and religious information were provided as additional types of information managed by two respondents.

The majority of the respondents did not report having any issues collection information about their children from third parties when needed. One respondent, however, commented that it was "hard to keep all the medical records straight [...] the doctors are not always willing to share the details [...] school records are better but still not great". The perceived difficulty of sorting, storing or retrieving their children's information is perceived to be low as only a quarter of the respondents (25.64%) reported having issues. The explanations provided by those who reported having issues point to problems dealing with the "overwhelming" amounts of information, the fact that so much of the information is paper-based and the fact-that several different accounts are needed to access all of the information.

Respondents receive a variety of educational information regarding their children. The most common types received were report cards, progress reports and assignments/ school work. When compared with the response to the question about how much educational information they choose to save, it was evident that most received information is retained, with the exception of correspondence and meeting invitations. Responses to questions regarding the types of educational information received were separated by parents of school-aged children and parents of pre-school-aged children and are presented in Figs. 3 and 4.

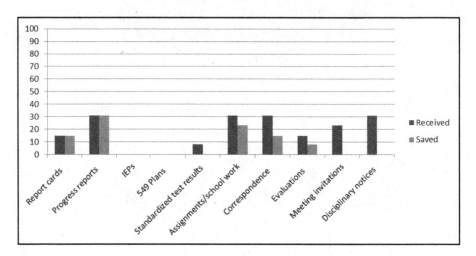

Fig. 3. Percentage of educational information received/retained by parents of pre-school-aged children

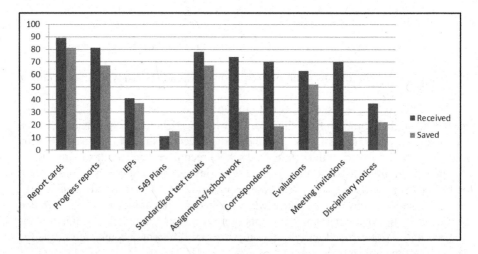

Fig. 4. Percentage of educational information received/retained by parents of school-aged children

Survey responses indicate that there is a mismatch between the ways parents currently receive educational information regarding their children and how they would prefer to receive the information (see Fig. 5). Approximately 80% of respondents receive this information as a hardcopy or printed report while nearly 85% would prefer to receive the information electronically. However, a significant number of parents prefer paper even when electronic options may be available; 63% of respondents preferred to receive the information in printed form.

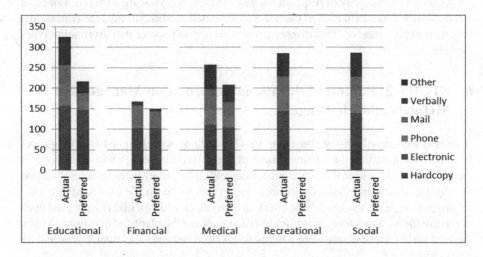

Fig. 5. Actual vs. Preferred methods of information receipt

Most respondents indicated that they would prefer to receive their children's financial and medical information electronically or online. Respondents were not asked to

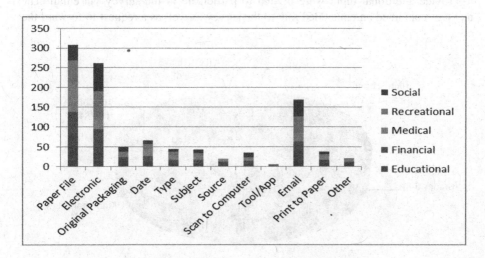

Fig. 6. Archive methods for received information

provide their preferred method of receipt for social and extracurricular information. Similarly to the results observed with educational information, a significant number of respondents also prefer to receive this information in hardcopy. Approximately half of the respondents keep the information indefinitely with the exception of extracurricular/recreational information. One respondent commented that extracurricular/recreational information is not kept because it changes each year, may be an indication for why other respondents also choose not to keep this information.

Although the majority of respondents would like to receive educational information electronically, more than 80% of them use paper-based methods to save the educational information they receive. This disparity was seen across most of the information types (see Fig. 6).

6   STUDY 2: Parental Educational Information Management Methods and Challenges

A second web-based survey consisting of 47 questions was designed to obtain input from parents regarding their management of, perceived challenges with and usage of their children's educational information specifically. The survey included a combination of multiple choice questions (with only one option to be checked), multiple choice questions (where respondents could check as many as they liked), Likert scales and open ended questions. The survey was pilot tested to improve the clarity of questions. Again, targeted survey participants were parents of children between less than 1 year and 18 years of age.

6.1   Demographics

Persons who indicated in their response to the initial survey that they would be willing to provide additional input were invited to participate in the survey via email. The message contained an embedded link to the survey as well as a request to forward the

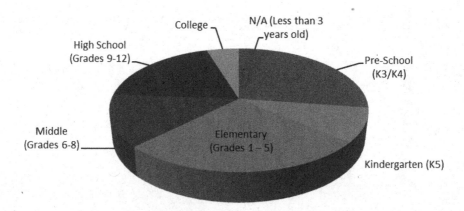

Fig. 7. Grade level distribution of the children of survey 2 respondents

invitation to other parents. During the period of data collection, 46 respondents met the selection criteria for completing the survey. The age and number of children of the respondents to the second survey aligned with the first survey respondents. Figure 7 reflects the grade distribution of the children of the survey respondents.

6.2   Results

Questions regarding the types of educational information parents receive, what they choose to retain and for how long they choose to retain the information were re-visited in the second survey. For these areas, the survey results were consistent with those from the first survey. The top five types of education information received by parents as indicated by 60% or more respondents are report cards, progress reports, correspondence, assignments/school work and meeting invitations. These types of data are retained indefinitely by approximately 43% of parents.

Again, survey results show evidence a mismatch between the ways parents currently receive education information regarding their children and how they would prefer to receive the information. Because most parents receive information in both electronic and hardcopy forms, they were asked what attempts they have made at combining the types of data received. Approximately 41% of respondents transfer hardcopy to electronic files for storage. However, 43% of respondents transfer electronic information to hardcopy for archive. Responses to questions regarding actual and preferred methods of information receipt and archive methods received were separated between those from parents of school-aged children and parents of pre-school-aged children and are summarized in Figs. 8 and 9 below.

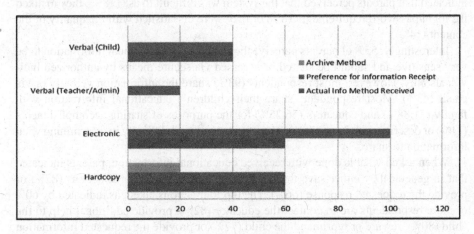

Fig. 8. Actual and preferred methods of educational information receipt and archive method of parents of pre-school-aged children

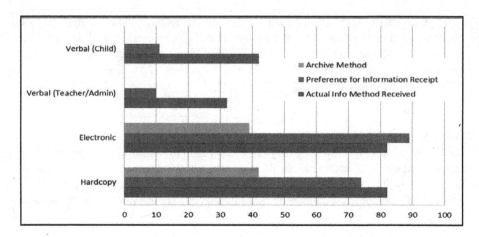

Fig. 9. Actual and preferred methods of educational information receipt and archive method of parents of school-aged children

An education management system (ex. ParentCONNECTTxp, SchoolMAX, Edline, etc.) is available to approximately 67% of the parents surveyed. The overwhelming majority, 90%, of parents use the available education management system. When asked what they liked most about the available education management system, 55% of parents stated the availability, 18% liked the ease of use and 14% noted the quality of the content. When asked what they liked least about the available system, 36% reported that there was not anything they did not like. This was the number one response. Other responses indicated that parents perceived that the system was difficult to use (18%), they disliked the login/password requirement (18%) or they were dissatisfied with the quality of the content (14%).

Interestingly, 55% of parents perceive their children's educational information to be very sensitive and should be shared or accessed via secure means by authorized individuals only. However, most respondents (93%) share the information verbally or via email (43%). Most respondents share their children's educational information with family (71.88%) and educators (56.25%) for the purposes of sharing accomplishments (71%) or describing an issue (75%). There is no perceived difficulty in determining what information to share.

When asked what is done with received educational information, parents indicated that in general they either save the information and take additional actions (82%) or provide the requested response (66%). The top four actions taken, as indicated by 60% or more respondents are to contact the educator (82%), provide additional help to the child (80%), reward or reprimand the child (77%) or provide the requested information or item (61%). Responses to questions regarding the types of information received and retained are summarized in Figs. 10 and 11 below.

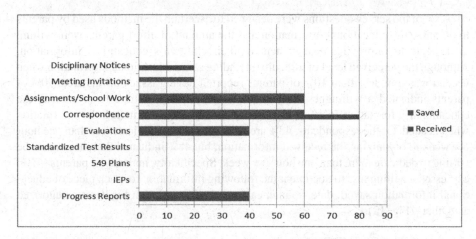

Fig. 10. Percentage of educational information received/retained by parents of pre-school-aged children

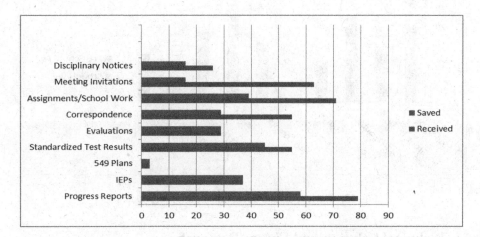

Fig. 11. Percentage of educational information received/retained by parents of school-aged children

The most prevalent methods of communicating with their children's schools as indicated by 50% or more respondents are via email (86%), in person (77%), verbally over the phone (68%) or via written notes or letters (57%). The majority of respondents do not perceive any issues communicating with the school. The top four purposes for which parents save educational information regarding their children as indicated by approximately 50% or more respondents are: use as supporting documentation when communicating with educators or others, to assist child in reviewing/studying material or as a teaching tool, show progress or decline in development and/or skill and as a memento; to remember a child's accomplishments at a particular age or grade.

A set of the survey questions were designed to ascertain the methods used by parents to organize the educational information and the amount of effort parents were willing to dedicate to improving management of their children's educational information. Although the perceived level of difficulty in finding saved educational information when needed was low, less than 10% of parents reported having issues in this area, 90% of parents indicated a willingness to dedicate some amount of time to organizing the educational information in effort to improve effectiveness in finding the information when needed. Of the respondents, 43% are willing or able to dedicate less than one hour per week to organizing the received information, but 48% indicated that they would be willing to dedicate more than one hour per week. Specifically, majority of parents (67%) expressed a willingness to document the following information for each piece of educational information saved; date, source, category and description for items categorized as 'Other' (Fig. 12).

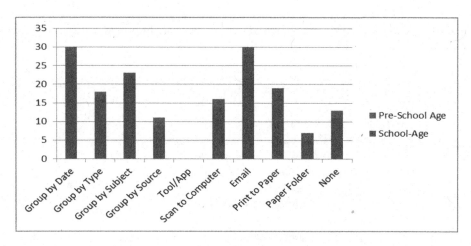

Fig. 12. Current organizational methods of respondents

7   Technical Solution and Future Research

A web portal/site for parents to use to manage information regarding their children's education will be developed. The basic web portal design will be based on functionality available in education management systems currently in use in Maryland public schools. SchoolMAX used in PG County Schools and ParentCONNETxp used in AA County in particular will be referenced. The features and functionality that differentiate the developed web portal/site from the existing school web-based software applications, however, are the additional pages, graphs and reports that are focused towards the needs of parents. The results of the studies will be used to create a list of information management needs of parents. The list of needs will be used to derive requirements that will drive the design of a technology solution to assist parents in the management of information regarding their children's education. This site will have four primary functions: monitoring, retrieving, communication and decision making. The monitoring function will enable the viewing of information provided/uploaded by the school via the site and enable the storage and viewing of educational information provided outside of the school's site. The retrieving function will allow parents to retrieve information regarding their child's education when needed. The communication function will enable allow parents to correspond with teachers and educators. The decision making function will allow parents to observe trends and anomalies in educational development.

Methods to integrate educational information received by parents will also be further explored. A study will be conducted where parents will be asked to complete tasks related to making decisions regarding their children's education using current methods and the new web portal tool. The results of the study will be used to determine where technology provides the most improvement in the effectiveness of parental information management.

8   Conclusions

The results of the first survey confirm that parents must manage are large volume of information regarding their children. The majority of issues related to this information management are associated with educational and medical information. Overall parents feel that the information regarding their children that they manage is sensitive, therefore privacy concerns must be considered when designing solutions to assist parents in managing this information. Per the survey results, few information management tools are used to manage the data in its categories.

Per the second survey results, no information management tools, outside of the educational management systems provided by the schools, are used by parents to manage the educational information of their children. Although the perceived difficulty with organizing educational information is low as indicated by survey responses, the willingness of the majority of participants to dedicate time each week to increasing the effectiveness of their current situation indicates that there is room for improvement.

With a better understanding of how parents receive and share information regarding their children as well as the purposes for which parents use the information technology can be developed to improve parental monitoring of the progress of their children, enable parents to identify of trends and anomalies in their children's development and improve the effectiveness of communications with providers and educators. The use of such technology by parents would enable them to get the most out of their position of influence as a major contributing factor in the development of children.

References

Anne Arundel County Public Schools. AACPS ParentCONNECTxp User Guide (2015). From AACPS: http://www.aacps.org/aacps/shared_docs/Elementary_ParentCONNECTxpUser Guide.pdf. Accessed 2 Sep 2015

Bishop, P.: Information and Communication Technology and School Leaders. In: Proceedings of the Seventh World Conference on Computers in Education. Australian Computer Society, Inc., Copenhagen (2002)

Bruce, H., Jones, W., Dumais, S.: Information behaviour that keeps found things found. Inf. Res., 207 (2004). http://InformationR.net/ir/10-1/paper207.html. Accessed

Buttfield-Addison, P., Lueg, C., Ellis, L., Manning, J.: "Everything goes into or out of the iPad": the iPad, information scraps and personal information management. In: Proceedings of the 24th Australian Computer-Human Interaction Conference, pp. 61–67. ACM, Adelaide (2012)

Callan, J., Allan, J., Clarke, C.L., Dumais, S., Evans, D., Sanderson, M., Zhai, C.: Meeting of the MINDS: an information retrieval research agenda. Newslett. ACM SIGIR Forum **41**, 25–34 (2007)

Crabtree, R.K.: The Paper Chase: Managing Your Child's Documents (1998). From Wrightslaw: http://www.wrightslaw.com/info/advo.paperchase.crabtree.htm. Accessed 14 Feb 2013

Excent: MyIEPmeeting Overview (2014). From supt.excent.com: http://supt.excent.com/products/myiepmeeting/. Accessed 9 July 2015

Jones, W., Anderson, K.M.: Many views, many modes, many tools ... one structure: towards a non-disruptive integration of personal information. In: Proceedings of the 22nd ACM Conference on Hypertext and Hypermedia, pp. 113–122. ACM, Eindhoven (2011)

Jones, W., Anderson, K.M.: Representing our information structures for research and for everyday use. In: CHI 2012 Extended Abstracts on Human Factors in Computing Systems, pp. 151–160. ACM, Austin (2012)

Jones, W., Dumais, S., Bruce, H.: Once found, what next? A study of 'keeping' behaviors in the personal use of web information. In: Proceedings of ASIST 2002, pp. 391–402. Information Today, Inc., Philadelphia (2002)

Karger, D.R., Jones, W.: Data unification in personal information management. Commun. ACM Pers. Inf. Manage. **49**, 77–82 (2006)

Kazai, G., Milic-Frayling, N., Haughton, T., Manola, N., Iatropoulou, K., Lempesis, A., Mikulicic, M.: Connecting the local and the online in information management. In: Proceedings of the 19th ACM International Conference on Information and Knowledge Management, pp. 1941–1942. ACM (2010)

Klein, E.: 5 Apps to Creatively Connect with Parents! 3 September 2013. From Scholastic.com: http://www.scholastic.com/teachers/top-teaching/2013/09/5-apps-creatively-connect-parents. Accessed 8 July 2015

Ma, Y., Fox, E.A., Goncalves, M.A.: Personal digital library: PIM through a 5s perspective. In: Proceedings of the ACM First Ph.D. Workshop in CIKM, pp. 117–124. ACM (2007)

Marcu, G., Tassini, K., Carlson, Q., Goodwyn, J., Rivkin, G., Schaefer, K.J., Kiesler, S.: Why do They still use paper? Understanding data collection and use in autism education, pp. 3177–3186. ACM (2013)

May, L.: Local mom-entrepreneurs create Seesaw app to help parents manage kids' lives, 10 January 2015. From WCPO Cincinatti: http://www.wcpo.com/money/local-business-news/local-mom-entrepreneurs-create-seesaw-app-to-help-busy-parents-manage-their-kids-lives. Accessed 9 July 2015

Oh, K.E., Belkin, N.J.: Cross analysis of keeping personal information in different forms. In: Proceedings of the 2011 iConference, pp. 732–733. ACM, Fort Worth (2011)

Patrikakou, E.N.: The Power of Parent Involvement: Evidence, Ideas, and Tools for Student Success. Center on Innovation & Improvement, Lincoln (2008)

Piper, A.M., D'Angelo, S.D., Hollan, J.D.: Going digital: understanding paper and photo documentation practices in early childhood education, pp. 1319–1328. ACM (2013)

Ponsford, N.: Five of the best apps that help teachers communicate with parents, 28 April 2015. From The Guardian: http://www.theguardian.com/teacher-network/2015/apr/28/five-best-apps-teachers-communicate-parents. Accessed 8 July 2015

Pratt, W., Unruh, K., Civan, A., Skeels, M.M.: Personal health information management. Commun. ACM Pers. Inf. Manage. **49**, 51–55 (2006)

Prince George's County Public Schools. Family Portal for Parents & Guardians Guide (2015). From PGCPS Student Information System - SchoolMAX: https://docs.google.com/document/d/1w-oBIgUCEsfYAP3uv_ZkyC-txiYk3zn06VVETt3SsK8/edit?pref=2&pli=1. Accessed 2 Sep 2015

Roshan, P.K., Jacobs, M., Dye, M., DiSalvo, B.: Exploring how parents in economically depressed communities access learning resources, pp. 131–141. ACM (2014)

Swanson, G.: Managing Individual Education Programs (IEP) on the iPad, 20 January 2012. From Apps in Education: http://appsineducation.blogspot.com/2012/01/managing-individual-education-programs.html. Accessed 8 July 2015

Teach.com, 28 January 2015. From 7 Innovative Apps for Parent-Teacher Communication: http://teach.com/education-technology/parent-teacher-apps. Accessed 8 July 2015

Trullemans, S., Signer, B.: From user needs to opportunities in personal information management: a case study on organisational strategies in cross-media informaiton spaces, pp. 87–96. IEEE (2014)

Turner, E.: Technolgoy use in reporting to parents of primary school children. SIGCAS Comput. Soc. **40**, 25–37 (2010)

Van Kleek, M., Smith, D.A., Packer, H.S., Skinner, J., Shadbolt, N.R.: Carpe data: supporting serendipitous data integration in personal information management, pp. 2339–2348. ACM (2013)

Wright, P., Wright, P.: The Special Education Survival Guide: Organizing Your Child's Special Education File: Do It Right! 21 July 2008. From Emotions to Advocacy: http://www.fetaweb.com/03/organize.file.htm. Accessed 14 Feb 2013

Purchasing Customer Data
from a New Sales Market

Kenta Nakajima, Hideyuki Mizobuchi[✉], and Yumi Asahi

Department of Management Systems Engineering, School of Information
and Telecommunication Engineering, Tokai University, Tokyo, Japan
{4bjm2108, 4bjml223}@mail.tokai-u.jp,
asahi@tsc.u-tokai.ac.jp

Abstract. A research about motorcycle purchases customers and its customer financial transactions. Current motorcycle features traditional Cr-MQ steel new material added (Titanium, Carbon, Aluminum, etc.) of highlights is suitable for development and technological innovation, dramatically increase performance of the motorcycle and the machine is called a sophistication and precision. You can read from the manufacturing of motorcycles that are considered the role of its usage, such as use as a hobby not only as a way to travel when you purchase a motorcycle from this customer using the exhilaration and sense of speed and motorcycle is that each person and each needs for motorcycle production. Thought the motorcycle worth increasing as customers to choose installment payments by the customer to buy is on the rise. However, customers could not pay the prescribed payment period even installment payments by the Government and the economy that status quo. Firms selling motorcycle that customers will continue to increase, and no longer is the recovery of the cost of production, could lead to a deterioration in business conditions. The find criteria aiming to minimize these problems, with motorcycle purchase customer data based on non-payment of past customer data gathering and analysis, identify the characteristics of customers that we can't continue to pay the customer. Customer's primary income or occupation, purchased from a motorcycle purchase customer usage data for payment and also reads the characteristics of those who cannot as a research method, motorcycle products, how to split payment, loans, split payment of 6 months within or payment within 12 months or 18 months overdue status data than was analyzed and then each group products, engine, etc. You could take the theory as a result of difficult to recall what customers are buying and manufacturing costs. Increase in motorcycle buyers, and value of higher than the result this time led models, while a steady cost recovery environment, the uncollected laid out plans to break the company's financial difficulties caused by possible related companies. Also led to started payment of product improvements, lower the rate of unpaid. I think it should create a model as any other leads from a variety of perspectives.

Keywords: Motorcycle customers date · Multinomial logistic regression analysis

© Springer International Publishing AG 2017
S. Yamamoto (Ed.): HIMI 2017, Part I, LNCS 10273, pp. 366–375, 2017.
DOI: 10.1007/978-3-319-58521-5_29

1   Introduction

We are using these data provided by motorcycle dealer. Than the data I got from it statistical analysis. First, asked for the number of customers for each product. As a result "K" all of 14304 customers found 6064 customers. It occupies all customer's 42.4%. Asked to become 6months bad for each product. As a result "K" is very much which models. Customer number of the "K" and "B" of 1.2 times the difference.[*1] But in 6months bad customer number difference is bubbling up to 2.5 times[*2] (Figs. 1 and 2).

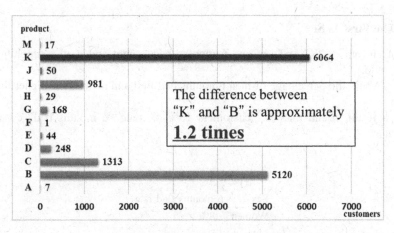

Fig. 1. Motorcycle product graph[*1]

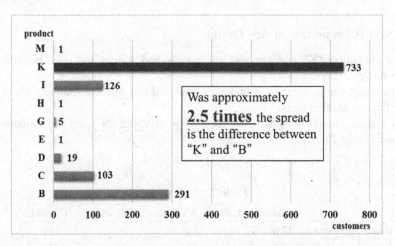

Fig. 2. Motorcycle product graph (6 months BAD)[*2]

I thought, there is our high "K" customer rate 6months bad customers. Because of that, "K" to focusing 6 months bad "of decided to examine the characteristics".
("K" is a small motorcycle of a certain motorcycle manufacturer.)

2   Result of Analysis

We advanced the analysis in this way.

Fast step is Extract "K" customer data from data. Second step are Each kind of extract customer number and Each kind of extract was 6 months on Bad customer number.

Final step is Each kind of customer number was 6months bad break Species each and number of customers, the proportion.

2.1   The First Is Sex

Data of customers "K" and sex and 6 months bad sought and used a 6months bad gender ratio.

As a result, the percentage of men 6months bad find and about 13% higher than in women.

As a result, found that "K" customers 13% of male "6 months bad" customer (Table 1).

Table 1. Sex ratio

Sex	6 months Bad rate
Women	8%
Men	**13%**
Total	12%

2.2   Next Is Proportion of Age Groups

Data of customers "K" and age and six months bad sought and used 6months bad gender ratio.

As a result, the percentage of under 29 years old 6months bad find and about 17% higher than in another ages.

As a result, found that "K" customers 17% of under 29 years old 6months bad customer (Table 2).

Table 2. Ages ratio

	6 months Bad rate	6 months Bad customer's	Customer's
Under 29 years old	**17%**	148	846
30s	15%	304	2087
40s	9%	151	1609
50s	8%	80	1059
60s	12%	48	393
Over 70 years old	10%	2	20
Total	12%	733	6014

2.3   The Percentage of Genera and Species

Data of customers "K" and "Genera and species and 6months bad sought and used 6months bad gender ratio".

As a result, the percentage of Single and Bereavement 6months bad find and about 13% higher than in another Genera and species.

As a result, found that "K" customers 13% of "Single and Bereavement 6 months bad" customer (Table 3).

Table 3. Genera and species ratio

Genera and species	6 months Bad rate	6 months Bad customer's	Customer's
Married	7%	31	418
Single	13%	657	4567
Bereavement	13%	11	73
Separation	11%	16	134
Divorce	11%	8	65
Marital life	9%	3	31
Total	12%	726	5288

2.4   Next Is the Percentage of Job Title

Data of customers "K" and job title and 6months bad sought and used 6months bad gender ratio. As a result, the percentage of farmers 6months bad find and about 18% higher than in another job title.

As a result, found that "K" customers 18% of farmers 6months bad customer (Table 4).

Table 4. Occupation ratio

Job title	6 months Bad rate	6 months Bad customer's	Customer's
Self-employed	16%	232	1176
Freelance	7%	5	63
Salaried employees	11%	384	3152
Civil servants	9%	49	494
Military personnel	15%	5	28
Farmers in - to peasant	18%	12	56
Businessman	6%	10	145
Pensioners	14%	29	172
Total	12%	733	5331

2.5   Next Is the Percentage of Living in State

It divided the cities of Latin America by a temporary name.

Data of customers "K" and Living in State and 6months bad sought and used 6months bad gender ratio.

As a result, the percentage of "**a state**" 6 months bad find and about 27% higher than in another Living in States.

As a result, found that "K" customers 27% of "a state" 6months bad customer.

3   Research Content and Result

3.1   Flow

As research content, first, purpose is to find out why customers cannot pay within 6 months. Second, in this case, using 6 months bad living in state customers to conduct Multinomial logistic regression analysis. At that time, objective variable user the highest percentage of the top three states. Third, determining future tasks and analysis contents from analysis result (Table 5).

Table 5. Each state ratio

Living in state	6 months Bad rate	6 months Bad customer's	Customer's
a	**27%**	13	49
b	**21%**	16	77
c	**21%**	51	245
d	18%	10	56
e	17%	16	95
f	16%	54	330
⋮	⋮	⋮	⋮
Total	12%	733	6044

Explain the outline of the top three states.
"a state" is the northern city of Latin America.
"b state" is a coastal city in the southeastern part of Latin America.
"c state" is the center city of Latin America.

3.2   Multinomial Logistic Regression Analysis

Multinomial logistics regression analysis is used when there are three or more objective variables of the nominal scale.

$$\log_e \left(\frac{P_A}{P_C} \right) = \alpha_A + \beta_{1A} x_1 + \beta_{2A} x_2 + \cdots \beta_{nA} x_x$$

$$\log_e \left(\frac{P_B}{P_C} \right) = \alpha_B + \beta_{1B} x_1 + \beta_{2B} x_2 + \cdots \beta_{nB} x_x$$

P_A, P_B and P_C represent the probability that each group will occur.

The formula below is a model expression for multinomial logistic regression analysis. Here, it is a model expression for three values (A group, B group, C group).

The first model equation expression expresses the likelihood of A to C. The second equation model expression expresses the likelihood of B to C. From this model expression, if the coefficient is +, it is interpreted that the group A tends to occur with respect to the group C, and if it is −, it is interpreted that the group A is unlikely to occur. By taking an exponent in the partial regression coefficient, the odds ratio (Exp (B)) of group A to group C is obtained.

As an example objective variable are Company A sales and Company B sales. Explanatory variables are advertising expenses(A) and personnel expenses(P).

Table 6 is the result of Company A sales. As an interpretation of this table, if the significance probability is 0.05 or less and the odds is 1 or more, there is an influence. Also, if the significance probability is 0.05 or more and the odds is 1 or less, there is no influence. In this case, advertising expenses(A) has influence on company A sales.

Table 6. Analysis result of company A sales

Speding	B (Regression coefficient)	Deviation	Wald	df	Singnificance probability	Exp(B)
A	2.6426	1.1982	2.2612	1	**0.02**	**1.708**
P	1.9865	1.3143	1.8762	1	0.62	0.708
Constant	....	....	...	...	...	...

Table 7 is the result of Company B sales. As an interpretation of this table, if the significance probability is 0.05 or less and the odds is 1 or more, there is an influence. Also, if the significance probability is 0.05 or more and the odds are 1 or less, there is no influence. In this case, the significance probability of personnel expenses(P) is 0.05 or less, but the odds are 1 or less. In other words, personnel expenses(P) have no influence on company B sales.

Table 7. Analysis result of company B sales

Speding	B (Regression coefficient)	Deviation	Wald	df	Singnificance probability	Exp (B)
A	1.9877	1.2323	2.2221	1	1.22	1.8822
P	2.1128	1.7635	1.9811	1	**0.045**	**0.7708**
Constant	....	....	...	...	...	...

3.3   Research Explanation

We divided the research by two plans.

(Plan1)

Introduce purpose variables and explanatory variables used for Multinomial logistic regression analysis. Objective variable is "a state", "b state", "c state". All 6 months bad "K" customers. Explanatory variables are Primary income, Item price, deposit, Division number, interest(%), interest amount and loan.

(Plan2)

Introduce purpose variables and explanatory variables used for Multinomial logistic regression analysis. Objective variable is "a state", "b state", "c state". All 6 months bad "K" customers. Explanatory variables are Primary income, Item price, deposit, Division number, interest(%), interest amount, loan, "FINANCIAL INSTITUTION A" score and "FINANCIAL INSTITUTION B" score.

3.4   Discrimination

As a discrimination method, Odds (Exp(B)) represent relationship with resident state 6months bad. High odds (Exp(B)) is consider to be 6 months bad.

3.5   Results of Multinomial Logistic Regression Analysis

(Plan1)

Looking at these analysis result Tables 8 and 9.

Table 8. Analysis result of "b state"

Resident state		B	Deviation	Wald	df	Singnificance probability	Odds (Exp(B))	Correct answer rate
b	Intercept	−263.744	27.059	95.004	1	.000		21.1%
	Primary income	−.004	.004	0.954	1	.329	.996	
	Item price	−0.719	.517	1.935	1	0.164	.487	
	Deposit	−0.327	.206	2.521	1	0.112	0.721	
	Division number	−0.582	0.006	10234.781	1	.000	.559	
	Interest(%)	.582	.005	11636.139	1	**.000**	**1.790**	
	Interest amount	.590	.000		1		1.804	
	Loan	−0.173	0.127	1.86527796	1	0.172016882	0.841	

Table 8 is the result of customers in "b state". Interest(%) is considered to be affecting because it meets the condition of significance probability and odds.

Item price, deposit, division number and loan has a significance probability of 0.05 or less. However, since odds are less than 1, they are not affected.

Table 9. Analysis result of "c state"

Resident state		B	Deviation	Wald	df	Singnificance probability	Odds (Exp(B))	Correct answer rate
c	Intercept	−149.936	97.555	2.362	1	.124		71.1%
	Primary income	−.002	.004	0.393	1	.531	.998	
	Item price	−0.673	.518	1.689	1	.194	.510	
	Deposit	−0.390	.200	3.789	1	.052	0.677	
	Division number	−0.359	0.204	3.112	1	.078	.698	
	Interest(%)	.361	.204	3.130	1	.077	1.434	
	Interest amount	.368	.206	3.176	1	.075	1.444	
	Loan	−0.193	.127	2.315	1	.128	0.824	

Table 9 is the result of customers in "c state". These explanatory variables are not affected because they do not satisfy the condition.

(Plan2)

Looking at these analysis result Tables 10 and 11.

Table 10. Analysis result of "b state"

Resident state		B	Deviation	Wald	df	Significance probability	Odds (Exp(B))	Correct answer rate
b	Intercept	−730.476	85.864	72.375	1	.000		29.4%
	Primary income	−.011	.006	2.813	1	.094	.989	
	Item price	−1.671	.017	10027.044	1	0.000	.188	
	Deposit	1.668	.017	9388.232	1	**0.000**	**5.301**	
	Division number	−2.758	1.673	2.717	1	.099	.063	
	Interest(%)	−.871	.420	4.297	1	.038	.419	
	Interest amount	−.584	.369	2.502	1	.114	.558	
	Loan	1.698	0.000		1		5.462	
	FINANCIAL INSTITUTION A	−.039	.025	2.416	1	.120	.962	
	FINANCIAL INSTITUTION B	.029	.018	2.511	1	.113	1.029	

Table 10 is the result of customers in "b state". Deposit is considered to be affecting because it meets the condition of significance probability and odds.

Item price and interest have a significance probability of 0.05 or less. However, since odds are less than 1, they are not affected.

Table 11. Analysis result of "c state"

Resident state		B	Deviation	Wald	df	Singnificance probability	Odds (Exp(B))	Correct answer rate
c	Intercept	−551.881	281.391	3.847	1	.050		61.7%
	Primary income	−.008	.006	1.675	1	.196	.992	
	Item price	−1.349	.672	4.031	1	.045	.259	
	Deposit	1.349	.671	4.044	1	**.044**	**3.853**	
	Division number	−3.092	1.704	3.293	1	.070	.045	
	Interest(%)	−.888	.412	4.642	1	.031	.411	
	Interest amount	−.700	.375	3.484	1	.062	.497	
	Loan	1.381	.686	4.051	1	**.044**	**3.978**	
	FINANCIAL INSTITUTION A	−.044	.025	3.101	1	.078	.957	
	FINANCIAL INSTITUTION B	.030	.019	2.564	1	.109	1.030	

Table 11 is the result of customers in "c state". Deposit and loan are considered to be affecting because they meet the condition of significance probability and odds. Item price and interest have a significance probability of 0.05 or less. However, since odds are less than 1, they are not affected.

(Plan1)

Table 12. Correct answer rate of plan1

	b	c	a
Correct answer rate	21.1%	71.1%	7.9%

Table 12 is the correct answer rate for each state. "a state" could not display the result because the correct answer rate was low. The coefficient of determination of this model is 45% to 55%.

(Plan2)

Table 13. Correct answer rate of plan2

	b	c	a
Correct answer rate	29.4%	61.1%	8.8%

Table 13 is the correct answer rate for each state. "a state" could not display the result because the correct answer rate was low. The coefficient of determination of this model is 58% to 66%.

4 Future Task

4.1 Summary

In plan1, 6 months bad "K" customers of "b state" are considered to be due to interest rate. In plan2, 6 months bad "K" customers of "b state" and 6 months bad "K" customers of "c state" are considered to be due to deposit. It seems that 6 months bad "K" customers of "c state" will become unpaid due to borrowing transactions.

4.2 Task

In the future task, Assigning sex, ages, and Job title of 6 months bad "K" customers from the top percentage items, to analyze Multinomial logistic regression analysis and others using them. Other models also find characteristics from same way. Increase the number of plans that will be useful for future strategy from this result.

References

1. Uchida, O.: Logistic regression analysis by SPSS. Omusya, Tokyo (2011)
2. Local Authority Internationalization Association: Share motorcycle in each country. Local Authority Internationalization Association, Tokyo (1989)
3. Miyagi, H.: Strength of Japan brand motorcycle overseas. Japan Automobile Manufacturers Association, Tokyo (2016)
4. Kazuhiro, T.: Challenge to The Market of An Electric Motorcycle and A Microminiature Mobility:—Collaboration with The Sightseeing Business—. Electrical Engineers, Tokyo (2016)
5. Fujii, H.: Read the market: overseas economy, monetary policy and signs of bottoming out in the Latin Americaian economy. Institute for financial and fiscal affairs, Tokyo (2014)
6. Nishikawa, T.: Latin Americaian economy of foreign internal illness. Overseas Foreign Exchange Trade Study Group, Tokyo (2013)
7. Mainichi newspaper company: Latin Americaian economy in danger. Mainichi newspaper company, Tokyo (2011)
8. Ninomiya, K.: Latin Americaian economy and the automobile industry. Japan automobile manufacturers association, Tokyo (2010)
9. Hamaguchi, N.: Latin Americaian economy, current situation and issues. In: Japan International Workshop, Tokyo (2006)
10. Kadokura, T.: The Latin Americaian economic frontier and relationship with Japanese companies. Hyogo economic study group, Kobe (2006)

Analyzing the Daily Meeting of Day Care Staffs Who Personalized Occupational Therapy Program in Response to a Care-Receiver's Pleasure

Chika Oshima[1(✉)], Yumiko Ishii[2], Kimie Machishima[1], Hitomi Abe[2], Naohito Hosoi[2], and Koichi Nakayama[1]

[1] Saga University, Saga, Japan
karin27@sa3.so-net.ne.jp
[2] Sodegaura Satsukidai Hospital, Sodegaura city, Chiba prefecture, Japan

Abstract. In the approach of the Yuzu-no-sato occupational therapy program (Yuzu-OTP), since each care receiver's program is personalized, even care receivers with severe dementia can develop a feeling of accomplishment and pleasure. Reflection meetings after the program is administered are important because they allow staff to become aware of what they have observed, experienced, and felt during the work occupation sessions, with a view to creating personalized programs. However, it is difficult for other facilities that hope to adopt Yuzu-OTP to hold such meetings; one reason for this is that staff at other facilities do not know how to conduct the meetings. Therefore, in this paper, we analyzed meetings that were part of the Yuzu-OTP and showed how staff members generated new knowledge concerning what each care receiver should do during the next occupational therapy session to elicit enthusiasm and a feeling of accomplishment.

1 Introduction

The lives of care receivers at the "Yuzu-no-sato [1]" severe dementia day care facility are mentally and physically balanced. It is rare for care receivers to refuse to come to this facility, and we think that "The approach of Yuzu-no-sato occupational therapy program (Yuzu-OTP)" helps them to feel calm, relaxed, and willing to stay [2]. Yuzu-OTP is carried out for one hour every day. Some care receivers paint a color to the sketch, another care receiver winds wool into a core of wrap film, the other winds small stockings piece around a hanger (making a hanger mop). Moreover, the staff at Yuzu-no-sato personalize each program in response to a care receiver's pleasure by selecting a suitable work for the care receiver to do and/or making arrangements for him or her to engage in suitable tasks [3]. Balance between skills and challenge occurs the flow experience which is the crucial component of enjoyment [4]. Thus, the care receiver can develop a feeling of accomplishment, and it has been established that such a feeling can be effective in alleviating the behavioral symptoms of dementia [5].

© Springer International Publishing AG 2017
S. Yamamoto (Ed.): HIMI 2017, Part I, LNCS 10273, pp. 376–387, 2017.
DOI: 10.1007/978-3-319-58521-5_30

A staff meeting for reflection is an important step in providing suitable work for each care receiver, because the suitable work is found from how the care receiver did the work. However, another day care facility that tried to conduct a Yuzu-OTP could not hold the meeting and arrange the work for each care receiver, as only one staff member prepared materials and provided work for the care receivers, and no reflection on the program was carried out [6]. This is a common phenomenon: Although clinical nurses routinely attend reflection meetings, we have learned that at least in Japan, care staff at day care facilities for elderly people with dementia rarely have such meetings. Multiple factors may prevent staff from having daily meetings. For instance, because the day cares suffer from chronic labor shortages, staff cannot take time away from providing care to gather for a meeting. Moreover, since most staff members work part time, they cannot afford to extend their work time to attend meetings. However, the leader of Yuzu-no-sato told us that such meetings are important to provide good care when we interviewed her. These meetings do not necessarily need to include all staff members or be scheduled at a structured time. It is permissible for only a few staff members to gather and spend a few minutes reflecting on how each care receiver performed.

The most important issue is that the staff at many day care facilities do not know how to conduct these meetings. In particular, when we interviewed to the director of another day care facility, we have learned that although staff members can report on care receivers' physical rehabilitation, bathing care, meal assistance, and toileting assistance, they are unaccustomed to reflecting on the occupational therapy program. These staff members do not know what they should observe and consider in the program, and therefore they have problems reflecting on it.

In collaboration with the leader of Yuzu-no-sato, we explained how Yuzu-OTP should be carried out to the director at day care facility X, which is seeking to provide an occupational therapy program to care receiver with dementia. Moreover, we observed the occupational therapy program at facility X [6]. At the same time, we externalized what the staff at Yuzu-no-sato consider in the occupational therapy program on a piece of paper and prepared a sheet on which staff at facility X could write down their observations. These materials were then provided to the facility X. As a result of the trial, it was difficult for staff at facility X to write down their observations on the sheet. Thus, they could never hold a meeting. We thought that staff at facility X did not have the willingness to hold the meeting, because they could not externalize their awareness.

We aim to actualize Yuzu-OTP at other day care facilities, including facility X, and to make Yuzu-OTP an integral part of good care for people with dementia. Therefore, we seek to construct a system that allows staff to conduct meetings to reflect on care receivers' performance in the occupational therapy program. In this paper, we describe the features of Yuzu-OTP and analyze the meetings that take place at Yuzu-no-sato.

2   Related Works

In past research, an application was developed for staff to enter their observations and photos on a tablet terminal and share this information with other staff members [7]. However, many staff at day care facilities were unfamiliar with a kind of tablet terminal, and would be difficult for them to take it out of their pocket during care. Thus, they would feel uncomfortable using the tablet terminal and writing down their observations on the screen. While there is also a smart voice messaging system available for staff to record their observations [8], which circumvents the need to write, this would also be uncomfortable for staff, as they would feel self-conscious in recording their notes in front of care receivers and their families.

3   Features of the Approach of Yuzu-no-sato Occupational Therapy Program

In this section, we introduce some of the features of Yuzu-OTP based on a previous work [3]. In the workroom at Yuzu-no-sato, there are tables set up throughout like islands, allowing several people to sit together. The staff members allocate where each care receiver will sit each day based on the care receiver's ability and compatibility with others.

As shown in Fig. 1, one of the features of Yuzu-OTP is that staff members talk to each care receiver and perform some works together during the program. In general, for occupational therapy programs at other facilities, the staff member initially explains how the work will affect the care receiver's physical function. Since the general program aims for the care receiver push through the work, the staff encourages him or her to persist. However, in some cases, no staff member talks to the care receiver during the program. In contrast, at Yuzu-no-sato, there is at least one staff member at each table. The staff asks the care receiver to carry out the work politely, for example, "Could you help me?" or "You are a very good worker. Could I ask for this work?" Since this elicits feelings in the care receiver that he or she is helpful for somebody, it is easy to persuade the care receiver to start the work, even if he or she has severe dementia. In this case, staff members direct their attention to the care receivers by engaging in conversation; the aim of this is to observe how each care receiver is doing, that is, his or her pleasure to complete the task, ability to carry out the work, fatigue, safety, and so on. The staff may change the care receiver's tool, chair, or cushion so that he or she can perform the work comfortably. When the staff observes that the care receiver is not willing to do the work despite efforts to engage him or her, the staff member lets the care receiver take a break or provides him or her with a new task.

This description demonstrates that Yuzu-OTP aims to make the facility comfortable for the care receiver. The staff at Yuzu-no-sato are not concerned with whether the care receiver completes his or her work. Rather, it is important for

Fig. 1. The staff talks to the care-receiver.

the care receiver to be willing to do the work and to develop a sense of accomplishment through the program. Furthermore, when the care receiver considers that his or her work is complete, the staff at Yuzu-no-sato teach him or her a method that the work becomes more expressive. Then, the work is brought to the next level and the care receiver's sense of accomplishment increases [3].

Yuzu-OTP involves many kinds of work. However, painting is the first activity for a new care receiver to engage in, and therefore this activity will be the focus in this work. In such a task, he or she receives a sample (a painted picture) and a sketch (a picture that only includes outlines). Then, he or she adds colors to the sketch (this is called "Iro nuri" or "Nurie" in Japanese). We analyzed what the staffs of Yuzu-no-sato observe in care receivers' work [3]; here, we provide a summary of what happens as the care receiver does Iro nuri. The following are questions that the staff members consider during the task:

- Can the care receiver understand what he or she is doing?
- How does he or she hold a color pencil?
- How does he or she paint the color on the sketch? Is the color different from the sample?
- What direction do his or her eyes follow when the staff member points during their conversation?
- How does he or she respond when the staff talks to him or her?
- Is he or she tired of the work?
- Does he or she have a bad posture?
- Is he or she doing the work with pleasure?
- Can he or she develop a feeling of accomplishment?

The staff member considers the care receiver's cognitive ability, grip, pressure on the pen, skill, visual/auditory ability, fatigue, pleasure, and sense accomplishment. These items are not meant to evaluate the care receiver's ability with numerical value; rather, the intention is to find the most suitable work for the individual care receiver.

4   Analysis of the Staff Meeting for Reflection

4.1   Aim

We sought to establish the importance of the meeting by analyzing the staff's conversation. We want to find how the staff verbalize their notice in the work program at the meeting.

4.2   Method

One of the authors participated in an evening staff meeting at Yuzu-no-sato and recorded it. Then, we analyzed the utterances of the staff. This study was approved by the Independent Ethics Committee of Faculty of Medicine at Saga University. We also obtained the consent of the hospital director at Sodegaura Satsukidai Hospital.

4.3   Transcript Symbols

We use the following transcript symbols [9] to express the staff utterances:

- A left bracket ([) indicates the point of overlap onset;
- An equals sign (=) indicates no break or gap;
- Numbers in parentheses (0.0) indicate elapsed time by tenths of seconds;
- A dot in parentheses ((.)) indicates a brief interval;
- Colons (::) indicate prolongation of the sound immediately prior. The longer the row of colon, the longer the prolongation;
- Parenthesized words ((*word*)) indicates that the transcriber was not really sure about what was said;
- Empty parentheses (()) indicate that the transcriber was unable to hear what was said;
- Parenthesized "h" indicates plosive; and
- Dollar signs ($ $) indicate that the speaker was smiling during the utterance.

4.4   Result

Excerpt 1 from the meeting, given below, is from the discussion of a novice occupational therapist (OT), an expert care worker (ES), the other staff (S), and the staff leader (SL) on how Care Receiver-A performed. "R" represents a staff member who was not present at this meeting. Although OT was a novice, she assumed the role of planning the next activity for each care receiver based on the reflection in the meeting. She tackled this role while receiving the leader and other staff members' instructions.

EXCERPT 1

01ES: A-san desu
02OT: demo nanka hamigakinotokini shijigahairanakute=
03ES: =utamo kashi yometenakatta A-san
04SL: a::so
05OT: suidonojaguchimo maekara ayashiitokoroga atta[kedo=
06ES: [attakedone
07OT:=kanzenni kyo mizuno dashikataga wakaranakute
snip
08SL: Kamioriwa dodattano?
09OT: Kamioriwa R-sankara zakkuri kiitandesukedo=
10SL:=yarudesyou [origamigatokui
11OT: [kanari[yappari
12ES: [aa nankamaene funeo ottemashitayo=
13OT:=[sonandesuyone? sutekina
14SL: =[anone ano (h) kamioriga sugoitokuinahitojanai?anohito. dakedo kyo=
15ES:=(   )wo ottyattandayone=
16SL:=so[soredewakattanndayone
17ES: [sagyonoshijiga hai[ranakutene
18SL: [origamiga   tokuinahazudattanoni.   kyo
kamiorinokouteiga zenzendamedattano. watashiga totyudemitandakedo
snip
19SL: sorede kamiorigasoredakedekinakunattekityattakara tukikkirininattyauyo
20OT: sodesune(.)orikeiwa.
(6.0)
21SL:aa::n?tte itteta.
22SL: a sokka(.)sokkatteittetakara honninmo tumatteirunoga wakarukara(.)ne.
23SL: moshikashitara soredakejanaihogaiinokamo(.)hanhanguraideiinokamo tuginosagyo.
(2.0)
24SL: sutoresutekina tokorowo kangaereba

English translation of Excerpt 1

01ES: The next is A-san.
02OT: So, when she brushed her teeth, she could not receive my instruction.=
03ES: =A-san also couldn't sing.
04SL: Oh, really?
05OT: She might confuse how to use the cock of a water supply from the past, [but=
06ES: [Yes, she did.
07OT:=She could not totally understand how to do it today.
snip
08SL: How about origami?
09OT: I heard how A-san did the origami from R-san.=
10SL:=Would she do it? [She is good at folding origami.
11OT: [Just as [I thought.
12ES: [Ah, she folded a ship previously.=
13OT:=[That's right. It was wonderful.
14SL: =[So (h) she is very good at folding origami, isn't she? But, today=
15ES:=She folded (   )=

16SL:=Yes. [We understood her cognitive state from her performance.

17ES: [She could not receive [my instruction.

18SL: [Although she should have been good at folding the origami, she was completely unable to understand the process of folding. I saw
her condition throughout the activity.
snip

19SL: Since she has been not able to understand the process of folding origami, the
staff will have to attend to her constantly.

20OT: Sure(.)About the origami series.

(6.0)

21SL: She said "u::m."

22SL: She said "aha(.)aha(.)" I think that she also can understand she
is stuck on folding the origami(.)isn't she?

23SL: I think that she should not do only origami(.)She should do
another work for half of the working time.

(2.0)

24SL: If we consider her stress.

In this meeting, first, OT talked about how Care Receiver-A appeared before
the program started (L.01–07). ES agreed with OT's opinion and reported that
she had observed the same thing, while SL listened and nodded. Then, SL asked
OT how Care Receiver-A appeared during the activity (L.08). Because SL was
also monitoring Care Receiver-A's appearance at this time, she wanted to report
her opinion to others (L.10, 14, 16, 18, 20, 22). SL suggested that OT should
reflect on Care Receiver-A's behavior while planning the next program activity
(L.19). However, OT did not answer (gap six seconds); therefore, SL gave OT a
clue to plan the next work (L.31–34).

In the next conversation, the staff discussed Care Receiver-B, who had
painted a water color during the program. This discussion is given in Excerpt 2.

EXCERPT 2

01SL: B-sanno hatuno suisaiwa dodattano?

02S: ano::nanka [onajitokoro nankaimo yattyau

03OT: [nankaimo kasanenuri zuttoyattemasita.=

04SL: =demokireiniwa nutteitayone?

05OT: [kanseishitemo.

06S: [nanka siroitokoroga nokotteitemo kinishinaindayone. dekokowo::tonankaika
susumerundakedo tyottoyosuwomite(.)honninwa kasenisiteiruto yappari
nuttenakute=

07ES: =ne

08S: un iroga nuttearutokoro[bakkari nuttyauno

09ES: [un kasaneru

(3.0)

10OT: [demo kyowa

11SL: [demo ajinoaru sakuhindane? sorewa soredene=

12OT: =[un

13ES: =[tyottone[kasanenuri shityatteiru

14S: [kasanenurishite::

15ES: demo::=

16SL: =sorewa sorede soyuu sakuhinna kanjiga suruyone?

17ES: so hanbunijowane:

18OT: un.

19ES: nantoka jibunde yarete mashitamonne?

20S: nanka kibun koyoshityatteitamitaide ahahatte[$waratteiru koegaookute$

21ES: [$so so$=

22SL: =waratteru $mitaina koedatta$

23ES: iyaja naindayone?=

24SL: =iyajanai.

25OT: nanka jibunde ko parettoni=

26ES: =sonanoyo=

27OT: =enogu tukerutte

28S: a::[dekinai dekinai

29OT: [dekinai?=

30ES: =dekinainoyo. sokoga dekinai[noyo

31S: [de fudega pasapasa[ninatte=

32ES: [so

33S: =torino ashiatomitai[ninattyatte

34ES: [so patapatatte nattyaukara [mata oomenitukete
motaseruto=

35S: [tuketeagete

36ES: =mata onajitokorowo.demo futoifudede yokattayo hosoiyori

37OT: hai

38ES: futoito kohanini iroga tukukara

(2.0)

39ES: demo anokata suisaimo ikeruyo?

40S: torikakariwa [biwaga ikerune.

41SL: [dareka tuiteite agerebane(.)chikakudene(.)suisaityuwa
tuiteiteagete.

42S: ne.

43SL: suisai chimude yattemireba iinjanai?

44OT: un.

English translation of Excerpt 2

01SL: How about B-san who tried to firstly paint in a picture in watercolors?

02S: Hmm. [She painted the same space many times

03OT: [It was many times, she repeated what she had already done before.=

04SL: =But she was painting neatly, wasn't she?

05OT: [Although the painting wasnt completed,

06S: [Hum, she was not concerned with the blank area, was she? I suggested that she
should paint a different area on several occasions. Then, I left it to her and watched
her state. However, she did not paint after all.=

07ES: =Yeah.

08S: Yeah, she painted only the place where have been [already painted.

09ES: [Yes, she did.

(3.0)

10OT: [But, today

11SL: [But, there was a taste in her painting, wasn't there? It was right, somehow=

12OT: =[Yes.

13ES: =[It was a little, [she over painted.

14S: [Over painting::

15ES: But::=
16SL: =It was all right. We can consider that it is such a work, can't we?
17ES: Yeah, it was considered more than half:
18OT: Yes.
19ES: She managed to paint by herself, didn't she?
20S: She was in high spirits. I heard "Ahaha" [$and her voice sounded amused$
21ES: [$Right$=
22SL: =$It was laughter.$
23ES: She didn't refuse to paint, right?=
24SL: =That's right. She did not refuse it.
25OT: So, she used the palette by herself in this way.=
26ES: =That is what I mean.=
27OT: =Did she put paint on the paintbrush?
28S: Ah::,[she could not, could not.
29OT: [Couldn't she do it?=
30ES:=Yes, she could not. She could not [it.
31S: [And her paintbrush got too
     [dry.=
32ES:[That's right.
33S: =It became a bird [footprints.
34ES: [Yeah, because she did pitter-patter painting,
     [I added more color to the paintbrush more and I let her have it.=
35S: [added a color...
36ES: =But, she painted the same area. However, the thick paintbrush was better than
a thin paintbrush for her.
37OT: I see.
38ES: The thick brush can place color on a broader area.
(2.0)
39ES: She can continue painting water colors, can't she?
40S: At first, [we can provide her a sample picture for painting, "Biwa."
41SL: [Someone should follow her(.)Near she(.)When she paints.
42S: Yeah.
43SL: Should she paints in "the water-color team?"
44OT: I see.

Care Receiver-B's spirits were high when she was painting a water color
(L.20). However, she painted the same space repeatedly, and she was unaware
that there were spaces that had not yet been painted (L. 02, 03, 06, 08, 09,
13, 14). The staff members who participated in the meeting spoke rapidly, and
many utterances overlapped. Each staff member observed how Care Receiver-
B was painting and how she externalized her awareness. Although most staff
member reported that Care Receiver-B painted only one area of the picture,
SL had a different viewpoint from the other staff members, as shown when she
commented, "But, she was painting neatly, wasn't she? (L.04)," "But, there
was a taste in her painting, wasn't there? (L.11)," and "It was all right. We
can consider that it is such a work, can't we? (L.16)." Thus, SL accepted Care
Receiver-B's work and asked the other staff members to appreciate it as well.
At this point, ES reported that Care Receiver-B could paint by herself (L.19),
and S reported that painting made Care Receiver-B happy (L.20). Finally, ES

concluded that Care Receiver-B did not hate painting, even if she could not carry out all aspects of the task.

OT, who had to plan the next activity for Care Receiver-B, asked ES and E whether Care Receiver-B could put color on the paintbrush from the palette by herself (L.25, 27, 29). ES and S did not say that Care Receiver-B was unable to do it; rather, they gave OT some ideas about how to set up the water-color painting activity for Care Receiver-B (L.28, 30–36, 38). Then, SL proposed that OT create a team - "the water-color team (L.43)" - consisting of care receivers who painted water colors. One of the staff members would attend to this team and assist them to paint.

5 Discussion

The Yuzu-OTP at Yuzu-no-sato day care involves scheduling each day based on the work process shown in Fig. 2. The steps involved in organizing this therapy are discussed below.

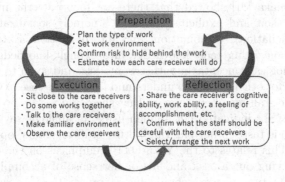

Fig. 2. Work process in Yuzu-OTP.

Preparation. First, the staff plan the type of work to be carried out by each care receiver. They arrange each care receiver's work based on his or her cognitive state, tastes, interests, job experience, and so on. On the day that the task is to be carried out, they set articles on tables and regulate the work environment. Moreover, the staff confirm a way of correspondence to each care receiver and risk to hide behind in each work. Then, the staff estimate how each care receiver will do his or her individual work.

Execution. During the work program, the staff members sit close to the care receivers, perform some works together, talk to them, and observe how they are carrying out their tasks (see Sect. 3) [3,6]. The staff write down their awareness [10] on the prepared sheet.

Reflection. After the care receivers leave the day care, the staff members attend a staff meeting. They report on how each care receiver did and reflect on his or her state. The staff's reflection leads to the next plan of the work that each care receiver can manage with enthusiasm and a greater feeling of accomplishment.

In the reflection step, the staff reported their observations in detail (see Sect. 4). Some staff jotted down what they had seen in about one sentence when they had a bit of free time. It is useful for the reflection meeting when staff write down their observations in advance; in this study, we found that these memos were sometimes discussed in the meetings. However, our previous research showed that in terms of the care staff at facility X, care staff receivers could not write down their observations [6]. Therefore, as future work, we are seeking to address how the system can be made more useful when it comes to allowing staff to write down their perceptions and connect to the reflection step (the meeting).

In the meetings, since the individual's perspective was conveyed to the other staff members, they could share their viewpoints, support the steps another co-worker had taken to encourage the care receiver, and create new thoughts and suggestions. Nonaka [11] showed that there are four patterns in the dynamic interaction of "tacit and explicit knowledge," namely socialization, externalization (or articulation), combination, and internalization. Externalization is the process of converting tacit knowledge into explicit knowledge. People use metaphors, analogies, concepts, hypotheses, models, and so on to translate their tacit knowledge for other people to understand [11]. In the case of Care Receiver-B, initially, some staff members thought that she could not paint well. However, after the leader (SL) indicated her opinion using an analogy, saying "Aji noaru sakuhin" [There is taste in her painting], other staff members' opinions became more positive. This relates to the Yuzu-OTP's emphasis on the care receiver's pleasure in carrying out a task and his or her sense of accomplishment when determining what type of work should be set up for the care receiver. In this way, during the meetings, the staff members generated new knowledge concerning what each care receiver should do during the next occupational therapy session to elicit enthusiasm; thus, they engaged in reflection.

6   Conclusion

In this paper, we analyzed meetings at the "Yuzu-no-sato [1]" day care facility for individuals with severe dementia. We found that the staff became aware of what they have observed, experienced, and felt during the work occupation sessions. In the meetings, staff members could share their viewpoints and create new thoughts and suggestions. In the future, we intend to construct a system that allows staff at other day care facilities to externalize their awareness easily. Moreover, we will record utterances that emerge not only in meetings but also when Yuzu-no-sato's staff are carrying out the preparation and the execution steps. We will then clarify features of Yuzu-OTP based on a conversation and gesture analysis [12].

References

1. Yuzu no sato. http://www.satsuki-kai.or.jp/kanjya/reha0102.html
2. Ishii, Y., Hosoi, N.: The process of determining the therapy program for users of severe dementia day care. In: Proceedings of the 32nd International Conference on of Alzheimer's Disease International (2017, in printing)
3. Machishima, K., Ishii, Y., Oshima, C., Hosoi, N., Nakayama, K.: The process of determining the occupational therapy program viable for users of severe dementia day care facility. J. Jpn. Soc. Dement. Care **15**(2), 503–512 (2016). (in Japanese)
4. Csikszentmihalyi, M.: Beyond Boredom and Anxiety. Jpssey-Bass, San Francisco (1975)
5. Kolanowski, A., Fick, D.M., Buettner, L.: Recreational activities to reduce behavioural symptoms in dementia. Geriatr. Aging **12**(1), 37–42 (2010)
6. Oshima, C., Ishii, Y., Machishima, K., Abe, H., Hosoi, N., Nakayama, K.: A process of instruction how to personalize occupational program according to individual's characteristics at day-care facilities for getting a feeling of accomplishment. SIG Technical reports, 2016-AAC-1(14) (2016). (in Japanese)
7. National Institute of Advanced Industrial Science and Technology: Dance care. http://unicus.jp/taxonomy/term/11
8. Uchihira, N., Choe, S., Hiraishi, K., Torii, K., Chino, T., Hirabayashi, Y., Sugihara, T.: Collaboration management by smart voice messaging for physical and adaptive intelligent services. In: Proceedings of PICMET 2013. IEEE (2013)
9. Jefferson, G.: Glossary of transcript symbols with an introduction. Pragmatics and Beyond New Series, vol. 125, pp. 13–34 (2004)
10. Buckler, B.: A learning process model to achieve continuous improvement and innovation. Learn. Organ. **3**(3), 31–39 (1996)
11. Nonaka, I., Takeuchi, H.: The Knowledge-Creating Company: How Japanese Companies Create the Dynamics of Innovation. Oxford University Press, New York (1995)
12. Hosoma, H.: Hands and knowledge. In: Motomura, Y., Butler, A., Bekki, D. (eds.) JSAI-isAI 2012. LNCS, vol. 7856, pp. 233–241. Springer, Heidelberg (2013). doi:10. 1007/978-3-642-39931-2_17

Designing User Interfaces
for Curation Technologies

Georg Rehm[1]([✉]), Jing He[2], Julián Moreno-Schneider[1], Jan Nehring[1],
and Joachim Quantz[2]

[1] DFKI GmbH, Alt-Moabit 91c, 10559 Berlin, Germany
{georg.rehm,julian.moreno_schneider,jan.nehring}@dfki.de
[2] ART+COM AG, Kleiststraße 23-26, 10787 Berlin, Germany
{jing.he,joachim.quantz}@artcom.de
http://digitale-kuratierung.de

Abstract. Digital content and online media have reached an unprecedented level of relevance and importance. In the context of a research and technology transfer project on Digital Curation Technologies for online content we develop a platform that provides curation services that can be integrated into concrete curation or content management systems. In this project, the German Research Center for Artificial Intelligence (DFKI) collaborates with four Berlin-based SMEs that work with and on digital content in four different sectors. The curation services comprise several semantic text and document analytics processes as well as knowledge technologies that can be applied to document collections. The key objective of this set of curation services is to support knowledge workers and digital curators in their daily work, i.e., to automate or to semi-automate processes that the human experts are normally required to do intellectually and without tool support. The goal is to help this group of information and knowledge workers to become more efficient and more effective as well as to enable them to produce high-quality content in their respective sectors. In this article we concentrate on the current state of a user interface that is currently under development at ART+COM, one of the SME partners in the project. A second, more generic, i.e., not domain-specific user interface is under development at DFKI. In this article we describe the technology platform and the two different interfaces. We also take a look at the different requirements for ART+COM's domain-specific and DFKI's generic user interface.

Keywords: Digital curation technologies · User centered design · Natural Language Processing

1 Introduction

Digital content and online media have reached an unprecedented level of relevance and importance, especially with regard to commercial, political and societal aspects, debates and collective decisions. One of the many technological

© Springer International Publishing AG 2017
S. Yamamoto (Ed.): HIMI 2017, Part I, LNCS 10273, pp. 388–406, 2017.
DOI: 10.1007/978-3-319-58521-5_31

challenges related to online content refers to better support and smarter technologies for data, information and knowledge workers, i.e., persons, who work primarily at and with a computer, who are facing an ever increasing incoming stream of heterogeneous information and who create, based on the specific requirements, demands, expectations and conventions of the sector they work in and also based on their job profiles and responsibilities, in a rather general sense, new information. For example, experts in a digital agency build mobile apps or websites for clients who provide the digital agency with documents, data, pictures, videos and other assets that are processed, sorted, augmented, arranged, packaged and then deployed. Knowledge workers in a library digitise a specific archive, augment it with additional metadata, maybe also critical edition information and publish the archive online. Journalists need to stay on top of the news stream including blogs, microblogs, newswires, websites etc. in order to produce a new article on a breaking topic, based on the information they collected, processed, sorted, evaluated, verified and synthesised. A multitude of examples exists in multiple different sectors and branches of media (television, radio, blogs, print journalism, investigative journalism etc.). All these different professional environments and contexts can benefit immensely from semantic technologies that support these knowledge workers, who typically work under high time pressure, in their respective activities: finding relevant information, highlighting important concepts, sorting incoming documents in multiple different ways, translating articles in foreign languages, suggesting interesting topics. We call these different semantic services, that can be applied in different professional environments that all have to do with the processing, analysis, translation, evaluation, contextualisation, verification, synthesis and production of digital information, *Curation Technologies*.

In the context of our research and technology transfer project Digital Curation Technologies (DKT), the German Research Center for Artificial Intelligence (DFKI) develops a curation platform that offers language- and knowledge-aware services such as semantic analysis, search, analytics, recombination and generation (e.g., thematic, chronological and spatial) for the curation of arbitrary types of digital content. The platform automates specific parts of the curation workflows that knowledge workers or digital curators typically follow. Semantic technologies can be used to assist the experts in data processing, in terms of efficiency, breadth, depth, and scope, ascertaining what is important, relevant, maybe even genuinely new and eye-opening. The common ground for all these tasks and challenges is the curation of digital information.

We mainly work with larger, self-contained document collections – however, our technologies can also be applied to dynamic content, news, search results, tweets, blog posts etc. The key objective is to shorten the time it takes knowledge workers to familiarise themselves with a potentially large set of documents by semantically extracting relevant data of various types and presenting the data in a way that allows the knowledge workers to be more efficient, especially in the situation when he or she is not a domain expert with regard to the topics of the document collection. In the project, DFKI works with data sets provided by the project partners, four SME companies active in different sectors:

- **ART+COM AG:** Museums and museum design, exhibitions, showrooms
- **Condat AG:** Television, web tv, radio, media
- **3pc GmbH:** Public archives
- **Kreuzwerker GmbH:** Print journalism

DFKI develops the curation technology platform and provides curation services to the SME partners through standard web interfaces. The SME partners integrate these curation services in their own domain-specific and sector-specific systems and applications. One of the key aspects of our project is to explore how far we can go, how much we can achieve with the rather *generic* curation services in the different *domain-specific* use case scenarios of the four SME partners, all of which have their own requirements, demands, constraints and peculiarities.

With regard to the technologies DFKI builds modular semantic Language Technology and Knowledge Technology components that can be arranged in pipelines or workflows. Based on the output of these Natural Language Processing (NLP) and Information Retrieval (IR) components, a semantic layer is generated on top of a document collection. It contains various types of metadata in the form of annotations on the documents that can be made use of in further processing steps, visualisations or graphical user interfaces.

In this article we concentrate on the collaboration between DFKI and the project partner ART+COM AG, a design studio with an extensive history in creating media-rich exhibition designs in cultural and commercial sectors, e.g., a zoo for micro-organisms (Micropia) in Amsterdam, The Netherlands, an experience centre on Viking history in Jelling, Denmark, or a Product Info Center for the car manufacturer BMW in Munich, Germany.[1] ART+COM employs a number of knowledge workers who can, in a way, be conceptualised as the prototypical textbook users of digital curation technologies. These knowledge workers need to be able and flexible enough to familiarise themselves with completely new topics and domains in a very short timespan. In order to support this highly complex task, ART+COM is experimenting with curation technologies, for example, to process materials in order to produce a project pitch, to plan a new museum from scratch or to plan individual museum exhibits. The goal is to help these digital curators to become more efficient and more effective as well as to enable them to produce high-quality content through generic curation technologies.

The remainder of this article is structured as follows. First, we describe the technology platform and some of the curation services in more detail (Sect. 2). After this description of the technical background we concentrate on the state of a user interface that is currently under development at ART+COM (Sect. 3). A second, more generic, i.e., not particularly domain-specific, user interface is under development at DFKI (Sect. 4). Finally, we take a look at the boundary and different requirements between DFKI's *generic* user interface and ART+COM's rather *domain-specific* user interface (Sect. 5).

---

[1] http://www.artcom.de.

2   Curation Technologies

In this section we briefly describe the current version of our curation platform [1,4,5,13]. The curation services exposed through RESTful APIs comprise modules that either work on their own or that can be arranged in the form of workflows. All current use cases at the four SME project partners (see above) revolve around the processing of document collections of almost arbitrary sizes, ranging from a few files to collections comprising millions of documents. The system is still under development.[2] The various NLP modules analyse documents and extract information to be used in several digital curation scenarios. Interoperability between the modules is achieved through the NLP Interchange Format (NIF) [11], i.e., all modules accept NIF as input and return NIF as output. The shared usage of NIF allows for the combination of web services in a decentralised way, without hard-wiring specific workflows or pipelines. In the following we present some of the curation services.

2.1   Named Entity Recognition and Named Entity Linking

First we convert every document to NIF and then perform Named Entity Recognition (NER). The NER module consists of two different approaches (additional ones to be added) that allow training the system with annotated data and/or to use lexicons and dictionaries. Afterwards the service attempts to look up the named entity on its (language-specific) DBPedia page using DBPedia Spotlight [12] to extract additional information using a SPARQL query. Similar queries can be used to retrieve additional information for different types of entities, e.g., for locations we point the service to Geonames in order to retrieve its coordinates.[3]

2.2   Temporal Expression Analysis

The temporal expression analyser is based on a regular expression based grammar that can process German and English natural language text. After the identification of temporal expressions, they are normalised to a shared machine readable format and added to the NIF representation. We also add document-level statistics based on the normalised temporal values. This analysis information can be used to position a document on a timeline.

2.3   Geographical Localisation Module

The geographical location module uses SPARQL to retrieve the latitude and longitude of a location as specified in its DBpedia entry (see above). The module also computes the mean and standard deviation value for latitude and longitude of *all* identified locations in a document. This analysis information can be used to position a document on a map visualisation.

---

[2] In a second paper at this conference [4], we focus upon the "Semantic Storytelling" curation service and provide more technical details regarding the Curation Platform. The platform itself is based on the FREME infrastructure [11].

[3] http://www.geonames.org.

2.4   Text Classification and Document Clustering

For the classification service we make use of the Mallet Toolkit[4] to assign topics or domains such as "politics" or "sports" to documents. The respective topic is stored within an RDF element in the NIF representation. Document clustering, or, rather, the clustering of all entities contained in a document or all documents, is performed with the help of WEKA.[5] The service is called from the interface in order to give users a clarifying view by groups of entities appearing in a collection, which can be useful as an exploratory tool.

3   Curation Technologies for Exhibition Design

The primary technical challenge of the project is the development of smart curation technologies that, already in their generic state, provide good results in terms of recall, precision, quality, and coverage, and that can be customised and configured to the four specific SME partners' use cases through domain adaptation and customisation capabilities. A second challenge relates to the – by definition domain-specific – design of the corresponding user interfaces (UI) under development by the SME partners. These UIs have their own requirements and constraints, depending on the respective domains, sectors, use cases and target users. In this paper we focus upon the sector of exhibition design. We explain, in detail, the user-centered design process, which has been guiding the implementation of the ART+COM user interface.

3.1   Initial User Studies

The UX design team at ART+COM began the user research process with in-depth interviews and surveys to learn about our potential users, the knowledge workers, their behavior, goals, motivations and needs. The initial user research was carried out in a relatively broad way, involving 12 knowledge workers in academic and commercial fields producing either scientific or creative work. The interviews were conducted in each interviewee's typical work environment, ranging from library, office to cafe and home. The interviews began with asking the interviewees general questions about their research process and goals. Then interviewees were asked to show us, on their computers, how they perform their research. This provided us with insights on the kinds of tools and environments each user is familiar with as well as extrapolating their usage patterns. Moreover, the team acquired an intuitive understanding of the different phases of their workflows, and the goals and expectations for each research step.

While the interviews gave us qualitative findings, the surveys provided a quantitative overview of the potential users. The questionnaire was based on the insights the design team gathered from the interviews, addressing the problem space identified in each key research phase. The 15 questions were split into

---

[4] http://mallet.cs.umass.edu.
[5] http://www.cs.waikato.ac.nz/ml/weka/.

"gathering information", "processing information", and "sharing information" phases. About half of the questions were multiple choice, with the option for embellishment, and the other half free-text. The questions included the kinds of existing tools and services they use and pain points they experience as well as the kind of data and information they gather, how they organise them and share their findings. Responses from 20 participants were received.

3.2 Personas

The qualitative and quantitative user research forms the basis for creating several personas. Personas can be used to synthesise real users' needs, behaviours, and mental models. Based on the results of the surveys and interviews a set of behavioral variables were identified, which can be used to create semantic differential scales [6]. During the persona workshops, the team collectively placed each user along the scales based on his/her responses and actions. Eventually, clusters began to emerge on the scales, from which primary and secondary personas were identified. Meet Julia, Kate, and Alex (Fig. 1).

Julia is our primary persona. She works at a creative agency as a content researcher. Constrained by time and budget, shes quick on her feet in gathering information for many short-term projects, often at the same time. Her research process is open, from one keyword branching into other possibly interesting topics, formulating and refining the "right" questions. Her goal is to be able to quickly grasp a general impression of a topic so that she can focus on meaningful key points to highlight and share with the team. During the research, she constantly weighs in on the validity of the sources found.

On the contrary, Alex is an academic researcher working on long-term rigorous academic research. When he is not writing, he is doing research in online archives or burying his head in books at the library. Alex works mostly alone. His research process is highly structured and iterative, taking his time to conduct thoroughly primary as well as secondary research.

Personas set the foundation for the following steps in the user-centered design process, helped us prioritise core features and to communicate them to the design, development and product management team.

3.3 User Scenarios, Task Analysis, Functional Requirements

Based on the knowledge about the personas, the team formulated user scenarios to understand the context and motivation behind users' interactions, one of which represents the most common usage pattern of Julia, our primary persona. The scenario describes that Julia has received a lot of material from the client for an exhibition about microbes. These materials include images and scientific papers about different micro-organisms, including their behaviors, interactions with their habitat, etc. Julia has a couple days to get an overview of the received information as well as to familiarise herself with the topic of microbiology. She has to effectively share her key findings with the design team in order to kick-start conceptual and creative brainstorm sessions.

Fig. 1. Primary and secondary personas

A task flow [7] is generated describing the individual steps Julia would take in order to complete this assignment. The tasks are described intentionally on a high level to focus on her actions rather than being distracted by the current technology she employs. Twelve steps have been defined, which are grouped in the phases "search", "evaluate", and "organise" of her entire workflow (Fig. 2). Having the persona in mind, the team then brainstormed on the user's functional

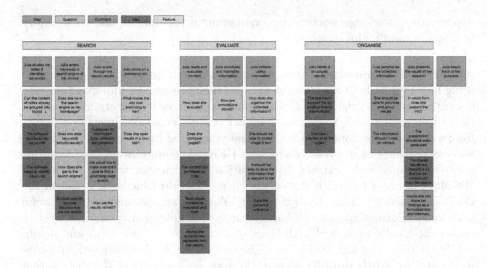

Fig. 2. User task flow

needs, required knowledge and optimal outcome for each step. For example, in step one Julia studies her notes and identifies keywords. Her functional needs at this stage could be having structured notes, an overview of keywords and the ability to identify keywords. However, since she is new to the topic of microbiology, it may not be easy for her to find relevant information at first.

After having gone through all the key tasks the user performs, the next iteration focused on translating the user's functional needs to functional requirements of the system. In order to fulfill his/her needs in the "search" step, the system could allow the user to import her notes and source materials, extract the keywords and display the keywords in a meaningful way, which could provide the user an immediate overview and understanding of the information at hand so that she can have a better start for her research.

In this first step, the design team has identified the user's need to acquire specific knowledge necessary to accurately make the right decision. In this case, familiarising herself with the topic of microbiology. The key pain point for our personas is the lack of an overview of the information they find and collect. Therefore, the team decided to prioritise the system functionalities which would optimise the user's task flow, namely impart the knowledge they need, and improve the information overview.

3.4   Minimum Viable Product

Based on the core features identified during the task analysis, we defined the major problem-space that we would like to tackle within the scope of the minimum viable product (MVP) [8]. The design of the MVP would only focus upon optimising the user's initial research phase of the entire workflow. The MVP would inform us how the curation services and visualisation techniques could improve the knowledge worker's understanding of the domain and their ability to discover meaningful insights.

Application Framework. Our prototype is a web application implemented using RESTful APIs. It allows users to begin their research by importing existing documents, such as briefing materials from the client, or by performing an explorative web search with keywords. Whether it's imported documents or results from web pages, the content is automatically analysed by the semantic curation services provided by our research partner DFKI. The application then performs a batch-lookup on the extracted information, for example, named entities, on Wikidata in order to enrich the entities (e.g., "Harald Bluetooth", "Gorm the Old", or "Sweden" in the context of the Viking experience center) with useful additional information. The Wikidata entry of a given entity can be used to enrich the locally presented with the date and place of one's birth and death, family relations and occupation, etc. The entities are further enriched with top-level ontology labels in order to give the user an overview of the distribution of information in categories, for instance, person, organisation, and location. Figure 3 shows the key screens implemented in the current prototype.[6]

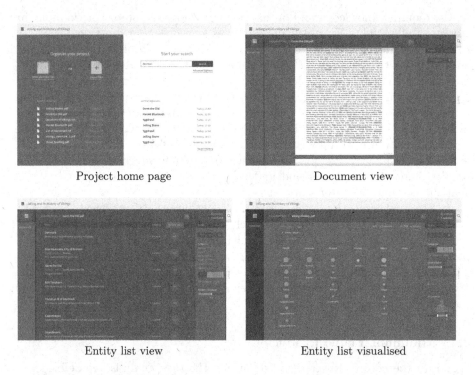

Project home page   Document view

Entity list view   Entity list visualised

Fig. 3. Prototype application for content curators developed by ART+COM

---

[6] A screencast of the prototype is available at https://vimeo.com/182694896.

Information Visualisation. Our second focus is to visualise the extracted information. We implemented the visualisations in D3, a Javascript library optimised for visualising data with HTML, SVG and CSS. The challenge is to provide intuitive and effective interaction modalities so that the users can gain a quick overview of a specific topic or drill down into the semantic knowledge base to explore deeper patterns or relationships.

We realised several visualisations including a network overview, semantic clustering, timelining and maps (Fig. 4). While a network is effective for exploring semantic relationships amongst extracted entities, semantic clustering provides a good overview of entities closely related to each other in groups. Timelines and maps, in addition, offer a geo-temporal overview of extracted entities. Combining all of the above mentioned visualisations for doing research on Harald Bluetooth, for example, the user can explore the places and people to which he is connected in the network visualisation, view his timespan of reign and family lineage along the timeline, and explore notable events that are highlighted on the map.

In terms of interaction modalities, the user can directly manipulate the graph by zooming and panning. On highlighting entities, tooltips appear to display entity properties found on Wikidata. Users can also select and focus on the connections between two entities to explore in depth how they are related. Harald Bluetooth's connection to Gorm the Old, for instance, is encoded with several connection possibilities. Harald is the son of Gorm, He also became the King of Denmark after his father.

Besides the direct interaction with the visualisation, we also implemented interactive filters in order for the user to effectively get to specific information needed. For instance, the category filter allows the user to filter entities which are only person or a combination of person, location, or other category labels that are deemed relevant to the user.

3.5   User Evaluation

The MVP is developed in an agile approach, in which the team at ART+COM iterates through design, development and user test cycles. We consistently invited our in-house curation workers to participate in the user tests.

Earlier Prototypes. In the first user test the user was asked to interact with a paper prototype (Fig. 5). The aim was to quickly find out if the overall navigation structure was sound. For instance, we learned that our users need to be able to quickly switch between projects and perform project-based searches. We took this insight and built our application so that the search history is part of a project property. Previously searched items show up in relevant project locations so that users don't lose track of their search progress when switching between projects.

This was followed by an interactive prototype implemented in Proto.io.[7] In this prototype users could perform basic interaction such as enter a keyword, scroll

---

[7] https://proto.io.

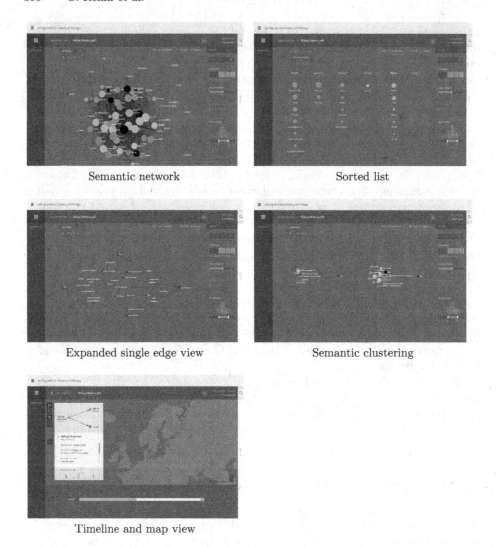

Semantic network   Sorted list

Expanded single edge view   Semantic clustering

Timeline and map view

Fig. 4. Visualisation types

through the page, drag and drop files. The interaction was limited, but the design was able to evaluate and conclude that the users understood the overall interaction framework. Furthermore, we were able to get the user's impression on the usefulness of contextual visualisation. All six users we interviewed understood that visualisations are used to summarise the content of a given page. Some found it "novel", while others could imagine the visualisations help them create new content and "make sense of data". Since the content of the user test was based on an existing project about Vikings in Denmark, one user raised the question how visualisations would evolve if the content is more scientific instead of historical.

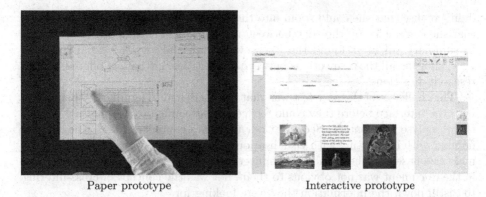

Paper prototype   Interactive prototype

Fig. 5. Earlier low-fi prototypes

Current Prototype. The last user test was conducted using the latest developed web application, described in Sect. 3.4. The design team focused on, one, evaluating the usefulness of semantically extracted entities and the information that enriches the given entities, and, two, user interaction with the visualisations.

We interviewed five knowledge workers. Each interview took about one hour. We first informed the users that our design studio has been invited to create a concept proposal for an interactive installation about the Italian artist Caravaggio for an art museum. Given this context, the user had a few minutes to glance through a printed document about the artist. The users were then asked to switch to the web application, in which we presented the printed document digitally with extracted entities highlighted. We asked them to focus on highlighted words and what they could mean. All the users were able to identify that the highlighted words were about people and places. One user questioned why only these words were highlighted while another user concluded that the people and places must all have a connection to Caravaggio.

The users were asked to navigate to the entity list view where the entities are listed based on number of occurrences, category types or alphabetical order. Each entity is assigned a top-level category and enriched with a short descriptive statement. We asked the users to explore the content and interface freely while thinking aloud. Here, the users perceived that the enrichment of the entities seem to come from the web, like "a condensed version of a browser search".

Throughout the evaluation, users were asked to keep in mind a few keywords that seemed interesting to them as they transition from the document view, to the entity list view, and finally to the visualisation view, in hope that the users can keep focus on exploring the content rather than feeling overwhelmed by being confronted with a new interface. In the visualisation view, the users could first begin with free exploration while thinking aloud. All of them started by directly manipulating the graph, i.e., dragging the nodes or highlighting nodes to see additional information in the tooltip. We then asked them to perform actions they missed during the free exploration phase. For example, one user didn't realise that she could zoom into the graph while another user didnt know that she could click on the edge between nodes to explore in depth the relation. In summary, all users found the list view most useful and the expanded edge view, showing all the connections between two entities, intriguing, offered further research directions.

The challenge of the user test was that the users had to familiarise themselves with the interface before they could feel confident enough to use the tool to help them analyse the content. Secondly, our users are content workers who are not familiar with interacting with visualisations. Changing the visual encoding of the node size based on the number of connections versus the number of occurrences in the document was not obvious to them, nor was the concept of cross-filtering to distill down the information they were looking for.

The users concluded that the application provides a good overview of the subject and that they would use the tool at the beginning of a project, particularly when confronted with massive amounts of text. However, some relevant information from the original text was missing and some extracted information seemed out of context. Regarding the usefulness of extracted information, they validated the relevance of the extracted names of people and places and that the enriched "general information" about each entity was useful. However, they wish for more relations between entities extracted from the document so that they could deepen their understanding through the document itself as well as through the, more generally defined, Encyclopedia-like information.

3.6 Next Steps

ART+COM will continue to improve the visualisation-based user interface, allowing a seamless browsing experience between entities and the content from which they are extracted. We will evaluate the approach with different knowledge domains as ART+COM's exhibition topics are quite diverse, ranging from historical to scientific. We already started exploring image classification as the knowledge workers often work with images. The web search so far is based on search queries from Bing and Wikipedia only. We could, in addition, include sources from Project Gutenberg, Archive.org or other structured knowledge bases.

Finally, "Queen" can be either an occupation or the name of a rock band. In order to offer our knowledge workers reliable enriched information that is context-specific, the team at ART+COM will, in close collaboration with DFKI, continue to improve the graph-service so that we can better resolve the intended meaning of ambiguous entities and provide more flexibility in the user-interface so that the system can also learn and adapt based on user's input and intent.

4 Between Domain-Specificity and General Applicability

So far we have described the digital curation platform (Sect. 2) and one specific use-case, the application of curation services, provided by the platform, in the domain-specific user interface designed and implemented by ART+COM

(Sect. 3). The curation platform itself provides RESTful APIs. Language and Knowledge Technology platforms such as this one do not typically come with a UI because their functionality is usually integrated in larger applications with concrete use cases and established user interfaces.

Nevertheless, there is a certain GUI approach that several Natural Language Processing applications share, especially systems that concentrate on text analytics such as part-of-speech tagging, Named Entity Recognition and relation extraction. These methods analyse text content and annotate information in the processed documents. There are several different ways of presenting and visualising the annotated information, i.e., using different text or background colours (of specific text segments), different fonts or font sizes, using pop-up menus or using additional graphs that are embedded into the document display. Additionally, an explanation of, for example, the different colours is usually shown to the left or right of the document view. To a certain extent this approach can be seen as an established interface convention and best practice in research and industry.

Several tools apply this interface metaphor. One of them is the General Architecture for Text Engineering (GATE), an integrated system that provides mechanisms and a graphical interface that allow putting together NLP pipelines in an easy way.[8] GATE has several technological properties that make its application in a general curation scenario a rather big challenge. For example, the inclusion of external storage, such as Virtuoso or Lucene, is possible but very difficult. GATE provides part of its functionality using the interface metaphor briefly described in the introduction of this section. A second tool that uses this metaphor is Open Calais, a commercial product by Thomson Reuters.[9] Open Calais can be tested through a web interface and also attempts to link entities to knowledge bases. Compared to these typical interfaces, ART+COM's user interface goes several steps further by providing customised features that are tailor-made to the requirements of their in-house knowledge workers and content curators, such as presenting different views that show the number of occurrences of entities in a document in order to make it easier to assess their respective relevance.

A type of software that comes close to what a generic curation user interface can or should be able to support, is the established software category of Content Management Systems (CMS). The primary function and use case of all CMS products is the management of individual content pieces including creation, editing and publishing. Many CMS tools also provide analytics functions but these only refer to typical key performance indicators such as web access statistics, advertisements, conversion rates and others. Only very few Content Management Systems provide features that resemble our curation services, i.e., actual semantic content analytics. However, many CMS products allow the integration of plug-ins, making it possible to integrate our curation services into an established CMS.

DFKI has been developing a more generic interface that we call "Curation Dashboard". It is meant to provide a GUI and testbed that makes available all

---

[8] https://gate.ac.uk.
[9] http://www.opencalais.com.

curation services developed by DFKI. The interface is used to test the curation platform with an immediately and intuitively usable interface, to evaluate certain curation services, to showcase the system (and project) to interested colleagues from research and industry as well as to experiment with concrete curation scenarios. Among others, we have already used the dashboard to experiment with four use cases not covered by our funded project (digital libraries [9,10], forensic linguistics [2], digital humanities [3] and investigative journalism).[10]

In contrast to ART+COM's interface, the DFKI curation dashboard (Fig. 6) is not meant for production use but as a tool that can be demonstrated at conferences, in industry exhibitions, presentations, or within project acquisition scenarios. There are many different use cases and sectors that could be interested to work with curation technologies. In addition to the ones already mentioned, these are, among others, healthcare, finance, trend detection, customer relationship management and research itself (citation analysis etc.).

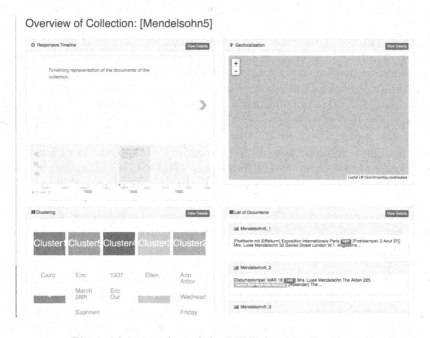

Fig. 6. Main interface of the DFKI Curation Dashboard

The main interface of the dashboard (Fig. 6) is composed of four parts that show a small preview of the available visualisations as a summary of the document collection: timelining (top left), geolocation (top right), entities clustering visualisation (bottom left) and document list view (bottom right). The current preview is limited. A visualisation of all documents in a collection can be accessed

---

[10] A screencast of the prototype: https://www.youtube.com/watch?v=TgP_TxoobuU.

through their own specific views (Figs. 7 and 8). These are bigger and offer better visualisation possibilities for larger numbers of documents.

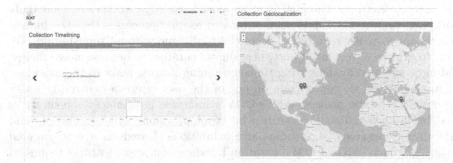

Fig. 7. Timelining (left) and geolocation (right) interfaces of the Curation Dashboard

The document view (Fig. 8) shows the output of the NLP processes through the annotations visualised within the text using the established best practice approach described above, i.e., among others, applying colours to mark specific metadata. In our case, the colours represent the type of analysis that created the annotations.

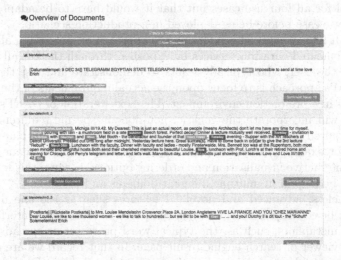

Fig. 8. Documents list interface of the Curation Dashboard

5   Summary and Conclusions

In the project Digital Curation Technologies we develop a platform that provides a set of generic curation services that can be integrated, via RESTful APIs, into sector-specific applications with their own sector-specific requirements and use cases. The services comprise, among others, several semantic text and document analytics processes as well as knowledge technologies that can be applied to document collections. The goal is to support knowledge workers in their daily work, i.e., to automate or to semi-automate routine processes that the human experts are normally required to do intellectually and without tool support. We want to explore if we can support these digital curators to become more efficient and more effective by delegating time-consuming routine tasks to the machine.

In this article we concentrate on one of the user interfaces currently under development in the project. ART+COM's interface is primarily meant to be used by in-house content curators who develop, among others, concepts and exhibits for museums, showrooms and exhibitions. Based on a user-centered design approach, ART+COM's curation interface comprises features requested and tailored to the requirements of their target users.

A more generic, i.e., not domain- or use-case-specific interface is under development at DFKI. This curation dashboard has a different purpose: it is meant as an environment so that services can be tested and evaluated. The interface is also used to showcase the platform to colleagues from research and industry as well as to assess the feasibility of other curation scenarios. DFKI recently used the system for experiments in four domains not covered by our project, i.e., digital libraries [9,10], investigative journalism, forensic linguistics [2], digital humanities [3]. These preliminary tests have shown that the dashboard has a lot of potential for all four use cases but that it would have to be adapted to the respective use case before being deployed in a production scenario.

While DFKI's dashboard is adopting the approach of showcasing all features of the implemented curation services by exposing, through the UI, all technical features to the user, who typically wants to demonstrate and test the system, ART+COM's approach is to focus upon the actual requirements of the intended target users in a production environment. The next iteration of DFKI's curation dashboard will incorporate the generic, non-domain-specific requirements and insights acquired by ART+COM during the user centered design phase of their interface, for example, presenting the respective frequencies of named entities including interactive visualisation and ordering options, because this feature can potentially be helpful in multiple different domains and use cases.

Nevertheless, advanced and novel UI features such as the one mentioned above must be considered unusual when compared to established interface types and visual metaphors, such as, the typical word processor or spreadsheet, the typical file viewer or search engine result page. In that regard we are exploring new visual metaphors and interaction concepts that bridge the gap between information and knowledge, whether through smart context-sensitive annotation features or non-linear information displays, from which patterns and insights can emerge. This boundary between established and experimental interfaces is dynamic and fluid. It is influenced by the experience users make with popular software tools and mobile apps, which in turn, shape their expectations with regard to the responsiveness and behaviour of an application. For example, due to the fact that all online search engines introduced the feature of automatically providing suggestions when typing in a query, users nowadays expect any search interface to provide suggestions as well.

Especially in a production environment, it can be a challenge to introduce novel interfaces and new visual metaphors – interfaces that are *too* novel or *too* avantgarde may require extensive training sessions, for example. Nevertheless, completely new functionalities require the development of new interfaces and the adoption of new metaphors. In that regard we are currently in the process of developing a new type of interface for a novel curation service called "semantic storytelling" that is meant to generate possible storylines for articles that deal with the content of a specific document collection [4]. As semantic technologies that are based on Artificial Intelligence methods have been making tremendous steps forward recently, so should the way knowledge workers and content curators experience information be transformed. Technology is slowly but surely becoming a co-curator of automatically processed or generated information, making innovative user interface design all the more relevant and important.

Acknowledgment. The project "Digitale Kuratierungstechnologien" (DKT) is supported by the German Federal Ministry of Education and Research (BMBF), "Unternehmen Region", instrument Wachstumskern-Potenzial (no. 03WKP45). More information: http://www.digitale-kuratierung.de.

References

1. Bourgonje, P., Moreno-Schneider, J., Nehring, J., Rehm, G., Sasaki, F., Srivastava, A.: Towards a platform for curation technologies: enriching text collections with a semantic-web layer. In: Sack, H., Rizzo, G., Steinmetz, N., Mladenić, D., Auer, S., Lange, C. (eds.) ESWC 2016. LNCS, vol. 9989, pp. 65–68. Springer, Cham (2016). doi:10.1007/978-3-319-47602-5_14
2. Bourgonje, P., Schneider, J.M., Rehm, G.: Digital curation technologies for forensic linguistics. In: 13th Biennial Conference of the International Association of Forensic Linguists, Porto, Portugal, July 2017, In print
3. Bourgonje, P., Schneider, J.M., Rehm, G.: Semantically annotating heterogeneous document collections – curation technologies for digital humanities and text analytics. In: CUTE Workshop 2017 -CRETA Unshared Task zu Entitätenreferenzen. Workshop bei DHd2017, Berne, Switzerland, February 2017, In print
4. Bourgonje, P., Schneider, J.M., Rehm, G.: Towards user interfaces for semantic storytelling. In: 19th International Conference on Human-Computer Interaction-HCI International 2017, Vancouver, Canada, July 2017, In print
5. Bourgonje, P., Schneider, J.M., Rehm, G., Sasaki, F.: Processing document collections to automatically extract linked data: semantic storytelling technologies for smart curation workflows. In: Gangemi, A., Gardent, C. (eds.) Proceedings of the 2nd International Workshop on Natural Language Generation and the Semantic Web (WebNLG 2016), pp. 13–16. The Association for Computational Linguistics, Edinburgh, September 2016
6. Osgood, C.E., Suci, G.J., Tannenbaum, P.H.: The Measurement of Meaning. University of Illinois Press, Urbana (1957)

7. Hackos, J.T., Redish, J.C.: User and Task Analysis for Interface Design. Wiley, New York (1998)
8. Manovich, L.: Lean UX. OReilly Media Inc., Sebastopol (2013)
9. Neudecker, C., Rehm, G.: Digitale Kuratierungstechnologien für Bibliotheken. Zeitschrift für Bibliothekskultur 027.7 4(2), November 2016. http://0277.ch/ojs/index.php/cdrs_0277/article/view/158
10. Rehm, G.: Flexible Digitale Kuratierungstechnologien für verschiedene Branchen und Anwendungsszenarien. In: Bienert, A., Flesser, B. (eds.) EVA Berlin 2016- Elektronische Medien & Medien, Kultur, Historie, Berlin, Germany, 23. Berliner Veranstaltung der internationalen EVA-Serie. 09–11 November, pp. 19–22, November 2016
11. Sasaki, F., Gornostay, T., Dojchinovski, M., Osella, M., Mannens, E., Stoitsis, G., Richie, P., Declerck, T., Koidl, K.: Introducing FREME: deploying linguistic linked data. In: Proceedings of the 4th Workshop of the Multilingual Semantic Web. MSW 2015 (2015)
12. Spotlight, D.: Dbpedia spotlight website (2016). https://github.com/dbpedia-spotlight/
13. Srivastava, A., Sasaki, F., Bourgonje, P., Moreno-Schneider, J., Nehring, J., Rehm, G.: How to configure statistical machine translation with linked open data resources. In: Proceedings of Translating and the Computer 38 (TC38), London, UK, pp. 138–148, November 2016

Developing a Common Understanding
of IT Services – The Case of a German University

Christian Remfert[✉]

University of Muenster, Muenster, Germany
christian.remfert@wi.uni-muenster.de

Abstract. IT service management is the prevailing standard for IT operations in practice. It is rooted in the so-called Information Technology Infrastructure Library, a best practice standard that proposes to look upon IT functions as a service provider that delivers IT services to the business. This idea of a service orientation has also attracted academic attention since the turn of the century. Although, the core concept of ITSM, the IT service itself, is still not clearly defined, and thus practitioners still struggle with this concept. Therefore, based on the ITIL and the academic literature, we developed an IT service definition that contains six unique characteristics. This definition has been tested in a case study that we conducted with the IT department of a German university. In this paper, we elaborate on the empirical validation and its results.

Keywords: IT service · IT Service Management · ITIL · Case study research · Evaluation research

1 Introduction

Since the 1970s, information technology has found its way into the daily business activities of companies, and over the years its importance has continued to rise. In today's society, companies of the so-called information age rely on IT in a way that a breakdown of the IT-based infrastructure quickly leads to severe problems. To prevent such a breakdown, it is necessary to professionalize IT operations. Such a professionalization is the aim of the so-called Information Technology Infrastructure Library (ITIL), a best practice standard which was first developed in the 1990s and is now in its third edition. It proposes looking upon an internal IT function as an IT service provider that provides services to the business units. This idea of a service orientation is not only used in practice but has also attracted academic intrigue since the turn of the century and is discussed here under the paradigm of "IT Service Management" (ITSM).

Research so far has focused on the diffusion of the ITIL in practice. Studies by Kemper et al. [1], Hochstein et al. [2], Tan et al. [3], Marrone and Kolbe [4] as well as Marrone et al. [5] document a broad adoption of the ITIL. The benefits that organizations associate with the implementation of the ITIL are, for example, a higher overall service quality, a higher first call resolution rate, and a reduction in downtimes. Remarkably, the benefits perceived seem to significantly diminish the higher level of maturity achieved [4]. Although the ITIL and ITSM in particular are widely adopted in practice,

© Springer International Publishing AG 2017
S. Yamamoto (Ed.): HIMI 2017, Part I, LNCS 10273, pp. 407–421, 2017.
DOI: 10.1007/978-3-319-58521-5_32

practitioners still struggle to understand the core concept of ITIL and ITSM – the IT service itself – as it is still not clearly defined and has yet to be researched in depth [6].

To counteract this gap, we conducted an in-depth literature review and developed an IT service definition, which is based on the few academic contributions in this field as well as the recommendations of the ITIL. This definition proposes six characteristics, which we believe, if taken together, fully capture an IT service in the sense of IT service management (for more details, see [7]). To evaluate our definition empirically, we have set up a research project with the IT department of a German university. In this paper, we will report on this research project and our evaluation approach as well as the results.

We will start in Sect. 2 with a brief overview about our six defining characteristics of an IT service. In Sect. 3, we will detail the case study and the research methods used, followed by an elaboration on the findings and results in Sect. 4. In the final section, we sum up our findings and provide an outlook on future research.

2   The Concept of an IT Service in the Academic Debate

In its broadest sense, the term "IT service" can refer to any service (somehow) related to Information Technology. Taxonomies that build on such an inclusive definition involve "software development projects", "hardware deployment", "hardware repair", "software maintenance", "software hosting", "systems integration" as well as "IT hotlines", "IT consulting", "IT training", and "IT outsourcing" [8–10]. Given this diversity, it is obvious that IT can play different roles in IT services.

The ITIL, as the de facto standard for IT service management, has a much narrower understanding of an IT service. Here, IT service is understood as a service that is "made up of a combination of information technology, people and processes" [11] and it "directly supports the business processes of one or more customers" [11]. This definition underlines that an IT service in the sense of the ITIL makes use of information technology to support the business of a customer. Therefore, IT is used as a means to produce an IT service but is not the outcome of the latter. Also, the direct support of the customer's business is highlighted. This stands in contradiction to some of the exemplary IT services mentioned above.

Beside the ITIL, a small number of academic authors have developed their own definitions of an IT service in the sense of ITSM. They range from those that focus on generated value ("what?"), to those that stress the technical implementation of an IT service ("how?"). For example, Zarnekow et al. [12] define an IT service as "a bundle of IT accomplishments to support a business process or business product of the customer to generate a value for him" and therefore focus the business support and the value generation of an IT service. With a more technical view, Ebert et al. [13] for example define an IT service as "as a bundle of components that supports business processes with information processing, provisioning and storage. Components (i.e. sub-services) of an IT service can constitute manual services, as well as technical services". They hence emphasize the technical implementation of an IT service. This variety of definitions might lead many organizations to struggle with the main ideas underlying IT service orientation. For example, a study by Winniford, Conger and Harris [6] found that IT executives, despite claiming to have successfully introduced the ITIL in their organization, had difficulties explaining what an IT service is and had trouble giving examples. Additional case studies and action research [14–16] reveal that organizations that adopt the ITIL do not necessarily understand and implement the underlying core concepts including, above all, that of an IT service. This is a devastating result, given that the IT service is the "nucleus of the entire ITIL" [17, 18].

A clear understanding of IT services is also a necessary prerequisite of any theory development on "*IT Service* Management". In fact, the IT service is the core theoretical term of ITSM. But so far, researchers have not been able to clearly define what exactly is meant by the term "IT service", thus the theoretical kernel of ITSM remains vague [19]. We took this situation as motivation to investigate the concept of an IT service as rooted in the ITIL and discussed deeper in ITSM. The objective of our research was to come up with a clear and substantial definition of "IT service", which is desperately needed for ITSM research. As a result of our research, we have developed a set of six defining characteristics of an IT service (for a more detailed explanation, see [7]):

Intangible

Services are bundles of activities, performed by a service provider and rendered to an external factor by the use of internal production factors [21]. This is called intangibility. For most IT services, the external factor is a so-called business process object: a process-shaping object that drives the process flow in that its status demands for the execution of specific processing functions (see [22]). Business objects are processed within customer business processes. For example, if the business process "Invoicing" is supported by an IT Service, one business process object would be the invoice itself. Some others further argue that the external factor of an IT service can also be a business product or service of an organization (see [12]).

Generating Customer Value

IT services are ordered by business organizations (the customers) that expect the service to generate a value for them by supporting the execution of business processes. Value may be generated for example, by shortening processing times or by raising the quality of the process outcome, thus resulting in cost reductions or higher customer satisfaction. Value generation through IT services require an employee of the organization (the user) to call upon the service. For example, an employee might use an IT service to create an invoice for a customer. This task requires them to fill in customer data and invoice positions before the invoice can be generated.

Produced by Means of an IT-based infrastructure

IT services are produced by means of an IT-based infrastructure. Such an IT-based infrastructure is the backbone of each service production and therefore also referred to as "production infrastructure" by Zarnekow et al. [12]. A production infrastructure is divided into layers for application systems and technical assets, like servers, basic software or network components. The higher-level components here use performances of the lower-level components. For example, the application systems use the performances of operating systems and hardware servers to provide the business logic for processing a business process object.

Produced in an industrial fashion

The idea of an IT-based production infrastructure is closely related to that of industrialization which implies that production processes are automated, specialized and standardized to reduce production costs, and increase the production speed and quality of the products. Automation refers to the substitution of manual labor by machines or technology in industrialized production processes. In effect, automation leads to production processes that are mainly executed, supported, and controlled by machines (the IT-based production infrastructure). Automation in turn furthers specialization by first dividing labor between machines and humans, and second by differentiating tasks and responsibilities of human actors. This results in human actors with dedicated skills performing highly specific tasks (the employees of the service provider). A third trait of industrial production is standardization. The idea is that reductions in unit cost are larger the higher the number of products produced (product standardization). Standardized products can be produced through standardized procedures that in turn allows for high levels of specialization and learning effects (economies of scale). Product standardization is particularly supported by the idea of composing IT services out of standardized technical component services, the so-called infrastructure services. The latter do not deliver any business value on their own, and thus are not offered directly to customers.

Mass Customized

The value generation for a customer and standardized production stand in contradiction to each other. As value is generated within the business processes of the customer, with each customer being unique, standardized services cannot suit the customers' needs the same way individually produced ones can. In the theory of industrial production, this challenge is addressed with the concept of mass-customization. Mass customization proposes combining standardized pre-fabrication and individualized assembly for offering products that match individual customer needs better than mass products but are at the same time much cheaper than individually manufactured products. At the heart of mass-customization is the concept of modularization; IT services as end-products are to be composed out of modules, that is standardized and reusable components.

Provided Care-free to customers

The production of an IT service is often very complex in terms of the work to be done and the necessary production infrastructure. Moreover, the service provider is responsible for operating and maintaining the production infrastructure and ensuring that it is working to produce a service. The customer who orders the services, however, should not be burdened with technical complexity and production details. Hence, the whole service provision should be transparent for him. In turn, the customer pays a service fee to the service provider for the service usage.

These six characteristics have been developed based on the ITIL and the academic literature that we found by an in-depth literature review. For an explanation of the whole literature review process and the development of our definition, see [7]. To validate our definition empirically and to find out if it helps practitioners better understand what an IT service is and how to define it, we set up a research project that we will report on in the next section.

3   Research Design

We are drawing on a case study regarding the central IT function of a German university, which is called UnIT here. Following the contributions of Flyvbjerg, case studies might also be a valid research method to do an in-depth evaluation of concepts, like our service definition [23]. In the next paragraph, we will give a short introduction of our research partner, followed by an overview about the research methods used.

3.1   The Project Partner UnIT

UnIT is the central data center of one of the biggest universities in Germany. It operates central IT infrastructures and provides accomplishments to members of the university (like students, scientific, and non-scientific employees). These accomplishments are intended to foster productivity and support members in their daily business activities, for example by providing internet access. While the daily business activities of non-scientific employees might be relatively homogeneous, research is an especially crea-tivity intensive process. It is therefore a very heterogeneous and non-standardized field of work. To support this heterogeneous work, a heterogeneous IT-based infrastructure is also necessary. As it would be almost impossible for UnIT to operate such a hetero-geneous infrastructure, which powers the work of over 40,000 students as well as more than 5,000 employees, the university established additional, decentralized IT functions (called DecentITs) for each faculty, that provide special accomplishments and support for faculty members. For example, DecentITs offer the workplaces that include also accomplishments of UnIT (like internet access). The DecentITs are therefore the single point of contact for employees.

UnIT therefore must deal with two types of "customers": on the one hand, they provide accomplishments directly to students and employees, whose technical affinity might vary from low to high. On the other hand, UnIT provides accomplishments to the decentralized IT functions, which combine them, and in turn provide them to their students and employees. It should be noted here that at the time of the project, a clear differentiation between UnITs responsibilities and those of the faculty IT functions was often not possible, and therefore responsibilities were overlapping in some points.

To deliver all accomplishments, UnIT has around 120 employees that are working in different departments: there are non-technical departments like administration or public relations, as well three departments responsible for the operation and maintenance of the IT-based infrastructure. Some of those departments were furthermore divided into teams. All of these teams are headed by a team leader and all departments have a depart-mental leader as well as a deputy. The departmental leaders stay in close contact with and report to the CEO of UnIT, which consists of UnITs CEO, a director as well as the deputy of the CEO. The top management, the departmental leaders and the team leaders together form the management board of UnIT.

The CEO and the director report directly to the rector and the chancellor of the university. Together with the rector and the chancellor as well as a small number of university employees, UnITs top management forms a steering committee of the university, which discusses strategic questions regarding the use of IT throughout the entire university. Moreover, this board is involved in developing an IT strategy every five years, which sets the directions for the IT functions.

In 2006, UnIT decided to introduce ITSM for the following reasons: first, the full range of provided accomplishments was requested to be made transparent by the central university administration. This might be due to the reason that the university was under high cost pressure due to changing laws: While in former times, the universities had been funded by the German state, since 2006, students had to pay tuition fees and the funding by the state has been reduced. Second, there was interest to clearly define the responsibilities of UnIT and the faculty's own IT functions. This was due to the fact that the borders between those two had blurred and the number of cases, in which nobody felt responsible, e.g. for a system breakdown, was increasing.

Therefore, a first attempt has been made to introduce ITSM at UnIT. This attempt was unsuccessful as we will report later. Even a second try did not achieve the former mentioned objectives. Until today, the introduction of ITSM did not happen. Therefore, UnIT asked us to help them. For this, we set up a joint research project in March 2016 to establish an IT service definition.

3.2   Research Method

As already mentioned, we designed the research project as a case study and began our project by identifying the problem to be addressed and setting an objective to achieve. For this, we first interviewed the CEO and director of UnIT in March 2016. Questions in this semi-structured interview focused on the main rationale for introducing IT service management and here, especially, an IT service catalogue. Furthermore, we asked questions on their previous experiences and why the former attempts of establishing services had failed.

Based on the interview responses, we designed a first workshop with the whole management board of UnIT, which was conducted in May 2016. The focus of this workshop was on gaining an understanding of how the board members perceived IT services and what they find difficult, when defining those. To gather this information, we used a group discussion approach (see [24]). This approach is characterized by the fact that the researcher provides key questions to stimulate and uphold a debate, while not being an active part of the discussion itself. To be more precise, his role is that of a moderator.

The key questions for the discussion were the understanding of services in general and IT services in special as well as a demarcation of IT services from each other.

The insights from this group discussions were then analyzed and aggregated. We used them to develop an UnIT-own service definition, which we presented in a second workshop in June 2016. This workshop was again done with the members of UnITs management board. We used this appointment for another group discussion, in which we presented the aggregated service definition based on the results of the first workshop as a stimulus. Key questions here were if the prepared definition reflects the understanding of the board members correctly and if they feel comfortable with it. This workshop gave us a unique chance to double-check and verify the interpretation of the results of the first workshop, and to extend our own understanding of the situation and challenges at UnIT. After closing the discussion and feedback round on UnITs own IT service definition, we asked the management board to create exemplary service descriptions based on it. We then analyzed the experiences the board members gained while they created these descriptions. This gave us further insights as to whether the self-developed definition is practically applicable or not.

Finally, we set UnIT's service definition in contrast to our own, literature-based one to get valuable feedback from the practitioners and to discuss our definition. We were hoping that the practitioners, especially due to their former experiences with IT services, could discuss our definition in a much more intensive and profound way. We also wanted the practitioners to use our definition and rework their service descriptions to validate the practicability of our definition. In the next section, we will report on the insights and results of the workshops and the feedback and applicability regarding our service definition.

4   Development and Evaluation of an IT Service Definition

After we agreed on a joint research project, in our first meeting with the CEO and the director of UnIT in March 2016, we conducted a semi-structured interview to identify the problem that we wanted to work on.

4.1   Motivation for Introducing IT Services

In the interview, we obtained information that UnIT's first attempts to introduce an IT service orientation were going back to 2003. We asked in more depth, why – around 13 years later – no final catalogue of services has been established and identified different reasons for that.

First, the CEO told us that not enough resources had been put into the effort. This meant that the department leaders were requested to write down "accomplishments" of their department, but had to do this alongside their daily work. This led to multiple delays in the submission. After every department leader had submitted their list of accomplishments, the aggregated portfolio was found to contain around 300 of those. In contrast to other organizations, where normally 30–70 services are in place, this a surprisingly high number. A deeper look into the portfolio of accomplishments revealed that the list showed a great variety of accomplishments, ranging from small, single (and often very technical) activities, up to the execution of complete business processes, besides the delivery of products, provision of user support, holding lectures or rental services for hardware assets. As we were astonished about this long list, the CEO explained us, that the portfolio has been perceived as documentation about the accomplishments delivered for external stakeholders (like the university administration) and therefore, every employee of UnIT had a high interest in being represented within the list, so as to not be critically scrutinized for what they actually do. Beside this fact, the CEO told us that the department leaders had another problem: they did not know exactly, what they should write down in the list, or to be more precise: what "accomplishment" means. At that point in time, the ITIL was on the rise in public and services seemed to be an appropriate way to encapsulate the accomplishments. Therefore, all department leaders as well as the CEO and the director attend an ITIL Foundation course and successfully passed the certification exam. The management board was optimistic that this would establish a common ground to work on and another attempt was made to define a list of delivered accomplishments, which were now called "services". When we questioned on the difference between "accomplishments" and "services", the CEO told us that for him and the management board "this is just a synonym". In former times, "everybody spoke on 'accomplishments and now it is 'services' – for me, there is no difference". While this might be doubted on a notional level, it made explicit – especially against the background of the former (very technical) portfolio – that the idea of leaving out technical details and taking a non-technical, customer-oriented perspective (as proposed by the ITIL and ITSM), had not been adopted thus far. When we questioned this and asked for general characteristics of a service, the CEO told us that this is a problem at UnIT, as the management board members do not have a common understanding of what an IT service is, even after being ITIL certified.

In a last step, we wanted to find out the goal, why UnIT wanted to introduce IT services. The CEO as well as the director told us there are two reasons: first, UnIT wanted to get an overview of the service delivered as there was not a complete list in existence. Such a list would be helpful in the future to analyze which services are not needed anymore and to stop providing them, as well as to question the scope of delivered services. Second, they wanted to assign clear responsibilities to the accomplishments. And third, they believed that service management would gain benefits: For example, that the standardization of production processes and services would ensure a steady quality.

4.2   Discussion and Development of an IT Service Definition

Based on what we discovered in the first interview, we set up a workshop focused on the different IT service understandings with the intention of developing a preliminary working definition. As mentioned above, we designed this workshop as a group discussion, stating the question, "what is the motivation for you (the practitioners) to introduce IT services?" at the beginning. From this, we gained different, interesting insights: first, one department leader told us that he has a personal interest in introducing IT services: As he is soon retiring, he wanted to finally structure his department before handing it over to his successor. He told us that IT services seem to be an appropriate means of structuring the departments' internal activities as it carves out, what activity should be done for which IT service. Based on this overview of activities, responsibilities could be assigned to the different activities or – even more – to the whole production of the service. He furthermore mentioned that such responsibilities are not given for his department currently and sometimes nobody feels responsible in case of a breakdown. He summarized that IT services are a vehicle to (re-)define the internal, organizational structures.

Such an introspective view was also shared by another department leader, who adds that such an assignment of responsibilities is not only meaningful within a department, but also to coordinate the work between the different departments and teams. In his opinion, this is necessary, as the responsibilities between the departments are not clearly defined, which in turn leads to a "vacuum situation", where nothing happens. IT services – in his opinion – would counteract this by clearly defining responsibilities within as well as between departments.

In addition to internal views, another department leader had a more external view and considered IT service more as a "marketing tool". He told us that IT services and an IT service catalogue would allow him to make visible for the users what accomplishments his department delivers. This "marketing" was important for him as his department is the main interface between the users and UnIT: it is responsible for user regarding the accomplishments which the users (students, employees) can directly receive from UnIT (like printing or internet access).

After questioning the motivation, we went over to their understanding of an IT service. We asked openly, what an IT service is, leading to a very extensive discussion, bouncing from one point to another. The whole discussion began with one department leader stating, that a service is, "when the user gets help from UnIT". This statement was influenced by a day-to-day understanding of "service" as being an activity of help or support. We took this statement and asked further, how it applies to the list of accomplishments the CEO told us about. The department leaders began to discuss and introduced another term to differentiate, the German word "Dienst". "Dienst" is the translation of "service" and this was quite interesting, because the department leaders factually used the same term to describe different things: "service" was used for activities regarding user support or help, while "Dienst" was used for – mainly technical – activities that the employees of UnIT were performing. Within the discussion, another department leader even introduced another term, "Dienstleistung", which can be translated as "rendering a service". Regarding his understanding, "Dienstleistung" is about the initial activities that are done to establish a "Dienst". He gave the following example: the provision of a network connection ("Dienst") would first require the installation of a network socket ("Dienstleistung"). In case of a breakdown (e.g. the network connection not working), the user gets help or support (the "service"). Even more interesting, the practitioners led the discussion to the point that they were asking each other things like: "But if I think about X, what is then the 'service', 'Dienst' and 'Dienstleistung'". This underlined that it was difficult to differentiate the terms from each other.

We pushed the discussion forward by asking who the former described accomplishments or activities were delivered for. This started a discussion about service recipients. Within this discussion, different possible recipients were mentioned: from the university administration, the building authority of the university (e.g. for the installation of network sockets) and the institutes or chairs, to the employees and students. The group started to discuss these recipients and developed a differentiation between a customer and a user: the customer as the person or organizational unit that pays for the service ("Dienst", "Dienstleistung") and the user, who really uses the latter.

The discussion continued to the point that some customers or users needed different variants of the same service. Therefore, the practitioners agreed that the provided services need to be differentiated. They underlined this fact with an example where some faculties need higher availability of systems than others. This is turn pushed the discussion to the point that – explained by the availability example – services should be normally provided in a standardized way, to achieve standardized results and therefore allow for the promise of a certain degree of quality, besides those case of special requirements. Stemming from this, the practitioners also agreed that the service has to have a value for the customer or user using it. Although they mentioned this, it was hard for them to describe what the value is in detail. The discussion was around the example of the network connection again, where some of the practitioners mentioned that the network socket would generate the value while other said that the network connection for a device that is provided over this socket, generates value. They were not able to clearly work out how the value can be determined but agreed on the fact that a service has a value "somehow".

The last question we asked was regarding the difference between a service in general and an "IT service". The first answer we got was: "It is called IT service because it is a service provided by us – the IT". This showed us that the understanding of an IT service is closely related to the providing organization. The same person substantiated this by telling us that, "for example financial services are provided by the financial department". However, this view was not shared by other department leaders, who argued that it is called "IT service" because it uses information technology. This in turn was countered by another person who said that "nowadays nearly everything is or includes IT". He furthermore questioned if it is necessary to differentiate the "amount of IT used" to demarcate if it is an "IT service" or a service in general. He underpinned his question with the example that UnIT also holds lectures on the use of application systems, like statistical software. He argued that there is also a considerable amount of IT "in it", but felt uncomfortable with calling those lectures an "IT service".

At the end of the discussion, the practitioners were confused about what an IT service is. Within the discussion, their own understanding had been questioned, either by us or their own colleagues. Their perception of an IT service had become blurred and therefore, at the end, they agreed upon the fact that it is difficult to establish a common understanding of an IT service.

After the first workshop, we took all the comments and analyzed them in detail to create a summary for the second workshop. In this summary, we worked out the key facts and intermediate results of the group discussion:

- IT services have a user help or support part,
- they are produced for a user and ordered by a customer,
- they generate a value,
- they are closely connected to technical accomplishments, which require initial activities (preparation) to be provided.
- IT services should be standardized and produced by an interplay of UnIT's different departments if possible, but
- should not neglect specific and special requirements of customers.
- Moreover, IT services use a large amount of information technology.

With these characteristics, we went back to UnIT and conducted the second workshop. We started this second workshop with an evaluation of whether we understood the practitioners correctly and if they agree upon the discussed characteristics. They confirmed that we understood them correctly and told us that since the first workshop, an internal debate on what an IT service is, had started again. The summary of the characteristics was a helpful first step towards a common understanding. After presenting these, the practitioners told us that – although they developed these features on their own – the explicit and condensed reproduction of what they discussed was helpful for them. We went over and showed them examples from their own list of accomplishments (or "service catalogue" as it had now been named) and asked them to reflect these against their characteristics, and to determine if they still believe that these are IT services. Within the discussion of these examples, the practitioners agreed that not everything in the service catalogue is an IT service. Furthermore, they concluded that they need to differentiate between general services and IT services. Services like "Provision of Handbooks" or "Camera Rental", as well as "Lectures" were no longer recognized as IT services but as services in general. They further recognized that information technology is nothing that is provided to the user, but what is used to provide an IT service (as a means of production).

For the practitioners, this was a big first step towards a common understanding of what an IT service is. They were now able to distinguish services in general and IT services. We further asked them to "test" their characteristics and use them to describe a sample set of services of their own department either for end-users (students and employees) or for technical organizations like the DecentITs. After this had finished, we analyzed the descriptions within the group and found that on first glance the services were described quite homogeneous due to the defined characteristics. However, they varied in terms of details in the individual descriptions: while some of the department leaders wrote down the used IT components in a very detailed way (down to software protocols used), others kept a very high level ("the service uses a webserver and the software X") description. The same happened for generated value. Here, some wrote "a network socket is provided" while others wrote "the user can print a document". The practitioners were quite happy with their characteristics "somehow" but asked us for our opinion.

4.3 Evaluation of Our Literature-Based IT Service Definition

We took this as a chance to evaluate our own definition as outlined in Sect. 2. To make our characteristics comparable to those of the practitioners, we analyzed the practitioners' characteristics and preliminary descriptions in terms of their meaning. We then related them to our characteristics, which led us to the comparison as depicted in Table 1.

As can be seen, the developed definition of the practitioners was quite close to ours. Only the business process object as the external factor was not mentioned by the practitioners. When we presented our definition and the comparison to UnIT's definition, the practitioners were happy that they were quite near to the "academic view" on IT services.

We then evaluated where their definition differed to ours by presenting the respective characteristic of our definition and asking the practitioners for their opinion in terms of their meaningfulness and practicability. We started with the business process object and explained what this means and how it is related to the generated value. The practitioners told us that it is obvious for them that a service has some "object" it renders to – although they never mentioned this in the discussions before and also never spoke of "business processes". But they nevertheless agreed that the business process object as well as business processes should be part of each IT service.

Table 1. Comparison of UnIT's and our IT service definition

	UnIT's definition	Our definition
Intangible	✘	✔
Generating customer value	✔	✔
Produced by means of an IT based infrastructure	(✔)	✔
Produced in an industrial fashion	(✔)	✔
Mass customized	(✔)	✔
Provided care-free to customers	✔	✔

The use of an IT-based production infrastructure as understood by us was very insightful for the practitioners. As outlined before, they struggled to answer the question, "how much IT" is used in an IT service and in which way. This is closely related to the degree of automation as proposed by industrialization. Although the practitioners did not talk about automation previously, after we explained the idea of automation in services, they agreed that the service is provided by information technology and the people around oversee setup, maintenance and support. Also, the other concepts of automation, standardization and specialization, were seen as meaningful by the practitioners. They agreed that the service production and the service results should be standardized (where possible) and that service production is done as a cooperation of multiple departments – what can be interpreted as specialization.

The characteristic of carefree provision was also mentioned by the practitioners in the workshop – although they understood it more in a way that the user obtains support in case of a breakdown. When we explained to them our understanding of a carefree provision – that the IT infrastructure used for the service is fully owned by the service provider – they told us that this is helpful for them to distinguish IT and non-IT services from each other.

For mass customization, the practitioners mentioned that services need to be offered in variants to meet individual requirements, but they did not go as far as mass customization goes. Therefore, they did not think of modules or technical services which are connected to each other to provide an IT service for the customer. Although they liked the idea of mass customization, they stated that this would be a future step for them as they first wanted to establish an initial list of services and just assign concrete IT components to those.

In the end, they agreed with what we explained to them and found our definition as a meaningful evolution to their own. To further validate our definition empirically, we asked the practitioners again to describe exemplary services from their department using our definition. We analyzed these descriptions and found that the generated value was now described in a more customer-oriented fashion. The only thing that was still complicating the matter was the concept of a business process object. Some of the practitioners seemed to have not correctly understood what such an object is. For example, the department leader, who specified the "e-mail communication service" wrote down that the mailbox of the user is the business process object. But in an e-mail service, the business process object is the e-mail itself that is being processed (created, sent and received) by the service. Interestingly, another department leader who had correctly understood what a business process object is, explained to his colleagues the concept, validating that the concept had been understood by some participants. They also validated that this characteristic is helpful. Furthermore, they also explained that they could figure out the customer value more easily by first identifying the business process object and then asking for the value that is generated by processing it.

5   Summary and Outlook on Future Research

Within the case study we gathered many interesting insights, which we distinguish into findings regarding the motivation for the use of IT services, the understanding of IT services before introducing our definition as well as the evaluation of the latter. The results are summarized in Table 2.

We were able to validate our definition within this project, but we also noticed that the concept of a business process object was quite difficult to understand for the practitioners. Also, the implementation of mass customization seems challenging. Here, different approaches from the literature (see for example [25]) might be considered and tested further.

The next step after service definition is to specify the services in a customer-oriented way for a service catalogue. We are currently doing this with UnIT and the initial results are promising. We intend to work on this further to open the "black box" around the concept of an IT service.

Table 2. Results of our case study

Motivation	• IT services help to structure the department's organization • IT services can be used as a marketing tool to make accomplishments transparent to external service recipients • IT services can be a lever to determine a complete overview of accomplishments • IT services can ensure standardized processes and results, and therefore a steady quality • IT services help to assign responsibilities within a department and in the interplay with other departments or external IT organizations
IT service understanding before	• Services are named along their providing organizational unit – hence, "IT services" are provided by the IT function • IT is used to provide an IT service or is the core of the service (i.e. hardware rental) • IT services are support activities • IT services have different recipients: end-users and other technical IT functions (like the DecentITs)
Intermediate IT service understanding after first workshop	• IT services have a user help or support part, • they are produced for a user and ordered by a customer, • they generate a value, • they are closely connected to technical accomplishments, which require initial activities (preparation) to be provided. • IT services should be standardized and produced by an interplay of UnIT's different departments if possible, but • should not neglect specific and special requirements of customers. • Moreover, IT services use a large amount of information technology.
Evaluation of literature-based IT service definition	• Practitioners agree that a service is rendered to an object that is a business process object in case of an IT service. Although, identifying the business process object was quite difficult for some of them • The generation of a customer value was unquestioned • The use of IT only as a production factor and not as core of an IT service helped practitioners to distinguish IT services from services in general • The idea of transferring industrial production traits to IT services was perceived as valuable, especially recognizing that standardization leads to standardized results and a steady quality • The combination of service modules to customer-oriented services using mass customization has been acknowledged theoretically, but has not and cannot be implemented yet • The provision of services in a carefree way was also unquestioned and helped the practitioners to distinguish IT services from general services like user support

References

1. Kemper, H.-G., Hadjicharalambous, E., Paschke, J.: IT-Servicemanagement in deutschen Unternehmen – Ergebnisse einer empirischen Studie zu ITIL. HMD - Prax. der Wirtschaftsinformatik, pp. 22–31 (2004)
2. Hochstein, A., Tamm, G., Brenner, W.: Service oriented IT management: benefit, cost and success factors. In: Proceedings of the European Conference on Information Systems (2005)
3. Tan, W.-G., Cater-Steel, A., Toleman, M.: Implementing IT service management: a case study focussing on critical success factors. J. Comput. Inf. Syst. Winter, 200 (2009)
4. Marrone, M., Kolbe, L.M.: Uncovering ITIL claims: IT executives' perception on benefits and business-IT alignment. Inf. Syst. E-bus. Manage. **9**, 363–380 (2011)

5. Marrone, M., Gacenga, F., Cater-Steel, A., Kolbe, L.: IT service management: a cross-national study of ITIL adoption. Commun. Assoc. Inf. Syst. **34**, 865–892 (2014)
6. Winniford, M., Conger, S., Erickson-Harris, L.: Confusion in the ranks: IT service management practice and terminology. Inf. Syst. Manage. **26**, 153–163 (2009)
7. Teubner, A., Remfert, C.: Towards a theoretical backing for IT services. In: Proceedings of the 19th International Conference on Human-Computer Interact (2017)
8. European Information Technology Observatory: ICT Market Report 2012/13 Definitions & Methodology (2013)
9. Statistisches Bundesamt: Erzeugerpreisindizes für Dienstleistungen: Informationen zum Preisindex IT-Dienstleistungen. DESTATIS, Wiesbaden (2013)
10. IDC: Europe, Middle East and Africa IT and Business Services (2015)
11. OGC: ITIL ® Glossary and Abbreviations. The Stationary Office Ltd., London (2011)
12. Zarnekow, R., Brenner, W., Pilgram, U.: Integriertes Informationsmanagement: Strategien und Lösungen für das Management von IT-Dienstleistungen. Springer, Berlin (2005)
13. Ebert, N., Uebernickel, F., Hochstein, A., Brenner, W.: A service model for the development of management systems for IT-enabled services. In: Proceeding of the Thirteenth Americas Conference on Information Systems, pp. 1–8. Keystone, Colorado (2007)
14. Hochstein, A.: Operations management and IS: using the SCOR-Model to source make and deliver IS services. In: Proceedings of the 12th Americas Conference on Information Systems (2006)
15. Becker, J., Pöppelbuß, J., Venker, D., Schwarze, L.: Industrialisierung von IT-Dienstleistungen: Anwendung industrieller Konzepte und deren Auswirkungen aus Sicht von IT-Dienstleistern. In: Proceedings of the 10th International Conference on Wirtschaftsinformatik, pp. 345–354 (2011)
16. Teubner, A., Remfert, C.: IT service management revisited - insights from seven years of action research. In: International Conference on Information Resources Management (2012)
17. Huppertz, P.G., Kresse, M., Swidlowski: IT Service Management Advanced Pocket Book. IT-Service - Kern des Ganzen. Serview GmbH (2006)
18. Lichtenstein, S., Nguyen, L., Hunter, A.: Issues in IT Service-Oriented Requirements Engineering. Australas. J. Inf. Syst. **13**, 176–191 (2005)
19. Peppard, J.: Managing IT as a portfolio of services. Eur. Manage. J. **21**, 467–483 (2003)
20. Teubner, A.: IT-Service Management in Wissenschaft und Praxis: Best Practice in der akademischen Diskussion und industriellen Umsetzung, German edn. VDM Verlag Dr. Müller, Saarbrücken (2008)
21. Maleri, R., Frietzsche, U.: Grundlagen der Dienstleistungsproduktion. Springer, Heidelberg (2008)
22. Rosemann, M.: Komplexitätsmanagement in Prozeßmodellen. Gabler, Wiesbaden (1996)
23. Flyvbjerg, B.: Five Misunderstandings About Case-Study Research. Qual. Inq. **12**, 219–245 (2006)
24. Bohnsack, R.: Das Gruppendiskussionsverfahren in der Forschungspraxis. Budrich, Opladen (2006)
25. Grawe, T., Fähnrich, K.-P.: Service Engineering bei IT-Dienstleistern. In: Fähnrich, K.-P., van Husen, C. (eds.) Entwicklung IT-basierter Dienstleistungen (2008)

Does the Visualization of the Local Problem Bring Altruism?

Yurika Shiozu[1(✉)], Koya Kimura[2], Katsunori Shimohara[2], and Katsuhiko Yonezaki[3]

[1] Faculty of Economics, Aichi University, 4-60-6 Hiraike-cho, Nakamura-ku,
Nagoya, Aichi 453-8777, Japan
yshiozu@vega.aichi-u.ac.jp
[2] Graduate School of Science and Engineering, Doshisha University, 1-3 Tatara Miyakodani,
Kyo-tanabe, Kyoto 610-0321, Japan
kimura2013@sil.doshisha.ac.jp, kshimoha@mail.doshisha.ac.jp
[3] Global Cooperation Institute for Sustainable Cities, Yokohama City University,
22-2 Seto, Kanazawa-ward, Yokohama 236-0027, Japan
kyonezak@yokohama-cu.ac.jp

Abstract. The purpose of this paper is to predict the demand for local public goods by local residents and to consider ways to promote diversification of cost burden on supply. We employ a questionnaire survey on issues of current interest from the viewpoint of the cost burden associated with the operation of a community bus service. From the survey results, it was established that there was almost no use of non-contact IC cards in the context of mobile phone usage. It was revealed that there was a certain level of support for collecting expenses through fares rather than through annual payments.

Keywords: Contingent Valuation Method · Option value · Non-contact IC card

1 Introduction

The purpose of this study is to predict the demand for local public goods, and to examine a method to promote the diversification of the expense burden of supply.

Nowadays public transport is non-existent in many areas of Japan. For person who is unable to drive cars including elderly people and children this is obviously detrimental in terms of mobility restrictions. However, there are cases where community bus operations have been attempted, and succeeded.

If the community bus is a local public good, and that bus service is run by affected residents, this amounts to the private supply of a local public good. According to Shiozu et al. [3] if a reciprocity motive works vis-à-vis the personal supply of local public goods, theoretically under an unsociable network, all members of the network incur a flat expense; more than the expense that social advantage should be in the situation.

However, efforts to instigate community bus services, are not guaranteed to succeed; for example, a consensus might not be established in its favor, or demand might be less than the expense.

© Springer International Publishing AG 2017
S. Yamamoto (Ed.): HIMI 2017, Part I, LNCS 10273, pp. 422–434, 2017.
DOI: 10.1007/978-3-319-58521-5_33

It is known that some people find value in knowing that community bus services will exist in the future when their mobility might be restricted. Oguma et al. calls this option value and suggests using the Contingent Valuation Method (CVM) for its measurement.

CVM is technique to measure the economic value of non-market goods and services; it has been applied widely in the academic literature, and moderately in actual decision-making contexts. Because subjects are asked to directly reveal their economic wants and desires, CVM is commonly referred to as an expressed preference technique.

Oguma et al. [2] points out that expressing value in this case-study context raises challenges because the operational cost of the bus service needs to be financed via fares. Assuming that travel expenses are covered by fare income, it is necessary to set fares accordingly or compensate to some degree with subsidies. Because many local governments are already financially challenged, the latter method is not realistic. Additionally, fairness of the cost burden is an important consideration.

In this study, we operationalized a questionnaire which contained questions regarding usage of mobile phone wallets (payment functionality on smart devices) and options for covering operational costs associated with maintaining a community bus service. We found that there was little use of mobile phone wallets. We show that they prefer to bear the cost by fare rather than annual fee and some of them find out the option value. In addition, the quantity of demand did not decrease substantively following fare hikes; but a non-marginal increase in demand is predicted where fare reductions occur. In consideration of the result from other survey which shows that the use of non-contact plastic IC card has been promoted, we suggest to introduce a plural fare system for collecting option value with the non-contact plastic IC card.

The remainder of the paper is organized as follows. In Sect. 2 we describe the survey district. Next, in Sect. 3 we survey the use situation of the wallet phone. In Sect. 4 we estimate community bus demand using the CVM. Finally, Sect. 5 concludes.

2 Survey District

The case-study area is Makishima, Uji-city, Kyoto prefecture. This area is located across suburbs of 3 big Japanese cities. The population of the district is 15,225 people in October 2016. It increases a little than last year. The elderly constitute 21.9% of the population, which is lower than the 26.7% average in Japan. Figure 1 is a map of Uji-city; the Makishima district is located in the northwestern part of the city. Two private railroads run in the district, and a bus operates in north and south directions. There is currently no east-west bus service; as such, the mobility of some residents is restricted.

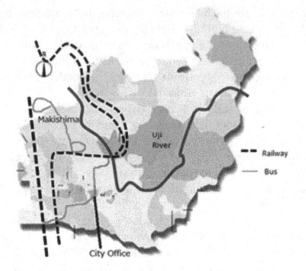

Fig. 1. Uji-city Map

3 Data

We gathered data, via a questionnaire survey, about usage of cellphone payment functionality, and preferences for bus operation. We denote the former as questionnaire test 1 and the latter as test 2.

3.1 Test 1: The Cellphone Questionnaire

We distributed this questionnaire via mail to 8,000 inhabitants in the survey area in February, 2012. The number of effective responses was 1956. The focal item concerned mobile phone electronic payment functionalities. The distribution of respondent ages in this sample is depicted in Fig. 2; the modal age interval therein is respondents in their 60s.

Table 1 expresses two-way frequency data pertaining to this sample in terms of age and the use of mobile phone wallet/QR code functionalities.

From Table 1, excepting people in their 80s, the choice "I have not used the mobile phone wallet or QR code" is the modal response for all age categories. There is a statistically significant difference in terms of usage of these functionalities if we compare people before 70s and after 70s.

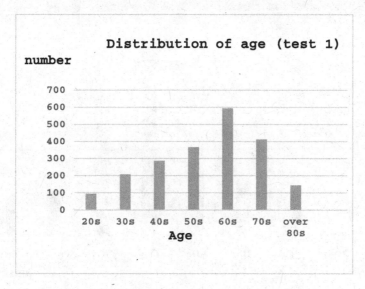

Fig. 2. Distribution of age (test 1)

Table 1. The use of mobile phone wallet/QR code functionalities by respondent's age

	Use of mobile phone wallet/QR code						Total number
	1	2	3	4	5	9	
20s	1	2	5	10	78	2	98
30s	0	2	8	35	157	2	204
40s	1	1	14	38	233	11	298
50s	0	3	3	18	319	25	368
60s	0	3	3	10	528	77	621
70s	0	0	5	6	220	85	316
Over 80s	0	0	0	2	24	25	51
Total number	2	11	38	119	1559	227	1956

1: three times or more per day 2: once or twice per day
3: several times per week 4: several times per month 5: none
9: do not have cellphone

3.2 Test 2: Bus Operation Survey

In the areas that we investigated vis-à-vis cellphone usage, we carried out a further survey about bus services on 1,400 inhabitants. The investigation period is from 15th October 2016 to November 15th. Survey items are about annual contribution payment amount and motivation when introducing a membership fee system when driving a bus, about fare payment amount and motivation when traveling without introducing membership system. The number of effective responses was 438. The distribution of respondent ages in this sample is depicted in Fig. 3.

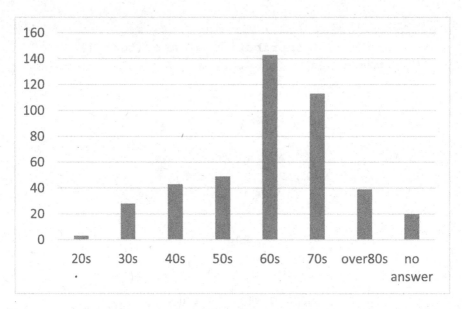

Fig. 3. Distribution of age for community bus survey

Comparing Fig. 3 with Fig. 2, there are more responses from elderly people. Because the focal item is a community bus service, people who have mobility restrictions could have higher propensities to complete the questionnaire because it relates to their well-being to a greater extent than those people without mobility restrictions.

Some areas have no bus services running to the station, city hall, or the hospital. Topographically, the area is flat, thus people without mobility problems can travel by bicycle and on foot. However, most inhabitants travel by privately owned cars.

3.2.1   Preferences for Contributing Toward Bus Operation Costs

To operationalize the CVM in this context, we asked respondents to express their fare payment intentions in monetary amounts; this was done in two phases based on a binary choice principle.

CVM is a method by which a researcher directly asks the subject about economic value. In particular, at first, the investigator presents the scenario to the subject, then the subject replies his/her willingness to pay. There are two ways to represent one's willingness to pay. One is the subject directly presents the amount of payment. The other is the subject just declares approval or disapproval of the amount of payment which the investigator shows. Because both methods do not ask the subject to pay the willingness to pay, it is well known that the former method overestimates the willingness to pay. Recently, the researchers usually adopt the latter method. To use the latter method, the case where the investigator asks once is called single bound, and the case of twice is called double bound.

In this case, to operate bus needs initial cost, for example, vehicle cost or installation cost of bus stop, and operation cost. Suppose a case where these fixed costs are procured by annual membership fee and a case where they are procured from fare. We asked subjects by survey questionnaire of the binary choice double bound method for intention to pay for annual fee and intention to pay for freight.

3.2.1.1. Preferences for Annual Payment

First of all, we asked respondents if they would agree to pay 1,500 yen annually per household with a part of bus travel expenses as local burden (First bid price). Next, would they agree to pay 2,000 yen per year (Second bid price 1). Where respondents did not agree to paying the initial amount, they were asked to pay an annual payment of 1,000 yen (Second bid price 2). The results are shown in Table 2. Respondents were also asked to explain the reasons why the burden was acceptable.

Table 2. Preferences for annual payment

	Payment	Yes	No	No answer
First bid price	1,500 yen	162	248	28
Second bid price 1	2,000 yen	101	52	9
Second bid price 2	1,000 yen	47	192	9

We asked the person who said that they would pay annual payment even a little for the reason. About half of the 279 people who responded were concerned for the mobility and well-being of others (Fig. 4).

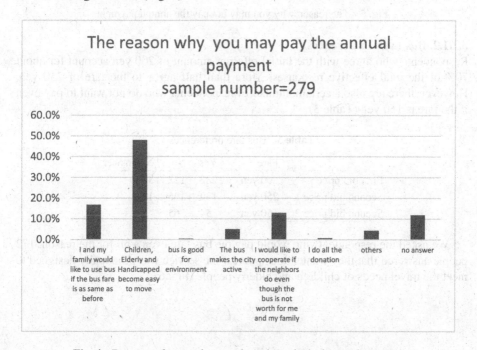

Fig. 4. Reasons why people agreed to a hypothetical annual payment

Where applicable, we also asked people to explain why they did not want to pay the burden of bus operation. As a result, 61.8% of respondents said that the passengers on the bus should pay. Moreover, 10.8% (17 people) answered that they cannot afford to pay the contribution See Fig. 5.

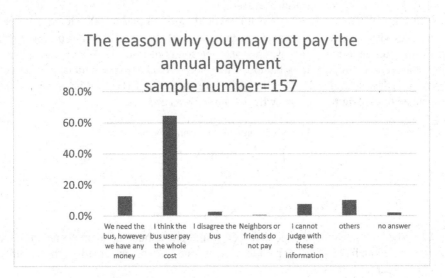

Fig. 5. The reason why you may not pay the annual payment

3.2.1.2. Bus Fare Preferences

Respondents who agree with the initial offering amount of 200 yen account for about 70% of the total effective responses. More than half agree to the fare of 250 yen. However, there are also a certain number of respondents who do not want to pay even if the fare is 150 yen (Table 3).

Table 3. Bus fare preferences

	Fare	Yes	No	No answer
First bid price	200 yen	282	122	34
Second bid price 1	250 yen	139	126	17
Second bid price 2	150 yen	54	65	3

We asked the respondent who would pay the bus fare even a bit for the reason. 172 people answered that they wanted to support if the service was principally designed to meet the travel needs of children and elderly people (Fig. 6).

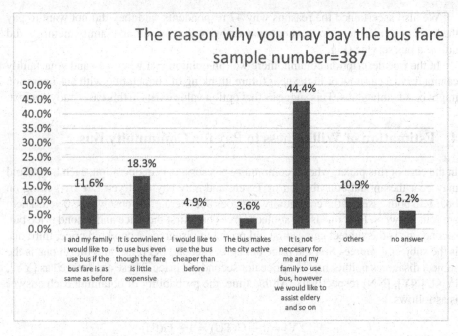

Fig. 6. The reasons why you may pay the bus fare

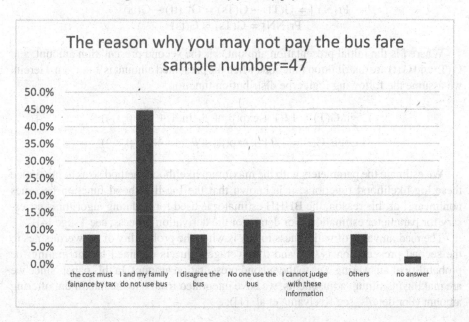

Fig. 7. The reasons why you may not pair the bus fare

We also ascertained the reasons why 47 respondents said they did not want to pay the bus fare at all; the most frequent answers were that myself and family members did utilize a bus service (Fig. 7).

In the free description column, there was an opinion that when you and your family cannot drive a car now or in the near future, thinking of cooperating with bus operation might be advantageous. This suggests that option value exists in this case-study context.

4 Estimation of Willingness to Pay for Community Bus

In the case of this paper, when a community bus service is in operation, each household may bear the annual contribution of T yen, and may pay the t yen fare by getting on board. In both cases, if the community bus does not operate, the cost will be 0 yen. There are four answers. First one is the subject agrees both first bid price and second price bid, second one is the subject agrees first bid price but disagrees second bid price, third one is the subject disagrees first bid price but agrees second bid price, and fourth one is the subject disagrees neither first bid price nor second bid price. These are denoted as [YY], [YN], [NY], [NN] respectively. At this time, the probability of obtaining each answer is as follows.

$$Pr[YY] = 1 - G(TU) = 1 - G(tU)$$
$$Pr[YN] = GU(TU) - G(Tf) = GU(tU) - G(tf)$$
$$Pr[NY] = G(Tf) - G(Ts) = GU(tf) - G(ts)$$
$$Pr[NN] = G(Ts) = G(ts)$$

Where f is the initial presentation amount, s is the second presentation amount, and G (T) and G (t) are distribution functions when the presented amount is T or t yen. Herein, we assume the following logit type distribution function.

$$\text{Logit } G(T) = 1/(1 + \exp(\beta_0 + \beta_T \ln T + \sum \beta_k x_k))$$
$$\text{Logit } G(t) = 1/(1 + \exp(\beta_0 + \beta_t \ln t + \sum \beta_k x_k))$$

We estimate the parameters with the maximum likelihood method so as to maximize these log-likelihood functions. It is known that the log-likelihood function becomes nonlinear. For this reason, the BHHH estimator is used for updating algorithms necessary for parameter estimation (For details of the derivation process, see Tsuge [4]).

The median value of willingness to pay is when the probability of answering Yes to the second presentation is 0.5, and the average value is obtained by integrating the probability of answering Yes to the second presentation amount. In this paper, since we are making maximum adjustments, we have integrated from 0 to the maximum offering amount (For details, see Kuriyama et al. [1]).

4.1   Estimation Results Concerning Annual Payment

From Fig. 8 and Table 4, the intention to pay an annual contribution for bus operation revealed a median value of 1,042 yen; and it was 1,134 yen on average when the maximum bid amount was set.

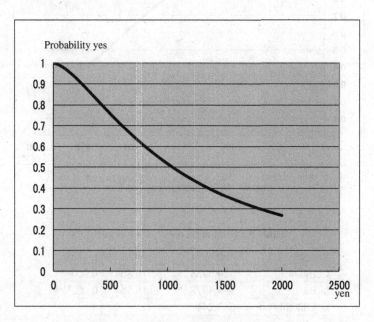

Fig. 8. Willingness to pay annual payments

Table 4. Estimation results for annual payments

Variable	Coefficient	t-value	p-value
Constant	10.7938	10.396	0.000***
ln(Bid)	−1.5532	−10.718	0.000***
Log-likelihood	−482.890		

n = 392; *** denotes significant at the 1% level.

4.2   Estimation Results Concerning Bus Fares

From Fig. 9 and Table 5, the median willingness to pay bus fare was 226; and it was 209 yen on average when the maximum offering amount was set.

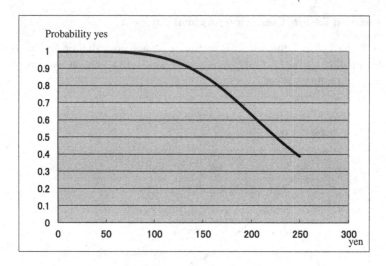

Fig. 9. Willingness to pay bus fare

Table 5. Estimation results for bus fares

Variable	Coefficient	t-value	p-value
Constant	24.3738	16.864	0.000***
ln(Bid)	−4.4978	−16.584	0.000***
Log-likelihood	−517.241		

n = 384; *** denotes significant at the 1% level.

4.3   Price Elasticity of Bus Fares

From the results in Table 2, nearly half of the respondents are opposed to paying annual contributions; this is justified in terms of bus users should pay the cost. Also, assuming the fare is an option from Table 3, even if a fare higher than the initial offering amount is favored, agreement is higher than opposition. This could reflect willingness to cooperate to support others.

Therefore, in this section, we examine how the number of passengers change when the fare changes, by invoking the price elasticity of demand. If the number of passengers does not change even if the fare is raised somewhat, the operation of the community bus can be said to be sustainable if the initial cost and fixed cost for bus operation are collected by freight. Conversely, if the bus fare is set high and the number of passengers is drastically reduced, it is necessary to examine the collection of the initial cost and fixed cost in another way.

The equation for calculating the price elasticity (ε_d) of bus demand is as follows. Where p is the fare after change, q is the number of passengers after the change, Δ p is the price difference, and Δq is the variation in the number of passengers.

$$\varepsilon_d = -(\Delta p/p)/(q/\Delta q)$$

Calculating by applying the values in Table 3, when the fare falls from 200 yen to 150 yen, the price elasticity becomes 2.07; as the fare for this bus service decreases, it is expected that demand substantively increases. By contrast, when the fare increases from 200 yen to 250 yen, the price elasticity becomes 0.22; as such, demand only decreases marginally.

Therefore, according to these results, it is expected that demand will increase significantly as the fare falls. If the fare rises, however, it can be posited that demand will not decrease so much.

5   Conclusion and Remarks

The result of the cellphone survey obtains the subjects do not have experience using electronic wallet and QR code functionalities. Recently, Felica Network undertook a similar survey in Tokyo based on a sample of residents 15 years or older between May 28–June 8, 2016. Therein, about 20% of the subjects used phone based electronic wallet functionalities. They asked questions pertaining to the usage of electronic money; women, adolescents and men over 60 years old were more likely to use physical, plastic debit/cards. In other words, it is thought that the people who are more likely to use community bus services are more likely to use plastic debit/credit cards.

From the result of the bus operation survey, we can estimate the median of the willingness to pay for annual payment is lower than first bid price. On one hand the median of the willingness to pay for bus fare is higher than first bid price. From this, we infer that subjects prefer the fare which includes whole cost to annual payment.

However, when all the initial expense is financed by the fare, it needs more number of passengers or higher bus fare.

From the price elasticity of bus demand, it can be said that the bus demand does not decrease so much if the bus fare is 50yen higher than first bid price, however, the bus demand increases much more if the bus fare is 50yen lower than first bid price.

Therefore, in order to realize the bus operation, it is supposed to suggest that the operator hands an IC chip card to the person who paid money of annual fee and apply the discount bus fare, or the system that user can pay financial reserve funds on the IC chip card little by little to prepare for future use.

We do not differentiate estimates of bus service payment intention amounts by age categories herein. We would try to estimate the amount of payment intention according to the generation. And we would like to consider the way of the expense burden that a bus service becomes sustainable by using a classification model.

We have collated GPS data from certain survey district residents; we hope to use the data in the future to further explore bus service demand.

Acknowledgement. In creating this paper, we appreciate the members of the specific NPO Corporation, Makishima Kizuna no Kai who gave us a lot of advice to make questionnaire. We would like to express our gratitude to the residents of the area who cooperated in the questionnaire survey. This research was subsidized by JSPS Graduate School Expenses JP 16 K 03718, JP 15 H 0 3364.

References

1. Kuriyama, K., Tsuge, T., Shoji, Y.: Introduction to environmental evaluation for beginner. In: Syoshinsya no tame no Kankyo Hyoka Nyuumon, pp. 109–173. Keiso-Shobo (2013). (in Japanese)
2. Oguma, H., Yokoyama, T., Nishimura, S., Moriyama, O., Kamiya, H.: Residents' evaluation of bus services in depopulated areas and policy issues. Transp. Econ. **75**(8), 57–71 (2015)
3. Shiozu, Y., Yonezaki, K., Shimohara, K.: Incentive structure of participation in community activity. In: Yamamoto, S. (ed.) HIMI 2013. LNCS, vol. 8016, pp. 259–268. Springer, Heidelberg (2013). doi:10.1007/978-3-642-39209-2_30
4. Tsuge, T., Kuriyama, K., Mitani, K.: New technique of evaluation for environment. In: Kankyo Hyoka no saishin technique, pp. 14–52. Keiso-Shobo (2011). (in Japanese)

Analysis to the Customer of the EC Site User

Takeshi Shiraishi[✉] and Yumi Asahi

School of Information and Telecommunication Engineering,
Department of Management Systems Engineering,
Tokai University, Tokyo, Japan
4BJM2117@mail.tokai-u.jp, asahi@tsc.u-tokai.ac.jp

Abstract. Now, in Japan business of clothes with E-commerce(EC) is done activity. Sales of direct sales store and outlets is decreasing, so a number of its store to close are increasing. It's expected that Sales with EC site and market size continue to increase from now on. In this circumstance, in order to develop EC site which scale shows a great growth, we have done a calculation of the factor score through the questionnaire items, and classification of customer with questionnaire date and customer's record to purchase. After this, we have grasped the characteristics of classified customer information, and compared some clusters. As a result, the characteristics of customer cluster regarded as "fashionable" must be gotten close to its not customer cluster. "Not fashionable" customers have higher average value of "frequency of purchase" and "expenses of purchase" per customers, therefore, it's expected increasing of sales and expand of its size.

Keywords: Service management · Business to customer · The individuality

1 Introduction

1.1 About E-Commerce

Now, the size of EC site is adopted B to C (business to customer) style is increasing year by year in Japan. In 2010, it was 7,780 thousand million yen, meanwhile in 2015 it was 1.37 billion yen and have grown year by year as Fig. 1 shows. From 2014 to 2015 its growth rate recorded 7.6%, it's expected to expand the market size from now on. The highest field of sales is field of "Product sales" which was recorded 7,239 thousand million in 2015 and occupied a half of market size. Sales of clothes in its field was registered 1,383 thousand million, and occupied about 20% of market size. However, the transition rate to EC site of sales of clothes is recorded 7.9% and low value, but in other words, there will be development of sales and market, which is a remarkable field in the future.

1.2 Fashion Market

The fashion market in Japan had declined since 1990's "collapse of bubble economy" In recent years, size of market has not widely changed, and decayed gradually. One of

© Springer International Publishing AG 2017
S. Yamamoto (Ed.): HIMI 2017, Part I, LNCS 10273, pp. 435–447, 2017.
DOI: 10.1007/978-3-319-58521-5_34

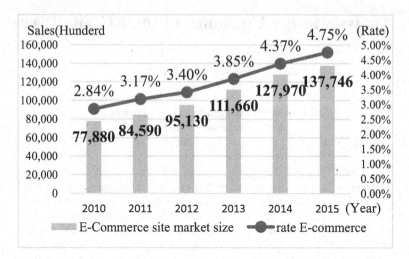

Fig. 1. E-commerce market size and conversion factor

some causes to lead to reduce its size is a major factor to decline sales of clothing field. Compared with sales in 2002, its sales declined 19 thousand million yen. And some markets like the shoes, cosmetics and accessory have declined likewise, but its size is not so big that decrease of its sales doesn't influence greatly the whole of fashion market. And surely there is downward tendency in the fashion market. However, it's expected the condition to increase sales with EC site will influence greatly the future fashion market (Fig. 2).

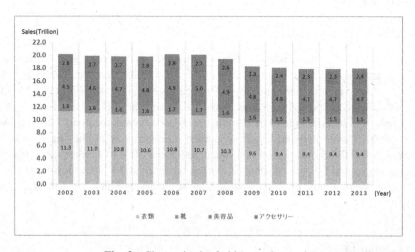

Fig. 2. Change in the fashion market scale

2 Data Used for the Analysis

In this study, we proceeded under purchase date of EC site and its related date. This date was provided in "date analysis competition" hosted Joint Association Study Group of Management Science in 2017.

2.1 Data Summary

The provided dates in this time are 6: Customer data, Questionnaire data, Favorite shop data, Order data, Order detailed data and Item data.

By the customer number, the dates are linked that Questionnaire data, Favorite shop data and Order detailed data.

By the order number, the dates are linked that Favorite shop data and Order data.

By the item code, the dates are linked that Order data and Item data.

By the shop number, the dates are linked that Order detail data and Item data.

To put the above into a diagram is following Fig. 3.

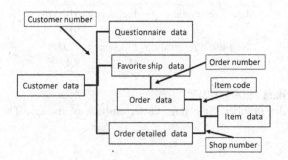

Fig. 3. Data combination

2.2 Purchasing Date of All Customers

Purchase observation terms: April 1, 2015–March 23, 2016
  Questionnaire terms: March 17, 2016–March 23, 2016
  Adopted the customer age and favorite shop data, as of March 17, 2016.
  Questionnaire respondent: 3,144 people
  Questionnaire non-respondent: 100,000 people

2.3 The Data Which Were Used for a Study This Time

Customer data (103,144)
  Variable: A questionnaire answer flag, A customer number, Gender and age.
  Question data (3,144)
  Variable: Customer number and Question item 103 (among 109)

The reason not making use of six data, because of a free description.
Questionnaire flag, 3,144 of 103,144
The gender ratio of questionnaire respondent: men 31.3%, women 68.7% (Table 1)

Table 1. The age ratio of questionnaire respondent

			Age						Sum
			10s	Early 20s	Late 20s	Early 30s	Late 30s	40s over	
Questionnaire	Non-answer	Frequency	4,395	16,378	19,308	20,182	18,117	21,620	100,000
		%	4.4%	16.4%	19.3%	20.2%	18.1%	21.6%	100.0%
	Answer	Frequency	112	290	498	631	622	991	3,144
		%	3.6%	9.2%	15.8%	20.1%	19.8%	31.5%	100.0%

Order data (557,476)
Variable: Customer number, Order number, Reservation flag and Purchase device
(Table 2).

Table 2. The age ratio of questionnaire respondent

Customer	Value	
Use a reservation	Frequency	510,378
	%	91.6
Non-use a reservation	Frequency	47,098
	%	8.4

Order detail data (1,009,022)
Variable: Order number, Sale flag, Order amount of money, The number of the
orders (Table 3).

Table 3. Ratio of which device customer use for a purchase

Puchase device	Value	
Smartphone	Frequency	179,975
	%	32.28
Cellphone	Frequency	374,480
	%	67
PC	Frequency	3,020
	%	0.54

3 Procedure of Analysis

3.1 The Purpose of this Study

The purpose this study "Fashionable customer increased". That purpose is intention of
data source. The data source site hype sales by-product. The definition about "fashionable" has various views. However, "The person good at own expression." and,

"Deep person of own understanding" to assume in this study. We were adopted that assume reason "fashionable sensibility is difference each person". Because, we can't figure "fashionable" objectively. However not, "fashionable" figure for other person. It established to own "fashionable" and, the people who grasp "fashionable" with own expression, an analysis was advanced to a principal axis.

First, questionnaire data have 3 question forms.

Question 1,7 and Question 8 were 1-0 answer.

Question 2, 3, 4 and Question 8 were 1–4 answer.

Question 9 was 1–5 answer.

1–4 and 1–5 answer were reverse item. Because, we reverse item processing was done.

The factor analysis preformed for the questionnaire data. The number of the calculated factors was 28. However, we chose8 in criteria of scree plot. 8 factor scores The varimax revolution gave to below are extracted.

The first factor is formed by only the life emphasis value. Therefore, this factor was regard as the life emphasis value (Table 4).

Table 4. The 1st factor

Question number	Factor score	Question contents
Q3_3	.785	The life emphasis value Achievement and fame (glory, honor, winning a prize and services)
Q3_4	.766	The life emphasis value Competition and victory (victory, victor and No1)
Q3_15	.736	The life emphasis value The rise (president, the part section chief and promotion)
Q3_9	.626	The life emphasis value Belonging (first-class university, getting a job and first-class enterprise)
Q3_18	.574	The life emphasis value Famous (celebrity, celebrity and celebrity)
Q3_17	.483	The life emphasis value Wealth (sum, assets, saving, extravagant spree and moneymaking)
Q3_8	.427	The life emphasis value Qualification (MBA, state qualification and bookkeeping)
Q3_10	.418	The life emphasis value Property (home, car and collection)
Q3_5	.390	The life emphasis value The personal ability (the communication power, the reading comprehension and the presentation power)

The second factor is formed by only the fashion change. Because, those question depend on the feeling. Therefore, this factor was regard as the feeling degree (Table 5).

Table 5. The 2nd factor

Question number	Factor score	Question contents
Q9_3G	.895	Fashion change The chance to buy fashion related goods and the number of times
Q9_4G	.872	Fashion change The price which begins to buy fashion related goods
Q9_1G	.844	Fashion change Interest to fashion
Q9_2G	.810	Fashion change The situation and the chance which pay regard to fashion
Q9_5G	.366	Fashion change The genre of the fashion which is often bought

The third factor is formed by only the sense of value in the fashion. It is a promise that those question are interesting in a fashion. Therefore, this factor was regard as the fashion interest degree (Table 6).

Table 6. The 3rd factor

Question number	Factor score	Question contents
Q8_13	.611	Sense of values in the fashion Fashion is a part of the lifestyle
Q8_25	.582	Sense of values in the fashion Clothes do one's value highly low
Q8_10	.541	Sense of values in the fashion Clothes to be one of the means to show personality
Q8_15	.524	Sense of values in the fashion Another person making a fashion check better
Q8_14	.505	Sense of values in the fashion Oneself minding how a fashion is seen from a person
Q8_8	.486	Sense of values in the fashion Fashion to be expression of one's identity
Q8_12	.457	Sense of values in the fashion I mind to choose the clothes in accord with the fashion show room surface
Q8_27	.326	Sense of values in the fashion There is a thing preparing the item which I liked by outlook on fashion oneself in different colors

The fourth factor is formed by only the purchase time. We can regard it a purchase opportunity. Therefore, this factor was regard as the serious consideration at an opportunity (Table 7).

Table 7. The 4th factor

Question number	Factor score	Question contents
Q6_6	.681	Purchase time When it was approached by need (the clothes which I liked without clothes to wear go bad)
Q6_3	.680	Purchase time When a person to contact changes (entrance into a school of higher grade, finding employment, change of job, start of the hobby)
Q6_7	.626	Purchase time A trip, an event
Q6_4	.591	Purchase time When I got tired of the clothes which oneself had
Q6_2	.565	Purchase time When a season changes
Q6_5	.426	Purchase time When there is money usable freely

The fifth factor is formed by only A fashion problem. Therefore, this factor was regard as the fashion problem (Table 8).

Table 8. The 5th factor

Question number	Factor score	Question child contents
Q7_1	.717	A fashion problem I do not understand the way of coordinates
Q7_4	.675	A fashion problem I do not know what oneself looks good with
Q7_3	.570	A fashion problem I do not understand the fashion
Q7_11	−.532	A fashion problem None
Q7_5	.503	A fashion problem I do not know what I should wear depending on the situation

The sixth factor is formed by the consciousness and the well-being. The antonym of the pessimism is optimism. Therefore, this factor was regard as the well-being for the life (Table 9).

Table 9. The 6th factor

Question number	Factor score	Question contents
Q2_13	.887	Consciousness It is pessimistic for one's present conditions (the private life, work)
Q2_14	.886	Consciousness It is pessimistic for one's future (the private life, work)
Q4	−.676	Well-being

The seventh factor is formed by only the life serious consideration value. The history and the specialty were strong in an impression of the study and associated a well-read image. Therefore, this factor was regard as the culture serious consideration (Table 10).

Table 10. The 7th factor

Question number	Factor score	Question contents
Q3_14	.649	Life serious consideration value The history (long-established store, tradition, remains, culture)
Q3_11	.645	Life serious consideration value Specialty (professor, shogi player, writer, professional)
Q3_12	.615	Life serious consideration value An ambition (adventure, ambition, dream)

The eighth factor is formed of the question item of the plural (Table 11).

Table 11. The 8th factor

Question number	Factor score	Question contents
Q8_6	.658	Outlook on fashion It is the rotation wearing clothes different from the person
Q8_7	.648	Outlook on fashion It is one not to be particular about in a conventional style and model
Q3_6	.476	Life serious consideration value Personality (originality, difference, exceptional talent, special straight fact)
Q2_8	.390	Consciousness I often customize it for oneself without being satisfied with a ready-made article

"I'd like to have a clothes different from the environment".
"I'm not particular about a conventional style".
"The individuality of the life emphasis value".
"A ready-made is customized".
The factor is possible to infer from those. It is showed the strength of the individuality.

3.2 Analysis of Characteristics of the Customer Based on Cluster Analysis

A cluster analysis is performed based on 8 factor scores obtained by the factor analysis. It was made to make it easy to compare three groups.

Group 1 was 54.3% of whole in 1,707 people. Group 2 was 20.1% of whole in 633 people. Group 3 was 25.6% of whole in 804 people. The one-way analysis variance was preformed based on the separated group number and 8 factor scores. A result was graphed and it was mentioned as Fig. 4.

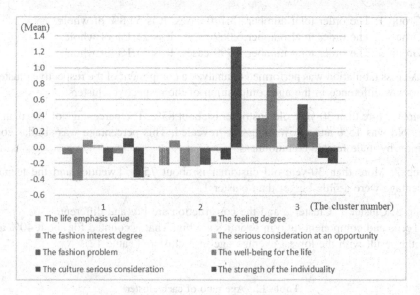

Fig. 4. As a result of the one-way analysis variance

The chart the one-way analysis variance the feature of each customer group are seen.

Group 1: "The feeling degree" and "The strength of the individuality" are reflected minus. "Culture emphasis" indicated the numerical value higher than other groups. It was possible to infer from this thing that the clothes which don't influence "The feeling degree" and "The strength of the individuality" are liked. In addition to there is also a face where the culture is emphasized. Therefore, it was understanding with a customer group of "uniform supreme principle".

Group 2: "The strength of the individuality" stand out more than other groups. Because, there are few fashion problems, they grasp their fashion suit well. A cluster of group 2 thought it was possible to change it according to the feeling. Therefore, Group 2 could infer that own expression was a good and fashionable group.

Group 3: "The life emphasis value", "The feeling degree" and "The fashion problem" stand out more than other groups. They are capricious from that things. However, it is decided clearly to make it important in a life. Thor, it was possible to infer that Group 3 is the customer group. They can't decide clothes when accorded in various situation.

3.3 Appointments of Customer and Other Data

Order data customer data are combined with questionnaire data and a feature was analyzed. Data combination was performed based on order data. Because, a customer of non-answer didn't belong to a customer group in analysis. So it was eliminated. Therefore, we increased in the number of data of a customer group in 24,038 lines from 3,144 lines.

Group 1: The order total number 13,170 cases. It is 54.8% of whole.
Group 2: The order total number 5,069 cases. It is 21.1% of whole.
Group 3: The order total number 5,799 cases. It is 24.1% of whole.

A cross tabulation was performed to analyze a component of the respective clusters. There was difference in the age composition of the respective clusters.

Group 1: More than 30-year-old customer is about 85%. The percentage of less than 20 years old was 15% and a low thing was revealed. This percentage was similar composition by male female commonness.

Group 2: More than 30-year-old customer is about 75%. Twenties and the teenage percentage were a little bigger than cluster 1.

Group 3: Cluster 1, Cluster 2 and the construction are big and different.
Teens and component ratio in twenties are big. That accounted for about 40% and was the result with the lowest average age in 3 clusters (Table 12).

Table 12. Age ratio of each cluster

			Age						Sum
			10s	Ealy 20s	Late 20s	Ealy 30s	Late 30s	Over 40s	
Cluster	1	frequency	77	256	1,274	2,122	2,222	3,227	9,178
		%	.8%	2.8%	13.9%	23.1%	24.2%	35.2%	100.0%
	2	frequency	28	284	404	621	886	1,383	3,606
		%	.8%	7.9%	11.2%	17.2%	24.6%	38.4%	100.0%
	3	frequency	156	593	723	655	858	1,118	4,103
		%	3.8%	14.5%	17.6%	16.0%	20.9%	27.2%	100.0%
sum		frequency	261	1,133	2,401	3,398	3,966	5,728	16,887
		%	1.5%	6.7%	14.2%	20.1%	23.5%	33.9%	100.0%

4 Result of Analysis

4.1 Analysis of Cluster 1

As a result of the one-way analysis variance, it shows that the factor of "felling degree" and "the strength of the individuality "are lower and "culture serious consideration "is higher, we interpret this group as "inform supremacy ". In addition, the age composition in the cluster is older, above all aged 30 or more, so it's expected member of this group has many chances to put their suit and their business attire. And The following average values of customers in this cluster is the highest values in the all cluster; expenses to order "333,333yen" and the number of order "224 items" and the number of times to use the discount sales "183 times" which are all per one customer. Most of customers in this group is older than other group, they may live a comfortable life with enough money and time. Therefore, it is expected this customer is the most frequently to order (Fig. 5).

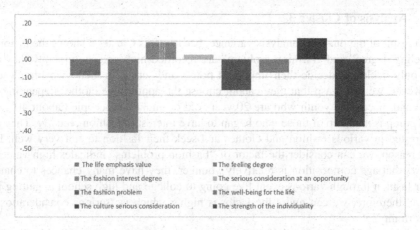

Fig. 5. As a result of the one-way analysis variance of Cluster 1

4.2 Analysis of Cluster 2

As a result of the one-way analysis variance, it shows that factor of "felling degree" is positive value and "the strength of the individuality" is above all high degree. So We guessed that this group is good at self-expression and stylish. Certainly Cluster 2 is a little similar to cluster 1 in term of the value of age composition, but to stress the individuality, it's expected customers of this group get most likely a creative job, which has no chance to put a suit and works while putting ordinarily clothes.

To get accustomed putting ordinary clothes any time, it's also expected they are familiar with what kind of clothes they suit good, and as a result, the factor of "Fashion problems" is lower than other clusters.

And in the same way, the following average values of customers in this cluster is the lowest values in the all cluster; expenses to order "191,048yen" and the number of order "106 items" and the number of times to use the discount sales "86 times". As they know their fashion to suit well, and purchase to select items carefully, we can grasp that their expense of order and the number of their order may be lower value (Fig. 6).

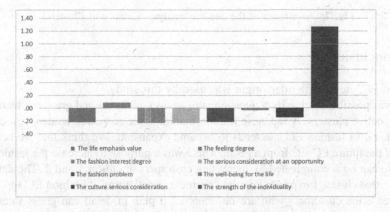

Fig. 6. As a result of the one-way analysis variance of Cluster 2

4.3 Analysis of Cluster 3

As a result of the one-way analysis variance, because this Cluster 3 shows the factor of "Feeling degree" and "Fashion problem" are recorded high values, probably they are not only fickle but decide their important points and senses in their own life clearly. However, we can grasp that they cannot choose the appropriate clothes depending on time and place. The youth who are 20 years old or under are occupied about 40%, so this group is made up of those who began to have interest in fashion recently. They are interested in various fashion and clothes and seek their fashion to suit very well. For that reason, we can consider the factor of "Fashion problems" indicates high value. It shows that age composition is relatively younger, they have many chances to change their fashion through various event like going to college and high school a, getting job move, therefore, we can guess the factor is higher which is "serious consideration at opportunity".

Likewise, we can grasp the following average values of customers in this cluster is in the middle values in the all cluster; expenses to order "211,840yen" and the number of order "114items" and the number of times to use the discount sales "102 times" (Fig. 7).

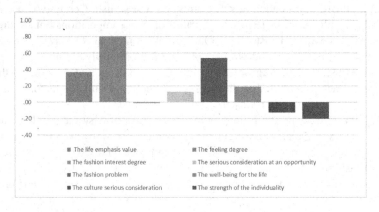

Fig. 7. As a result of the one-way analysis variance of Cluster 3

5 Conclusion

Fashion EC site of data offer origin was used by this study.

It was possible to classify a questionnaire answer customer and grasp the feature of the respective clusters. A Japanese fashion market is the reduction tendency, recently. A market of a fashion EC site tends to became expansion. We think that we help the sales of the future EC site from a result. There was a purpose to increase the fashion EC site. We can be accomplished by increasing customers of cluster 1 and 2. The detail of plan are that cluster 1 expands favorite "business casual attire". "Fashion EC site wants to increase the customers who are fashionable" a plan in detail can guess sales promotion activity to a customer of cluster 3 to be effective.

We make the problem of their fashion dear. And, we find out the clothes looking good with them. Depending on sales promotion activity. Cluster 3 has high possible which become an excellent customer from now on became there are a lot of young customers.

6 Further Task

In this study we proceeded the analysis which is focused on a questionnaire answers by customers, but this study has problems, which is needs of expansion of analysis range to respondents. In addition, we can't make use of same dates like date of purchase items. So with date of purchase product of customer included no-respondents, also we need to calculate "Lift values" and device the relationships to several products. We consider to suggest the new promotions and sales activities every Customers cluster from "Lift values".

References

1. Hamada, K.: Fashion Association, Hukusousyakaigaku to syakaigaku [Fashion Sociology and Sociology] (2007)
2. Takada, Y.: Bulletin of Toita Women's College 56, Aidenthithixi to fashion no kanrensei ni tuite no kousatu [Consideration about the association of identity and the fashion] (2013)
3. Hamada, K.: Fashion industry society article magazine 1 (1995-1), Gendaisyakai to hukusou ni kansuru iti kousatu – syakaigakuteki apurouti no teian [The Modern Society and Fashion – A Proposal for Sociological Approach] (1995)

Giving IT Services a Theoretical Backing

Alexander Teubner and Christian Remfert[(⊠)]

ERCIS Research Group on Strategic Information Management,
Muenster, Germany
{alexander.teubner, christian.remfert}@ercis.org

Abstract. The Information Technology Infrastructure Library (ITIL) is the prevailing standard for managing Information Technology (IT) operations in practice. What is revolutionary about the ITIL is that it proposes to conceive of IT not (only) as a technology, but rather as a means of providing services to businesses. This idea has gained considerable attention in academia, and has given rise to identifying "IT Service Management (ITSM)" as a new management paradigm and field of research. Unfortunately, the concept of an IT service has been poorly elaborated the within ITIL, and remains elusive in the academic debate surrounding ITSM. With this paper, we set out to resolve the vagueness surrounding the notion of an IT service based on an extensive literature review. We conclude a set of six defining features that we believe, if taken together, fully capture the concept of an IT service. We also substantiate these features with underlying theories. Finally, we illustrate the potential of our definition with an exemplary IT service that we defined for a German publishing company in the context of an ITSM research project we recently conducted.

Keywords: Information Technology Infrastructure Library (ITIL) · IT Service Management (ITSM) · ITility Service · IT service specification

1 Introduction

Information Technology Service Management (ITSM) is a paradigm for the management of Information Technology (IT) and Information Systems (IS) that promotes the idea of looking upon the IT organization as a service organization. ITSM is rooted in the Information Technology Infrastructure Library (ITIL), a best practice framework initially composed in the 1980 s by the British Central Computing and Telecommunications Agency (CCTA). A second edition, issued in 2001, was broadly perceived in practice and made the ITIL a de-facto standard. The third edition of the ITIL, issued in 2007 and updated in 2011, even found its way into the ISO/IEC 20000 making the ITIL a somewhat de-jure standard on an international scale. Hardly any other standard has influenced the practice of IT management in general and IT operations in particular to the extent the ITIL did. It is not surprising then that the ITIL has found its way into academic IS curricula and stimulated an academic debate [1].

Research so far has focused on the diffusion of the ITIL in practice. Studies by Kemper et al. [2], Hochstein et al. [3], Tan et al. [4], Marrone and Kolbe [5] as well as Marrone et al. [6] document broad adoption of the ITIL. The benefits that organizations associate with the implementation of the ITIL are, for example, a higher overall service

© Springer International Publishing AG 2017
S. Yamamoto (Ed.): HIMI 2017, Part I, LNCS 10273, pp. 448–468, 2017.
DOI: 10.1007/978-3-319-58521-5_35

quality, a higher first call resolution rate, or a reduction of downtimes. Remarkably, the benefits perceived seem significantly diminish with the level of maturity achieved [5].

In addition, studies that dive deeper into organizational practices reveal that many of the organizations still struggle with the main ideas underlying IT service orientation. For example, a study by Winniford, Conger and Harris [7] found that IT executives, despite claiming to have successfully introduced the ITIL into their organization, had difficulties explaining what an IT service is and struggled to give examples. Additional case studies and action research [8–10] reveal that organizations that adopt the ITIL do not necessarily understand and implement the underlying core concepts including, above all, that of an IT service. This is a devastating result, given that the IT service is the "nucleus of the entire ITIL" [11, 12].

A clear understanding of IT services is also a condition sine qua non for any theory development on "*IT Service* Management". In fact, the IT service is the core theoretical term of ITSM. But so far, researchers have not been able to clearly define what exactly is meant by the term "IT service", so that the theoretical kernel of ITSM remains vague [13].

We take this situation as the motivation to investigate the concept of an IT service as rooted in the ITIL and discussed in ITSM in more depths. The objective of our research is to come up with a clear and substantial definition of "IT service", which is desperately needed for ITSM research. In this paper, we lay out core findings from our research. We start with a theoretical investigation and with a literature review on the definitions of the term "IT service" given in the professional and academic literature in Sect. 2. Using this as a starting point, we dive deeper into the academic discussion on ITSM and the ideas underlying the IT service concept in Sect. 3. Here is where we carve out the distinguishing characteristics of IT services. To demonstrate the definitional power and practicality of our definition, we illustrate its applicability with a real-world example taken from one of our research projects on ITSM (Sect. 4). We close the paper with a short summary and an outlook on future research.

2 IT Services – Omnipresent but Still Ambiguous in the Literature

The empirical basis of our research is a literature review on the IT service concept as used in the academic debate on ITSM. Following the taxonomy of literature reviews proposed by Cooper [14], our review can be characterized as being *focused on research outcomes* with the *goal* of understanding a central issue, namely what is meant with IT service in ITSM, by *integrating* the current academic debate. We do this by synthesizing and consolidating the conceptions we find in the literature. Hence, the *organization* of our review is *conceptual*. We do this without biasing our perspective ex ante. Rather, we are open to any interpretation used in academia. The *coverage* of our literature review is broad. Although it is hardly possible to claim completeness for any literature review, we intended to be as *exhaustive* as possible in the coverage of the literature. The target *audience* is, first *specialized scholars* working on theoretical foundations of ITSM. Second, our research is of value for *practitioners* struggling with the definition of IT services in their concrete business settings.

In the next subsections, we provide insights into the findings from our literature review. We start with a short introduction into what is understood by the term "IT service" in general before we introduce a more in depth picture of its understanding in the academic debate on ITSM.

2.1   IT Services in General

In the literature, the term "IT service" is used to refer to a broad set of "services" that are (somehow) related to Information Technology. For example, publications in the context of SOA and Web Services tend to define an IT service in a technical way [15–18]. Other publications that deal with IT Services in an outsourcing and offshoring context use IT service to refer to solutions provided by IT outsourcing providers in general [19–24]. Similar definitions are found in publications on the IT service market, which also refer to a diverse set of offerings even including IT consulting, training, and software development as services [22, 25–30]. The diversity of IT services we found is also reflected in common IT service taxonomies used for statistical purposes [31–33]. These include a diverse mix of activities including "software development projects", "hardware deployment", "hardware repair", "software maintenance", "software hosting", "systems integration" as well as "IT hotlines", "IT consulting", "IT training", and "IT outsourcing". Given this diversity, it is obvious that IT can play different roles in IT services. In addition, many authors do not explain why they look at a "software development project" or a "hardware deployment" as a service. Other authors, in contrast, explain their service understanding in more detail, often by referring to service theory in general [9, 34–37]. This is particularly true for the academic debate on Service Science which builds strongly on the foundations of service theory in general next to theories from management studies and engineering [38, 39]. We also see the value of applying the perspective of the general theory of services (GTS) to IT services. It turned out to be particularly helpful in making sense of the different interpretations of IT services that we found in the literature and in explaining how they differ.

GTS looks upon services, above all, as immaterial and intangible goods. Immateriality is the reason that software is often subsumed under the roof of "IT services" [32]. However, the intangibility of services requires a physical object for the service to manifest. GTS refers to this object as the "external factor". External factors can be the service customer herself as well as people in her aegis or goods in her property. Everyday examples are a haircut, gardening services or a carwash. In many cases, the term "IT service" refers to services that have information technology facilities in the property of the recipient as external factors [26, 29, 40–43]. A simple example is a computer repair, with a broken computer being the external factor. Two further examples are an individual software development project and IT consulting. In the first case, the external factor is a customer problem defined in a software requirements specification. In the second case, the external factor is a management need to be addressed in a specific business context.

An immediate consequence of intangibility is that services cannot be stored so that the production and use of a service are coincidental. This condition, the so called "uno-actu-principle", requires that a service provider needs to hold available all the production factors necessary to render the service on demand for service customers. GTS refers to these internal production factors as "potential factors". Business Process Outsourcing (BPO) or Software as a Service (SaaS) may serve as examples [32, 33]. In both cases, IT systems are the core production factor deployed to deliver the service, i.e. to execute business processes automatically or to provide a user with software functionality. Such IT services that make use of hard- and/or software as potential factors are often referred to as "IT-based services" in the literature [37, 44].

2.2   IT Services in the Context of ITSM

Equipped with a GTS-based understanding of IT services, we analysed in more detail academic publications in the field of ITSM and ITIL. We identified the Information Systems discipline as central to the debate on ITSM. Hence, we sought for academic publications in Information Systems and its "mother disciplines" Business Administration and Computer Science. We chose the EBSCO databases "Academic Search Premier", "Business Source Premier", "EconLit with fulltext" and "Information, Library and Technology Abstracts" (that include also the Senior Scholars Basket of Eight) for the IS and BA disciplines, as well as ScienceDirect, EmeraldInsight, ABI/Informs and Springer to get access to relevant publications in these disciplines. In addition, for a better coverage of publications from Computer Science, we also included IEEExplore. Finally, the ECONIS catalogue of the German National Library was used to complement journal and conference publications with book publications in the field of IS. We searched these data bases very broadly for occurrences of the term "IT service" in different notations using the search string <"IT-service" | "IT service" | "IT-Service" | "IT Service" > in title and/or abstract. This search led to a sample of 328 results that we checked manually for being related to ITSM or not. This way, we excluded, for example, technical contributions on Service Oriented Architectures (SOA) or web services as well as general publications on IT outsourcing and the IT market. This left us with a remaining subsample of 178 publications that could be of relevance for our topic. Of these, the majority was published on conferences (49%) and on smaller workshops (13%). The fact that only 2% of the publications had found entrance into the journals can be seen as an indication for a preliminary state of theory development on ITSM. In addition, we found that the academic debate on ITSM is more vivid in middle Europe and Scandinavia than in the USA and the UK.

Our literature review revealed that most publications (77%) totally omit defining what they mean by an IT service [5, 56–59]. Other publications (4%) simply refer to the definition given in the ITIL [7, 60–64]. This left us with only 13 out of 178 publications that have a dedicated definition of "IT service". However, a short look at Table 1 reveals that these definitions are neither unambiguous nor concise, but differ substantially in both definiendum (IT product, IT performance) and definiens (IT functions, performances, service components). In Table 1, we have organized the definition on a continuum depending on whether they emphasize more "what" IT services are "good for" while others try to explain "how" IT services are "composed or produced" as indicated on the left of the table.

Table 1. IT service definitions in the literature

What?	■ "An IT service is a bundle of IT accomplishments to support a business process or business product of the customer to generate a value for him" [45]
↑	■ "A service can be described as a clearly definable service, based – at least partly – on information technology (IT). It is offered by a service provider on the request of a service customer" [46]
	■ "[…] IT service [are] understood as business process supporting IT functions, which are represent themselves to the user as closed, application-oriented units." [2]
	■ "IT Services that consist of internal and external services and non-cash benefits are provided by IT organization for customers, where time range, quality and costs of the IT service provision are contracted between the related parties by so-called Service Level Agreements (SLA)." [47]
	■ Teubner [48] characterizes IT services in the sense of ITSM as being "managed services" in the sense that the service provider takes full responsibility for generating a value to the customer. This includes the information technology applied and the related production processes alike.
	■ Hallek [49] and Kozlova, Hasenkamp and Kopanakis [50] refer to GTS and defines IT services by a set of characteristics around the value generation for the customer by the use of IT resources and activities.
	■ "Service components are granular service modules that can be reused due to their abstraction and configurability. Service products are saleable services, which are assembled from a defined set of service components." [44]
	■ "We define a service as a functionality that is provided with a certain quality and cost as a Service Access Point (SAP)"[51, also amended by, 52]
	■ "IT services are IT performances and bundles of IT performances, which are related with the provision and/or the use of performance potential. Internal and extern factors are set in relation to each other in a performance provisioning process by the combination of humans, tasks and technology. The combination of the factors pursues the goal to generate a value adding effect on the external factor." [53]
	■ "A Service is a logical grouping of functionality that is made available through the combination and specific configuration of hardware and software." [54]
↓	■ "We define an IT service as a bundle of components that supports business processes with information processing, provisioning and storage. Components (i.e. sub-services) of an IT service can constitute manual services, as well as technical services." [55]
How?	

The least common denominator of the definitions in Table 1 is perhaps that they assign "IT" or related concepts such as "IT components", "IT functions", or "IT performances" the role of a potential factor. Hence, to use the terms of Böhmann and Grawe and Fähnrich [37, 44], IT services are always "IT-based services". However, the scope of IT-based services is still large: a data centre service, a computer-supported health check and market research supported by databases and software for statistical analysis are included alike.

In the next section, we set out to distinguish the concept of "IT services" in ITSM from other, broader interpretations. For this purpose, we will refer to this concept with the term "ITility Service" in the following chapters. We have chosen this term because of its phonetic picture that corresponds to that of the term "utility". This correspondence is intended to emphasize two basic features: First, ITility Services are utilities in the sense that they are useful and generate (business) value for a service customer. Second, the way that customers are served with ITility Services is sometimes envisioned in ways that are similar to how utility companies serve their customers with gas, water, and electricity [65]. And as a nice side effect, "ITility" can also be associated with the ITIL as the initiator and stimulator this field of research. In the next section, we introduce the characteristics of ITility Services and relate them to discussions in the academic literature.

3 Towards a Concise Definition

In this section, we put forward six characteristics that we believe make a concise and relevant definition. We demonstrate how each characteristic is more or less rooted in the ITIL, and go on by substantiating it with the academic discussion on ITSM and emerging theory development.

3.1 Intangible

Above all, a service is intangible, so that it requires an external factor to manifest itself and generate a business value. This important characteristic of ITILity services is broadly shared throughout the academic literature on ITSM [2, 11, 45, 49, 55]. Yet there is little consensus on what this external factor actually is. The ITIL does not explicitly elaborate on this, but simply says that an IT service "[...] supports the business processes of one or more customers" [66]. However, it is misleading to look upon the business process itself as an external factor since ITility Services do not transform business processes (as opposed to, for example, change management consulting services). Rather than being altered through an ITility Service, business processes themselves transform information objects. These objects are already well known from business process management research where they are called "business process objects". Rosemann [67] characterizes business process objects as "process-shaping objects" that "drive the process flow" in that their status demands for the execution of specific processing functions. Invoice processing is a good example with the invoice being the formative (information) object for the whole business process. A typical ITility Service in this example could entail the processing of a customer master data record together with ordering data for writing invoices.

In line with the ITIL, most researchers agree on the fact that ITility Services support business processes, thus implicitly pointing to business process objects as the external factor. Zarnekow et al. [45] go one step further when also considering the products that an organization offers to its customers as external factors of ITility Services. They give the example of an electronic railway ticket which is part of a railway company's end customer product/service. The authors argue for the relevance of *business product objects* as external factors by highlighting the immediate value contribution to the company's products and services. We acknowledge that the external factor of an ITility Service can be both a business process or business product information object. Hence, we refer to this object more broadly as *business object*.

3.2   Generating Customer Value

ITility Services generate value by processing business objects. The ITIL explains that this value is produced "[…] by facilitating outcomes customers want to achieve" [66]. Service customers are the organizations or organizational units that order and use the ITility Services. But how can organizations profit from an ITility Service? In most cases, it is through human actors that perform business task and execute business processes on behalf of the customer organization. In the ITIL, these human actors are referred to as "users" of an ITility Services [68]. Users invoke an ITility Services, for example, by pressing a button or entering a command [69]. In some cases, they must feed in information manually before they can invoke the service, for example by filling an entry mask. In very rare cases, where business processes are fully automated, the actors invoking an ITility Service can also be machines.

Irrespective of how an ITility Service is triggered, it is on behalf of a customer organization and to its benefit. An ITilty Service may be utile in the eyes of a user or a group of users. These users act on behalf of a customer organization that ultimately appropriates the business value from the ITility Service.

3.3   Provided by Means of an IT-Based Infrastructure

Our analysis so far has told us that the external factors of ITility Services are information objects. Users play an important role in feeding in information objects and triggering their processing. But what is the role of "IT" in rendering ITility Services? The ITIL uses the term "IT" as an umbrella term for a broad set of components including "computers, telecommunications, applications and other software" [66]. Zarnekow et al. [45] distinguish these components in more detail into application systems, servers, storage media, wireless and wired networks as well as desktop systems. These components are "executing" service [70]. Moreover, researchers highlight that these components are highly interrelated and strongly interact with each other to produce the intended service outcomes. It is for this reason that Zarnekow et al. refer to these IT components as "production infrastructure" [45]. They propose to arrange this infrastructure into homogenous layers, with lower-level components providing inputs to higher-level components. On the lowest layers they see the technology resources like server hardware and storage components, which in turn can be used by system software components including middleware and operating systems. These in turn provide services to application platforms (e.g. workflow management and data management systems) and application systems (e.g. enterprise resource planning, office) which implement the business logic for processing information objects.

3.4   Produced in an Industrial Fashion

The ITIL explains that ITility Services are produced "by information technology" in combination with human actors ("people") within defined "processes" [66]. Rodosek [51] looks upon IT facilities and people as the "elements" that (ITility) services are made of. Accordingly, IT and people can be looked upon as the essential "potential factors" in the production of an ITility Service. This is analogous to industrial production, with IT representing the production equipment and the "people" representing the workforce needed to operate and supervise the technical equipment. In addition, the idea of industrialization is associated with production processes that are standardized, automated and specialized in order to reduce production costs and to increase the production speed and the quality of the products [71]:

- *Automation* refers to substitution of manual labour by machines or technology in industrialized production processes. In effect, automation leads to production processes that are mainly executed, supported, and controlled by machines. In the case of ITSM, these machines are represented by the IT-based production infrastructure introduced in the above section.
- Automation in turn furthers *specialization* by first dividing labour between machines and humans and second by differentiating the tasks and responsibilities of human actors. Specialization results in human actors with dedicated skills performing highly specific tasks.
- A third trait of industrial production is *standardization*. The idea is that reductions in unit cost are bigger the higher the number of products produced (product standardization). The reason is that standardized products can be produced through standardized procedures, which in turn allow for high levels of specialization and learning effects (economies of scale).

The ITIL supports the idea of product standardization by distinguishing between "business services" (that are assumed to deliver "products" to end users and customers) on the one hand and "infrastructure services" (that can be compared to "upstream products" or technical "product components" in industrial production) on the other hand. The ITIL also promotes the standardization of processes. Well-known processes put forward by the ITIL are "Technical Management", "Application Management", "Event Management", "Incident Management", or "Problem Management". The ITIL also proposes specialized job profiles with dedicated responsibilities and skill requirements such as "Capacity Manager", "Incident Manager", "Continuity Manager" or "IT Operator".

While the ITIL does not explicitly highlight the "industrial production" of IT services as a definitional feature, this characteristic is among the most prominent ones in the academic discussion on ITSM [9, 72, 73]. Hochstein [74] proposes processes for planning ITility Services in an industrial fashion based on the assumption that these services can be standardized and that their production can be automated. Zarnekow [75] shares these assumptions and proposes to furthermore apply methods for industrial production planning and control to tasks such as the planning of production sites, programmes, and for adjusting production volumes. Traugott [76] and Hallek [49] further propose to apply techniques from industrial production planning such as service trees, part lists, and working plans to the production of ITility Services. Moreover, Probst [77] as well as Hallek [49] propose semi-formal models to describe standardized ITility Service processes. These works culminate in the proposition of an excellence model for producing ITility Services in an industrial fashion [78] and give rise to the vision of an "IT factory" [65]. However, this research largely remains on a conceptual level and fails to provide much empirical evidence for the efficacy or at least the feasibility of the propositions made. In fact, empirical studies indicate that practice is far from implementing such concepts [9, 74].

3.5   Mass-Customized

Customer orientation on the one hand (Sect. 3.2) and industrialization of ITility Services on the other (Sect. 3.4) involve an inherent contradiction: meeting individual customer needs and standardizing ITility Services (and their production) are conflicting goals. The ITIL does not give much guidance on how this immanent conflict can be resolved. Fortunately, this conflict is already well-known in industrial production and has been successfully addressed with an approach called "mass-customization". This approach has been introduced by Davis [79] and further developed by researchers like Hart and Taylor [80]. The central idea of mass customization is to combine standardized pre-fabrication and individualized finishing to be able to offer end-products to customers that match their individual needs better than mass products but that are at the same time much cheaper than custom-made products.

At the heart of mass customization lies the concept of modularization, that is mass-customized products are to be composed of standardized components. These components, called modules, are supposed to be combined flexibly in ways that allow for tailoring end-products to the specific needs of individual customers. There are two dominant approaches to achieve this: One is the *flexible combination* approach which entails much complexity as it necessitates predefined and standardized interfaces of each module. Hence, this approach quickly encounters technical limits [81, 82]. The other approach assumes a common core product, the so-called product platform, that is extended with add-on functionality by attaching optional modules. Compared to the flexible combination approach, the *platform approach* is less flexible but more manageable and thus more practicable. Both approaches have been applied to ITiltiy Services.

Rudolph [53] builds on a platform approach for mass-customization. She looks upon ITility Services as bundles of so-called "service modules" which she further distinguishes in "standard modules" and "optional modules". Moreover, she suggests that an ITility Service includes at least one standard module as a core which can also be thought of as a service platform. This core (or platform) can be enriched by a set of optional modules that allow for tailoring ITility Services to the specific needs of customers. Grawe and Fähnrich [44], in contrast, favour the approach of flexible combination. They propose to compose ITility Services out of reusable components and postulate detailed guidelines for product composition to ensure a demanded quality, meet capacity requirements, and to enforce technical compatibility. The authors call this approach "mass configuration". Brocke, Uebernickel and Brenner [83] consider both the platform and flexible combination approach with respect to their applicability to the mass-customization of ITility Service level agreements. They also discuss possibilities to combine both approaches.

The academic debate on the industrialization and mass-customization in ITSM is closely linked to Service Science and, in particular, Service Engineering. The latter is a research field within Service Science concerned with the application of systematic, engineering-like methods to the design of services and service systems [84–86]. Service Engineering does not specifically focus on ITility Services, but has a broader interest in the use of IT for delivering services. Hence, some authors look upon ITSM as being "a subset of Service Science" [57]. However, many researchers in this field have a specific interest in IT-based services [37, 44, 87]. Some of their ideas and propositions concerning the standardization of service products, the reuse of service modules, or modular service architectures have also been adopted to ITility Services.

3.6   Provided Carefree to the Customer

The production of ITility Services is a complex process that involves multiple IT facilities and a large set of professional personnel operating it (Sects. 3.3 and 3.4). However, the customer should not be burdened with this complexity. Instead, he should be able to take advantage of the services "without the ownership of costs and risks" [66]. This in turn makes rendering ITility Services "carefree" for the customer. The provider must deal with the challenges, costs and risks of producing them. In return, the provider is entitled to charge the customer with a service fee that accounts for the costs and risks of service production and may also include a profit margin.

In line with the ITIL, researchers in the field of ITSM share the assumption that the production of ITility Services should be transparent to the customer and the users. Jouanne-Diedrich, Zarnekow, and Brenner hold the view that the business departments which order the service "are not interested in how these are provided but only in that they generate a value at reasonable costs" [73]. Rudolph adds that "technical details such as the equipment used and the configuration of application or database servers does not matter and thus does not need not to be exposed to customers and users who should instead be well informed about the service functionality and potential contributions to the business" [53]. Zarnekow et al. even demand that "(...) those who receive the services should be shielded from the technological complexity underlying the production of the services" [45]. Only the provider of the service needs to have authorization and an overview over the equipment and processes involved in service production since he bears the risks of service production [48].

The idea of carefree ITility Services is also supported by the postulate of a single face to the customer [44]. Neither the customer nor the users of ITility Services want to get burdened with technical details and multiple contact persons, but they want to have one contact point which is, according to the ITIL, a responsible service manager and, respectively, the central service desk [66].

4   Implications for Developing IT Service Level Agreements

Our understanding of an ITility Service as put forward in the previous section has an immediate impact on the development of Service Level Agreements. In general, a Service Level Agreement (SLA) is an agreement between a customer and a provider on the provision of a service. A SLA is output based in the sense that it defines what kind of service (service subject) the customer will receive in which quality (service levels) rather than how the service is rendered. Karten [88] defines a SLA as "a formal negotiated agreement which helps to identify expectations, clarify responsibilities, and facilitate communication between a service provider and its customers." SLAs can be used between two legally independent parties or by two different parties within the same organization. In the latter case of external SLAs, formal contracts are written up and hence include legal regulations.

In very general terms, an IT SLA is characterized by the fact that one party in the agreement is an IT service provider. In more detail, Berger [89] defines an IT SLA as a formal and written agreement between a service customer and a service provider for a defined period of time. The provider confirms rendering a service specified in scope and quality while the customer, in response, agrees to make a compensation payment.

However, despite their huge practical importance, research so far has not paid much attention to IT SLAs [89]. Recommendations on what to include in an IT SLA are scant [89–93]. Table 2 presents an overview of three recommendations that go beyond simple lists of attributes and also suggest a structure.

Table 2. Contents of IT SLAs in the academic literature

Berger (2005)	Goo (2008)	Gadatsch/Mayer (2010)
Service elements covering the subject of the service and its quality. Quality is defined in terms of minimum performance levels (service levels) to be achieved, separately for core service and support. Core service metrics include service hours, availability, recovery times, performance, stability, etc. Support metrics include support hours, availability, competencies, etc. **Management elements** covering service monitoring (e.g. practices for monitoring the service levels) as well as the communication between provider and customer (e.g. policies for solving conflicts) **Communication elements** describing the versions and changes of the SLA document itself	**Foundations**: General assumptions of customer and provider, general service descriptions and responsibilities **Changes**: Demand management, changes, feedback and innovation plans **Governance**: Communication plans, measurement charter, conflict arbitration, and contract enforcement	**Service specification** including service subject and scope **Dates and time frames:** For example, service monitoring reporting intervals or troubleshooting times for the service. **Terms** for compensation and penalties of successful/ non-successful service provision. **Organizational** policies for the cooperation between provider and customer. Includes support hours and channels (e.g. telephone, e-mail). Service **reporting** by the provider **Tolerance levels** for services/outages **Consequences** of service outages **Actions** to be taken in case of a service outages (e.g. price cutting)

The recommendations in Table 2 differ significantly in how they structure an IT SLA and in the attributes they include. This diversity is partly owed to the different types of IT services that can be subject to an SLA (Sect. 2.1). Unfortunately, specific recommendations for designing SLAs in an ITSM context are still missing. The only source of advice for practitioners is an example from the ITIL [94], which does not recommend any structure, but simply provides a long list of attributes without justifying them.

Moreover, as a closer look reveals, some attributes seem to be selected randomly. For example, attributes like "batch operating times" or "printing" are relevant only in specific cases where batch processing and printers are involved. Moreover, attributes such as "continuity", "security", "change management", and "reporting and review" are defined in terms of the processes executed by the provider rather than in terms of what the customer receives. However, a certain procedure for "change management" on the provider side cannot be immediately translated into certain service quality for the customer.

More fundamentally even, the ITIL example does pay only little attention to defining the service itself. It recommends to give a short service description without giving much guidance on how to define the service concisely. The ITIL simply suggests describing the "key business functions" and "deliverables" without giving further explanations. Only "if appropriate", these shall be complemented with a description of the "minimal functionality to be provided". Hence, with respect to the service definition, the ITIL does not give any specific advice for specifying ITility services if compared to the general IT SLA recommendations (Table 2).

As opposed to the little attention payed to defining IT services in the literature, an empirical study by Trienekens, Bouman and van der Zwan [95] indicates that practitioners often struggle with clarifying the subject of an IT service in SLAs. We look upon this problem as being particularly severe for ITility services which are more difficult to grasp because of their supporting nature (Sects. 3.1 and 3.2) and technical transparency (Sect. 3.6). Hence we propose to start the SLA with a detailed definition of the **service subject** comprised of four attributes. Here, we propose to start with defining the *business processes* or *products* supported by the ITility Service (Sect. 3.1). This attribute easily allows customers to figure out whether the service can be used in their organization and if so, where it can be used. ITility services provide value to the customer by supporting the business. Hence, after the business processes targeted by the service have been determined, we propose to specify the *value* provided by the service in more detail (Sect. 3.2). For example, an ITility service that supports writing invoices might have value to the customer organization by speeding up the billing process, reducing errors, and facilitating invoice and payment tracking. A further clarification of the service can be achieved by determining the *business objects* processed (Sect. 3.1). In the invoice example, these objects are, above all, a customer data set, a delivery data set, and the invoice as an outcome. Finally, to complete the description of the service, we recommend providing more detailed information on the *functionality* provided by the service. In the example above, core functions might be composing invoices, printing invoices, and tracking the payment process. A negative delimitation of the functionalities not included in the service might also help to clarify the scope of the service (compare Berger [89]).

The service subject (what?) is the point of reference for defining the **service quality** (how good?). The IT SLA literature (Tables 2 and 3) suggests a set of quality attributes such as, above all, service hours, response time, processing capacity, availability, reliability, recovery period, security. However, the proposals do not distinguish quality attributes in the three different service dimensions (Sect. 2.1), namely the result dimension, the process dimension, and the dimension of potential factors. In Sect. 3.6 we have argued that ITility services emphasize the results dimension (i.e. what the customer gets) over the process and potential factor dimensions (i.e. how the service is produced). In line with this, an SLA for an ITility service should favour result-oriented quality levels such as service hours, availability, reliability, response and processing time. The process-oriented quality attributes that are prominently featured in the ITIL example (e.g. security, continuity, change management etc.), should only be included in particular cases and for specific reasons. They can help in facilitating the co-operation between customer and provider (e.g. to foster common working practices) or in ensuring compliance. The same is true for potential-oriented quality attributes (e.g. compliance with security standards or professional qualifications).

Table 3. Sample SLA from the ITIL

- **Parties involved** in the SLA: Customer and Provider and duration of the agreement.
- **Service description**: Key business functions, deliverables and all relevant information to describe the service and its scale, impact and priority for the business.
- **Scope of the agreement**: What is covered by the agreement and what is excluded?
- **Service hours**: Hours the customer can expect the service to be available
- **Service availability:** Target availability levels, normally expressed as percentages (e.g. 99%), measurement periods, methods and calculations.
- **Reliability:** The maximum number of service breaks that can be tolerated within an agreed period, e.g. mean time between failure.
- **Customer support:** How, when and where to access the Service Desk, support hours, support metrics, and measurement.
- **Point of contact and escalation:** Coordinates of the persons involved in executing the SLA including escalations.
- **Service performance:** Response times for the IT service (targeted, maximum, average) including, for example, indications for traffic volumes, throughput activity, constraints, and dependencies.
- **Batch turnaround times:** When are batch jobs executed and result available?
- **Functionality:** Minimal functionality to be provided and number of errors tolerated.
- **Change Management:** Change management procedures to be followed and targets for managing Change Requests.
- **Service Continuity:** Provider's plans for insuring continuity, accounting for possible impacts on service quality.
- **Security:** Security policies of the provider.
- **Printing:** Special conditions relating to printing and printers.
- **Responsibilities:** Responsibilities of the various parties involved within the service including provider, customer, and users.
- **Charging:** Charging formulas used, charging periods together with invoicing procedures and payment conditions (if applicable).
- **Service reporting and review:** Contents and periods of service reporting, report distribution, frequency of SLA review meetings.
- **Glossary** of terms and abbreviations used.
- **Amendment sheet:** Record of agreed amendments.

Table 4. SLA stub for an ITility service

Service header

- **Name** of the service: *A unique name for the service, e.g. "Managed Invoice Processing Service"*
- **Short description:** *A summary of the service subject, e.g.: "The service supports debtor accounting, in particular the creation, control and dunning of invoices".*
- **Customer** and **user groups:** *Intended addressees of the service, e.g. Head of Financial department as customer and financial accountants and clerks as users*

Core service

Service subject

- **Business processes** *supported by the service, e.g. invoicing and payment tracking*
- **Value** *that is generated for the customer, e.g."The service speeds up invoice processing and lowers billing costs."*
- **Business objects** *processed in the business processes, e.g. customer master data, delivery note, invoice*
- **Functionalities** *provided by the service (also those not included, if appropriate), e.g. create, edit and cancel invoices; print invoices; send invoices via e-mail, check payments and create duns*

Service variants

- **Versions**: *Pre-configured extensions of the base service that provide additional functionality, such as an integration with online banking*
- **Options**: *Additional functions that can be selected freely as extensions to the base service, e.g. automatic dunning.*

Core service quality

Quality levels

- **Service Times**: *Hours the service is available to customers, e.g. from 8 am – 6 pm on working days*
- **Performance attributes related to the service outcome** *such as availability, response time, processing time, failure rates, mean time between failures, mean time to recover.*
- **Additional quality attributes related to processes and potential factors (if required),** *for example compliance to standards, update-to-dateness of accreditations, audit periods to be observed, minimum processing capacities to be maintained*

Quality variants

- **Versions**: *Pre-configured extensions to the service quality, e.g. power processing package that guarantees a higher processing speed and capacity*
- **Options**: *Single selectable enhancements to the service quality, e.g. higher availability (for example 24 h a day) or shorter response times.*

Support service quality

Quality levels

- **Support times**: *Hours that the support is available to customers, e.g. each working day from 8 am to 6 pm*
- **Performance attributes** *such as response time, ticket processing duration, problem resolution time.*

Quality variants

- **Versions**: *Pre-configured support packages with different support times and performance requirements, in practice often termed gold, silver and bronze service*
- **Options**: *Freely selectable enhancements for the support, for example German as an additional support language*

Both the service subject and the quality attributes introduced so far relate to the core ITility service which is automated (Sect. 3.4) and produced by means of an IT-based infrastructure (Sect. 3.3). In addition, the SLAs summed up in Tables 2 and 3 include attributes that refer to the support provided to the users of the core services. Support, however, is an add-on to the core service that facilitates its use. As such, it is largely independent from core service (also see [89]). This can easily be seen from the fact that different support conditions can be applied to one and the same core service and the same support conditions can be applied to multiple core services. Hence, we propose to specify the **support service** in a separate section of the SLA. The literature assumes that the subject of support (assistance in using the service, support in case of service breakdowns) is well-known and does not need further elaboration in an SLA. But irrespective of whether the subject of support needs further clarification or not, there is still the need to define the quality expected from the support. The support quality should again focus on the result-dimension of the service. Typical attributes proposed in the literature are availability, response time, resolution times etc.

So far, we have introduced a very basic service. According to the ITSM paradigm, such a basic service should be further adaptable to the specific needs of different customer groups. The method of choice for this purpose is mass-customization, which can be achieved either through preconfigured versions or as optional modules to the base service (Sect. 3.5). Mass-customization can be applied to the service scope as well as to the quality of the core service and of support. Accordingly, our SLA allows for **variants** in all three SLA sections introduced so far.

The three SLA sections "Core Service", "Core Service Quality", and "Support Service Quality" allow for a thorough specification of an ITility service. Irrespective of this, customers need additional support in figuring out whether services fit to their needs or not. ITSM suggests developing IT Service Catalogues for this purpose [94]. Such catalogues should give a carefully curated and organized overview over services that might be of interest to the customer. We support the view that customers cannot be expected to read complete SLAs just for the purpose of finding out whether a service might be of interest to them or not. Hence, the necessity to assist the development of Service Catalogues as well as the general ITSM postulate of customer-orientation has led us to include a **"Service Header"** in an SLA upfront. This header is intended to give a quick orientation by expressing the essence of the SLA. It can be compared to a concise management summary, which answers questions like: Is the service relevant for my organization? Does it meet my business needs? Who are the users addressed by the service? The header includes a unique name for the service, a short description of the service subject and scope, as well as the targeted customer and user groups.

Table 4 displays the IT SLA stub resulting from our theory-based understanding of an ITility service. Our stub provides a clear structure and, as a comparison with Table 2 reveals, covers the central SLA attributes discussed in the literature. What is not included in our SLA stub are attributes referring to the communication and cooperation between service provider and customer (e.g. points of contact, reporting and escalation procedures). We have left out these attributes because our interest was first of all in demonstrating the impact of our specific understanding of ITilty services, which is not immediately related to communication and cooperation. Further SLA attributes that we did not dwell on such as document versioning and a glossary relate to the SLA document itself. Our SLA stub also does not include pricing and legal aspects. The reason is that these apply only in the specific case of external SLAs, where the provider is outside of the customer's organization.

5   Conclusions and Future Research

In this paper, we have put to discussion a definition of IT services for the particular context of IT Service Management (ITSM). For the purpose of distinguishing them from IT services in other contexts, we refer to such IT services with the artificial term "ITilty services". Based on both the general theory of services and the theories of industrial production we have proposed six distinguishing features of ITility services: They are intangible, provide a value to customers, are produced in an industrial fashion by means of an IT-based infrastructure, their production is transparent to the customer, and they are mass-customized to better meet customer needs.

To demonstrate the impact and relevance of our definition, we have applied it to the definition of a Service Level Agreement. The results document that our definition makes a difference: The ITility SLA stub proposed in Table 4 clearly marks itself off from the IT SLAs proposals given in the academic literature. It provides a clear structure and distinguishes explicitly between the core services and support. It also favours defining service outcomes over the processes and potentials factors used for rendering the service. Finally, it accounts for a sophisticated customization of the service scope, service quality, and support.

We have also been able to assess the practicability of our definition in industry. We applied our definition of an ITility Service in a German publishing company that worked on the definition of a company-wide IT Service Catalogue. In this project, we were able to define 32 ITility Services that finally found their way into the catalogue. Motivated by the success of this project, we are currently assessing our ITility Service definition on a broader scale in a project with a German University. The central IT unit of this university has been working on initiatives to develop a university-wide service catalogue from 2010 on. The major motivation for developing such a service catalogue was to get an overview of the spectrum of IT offerings and services across the university, including the central university data centre and decentral IT units. An additional motivation was to ensure a high service quality and to be able to demonstrate it to customers and users. However, the central IT unit's initiatives encountered severe difficulties in establishing consensus on what actually an IT service is or should be. These can be exemplified by IT services from the initial service catalogue like "Lectures on Office Applications", "Provision of LAN nodes", "Distribution of IT Handbooks" or "Rental of Photo Cameras". Given these difficulties, we started a joint research project in 2016. By now we have been able to identify a set of 30 core services for the university with the help of our definition. We are currently working on the negotiation of these services in SLAs with different departments and user groups in the university. We used a template similar to that displayed in Table 4 for this purpose. The project is still running, but is encouraging so far [96]. Our experiences suggest that our definition of an ITility Service is very helpful for practitioners to better understand the nature of ITility Service. It also seems to be conducive in identifying service candidates and agree upon them in SLAs.

References

1. Cater-Steel, A., Zarnekow, R., Wulf, J.: IT service management in the academic curriculum - Comparing an Australian and German experience. In: Proceedings of 15th Pacific Asia Conference on Information Systems (PACIS 2011) (2011)
2. Kemper, H.-G., Hadjicharalambous, E., Paschke, J.: IT-Servicemanagement in deutschen Unternehmen – Ergebnisse einer empirischen Studie zu ITIL. HMD - Prax. der Wirtschaftsinformatik, pp. 22–31 (2004)
3. Hochstein, A., Tamm, G., Brenner, W.: Service oriented IT management: Benefit, cost and success factors. In: Proceedings of the European Conference on Information Systems (2005)
4. Tan, W.-G., Cater-Steel, A., Toleman, M.: Implementing IT service management: A case study focussing on critical success factors. J. Comput. Inf. Syst. Winter **50**(2), 1–12 (2009)
5. Marrone, M., Kolbe, L.M.: Uncovering ITIL claims: IT executives' perception on benefits and business-IT alignment. Inf. Syst. E-bus. Manag. **9**, 363–380 (2011)
6. Marrone, M., Gacenga, F., Cater-Steel, A., Kolbe, L.: IT service management: A cross-national study of ITIL adoption. Commun. Assoc. Inf. Syst. **34**, 865–892 (2014)
7. Winniford, M., Conger, S., Erickson-Harris, L.: Confusion in the ranks: IT service management practice and terminology. Inf. Syst. Manag. **26**, 153–163 (2009)
8. Hochstein, A.: Operations management and IS: Using the SCOR-Model to source make and deliver IS services. In: Proceedings of the 12th Americas Conference on Information Systems (2006)
9. Becker, J., Pöppelbuß, J., Venker, D., Schwarze, L.: Industrialisierung von IT-Dienstleistungen: Anwendung industrieller Konzepte und deren Auswirkungen aus Sicht von IT-Dienstleistern. In: Proceedings of the 10th International Conference on Wirtschaftsinformatik, pp. 345–354 (2011)
10. Teubner, A., Remfert, C.: IT service management revisited - insights from seven years of action research. In: Proceedings of the International Conference Information Resources Management (2012)
11. Huppertz, P.G., Kresse, M., Swidlowski: IT Service Management Advanced Pocket Book. IT-Service - Kern des Ganzen. Serview GmbH (2006)
12. Lichtenstein, S., Nguyen, L., Hunter, A.: Issues in IT service-oriented requirements engineering. Australas. J. Inf. Syst. **13**, 176–191 (2005)
13. Peppard, J.: Managing IT as a portfolio of services. Eur. Manag. J. **21**, 467–483 (2003)
14. Cooper, H.M.: Organizing knowledge syntheses: A taxonomy of literature reviews. Knowl. Soc. **1**, 104 (1988)
15. Zeng, J., Lin, I.J., Dispoto, G., Hoarau, E., Beretta, G.: On-demand digital print services: A new commercial print paradigm as an IT service vertical. In: Proceedings of the - 2011 Annual SRII Global Conference SRII 2011, pp. 120–125 (2011)
16. Shao, X., Chai, T.Y., Lee, T.K., Ngoh, L.H., Zhou, L., Kirchberg, M.: An integrated telecom and IT service delivery platform. In: Proceedings of the 3rd IEEE Asia-Pacific Services Computing Conference APSCC 2008, pp. 391–396 (2008)
17. Mayerl, C., Vogel, T., Abeck, S.: SOA-based integration of service management applications integrated IT service management. In: International Conference on Web Services (2008)

18. Cai, H.: A two steps method for analyzing dependency of business services on IT services within a service life cycle. In: 2006 IEEE International Conference on Web Services, pp. 877–884 (2006)
19. Dhar, S.: From outsourcing to cloud computing: Evolution of IT services. In: IEEE International Technology Management Conference, pp. 1–5. IEEE (2011)
20. Kuo, P., Hsieh, C., Road, T.: Service competition for IT service outsourcing, pp. 1–4 (2008)
21. Su, N., Levina, N.: Global multisourcing strategy: Integrating learning from manufacturing into IT service outsourcing. IEEE Trans. Eng. Manag. 58, 717–729 (2011)
22. Xi, C.: The theoretical research on contracts in IT service industry, pp. 3274–3276 (2007)
23. Noroozi, F.: Outsourcing of IT services and its affect on IT development in Iran shahkoohg. In: 2006 International Conference on Information and Communication Technologies and Development (2006)
24. Jonsson, N., Möller, O., Lilliesköld, J.: Reasons for not offshoring IT services in Swedish banks. In: Portland International Conference on Management of Engineering and Technology, pp. 1451–1455 (2007)
25. He, T., Jiang, H., Zhang, L.: Capacity expansion for an IT service firm under exponential demand growth with skilled workforce. In: 2010 International Conference on Modelling, Identification and Control, pp. 617–622 (2010)
26. Lee, K., Park, T.Y., Krishnan, R.T.: Catching-up or Leapfrogging in the Indian IT service sector: Windows of opportunity, path-creating, and moving up the value chain. Dev. Policy Rev. 32, 495–518 (2014)
27. Jeong, E.J., Jeong, S.R.: A checklist for assessment of risks involved in IT service project contract. J. Internet Comput. Serv. 170, 57–65 (2014)
28. Woodside, J.M.: Managing IT innovation: Recessionary service and staffing model perspectives. In: IEEE International Technology Management Conference, pp. 4–7 (2011)
29. Bharati, P.: India's IT services industry: A comparative analysis. Computer (Long Beach Calif.) 38(1), 71–75 (2005)
30. Witmeur, O., Fayolle, A.: Developing and testing a typology of growth strategies of entrepreneurial IT service firms. Solvy Brussels School of Economics and Management, Brussel (2010)
31. European Information Technology Observatory: ICT Market Report 2012 / 13 Definitions & Methodology (2013)
32. Statistisches Bundesamt: Erzeugerpreisindizes für Dienstleistungen: Informationen zum Preisindex IT-Dienstleistungen. DESTATIS, Wiesbaden (2013)
33. IDC: Europe, Middle East and Africa IT and Business Services (2015)
34. Nieminen, P., Auer, T.: Packaging of IT Services (1998)
35. Harmon, R., Auseklis, N., Reinoso, M.: From green computing to sustainable IT: Developing a sustainable service orientation, pp. 1–10 (2010)
36. Hintsch, J., Kramer, F., Turowski, K.: ERP systems' usage in the German IT service industry: An exploratory multi-case study. In: Proceedings of the - IEEE International Enterprise Distributed Object Computing Work, EDOCW 2015, pp. 169–178, November 2015
37. Böhmann, T.: Modularisierung von IT-Dienstleistungen: Eine Methode für das Service-Engineering. Deutscher Universitäts-Verlag, Wiesbaden (2004)
38. Buhl, H.U., Heinrich, B., Henneberger, M., Krammer, A.: Service Science. Wirtschaftsinformatik, vol. 50 (2008)
39. Hefley, B., Murphy, W. (eds.): Service Science, Management and Engineering Education for the 21st Century. Springer, Boston (2008)

40. Cheng, Y.: Information security risk assessment model of IT outsourcing managed service. In: 12th International Conference on Management e-Commerce e-Government, pp. 116–121 (2012)
41. Bhamidipaty, A., Lotlikar, R., Banavar, G.: RMI: A framework for modeling and evaluating the resiliency maturity of IT service organizations (2007)
42. Deshpande, P.M., Garg, D., Suri, N.R.: Auction based models for ticket allocation problem in IT service delivery industry. In: Proceedings of the 2008 IEEE International Conference on Services Computing, vol. 1, pp. 111–118 (2008)
43. Dube, P., Grabarnik, G., Shwartz, L.: SUITS: How to make a global IT service provider sustainable? In: Proceedings of the 2012 IEEE Network Operations and Management Symposium NOMS 2012, pp. 1352–1359 (2012)
44. Grawe, T., Fähnrich, K.-P.: Service engineering bei IT-Dienstleistern. In: Fähnrich, K.-P., van Husen, C. (eds.) Entwicklung IT-basierter Dienstleistungen, pp. 281–301. Springer, Heidelberg (2008)
45. Zarnekow, R., Brenner, W., Pilgram, U.: Integriertes Informationsmanagement: Strategien und Lösungen für das Management von IT-Dienstleistungen. Springer, Heidelberg (2005)
46. Meister, V.G., Jetschni, J.: Towards a semantic information system for IT services. In: 2012 Eighth International Conference on the Quality of Information and Communications Technology (2012)
47. Schomann, M., Röder, S.: Chancen und Grenzen der Industrialisierung von IT-Services. In: Keuper, F., Wagner, B., Wysuwa, H.-D. (eds.) Managed Services, pp. 66–90. Springer, Wiesbaden (2009)
48. Teubner, A.: IT-Service Management in Wissenschaft und Praxis: Best Practice in der akademischen Diskussion und industriellen Umsetzung (German Edition). VDM Verlag Dr. Müller, Saarbrücken (2008)
49. Hallek, S.: Produktionsplanung und -steuerung für IT-Services. Logos (2009)
50. Kozlova, E., Hasenkamp, U., Kopanakis, E.: Use of IT best practices for non-IT services. In: Annual SRII Global Conference SRII, pp. 725–734 (2012)
51. Rodosek, G.D.: A generic model for IT services and service management. In: Goldszmidt, G., Schönwälder, J. (eds.) Integrated Network Management VIII. ITIFIP, vol. 118, pp. 171–184. Springer, Boston (2003). doi:10.1007/978-0-387-35674-7_24
52. Brocke, H., Uebernickel, F., Brenner, W.: Customizing IT service agreements as a self service by means of productized service propositions. In: Proceedings of the Annual Hawaii International Conference on System Science (2011)
53. Rudolph, S.: Servicebasierte Planung und Steuerung der IT-Infrastruktur im Mittelstand. (2009)
54. Silva, E., Chaix, Y.: Business and IT governance alignment simulation essay on a business process and IT service model. In: Proceedings of the Annual Hawaii International Conference on System Sciences, pp. 1–11 (2008)
55. Ebert, N., Uebernickel, F., Hochstein, A., Brenner, W.: A service model for the development of management systems for IT-enabled services. In: Proceeding of the Thirteenth Americas Conference on Information Systems, Keystone, Colorado, pp. 1–8 (2007)
56. Wui-Ge, T., Cater-Steel, A., Toleman, M.: Implementing IT service management: A case study focusing on critical success factors. J. Comput. Inf. Syst. 50, 1–12 (2009)
57. Galup, S.D., Dattero, R., Quan, J.J., Conger, S.: An overview of IT service management. Commun. ACM 52, 124 (2009)
58. Jin, K., Ray, P.: Business-oriented development methodology for IT service management. In: Proceedings of the 41st Annual Hawaii International Conference on System Sciences, p. 99 (2008)

59. McNaughton, B., Ray, P., Lewis, L.: Designing an evaluation framework for IT service management. Inf. Manag. **47**, 219–225 (2010)
60. Braun, C., Winter, R.: Integration of IT service management into enterprise architecture. In: Proceedings of the 2007 ACM Symposium on Applied Computing - SAC 2007 (2007)
61. Lucio-Nieto, T., Colomo-Palacios, R., Soto-Acosta, P., Popa, S., Amescua-Seco, A.: Implementing an IT service information management framework: The case of COTEMAR. Int. J. Inf. Manage. **32**, 589–594 (2012)
62. Valiente, M.-C., García-Barriocanal, E., Sicilia, M.-Á.: Applying ontology-based models for supporting integrated software development and IT service management processes. IEEE Trans. Syst. Man Cybern. Part C – Appl. Rev. **42**, 61–74 (2012)
63. Iden, J., Langeland, L.: Setting the stage for a successful ITIL adoption: A delphi study of IT experts in the norwegian armed forces. Inf. Syst. Manag. **27**, 103–112 (2010)
64. Wegmann, A., Regev, G., Garret, G.-A., Marechal, F.: Specifying services for ITIL service management. In: International Workshop on Service-Oriented Computing: Consequences for Engineering Requirements, 16th IEEE International Requirements Engineering Conference (2008)
65. Abolhassan, F.: Der Weg zur modernen IT-Fabrik. Springer, Heidelberg (2013)
66. OGC: ITIL ® glossary and abbreviations. The Stationary Office Ltd., London (2011)
67. Rosemann, M.: Komplexitätsmanagement in Prozeßmodellen. Gabler, Wiesbaden (1996)
68. OGC: ITIL Service Strategy. The Stationery Office Ltd., London (2011)
69. Huppertz, P.G.: IT-Service-Verträge im Mittelstand – Kontrollierte Beauftragung durch eindeutige & vollständige Service- Spezifikation. Schriften zur Angew, Mittelstandsforsch (2010)
70. Mendes, C., Ferreira, J., Da Silva, M.M.: Using DEMO to identify IT services. In: Proceedings of the - 2012 International Conference on the Quality of Information and Communications Technology, QUATIC 2012, pp. 166–171 (2012)
71. Adam, D.: Produktions-Management. Gabler, Wiesbaden (1998)
72. Walter, S.M., Böhmann, T., Krcmar, H.: Industrialisierung der IT – Grundlagen, Merkmale und Ausprägungen eines Trends. Prax. der Wirtschaftsinformatik **256**, 6–16 (2007)
73. von Jouanne-Diedrich, H., Zarnekow, R., Brenner, W.: Industrialisierung des IT-Sourcings, pp. 18–27 (2005)
74. Hochstein, A.: Planerische Prozesse eines industrialisierten Informationsmanagements (2006)
75. Zarnekow, R.: Produktionsmanagement von IT-Dienstleistungen. Springer, Heidelberg (2007)
76. Traugott, M.: Praxisbericht: IT-Industrialisierung mit Servicebäumen, pp. 85–92 (2006)
77. Probst, C.: Referenzmodell für IT-Service-Informationssysteme. Logos, Berlin (2003)
78. Uebernickel, F., Hochstein, A., Schulz, V., Brenner, W.: Excellence-Modell der Industrialisierung des Informationsmanagements. HMD - Prax. der Wirtschaftsinformatik. **256**, 17–26 (2007)
79. Davis, S.: Future Perfect. Addison-Wesley, Reading (1987)
80. Hart, C.W., Taylor, J.R.: Value creation through mass customization. In: Achieving Competitive Advantage Through Mass Customization (1996)
81. Piller, T.F.: Mass Customization (2006)
82. Duray, R.: Mass customization origins: Mass or custom manufacturing? Int. J. Oper. Prod. Manag. **22**, 314–328 (2002)
83. Brocke, H., Uebernickel, F., Brenner, W.: Mass customizing IT-service agreements - Towards individualized on-demand services. In: 18th European Conference on Information System ECIS 2010 (2010)

84. Scheer, A.-W., Grieble, O., Klein, R.: Modellbasiertes Dienstleistungsmanagement. In: Bullinger, H.J., Scheer, A.W. (eds.) Service Engineering - Entwicklung und Gestaltung innovativer Dienstleistungen, pp. 19–51. Springer, Heidelberg (2006)
85. Bullinger, H.J., Fähnrich, K.P., Meiren, T.: Service engineering - Methodical development of new service products. Int. J. Prod. Econ. **85**, 275–287 (2003)
86. Spohrer, J., Maglio, P.P.: Service science: Toward a smarter planet. In: Introduction to Service Engineering, pp. 1–30. Wiley (2009)
87. Böhmann, T., Krcmar, H.: Modularisierung: Grundlagen und Anwendung bei IT-Dienstleistungen. In: Herrmann, T., Kleinbeck, U., Krcmar, H. (eds.) Konzepte für das Service Engineering, pp. 45–83. Physica-Verlag, Heidelberg (2005)
88. Karten, N.: How to Establish Service Level Agreements. Naomi Karten, Randolph (1997)
89. Berger, T.G.: Konzeption und Management von Service-Level-Agreements für IT-Dienstleistungen. University of Darmstadt (2005)
90. Van Grembergen, W., De Haes, S., Amelinckx, I.: Using COBIT and the balanced scorecard as instruments for service level management. Inf. Syst. Control J. **4**, 56–62 (2003)
91. Paschke, A., Schnappinger-Gerull, E.: A categorization scheme for SLA metrics. In: Proceedings of the Multikonferenz Wirtschaftsinformatik 2006, pp. 25–40 (2006)
92. Goo, J.: Structure of service level agreements (SLA) in IT outsourcing: The construct and its measurement. Inf. Syst. Front. **12**, 185–205 (2010)
93. Gadatsch, A., Mayer, E.: Masterkurs IT-Controlling Grundlagen und Praxis. Vieweg, Wiesbaden (2006)
94. OGC: ITIL Service Design. The Stationery Office Ltd., London (2011)
95. Trienekens, J.J.M., Bouman, J.J., van der Zwan, M.: Specification of service level agreements: Problems, principles and practices. Softw. Qual. J. **12**, 43–57 (2004)
96. Remfert, C.: Developing a common understanding of IT services – A case study of a German university. In: Proceedings of the 19th International Conference on Human-Computer Interaction, Vancouver (2017)

Analysis of the Consumption Action Behavior that Considered a Season

Saya Yamada[1](✉) and Yumi Asahi[2]

[1] School of Information and Telecommunication Engineering,
Course of Information Telecommunication Engineering,
Tokai University, Tokyo, Japan
yamada.s.3849@gmail.com
[2] School of Information and Telecommunication Engineering,
Department of Management System Engineering,
Tokai University, Tokyo, Japan
asahi@tsc.u-tokai.ac.jp

Abstract. In 2015, Internet use rate in Japan exceeded 82%, smartphone penetration rate exceeded 64%. And, utilization of online shopping was the third in the Japanese ICT services usage. In all ages, its utilization rate exceeded 68%. In the 2011 data that smartphones like iPhone and Android mobile phones began to spread, the use of net shopping was also the third most common. However, attention to utilization ratio, it is 64% in the 20s to 40s, slightly lower than in 2015. In the 50s, it is 51.5%, more than 10% lower. In the 60s and over, it is 36.7%, which is about half as low as 2015. Internet and smartphones popularized, and online shopping became familiar. Net business has become a big market in Japan. To the extent it can not be ignored. This report used purchase data of the Internet shopping site. From the basic statistics we found the following. Users are 65.9% for females and 34.1% for men. There are so many women to use. About the user's age, the over 40's (21.9%) is the most. Next was the result of early 30s (20.2%) and late 20s (19.2%). The population of Japan in 2015 is 59.00% in the over 40s. On the other hand, 5.99% in the early 30s and 5.40% in the latter half of the 20s. It is thought that users increase if the population number is large. Therefore, the main target is not over 40's, it is considered to be in the early 30's and the latter half of 20's. About the time when it is selling. The month with the highest sales is January which accounts for 13.4% of the total. The month with second sales is 11.1% in February, the third is 9.2% in December. Conversely, the month with the lowest sales is May and September, 5.8% of the total. The second is 6.2%, which is April. From this fact, it would be considered sell well are those in the winter season. About customer information. By prefecture, the largest number of Tokyo is 17.5%. It is about 50% of the total in the top six prefectures including that Tokyo. (Kanagawa prefecture 8.4%, Osaka prefecture 7.9%, Saitama prefecture 5.5%, Aichi prefecture 5.5%, Chiba prefecture 4.9%). This is the same ranking as the population ranking by prefecture in Japan. The largest number of registrants to the population is Tokyo. Besides, Kanagawa, Osaka and Kyoto prefectures were more than other prefectures. These four prefectures are the center of the west and east city. The method used covariance analysis and factor analysis. We modeled it about seasonal consumption behavior. The axis of analysis is "When do people buy things?"

© Springer International Publishing AG 2017
S. Yamamoto (Ed.): HIMI 2017, Part I, LNCS 10273, pp. 469–477, 2017.
DOI: 10.1007/978-3-319-58521-5_36

Keywords: Big data · Marketing · Season · Internet business · Shopping site · Fashion

1 Introduction

We used the data that is purchase data of one net shopping site for one year. It deals mainly with clothing. Users are 65.9% for females and 34.1% for men. There are so many women to use (Figs. 1 and 2).

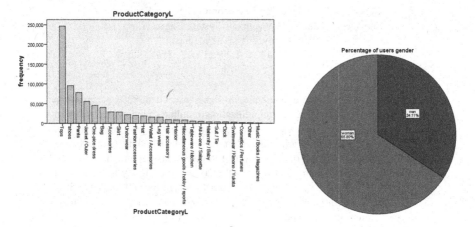

Fig. 1. Sales by item for each year   **Fig. 2.** User's ratio

On total sales, Tops' sales are the most common with 32.2%. The second is shoes (12.6%), the third is pants (10.2%). It is 5 items including jacket/outer and one piece, which is 68.1% of the total sales. Products are classified in 25 items including others. Of those, 14 items corresponding to 56% are not related to clothing. We handle fashion items other than clothing (shoes, bags, accessories, hats etc.). That is one of the reasons why sales are growing. Products such as dresses and skirts, hair accessories, maternity, baby, etc. are enriched because of the large number of female users.

2 About the User's Age

About the user's age, the over 40's (21.9%) is the most. Next was the result of early 30s (20.2%) and late 20s (19.2%). The population of Japan in 2015 is 59.00% in the over 40s. On the other hand, 5.99% in the early 30 s and 5.40% in the latter half of the 20s. It is thought that users increase if the population number is large. Therefore, the main target is not over 40's, it is considered to be in the early 30's and the latter half of 20's (Figs. 3 and 4).

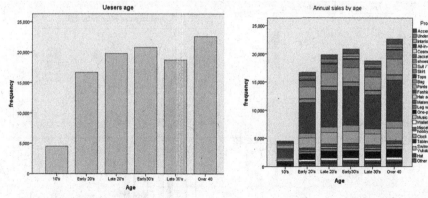

Fig. 3. Period of user's age

Fig. 4. Annual sales by age

Regarding sales by age, "Tops" is most bought at any age and is around 32%. The second is shoes, the third is pants. This is the same as the overall result (Figs. 5 and 6).

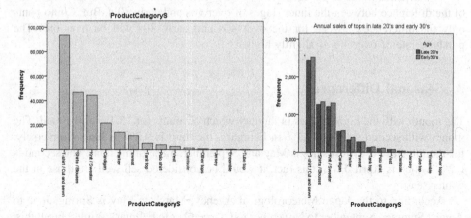

Fig. 5. Total sales of "Top"

Fig. 6. Annual sales of tops in late 20's and early 30's

"Tops" is the most popular product in annual sales, T - shirts/cutsaws are 38.4%. This is the same result even in the whole case, even in the main target that half of my 20s and early 30s. T-shirt/cut-saw category has sales of about 40% or more. Next, shirts/blouses (19.3%) and knit/sweaters (18.6%) are well selling. The top three are selling well (Figs. 7 and 8).

Shoe categories are mostly purchased mainly by people over 40 years old in most items. However, the purchase of rain shoes in the late 30s and early 30s is somewhat larger than in other age. Moccasin/deck shoes are almost flat except for teens. The beach sandals are slightly larger in the early 20s to the late 30s.

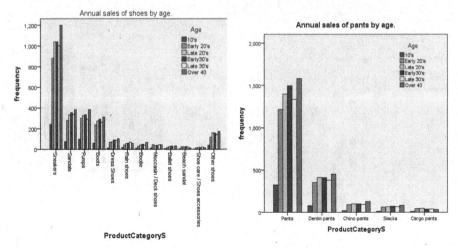

Fig. 7. Annual sales of shoes by age.

Fig. 8. Annual sales of pants by age.

As for pants, items of pants, denim trousers, slacks and cargo pants are within 3% of the difference between the inner stages of over 40s and early 30's. But, Chino pants only the difference between for the over 40s and early 30s will be over 6%. The purchase rate of over 40s is slightly higher.

3 Seasonal Difference

The month with the highest sales is January which accounts for 13.4% of the total. The month with second sales is 11.1% in February, the third is 9.3% in June. Conversely, the month with the lowest sales is May and September, 5.8% of the total. The second is 6.2%, which is April. From this fact, it would be considered sell well are those in the winter season

According to the Japan Meteorological Agency, March to May is Spring, June to August Summer, September to November fall, December to February Winter. From this, it can be said that things are selling well during the winter and the summer season. Japanese long vacations are mainly year-end and New Year holiday, spring break in March, summer vacation in August. Especially, the sales are good when in February and July before spring vacation in March and the summer vacation in August (Figs. 9 and 10).

Spring and autumn are seasons when sales fall. In Japan, spring (April) is the new fiscal year, and autumn (September) is the new term. Regarding Spring, sales are suddenly dropped while sales are favorable until March. Because the people buy clothes as preparations for the new fiscal year, it seems that sales in March become many. I think that preparations have been completed in the previous month, or there are not need to buy clothes, or there spent money in preparation in the previous month. Annual sales by season, "Tops" is the most common in around 32%. It is similar to the whole data. The second is shoes, the third is pants. (Figs. 11, 12 and 13)

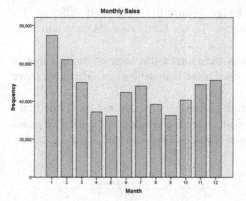

Fig. 9. Monthly sales

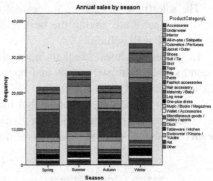

Fig. 10. Annual sales by season

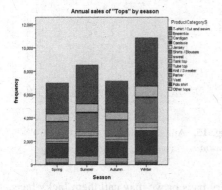

Fig. 11. Annual sales of "Tops" by season

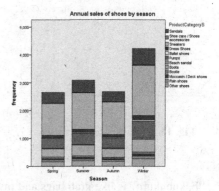

Fig. 12. Annual sales of shoes by season

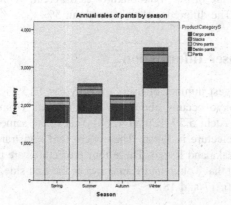

Fig. 13. Annual sales of pants by season

The sales ratio of each item does not change, even if the seasons are different. T -
shirts/cut - sews are among the best selling in 'Tops'. Next, shirts/blouses and knit/
sweaters are well selling.

In genres of shoes, sneakers have about three times the sales of sandals that is
second selling. Sandals, pumps and boots have more than 10% sales. There are more
characteristic than other items.

In the group of pants, "pants" that includes all things that can not be divided into
items such as denim pants and chino pants with patterns and colors items are sold most.
"Pants" is about 3.5 times the sales of denim trousers. (Figs. 14 and 15)

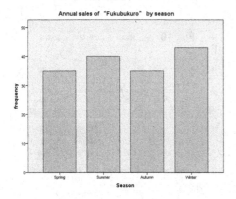
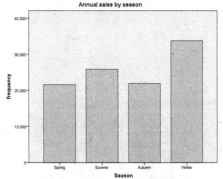

Fig. 14. Annual sales by season   **Fig. 15.** Annual sales of "Fukubukuro" by
season

"Fukubukuro" is like grab bags and mystery bags or we may call them lucky bags.
These usually contain variety of goods that are much more valuable than the price of
the bag.

We made comparison between total sales and sales of "Fukubukuro". Its winter
sales are 32.7% and in the spring is 20.9% of the total. There is a difference of about
12%. However, the genre of the "Fukubukuro" is different. Winter's sales are 28.1%
and spring is 22.9%. The difference shrinks to about 5%.

4 About Purchaser Information

By prefecture, the largest number of users in Tokyo is 17.5%. And the top six prefectures including Tokyo occupy about 50% of the total. (Kanagawa 8.4%, Osaka
7.9%, Saitama 5.5%, Aichi 5.5%, Chiba 4.9%) This is the same ranking as the population ranking by prefecture in Japan. There were four registrants to the population,
Tokyo, Kanagawa, Osaka and Kyoto. These four prefectures are the center of the west
and east. We analyzed that Tokyo and Kanagawa as the east side, Osaka and Kyoto as
the west side (Figs. 16, 17 and 18).

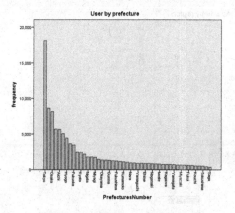

Fig. 16. User by prefecture

The total sales is overwhelmingly in the eastern side of Tokyo and Kanagawa. But, even if the regions are different, the ranking of the top does not change. The top selling is "Tops". The second is shoes, third is pants. There is a little difference from the 7th. However, the difference is at most 4 ranks. (Figs. 19, 20 and 21)

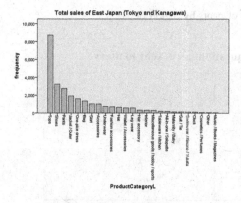

Fig. 17. East side user

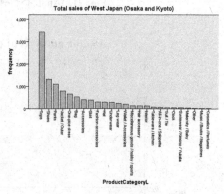

Fig. 18. West side user

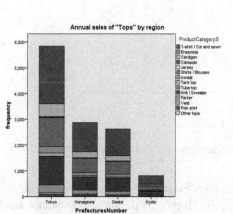

Fig. 19. Annual sales of "Tops" by region

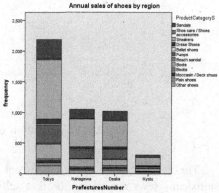

Fig. 20. Annual sales of shoes by region

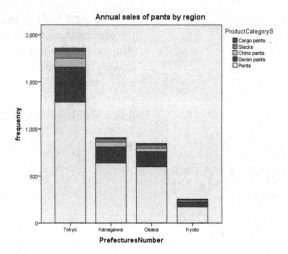

Fig. 21. Annual sales of pants by region (left)

Factor analysis of questionnaires sent to users

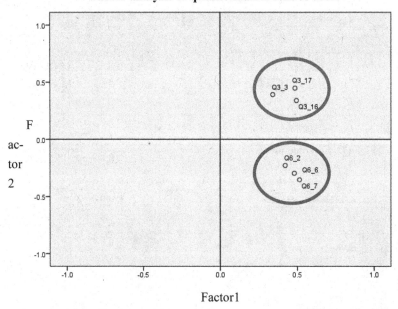

Fig. 22. Factor analysis of questionnaires sent to users

The sales ratio of each item does not change, even if the regions are different. T - shirts/cut - sews are among the best selling in 'Tops'. Next, shirts/blouses and knit/ sweaters are well selling.

In any region, and in the genre of shoes, sneakers are the first and sandals are sold second. However, in Kyoto only, the third are boots and the fourth are pumps.

This rank has been reversed the comparison between this and the other. Sandals, pumps and boots have sales of more than 10% in any area.

Pants were in the same order as the whole data, too.

We analyzed the factor of the questionnaire that we went to the user. Blue circle is a person who cares about fashion for his title in life value. Red circle are those who purchase clothes and the like as they are forced to need seasons and events (Fig. 22).

5 Discussion/Summary

We analyzed the data from the viewpoint of age, season, month and region. However, we did not see a big difference in the inside of the products we purchase. There were minor differences. It did not significantly affect the overall data.

There is bias in purchase number by season and month, many items record high sales in winter. There have a big difference in sales with other seasons. However, the "Fukubukuro" had little difference in seasonal sales. From this, we think that if we use a means the "Fukubukuro" in spring and autumn when less sales, we might be able to sell more.

References

1. http://www.soumu.go.jp/johotsusintokei/whitepaper/ja/h24/html/nc243130.html. Accessed 9 Feb 2017
2. http://www.soumu.go.jp/johotsusintokei/whitepaper/ja/h27/html/nc122200.html. Accessed 9 Feb 2017
3. http://www.jma.go.jp/jma/kishou/know/yougo_hp/toki.html. Accessed 10 Feb 2017
4. http://d.hatena.ne.jp/keyword/%CA%A1%C2%DE. Accessed 10 Feb 2017

Multimodal and Embodied Interaction

Research on High Fidelity Haptic Interface Based on Biofeedback

Katsuhito Akahane[1(✉)] and Makoto Sato[2]

[1] Tokyo Institute of Technology, Yokohama, Japan
kakahane@hi.pi.titech.ac.jp
[2] Tokyo Metropolitan University, Tokyo, Japan
mktsato@gmail.com

Abstract. In this paper, we propose a high fidelity haptic interface based on biofeedback. When we interact with a very stiff virtual object in the virtual world by a haptic interface, the haptic interface frequently becomes unstable. We cannot feel the virtual object stably. On the other hand, when we interact with a real object in the real world, the dynamics of our fingers and arm always change and adjust to the appropriate value for the real object. We can feel the real object stably. By using the adaptation, we aimed for achieving the high fidelity haptic interface. In this study, the proposed system measured the grasping force generated by the user interacting with a virtual object by the haptic interface. The system also controlled the coupling impedance between the virtual object and the haptic interface by using the grasping force as biofeedback. In order to measure the grasping force, we developed a new end effector for a string based impedance haptic device SPIDAR-G. We conducted evaluation experiments about the proposed system. The experimental results indicate that the proposed system improved the maximum stiffness of the virtual coupling, and achieved both stability and fidelity by using biofeedback.

Keywords: Haptic interface · Impedance control · Biofeedback

1 Introduction

In recent years, the performance of computers has improved and systems that interact with virtual reality (VR) are researched and developed. A Haptic interface is a device that lets a user touch, feel, and manipulate objects in the VR world created on the computers. When a user interacts with the virtual object using a haptic interface, the haptic interface measures the position and orientation of the end effector as input information from the user. The haptic interface also generates the force that is calculated by a physics simulation, spring-damper mode, etc. to the end effector. the user can feel the haptic sensation through the end effector. The stability range of the impedance (Z-width) is one of the most significant properties of a haptic interface. The wide stability range enables us to interact with a variety of virtual objects such as very soft objects, very stiff objects, etc. In the haptic control loop, the state of the user who operates the end effector influences the stability and fidelity of the system. The impedance of the user differs

S. Yamamoto (Ed.): HIMI 2017, Part I, LNCS 10273, pp. 481–491, 2017.
DOI: 10.1007/978-3-319-58521-5_37

between when the user strongly grasps the end effector and when the user weakly grasps it. The change of grasping force causes the change of dynamics of the whole system. The viscosity of the user who strongly grasps end effector absorbs extra energy generated by the haptic interface that displays the very stiff virtual object. In addition, the effect of the dissipation of the energy is considered to be more effective if the viscosity of the device is sufficiently smaller than the viscosity of the user.

In order to measure a user state and feed back to a system, electroencephalogram, electromyogram, electrocardiograph, etc. have been presented. The human interfaces using them have also been researched and developed [1–6]. However, they have some problems of requiring a large-scale device to use them, usability, etc.

In this research, we aimed for the high definition haptic interface that measures the grasping force of the user and estimates the user impedance in real time. The system also controlled the coupling impedance between the haptic interface and the virtual object based on the grasping force of the user as biofeedback for both stability and fidelity.

2   Impedance Control Haptic Interface

An impedance control haptic interface measures the position and orientation of the end effector and displays the force and torque to the end effector. The user can feel haptic sensation through the end effector. Many such devices have been developed.

2.1   String Based Haptic Interface

A string based haptic interface SPIDAR-G (Fig. 1) is an impedance control haptic interface [7, 8]. The device consists of high precision coreless direct current (DC) motors with rotary encoder, pulleys, strings, grip, and frame. The DC motor with rotary encoder is installed in the frame. The eight strings are connected to the end effector, and each string is driven by DC motor with pulley. The device measures the length of strings with

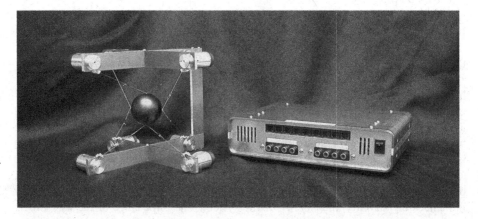

Fig. 1. String based haptic interface SPIDAR-G (6 degrees of freedom, impedance control)

the rotary encoder and calculates the 6 degrees of freedom (DOF) of the position and orientation of the end effector. By controlling the tensions of all strings with the DC motor, the force and torque of 6DOF are displayed to the end effector. The user can feel haptic sensation by grasping the end effector.

2.2 Virtual Coupling

Colgate etc. [9] introduced virtual coupling, which is a connection between a haptic interface and a virtual object by virtual impedance (Fig. 2). The virtual coupling between an impedance haptic interface and a virtual object is given by the Eqs. (1, 2). Where $f_h(s)$ is the force to the end effector in frequency domain, $f_e(s)$ is the force to the object, $v_h(s)$ is the velocity of the end effector, and $v_e(s)$ is the velocity of the object. The coupling impedance $Z_c(s)$ consists of stiffness K and viscosity B. The property of the virtual coupling depends on the coupling impedance which enables the coupling between the haptic interface in the real world and the virtual object in the virtual world. In order to increase the fidelity of the operation, it is necessary to increase the coupling impedance. However, the coupling impedance is increased much higher, the passivity of the system is not maintained and the system becomes unstable. Because the virtual stiffness is not a passive element in the temporal and spatial discrete system by digital computer. It is important to increase the coupling impedance. However, we have to decrease the coupling impedance to maintain stability. Both fidelity and stability of haptic interface have been discussed in various viewpoints [10–13]. In this research, we aimed to achieve both fidelity and stability by controlling the coupling impedance dynamically based on biofeedback.

$$f_h(s) = -f_e(s) = Z_c(s)(v_e(s) - v_h(s)) \tag{1}$$

$$Z_c(s) = K/s + B \tag{2}$$

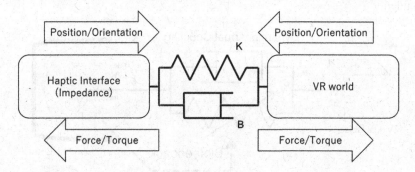

Fig. 2. Virtual coupling

3   Proposed System

3.1   Stability of Haptic Interface

Focus on energy generated by the virtual stiffness used in the virtual coupling. The force calculated by the virtual stiffness is discretely increased and decreased by squeezing and releasing in the temporal and spatial discrete system. There is a difference between the charged energy and the discharged energy. The discharged energy is greater than the charged energy. It means that energy conservation low is not satisfied in the virtual coupling in the discrete system. The higher stiffness is displayed the more extra energy is generated. The extra generated energy is absorbed by the viscosity of haptic interface and the user. However, the amount of the extra generated energy is greater than the amount of consumption by the viscosity of haptic interface and the user, the whole system becomes active and can be unstable.

3.2   System Configuration

The higher coupling impedance provides the smaller error between the VR object and the end effector. It is also possible to display force and torque close to the real object and to directly operate the virtual object. However, if the impedance is always very high to increase the fidelity, the extra energy generated by the impedance and the system can be unstable.

   We propose a method to control the coupling impedance according to the impedance of user that is estimated from the grasping force (Fig. 3) and a mapping between the grasping force and the coupling impedance (Fig. 4). If the grasping force is weak, the system reduces the coupling impedance within the range of maintaining interaction in VR world to achieve high stability. If the grasping force is strong, the system increases the coupling impedance within the range of maintaining stability in the system to achieve high fidelity.

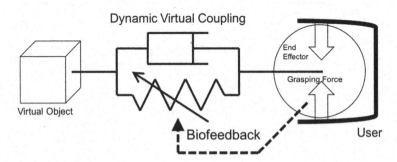

Fig. 3. Dynamic virtual coupling with biofeedback

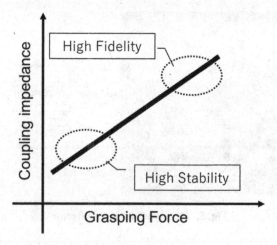

Fig. 4. Relationship between grasping force and coupling impedance

3.3 Prototype of End Effector

In order to design the end effector that allows measurement of the grasping force without deteriorating performance of haptic sensation, it must be lightweight, compact, and rigid. The end effector receives force not only from a user's hand but also from the tension of all strings in SPIDAR-G. The proposed end effector needs to separate these two forces. We designed the new end effector for SPIDAR-G (Fig. 5). The end effector consists of a main plate, two sheet force sensors and two half sphere grips. The main plate is connected to all strings from DC motors in SPIDAR-G. Each force sensor on the center of the main plate only measures the vertical force from the half sphere grip. The new end effector measures the grasping force that is generated by user holding the both half sphere grips by using Eqs. (4, 5, 6, 7) where f_{sens0} and f_{sens1} are the sensor values of the force sensors on both sides of the main plate, f_{grasp0} and f_{grasp1} are the grasping forces to the end effector, F_{dispZ} is the vertical force from strings to the main plate and f_{grasp} is the grasping force.

$$f_{sens0} = f_{grasp0} + F_{dispZ} \qquad (3)$$

$$f_{sens1} = f_{grasp1} - F_{dispZ} \qquad (4)$$

$$f_{grasp} = (f_{grasp0} + f_{grasp1})/2 \qquad (5)$$

$$f_{grasp} = (f_{sens0} + f_{sens1})/2 \qquad (6)$$

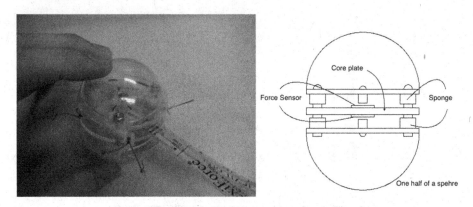

Fig. 5. Prototype of the end effector

The values of force sensors are converted into voltages by the analog amplifier circuit. The voltage is taken into the PC by the A/D converter on the haptic controller via USB2.0. The sensing frequency synchronize with the control frequency of the haptic interface.

4   Experiment

4.1   Measurement of Grasping Force

The grasping force of the user interacting with a virtual object in virtual world by the haptic interface SPIDAR-G was measured.

A rigid body of a sphere and a rigid surface were placed in the virtual world (Fig. 6). The virtual world was simulated by Open Dynamics Engine [14] that is a real-time physics simulator of rigid body. In this measurement, the simulation frequency was about 333 Hz and the update frequency of the haptic interface was 1 kHz. The coupling impedance that was reasonable value to interact with the virtual object stably was $K = 1200$ N/m and $B = 20$ N/ms^{-1} in this experiment. The subject was five adult males. The measurement was as follows:

Step1.   A subject moved the haptic cursor without coupling objects in free space.
Step2.   The subject moved the coupling object in free space.
Step3.   The subject moved the coupling object to the virtual surface.

The grasping force of the subject was measured at each step. The result is shown in the Table 1. The grasping force on the Table 1 is the average of the grasping force of 5 subjects during each step. The results show that the minimum grasping force was measured when the subject moved the haptic cursor without coupling objects in free space, the slightly increasing grasping force was measured when the subject moved the coupling object in free space, and the maximum grasping force that was much greater than the others was measured when the subject moved the coupling object to the surface. The state of the subject in the manipulation caused the change of the grasping force. The

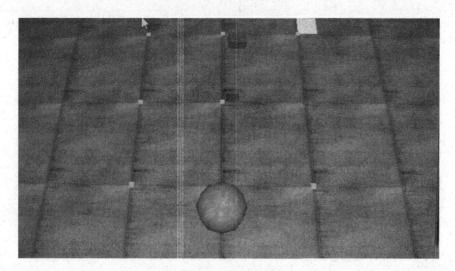

Fig. 6. VR world

subjects adjusted their grasping force according to the situation. It was suggested that the grasping force, which is adjusted by capability of the user, enables biofeedback.

Table 1. Average of grasping force.

Step	Grasping force (N)
1. Moving the haptic cursor in free space	0.222
2. Moving the coupling object in free space	0.373
3. Moving the coupling object to the virtual surface	1.849

4.2   Measurement of Coupling Impedance Range

In order to control the coupling impedance by the grasping force as biofeedback, the controllable range of coupling impedance was measured. The upper limit of the range was measured when a subject grasped maximum force and interacted with a virtual object stably. The lower limit of the range was measured when the end effector with weight fell down and became stable on the virtual surface. Because the lower limit of the impedance assures the maximum coupling impedance without grasp by a subject on the end effector and the interaction with a virtual object stably. The stability of the system is specially disturbed by the update frequency of the system. Especially in the VR world that is executed in a PC with non-real-time operating system, the update frequency is disturbed by computational load. In order to show that the proposed method is an effective method even if the update frequency of the VR world is changed, we measured impedance at the simulation update frequency 1 kHz, 500 Hz, and 333 Hz, respectively. The update frequency of the haptic interface was 1 kHz in this measurement.

Figure 7 shows experiment result of measurement of coupling impedance range. The upper limit of the impedance is indicated by a solid line and the lower limit of the impedance is indicated by a dotted line. At each update frequency in the VR world, increasing of viscosity B enables increasing of stiffness K, and increasing of viscosity B exceeding a certain value causes decreasing stiffness K sharply.

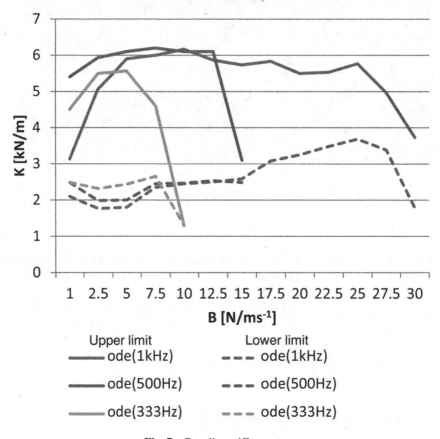

Fig. 7. Coupling stiffness range

4.3 Measurement of Maximum Impedance by Biofeedback

Based on the coupling impedance range in Fig. 7, the relationship between the grasping force and the coupling stiffness was implemented. In this study, the viscosity coefficient was fixed at $B = 5$ N/ms^{-1} where the stiffness K was high at all the measured frequencies in Fig. 7. The relationship between the normalized grasping force and the coupling stiffness corresponded by the linear function shown in Fig. 8. The proposed system estimated the appropriate coupling impedance by using the coupling stiffness range in Fig. 7 and the relationship between the grasping force and coupling stiffness in Fig. 8. We examined whether the stiffness K in the proposed system is adjusted by biofeedback in the several control frequencies and it is possible to increase the stiffness K compared with the traditional system which the stiffness is fixed in. In the traditional system, the stiffness was fixed maximum stiffness that enabled interaction with the virtual object.

In the proposed system, the stiffness was controlled by biofeedback. The other experiment setups were the same as the former experiment.

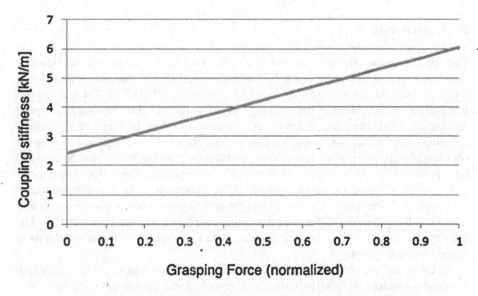

Fig. 8. Relationship between grasping force and coupling stiffness

Table 2 shows the results that are the maximum impedance of the proposed system and the static impedance of the traditional system, and improvement rate between the proposed system and the traditional system. The result in Table 2 indicates that the proposed system achieves higher stiffness than the traditional system in all simulation update frequencies. The improvement rates in each control frequency are 16.7%, 21.0%, and 21.6%, respectively.

Table 2. Maximum stiffness and improvement rate.

	333 Hz	500 Hz	1 kHz
Proposed (kN/m)	6.5	7.5	7.5
Traditional (kN/m)	5.57	6.2	6.17
Improvement rate	16.7%	21.0%	21.6%

This is because the maximum stiffness in the traditional system is not necessarily the maximum stiffness that becomes stable while the virtual object contact on the virtual surface. The traditional system that uses the fixed coupling impedance reduces the maximum stiffness that allows user to stably interact with the virtual object at all times. The proposed system that uses the dynamic controlled coupling impedance based on biofeedback achieves the maximum stiffness higher than the traditional system in the all conditions. When the virtual object that is operated by a user touches the other virtual object, the grasping force of the user is increased. The increase of the grasping force is caused by the increase of the impedance of the user, which enables the maximum stiffness higher than the traditional system.

5   Conclusion

This paper addressed dynamic control of coupling impedance between the haptic interface and a virtual object by using biofeedback based on the grasping force of user improved both fidelity and stability with haptic interface SPIDAR-G. The end effector that enabled measurement of the grasping force of a user for SPIDAR-G was designed and implemented. The grasping force was measured at moving the haptic cursor without coupling object in free space, moving the coupling object in free space, and moving the coupling object to the surface. It was suggested that the grasping force, which is adjusted by capability of the user, enables biofeedback. The impedance range that was dynamically controlled was measured in several update frequencies. The dynamic control of the coupling stiffness, which proportioned the grasping force was implemented. It was found that the maximum stiffness of the virtual coupling improved by about 20%. The validity of biofeedback based on the grasping force has been shown by the development of the proposed system.

In the future, the control method of dynamic coupling such as viscosity coefficient, mapping coefficient also need to be discussed in more detail. To further verify the results, we will carry out subjective evaluation by users.

References

1. Shin, D., Kim, J., Koike, Y.: A Myokinetic arm model for estimating joint torque and stiffness from EMG signals during maintained posture. J. Neurophysiol. **101**, 387–401 (2009)
2. Yoshimura, N., DaSalla, C.S., Hanakawa, T., Sato, M., Koike, Y.: Reconstruction of flexor and extensor muscle activities from electroencephalography cortical currents. Neuroimage **59**(2), 1324–1337 (2012)
3. Watanabe, M., Yamamoto, T., Kambara, H., Koike, Y.: Evaluation of a game controller using human stiffness estimated from electromyogram. In: IEEE EMBS Conference 2010, pp. 4626–4631 (2010)
4. Kawase, T., Kambara, H., Koike, Y.: A power assist device based on joint equilibrium point estimation from EMG signals. J. Robot. Mechatron. **24**(1), 205–218 (2012)
5. Ahi, S.T., Kambara, H., Koike, Y.: A dictionary-driven P300 speller with a modified interface. IEEE Trans. NSRE **19**(1), 6–14 (2011)
6. George, L., Marchal, M., Glondu, L., Lécuyer, A.: Combining brain-computer interfaces and haptics: detecting mental workload to adapt haptic assistance. In: Isokoski, P., Springare, J. (eds.) EuroHaptics 2012. LNCS, vol. 7282, pp. 124–135. Springer, Heidelberg (2012). doi: 10.1007/978-3-642-31401-8_12
7. Ishii, M., Sato, M.: A 3D interface device using tensed strings. Presence Teleoper. Virtual Environ. **3**(1), 81–86 (1994)
8. Kim, S., Hasegawa, S., Koike, Y., Sato, M.: Tension based 7-DOF force feedback device: SPIDAR-G. In: Proceedings of the IEEE Virtual Reality 2002 (2002)

9. Colgate, J.E., Stanley, M.C., Brown, M.J.: Issues in the haptic display of tool use. In: Proceedings of IEEE/RSJ International Conference on Intelligent Robots and Systems, vol. 3, pp. 140–145 (1995)
10. Colgate, J.E., Crafing, P.E., Stanley, M.C., Schenkel, G.: Implementation of stiff virtual walls in force-reflecting interface. In: IEEE VR Annual International Symposium, pp. 202–208 (1993)
11. Baraff, D.: Analytical methods for dynamic simulation of non-penetrating rigid bodies. In: Proceedings of SIGGRAPH 1989, CG, vol. 23, pp. 223–232 (1989)
12. Mehling, J.S., Colgate, J.E., Peshkin, M.A.: Increasing the impedance range of a haptic display by adding electrical damping. In: World Haptics 2005, pp. 257–262 (2005)
13. Akahane, K., Hamada, T., Yamaguchi, T., Sato, M.: Development of a high definition haptic rendering for stability and fidelity. In: Jacko, Julie A. (ed.) HCI 2011. LNCS, vol. 6762, pp. 3–12. Springer, Heidelberg (2011). doi:10.1007/978-3-642-21605-3_1
14. Open Dynamics Engine. http://opende.sourceforge.net/

An Intuitive Wearable Concept for Robotic Control

Lisa Baraniecki[1(✉)], Gina Hartnett[2], Linda Elliott[3], Rodger Pettitt[3],
Jack Vice[1], and Kenyon Riddle[4]

[1] AnthroTronix, Inc., Silver Spring, MD, USA
{Lisa.Baraniecki,Jack.Vice}@atinc.com
[2] Army Research Laboratory, Human Research and Engineering Directorate,
Fort Rucker, AL, USA
Regina.A.Hartnett.Civ@Mail.Mil
[3] Army Research Laboratory, Human Research and Engineering Directorate,
Fort Benning, GA, USA
{Linda.R.Elliott.Civ,Rodger.A.Pettitt.Civ}@Mail.Mil
[4] Aptima, Inc., Performance Assessment and Augmentation Division, Orlando, FL, USA
KRiddle@aptima.com

Abstract. In this study we explore the concept of gesture-based robot control for maneuver and manipulation, using a prototype system by AnthroTronix [1]. For the task, 24 Soldier-participants were asked to tele-operate the robot through a course containing several tight turns and obstacles. They were then asked to simulate "planting a breaching charge" by approaching a target with a marker attached to the end of the manipulator arm. They were provided with video feedback via a camera mounted to the chassis of the robot. Performance on the task was defined as time to navigate to the intended target, time to manipulate the arm to the target, and accuracy of the manipulation task. Results suggested that the use of the instrumented glove reduced the time needed to maneuver the manipulator arm as compared to the use of the handheld controller.

Keywords: Robot control · Instrumented glove · NuGlove · Wearable concept · Human-robot interaction

1 Introduction

A future vision of the use of autonomous and intelligent robots in dismounted military operations has Soldiers interacting with robots as teammates, with an interim goal of having the robot able to execute tactics much like a military working dog or robotic wingman [2–4], with increasing levels of autonomy—and corresponding issues [5]. Soldiers would no longer have to continuously tele-operate every movement of the robot. Instead, Soldier–robot interactions would be more tactical, bidirectional, and naturalistic [6]. Gesture-based commands to robots are one such means to more naturalistic control, and have been used in a variety of different settings, such as assisting users with special needs [7], assisting in grocery stores [8], and home assistance [9]. Examples of gestural commands in these settings include "Follow me", "Go there", or "Hand me that".

© Springer International Publishing AG 2017
S. Yamamoto (Ed.): HIMI 2017, Part I, LNCS 10273, pp. 492–503, 2017.
DOI: 10.1007/978-3-319-58521-5_38

In this report, we describe progress regarding use of an instrumented glove to detect and transmit hand and arm signals to maneuver and manipulate a small ground robot and robotic arm, without the use of speech or visual interface icons. This research effort was performed to examine the concept of instrumented gloves as a means for gesture based HRI control. Instrumented gloves were used to investigate aspects of gesture-based controls compared to a handheld controller. The system was developed through an Army Small Business Innovative Research (SBIR) program, led by Army Research Laboratory Human Research and Engineering Directorate in collaboration with Anthro-Tronix, Inc (ATinc), building upon previous efforts regarding wearable computers and robotic platforms [1, 10].

1.1 Purpose

The current effort seeks to investigate an advanced concept in intuitive interfaces to reduce cognitive, physical, and temporal demands and enhance robot control. Instrumented gloves were adapted to aid in robot control for driving and robotic arm manipulation. In this experiment, soldiers used the instrumented glove or a handheld controller to navigate around obstacles and manipulate the robotic arm.

2 Robot Control

2.1 Gestures for Robot Control

Instrumented gloves are the most common instantiation of wearable, instrumented systems for robot control [11]. The glove concept is congruent for many work situations where operators may already have to wear gloves. For robot control, glove-based approaches are usually stand-alone, with the glove sending signals to robotic intelligence software for recognition, interpretation, and translation into computationally understandable and executable robotic behaviors.

Gesture recognition is accomplished through the mathematical interpretation of human body movements. Hand and body gestures can be transmitted from a controller mechanism that contains inertial measurement unit (IMU) sensors to sense rotation and acceleration of movement, or in other instances via camera vision-based technologies. Inertial measurement unit (IMU) sensor technologies placed on the body provide an alternative, technically-feasible, near-term approach to gesture recognition within uncontrolled environments. ATinc has demonstrated IMU-based hand and arm signal gesture recognition accuracy of 100% [10] via a custom instrumented glove interface. They have previously integrated with unmanned ground vehicles (UGVs) to demonstrate intuitive forms of control and communication.

2.2 Robot Control

Robot control is traditionally accomplished using handheld controllers, much like a gamepad or joystick form factor. Use of instrumented gloves to accomplish simple movement commands have been demonstrated across a number of situations [11]. There are several examples of using gestures for control of a robot [12, 13]. A strong advantage to a multi-use instrumented glove to a dismount Soldier is that sensors can be embedded within a standard Army field glove normally worn by Soldiers, thus eliminating the need to carry a handheld controller, and allowing easier access to their weapon.

While it is easy to think of single commands (e.g., stop, move forward, turn left) as simple commands, one should keep in mind it is not the command per se, but the distinguishability and the intuitive nature of the gesture that determines ease of use and recognition. When the gesture set is small, recognition rates have been high, across many glove-based approaches [11].

2.3   Remote Manipulation

Ground-based mobile robots are often used for remote manipulation of objects. In combat situations, this capability is often used for explosive ordinance disposal (EOD) [14]. Several efforts have been reported where gestures have been developed for remote manipulation. Several of these regard the development of service robots designed to assist people in locations such as offices, supermarkets, hospitals, and households. Other efforts focus on assisting users in more dangerous environments such as hazardous areas or space, using telepresence and teleoperation (see [15] for a review of teleoperation issues).

3   Equipment

3.1   Instrumented Glove for Robot Control

Participants used a single instrumented glove for robotic maneuvering and manipulation developed by ATinc, called the NuGlove. The single-glove configuration allowed for the switching between robot driving and robotic arm manipulation. The glove contained ten 9-axis sensors (3-axis accelerometer, 3-axis gyroscope, and 3-axis magnetometer). Data from the glove sampled at a rate of 100 Hz. The glove was tethered to a smartphone, which was used to transmit the wireless command signal (Fig. 1).

Fig. 1. AnthroTronix NuGlove

In addition to the instrumented glove, the robot was controlled via a traditional gamepad controller commonly used for robotic control and gaming. This gamepad, the

Xbox 360 controller (shown in Fig. 2), is familiar to most video gamers and was integrated with the handheld computer via wireless protocols.

Fig. 2. X-box controller

3.2 Robot

The robot used for this evaluation was a Jaguar V2 Robot implemented with a three degree of freedom (DOF) manipulator arm (shown in Fig. 3), which is a commercially available off-the-shelf mobile robotic platform. It is rugged, lightweight (<25 kg), and compact, as well as weather and water resistant. It has a chassis with two flippers for completing mobility tasks and had a commercial-off-the-shelf (COTS) manipulator arm mounted to the upper chassis housing. A felt tip marker was attached to the end of the manipulator arm to enable accuracy measurements for the dexterous task of touching a paper target.

Fig. 3. Robotic platform & manipulator arm

4   Experimental Methods

4.1   Participants

Twenty-four Soldiers participated in this study. They were recruited from the Officer Candidate School at Fort Benning, GA. All participants had a BS degree or higher—two had PhDs. Age ranged from 22 to 32 (average = 26.04). Twelve were female. Three participants were left-handed. Uniform size ranged from XS to L.

4.2   Robot Control Procedures

Soldier-participants were briefed on the purpose of the robot control experiment. They were told they would be trained on two controllers (i.e., gamepad, instrumented glove). After two training runs, each Soldier accomplished robot navigation and manipulation twice, once with each controller. Performance data was collected through trained observers. After each performance session, each Soldier filled out a NASA TLX self-report of workload. After both performance sessions were complete, they filled out a questionnaire pertaining to each controller.

4.3   Robot Control Training

Participants were trained on the different controllers prior to completing the task. The trainers described the general task demands throughout the robot control course, and explained that the goal of the task was to tele-operate the robot through the course while avoiding all obstacles and staying within the barriers. Participants were then shown the robot that they would be operating, including the chassis and three degree of freedom arm. They were told to navigate using only the camera for visual feedback, and for the task they must drive the chassis through the course and touch the target using the arm. They were told that they would be using two different control methods to operate the robot.

For the handheld controller condition, participants were shown the layout of the joystick and button controls. They were told to regard the arm as they would a human finger, given that it had the same number of joints and segments. They were shown how to use the handheld controller buttons to move the joints of the arm. They were also shown how to control robot maneuvers and movements, via the camera feedback. Participants then completed a test run once all questions of theirs were addressed.

For the glove condition, participants were shown the Android interface that was used in conjunction with the glove to operate the robot. The app interface consisted of "Drive", "Arm", and "Lock" buttons. This was used to toggle between driving (Drive) mode and manipulation (Arm) mode, as well as the option to completely stop operation of the robot (Lock). As in the controller condition, participants were encouraged to regard the manipulator arm as they would the human finger. Movement of the arm mapped directly to the index finger on the glove. Participants were then shown how to use the glove to control the chassis drive. They were asked if they had any questions and asked to complete a test run.

4.4   Robot Control Route and Task Demands

There were two options for robot control setup: single-glove control in which control was switched from the chassis to the manipulator arm and gamepad control in which one joystick controlled the chassis and the button pad was used to control the manipulator arm. A marker was attached to the end of the robotic arm to indicate where the participant planted the target. A camera was attached to the robot chassis for video feedback during teleoperation.

Obstacle locations were systematically varied for the three performance conditions (e.g., training, glove, gamepad) to minimize practice effects. To begin each trial, the robot is placed at the start point. The operator maneuvered the robot along the path, taking care to avoid obstacles and stay within line boundaries. At the end of the route, they deployed the manipulator arm, and made contact with a target on the door. The target was clearly visible via the robot's camera. Figure 4 shows the robot system along with the simulated path. Soldiers were given 25 min to complete the building-clearing task. Each condition took approximately 1 h to train, perform and provide feedback.

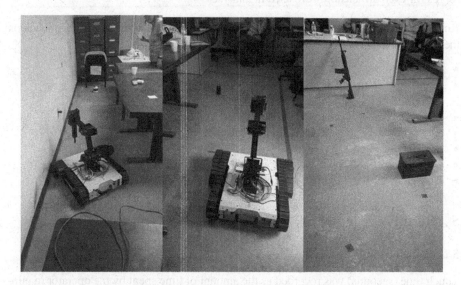

Fig. 4. Robotic platform & manipulator arm & course

4.5   Robot Control Performance Measures

For each of the conditions, drive time was collected as the total recorded time to complete navigation of the robot from the starting position to the intended target. This only included the task time to drive the robot chassis, and not to manipulate the robot arm. Touch time was also recorded and was the total time recorded to complete the manipulation portion of the task. It was the total time that participants spend within the manipulation mode to manipulate the robot arm to the placed target. Distance in inches of the final mark made by the operator from the intended target was noted, as well as the number of times the robot hit or crossed one of three aspects of the course: boundary lines, boundary posts (a table), or a simulated IED obstacle.

Mechanical Failures

Due to power draw issues, the unmanned ground vehicle used for the experiment sporadically dropped wireless connectivity. During one of the participants' runs, the robot collided with one of the barriers, causing a gear to snap. The motor was switched out for a spare motor. These issues delayed a few experimental runs, but were quickly resolved.

4.6   Robot Control Subjective Measures (Workload and Feedback)

Subjective measures included:

NASA TLX - the NASA TLX is a multi-dimensional rating scale for operators to report their mental workload. It uses six dimensions of workload to provide diagnostic information about the nature and relative contribution of each dimension in influencing overall operator workload. Operators rate the contribution made by each of six dimensions of workload to identify the intensity of the perceived workload [16]. Unweighted scores for each dimension were used in analyses.

Robot Control Questionnaire - participants were asked to provide open feedback on the following aspects of the overall system and experiment.

- Ease of training of the two controllers
- Comfort/fit of the glove
- Any problems experienced with the glove
- Control scheme of the gamepad controller
- Any problems experienced with the controller
- Which controller was preferred
- Overall glove controller concept
- Ways to improve the glove system

5   Results

5.1   Touch Time

Touch time (seconds) was recorded as the amount of time spent by the operator manipulating the robotic arm **to** 'touch' the intended target at the end of the pathway. Paired-comparison t-test of this difference was significant (t = 2.394, df = 36, p = 0.022). Figure 5 and Table 1 show the results for touch time (Fig. 7).

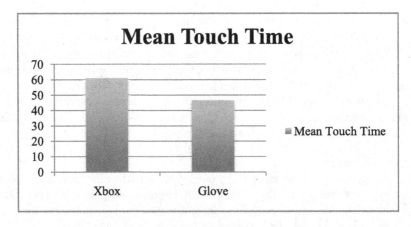

Fig. 5. Mean touch time (seconds)

Table 1. Touch time for both conditions

	Mean (seconds)	N	Std. deviation	Std. error mean
Xbox_touch time	61.08	37	33.694	5.539
Glove_touch time	46.73	37	24.519	4.031

5.2 Drive Time

The amount of time, in seconds, spent by the operator driving the robot before switching to manipulator mode was recorded during **each** run. Drive times for the Xbox and glove control conditions are indicated in Figs. 6, 7 and Table 2. Paired-comparison t-test of this difference was significant (t = − 3.14, df = 36, p = 0.003).

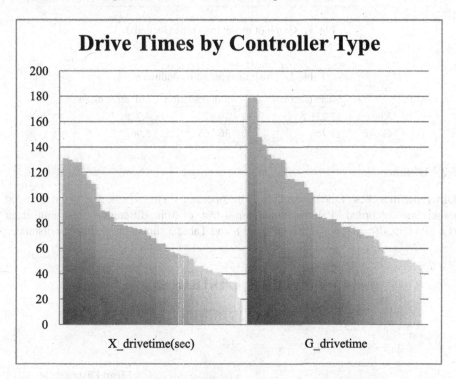

Fig. 6. Drive times (seconds) by controller type across subjects

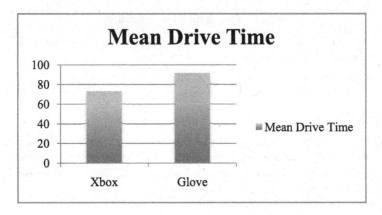

Fig. 7. Graph of mean drive time (seconds)

Table 2. Drive time for both conditions

	Mean (seconds)	N	Std. deviation	Std. error mean
Xbox	73.22	37	29.977	4.928
Glove	91.76	37	36.263	5.962

5.3 Distance

Difference in inches of the mark made by the operator via the robotic arm to the intended target was recorded. Paired-comparison t-test of this difference was significant ($t = -4.035$, $df = 37$, $p = 0.000$). Figure 8 and Table 3 shows the results for distance.

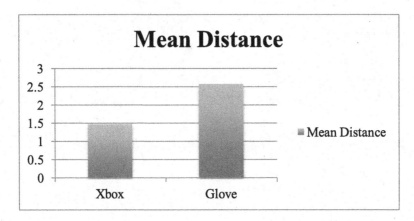

Fig. 8. Mean distance

Table 3. Distance for both conditions

		Mean	N	Std. deviation	Std. error mean
Pair 1	Xbox_distance	1.4724	38	1.04614	.16971
	Glove_distance	2.5803	38	1.53308	.24870

Other measures collected related to the number of times the robot hit either the barriers or obstacles of the course. However, the difference in means of the two conditions was not statistically significant.

5.4 Subjective Feedback

After completion of the robotic control task, participants were asked to provide feedback of the training, glove, gamepad controller, system preference, glove controller as a concept, and suggestions to improve the system. Overall, the gamepad controller had greater positive feedback, mostly due to familiarity with the system in commercial applications (i.e. home video-gaming). However, the glove was viewed as an intuitive interface for maneuver, but less for arm manipulation. Negative feedback relating to either system corresponded mostly to how the controller (glove or gamepad) was implemented with the robot. When asked which system participants preferred, 9 responded that they prefer the gamepad controller, mainly due to their familiarity with the system. Of the remaining 9 participants whose responses were recorded, 8 preferred the glove and reported it as easier to use and quicker to learn. One participant responded that they did not have a preference of system. Other comments on the overall system included ones regarding the camera for feedback.

6 Conclusion

Given that the glove condition showed better performance, in the form of faster completion times, for the touch time than for the drive time, we can conclude that the glove is better suited for faster completion of manipulation tasks. However, it should be noted that the accuracy for the task was lower in the glove condition. Since the gamepad style controllers are a common consumer product, additional user training with the glove controller may increase the glove controller performance compared to the gamepad for chassis control and/or manipulator arm accuracy. Additionally, alternate control mappings of glove sensor input to robot motor activation may show higher performance. The index finger mapping was selected as the most intuitive, however, other approaches might be more effective for manipulation speed and accuracy.

The results of the drive time by controller type show similar distributions, with the exception of two outlier data points for the glove control condition which if eliminated, would significantly reduce the difference between the mean values of the Xbox and glove controller. Depending on the task, speed may take priority over accuracy, or vice-versa. For example, during a building reconnaissance, deployment of a camera payload that is mounted to a manipulator arm may require speed over accuracy due to the nature of the mission in progress.

Soldier feedback on the instrumented glove was of most interest in this preliminary evaluation. Some issues were anticipated due to having a single glove size. Additional feedback from the Soldiers with regard to glove-robot-camera integration will aid in further refinement of the glove as a viable option in operational settings.

Because the glove technology integrates into existing combat attire, the glove control solution provides an overall weight reduction to the soldier's combat load as it eliminates the need for a dedicated controller. Current ruggedized operator control units (OCUs) are bulky and add extra weight to the soldier's load. The sensors in the glove controller add approximately 70 grams of weight, in comparison to about 205 grams for an Xbox controller. Additionally, unlike holding a game controller, the soldier using the glove controller can quickly and easily transition from robot control to individual rifle deployment, thus maintaining a higher level of defensive posture.

Acknowledgments. This research effort was in support of Army Research Laboratory Contract W911NF-13-C-0071. The team would like to acknowledge Dr. Anna Skinner, Josh Nichols, and the volunteer staff for their support of the effort.

References

1. Lathan, C.E., Tracey, M.R., Vice, J.M., Druin, A., Plaisant, C.: U.S. Patent No. 6,895,305, U.S. Patent and Trademark Office, Washington, DC (2005)
2. Phillips, E., Ososky, S., Swigert, B., Jentsch, F.: Human-animal teams as an analog for future human-robot teams. In: Proceedings of the Human Factors and Ergonomics Society 56th Annual Meeting, vol. 56(1), pp. 1553–1557 (2012)
3. Redden, E., Elliott, L., Barnes, M.: Robots: the new team members. In: Coovert, M., Foster, L., (eds.) The Psychology of Workplace Technology. Frontier Series. Society for Industrial and Organization Psychology, Bowling Green (OH) (2013)
4. Barnes, M., Chen, J. Hill, S. Humans and autonomy: implications of shared decision-making for military operations. Technical report No. ARL-TR-7919. Army Research Laboratory Human Research and Engineering Directorate, Aberdeen Proving Ground, MD
5. Nahavandi, S.: Trusted autonomy between humans and robots: toward human-on-the-loop in robotics and autonomous systems. IEEE Syst. Man Cybern **3**(1), 10–17 (2017)
6. Goodrich, M., Schultz, A.: Human-robot interaction: a review. Found. Trends Hum. Comput. Interact. **1**(3), 203–275 (2007)
7. Jung, B., Sukhatme, G.S.: Real-time motion tracking from a mobile robot. Int. J. Soc. Robot. **2**(1), 63–78 (2010)
8. Corradini, A., Gross, H.M.: Camera-based gesture recognition for robot control. In: Proceedings of the IEEE-INNS-ENNS International Joint Conference on Neural Networks, IJCNN 2000, vol. 4, pp. 133–138. IEEE (2002)
9. Muto, Y., Takasugi, S., Yamamoto, T., Miyake, Y.: Timing control of utterance and gesture in human-robot interaction. In: RO-MAN (2009)
10. Lathan, C., Vice, J.M., Tracey, M., Plaisant, C., Druin, A., Edward, K., Montemayor, J.: Therapeutic play with a storytelling robot. In: CHI 2001 Extended Abstracts on Human Factors in Computing Systems, pp. 27–28. ACM, March 2001
11. Elliott, L., Hill, S., Barnes, M.: Gesture-based controls for robots: overview and implications for use by Soldiers. ARL Technical report 7715. Army Research Laboratory Human Research and Engineering Directorate, Aberdeen Proving Ground, MD (2016)

12. Rogalla, O., Ehrenmann, M., Zollner, R., Becher, R., Dillmann, R.: Using gesture and speech control for commanding a robot assistant. In: Proceedings of 11th IEEE International Workshop on Robot and Human Interactive Communication, pp. 454–459. IEEE (2002)
13. Waldherr, S., Romero, R., Thrun, S.: A gesture based interface for human-robot interaction. Auton. Robots **9**(2), 151–173 (2000)
14. Axe, D.: War Bots: How US Military Robots are Transforming War in Iraq, Afghanistan, and the Future. Nimble Books, Ann Arbor (2008)
15. Basañez, L., Suárez, R.: Teleoperation. In: Nof, S.Y. (ed.) Springer Handbook of Automation, pp. 449–468. Springer, Heidelberg (2009)
16. Hart, S.G., Staveland, L.E.: Development of NASA-TLX (Task Load Index): results of empirical and theoretical research. Adv. Psychol. **52**, 139–183 (1988)

Feasibility of Wearable Fitness Trackers for Adapting Multimodal Communication

Daniel Barber[✉], Austin Carter, Jonathan Harris, and Lauren Reinerman-Jones

Institute for Simulation and Training (IST), University of Central Florida (UCF),
Orlando, FL 32826, USA
{dbarber,acarter,jharris,lreinerm}@ist.ucf.edu

Abstract. In addition to efforts to increase the intelligence and perception capabilities of robots to enable collaboration with human counterparts, there is also a focus towards improving interaction mechanics. Multimodal communication is one such tool under investigation due to its dynamic ability to select explicit and implicit communication modalities with the aim of facilitating robust exchanges of information. Although there is extensive research in the domain of explicit communication using auditory, visual, and tactile interfaces, investigations into systems that incorporate implicit methods, or actually adapt and select appropriate modalities for reporting data from a robot to human is limited. Furthermore, a missing piece is identifying how and when to trigger these changes. A novel strategy to accomplish adaptation is through identification of teammate's physiological state. From the literature, one can find examples of researchers using high fidelity systems to measure physiological response and predict user workload, but many of these technologies are prohibitively expensive or not suitable for use in many domains of interest for human robot interaction such as dismounted infantry operations. Recent advancements in wearable consumer technologies, specifically fitness trackers supporting integration with third party software, are making it possible for incorporation of low cost systems in a variety of novel applications. A logical extension of these applications being physiological state measurement to drive adaptive automation in the form of multimodal interfaces. This paper describes the results of a study to assess the feasibility of using data from a wearable fitness tracker in an adaptive multimodal interface for squad-level human-robot interaction.

Keywords: Fitness trackers · Physiological assessment · Human-robot interaction · Multimodal communication · Adaptive automation

1   Introduction

A growing body of research and added commercial interest is pushing intelligence and perception capabilities of robots into new areas of collaboration with human counterparts. Through congressional mandate and funded research efforts, robots are no longer seen as remote control tools, but teammates capable of taking on different roles and responsibilities to accomplish a shared objective [1–3]. In addition to making robot teammates smarter, there is also a strong focus towards improving interaction mechanics

© Springer International Publishing AG 2017
S. Yamamoto (Ed.): HIMI 2017, Part I, LNCS 10273, pp. 504–516, 2017.
DOI: 10.1007/978-3-319-58521-5_39

for seamless integration with end users within mixed-initiative teams. Within the mixed-initiative paradigm, teams employ flexible interaction strategies where each agent (human or robot) contributes what is best-suited at the most appropriate time [4]. At the root of any interaction between humans and robots is the exchange of information using auditory, visual, and tactile modalities. Appropriately using these modalities is required for effective communication, with interactions tailored to human expectations, demands, and mental models [5]. Multimodal communication is a framework and tool under investigation to meet this need due to its support for the flexible selection of explicit and implicit communication modalities to enable robust exchange of information when compared to single modalities [6–8]. Although there is extensive research in the domain of explicit communication using auditory, visual, and tactile interfaces, investigations into systems that adapt and select appropriate modalities for bi-directional interaction with human teammates is limited.

1.1 Adaptive Automation for Human Robot Interaction

The environments todays soldiers interact within are inherently complex. Working within teams, regardless of the presence of a robot, includes multitasking during which soldiers must pay attention to their own task execution and their teammates. For example, a cordon and search operation, one of the most frequently used tactics dismounted soldier teams use in complex urban environments, requires reconnaissance, enemy isolation and capture, and weapons and material seizures [9]. With the inclusion of robots to assist in cordon and search or other operations, there is potential for an increase in soldier workload due to the superhuman information gathering capabilities of robots. Robot teammates equipped with cameras, LIDAR, SONAR, and other sensors have the ability to capture and aggregate a multitude of data, which could negatively impact a soldier's situational awareness and workload if not delivered appropriately.

Adaptive automation refers to a system capability that enables task sharing between a human operator and a system [10, 11]. With robots and their interfaces becoming more capable and independent, adaptive automation is well suited to enabling mixed-initiative squad-level team concepts. Previous efforts at using adaptive automation in ground robot teaming scenarios have shown performance benefits [10, 12]. Extending this work to adapt multimodal communication is henceforth likely to improve team communication performance. In such a scenario, automation built within human robot interfaces can select the appropriate modality, or combination thereof, to deliver messages to soldiers in a way that does not increase cognitive demand or interfere with tasks using conflicting visual or auditory resources.

1.2 Implicit Communication for Adaptive Strategies

In addition to understanding what single or combination of modalities will result in the most effective exchange of information, a critical piece of the puzzle is identifying how and when to trigger these changes. Situational context when directly interacting with a robot is one method of triggering these changes, but an alternative strategy of interest from the domain of implicit communication is the identification of teammate physiological states [13]. From the literature, one can find examples of researchers using electroencephalograms (EEG), electrocardiograms (ECG), eye tracking, and other sensors in combination to measure physiological response to classify a participant's level of workload [13–16]. By employing physiological sensors to classify a user's state, automation within an interface can trigger different multimodal communication strategies to maintain a baseline level of performance. For example, when a soldier is experiencing high workload; a multimodal interface may chunk auditory reports together or pair with tactile feedback to ensure messages are received. Teo, et al. [13] developed a closed-loop system that demonstrated this exact concept by using a combination of physiological sensors to trigger automation in a remote supervisory reconnaissance and surveillance mission with a ground robot.

1.3   Wearable Fitness Trackers for Implicit Communication

Although using physiological sensors to measure a person's state is a promising technique, many of the technologies, are prohibitively expensive or not suitable for use in squad level human robot teaming. Within this domain, users are on the move, and current physiological sensing devices would interfere with operations or disrupt their wearing of other equipment. Recent advancements in wearable consumer technologies, specifically fitness trackers supporting integration with third party software, are closing this gap, making it possible for incorporation of low cost, non-disruptive systems in a variety of novel applications. The Microsoft Band 2, Fig. 1, is an example of a wrist-worn device that supports real-time collection of heart rate, inter-beat interval, heart rate variability, skin temperature, ambient temperature, and galvanic skin response (GSR) over a Bluetooth connection on multiple operating systems [17].

Fig. 1.   Microsoft band 2 wearable fitness tracker.

These sensors, in particular the optical heart rate monitor and GSR, provide similar measures to those used in previous efforts such as Teo, et al. [13]. However, the feasibility of fitness trackers for triggering adaptive communication is unclear, as the manufacturers did not design them with this purpose in mind and may not have the required sensitivity and saliency for accurate physiological state classifications.

1.4 Adaptive Multimodal Interfaces

Accomplishing the vision of adaptive multimodal communication interfaces for soldiers and robots requires a systematic investigation into the performance costs and benefits of single versus multiple modalities and physiological response within different mission contexts and environmental demands. However, a review of the literature shows a limited number of studies to date investigating multimodal communication within mixed-initiative infantry operations [18], with the majority focused on teleoperation [19, 20], humanoid robot assistants [7, 21], and vehicle driving scenarios [22–24]. Few meta-analyses have surveyed the performance costs and benefits of redundant versus single-modality presentation for an interrupting and ongoing task [22, 23]. Moreover, conflicting results across studies demonstrate unclear effects of modality switching on vision-based signal detection tasks like those of cordon and search operations [25]. The goal for this effort is to address this gap by beginning to understand independent and redundant communication modalities and adaptive strategies in squad-level human robot interactions. Specifically, the aim for this paper is to assess the feasibility of using wearable fitness trackers as a means of state identification for adapting multimodal communication.

2 Method

2.1 Participants

A total of 56 (34 males, 22 females) participants between the ages of 18 and 40 (M = 19.29, SD = 2.29) participated in the study. All participants received credit for their psychology courses for completing the study. Participants were asked not to consume alcohol or any sedative medication for 24 h or caffeine for two hours prior to the study.

2.2 Equipment and Simulation Environment

As previously mentioned, cordon and search is one of the most common operations a squad may perform in an urban environment. It also contains enough complexity to make it well suited for investigating the challenges of mixed-initiative teaming between humans and robots. For the present effort, a custom 3D simulation using the Unreal 4 Game Engine [26] was created, Fig. 2. Within the simulation, participants took the role of a squad leader performing the outer cordon task. This outer cordon activity replicated a signal detection task, [27], where participants were required to look for insurgents walking in front of and around a building at different event rates. If participants detected an insurgent, they used a mouse to click on the character, which the software logged. A 30" monitor with a resolution of 2560 × 1600 pixels was used to present the environment.

Fig. 2. Unreal 4 game engine simulation used in experiment. Image represents the 3D field of view participants experienced while executing an outer cordon operation. Characters in the environment were animated and walked on and off screen and variable event rates. At the top center is an overlay of the multimodal interface visual display when present.

In addition to the outer cordon signal detection task, participants received information from two virtual robot teammates performing the inner cordon task (not within the participants' field of view). A modified version of the multimodal interface (MMI)

Fig. 3. Multimodal interface (MMI) visual display. Display is comprised of three main areas: semantic map (left) showing robot location and icons of objects found, video/camera (top right), and status (bottom right) illustrating the current command the robot is executing and the most recent report (in text) of what the robot detected.

developed by Barber et al. [5] was used to deliver auditory and visual reports from robot teammates. The visual display of the interface, illustrated in in Fig. 3, appeared on top of the 3D simulation at the top center area of the screen at a resolution of 602 × 377 pixels, Fig. 2. The resolution and size of the visual display was scaled to match 1:1 to the physical size of the Toughpad FZ-M1 tablet used in [5] when shown on the 30″ monitor used in the study. For each visual report, the display was present for 10 s before being hidden off screen. For the auditory modality, text reports were converted to speech using Microsoft Speech Platform SDK version 11 text-to-speech (TTS) and the default male voice of the Windows 10 operating system, [28].

For physiological data capture, the Microsoft Band 2 was used [17]. The Microsoft Band 2 was selected because it provided sensor data corresponding with previous research efforts for classifying physiological state (e.g. interbeat interval (IBI)), and Microsoft providing a Windows software development kit (SDK) enabling real-time capture of data during the simulation. A custom software application using the provided SDK captured and recorded data from the device.

2.3 Design

A 3 (Adaptive Strategy: Constant, MMI, User) × 3 (Modality: Auditory, Visual, Auditory and Visual) × 2 (Environmental Demand: High, Low) repeated measures design was employed. For adaptive strategy, constant (C) meant that no adaptation to communication modality occurred, MMI indicated that the multimodal interface triggered changes to modality, and for user (U), the participants triggered which modality was

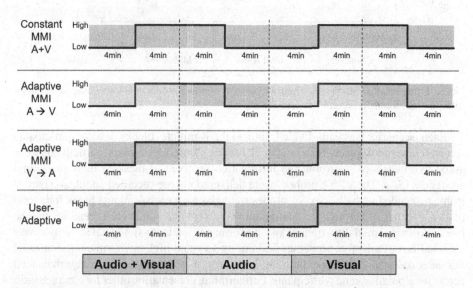

Fig. 4. Scenario design for the experiment. Four scenarios were created for each participant, one constant adaptive strategy (both visual and audio reports), two MMI adaptive (audio to visual and visual to audio), and one user-adaptive. Event rate (high/low) for the signal detection task is indicated by the square wave function, with report periods divided into 4 min blocks.

used with the spacebar key on the keyboard. Two modalities were used auditory (A) and visual (V) and depending on the adaptive strategy were presented standalone or redundantly. Environmental demand during scenarios was either high (H) or low (L). To manipulate environmental demand, event rates of 15 events/minute and 60 events/minute on the signal detection task were used corresponding to low and high task load respectively. Selection of these event rates was taken from Abich et al. [29], which established event rates for a similar signal detection task that elicited distinct levels of low and high workload as reported by the NASA-TLX.

A total of four scenarios were created to capture the experimental design and collect an equal amount of data across adaptive strategy, communication modality, and environmental demand (event rate), illustrated in Fig. 4.

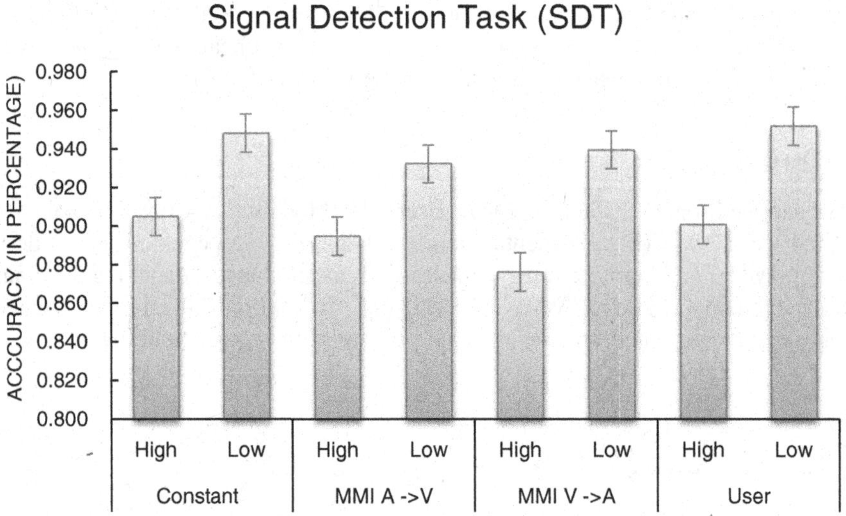

Signal Detection Task (SDT)

Fig. 5. Comparison of IBI between high and low environmental demands across adaptive strategy scenarios. Error bars represent standard error.

Each scenario was sub-divided into eight 4-minute blocks where participants received nine reports each, for a total of 72 reports. After three reports, participants were asked two questions regarding the information received to measure their situational awareness (SA). These "SA probes" were delivered via pre-recorded audio, and participants responded verbally. Six SA probes were given for each 4-minute block for a total of 48 per scenario. Through the manipulation of event rate within each scenario, and the break down of modality transitions, performance and physiological response was captured across adaptive strategies and during low and high environmental demands. For each scenario, a different building location was used which was counterbalanced across manipulations and participants. Furthermore, presentation order for each scenario was randomized and counterbalanced across participants as well.

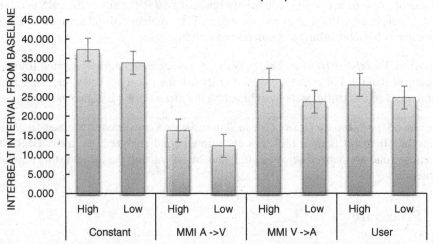

Fig. 6. Comparison of HRV between high and low environmental demands across adaptive strategy scenarios. Error bars represent standard error.

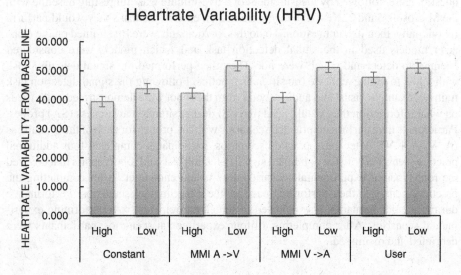

Fig. 7. Comparison of GSR between high and low environmental demands across adaptive strategy scenarios. Error bars represent standard error.

Dependent Variables

Signal Detection Task (SDT). The accuracy of participants in identifying enemy insurgents [27]. For each time period analyzed, the total number of correctly identified insurgents was divided by the total number of insurgents presented to obtain an accuracy percentage.

Interbeat interval (IBI). Interbeat interval as reported from the Microsoft Band 2, measured as the time in milliseconds between heartbeat RR peaks of the QRS complex [30]. For each time period analyzed, the mean IBI was calculated and normalized across participants by subtracting the mean resting baseline value.

Heartrate Variability (HRV). The variance of the interbeat interval reported from the Microsoft Band 2. For each time period analyzed, the mean HRV was calculated and normalized across participants by subtracting the mean resting baseline value.

Galvanic Skin Response (GSR). Mean skin resistance converted to Siemens reported from the Microsoft Band 2 [30]. For each time period analyzed, the mean GSR was calculated and normalized across participants by subtracting the mean resting baseline value.

3   Procedure

Upon arrival, participants first completed an informed consent document, and then were equipped with the Microsoft Band 2 on the wrist of their non-dominant hand after the area was cleaned with an alcohol pad. Participants then completed a demographics questionnaire, followed by measurement of a five-minute wakeful resting baseline with the Microsoft Band 2. Next, they were trained on each of the tasks they would perform individually, then in combination. To do this, participants were first trained on the character models used in the signal detection task and which models were considered enemies to detect and which were not. They then performed the signal detection task with a low to high event rate transition as practice. Following the signal detection task training, example visual and audio reports from the robot were demonstrated, with focus on what information they would need to recall during situation awareness (SA) probes. Participants than performed practice scenarios with SA probes for each of the modalities (A, V, A + V). After these practice scenarios, participants completed four additional practice scenarios with the combined signal detection task and robot reports that covered the four types of experimental scenarios they would encounter. After completing the practice scenarios, they performed each of the experimental scenarios. Performance during practice scenarios was not used to screen participants from performing experimental scenarios. After completing all four experimental scenarios, participants were debriefed and dismissed.

4   Results

4.1   SDT

A 4 (Adaptive Strategy: Constant, MMI Audio to Visual, MMI Visual to Audio, User) × 2 (Environmental Demand: High, Low) repeated measures ANOVA was performed for performance on the signal detection task revealing a significant main effect for adaptive strategy ($F(2.50, 97.33) = 3.30, p = .03, \eta2 = .08$), Fig. 8. A pairwise comparison with a Bonferroni correction indicated that participants in the constant adaptive strategy ($M = 0.94$, $SD = 0.04$) identified insurgents more accurately than participants in the audio to visual adaptive strategy ($M = 0.92$, $SD = 0.05$, $p = .002$). A significant main effect for environmental demand ($F(1, 42) = 88.13$, $p < .001$, $\eta2 = .68$) Fig. 8, was also found, such that performance was higher in a low event rate ($M = 0.96$, $SD = 0.04$) than in a high event rate($M = 0.91$, $SD = 0.05$).

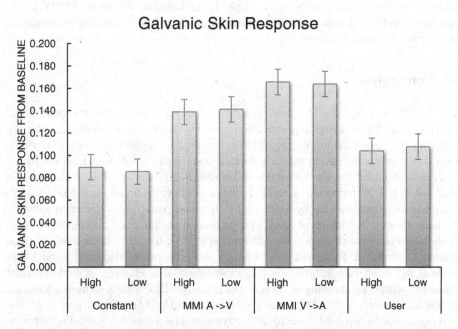

Fig. 8. Comparison of SDT between high and low environmental demands across adaptive strategy scenarios. Error bars represent standard error

4.2 IBI

A 4 (Adaptive Strategy: Constant, MMI Audio to Visual, MMI Visual to Audio, User) × 2 (Environmental Demand: High, Low) repeated measures ANOVA was performed and showed no significant main effect for mean IBI between adaptive strategies or environmental demand, Fig. 5.

4.3 HRV

A 4 (Adaptive Strategy: Constant, MMI Audio to Visual, MMI Visual to Audio, User) × 2 (Environmental Demand: High, Low) repeated measures ANOVA was performed and showed no significant main effect HRV for adaptive strategy. There was however a significant main effect for environmental demand, ($F(1, 36) = 27.66$, $p < .001$, $\eta2 = .44$), such that HRV during high demand ($M = 42.49$, $SD = 37.56$) was lower than during low (M = 49.367, SD = 36.06), Fig. 6. No significant interaction between adaptive strategy and modality was shown.

4.4 GSR

A 4 (Adaptive Strategy: Constant, MMI Audio to Visual, MMI Visual to Audio, User) × 2 (Environmental Demand: High, Low) repeated measures ANOVA was performed and revealed no significant effects for mean GSR between adaptive strategies or high and low task demands, Fig. 7.

5   Conclusion

The present study described a starting point in the advancement of dynamic multimodal interfaces capable of changing presentation format to ensure robust communication. An experimental design demonstrating different adaptive strategies and levels of environmental demands was used to measure impacts on task performance and the sensitivity of a commercial-off-the-shelf wearable (Microsoft Band 2) to detect these changes. An analyses of task performance on an SDT supported previous findings related to manipulation of event rate reported by Abich et al. [29], where participants' detection accuracy decreased during higher event rates. Furthermore, a performance difference was also revealed for adaptive strategy type, with highest SDT performance in the constant (dual modality) condition. Following these findings, analyses of the Microsoft Band 2 data showed that heart rate information was most sensitive to changes in environmental demands, with GSR showing no effects. Specifically, HRV results showed significant differences between low and high task demand within adaptive strategies, such that HRV was higher during low, and lower for high environmental demand. This finding supports previous research correlating HRV and workload, [31]. Although promising, further work is still needed to determine if these findings are consistent across different task types within this domain before attempting to dynamically change modalities. Furthermore, although differences in performance on the SDT were shown between adaptive strategies, more analyses are still required to understand impacts of these strategies on working memory and situational awareness on longer duration exercises, and whether when you adapt the modality during changes to environmental demand matters.

Acknowledgments. This research was sponsored by the Army Research Laboratory and was accomplished under Cooperative Agreement Number W911NF-10-2-0016. The views and conclusions contained in this document are those of the author's and should not be interpreted as representing the official policies, either expressed or implied, of the Army Research Laboratory or the U.S. Government. The U.S. Government is authorized to reproduce and distribute reprints for Government purposes notwithstanding any copyright notation herein.

References

1. Phillips, E., Ososky, S., Grove, J., Jentsch, F.: From tools to teammates: toward the development of mental models for intelligent robots. In: Proceedings of the Human Factors and Ergonomics Society 55th Annual Meeting (2011)
2. U.S. Congress, National Defense Authorization Act for Fiscal Year 2001, Washington, D.C. (2001)
3. U.S. Army Research, Laboratory, Robotics, 1 June 2011. http://www.arl.army.mil/www/default.cfm?page=392. Accessed 10 Feb 2017
4. Hearst, M., Allen, J., Guinn, C., Horvitz, E.: Mixed-initiative interaction: trends & controversies. In: IEEE Intelligent Systems, pp. 14–23 (1999)
5. Barber, D.J., Abich, J., Phillips, E., Talone, A., Jentsch, F., Hill, S.G.: Field assessment of multimodal communication for dismounted human-robot teams. In: Proceedings of the Human Factors and Ergonomics Society Annual Meeting (2015)
6. Lackey, S.J., Barber, D.J., Reinerman-Jones, L., Badler, N., Hudson, I.: Defining next-generation multi-modal communication in human-robot interaction. In: Human Factors and Ergonomics Society Conference, Las Vegas (2011)
7. Bischoff, R., Graefe, V.: Dependable multimodal communication and interaction with robotic assistants. In: 11th IEEE International Workshop on Robot and Human Interactive Communication (2002)
8. Partan, S., Marler, P.: Communication goes multimodal. Science **283**(5406), 1272–1273 (1999)
9. Sutherland, J., Baillergeon, R., McKane, T.: Cordon and search operations: a deadly game of hide and seek. Air Land and Sea Bulletin: Cordon and Search, pp. 4–10 (2010)
10. Cosenzo, K., Chen, J., Reinerman-Jones, L., Barnes, M., Nicholson, D.: Adaptive automation effects on operator performance during a reconnaissance mission with an unmanned ground vehicle. In: Proceedings of the Human Factors and Ergonomics Society 54th Annual Meeting, Los Angeles, CA (2010)
11. Parasuraman, R., Hancock, P.: Adaptive workload and control. In: Workload and Fatigue, Mahwah, NJ, USA, pp. 305–320. Lawrenc Erlbaum Associates (2001)
12. Taylor, G.S., Reinerman-Jones, L., Szalma, J.L., Mouloua, M., Hancock, P.A.: What to automate: addressing the multidimensionality of cognitive resources through system design. J. Cogn. Eng. Deci. Making **7**(4), 311–329 (2013)
13. Teo, G., Reinerman-Jones, L., Matthews, G., Barber, D., Harris, J., Hudson, I.: Augmenting robot behaviors using physiological measures of workload state. In: Human Computer Interaction International, Toronto, CA (2016)
14. Barber, D., Reinerman-Jones, L., Lackey, S., Hudson, I.: Augmenting robot behaviors using physiological measures. In: Schmorrow, D.D., Fidopiastis, C.M. (eds.) FAC 2011. LNCS, vol. 6780, pp. 567–572. Springer, Heidelberg (2011). doi:10.1007/978-3-642-21852-1_65
15. Abich, J., Reinerman-Jones, L.R., Taylor, G.S.: Investigating workload measures for adaptive training systems (2013)
16. Mercado, J., Reinerman-Jones, L., Barber, D., Leis, R.: Investigating workload measures in the nuclear domain. In: Proceedings of the Human Factors and Ergonomics Society Annual Meeting (2014)
17. Microsoft, Microsoft Band Features, Microsoft. https://www.microsoft.com/microsoft-band/en-us/features. Accessed 10 Feb 2017
18. Redden, E., Elliot, L.: Robotic control systems for dismounted soldiers. In: Jentsch, F.G., Barnes, M.J. (eds.) Human-Robot Interactions in Future Military Operations, pp. 335–352. Ashgate (2010)

19. Pettitt, R., Redden, E.S., Carsten, C.: Scalability of robotic controllers: speech-based robotic controller evaluation (ARL-TR-4858). Aberdeen Proving Ground, MD: US Army Research Laboratory, pp. 1–46 (2009)
20. Oron-Gilad, T., Redden, E.S., Minkov, Y.: Robotic displays for dismounted warfighters. J. Cogn. Eng. Decis. Making 5(1), 29–54 (2011)
21. Bennewitz, M., Faber, F., Joho, D., Behnke, S.: Fritz - a humanoid communication robot. In: The 16th IEEE International Symposium on Robot and Human interactive Communication (2007)
22. Wickens, C.D., Prinet, J., Hutchins, S., Sarter, N.B., Sebok, A.: Auditory-visual redundancy in vehicle control interruptions: two meta-analyses. In: Human Factors and Ergonomics Society 55th Annual Meeting, Santa Monica, CA, USA (2011)
23. Wickens, C.D., Gosney, J.: Redundancy, modality, and priority in dual task interference. In: Proceedings of the Human Factors and Ergonomics Society 47th Annual Meeting, Santa Monica, CA, USA (2003)
24. Lu, S.A., Wickens, C.D., Prinet, J.C., Hutchins, S.D., Sarter, N., Sebok, A.: Supporting interruption management and multimodal interface design: three meta-analyses of task performance as a function of interrupting task modality. Hum. Factors 55(4), 697–724 (2013)
25. Reinerman-Jones, L.R., Taylor, G., Sprouse, K., Barber, D., Hudson, I.: Adaptive automation as a task switching congruence challenge. In: Proceedings of the Human Factors and Ergonomics Society Annual Meeting (2011)
26. Epic Games, Unreal Engine, Epic Games. https://www.unrealengine.com/what-is-unreal-engine-4. Accessed 10 Feb 2017
27. Green, D.M., Swets, J.A.: Signal Detection Theory and Psychophysics. Wiley, New York (1966)
28. Microsoft: Microsoft Speech Platform - Software Development Kit (SDK) (Version 11), Microsoft. https://www.microsoft.com/en-us/download/details.aspx?id=27226. Accessed 10 Feb 2017
29. Abich, J., Taylor, G., Reinerman-Jones, L.: Establishing workload manipulations utilizing a simulated environment. In: Human Computer Interaction International, Las Vegas, NV, USA (2013)
30. Microsoft: Microsoft Band SDK. https://developer.microsoftband.com/Content/docs/Microsoft%20Band%20SDK.pdf. Accessed 10 Feb 2017
31. Matthews, G., Reinerman-Jones, L., Barber, D., Abich, J.: The psychometrics of mental workload: multiple measures are sensitive but divergent. Hum. Factors 57(1), 125–143 (2015)

The Vibropixels: A Scalable Wireless Tactile Display System

Ian Hattwick[1,2]([✉]), Ivan Franco[1,2], and Marcelo M. Wanderley[1,2]

[1] Input Devices and Music Interaction Lab,
McGill University, Montreal, QC, Canada
{ian.hattwick,ivan.franco}@mail.mcgill.ca,
marcelo.wanderley@mcgill.ca
[2] Centre for Interdisciplinary Research in Music Media and Technology,
Montreal, QC, Canada

Abstract. This paper presents a wearable, wireless tactile display system which consists of individually controllable vibrotactile actuator devices, called Vibropixels. The design of the system is easily scalable and reconfigurable, allowing for implementation in a variety of applications. The system removes any limit on the number of actuator devices by avoiding both hand-shaking and packet acknowledgement functionality. The number of control messages required is minimized through the use of a exible two-part addressing scheme as well as functions allowing for the generation of multiple actuator envelopes on the devices. Created within an interdisciplinary art-science research project, 145 Vibropixels were utilized in the premier of the artistic installation *Haptic Field*. Recognizing that the artistic creation process often involves utilizing systems beyond their intended application, we designed our system to allow our collaborators to interact with and potentially modify the system on a hardware, firmware, or software level. Through interviews with our collaborators, we evaluated our system's ability to support the artistic creation process in light of Shneiderman's principles for creativity support tools. While our collaborators mostly used and modified the highest level software tools provided to them, we argue that supporting lower level modifications may still be useful depending upon available time and the knowledge of the user.

Keywords: Tactile display · Artistic creation · Wireless network

1 Introduction

The Vibropixels are a scalable, wireless tactile display system whose reconfigurable nature allows for use in a wide variety of applications. While the system was initially developed for use in professional artistic productions, it also suitable for use in other applications, including tactile notification systems and virtual reality environments.

This paper consists of two sections. In the first, we describe the Vibropixels tactile display system as it was used in the artwork *Haptic Field*. We will briefly

© Springer International Publishing AG 2017
S. Yamamoto (Ed.): HIMI 2017, Part I, LNCS 10273, pp. 517–528, 2017.
DOI: 10.1007/978-3-319-58521-5_40

review tactile display applications and implementations, and review the requirements of the creation of a system designed for use in professional artistic productions.

In the second section of the paper, we discuss the use of the system in the artistic creation process. As the system was designed in a collaborative research projects with professional artists, one of our interests was facilitating the exploration of the system throughout its development stages. One way in which we approached this was allowing for easy access to and modification of the system's hardware, firmware, and software components. Our intention was to allow transparent access to the system's functionality as well as avoiding predefined limits on the its use. While our primary concern in this project was the creation of an artistic work, the flexibility provided by these design decisions may also facilitate the system's use in other applications.

2   The Technical Development of the System

The first public use of the Vibropixels was in the artwork *Haptic Field*, which premiered at the Chronus Art Center in Shanghai, China from July 9–September 6, 2016. Created by Chris Salter and Tez in collaboration with Ian Hattwick, *Haptic Field* is an immersive multisensory art installation based upon an earlier work by the collaborators, *Ilinx*, with visual, sonic, and tactile elements [3].[1] In *Haptic Field*, visitors wear a garment with seven Vibropixels attached and navigate a large, dark space while experiencing a variety of tactile patterns.

In this section we review wearable tactile display systems and implementations, the requirements placed upon the design of the Vibropixels by their intended use in professional artistic productions, and a technical description of the system as used in the premiere of *Haptic Fields*.

2.1   Wearable Tactile Displays

Tactile displays systems have been created for a wide variety of applications, including navigational assistance [2], sensory substitution [1], and enhancing interaction with virtual environments [5]. Many tactile displays are either embedded in handheld devices [7] or in wearables limited to one segment of the body, such as a ring, glove, or belt [12]. Other displays are able provide stimuli over a large portion of the body, frequently taking the form of a jacket or vest [4]. However, it is difficult to create such a system that is both robust enough for use in public presentations and also inexpensive enough to scale easily.

Another challenge is that tactile display applications often have specific requirements for actuator locations. Lindeman presents a vest created to provide feedback to participant's interacting with a virtual environment [5]. One of

---

[1] For a detailed description and video of *Haptic Field*, visit: http://ianhattwick.com/haptic-field/.

their requirements was to provide feedback when an avatar collides with door-frames, necessitating actuators placed on those parts of the body most likely to contribute to such collisions such as the outer shoulders.

The use of tactile displays in wearable form factors suggests the systems be embedded within a garment. Frequently, actuators will be distributed within the garment with wired connections to electronics which provide signals for driving the actuators as well as which allow for communication for a remote computer to control the display [11, Chap. 4, p. 11]. This architecture presents several problems for prolonged use. First, the wiring greatly impacts the garment's bulk, weight, and flexibility. Secondly, the wiring present potential points of failure as it often will be exposed to stress both when the garment is put on as well as in normal movements. Third, this construction can be time-consuming and expensive. Lastly, this architecture tends to locate the weight and bulk of the battery and wireless communications at a single point.

By switching to a system comprised of a monolithic, self-contained devices many of these problems are eliminated. However, the tradeoff is the increased size of the hardware at each actuator location. Therefore, ideal applications for the Vibropixels will be those which require a coarse distribution over the body rather than high spatial resolution.

2.2 Requirements for Use in Professional Artistic Productions

The requirements which shaped the design of the Vibropixels grew out of our intended application of use in professional artistic productions.

One primary requirement was that the system be able to accommodate large numbers of actuators, allowing for the distribution of tactile stimuli across many simultaneous participants. The cost of developing and manufacturing the devices therefore became a priority. We also had an interest in supporting the social context of this kind of artistic experience. One way of doing so was the integration of LED lighting in order to allows participants to get a sense of the tactile stimuli being experience by other participants. Another was the integration of motion sensing which would allow future applications which transmit tactile information regarding other participant's movements.

Another primary concern in the systems design was both its robustness and ease of use. Artistic installations which last for weeks or months are often maintained day-to-day by untrained staff. The system should be not only robust enough to endure constant use throughout this timeframe, but also should not require any specialized knowledge to run, maintain, and repair in the case of failures.

Finally, we also had an interest in supporting the system's use for a wide variety of artistic works. Many applications for tactile displays may go unexplored due to the difficulty of creating such systems. Our intention was to create a system which would allow for easy reconfigurability, supporting a variety of applications both within artistic contexts as well as within the broader research community.

2.3   System Overview

The Vibropixel system consists of four primary elements: the hardware implementation, the embedded firmware, the wireless communication implementation, and software tools for generating control messages. In this section we will discuss the first three elements; in Sect. 3.2 we discuss the creation of software tools and user interfaces for use with the system.

The electronic hardware is built around an ATmega328PB microcontroller running at 8MHz, as shown in Fig. 1. For reasons described in Sect. 2.2, we also integrated four individually-controllable WS2812b RGB LEDs as well as a Freescale Semiconductor MMA8652 3-axis accelerometer. A Nordic Technologies nRF24L01+ 2.4 GHz transceiver provides for wireless communication.

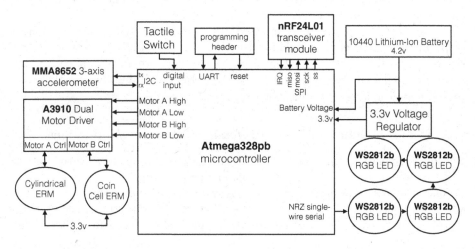

Fig. 1. A system overview showing the hardware configuration of a single Vibropixel.

As the creation of vibrotactile stimuli was our primary concern, we examined a variety of tactile actuators in order to identify a solution that would be power-efficient, generate strong vibrations, allow for the creation of a variety of stimuli, and be cost-efficient. Our final design utilizes two different kinds of eccentric-rotating mass (ERM) actuators which possess very different characteristics. The first is a pancake-type actuator that is highly-efficient in terms of power consumption and efficiency, and which creates a reasonable amplitude of vibration. We have found, however that this kind of actuator often responds very slowly, with a rise- and fall-time frequently exceeding 100 ms.

In order to allow for the generation of stimuli which require faster response times, the Vibropixels also utilize a cylindrical-style ERM actuator. These actuators tend to be much less power-efficient, drawing three to four times as much current. However, they also respond much faster and are able to generate a higher peak amplitude of vibration.

2.4 Firmware Overview

The embedded firmware on each Vibropixel consists of software modules for actuator control, LED control, power management, wireless communications (discussed in Sect. 2.5), and system management. A module for use with the accelerometer is under development for future applications. The firmware was programmed in the Arduino IDE, which provides for an easy-to-install and easy-to-use hardware programming interface.

Signals for controlling the actuators are created onboard the Vibropixels using an actuator envelope generator with controls for attack time, sustain time, amplitude, and decay time. A secondary function we refer to as *oscillation generation* helps with minimizing wireless transmissions as well as providing for the creation of more complex stimuli. The oscillation function allows for retriggering the actuator envelope generator at frequencies ranging from 0.01 to 30 Hz. Oscillation envelope controls allow for shaping the amplitude of the output from the actuator envelope generator, with controls for attack time, decay time, and overall length of oscillation.

As the primary function of the LEDs is to provide a visual reference of the current amplitude of vibration, controls are provided for selecting the LED colour as well as for scaling the brightness of the LEDs relative to the vibration amplitude. Figure 2 shows a sample user interface which provides controls for the actuator envelope generator, the oscillation parameters, and the LED parameters. The interface also provides a simple visual feedback regarding the expected output of the current settings.

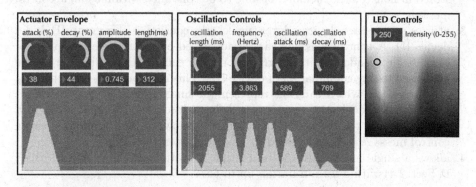

Fig. 2. A sample user interface which provides access to the control parameters used in *Haptic Field*, as well as visual feedback regarding the current settings.

2.5 Wireless Communication Implementation

The design of our wireless network grew out of the requirements of creating a highly scalable system with no limit on the number of receivers. To accomplish this, our system consists of Vibropixels which act as passive receivers and transmitters which relay control messages from a central computer. One of our

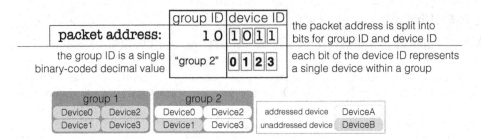

Fig. 3. A simplified depiction of the Vibropixel addressing scheme. In this example, the 6-bit address 101011 indicates the message is addressed to devices 0, 2, and 3 in group 2.

primary concerns was to minimize the number of wireless transmissions as our target applications could require many hundreds of receivers. To accomplish this, the system we created:

1. does not require hand-shaking between client and server devices in order to establish the network.
2. does not utilize packet acknowledgement capabilities which allow for confirmed packet transmission. Due to the fact that there is no guarantee that a particular control message will be received by its intended recipients, our implementation requires that each control message be entirely self-contained. All device settings and parameters are either set in firmware, permanently stored in non-volatile memory, or able to be contained within a single control message.
3. utilizes a two-stage device addressing scheme consisting of a group ID and a device ID. A control message can be addressed either a single group ID, or can also be broadcasted to all groups. Within each group, a message can be addressed to any combination of device IDs. This is accomplished by utilizing a device ID in which each bit represents a single device. If that bit is set high then the device it represents is being addressed; if the bit is set low, the device is not addressed. This scheme, as shown in Fig. 3, allows a single control message to be addressed to several devices.
4. allows a single message to create multiple vibration envelopes (as described in Sect. 2.4) with a total duration up to 65 s.

3   Artistic Creation with the Vibropixels

Many considerations affect the ability of a hardware system to support the artistic creation process. In this section, we will discuss these considerations, the artistic creation process in *Haptic Field*, and our ongoing work to facilitate the use of the Vibropixels in other artistic contexts.

3.1   Artistic Creation with Digital Hardware Systems

One of the primary challenges of designing hardware systems for artistic applications is the definition of design requirements. In their overview of software engineering practices in the creation of interactive art, Trifonova et. al found that frequently "requirements are difficult to capture, vague at the beginning and frequently changeable" [10]. This is largely due to the exploratory nature of much of the artistic creation process, in which inspiration comes as much from the unanticipated consequences of a system's behaviour as from the intended results. One consequence of this, as Trifonova et. al found, is that artists are often interested in expanding their knowledge of software engineering in order to increase their ability to experiment with digital systems.

Considering that many artists will not possess the technical knowledge to program a system directly, Colin Machin argues that one way of facilitating artistic exploration is the creation of simple application-specific programming languages [6]. These can serve as a kind of middle-layer, providing the artist with the ability to change the system's parameters while shielding them from the underlying complexity. While Machin described these languages as potentially being structured like the BASIC programming language, in our experience developing application-specific tools in common new media programming languages such as Max/MSP or Processing can serve the same function of shielding the user from the system's complexity while also allowing them to control the system's parameters algorithmically.

However, the creation of these tools is a research area in itself. Ben Shneiderman argues that the proper design of software tools can facilitate the creative process, and proposed a set of design principles to assist in this, which include supporting exploratory search, providing rich history-keeping, and designing with low thresholds, high ceilings, and wide walls [9]. While Shneiderman's work is focused on the creation of software systems, these principles also suggest ways of structuring interactions with hardware tools. Supporting exploratory search, for example, might suggest the creation of multiple representations of system parameters, encouraging different perspectives on working with it. Providing rich history-keeping is particularly important for exploratory processes, giving the ability to locate and recall the results of earlier explorations.

Shneiderman's principle of designing with low thresholds, high ceiling, and wide walls corresponds most closely with the arguments of Machin and Trifonova et al. This principle suggests that a system should provide for interaction and control of the system which is commensurate with the knowledge and intention of the user. In order to accommodate a wide range of users, it is common to attempt to provide an entry point for users with little technical skill, but also allow for access to lower-level parameters and functionality when required. Wide walls refers to a system providing a range of functionality for solving application-specific challenges, minimizing the need for the use of additional systems to fulfill application requirements.

One example of the support of these principles in the music domain is *libmapper*, a software tool for creating relationships between sensor data from hardware control interfaces and music synthesis parameters [8]. A complete set of these relationships is often referred to as a *mapping*. In this software, available input and output parameters automatically populate the left and right sides of a GUI, respectively, and users are able to create arbitrary connections between them using click-and-drag techniques. While creating effective mappings is a challenging task, the software GUI allows for quickly and easily iterating through possible combinations of input and output parameters. In addition, once a connection has been made, an additional set of advanced parameters allow for mathematical and algorithmic transformations of the data between the input and output devices.

In the next sections, we will consider the ways in which the concepts described above manifest in how artists are able to interact with the Vibropixels.

3.2   The Creation of *Haptic Field*

As our primary focus is not user interaction design but rather hardware system development, and our collaborators are fluent with new media software creation tools, we chose to focus on making the system easy to modify rather than attempting to create a fixed user interface. As described in Sect. 2, the system utilized in the creation of *Haptic Field* is comprised of four elements: the hardware architecture, the firmware, the communication protocol, and software tools for generating control messages. Many of the design decisions for each of these components were made explicitly to facilitate modification and programming of the system by our collaborators: the user interface was created in the popular multimedia programming language Max/MSP; the communications protocol was documented and communicated to our collaborators so that they could program alternative user interfaces for generating control messages; and the firmware was programmed in the Arduino IDE as many artists are familiar with working in that environment.

Following the initial public presentation of *Haptic Field*, we interviewed our artistic collaborators in order to ascertain how they interacted with the system's components and the software tools we provided. In particular, we were interested in when components were used as-is, and when they were used as the basis for modifications. The components and tools we provided them and their use is as follows:

1. *Hardware implementation:* Various iterations of the Vibropixels throughout the prototyping and development stages.
   Use: The Vibropixel hardware was not presented to our collaborators as a development platform, but as a fixed hardware configuration, and in general was used as such in the creation of the work. However, for the final artwork 12 Vibropixels were modified to create permanently installed ambient lighting. For this purpose, they were modified to accept power from a DC power supply, and hung from the ceiling of the installation space.
2. *Firmware:* Various iterations of the Vibropixel firmware developed in the Arduino IDE were provided.

Use: While our collaborators did look at the firmware provided to them, they did not modify it or use it to increase their understanding of the system.

3. *Written Documentation:* Written documentation of the wireless protocol and the control message structure.

   Use: The documentation was used to help conceptualize the structure and capabilities of the system. While the description of the control messages did aid in the creation of control messages without using the provided GUI, our collaborators added that conversations with the system's developers were perhaps more helpful in that task. It is clear, however, that the majority of the control messages were created with the software GUI as described below.

4. *Software Tool:* A software abstraction programmed in Max/MSP which accepted control messages and formatted them correctly for wireless transmission.

   Use: Used as intended, and not modified.

5. *Software Tool:* A simple software GUI programmed in Max/MSP for changing control parameters for the Vibropixels. The GUI provided for the development of *Haptic Field* was similar to that shown in Fig. 2, but without any visual representation of the envelopes and oscillation.

   Use: Used as the primary interface for exploring the functionality of the system as well as for creating control messages in the final composition. Various modifications were made during the creation process, including: adding support enabling a MIDI keyboard to control device parameters and send control messages to individual Vibropixels; adding algorithmic processes to transform device parameters over time; and adding functionality for receiving control messages from external software controlling the progression of the composition.

6. *Software Tool:* A software GUI programmed in Max/MSP for generating device addresses in the format described in Sect. 2.5.

   Use: Used as-is to generate device addresses for both the creation of the work and in the final composition. Modifications were made to allow for algorithmic generation of device addresses, and for receiving control messages from external software controlling the progression of the composition.

From these responses we can see that our collaborators primarily interacted with the highest level software tools provided to them. While the documentation of the control message structure did aid in their understanding of the system and the creation of some control messages, time pressure led them to revert to using the provided GUI and directly asking for help. As one of our collaborators reported, "we did look at the documentation but I think at that point we were just trying to get things going and just wanted something as intuitive as possible." Our other collaborated concurred, saying "when there is so little time ... you want to just see things working and you don't want to spend so much time on the software." However, he also mentioned that, given the right context, the ability to work with different layers would be appealing, saying "when you have more time, you're relaxed, and you want to think of something new then I would definitely go and try .. to modify the software and the source code."

While part of our strategy for creating wide walls and high ceilings remains providing direct access to each of the system's components, it is clear that many factors will affect the ability of users to take advantage of that access. Time pressure is one main concern, driving users to use those tools which provide the most immediate access to control of the system, however limited. In addition, users will often utilize those tools which most closely match with their existing knowledge and preferences. However, the ability of a simple modification to the hardware to remove the need for a separate system to provide ambient lighting suggests that access to the individual components remains valuable, but the ability to take advantage of this access is contingent upon time, knowledge, and the complexity of any necessary modifications.

The desire for lower thresholds for getting started with the system was common. One of our collaborators indicated a desire for help documentation such as that provided by Max/MSP, providing small single-function abstractions which would enable him to "copy a little piece and then you change it ... that is the way I'm used to learn things ... [I would like it] if there is a way to make it simpler to approach at first." However, shortly after he added that there is also a need for an interface which allows access to all of the system's parameters, saying "but of course you end up using the big thing because that's what makes it juicy."

Understanding the functioning of the system conceptually presented a challenge. Being presented with a UI which exposes all of the parameters of the system made it so that "you have to really understand the bigger mechanism." While one collaborator said "I remember looking at the documentation very carefully in the beginning... in order to understand how that worked and it was very clear and very important to understand," he continued by saying that it was less useful in the creation process – "and then after it was more like a practical thing, and we were also [working together in the same room]... so I kind of forgot about the documentation, I was looking at the patch and how it worked and just trying things out in the patch."

Our collaborators suggested that one way of helping resolve this challenge would be to provide visualizations of system behaviour, saying as that "it would be useful to have some way of understanding the correlations between the different envelope parameters", a problem we addressed in the creation of the GUI shown in Fig. 2, and also asking for a "visualization of groups ... a top-down representation" of the current state of the system.

Comments such as these made it clear that the lack of visual representations of the system's behaviour as well as the layout of the software tools negatively affected the user's exploration of the system – "the tools at the software level could have been more intuitive in framing the paradigm ... some of the stuff could have remained under the hood ... and the more generalizable parameters, amplitude, colour, intensity of the RGB channels, the oscillation features, those things could have been marked out more clearly to use them more creatively."

3.3   Facilitating Use of the System in Other Artistic Works

One of our goals was for the system to be suitable for use in a variety of artistic and research applications, and several such projects have been on-going since the initial public presentation of *Haptic Field*. Development of the various components of the system is ongoing, and our goal is to build upon our prior experience to enhance the system's ability to support these projects. In this section we will discuss several development strategies and the ways in which they engage with Shneiderman's principles.

The creation of a new software GUI to lower the barrier to entry is one ongoing development. Figure 2 shows the current implementation, which takes into account our collaborators' requests for visual feedback of the interactions between actuator envelope and oscillation parameters, and also groups the controls in a way which makes their relationships clearer. While we remain focused on hardware development, we are also working with our collaborators on the creation of visualizations to provide feedback regarding the spatial distribution of multiple Vibropixels, and to provide a real-time visualization of vibration amplitude for the whole system.

Several aspects of the Vibropixel hardware are in development, including independent control of the two motors as well as the use of the accelerometer. While we are striving to use conceptually simple implementations for these aspects, their interaction with other aspects of the system can lead to complex behaviours. To assist in their use, we are planning on creating presets fixed in firmware which provide immediately useable settings. In addition, we are going to provide software tools providing access to each aspect's parameters as well as providing visual feedback regarding the current state of the system.

As we saw in *Haptic Field*, simple hardware modifications can allow for implementing functionality outside of the Vibropixel's intended use, preventing users from needing to integrate additional systems into their application. To assist in this, we are planning on a hardware revision which provides access to unused microcontroller pins, providing additional analog inputs for reading external sensors and allowing for communicating with other digital modules using protocols such as I2C and UART. While most applications using these pins will need firmware revisions, we also plan on building into the standard Vibropixel firmware support for basic functionality, such as using analog sensor data to control actuator vibration.

4   Conclusion

In this paper we have presented a description of the Vibropixel system as used in the artwork *Haptic Field*, and a discussion of the ways in which the system supports the artistic creation process. While our focus has been on artistic applications, much of the discussion is equally applicable to other research applications which could utilize a tactile display system. In particular, Shneiderman's principles which we have focused on arose out of work on creativity and innovation across disciplines including engineering, research, and media [9]. The observations we have made regarding our collaborator's use of our system, therefore, should be of interest to the designers of tactile display systems in other collaborative contexts.

Acknowledgment. This research was funded by a grant from the Quebec Fonds Société et culture, a Natural Sciences and Engineering Research Council of Canada grant for the second author, and the Centre for Interdisciplinary Research in Music Media and Technology.

References

1. Bach-y-Rita, P., Kercel, S.W.: Sensory substitution and the human-machine interface. Trends Cogn. Sci. **7**(12), 541–546 (2003)
2. de Vries, S.C., van Erp, J.B.F., Kiefer, R.J.: Direction coding using a tactile chair. Appl. Ergon. **40**(3), 477–484 (2009)
3. Lamontagne, V., Hattwick, I., Franco, I., Giordano, M., Egloff, D., Martinucci, M., Salter, C., Wanderley, M.M.: The Ilinx Garment: whole-body tactile experience in a multisensorial art installation. In: Proceedings of the International Symposium on Electronic Arts (2015)
4. Lemmens, P., Crompvoets, F., Brokken, D., Eerenbeemd, J.V.D., Vries, G.J.D.: A body-conforming tactile jacket to enrich movie viewing. In: Proceedings - 3rd Joint EuroHaptics Conference and Symposium on Haptic Interfaces for Virtual Environment and Teleoperator Systems, World Haptics, pp. 7–12 (2009)
5. Lindeman, R.W., Page, R., Yanagida, Y., Sibert, J.L.: Towards full-body haptic feedback: the design and deployment of a spatialized vibrotactile feedback system. In: Proceedings of the ACM Symposium on Virtual Reality Software and Technology, pp. 146–149 (2004)
6. Machin, C.H.C.: Digital artworks: bridging the technology gap. In: Proceedings of the IEEE Eurographics UK Conference, pp. 16–23 (2002)
7. MacLean, K.E.: Haptic interaction design for everyday interfaces. Rev. Hum. Factors Ergon. **4**(1), 149–194 (2008)
8. Malloch, J., Sinclair, S., Wanderley, M.M.: Distributed tools for interactive design of heterogeneous signal networks. Multimedia Tools Appl. **74**(15), 5683–5707 (2014)
9. Shneiderman, B.: Creativity support tools: accelerating discovery and innovation. Commun. ACM **50**(12), 20–32 (2007)
10. Trifonova, A., Jaccheri, L., Bergaust, K.: Software engineering issues in interactive installation art. Int. J. Arts Technol. **1**(1), 43–65 (2008)
11. Van Erp, J.B.F., Self, B.: Tactile displays for orientation, navigation and communication in air, Sea and land environments. Technical report, NATO Research and Technology Operation, Neuilly-Sur-Seine, France (2008)
12. van Erp, J.B.F., van Veen, H.A.H.C., Jansen, C., Dobbins, T.: Waypoint navigation with a vibrotactile waist belt. ACM Trans. Appl. Percept. **2**(2), 106–117 (2005)

Image-Based Active Control for AEM Function of ARM-COMS

Teruaki Ito[1]([⊠]) and Tomio Watanabe[2]

[1] Tokushima University, 2-1 Minami-Josanjima, Tokushima 770-8506, Japan
`tito@tokushima-u.ac.jp`
[2] Okayama Prefectural University, 111 Tsuboki, Souja, Okayama 719-1197, Japan
`watanabe@cse.oka-pu.ac.jp`

Abstract. This study has proposed an idea of remote individuals' connection through augmented tele-presence systems called ARM-COMS (ARm-supported eMbodied COmmunication Monitor System). ARM-COMS is composed of a tablet PC and a desktop robotic arm. The table PC in ARM-COMS is a typical ICT (Information and Communication Technology) device and the desktop robotic arm works as a manipulator of the tablet. ARM-COMS has three types of functions; namely, autonomous positioning (AP), autonomous entrainment movement (AEM), and autonomous entrainment positioning (AEP), which are the key to connect the remote individuals. This paper mainly focuses on AEM function, which was implemented using a three-steps of control approach, including face detection, landmark detection and face orientation estimation. Reviewing the experimental results using a prototype system based on the three-step approach, the feasibility of this control procedure will be discussed.

Keywords: Embodied communication · Augmented tele-presence robotic arm manipulation · Face detection · Landmark detection · Face orientation

1 Introduction

ICT (Information and Communication Technology) technologies has the potential to further enhance a good communication. TV phone is regarded as a tool in SF movies in the old days. However, the time changed so fast that WiFi based video communication tool is one of the convenient tools which can be available to any of us [1]. On the other hand, it addresses the two types of critical issues, or the lack of tele-presence feeling and the lack of relationship feeling in communication [4].

One of the solutions to the former issue is proposed by several ideas of robot-based remote communication systems; such as physical telepresence robots [8, 21], or an idea of anthropomorphization [13]. Distance communication is supported by the basic functions of physical tele-presence robots, such as face image display of the operator [14], as well as tele-operation function such as remote-drivability to move around [9], or tele-manipulation [9]. However, it is recognized that a gap between robot-based video communication and face-to-face one have not been narrowed yet.

S. Yamamoto (Ed.): HIMI 2017, Part I, LNCS 10273, pp. 529–538, 2017.
DOI: 10.1007/978-3-319-58521-5_41

Recently, a new challenge has been undertaken by an idea of robotic arm-typed systems [24]. For example, Kubi [11], which is a non-mobile arm type robot, allows the remote user to "look around" during their video communication by way of commanding Kubi where to aim the tablet with an intuitive remote control over the net. Furthermore, an idea of enhanced motion display has also been reported [15] to show its feasibility over the conventional display. However, the movement of human body as a non-verbal message from a remote person is still an open issue on robotic arm-typed systems.

Considering the physical entrainment motion in human communication [23], this research challenges the two issues, which are the lack of tele-presence feeling and the lack of relationship in communication [5]. This paper focuses on AEM function, which was implemented using a three steps of control approaches, including face detection, landmark detection and face orientation estimation, of which procedure is also presented in this paper. Reviewing the experimental results using a prototype system, the feasibility of this control procedure will be discussed.

2   Overview of ARM-COMS(ARm-Supported eMbodied COmmunication Monitor System)

2.1   System Overview

ARM-COMS is composed of a tablet PC and a desktop robotic arm. The table PC in ARM-COMS is a typical ICT (Information and Communication Technology) device and the desktop robotic arm works as a manipulator of the tablet, of which position and movements are autonomously manipulated based on the behavior of a human user. This autonomous manipulation is controlled by the head movement of a master person, which can be recognized by a portable device, such as a Kinect [10] sensor, or a general USB camera, and its detected signals are transferred to the PC under which ARM-COMS is controlled.

A prototype system of ARM-COMS is shown in Fig. 1, where a 5-DOF robotic arm is the key manipulator which controls the movement of table PC. The robotic arm can be controlled by the acceleration sensor attached to the human subject [6]. Feasibility experiments in remote communication with/without ARM-COMS were conducted and its positive effects were recognized. Since the physical sensor was attached to the human subject in this prototype, non-contact type of motion sensor was also tested based on the hand gesture manipulation [7]. Using a hand gesture, which is based on more wide range of movement, motion control of ARM-COMS was analyzed. As the result of experiments, ARM-COMS could mimic the hand gesture motion based on the motion sensor control, using the three types of hand gestures which shows nodding, head-shaking, and head-tilting of head gesture.

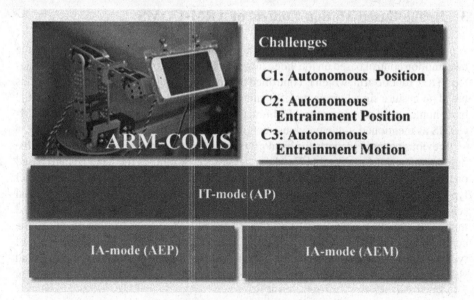

Fig. 1. Overview of ARM-COMS

2.2 IT/IA Modes with AP/AEM/AEP Functions of ARM-COMS

ARM-COMS operates as an intelligent ICT system in *IT-mode* as well as an intelligent avatar system in *IA-mode* (Fig. 1).

Considering the user's physical position, AP (Autonomous Position) function of *IT-mode* enables the tablet PC autonomously and automatically to take an appropriate position towards the user (Challenge 1). For example, ARM-COMS moves the tablet PC closer to the user when a phone call comes in.

ICT devices allow us to communicate with others over the network. However, there is a significant difference in communication between the face-to-face communication and the video communication. It is reported that sharing the same physical space and atmosphere among the participants typically plays a key role in human communication. Since the entrainment is associated with physical movement of a person [20], AEM (Autonomous Entrainment Motion) function of *IA-mode* enables physical movement of the tablet PC during remote communication for entrainment acceleration by mimicking the head movement of its master person (Challenge 2).

In addition to the head movement of a remote person, AEP (Autonomous Entrainment Position) function of IA-mode enables to express of relationship between the persons by the determination of appropriate distance (Challenge 3).

3   Image-Based Motion Control of ARM-COMS

A prototype of ARM-COMS system has been developed to study the feasibility of the head motion control based on the video image [18]. The prototype system adopts a table-top 5 DOF robotic arm, which is controlled by a microcontroller using simple commands based on gesture signals from an USB camera. The prototype is designed to mimic the basic human head motion as the AEM function, which is one of the challenges of ARM-COMS as mentioned in the previous session.

Previous paper [7] reports the hand gesture motion using ARM-COMS based on the finger motion sensor control [12], where ARM-COMS mimics the hand gesture based on the signals from the sensor. This type of finger motion control sensor is a non-contact type and easy to use. However, it is not so convenient for the user to prepare a special sensor, which is required to detect the hand motion. Therefore, in this experiments, head motion of a human subject was traced by a general USB camera, which generates the control code of AMR-COMS to mimic the head motion. Focusing on the two types of typical human head gestures, namely, nodding motion for affirmative meaning and head shaking motion for negative meaning, the experimental setup was designed as shown in Fig. 2.

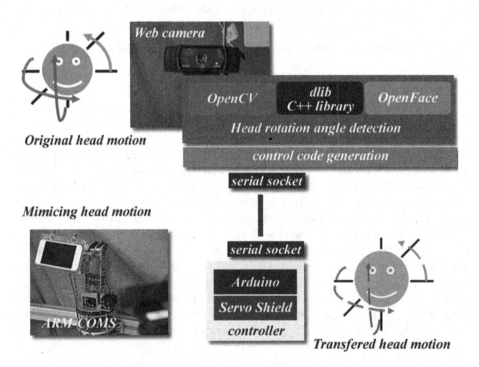

Fig. 2. Configuration of ARM-COMS prototype

Face detection procedure of a prototype of ARM-COMS is based on the algorithm of FaceNet [19], which includes image processing library OpenCV 3.1.0 [16], machine learning library dlib 18.18 [2], and face detection tool OpenFace [17] which were installed on a control PC with Ubuntu 14.04 [22] as shown in Fig. 2. Using the input image data from USB camera, landmark detection is processed.

The control procedure is based on the following three steps, which include the face detection, the landmark detection and the face orientation estimation.

The face detection narrows the face area captured by the USB camera. Using an extracted face image by open CV library [16], outline contour of the face is generated as shown in Fig. 3, which is used in landmark detection in the second step.

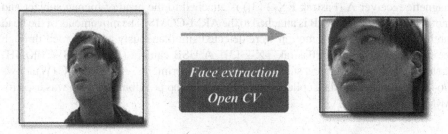

Fig. 3. Face extraction

The landmark detection captures the 68 landmarks defined the face as shown in Fig. 4. This facial landmark detection of 68 points is detected using dlib library [2].

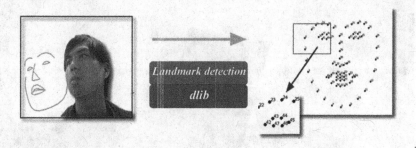

Fig. 4. Landmark detection

The face orientation estimation determines the orientation of the face. OpenFace [17] enables the calculation of rotational angles of roll-pitch-yaw by three dimensional co-ordinates of landmark points based on a perspective n-point (PnP) techniques as shown in Fig. 5.

Then control codes using roll-pitch-yaw angles are sequentially generated and transferred to ARM-COMS via serial sockets connecting the PC and the controller.

Head-motion of a human subject is detected and traced according to the movement of the subject. In order to evaluate the traceability of ARM-COMS, motion control

Fig. 5. Face orientation

experiments were conducted. Figure 6 shows the snapshot of experimental set-ups. A magnetic receiver A (Fastrak RX-2 [3]) is attached to the head of human subject and another magnetic receiver B is attached to the ARM-COMS. The movements of the head motion and ARM-COMS motion were detected simultaneously and recorded through the magnetic transmitter (Fastrak TX-2 [3]). A USB camera (Buffalo BSW20K04H) captures the image of human subjects during the experiments. A desktop PC (Windows 7/64) was used for the data collection, whereas a laptop pc (Ubuntu 14.04) was used for ARM-COMS control.

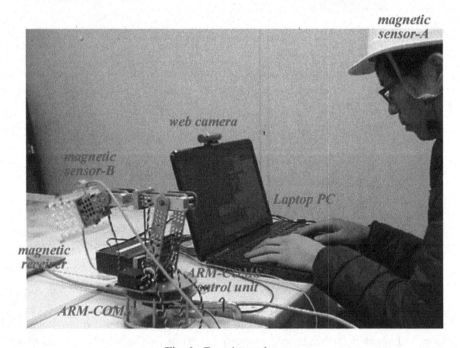

Fig. 6. Experimental setup

Experimental procedure:

Step 1:   Three nodding with over a period of one second each, followed by another three nodding with over a period of two seconds each, and another three nodding with over a period of three seconds each.

Step 2:   Three head shaking with over a period of one second each, followed by another three head shaking with a period of two seconds each and another three head shaking with a period of three seconds each.

Figure 7 shows the nodding gesture in head motion. The red line shows the time series variation of head angles in nodding gesture conducted three times in a consecutive manner, whereas the green line shows time series variation of pitch angles of the corresponding ARM-COMS motion. The graph shows that ARM-COMS mimics the head nodding motion quite well.

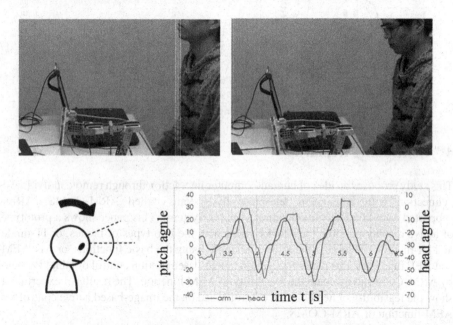

Fig. 7. Analysis of nodding motion (Color figure online)

Figure 8 shows the head shaking gesture of head movement. The red line shows the time series variation of head shaking gesture conducted three times in a consecutive manner, whereas the green line shows the time series variation of corresponding ARM-COMS motion. As seen from the graph, the ARM-COMS mimics the head shaking motion very smoothly.

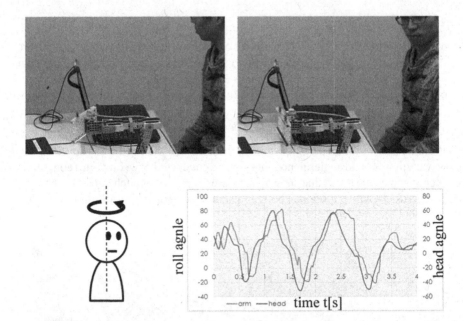

Fig. 8. Analysis of head shaking motion (Color figure online)

4   Concluding Remarks

This study proposes an idea of human-computer interaction through remote individuals' connection with augmented tele-presence systems called ARM-COMS (ARm-supported eMbodied COmmunication Monitor System). This paper shows a prototype of active display monitor for ARM-COMS with the two types of modes, or IT-mode and IA-mode. Considering the three challenges using the basic functions, or AP, AEM and AEP functions, this paper focuses on image-based motion control of tablet PC held by ARM-COMS to evaluate the feasibility of AEM function. The results of experiment show the feasibility of head motion control based on the image-based active control for AEM function of ARM-COMS.

Acknowledgement. This work was supported by JSPS KAKENHI Grant Numbers JP16K00274, JP26280077. The author would like to acknowledge Hiroki KIMACHI, and all members of Collaborative Engineering Labs at Tokushima University, and Center for Technical Support of Tokushima University, for their cooperation to conduct the experiments.

References

1. Abowdm, D.G., Mynatt, D.E.: Charting past, present, and future research in ubiquitous computing. ACM Trans. Comput. Hum. Interact. (TOCHI) **7**(1), 29–58 (2000)
2. Dlib c ++ libraty. http://dlib.net/
3. FASTRK. http://polhemus.com/motion-tracking/all-trackers/fastrak
4. Greenberg, S.: Peepholes: low cost awareness of one's community. In: Conference Companion on Human Factors in Computing Systems: Common Ground, Vancouver, British Columbia, Canada, pp. 206–207 (1996)
5. Ito, T., Watanabe, T.: Three key challenges in ARM-COMS for entrainment effect acceleration in remote communication. In: Yamamoto, S. (ed.) HCI 2014. LNCS, vol. 8521, pp. 177–186. Springer, Cham (2014). doi:10.1007/978-3-319-07731-4_18
6. Ito, T., Watanabe, T.: ARM-COMS for entrainment effect enhancement in remote communication. In: Proceedings of the ASME 2015 International Design Engineering Technical Conferences & Computers and Information Engineering Conference (IDETC/CIE2015), August, Boston, USA, DETC2015-47960 (2015)
7. Ito, T., Watanabe, T.: Motion control algorithm of ARM-COMS for entrainment enhancement. In: Yamamoto, S. (ed.) HIMI 2016. LNCS, vol. 9734, pp. 339–346. Springer, Cham (2016). doi:10.1007/978-3-319-40349-6_32
8. Kashiwabara, T., Osawa, H., Shinozawa, K., Imai, M.: TEROOS: a wearable avatar to enhance joint activities. In: Annual conference on Human Factors in Computing Systems, pp. 2001–2004 (2012)
9. Kim, K., Bolton, J., Girouard, A., Cooperstock, J., Vertegaal, R.: TeleHuman: effects of 3D perspective on gaze and pose estimation with a life-size cylindrical telepresence pod. In: Proceedings of CHI2012, pp. 2531–2540 (2012)
10. Kinect. https://dev.windows.com/en-us/kinect
11. Kubi. https://www.revolverobotics.com
12. Leapmotion. https://www.leapmotion.com/
13. Osawa, T., Matsuda, Y., Ohmura, R., Imai, M.: Embodiment of an agent by anthropomorphization of a common object. Web Intell. Agent Syst. Int. J. **10**, 345–358 (2012)
14. Otsuka, T., Araki, S., Ishizuka, K., Fujimoto, M., Heinrich, M., Yamato, J.: A realtime multimodal system for analyzing group meetings by combining face pose tracking and speaker diarization. In: Proceedings of the 10th International Conference on Multimodal Interfaces (ICMI 2008), Chania, Crete, Greece, pp. 257–264 (2008)
15. Ohtsuka, S. Oka, K.K., Tsuruda, T., Seki, M.: Human-body swing affects visibility of scrolled characters with direction dependency. In: Society for Information Display (SID) 2011 Symposium Digest of Technical Papers, pp. 309–312 (2011)
16. OpenCV. http://opencv.org/
17. OpenFace API Documentation. http://cmusatyalab.github.io/openface/
18. Sato, T., Kanbara, M., Yokoya, N., Takemura, H.: Dense 3-D reconstruction of an outdoor scene by hundreds-baseline stereo using a hand-held video camera. Int. J. Comput. Vis. **47**(1–3), 119–129 (2002)
19. Schoff, F., Kalenichenko, D., Philbin, J.: FaceNet: a unified embedding for face recognition and clustering, In: IEEE Conference on CVPR 2015, pp. 815–823
20. Sirkin, D., Ju, W.: Consistency in physical and on-screen action improves perceptions of telepresence robots. In: HRI 2012 Proceedings of the Seventh Annual ACM/IEEE International Conference on Human-Robot Interaction, pp. 57–64 (2012)

21. Tariq, A.M., Ito, T.: Master-slave robotic arm manipulation for communication robot. In: Proceedings of 2011 Annual Meeting on Japan Society of Mechanical Engineer, Vol. 11(1), p. S12013, September 2011
22. Ubuntu. https://www.ubuntu.com/
23. Watanabe, T.: Human-entrained Embodied Interaction and Communication Technology. In: Fukuda, S. (ed.) Emotional Engineering, pp. 161–177. Springer, New York (2011)
24. Wongphati, M., Matsuda, Y., Osawa, H., Imai, M.: Where do you want to use a robotic arm ? And what do you want from the robot ? In: International Symposium on Robot and Human Interactive Communication, pp. 322–327 (2012)

Effect on Postural Sway of the Invasion to Preferable Interpersonal Distance

Yosuke Kinoe[(✉)] and Saki Tatsuka

Faculty of Intercultural Communication, Hosei University,
2-17-1, Fujimi, Chiyoda City, Tokyo 102-8160, Japan
kinoe@hosei.ac.jp

Abstract. This paper proposed a methodology which allows the detection of characteristic postural sways which relate to the invasion to preferred interpersonal distance. The result of empirical study revealed that, at least in most cases under the condition of standing posture, the characteristic change points of postures which are caused by bodily sway can be identified based on the analysis of body pressure distribution using the biomechanical reference models. This methodology based on non-verbal behavior is also expected to be helpful to analyze problematic phenomena of the invasion to personal space of individuals who have the difficulties of linguistic behavior.

Keywords: Interpersonal distance · Personal space · Methodology · Non-verbal behavior · Body pressure distribution

1 Introduction

The personal space concept is a useful tool to investigate human spatial behavior, and still well established especially in the literature of environmental psychology [3] and related areas. Various attempts are made to broaden the application of personal space. With more than thousand studies reported on personal space, however, many aspects of its details including the relationship with physiological behaviors, are still not clear.

1.1 Intrusion to Preferred Interpersonal Distance

It is well known that unwanted intrusion into personal space leads to psychologically discomfort and then results in a physically explicit behavior such as an unpleasant facial expression and a withdrawal tendency [13]. The question is what happens to individual prior to explicitly expressing unpleasantness.

Preferred, Explicitly Uncomfortable, Intolerable Interpersonal Distances. The present study distinguished the following three different interpersonal distances:

(A) minimum interpersonal distance that individual feels preferable and comfortable,
(B) interpersonal distance that individual begins feeling discomfort consciously and explicitly,

S. Yamamoto (Ed.): HIMI 2017, Part I, LNCS 10273, pp. 539–553, 2017.
DOI: 10.1007/978-3-319-58521-5_42

(C) interpersonal distance that individual begins demanding its withdrawal if other approaches closer (ref. *flight distance* [6]).

Between three characteristic interpersonal distances above, two different types of boundary zones can be defined: (1) the boundary zone AB where individual feels some strange with the distance to the other but doesn't feel discomfort explicitly and (2) the boundary zone BC where individual feels discomfort explicitly but doesn't yet demand withdrawal. Our study focuses on the area where the preferred interpersonal distance is invaded, but individual doesn't yet demand its withdrawal (i.e. between A and C). Especially, we shed light on the boundary zone AB, an important area of maintaining the comfortability.

Non-verbal Method for Capturing Invasion to Preferred Interpersonal Distance. The most commonly used methods to measure personal space are based on stop-distance methods and naturalistic observation methods, which had been widely used and evaluated as feasible techniques for experimental and naturalistic filed studies, respectively [5]. In the use of the stop distance procedure, the subjects are instructed in which an experimenter initially stands two meters from the subject and then slowly walks toward the subject until the subject becomes uncomfortable and halts the experimenter's approach by saying stop. This method is useful to estimate the second category of interpersonal distance (explicitly uncomfortable) and to analyze phenomena in the boundary zone BC. Naturalistic observation methods can be employed to estimate the third category of interpersonal distance (intolerable) which allow the detection of the timing of withdrawal. On the other hand, as for the boundary zone AB in which individual doesn't begin feeling unpleasant explicitly and consciously, it is difficult to analyze spatial behavior by employing naturalistic observation methods which require an observable behavior or the stop-distance method which demands conscious verbal behavior. A non-verbal methodology is expected as a useful approach for investigating phenomena which occur especially in the boundary zone AB.

Objectives. The purpose of our study is to propose a methodology which allows the detection of phenomena which relates to the invasion to preferred personal space by employing a non-verbal method. Especially, we will shed light on phenomena which occurs in the boundary zone AB where individual feels some strange with the distance to the other but isn't aware of feeling discomfort consciously and explicitly.

This basic research is also expected to develop interesting potential applications. In particular, this methodology based on non-verbal behavior will be helpful for us to analyze undiscovered phenomena which relate to the invasion to personal space of person with difficulties of linguistic behavior, or of older elderlies. It also provides a useful basis for developing a technology that improves proxemic behavior of mobile social assistive robots, one of the important design aspect of mobile robots.

1.2   Our Approach

Postural Sway and Body Pressure Distribution at Foot and Buttock. In order to analyze phenomena in the boundary zone AB and BC, we focused on postural sway.

Postural sway was captured by applying body pressure distribution at feet (while standing upright) and buttocks (while sitting) (Fig. 1). By using a pressure sensor array, the body pressure distribution system tracks the center of pressure (CoP) and measures the pressure distribution between human body and support surfaces such as seats and insoles of shoes. Human bodily moves of surface level such as foot and buttock can be analyzed based on the change of pattern of body pressure distribution.

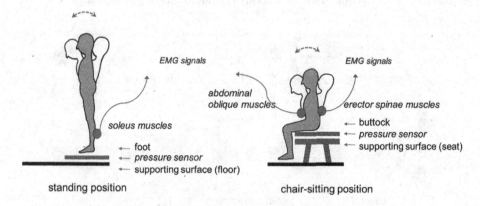

Fig. 1. Sensing postural sway (body pressure distribution and EMG signals)

Pressure distribution technology had been applied to various domains including a posture analysis during exercise and risk evaluation of pressure ulcers based on stress distribution in the gluteus muscles and enveloping fat in the buttocks during sitting for prolong time [2]. The challenge of the present study is to identify dynamic phenomena of very small bodily moves that occur and disappear in a moment.

EMG Signals from the Muscles that Maintain the Posture. Posture maintenance and control are fully dynamic process. The upright or sitting body is an inherently unstable system. In order to capture the electrical signals corresponding to muscle movements of the subject during a postural sway, Electromyography (EMG) was employed. EMG measures electrical activity in response to a nerve's stimulation of the muscle.

We focused on lower-limb muscles (soleus muscle) in a standing position, and back muscles (erector spinae muscle) and abdominal muscles (external abdominal oblique muscle) in a chair-sitting position (Fig. 1). These muscles were selected because they perform a range of functions which contribute the posture maintenance of standing or chair-sitting positions. For example in human standing, as gravity acts on the body to topple the person forwards, the whole body center of mass is typically maintained at a short distance in front of the ankle joints. Two muscles in the back of lower-limb, soleus and gastrocnemius, actively oppose the toppling effect of gravity [9].

Focusing on Standing and Chair-sitting Positions. By taking account into potential applications to situations of social assistance such as a care services for elderlies, we focused on both standing position and chair-sitting position.

Distinction of Different Combinations of Bodily Orientation. Because size and shape of interpersonal distance that individual permits has anisotropy [3, 7], the combinations of bodily orientation and approach angles were controlled and distinguished. Interpersonal distance was measured with the "center-center" model [8] which employs the distance between the vertexes of a participant and an approacher. Figure 2 describes the measurement of interpersonal distance based on the center-center model and the relationship between combinations of bodily orientations and approach angles.

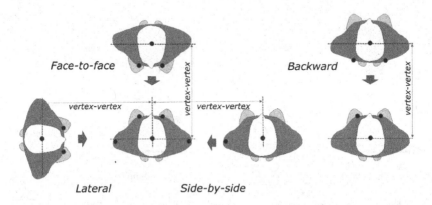

Fig. 2. Measurement of interpersonal distance in each combination of bodily orientation.

1.3 Our Hypotheses

The following hypotheses have been established prior to the present study.

1. When the other intrudes into individual preferred interpersonal distance, individual feels discomfort to current interpersonal distance, and causes a characteristic postural sway other than a verbal report and/or explicit physical behaviors such as an escape or unpleasant facial expression.
2. Postural sways above, verbalization of asking to stop approaching in the use of stop-distance method, and explicit physical behaviors such as an escape can occur at the different timings. Especially, postural sways possibly occur prior to the others.
3. The occurrence of postural sway above can be captured as a characteristic change pattern of CoP (center of pressure) and of body pressure distribution.
4. The occurrence of postural sway above can be captured as a characteristic change of muscular activities of postural maintenance.

2   Empirical Study I

The study I investigated how individual of chair-sitting position causes a postural sway when his or her preferred interpersonal distance is intruded. Body pressure mapping was employed. The experimental design of the study I is shown in Table 1. Under the condition of chair-sitting position, mainly hypotheses 1 and 3 were examined.

Table 1. The experimental design of the study I

Factor		Level	
Within subjects	Combination of posture	2	sitting(*)-sitting, sitting(*)-standing
	Combination of bodily orientations	4	face-to-face, backward from front, lateral direction(**), side-by-side (**)

Note (*): Posture of the evaluator (participant) indicated with (*).
Note (**): The participants were approached from a lateral of dominant hand.

2.1 Method

Participants. Eight healthy university students (3 males, 5 females, age range: 21–23 years) participated. The participants were recruited individually and were informed that the study dealt with spatial preferences. They gave their informed consent before participation in the study.

Setting. The data collection was carried out during daytime, in an empty and quiet class room (6.3 m × 5.5 m with a ceiling height of 3.0 m) of a university located in Tokyo metropolitan area. The brightness was appropriately maintained with an indoor lighting instead of natural light from outside. It took approximately one hour per participant.

Measurements and Experimental Arrangement
Interpersonal Distance. The inter-personal distance between vertexes of a participant and of an approacher was measured by using a laser range finder (BOSCH GLM7000), with the "center-center" model which is described in previous section.

   Body Pressure Distribution. Pressure mapping technology was used to visualize the distribution of contact pressure between human body and a supporting surface of a seat. In study I, each participant was seated in a sheet of fabric on a chair. A sensor sheet of the body pressure recording system (NITTA BIG-MAT, 44 × 48 cm) was interposed between them. The sheet surface was positioned parallel to the ground. Pressure data were originally sampled at 80 Hz, digitalized at 8 bits, then stored by the pressure recording system (NITTA BPMS).

Procedure. According to the experimental design of study I, eight data (2 × 4, see Table 1) under different experimental conditions were obtained per each participant. In each condition, according to the stop-distance procedure, an assistant experimenter initially stood 2.5 m from the participant and then approached the participant, in small steps, at a constant slow velocity (approx. 20 cm/s), one step per two seconds, until the participant began to feel discomfort about the closeness. By saying stop, the assistant experimenter's approach halted. In order to minimize a measurement error, the participant was allowed to make fine re-adjustment of their positions. The distance remaining between the vertexes of the participant and the assistant experimenter was measured. During each session of data collection, a continuous measurement was made from 10 s before the beginning of approach and continued until 10 s after the halt of approach, which lasted for approximately one minute. Each dyad of a participant and an assistant experimenter was not acquaintances. Data collection was performed in November and December 2016.

2.2 Data Analysis

Data collected from eight participants under eight different experimental conditions were analyzed. Each data consisted of a set of (a) interpersonal distance according to the stop-distance method, and (b) pressure distribution between a participant's buttock and a supporting surface of a chair. Pressure distribution data were stored by the recording system for the analysis of pressure mapping including CoP tracking.

2.3 Results

Mean of all the interpersonal distances obtained from all the conditions is 77.05 cm (SD = 24.73). The observed data ranged between 28.0 (sitting-standing, lateral) and 158.0 (sitting-sitting, face to-face). Body pressure mapping system visualized the pressure distribution at a participant's buttocks. Figure 3 shows examples of body pressure mapping under the condition of face-to-face (left) and side-by-side (right), which were captured at the different timings: when a participant said "stop approaching" (namely, *ts*), ts-0.3, and ts-4.0 s for face-to face (Fig. 3-a); ts, ts-4.0, ts-8.0 s for sitting-sitting (Fig. 3-b).

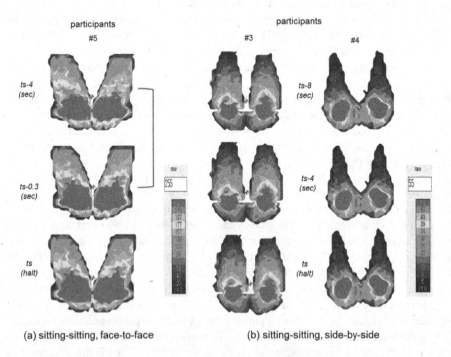

Fig. 3. Body pressure mapping at several timings (face-to-face, side-by-side).

The results of study I revealed that: (a) at least under a specific condition, significant changes of body pressure distribution were observed, for example, between the timings of ts-0.3 and ts-4 s (e.g. participant#5: {sitting-sitting, face-to-face}); (b) in some cases, the above significant changes were identified even before a participant said "stop approaching". In other cases, the above changes were not always observed based on pressure mappings (e.g. participant#3,4: {sitting-sitting, side-by-side}). No characteristic move pattern of CoP could be identified.

3   Empirical Study II

The study II investigated how the invasion of preferred interpersonal distance causes postural sway, based on body pressure distribution and EMG activity. The settings were enhanced to capture postural sway during sitting and standing upright. Hypotheses 1 to 4 were examined. The experimental design of the study II is shown in Table 2.

Table 2. The experimental design of the study II

Factor		Level	
Between subjects	Combination of gender	4	male(*)-male, male(*)-female, female(*)-male, female(*)-female
Within subjects	Combination of posture	3	sitting(*)-sitting, sitting(*)-standing, standing(*)-standing
	Combination of bodily orientations	2	face-to-face, side-by-side (the participants were approached from a lateral of dominant hand)

Note (*): The condition of a participant is described on the left of each pair.

3.1   Our Approach

Biomechanical Reference Model. We developed two biomechanical reference models of the foot and the buttock (Fig. 4) to analyze the relationship between body pressure mapping and a participant's bodily move based on biomechanical structure.

The foot has highly complex structure and functions. Based on MRI/CT scan images (e.g. [1]), subject-specific 3D finite element models of the foot were built to simulate the biomechanical behavior, for example, in order to predict the area characterized by excessive stresses on the plantar surface (e.g. [4]). A contact surface of the foot was first divided based on previous biomechanical studies [10], furthermore, its division was modified with an emphasis on the function of individual digit and plantar arch. Our reference model of the feet (ver. 1) consists of sixteen sections for both sides: big toe (T1); 2nd, 3rd, 4th and 5th toes (T2); forefoot medial (F1); forefoot intermediary (F2); forefoot lateral (F3); midfoot (M); heel (H); and plantar arch (A) (Fig. 4-a).

Some clinical researches recently employed subject-specific 3D finite element models of the buttock based on MRI/CT scan images to study the influence of material stiffness, soft tissue thicknesses and postures onto internal strains (e.g. [2]). The main

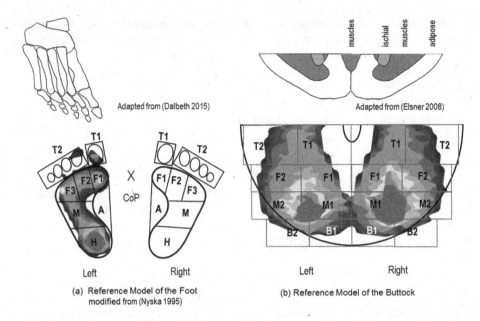

Adapted from (Dalbeth 2015)   Adapted from (Elsner 2008)

(a) Reference Model of the Foot
modified from (Nyska 1995)

(b) Reference Model of the Buttock

Fig. 4. Reference model and biomechanical sections of the foot and the buttock

structures constitute the surfaces of the skin, fat, and muscles and bone (ischial). Based on structural analysis, a contact surface of a buttock was divided into biomechanically useful sections, especially with an emphasis of the position of ischial. Our biomechanical reference model of the buttock (ver. 1) consists of sixteen sections (Fig. 4-b).

Body pressure distribution is calculated according to those biomechanical reference models. Those models can be adjusted to each subject by analogously transforming according to the size and shape of individual feet and buttock.

EMG Activities of the Muscles related to Posture Maintenance. EMG activity on both sides of lower-limb muscles (i.e. *soleus muscle*) in a standing position, and EMG activity on both sides of back muscles (i.e. *erector spinae muscle*) and abdominal muscles (i.e. *external abdominal oblique muscle*) in a chair-sitting position were recorded.

3.2   Method

Participants. Twelve healthy university students (5 males, 7 females, age range: 19–23 years) participated. They reported being usually moderately active. The participants were recruited individually and were informed that the study dealt with spatial preferences. They gave their informed consent before participation in the study.

Setting. The data collection was carried out during daytime, in an empty and quiet class room (6.3 m × 5.5 m with a ceiling height of 3.0 m) of a university located in Tokyo metropolitan area. The brightness was appropriately maintained with an indoor lighting instead of natural light from outside. It took approximately one hour per participant.

Measurements and Experimental Arrangement

1. *Interpersonal Distance.* The inter-personal distance between vertexes of each dyad of participants was measured with the "center-center" model which is described in previous section. The distance was measured by using a laser range finder (BOSCH GLM7000, measurement accuracy ±1.5 mm).
2. *Body Pressure Distribution.* Under the condition of standing position, a participant stood upright barefoot on a sheet on a floor. A sensor sheet of the body pressure recording system (NITTA BIG-MAT, 44 × 48 cm, spatial resolution 10 mm, sensor points 2112) was interposed between a participant's bare feet and supporting surface of a floor. The sheet surface was positioned parallel to the ground. Under the condition of chair-sitting position, the same experimental arrangement of the study I was applied. Body pressure data were sampled at 80 Hz, digitalized at 8 bits, then stored by the pressure recording system (NITTA BPMS) for subsequent analysis. Calibration of the pressure recording was made by the change of bodily positions.
3. *EMG Activity.* Pairs of disposable electrodes were attached over the bellies of the six different muscles. Electrodes over soleus muscles, erector spinae muscles and external abdominal oblique muscles were positioned 2.0 cm apart. The electrodes were connected to a biological amplifier (Guger Technologies g.USBamp). EMG signals were sampled at 1200 Hz, bandpass filtered (5–500 Hz), then stored for subsequent analysis, in addition to REF/GND. Due to a sufficient length of cables, participants' movement was not restricted by the recording apparatus.

Procedure. The data collection was performed by six different pairs of participants (A and B). They were not acquaintances. At first, one of participants (A) took a role of an evaluator and the other participant (B) took a role of an assistant experimenter (approacher). According to the experimental design, a set of six data (3 × 2, see Table 2) under different conditions were obtained per each participant. After all the data was obtained from a participant A, the participants exchanged their roles.

The stop-distance method was employed to measure interpersonal distances. At first, an assistant experimenter initially stood 2.5 m from an evaluator and then approached an evaluator, in small steps, at a constant slow velocity (approx. 20 cm/s), one step per two sec., until an evaluator began to feel discomfort about the closeness. By saying stop, an assistant experimenter's approach halted. In order to minimize a measurement error, an evaluator was allowed to make fine readjustment of their positions. The remaining distance between the vertexes of the evaluator and the approacher was measured. During each session of data collection, a continuous measurement was made from 10 s before the beginning of approach and continued until 10 s after the halt of approach, which lasted for approximately 1.0 min. The data were collected in January and February 2017.

3.3 Data Analysis

Data collected from twelve participants under six different experimental conditions were analyzed. Each data of participant's bodily movement consisted of a set of (a) interpersonal distance, and (b) body pressure captured between a participant's buttock and a chair or between his or her feet and a floor, and (c) EMG signals from the soleus muscles, and erector spinae muscles and external abdominal oblique muscles. Body pressure data were analyzed based on pressure distributions/mapping according to the reference models, CoP tracking, averaged, and temporal reporting.

3.4 Results

Mean of all the interpersonal distances obtained from all the conditions is 75.06 cm (SD = 20.51). The observed data ranged between 36.0 (female-female pair, sitting-standing, side-by-side) and 128.3 (female-male pair, standing-standing, face to-face). Statistical analysis such as ANOVA was performed, however, that is out of scope of the paper.

Figures 5 and 6 show the composite summary charts based on the synchronized data obtained from the participants #5 and #8, under the condition of {standing-standing, face-to-face}. Figure 7 shows the composite summary chart based on the synchronized data obtained from the participant #8, under the condition of {sitting-sitting, side-by-side}. Each chart consists of tracks of elapsed time, interpersonal distance, snapshots of pressure mapping of their feet or buttocks at the timing of characteristic change points, and EMG signals. Figures 5 and 6 include temporal reports of EMG obtained from both sides of soleus muscles, whereas Fig. 7 involves EMG obtained from both sides of erector spinae muscles and external abdominal oblique muscles.

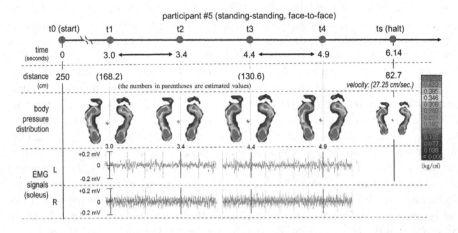

Fig. 5. Temporal change of distance, pressure mapping and EMG signals (participant #5)

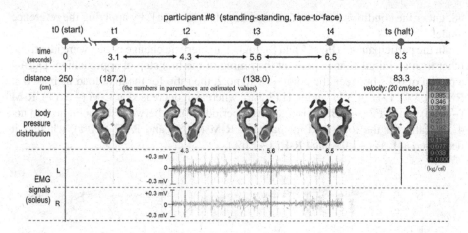

Fig. 6. Temporal change of distance, pressure mapping and EMG signals (participant #8)

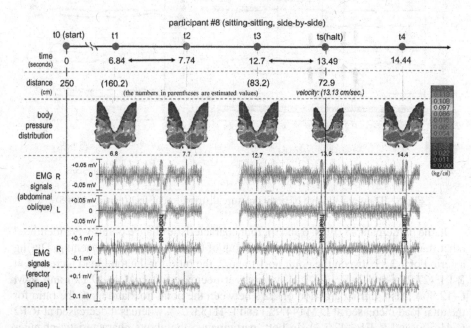

Fig. 7. Temporal change of distance, body pressure mapping and EMG signals (participant #8)

Analysis of Body Pressure Distribution. The characteristic change points of body pressure distribution were identified by detecting the points where the magnitude of the change or the change ratio of load ratio of each biomechanical section for the total load, had significantly increased or decreased during a short period.

Pressure Distribution of Feet While Standing. Figures 8 and 9 show temporal change of body pressure distribution of biomechanical sections of feet of the participants #5 and

#8, under the condition of {standing-standing, face-to-face}, by applying the reference model.

In the participant #5 (Figs. 5 and 8), four characteristic change points were identified other than an initial change point at the timing of the first step of approaching. During a period of 0.4 s between the point no.1 to no.2, the ratio for the total load increased at R-F1 (6.8%), L-H (4.3%), and R-H (3.2%), whereas it decreased at L-M (−6.6%), R-M (−4.0%) and R-F2 (−3.2%). Also, during a period of 0.5 s between the point no.3 to no. 4, the ratio for the total load increased at R-M (2.9%) and R-F2 (1.0%), whereas it decreased at L-H (−1.0%) and R-F1 (−1.6%).

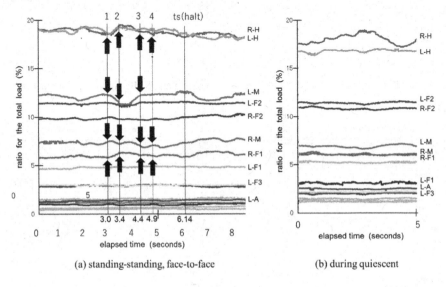

Fig. 8. Temporal change of body pressure distribution of feet (participant #5)

In the participant #8 (Figs. 6 and 9), four characteristic change points were identified other than an initial change point at the timing of the first step of approaching. During a period of 1.2 s between the point no.1 to no.2, the ratio for the total load increased at R-F1 (27.2%) and R-F2 (24.7%), whereas it decreased at L-M (−19.1%) and R-M (−12.8%). Also, during a period of 2.2 s between the point no.2 and no.4, the ratio for the total load increased at L-M (44.9%) and L-H (33.7%), whereas it decreased at R-F2 (−41.5%) and R-F1(−42.7%). In both participants, the above characteristic changes occurred in relatively short period whereas it smoothly changed in longer period while being quiescent (Figs. 8-b and 9-b).

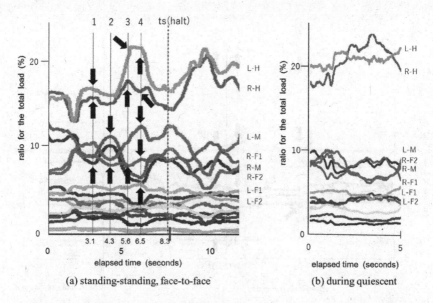

ratio for the total load (%)

elapsed time (seconds)

(a) standing-standing, face-to-face

(b) during quiescent

Fig. 9. Temporal change of body pressure distribution of feet (participant #8)

Pressure Dstribution of Buttocks While Sitting. Figure 10 shows temporal change of body pressure distribution of biomechanical sections of the buttocks of the participants #8, under the condition of {sitting-sitting, side-by-side}, by applying the reference model of the buttock. In the participant #8 (Figs. 7 and 10), four characteristic change points were identified other than an initial change point at the timing of the first step of approaching. During a period of 0.9 s between the point no.1 to no.2, the ratio for the total load increased at L-B1 (28.6%), L-M1 (3.2%), R-M2 (3.1%) and R-M1 (2.2%), whereas it decreased at L-F2 (−9.6%) and R-F2 (−7.5%). Also, during a period of 1.7 s between the point no.3 to no.4, the ratio for the total load increased at L-F2 (10.9%), R-F1 (6.3%) and R-F2 (3.3%), whereas it decreased at R-B2 (−14.3%), L-B2 (−15.4%), R-B1 (−10.5%) and R-M2 (−7.6%). On the other hand, it was almost flat while being quiescent (Fig. 10-b).

Analysis of EMG. Several identifiable characteristic patterns of EMG were found, for example, at soleus muscles, around t3 in Fig. 5, and around t3 in Fig. 6. They were very small changes in EMG activities in short period. Further analyses including frequency analysis are needed to elaborate the criteria of a characteristic pattern of EMG activity during postural sway. Examination of the other group of muscles can also be considered.

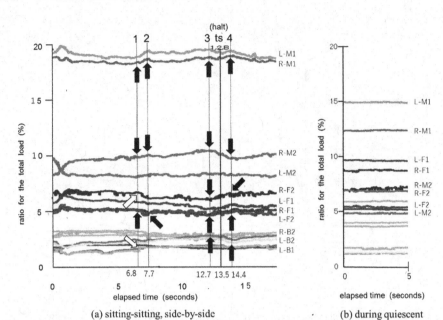

Fig. 10. Temporal change of body pressure distribution of buttocks (participant #8)

4   Discussion

The postural sways observed prior to the verbalization of "stop" involved a very small bodily move that occurred and disappeared in short period. In order to clarify the criteria of detecting a characteristic change of posture during approaching, further detailed analyses of the composite synchronized data based on multiple measurements including video and EMG will be effective. This integrated analysis approach will be also useful to investigate the detailed characteristics and mechanism of the occurrence of small characteristic postural sways during approaching and the emergence of a sort of mild affective state including feelings of discomfort, which are caused by the invasion to preferred interpersonal distance. Our future work involves a further characterization or segmentation of the boundary zone AB (between preferred and explicitly uncomfortable interpersonal distances) and a comparison with methods based on other non-verbal signs such as eyeblinks [11] and cardiovascular parameters including heart rate [12].

5   Concluding Remarks

This paper proposed a methodology which allows the detection of characteristic postural sways which relate to the invasion to preferred personal space. It employed body pressure distribution and EMG.

The results of our empirical study revealed that, at least in most cases under the condition of standing posture, the characteristic change points of postures which are caused by bodily sway can be identified based on the analysis of body pressure distribution using the biomechanical reference models of feet and buttocks. The characteristic change points of body pressure distribution were identified prior to and around the timing of verbalization of asking to stop approaching in the use of stop-distance method, and explicit physical behaviors such as an escape. The present study suggested body pressure distribution is a useful for identifying the effect on postural sway of the invasion to preferable interpersonal distance, however, it was very small bodily move that occurred and disappeared in short period. Further analyses will be needed to elaborate the criteria of detecting a characteristic change of posture during approaching and to verify the mechanism of the occurrence of small postural sway and the emergence of a sort of mild affective state including feeling uncomfortable, which are caused by the invasion to preferred interpersonal distance. This basic research is expected to provide a tool for identifying problematic phenomena of the invasion to personal space of individuals who have the difficulties of linguistic behavior.

Acknowledgments. We thank all the study participants and our lab. members 2016. We thank E. Matsuzaka who devotedly supported for conducting our experiments.

References

1. Dalbeth, N., Deacon, M., Gamble, G.D., et al.: Relationship between tissue stress during gait in healthy volunteers and patterns of urate deposition and bone erosion in gout: a biomechanical computational modelling study. RMD Open (2015). http://dx.doi.org/10.1136/rmdopen-2015-000101
2. Elsner, J.J., Geffen, A.: Is obesitya risk factor for deep tissue injury inpatients with spinal cordinjury? J. Biomech. **41**, 3322–3331 (2008)
3. Gifford, R.: Environmental Psychology, 5th edn. Optimal Books, Colville (2014)
4. Guiotto, A., Sawacha, Z., Guarneri, G., et al.: 3D finite element model of the diabetic neuropathic foot: a gait analysis driven approach. J. Biomech. **47**, 3064–3071 (2014)
5. Hayduk, L.A.: Personal space: Where we now stand. Psychol. Bull. **94**(2), 293–335 (1983)
6. Hediger, H.: Wild Animals in Captivity. Dover Publications, New York (1964)
7. Kinoe, Y., Mizuno, N.: Situational transformation of personal space. In: Yamamoto, S. (ed.) HCI 2015. LNCS, vol. 9173, pp. 15–24. Springer, Cham (2015). doi:10.1007/978-3-319-20618-9_2
8. Kinoe, Y., Mizuno, N.: Dynamic characteristics of the transformation of interpersonal distance in cooperation. In: Zhou, J., Salvendy, G. (eds.) ITAP 2016. LNCS, vol. 9755, pp. 26–34. Springer, Cham (2015). doi:10.1007/978-3-319-39949-2_3
9. Loram, I.D., Maganaris, C.N., Lakie, M.: Paradoxical muscle movement in human standing. J. Physiol. **556**, 683–689 (2004). http://doi.org/10.1113/jphysiol.2004.062398
10. Nyska, M., McCabe, C., Laing, P., et al.: Effect of the shoe on plantar foot pressures. Acta Orthop. Scand. **66**(1), 53–56 (1995)
11. Omori, Y., Miyata, Y.: The effect of interviewer distance on eyeblinks and heart rates of interviewee. Jpn. J. Psychol. **69**(5), 408–413 (1998)
12. Sawada, Y.: Blood pressure and heart rate responses to an intrusion on personal space. Jpn. Psychol. Res. **45**, 115–121 (2003)
13. Sommer, R.: Personal Space: The Behavioral Basis of Design, Updated edn. Bosko Books, Bristol (2008)

Effective Voice-Based Vibration Patterns for Tactile Interfaces

Daiji Kobayashi[✉] and Shun Washio[✉]

Chitose Institute of Science and Technology, Chitose, Hokkaido, Japan
{d-kobaya,b2131880}@photon.chitose.ac.jp

Abstract. Vibration patterns are used for presentation by tactile interfaces such as those of mobile phones. Our previous research clarified the perceptual characteristics of perceivable vibration patterns for the elderly. Then, we proposed application software for creating on/off controlled vibration patterns by tapping the touch screen of a smartphone to enable the user to create identifiable customized vibration patterns. Although Japanese elderly persons found the user interface difficult to use because of their reduced motor ability, our study concluded that the vibration patterns characterized by the pronunciation of the message were easily recognizable by users regardless of their age. This prompted us to develop an easy way to create vibration patterns based on the user's speech. The voice-based vibration pattern, which includes characteristics of the user's pronunciation, was more effective from the viewpoint of the memorability and learnability of the vibration pattern. However, the memorability of a voice-based vibration pattern could be reduced by specific characteristics of pronunciation such as monotonous speech. Hence, this study proposes two additional types of modified voice-based vibration patterns by emphasizing the characteristics of the user's pronunciation. Further, these two new types of vibration patterns were evaluated experimentally in comparison with the conventional type from in respect of memorability. As a result, we found that the user's pronunciation and/or recognition ability rather than the characteristics of the type of vibration patterns could affect the user's performance.

Keywords: Tactile interface · Vibration pattern · Identifiability · Memorability

1 Introduction

In the last decades, tactile and haptic interactions have been studied actively in the discipline of human-computer interaction. In recent years, especially, tactile devices have been developed for musicians to use when interacting with other players or instruments [2, 8]. These studies aimed to determine an effective communication method using tactile devices from which the information is distributed with the aid of the vibration patterns. Further, vibration patterns were considered for using navigation devices to inform the user of the direction [9]. In these studies, the tactile stimuli were two-dimensional and included dimensions such as the intensity and duration of vibrations. On the other hand, Geldard's research involved studying the perceptual characteristics of

© Springer International Publishing AG 2017
S. Yamamoto (Ed.): HIMI 2017, Part I, LNCS 10273, pp. 554–566, 2017.
DOI: 10.1007/978-3-319-58521-5_43

vibration stimuli, referred to as vibratory intensity discrimination, temporal discrimination, and learning curves for communication using "vibratese language" [1]. The letters or some prepositions of the "vibratese language" were formed by using five thoracic buzzes representing vibration stimuli composed of two dimensions such as intensity and duration. In this way, the researchers focused on improving the efficiency of the communication through tactile and haptic sensory modalities. Another important point to consider is the context of use in our daily life. In the case of using vibration stimuli as messages, the user would be required to learn the correspondence between the vibration stimuli and its meanings as well as the situation in which letters are sent by vibration patterns. The larger the number of multiple vibration patterns used, the more learning would be required. However, from the viewpoint of usability and accessibility, the minimization of cognitive fatigue to improve the learnability and discriminability, should consider designing the vibrations according to the ISO/FDIS 9241-940 standard [3]. In addition, the standard recommends "Where available, well known tactile/haptic patterns, which are familiar in daily life, should be used for presenting information." Based on this point, our series of studies about a tactile interface addressed creating more identifiable and memorable vibration patterns [4–7]. We subsequently found that vibration patterns reflecting the user's pronunciation of messages could be the desirable type of vibration pattern. However, creating such a vibration pattern should be easy; therefore, our challenge was to convert vocal sounds into vibration patterns we named voice-based vibration patterns.

2 Creating the Modification of Voice-Based Vibration Patterns

2.1 System for Activating Vibration Mouse

In our previous study, we proposed voice-based vibration patterns using a vibration mouse and our custom converter [9]. This required us to compare the voice-based vibration patterns with the modified types of the vibration patterns. Therefore, the experimental system we used for creating the new voice-based vibration patterns was also built for the previous study and is shown in Fig. 1. The system for generating vibratory stimuli by the vibration mouse consisted of a capacitor microphone (SONY ECM-PCV80U), a personal computer (DELL XPS8300), the converter we had developed, and the vibration mouse.

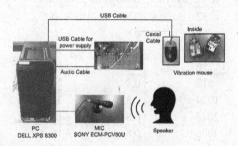

Fig. 1. System for generating vibratory stimuli by the vibration mouse.

The vibration mouse can generate a vibration wave with a larger amplitude than the vibration wave generated by mobile devices such as smartphones, because the vibration mouse was equipped by attaching a vibrating motor (S.T.L. JAPAN CL-0614-10250-7) to a computer mouse (DELL MO56UOA) and can present relatively strong vibration stimuli with an averaged vibrational wave velocity of 2.3 mm/s. The power voltage for activating the vibrating motor attached to the mouse was controlled using the converter and a personal computer running Windows 10 Pro Japanese edition. In addition, the vibration mouse simultaneously functioned as the computer mouse with two buttons and a scroll wheel.

The converter was driven by both the audio signal from the headphone jack and supply voltage (5 V) from the USB (universal serial bus) port of the personal computer. The circuit of the converter was a modification of the circuit of a sound level meter. The audio signal was output by playing a recorded audio file using our custom software and the microphone. Thus, the user had to record his/her pronunciation of notification messages and create the audio files in advance before presenting the vibration patterns as described later. The audio file consisted of data produced by analog-to-digital conversion at a sampling rate of 44.1 kHz with a 16-bit quantization bit rate. The voltage applied to the vibrating motor was supplied from the output jack of the converter.

2.2 Producing Two Types of Modified Voice-Based Vibration Patterns

Our original voice-based vibration patterns were generated by the system described above; however, it was pointed out that the memorability of a voice-based vibration pattern could be reduced by the specific characteristics of pronunciation such as monotonous speech. Therefore, we used the following two approaches to emphasize the characteristics of pronunciation.

The first approach involved playing the pronunciation of notification messages by adjusting the voice-frequency signal of each frequency range. Although we previously tried to emphasize the frequency band of vocals and consonants, i.e., 125 Hz for male speakers and 250 Hz for females at first, greater amounts of surrounding noise was

Table 1. Adjusted frequency bands and the associated gain.

Frequency, Hz	Bandwidth	Gain, dB
32	0.8	−16
64	0.8	−16
128	0.8	−16
256	0.8	−16
512	0.8	24
1024	0.8	32
2048	0.8	−16
4096	0.8	−16
8192	0.8	32
16384	0.8	32

included in the recorded audio files instead and the vibration patterns became indistinctive. Hence, we specially adjusted each frequency range of the voice-frequency signal to emphasize the accent of the pronunciation of notification messages by a few participants. As a result, the frequency ranges were adjusted in accordance with Table 1 for any speakers using our custom software and we named the adjusted vibration pattern the "accent-based vibration pattern."

Another way to emphasize the characteristics of pronunciation was to clarify each phrase included in the pronunciation of notification messages. In other words, we devised a way to ensure that the vibratory length of each phrase became clear. Concretely, data of an audio signal level exceeding the threshold level were converted into data with a frequency of 750 Hz and the amplitude of the frequency was maintained at a constant level using our custom software. In addition, the threshold was adjusted in tune with the loudness of the voice at the time. Therefore, we named this type of voice-based modification a "phrase-based vibration pattern."

The amplitude of the vibrational wave velocity of conventional voice-based, accent-based, and phrase-based vibration patterns was compared by measuring the vibration at the surface of the vibration mouse accordingly as follows. Observing the amplitude of the vibrational waveform, a vibration sensor of a vibrometer (MotherTool VB-8205SD) connected to a digital oscilloscope (Tektronix DPO2024B) was attached to the surface of the vibration mouse as shown in Fig. 2.

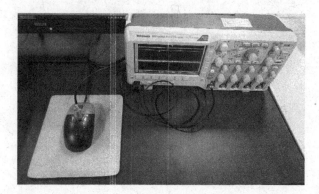

Fig. 2. Apparatus for observing the amplitude of the vibrational waveform presented by the vibration mouse.

Accordingly, we recognized that the vibrational waveform of the voice-based vibration pattern represented the pattern of the speech of messages in contrast to the waveforms of the other types of patterns. Thus, the accent-based waveform seemed to emphasize the pronunciation of the speech as well as the phrase-based waveform as shown in Fig. 3. Further, the amplitude of the vibrational phrase-based waveform seemed to be nearly constant.

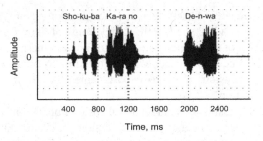

(a)   Voice-based vibration pattern

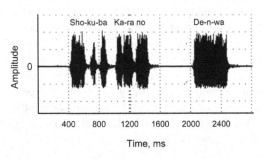

(b)   Accent-based vibration pattern

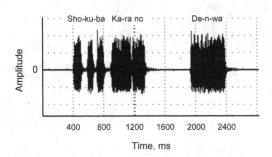

(c)   Phrase-based vibration pattern

Fig. 3. Example of three types of vibrational waveforms on the surface of the vibration mouse that were created from the same speech.

3 Evaluation of the Modified Vibration Patterns

3.1 Method

Overview. We compared the effectiveness of the voice-based, accent-based, and phrase-based vibration patterns in terms of memorability by evaluating these vibration patterns in experiments involving 24 young individuals. Specifically, the participants tried to create the three types of vibratory messages made from the common seven notification messages using the vibration mouse system in advance. The memorability of the respective vibration patterns was measured as follows. The participants tried to correlate the notification messages with the vibratory messages that were randomly presented by the vibration mouse to select an answer from the seven notification messages indicated.

Apparatus. The apparatus consisted of the vibration mouse system described above. However, for the experiments, the noise produced by the vibration mouse was reduced by wrapping the vibration mouse in a blanket on which the participants placed their dominant hand. The participants were then required to listen to white noise with a headphone.

Vibratory Notification Messages for Experiment. The experiment included a step in which a set of voice-based vibration patterns, including the seven notification messages, was created in advance. Considering the context in which vibratory messages are used in our daily life, we decided to produce the seven notification messages for smartphones and consisted of Japanese sentences representing the following: "Call from a friend," "Call from your office," "Call from your home," "You've got mail," "An earthquake," "The appointed time," and "It's going to rain." Especially, the Japanese pronunciation of each of the three notification messages "Call from a friend," "Call from your office," and "Call from your home" is highly similar. Thus, the software described above was used to modify the vibratory messages of the accent-based and phrase-based vibration patterns such that they differed from those of the voice-based vibration patterns.

Participants and Experimental Design. We selected 22 male students ranging from 20 to 24 years of age and two female students who were both 22 years of age as participants and all participants gave their informed consent for participation in advance. In addition, we confirmed that the participants could perceive the test vibration pattern correctly using the vibration mouse in advance. Although the experiment was applied within-subjects design, the 24 participants were divided into six groups including four members for counterbalancing against the order effect. Therefore, in the experiment, the respective groups attempted the voice-based, accent-based, and phrase-based vibration patterns in a different order.

Experimental Procedure. We assumed that creating vibratory messages from the user's voice would be required for using multiple vibratory messages by a smartphone. In this case, a user trying to identify vibratory messages could learn the appropriate way of pronunciation by increasing their experience. In this regard, we surmised that the participant's own way of pronunciation had a profound effect on the memorability of the vibration patterns for the participant. Thus, in this study, we expected the participants to create the desirable vibration messages included in the respective type of vibration patterns. The procedure followed during the trial in which a type of vibration pattern was used, consisted of the following three steps.

First, using the recording window shown in Fig. 4, participants were required to create seven vibratory messages of voice-based vibration patterns as identifiable and/or memorable as possible. Therefore, participants uttered the notification messages separately into the microphone to create the voice recordings. After recording a notification message, the participants were expected to click the check-marked button on the recording window to confirm the memorability of the vibratory message that was produced from their recorded voice. The vibratory message was presented on the vibration mouse. Then, the participants could record their voice again by clicking the microphone symbols included in the recording window if they wanted or tried to create a more identifiable and/or memorable vibration message. In this regard, the notification message the participant was required to pronounce was randomly selected and indicated on the microphone symbol in the recording window.

Fig. 4. Window for recording a notification message as a feature of our custom software. The Japanese notification message on the buttons are presented in the English alphabet for descriptive purposes.

Second, the participants were expected to learn the extent to which the notification messages corresponded to the vibration patterns by using the learning window indicated by the software. The learning window included seven buttons indicating the different notification messages and a "Next" button in the lowest part of the window as shown in Fig. 5. Using this window, the participant could present the vibratory message on the vibration mouse by using the mouse to select a button on the screen. Participants could learn the correspondence between the vibratory message and the notification message repeatedly until they internalized the relations. After the learning procedure, the participants clicked the "Next" button to progress to the last step upon which the learning window on the screen was replaced with the trial window as shown in Fig. 6.

After allowing participants to relax for a while, the seven vibration patterns were randomly presented to each of the participants separately. The participants tried to correlate the messages with the vibration patterns by using the vibration mouse to select the answer from seven notification messages as shown in Fig. 6. Participants' answers were recorded by the software and their opinions about the memorability of the respective vibration patterns were further assessed in an interview after all the trials.

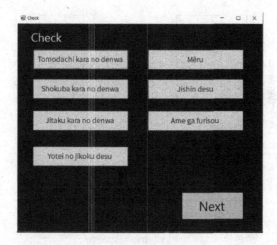

Fig. 5. Window for learning seven different notification messages. The respective Japanese notification messages on the buttons are presented in the English alphabet for descriptive purposes.

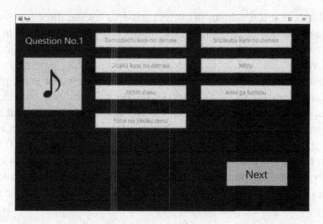

Fig. 6. Trial window for testing seven vibratory messages. The respective Japanese notification messages on the buttons are presented in the English alphabet for descriptive purposes.

3.2 Results

Number of Correct Answers. We measured the memorability of the notification message of the vibration pattern by counting the number of correct answers by the participants under three conditions, namely the use of voice-based vibration patterns, the use of accent-based vibration patterns, and the use of accent-based vibration patterns using the results of the trials conducted on the first day. As a result, the average number of correct answers using the respective vibration patterns was distributed as shown in Fig. 7.

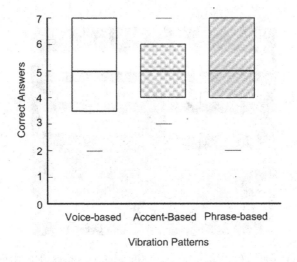

Fig. 7. Distribution of the number of correct answers using three types of vibration patterns.

Figure 7 shows that the median of correct answers for the three types of vibration patterns is almost the same. In addition, the number of correct answers in the case of using voice-based vibration patterns averaged 4.96 (SD = 1.76), although the number of correct answers in the case of using accent-based vibration patterns averaged 4.88 (SD = 1.45). Further, the number of correct answers in the case of using phrase-based vibration patterns averaged 5.17 (SD = 1.63). The result of multiple comparisons among these averages, i.e., the difference between the averages of any two conditions was not statistically significant, although each distribution of the number of correct answers was not a normal distribution statistically for a level of significance of 0.05. Thus, we concluded that the memorability of the three types of vibration patterns was almost the same. However, the average number of correct answers under the respective conditions was higher than the result of the previous study despite us including similar and complicated vibratory messages in each vibration pattern.

Participants' Opinions. The results of interviewing the participants indicated that identifiable and memorable vibration patterns largely depended on individuals rather than on the characteristics of vibration patterns. For instance, some participants tried to recognize a vibratory message by counting the phrases included in the vibration patterns. For these participants, the number of correct answers in the case of the phrase-based vibration pattern exceeded those of the other types of vibration patterns. Thus, it is necessary to discuss the perceptual characteristics of the participants and/or the manner in which the memorability of the vibration patterns is affected.

3.3 Discussion

The above results led us to assume that the desirable or identifiable type of vibration pattern was very much in accordance with the participant's characteristics such as their perception and way of recognizing. Thus, we classified the participants into the following three groups: Group A consisted of participants with the highest number of correct answers in the case of recognizing voice-based vibration patterns. Group B consisted of participants with the highest number of correct answers in the case of recognizing accent-based vibration patterns. Group C consisted of participants with the highest number of correct answers in the case of recognizing phrase-based vibration patterns. The number of participants in Group A, B, and C was 9, 7, and 8, respectively, and the number of correct answers for the respective vibration patterns was as shown in Fig. 8.

Figure 8 shows that six out of the nine participants of Group A could answer correctly for all the voice-based vibration patterns, although most of the participants could not recognize all the vibratory messages in the other vibration patterns. Meanwhile, three out of the seven participants could recognize the accent-based vibration patterns correctly and six out of the eight participants in Group C could recognize all the vibratory messages of the phrase-based vibration pattern. In this regard, Group C includes the two participants who could recognize all the vibratory messages in each of the vibration patterns. Except for these two participants, therefore, Fig. 8 indicates that the identifiable and/or memorable vibration patterns varied for most of participants. A participant of Group A said, "I tried to recognize the cadence of the vibratory message as for my speech, but the accent-based and phrase-based vibration patterns have fewer character-istics of the cadence of my speech. So, I was unable to identify these vibration patterns." Based on this participant's opinion, we concluded that the participants who tried to recognize the vibratory message from the cadence of their own speech would not be able to successfully recognize the monotonous phrase-based vibration patterns. On the other hand, three participants of Group C said, "I recognized the difference between vibratory messages by counting the number of phrases." This opinion suggested that it would be difficult for the participants of Group C to grasp the features of the respective vibratory messages by voice-based or accent-based vibration patterns. The participants of Group B said, "In the case of accent-based vibration patterns, the accent of speech was clear and most identifiable." Thus, the participants of Group B could use the accent of speech as a cue to recognizing the vibratory message.

Consequently, the above results suggest that the characteristics of the participant or manner of recognizing the vibratory message could vary and the way of pronunciation for creating the vibratory message could be improved by increasing their experience in any voice-based vibration patterns.

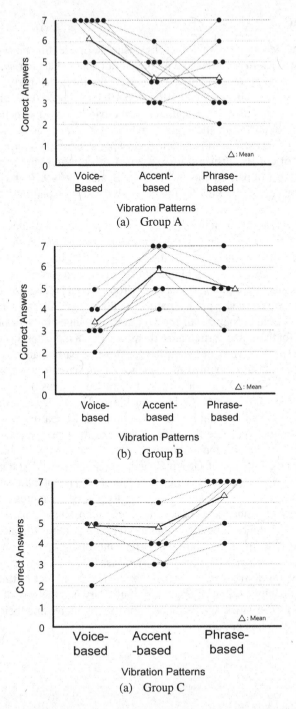

Fig. 8. Number of correct answers by the respective members of Group A, B, and C.

4   Conclusion

The aim of this study was to modify the conventional voice-voice-based vibration pattern to create more identifiable and memorable vibration patterns. Then we proposed two types of vibration patterns by emphasizing the characteristics of pronunciation, i.e., the accent-based vibration pattern, which emphasized the accent of pronunciation, and the phrase-based vibration pattern, which was formed by extracting phrases from recorded speech to produce vibration patterns with constant amplitude. Although the characteristics of these types of vibration patterns differed, we evaluated the memorability of these vibration patterns to compare these metrics with the conventional voice-based vibration pattern through recognition experiments. As a result, we found that the difference among the average number of correct answers when using the three types of vibration patterns was not statistically significant; however, the memorability with respect to the vibration patterns differed among the subjects as well. In other words, the perpetual characteristics of a participant's perception and/or the manner in which they created identifiable or memorable vibration patterns, rather than the characteristics of the vibration pattern, appeared to be effective. Therefore, new types of vibration patterns could be effective for appropriate users. In addition, allowing the user to choose the type of voice-based vibration pattern according to his/her needs seemed to be more effective.

The experimental results revealed that the number of vibratory messages based on a voice-based vibration pattern could be around five. Therefore, our approach to converting speech to a vibration pattern is expected to continue for application to daily contexts in our future work.

References

1. Geldard, F.A.: Adventures in tactile literacy. Am. Psychol. **12**, 115–124 (1957)
2. Giordano, M., Wandeley, M.M.: Follow the tactile metronome: vibrotactile stimulation for tempo synchronization in music performance. http://smcnetwork.org/system/files/SMC 2015_submission_4.pdf
3. ISO/FDIS 9241-940: 2017: Ergonomics of human-computer interaction — Part 940: Evaluation of tactile and haptic interactions (2017)
4. Kobayashi, D., Mitani, H.: Designing memorable tactile patterns. In: Yamamoto, S. (ed.) HIMI 2015. LNCS, vol. 9172, pp. 396–404. Springer, Cham (2015). doi: 10.1007/978-3-319-20612-7_38
5. Kobayashi, D., Nakano, M.: Designing memorable tactile patterns for older adults. In: Proceedings 19th Triennial Congress of the IEA (2015)
6. Kobayashi, D., Takahashi, K.: Designing understandable vibration patterns for tactile interface. In: Yamamoto, S. (ed.) New Ergonomics Perspective, pp. 259–266. CRC Press, London (2015)
7. Kobayashi, D., Nakamura, R.: Designing effective vibration patterns for tactile interfaces. In: Yamamoto, S. (ed.) HIMI 2016, Part I. LNCS, vol. 9734, pp. 511–522. Springer, Cham (2016). doi:10.1007/978-3-319-40349-6_49

8. Schumacher, M., Giordano, M., Wandeley, M.M., Ferguson, S.: Vibrotactile notification for live electronics performance: a prototype system. In: Proceedings of the 10th International Symposium on Computer Music Multidisciplinary Research, Marseille, France, 15–18 October 2013
9. Pielot, M., Poppinga, B., Boll, S.: PocketNavigator: vibro-tactile waypoint navigation for everyday mobile devices. In: MobileHCI 2010, 4 pp. (2010). https://pdfs.semanticscholar.org/2838/7229e7fcf038e48978fb02abcf015980e68b.pdf

Functional Balance and Goal-Directed Eye-Hand Coordination After Exogenous or Endogenous Visual-Vestibular Perturbation: Current Findings and Recommendations for Portable or Ambulatory Applications

Ben D. Lawson[1(✉)], Amanda A. Kelley[1], Bethany Ranes[2],
J. Christopher Brill[3], and Lana S. Milam[1,4]

[1] U.S. Army Aeromedical Research Laboratory (USAARL), Building 6901,
Fort Rucker, AL 36362, USA
Benton.d.lawson.civ@mail.mil
[2] Hazelden Betty Ford Foundation, PO Box 11, BC4, Center City, MN 550122, USA
[3] 711th Human Performance Wing, Air Force Research Laboratory,
Wright-Patterson Air Force Base, Dayton, OH 45433, USA
[4] Laulima Government Solutions LLC, 12565 Research Pkwy #300, Orlando, FL 32826, USA

Abstract. Orientation and balance can be disrupted by a sensory integration or sensorimotor challenge of exogenous origin, including rhythmic alterations in G-force and direction that occur during turbulent flight or travel by sea, as well as a visual-vestibular-somatosensory rearrangement caused by exposure to a moving vehicle simulator or virtual environments. Balance can also be disrupted by an endogenous challenge associated with an inner-ear disease or a head injury affecting peripheral or central balance systems. We sought to determine whether operationally relevant psychomotor performance (a dynamic simulated shooting task) was sensitive to a functional balance challenge caused by the aftereffect of unusual vestibular stimulation or blast/concussion. Seventy healthy subjects and 30 mild traumatic brain injury (mTBI) patients were evaluated with a shooting simulator used for military training. They performed four new shooting tests designed to quantify marksmanship speed and accuracy during tasks similar to established clinical gait challenges. Our exploratory tasks were assessed for their sensitivity to a temporary exogenous challenge (the aftereffect of spinning healthy subjects in a rotating chair to simulate vestibular vertigo) and their sensitivity to imbalance associated with the lingering effect of mTBI. The task that was the most reliable and most sensitive to an exogenous balance challenge was kneeling while shooting at targets to the left and right of the frontal visual field. This test merits further development. We present recommendations for developing this test further and for making the large testing apparatus portable, robust, and capable of expanded quantification of shooting performance, rifle kinematics, and postural sway.

© Springer International Publishing AG 2017
S. Yamamoto (Ed.): HIMI 2017, Part I, LNCS 10273, pp. 567–578, 2017.
DOI: 10.1007/978-3-319-58521-5_44

Keywords: Balance · Vestibular · Shooting · Performance · Concussion · Traumatic brain injury

1 Introduction

Body orientation and balance are maintained by the integration of information from multiple sensory systems. Altered integration of this multisensory information can be elicited by endogenous maladies that alter established sensorimotor relationships (e.g., vestibular injury, disease, or aging), by exogenous alterations of the gravitoinertial force environment (e.g., aircraft flight, travel by sea, acceleration in laboratory acceleration devices, or spaceflight), or by visual-vestibular rearrangements (e.g., exposure to driving or flying simulators). Regardless of which challenge causes altered sensation and control of body orientation and motion, there is an initial period of disruption of functional abilities, leading to disorientation, imbalance, disruption of gaze control, and/or motion sickness symptoms. The process of disruption and subsequent adaptation is similar for patients recovering from certain kinds of endogenous vestibular or balance pathology as for healthy people adapting to the exogenous vestibular challenge posed by exposure to a vehicle simulator or a prolonged voyage at sea or into space [16]. Once adaptation is achieved by sensorimotor recalibration to these new processing demands, coordination and well-being is restored.

We sought to determine whether an exogenous balance perturbation (the aftereffect of body rotation followed by a sudden stop) or an endogenous balance perturbation (the effects of concussion followed by lingering dizziness) would degrade performance of an applied psychomotor performance task requiring postural equilibrium during goal-directed activity. The exogenous rotation perturbation we employed is a challenge to vestibular and balance functioning familiar to any child and has been studied at least since the time of Erasmus Darwin. The endogenous challenge we studied (variously called concussion or mTBI) is strongly associated with dizziness and imbalance in ways described by Lawson et al. [12–14].

The task chosen for study was simulated rifle shooting. While shooting has many degrees-of-freedom as a performance task and is susceptible to learning effects, it is a fundamental skill in many military occupational specialties. While negative findings for shooting performance can be difficult to interpret, when performance decrements are detected for shooting, there is a more direct intellectual pathway to the interpretation of operational or functional significance of the decrement than there is for most other psychomotor tests. Shooting is also a suitable analogue of goal-directed activity requiring balance plus psychomotor or "eye-hand" coordination. The shooting tasks and other methods are described below.

2 Methods

2.1 Participants

Volunteers were evaluated in two studies of exogenous (Study 1) and endogenous (Study 2) balance perturbation. Study 1 included 60 healthy participants (without history of head injury or pathologies affecting balance functioning) from Fort Rucker, AL (mean age 27, SD 5.4; 56 men and 4 women) asked to shoot immediately after a 20-second period of rotation at a constant velocity of 180 degrees-per-second, a stimulus intended to produce a vestibular aftereffect on balance and shooting.[1] Study 2 of endogenous balance perturbation included 40 participants from Fort Benning, GA (mean age 33, SD 6.9; 38 men and 2 women). Thirty of the 40 Fort Benning participants had been patients of a traumatic brain injury treatment center, who had a documented diagnosis of mTBI [1]. Diagnosis was confirmed by their medical history (DD Form 2807) and an interview with our study physicians (Major Timothy Cho and Dr. John Campbell). The remaining 10 Fort Benning participants were healthy (no history of head injury or balance pathologies). While our plan was to compare the Study 1 (healthy Fort Rucker) participants to the Study 2 (mTBI Fort Benning) participants, we included 10 healthy Fort Benning participants as a site-of-recruitment check. To ensure that participants were familiar with military marksmanship, the study recruited U.S. Army active-duty Soldiers, Natural Guard/Reserve Soldiers, or civilians with recent military experience.

2.2 Apparatus

The Engagement Skills Trainer 2000 was employed to evaluate performance following exogenous or endogenous balance perturbation (Fig. 1). The device is a small arms simulator used throughout the U.S. Army for rifle marksmanship training [2]. Shooting was performed with an M4 carbine using iron sights and pneumatically simulated recoil [2]. In the Army marksmanship qualification test using the EST, standard targets appear at virtual distances between 50–300 m, with the furthest targets subtending approximately 0.93° of visual angle. Our dynamic shooting-while-moving tasks were more challenging, so we employed virtual shooting distances of 15–75 m (with the furthest targets subtending approximately 3.72°). This approach made speed of performing accurately our focus rather than raw accuracy and minimized speed-accuracy trade-offs [10]. This approach also was more representative of dynamic, short-range, fast reaction shooting (e.g., during breaching) than long-range shooting would be.

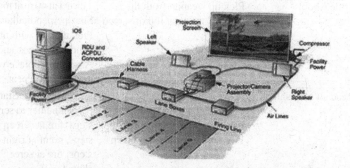

Fig. 1. The EST 2000 apparatus [2].

---

[1] This is a semicircular canal aftereffect that triggers transient post-rotation nystagmus and an illusion of head-reference yaw rotation velocity opposite the direction of chair rotation.

2.3 Psychomotor Performance Tasks

The participants executed four dynamic marksmanship tasks (Table 1) that were designed to be a compromise between the body movements known to challenge postural balance in established clinical balance gait tests and the skills needed to perform operationally relevant military weapons handling tasks. For example, established clinical assessments such as the Berg Balance Scale [3] and the Dynamic Gait Index [19] respectively challenge a patient's ability to pick up objects from the floor or walk forward while turning his/her head in yaw. Similarly, we designed a task requiring participants to pick up a rifle and shoot at a target (called "pick up rifle and shoot"), and a task requiring participants to walk forward and pivot (in yaw) to shoot to the side (called "walk, head-swivel, and shoot"). The full set of tasks is shown in Fig. 2. The initial development of the four tasks and their test properties is detailed in Grandizio et al. [6]. The tasks were designed to challenge balance similarly to established balance tests, but to add a readily quantifiable goal-directed psychomotor performance task of clear military relevance, i.e., shooting. The main measure of shooting performance was shooting throughput, or number of accurate shots per minute. Details concerning the collection and analysis of this measure and the other performance variables collected in our shooting studies is provided in Lawson et al. [17].

Table 1. The four dynamic marksmanship tasks

Task name	Overview	Task description
1. Kneel & shoot	While in a narrow kneeling stance, shoot at virtual targets to the left and right in the frontal visual field	Kneel 229 cm (90 in). from screen, rear knee near front heel. Engage left target, swivel ~30° to engage right target (then left – 10 targets total). Targets at 75 m. Each target visible for 2 s and 2 s elapse between targets
2. Pickup rifle, shoot	Pick up weapon from floor, shoot at target at top of screen	1 target at 40 m at top of screen. Start perpendicular to screen. Pick up rifle with natural bending of neck and head. After firing, place weapon on ground and repeat
3. Walk, head swivel, shoot	Walk while making 90° horizontal plane (yaw) head/rifle turn on every second step. Fire whenever facing screen	Target at 15 m. Start perpendicular to screen, take 2 steps, fire at screen to left, 2 steps, point at right wall, 2 steps, fire at screen to left (2 shots total)
4. Traverse beam, shoot	Walk quickly across the beam while hitting all 4 targets in succession	4 targets at 25 m. Stay on wooden plank 244 cm (96 in) long, 20 cm (8 in) wide, and 2 cm (0.8 in) tall

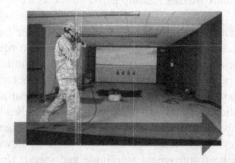

Fig. 2. The shooting tasks, from top to bottom: kneel and shoot; pickup rifle and shoot; walk, turn, and shoot; traverse beam and shoot (cable was kept clear of participant's feet by a metal guide rod not depicted).

2.4 Self-report Data

2.4.1 Perceived Workload
The National Aeronautics and Space Administration Task Load Index (NASA TLX) provides a workload assessment based on ratings for six dimensions, viz., mental demands, physical demands, temporal demands, own performance, effort, and frustration. It was used to assess perceived workload immediately after performing each shooting task. Detailed instructions can be found in the test administration guide [18]. A raw TLX scoring procedure was used [5, 7].

2.4.2 Dizziness
Participants completed the Dizziness Handicap Inventory (DHI). The DHI is a validated questionnaire that estimates functional disabilities related to vestibular dysfunction [8]. The questionnaire consists of 25 items related to the effects of dizziness, including physical (e.g., *Do quick movements of your head increase your problem?*), functional (e.g., *Because of your problem, do you have difficulty reading?*), and emotional effects (e.g., *Because of your problem, are you embarrassed in front of others?*). Answers are scored as *no* = 0, *sometimes* = 2, and *yes* = 4. The highest score possible is 100, with higher scores indicating a greater impairment. These data allowed us to characterize the participants' general daily problems with dizziness.

2.5 Procedures

The study protocol was approved by the Headquarters, U.S. Army Medical Research and Materiel Command Institutional Review Board. Written informed consent was obtained, after which the participants filled out questionnaires concerning daily dizziness etc., before being introduced to the EST weapons simulator. Participants first zeroed the rifle, calibrating the laser sensor to the direction the rifle was pointing. They then completed the Army's standard, relatively static marksmanship qualification test (involving shooting from the standing, kneeling, and prone positions). This permitted them to refamiliarize themselves with basic weapons handling and sight usage, and allowed us to use their static marsksmanship performance as a covariate during subsequent analyses.

Finally, the participants were introduced to the new dynamic marksmanship tasks. A member of the research team instructed participants in the proper execution of each task. Participants then practiced each shooting task prior to obtaining baseline performance data. The ultimate purpose of the shooting tests was to detect abnormal exogenous or endogenous vestibular/balance function, while avoiding sensitization or adaptation of concussion/mTBI patients. It was deemed important to limit head movement among mTBI participants, to avoid triggering unwanted symptoms. Therefore, while three sessions of practice were completed, the first was done at slower speed and with conscious limitation of head movement amplitude and speed. Upon completing the practice sessions, participants performed the dynamic marksmanship tasks. NASA TLX workload ratings were collected immediately following each of the shooting tasks. The performance order of the tasks in the dynamic battery was balanced.

3   Results

The main findings from these studies are summarized as follows:

3.1   We Identified the Most Reliable of the Shooting Tasks

The most reliable task of the four tasks assessed was kneeling while shooting at targets presented to the left and right (~30-degree sweep) of the visual field (test-retest Pearson $r = 0.54$) (Fig. 2).

3.2   We Identified the Shooting Task that Was Most Sensitive to Exogenous Balance Perturbation

Kneeling while shooting was the task that was most sensitive to changes in shooting performance caused by a brief period of rotation-induced dizziness followed by a sudden stop and an immediate shooting challenge (Pseudo R^2 variance accounted = 0.54).

3.3   We Failed to Identify a Shooting Task that Was Sufficiently Sensitive to Shooting Performance Degradation Associated with Endogenous Balance Perturbation

Standard range qualification score (the number of accurate hits recorded during a standard or non-dynamic simulated range qualification task) was included as a covariate in each analysis to help account for individual marksmanship ability among the participants. Preliminary analyses of the dynamic shooting data found that when correcting for standard marksmanship ability, a significant effect [($F(7, 68) = 3.07$, $p = .007$)] remained for the site at which the data was collected (Fort Rucker versus Fort Benning). Therefore, data collection site was also included as a covariate in the analyses. After correcting for variance due to initial (static) marksmanship qualification scores and site differences, a one-way MANCOVA nevertheless failed to detect an mTBI-specific difference in performance, with the overall main effect falling well short of significance [$F(7,68 = 1.42$, $p = 0.13$)].

Despite the failure to find a performance degradation due to the endogenous balance challenge we studied, the mTBI patients did feel dizzier than normal subjects while shooting and reported having to work harder to achieve a level of shooting performance that was comparable to normal subjects. These dizziness and workload findings are summarized below.

A one-way analysis of variance (ANOVA) demonstrated that DHI scores were significantly higher in the injured group than in the uninjured group [($F(1, 79) = 161.56$, $p < .001$)]. Mean and standard error values for both groups are represented in Fig. 3 (note that the values are too small in the uninjured group to be visible in the Figure). The findings confirmed that the injured group was experiencing significantly greater dizziness-related handicaps during their daily activity, according to this established clinical instrument. In the uninjured group, participants' DHI scores suggested no

574   B.D. Lawson et al.

functional impairment (according to DHI clinical cut-offs), whereas DHI scores for the injured group suggested mild-to-moderate impairment.

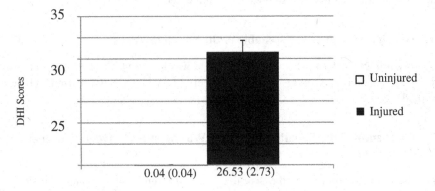

Fig. 3. Mean and standard error for dizziness handicap index (DHI) scores by injury condition. The DHI characterizes dizziness-related impairment during various activities of daily living. Mean DHI Scores by Group were 0.04 (SEM 0.04) for the uninjured group and 26.53 (SEM 2.73) for the injured group.

The mTBI group felt they needed to work harder than the healthy group to achieve comparable shooting scores. There was a significant overall between-subjects effect on subjective workload by condition demonstrating that, in general, injured participants reported significantly higher subjective workload scores than uninjured participants [$F(1, 78) = 14.77$, $p < .001$]. The main effect for condition is represented in Fig. 4.

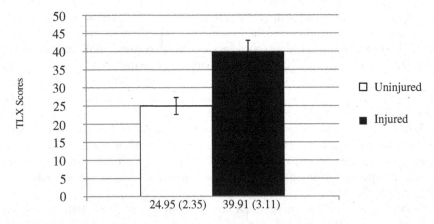

Fig. 4. Mean and standard error for NASA TLX scores by injury condition. Mean NASA TLX scores by group were 24.95 (SEM 2.35) for the uninjured group and 39.91 (SEM 3.11) for the injured group.

4 Discussion

4.1 Conclusions from the Present Study

We developed a prototype battery of dynamic shooting tasks that was intended to quantify goal-directed psychomotor performance during postural balance challenges and to pose a more realistic, operationally relevant balance challenge than traditional, static range marksmanship qualification tests. We then successfully identified a shooting task that was sufficiently reliable and sensitive to an exogenous balance perturbation to merit further refinement and study for potential future testing applications. However, more controlled research will be necessary to determine whether this or any of our other tests can distinguish healthy subjects from those affected by an endogenous balance challenge. The main limitation of our endogenous perturbation research was that our mTBI subjects were drawn from one site and most of our healthy subjects from another. We did not have access to mTBI subjects at our home site of Fort Rucker while initially developing the shooting tests, so we had to recruit our mTBI-affected subjects at Fort Benning during a second study. Unfortunately, the two groups could not be assumed to be from the same population (see Results), probably because the Fort Rucker participants were mostly aviation personnel, while the Fort Benning participants were mostly infantry personnel, who tend to be more practiced at rifle marksmanship.

4.2 Lessons Learned During Experimentation Which Are Relevant to Future Portable or Ambulatory Testing Applications

While the development of portable or ambulatory tests was not the purpose of this particular aspect of our research program, we learned useful lessons during the current study that are relevant to the future development of such portable systems. While the EST 2000 offers a versatile range of fairly realistic range training simulations and is highly relevant to military shooting performance, it required a fair amount of training and practice to use. It also required a utility van and several people to transport, and a large operating space within which to deploy. Furthermore, it required some troubleshooting and repairs during our studies. A portable or ambulatory application would not necessarily have the same level of onsite support and labor.

Several modifications were necessary to adapt the system to dynamic and ambulatory shooting research [9, 15], which were outside the EST's designed purpose. These included the addition of programs to permit sophisticated analyses of performance, repositioning of virtual targets (to increase subject movement), modification of the physical layout of the room to reduce trip hazards during ambulatory tests, increasing the spacing between subsequent targets to force the subjects to make larger head movements between shots, and the addition of an extended rifle cable and of a guide rod to direct the pneumatic cable away from the shooter's feet. These modifications permitted the EST to yield some interesting findings concerning dynamic shooting. Nevertheless, the design purpose of the EST is to simulate range marksmanship training, rather than to support formal experiments requiring the analysis of dynamic shooting performance during rapid body/rifle movement or ambulatory shooting. While the company was supportive and the EST was adapted successfully to support the present experiment and to make interesting inferences concerning rifle kinematics during rifle movement and aiming [17], we found that some data could be lost during the rapid or large-amplitude rifle movements required by our research, due to the way the EST sampling algorithm prioritizes different channels of the incoming data. A research-focused dynamic shooting device would need to have high sampling rates to ensure all rifle kinematics data is acquired without gaps. Finally, while the EST measured goal-directed psychomotor activity (shooting) and could be adapted to indirectly infer a disruption in postural equilibrium in the present study, it was not designed to measure postural balance directly. A research-focused dynamic shooting device designed to challenge balance should include a dedicated measure of postural sway.

The optimal device for assessing dynamic shooting-while-moving in a situation that challenges balance would be small (or even portable or ambulatory), user-friendly, and robust. A small system would be advantageous because it could be rapidly transported and deployed to classroom or field settings using a mid-sized vehicle and without the need for multiple support personnel. A highly usable system would require less training time and less set-up time. Finally, a robust system would experience less down-time and require less time spent on troubleshooting or repair. Increased robustness might be obtained by reducing the number and variety of electrical and mechanical machines which make up the shooting simulator, for example, by sacrificing or redesigning the pneumatically driven mechanical simulation of rifle recoil.

We envision the future integration of a small part-task shooting simulator with an objective indicator of postural sway. The simulator could consist of a virtual headset display with appropriate targets and a rifle that is suitably realistic. The simulator would present targets requiring head and rifle movement and yield a measure of one's speed of accurate shooting. The shooting simulator would be coupled with a direct, objective indicator of postural sway, such as an off-body motion tracking system or a body-mounted accelerometer package.

Some initial strides towards a dynamic moving-while-balancing shooting simulator could be made relatively rapidly by focusing solely upon our best-performing task, which was kneeling-while-shooting and engaging targets to the left and right. Since the subject would not be walking around the room during this test, room-mounted tracking systems or body-worn accelerometers would not be needed. All that would be required for postural sway measurement would be either a commercial camera system (such as was developed long ago by Kennedy [11] and more recently by Mortimer and colleagues, [4, 20]), or a balance platform capable of measuring center-of-pressure (of which, several small models have been developed, Lawson et al. [14]). Such a device would permit rapid testing, evaluation, and application of the best-performing test from the current study. However, a fully ambulatory balance and gait measurement system would be needed to obtain objective gait data when multiple steps are required across a large space. Ultimately, this would consist of a rifle, virtual display, and accelerometer/GPS-based wearable motion tracker. The tracker would need to be sophisticated enough to avoid the tracking errors that have been seen in some past models of wearable balance tracking systems [14].

Acknowledgements. This work was sponsored by the U.S. Army Medical Research and Materiel Command. The authors thank Drs. Heber Jones and Marlin Wolf for their advice and support with the apparatus and recruitment, respectively. This work was supported in part by two appointments to the post-graduate program at the U.S. Army Aeromedical Research Laboratory administered by the Oak Ridge Institute of Science and Education fellows through an interagency agreement between the U.S. Department of Energy and the U.S. Army Medical Research and Material Command. The views, opinions, and/or findings in this report are those of the authors and should not be construed as official Department of the Army positions, policies, or decisions, unless so designated by other official documentation. Citation of trade names in this report does not constitute an official Department of the Army endorsement or approval of the use of such commercial items. Mention of persons or agencies in this report does not imply their agreement with the contents of this report unless specifically stated by the authors.

References

1. American Congress of Rehabilitation Medicine: Definition of mild traumatic brain injury. J. Head Trauma Rehabil. **8**(3), 86–88 (1993)
2. Anthony, D.: EST 2000: Engagement Skills Trainer. Cubic Defense Application, Orlando (2006)
3. Berg, K.O., Wood-Dauphinée, S., Williams, J.I.: The balance scale: reliability assessment with elderly residents and patients with an acute stroke. Scand. J. Rehabil. Med. **27**, 27–36 (1995)
4. Mortimer, B.J.P., McGrath, B.J., Mort, G.R., Zets, G.A.: Multimodal feedback for balance rehabilitation. In: Antona, M., Stephanidis, C. (eds.) UAHCI 2015. LNCS, vol. 9177, pp. 322–330. Springer, Cham (2015). doi:10.1007/978-3-319-20684-4_31
5. Cao, A., Chintamani, K.K., Pandya, A.K., Ellis, R.D.: NASA TLX: software for assessing subjective mental workload. Behav. Res. Methods **41**, 113–117 (2009)
6. Grandizio, C., Lawson, B., King, M., Cruz, P., Kelley, A., Erickson, B., Livingston, L., Cho, T., Laskowski, B., Chiaramonte, J.: Development of a Fitness-For-Duty Assessment Battery for Recovering Dismounted Warriors. U.S. Army Aeromedical Research Laboratory, Fort Rucker (2014). USAARL Report No. 2014-18
7. Hart, S.G.: NASA-task load index (NASA-TLX); 20 years later. In: Proceedings of the Human Factors and Ergonomics Society 50th Annual Meeting, pp. 904–908. Human Factors and Ergonomics Society, Santa Monica (2006)
8. Jacobson, G.P., Newman, C.W.: The development of the dizziness handicap inventory. Arch. Otolaryngol.-Head Neck Surg. **116**, 424–427 (1990)
9. Jones, H., King, M., Gaydos, S.: A Novel Application of the Point of Aim Trace Feature for the Engagement Skills Trainer 2000. United States Army Aeromedical Research Laboratory, Fort Rucker (2011). USAARL Report No. 2011-14
10. Kane, R.L., Kay, G.G.: Computerized assessment in neuropsychology: a review of tests and test batteries. Neuropsychol. Rev. **3**(1), 1–117 (1992)
11. Kennedy, R.S.: Defense modeling simulation office. In: The Official Proceedings of Virtual Reality and Medicine-the Cutting Edge Conference and Exhibition, 8–11 September 1994, the New York Hilton, p. 111. SIG-Advanced Applications, Incorporated (1994)
12. Lawson, B.D., Rupert, A.H.: Vestibular aspects of head injury and recommendations for evaluation and rehabilitation following exposure to severe changes in head velocity or ambient pressure. In: Bos, J. Stark, J., Colwell, J. (eds.) Peer-Reviewed Proceedings of the International Conference on Human Performance at Sea, pp. 367–380. University of Strathclyde, U.K. (2010)

13. Lawson, B.D., Rupert, A.H., Cho, T.H.: Functional screening of vestibular and balance problems soon after head injury: options in development for the field or aid station. J. Spec. Oper. Med. **13**(1), 42–48 (2013)
14. Lawson, B.D., Rupert, A.H., Legan, S.M.: Vestibular Balance Deficits Following Head Injury: Recommendations Concerning Evaluation and Rehabilitation in the Military Setting. U.S. Army Aeromedical Research Laboratory, Fort Rucker (2012). Report No. 2012-10, 102 p.
15. Lawson, B., Ranes, B., Kelley, A., Erickson, B., Milam, L., King, M., Wrobel, C., Chiaramonte, J., Cho, T., Laskowski, B., Campbell, J., Thompson, L.: Mild Traumatic Brain Injury and Dynamic Simulated Shooting Performance. U.S. Army Aeromedical Research Laboratory, Fort Rucker (2016). Report No. 2016-16, 35 p.
16. Lawson, B.D., Rupert, A.H., McGrath, B.J.: The neurovestibular challenges of astronauts and balance patients: some past countermeasures and two alternative approaches to elicitation, assessment and mitigation. Front. Syst. Neurosci. **10** (2016). doi:10.3389/fnsys.2016.0096
17. Lawson, B.D., Ranes, B.M., Thompson, L.B.I.: Smooth moves shooting performance is related to efficiency of rifle movement. In: Proceedings of the Human Factors and Ergonomics Society Annual Meeting, vol. 60, no. 1, pp. 1524–1528. SAGE Publications, September 2016
18. National Aeronautics and Space Administration (NASA) AMES Research Center. NASA Task Load Index (TLX) Version 1.0 (n.d.). http://humansystems.arc.nasa.gov/groups/TLX/paperpencil.html
19. Shumway-Cook, A., Wollacott, M.: Motor Control: Theory and Practical Applications. Williams and Wilkins, Baltimore (1995)
20. Zets, G., Mortimer, B.: Enhanced System and Method for Assessment of Disequilibrium Balance and Motion Disorders. U.S. Patent and Trademark Office, Washington, DC (2015). U.S. Patent No. 9,149,222

Proposal of Interaction Used Umbrella for Smartphone

Sohichiro Mori and Makoto Oka[✉]

Tokyo City University, Tokyo, Japan
07o21classsuzu@gmail.com, moka@tcu.ac.jp

Abstract. In recent years, the hazards of operating on the smartphone while walking has become common knowledge today, and the behavior has become an object of public concern, frequently causing collisions between individuals and bicycles or cars. People operating on the smartphones while walking will inevitably gaze downward. Not being able to see what is in the front, they become involved in collisions.

In this study, we will make it possible to operate smartphones using umbrellas. For this purpose, we will develop a system and interaction that will turn the umbrella into smartphones (allow the umbrella to perform the input and output operations of the smartphones). Our aim is to suggest and validate the interaction between the user and his/her umbrella. By using the umbrella as a display, users will be able to face forward while walking. We will validate through several apps whether it is possible to operate the smartphone using an umbrella.

Keywords: Smartphone · Mobile phone · Cell phone · Texting while walking · Interaction · Umbrella

1 Introduction

The hazards of operating on the smartphone while walking has become common knowledge today, and the behavior has become an object of public concern, frequently causing collisions between individuals and bicycles or cars. This is because smartphone users tend to concentrate on their phones and not notice the approaching cars.

Today, meeting others without a smartphone is unthinkable. When meeting outside of their homes, people try to meet by communicating with each other. There is no guarantee they will be able to meet without operating on their smartphones while walking. For this reason, there is no end to collisions caused by users looking at their phones.

Moreover, on rainy days, one hand would be taken with the umbrella. Holding the smartphone in the other hand for contacting others will fill up both hands, and the hands will not be available for other purposes. To perform other tasks, individuals would have to hold both the umbrella and the smartphone in the same hand, which makes it difficult to operate on the phone.

People operating on the smartphones while walking will inevitably gaze downward. Not being able to see what is in the front, they become involved in collisions. In addition if they are wearing headphones they will not be able to hear, and the risk of causing an accident becomes even more elevated. However, although smartphone operation while

© Springer International Publishing AG 2017
S. Yamamoto (Ed.): HIMI 2017, Part I, LNCS 10273, pp. 579–588, 2017.
DOI: 10.1007/978-3-319-58521-5_45

walking is a known hazard, the numbers of these accidents do not decrease. On the other hand, it is impossible to prevent people from using their devices while walking. Taking these points into account, the solution would be to make it possible for smartphone users to operate on their phone whilst directing their attention to their surroundings. The risk would decrease drastically if individuals could operate their phone facing forwards, for example, by displaying the smartphone screen on the umbrella. Additionally, even in the rain, users would be able to hold the umbrella without using up both hands. If smartphones could be operated using the umbrella, users will not need to look down at the smartphone screen in their hands.

2   Related Work

Wang et al. noticed that smartphone users cross the road while operating on their phones [1]. Those who cross the road and operate on their phones simultaneously are in more danger than those who don't. Thus, Wang et al. developed "WalkSafe" to support those who operate on their phones while walking. WalkSafe photographs the surrounding scenery on the smartphone camera. The system uses machine learning on the photographed images and detects approaching cars. When cars are approaching, the system will warn the user through sounds and vibrations.

Kodama et al. have pointed out that although people are aware that smartphone operation while walking is dangerous, they are unable to stop [2]. In order to make this operation safer, they suggested a support system that uses an image sensor (Fig. 1). Their support system obtains the frontal image via a range image sensor, and shows the surrounding elements of danger in the overlay display on the upper part of the smartphone screen. When the distance between the user and the object is close, the color will be red, and when there are no objects approaching the user, the color will be blue. For example, if the user's left side is closer to the object, then the color on the smartphone's

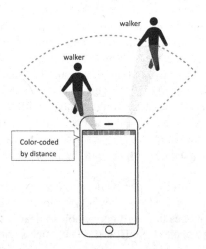

Fig. 1.   Safe-walking support system [2]. (Color figure online)

upper left will be red, and if there are no objects in front of the user, the upper center of the smartphone will be blue. The system warns the user using color and location on the screen.

Ito et al. assumed smartphone use by motorbike riders [3]. They attached an accelerometer on riding gloves, and suggested controlling the smartphone by detecting the hand gestures. The results of the operation would be outputted by sound or voice, and users would not need to stare at the smartphone during input or output. Their experiment demonstrated that acceleration is not influenced by vibration during the motorbike ride. The system detected accelerations without problem, and the user was able to operate the smartphone.

National Geographic conducted a study where a part of the sidewalk was experimentally converted into a "smartphone operators only lane." [4] The left side of the sidewalk was designated to smartphone users, and the right lane to other pedestrians. (Fig. 2) Results showed that very few people changed lanes while walking. Although many people operated on their phones while walking, they were so absorbed in the smartphone screen that they did not notice the smartphone users' lane.

Fig. 2. Cellphones lane [4]

In this study, we will make it possible to operate smartphones using umbrellas. For this purpose, we will develop a system and interaction that will turn the umbrella into smartphones (allow the umbrella to perform the input and output operations of the smartphones). Our aim is to suggest and validate the interaction between the user and his/her umbrella. By using the umbrella as a display, users will be able to face forward while walking. Since users will be operating their phones by tilting or moving the umbrella, they will not hold anything besides the umbrella. We will validate through several apps whether it is possible to operate the smartphone using an umbrella.

3   Examples of Application

In this study, we will not implement the OS functions for activating the app. (rancher functions), and assume that each application has been activated, and is ready for use. This time, we will make validations regarding the below apps.

3.1   Communication Apps Such as SNS

We validated using communication apps such as LINE and iMessage. Each communication consists of one screen per dialogue partner, with screens connected horizontally. Additionally, in each communication, older conversations exist in the upper section, and the newest conversation in the lowest section.

Switching between conversation partners is done by scrolling the screen horizontally with the left and right movements of the umbrella. Scrolling within each conversation will be done by the front and backward movement of the umbrella. The functions will mainly be for browsing, and not for input.

3.2   Map Apps

The map app will display the map surrounding the present location, and users will be able to scroll by moving the umbrella forwards, backwards, left, and right. Moving the umbrella upwards will reduce, and drawing it downwards will enlarge the size of the map (Fig. 3)

Fig. 3.   Map application on the canopy of umbrella

3.3   Movie and Music Player Apps

The display will consist of 3 panes. On the right 1/4 of the display, thumbnails of videos and music will be displayed vertically. User will be able to switch between videos by swaying the umbrella front and backwards. The left side of the display will be divided into the upper and lower halves, with SeekBar on the lower half. By swaying the umbrella left and right, user will be able to designate the section of the video they wish to watch. The upper left section will be for displaying the videos. User can control the volume (sound) by swaying the umbrella up and down.

4   Interaction Models

In utilizing the umbrella as a mobile device, the canopy would be the part suitable for the display. On the other hand, it is not realistic to connect a keyboard or a mouse to the umbrella for input purposes. Furthermore, having to touch the canopy as one would the screen of the smartphone will not be a fundamental improvement. Therefore, we will display the screen on the canopy and use the movement of the umbrella for input. With an umbrella used for input, it would be difficult to perform diverse operations like on the phones, since we would not be able to recreate the multi touch operations people perform with their fingers.

In order to come up with an interface that remains practical even with simplified operations, we will consider an interaction designed especially for umbrellas, which would be different from that for smartphones. Thus, we designated the selection (direction), decision, and cancel operations to different movements of the umbrella. Rocking of the umbrella to the front, back, left, and right will correspond to actions for pointing to directions such as the flick and slide on the smartphone. Input action for decision will be lifting the umbrella or hitting the shaft. Users can go back to the previous action by pulling the umbrella downwards.

Apps will be developed according to this interaction model. However, some of the apps may have their own individual interactions not necessarily be based on this model.

5   Implementation

The suggested interactions will be used in specific apps. The reactions to each action will depend on the app, but the basic actions will depend on the interaction model.

We used the following devices in creating the system.

5.1   Umbrella

We used a white umbrella with 92 cm length, 116.5 cm diameter, and 324 g weight. To create the system, we used an umbrella larger than normal. When the length of the umbrella is shorter, the focal length of the projector will be shorter, and thus the displayed image would be smaller. By using a short focus projector, we will be able to display large enough images.

5.2 PC

We used pc where in real-life situation smartphones would be used. With a smartphone, we would be able to use the built-in accelerometer. Since PCs do not have a built-in accelerometer, we connected the PC to an accelerometer using Arduino. The PC converts the values from the accelerometer into inputs, and processes them as operation on the app being displayed on the screen. The system should display the smartphone screen, but for the prototype, the PC screen will be displayed.

5.3 Acceleration Sensor

We used a 3-axis accelerometer. Although accelerometer would be enough in itself, adding a 3-axis gyro sensor may improve the accuracy of acceleration measurement. However because we were aiming for a simple system, we used the accelerometer only.

5.4 Projector

We selected a 168 g light-weight projector. Because the projector is light, it will not add too much weight to the umbrella once attached (Fig. 4). The projector has a built-in battery, and does not need an electrical power source. The compact projector has short focus distance, and can display a 37 inch image from 1.0 m distance.

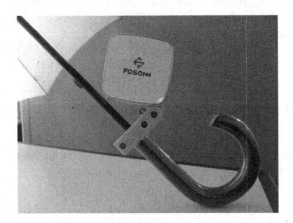

Fig. 4. Projector attached to umbrella

5.5 Arduino

The accelerometer will be attached to the tip of the umbrella, and will be connected to Arduino. Arduino outputs the acceleration values to the PC. Although we used the affordable Arduino Uno, a more compact Arduino or WiFi could be used.

6   Experiment of Movement Identification

6.1   Experiment Method

This system will be used while walking. When the user walks, naturally the umbrella will rock. The system needs to distinguish between the natural and the unnatural (deliberate operation by the user) rock. In order to distinguish between the two, we conducted an experiment. We attached the accelerometer to the tip of the umbrella, and asked 13 participants to move the umbrella. From the observed acceleration values, we aimed to calculate the acceleration values that would differentiate walking and deliberate operation.

The coordinate system for the accelerometer in this study is as follows: the back and forth movements will be shown on the x axis (the backward movements represented as positive values), the left and right movements will be shown on the y axis (left movements will be represented as positive values), and the up and down movements, on the z axis (downward movements will be represented as positive values). The reason the axes are inverted is because the accelerometer was attached to the umbrella tip in a vertically inverted position.

6.2   Result

The Fig. 5 shows the acceleration for the 5 times when participants rocked the umbrella forwards. We measured the acceleration at 30 Hz sampling rate. Dotted line stands for the acceleration on the x axis, the broken line, on the y axis, and the solid line, on the z axis.

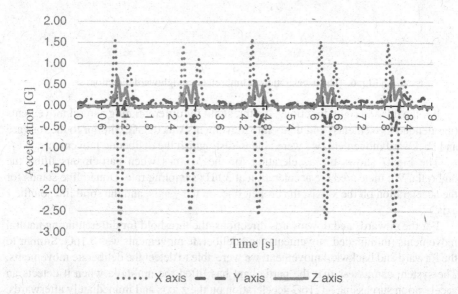

Fig. 5. The acceleration of umbrella in a forward direction.

For the forward and backward directions, the threshold for differentiating natural movements (unintended movements) and deliberate movements was 0.33G. If the accelerometer senses acceleration surpassing 0.33G on the x axis and immediately afterwards detect acceleration surpassing −0.33G, the system will assess that the umbrella was rocked forwards by the participant. Backward rocking can be detected in the same manner.

The Fig. 6 shows the acceleration for the 5 times when participants rocked the umbrella towards the right. We measured the acceleration at 30 Hz sampling rate. Dotted line stands for the acceleration on the x axis, the broken line, on the y axis, and the solid line, on the z axis.

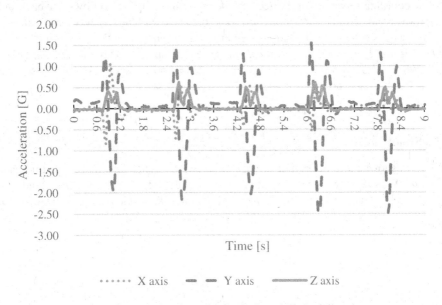

Fig. 6. The acceleration of umbrella in a rightward direction.

For the left and right directions, the threshold for differentiating natural movements (unintended movements) and deliberate movements was 0.33G. Similar to the forward and backward movement, we were able to distinguish the deliberate movements.

The Fig. 7 shows the acceleration for the 5 times when participants lifted the umbrella. We measured the acceleration at 30 Hz sampling rate. Dotted line stands for the acceleration on the x axis, the broken line, on the y axis, and the solid line, on the z axis.

For the upwards and downwards directions, the threshold for differentiating natural movements (unintended movements) and deliberate movements was 0.16G. Similar to the forward and backward movement, we were able to detect the deliberate movements. The system can assess that the participant has lifted the umbrella when it detects an acceleration surpassing −0.16G acceleration on the z axis and immediately afterwards, acceleration that surpasses 0.16G in the opposite direction on the same axis. Acceleration surpassing 0.16G is detected when the umbrella is rocked in the forward direction, but

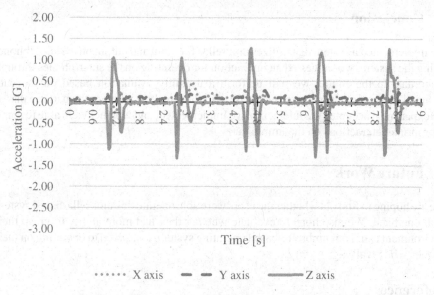

Fig. 7. The acceleration of umbrella in an upward direction.

because in this case the acceleration in the opposite direction will not be detected immediately afterwards, distinction between forward movement and upward movement is possible.

7 Evaluation Experiment

In the future, we will conduct an evaluation experiment following the below procedures. Ideally we should conduct the experiment outdoors in rainy weather. However, because our prototype is not waterproof, we are planning to conduct the experiment indoors.

We will explain the operation procedures to the participants of the experiment. We will explain them how to perform operations for each app. Participants will operate the umbrella and attempt to complete the goals we have set, such as turning the volume down 3 notches on music player, or displaying destination on the map app, etc. Participants will complete the goals through trial and error.

We will be recording the acceleration of the umbrella during the experiment. The participants will be asked to voice the intent for moving the umbrella. We will record the intent of the participant, the operation the participant made in order to realize the intent, and the results of the movement. Lastly, we will evaluate the results, including whether the participant was able to achieve the goal. We will conduct a questionnaire survey after the experiment and perform subjective evaluation.

Furthermore, we will calculate the movement of the umbrella based on the acceleration data attained, and analyze the participants' intent and the movement of the umbrella.

8   Conclusion

We implemented a system that utilizes umbrellas for input and output on the smartphone. Using the system, we suggested an interaction for operating on the smartphones through umbrellas. In the future, we will perform a usability evaluation based on the data obtained in the evaluation experiment. We will then analyze whether the participants of the experiment accepted the interaction we implemented, and whether were able to recall appropriate interactions on the umbrella.

9   Future Work

We are hoping to find out whether the users were able operate this umbrella-based system with one hand. We also hope to evaluate whether they had more ability to grasp their environment using our umbrella-based operating system, compared to operating on their phones while walking.

References

1. Wang, T., Cardone, G., Corradi, A., Torresani, L., Campbell, A.T.: WalkSafe: a pedestrian safety app for mobile phone users who walk and talk while crossing roads. In: HotMobile 2012 (2012). doi:10.1145/2162081.2162089
2. Kodama, S., Enokibori, Y., Mase, K.: Examination of safe-walking support system for "texting while walking" using time-of-flight range image sensors. In: UbiComp/ISWC 2016, pp. 129–132 (2016). doi:10.1145/2968219.2971407
3. Ito, A., Yamabe, T., Kiyohara, R.: Study of smartphone operation UI for motorcycles using acceleration sensor. In: DPSWS 2014, pp. 109–114 (2014). (in Japanese)
4. Cellphone Talkers Get Their Own Sidewalk Lane in D.C. https://www.yahoo.com/tech/cellphone-talkers-get-their-own-sidewalk-lane-in-d-c-92080566744.html

Factors and Influences of Body Ownership Over Virtual Hands

Nami Ogawa[1(✉)], Takuji Narumi[2], and Michitaka Hirose[2]

[1] Graduate School of Interdisciplinary Information Studies, The University of Tokyo,
7-3-1 Hongo, Bunkyo-ku, Tokyo 113-8656, Japan
ogawa@cyber.t.u-tokyo.ac.jp
[2] Graduate School of Information Science and Technology, The University of Tokyo,
7-3-1 Hongo, Bunkyo-ku, Tokyo 113-8656, Japan
{narumi,hirose}@cyber.t.u-tokyo.ac.jp

Abstract. The sense that one's own body belongs to oneself is called "Body Ownership". Until now, body ownership is investigated in a psychology field. However, the investigation of the origins and functional role of the sense of one's own body not only explores the philosophical question, but it also examines the issues that should be investigated before VR becomes widely used in our daily life. In this paper, we surveyed the existing literature on body ownership and categorized factors into bottom-up and top-down processes. We also identified the perceptual, cognitive, and behavioral influences of body ownership. We then discussed some promising areas for future research in the VR field. As for factors, it is promising to consider the interaction between the body and the external world, and to develop a unified evaluation standard and theoretical framework for research in this field. As for influences, it is promising to consider the higher, longer-term cognitive influences in the social context, and to apply them in the context of body augmentation in the real world.

Keywords: Body ownership · Virtual reality · Rubber hand illusion · Body augmentation · Multimodal integration

1 Introduction

With the development of Virtual Reality (VR) technology, we perceive the spaces of computer graphics (CG) projected on displays as if they exist before us. Furthermore, VR has enabled us to even present sensations that our bodies are actually immersed in the virtual environment with startling reality by using virtual CG hands. However, the creation of artificial virtual bodies involves the exploration of more profound questions than to merely artificially create the virtual environment. That is, because virtual bodies are exactly identical to the virtual self, it is impossible to create virtual bodies without knowing what the virtuality of the self, in other words, the self's self is.

"The virtuality of the self" may be considered as too philosophical. However, what if you hear that putting yourself in the particular virtual avatar changes subsequent attitudes or behaviors in the real world, such as reduces racial biases [1] or leads to helping behavior [2]. The sense that one's own body belongs to oneself, called "Body Owner-ship" affects perception, cognition, and behavior.

However, it is natural to think it can also affect these factors negatively. Furthermore, most of the effects are implicit and we are influenced without being aware of it. Thus, the investigation of the origins and functional role of the sense of one's own body not only explores the philosophical question, but it also examines the issues that should be investigated before VR becomes widely used in our daily life.

In this paper, we survey the existing literature on body ownership and summarize it into factors and influences. We then discuss the promising areas for future research in the field of VR.

2   Factors for Inducing Body Ownership

2.1 Rubber Hand Illusion

Actually, head-mounted displays are not necessary for creating virtual bodies artificially. Rubber hand illusions (RHI) are well known as the simple experiment that reveals the extent of body ownership over external objects [3]. In the field of psychology, neuro-science, and cognitive science, "the bodily self" is pursued by investigating the factors inducing body ownership using RHI. In RHI, watching a rubber hand being stroked synchronously with one's own unseen hand causes the rubber hand to be attributed to one's own body, such that it feels like one's own hand. It is known that RHI does not occur when the rubber hand is stroked asynchronously with the real hand. Thus, body ownership is induced by synchronous multisensory stimulation, but it is not sufficient. It does not occur for objects that do not resemble body parts. In fact, RHI is not induced when the rubber hand is replaced by a non corporeal object such as a wooden stick [4].

In summary, multisensory integration in the interaction with internal models of the body is necessary for the development of body ownership [5]. Multisensory integration and the internal models of the body are also referred as bottom-up processes and top-down influences [4] or multimodal triggers and semantic constraints [6]. While the former pertains to the integration of continuously updated current sensory inputs and motor information, the latter is the cognitive process that is contributed to by our semantic memories and knowledge.

2.2 Bottom-Up Factors

The classic RHI uses a paintbrush to provide synchronous visuotactile stimulation, but body ownership can also be induced by only synchronous visuomotor stimulation, in the absence of tactile stimulation. For example, both active motor control over the artificial hand [7] and a data-glove that uses sensors transmitting the positions of fingers to a virtually projected hand [8] induce body ownership. Body ownership occurs over a wide range of body parts when both real and fake bodies move homologous body parts at the same time, for example, fingers [9], arms [10], upper body [11], legs [12], and full body [13]. For both pairs of multimodal stimuli, spatial [7] and temporal [14, 15] corre-spondence is necessary.

2.3 Top-Down Factors

Not only the continuously updated bottom-up information, but body ownership is also influenced by higher-order top-down cognitive processes. Our semantic memories and knowledge contribute to the shaping of internal models of the body that contains information about the general and not self-specific visual, postural, and structural properties of the human body [6]. Kilteni et al. regarded top-down factors as semantic constraints and classified the important semantic feature of the fake body into shape, texture, the anatomical plausibility of their spatial configuration, and the anatomical plausibility of their internal structure [6].

Top-down semantic information has been proposed to be an important feature of general multisensory integration. For example, a visual stimulus showing a dog is semantically congruent with a barking but not with a meowing sound [16]. In this case, the semantic congruence of the audiovisual stimuli speaks in favor of a common underlying cause: a dog. Several studies have shown that the integration of crossmodal stimuli is enhanced when these are semantically congruent [17].

3 Issues for Future Research in Regard to Factors

The factors described above are important, but the relative influence remains unclear and debatable. In particular, the strength of influences is different depending on the types of multisensory triggers, that is, visuotactile or visuomotor. On the whole, body ownership tends to occur over a wide range of targets when induced by visuomotor correlations than by visuotactile correlations. That is, using VR, body ownership can even occur over the targets that are not induced by classic RHI. Particularly, with the development of VR technologies, it becomes possible to precisely synchronize visual and motor information across the whole body. It is reported that by utilizing VR that enables visuomotor correlations with high accuracy, body ownership occurs over semantically far different bodies such as six fingers [18] or very long fingers [19]. In fact, body ownership is strongly influenced by sense of agency rather than the similarity of the appearance of hands [20].

However, even though numerous studies about body ownership have been reported after Botvinick and Cohen first used RHI in 1998, visuomotor stimuli are much less used as compared to visuotactile stimuli. It can now be said that the investigation of body ownership over virtual hands has only just begun. Therefore, we point out the following three issues for future research, which comprised the characteristic features of body ownership research using VR.

3.1 Interaction Between the Body and the External World

Using VR, virtual hands can easily interact with external objects in virtual environments. Very few studies have investigated body ownership in regard to bodily interaction [21] despite the fact that the function to interact is one of the most important characteristics of the body. Interactive influences have rarely been investigated due to implementation limits. For example, the influences of incongruence in physical laws when interacting (e.g., penetration of virtual hands into a wall, lack of real haptic feedback) remains uninvestigated. However, these aspects can now be easily investigated thanks to the recent VR advances.

3.2 Unified Evaluation Standards

The intensity of the body ownership illusion is commonly measured by the subjective scores collected through questionnaires [3] in synchronous conditions versus asynchronous conditions. There are other objective measures such as skin conductance response (SCR) [22] and proprioceptive drifts [23]. For instance, when the rubber hand was "injured" by a knife, subjects displayed a strong SCR even though nothing was done to the real hand. Participants also perceived the position of their hand to be closer to the rubber hand than it really was (proprioceptive drifts). Interestingly, the prevalence of illusion over time [3] and the subjective intensity, as assessed through questionnaires [23], are positively correlated with proprioceptive drifts.

However, in case of body ownership illusions using VR, these objective measures cannot be used. Proprioceptive drifts are unavailable because virtual hands and participants' real hands are normally located in the same subjective position. SCR needs to be measured in a rest state and is unsuitable for virtual hands because participants' active movements of their hands produce substantial noise signals. Considering the current circumstances that different response variables are used by different experimenters, multiple and unified standard measurement methodology and experimental schemes that suit research on virtual hands' body ownership need to be developed in the future.

3.3 Theoretical Framework

Recently, theoretical frameworks for accounting mechanisms of body ownership have been developed, such as predictive coding [24], the causal inference models [25] and the connectionist models [26]. These models have been somewhat successfully applied in the field of multisensory integration and they are partially consistent with existing experimental approaches.

These approaches can be extended to account for a more holistic view of our own body perception. Therefore, experimental validation of such theoretical models is recommended in future work [6].

4 Influences of Body Ownership Illusion

Virtual reality techniques can be used to produce a strong ownership illusion over a virtual body even when there are radical semantic changes in comparison to the true body (e.g., the illusion of a dramatic increase in belly size [27], another person's body [28]). Since the body plays an important role in perception, cognition, and behavior, such changes in body images can induce consequences for these various functions.

4.1 Perceptual Influences

Spatial Integration. The inherent tendency of human to eliminate multisensory conflicts and to bind information across the senses into meaningful percepts [29] induces a perceptual fusion of visual, tactile, and proprioceptive signals into a unified perception of a single owned body that constitutes the physical self. This process involves the recalibration of all body-centered representations of space [30], such as tactile spatial remapping [31, 32] and proprioceptive drifts.

Tactile spatial remapping combines information about the location of the stimulus on the skin surface with proprioceptive information about the spatial location of body parts and internal models of the body in order to perceive the location of a tactile stimulus in the external space. In RHI, the location of the tactile stimuli applied onto participants' real hands is perceived to be on the artificial hands because proprioceptive information is drifted.

Proprioceptive drifts is well known as an induced change in the perceived location of the participant's own hand towards the rubber hand, but according to a recent report, the perceived positions of the real and artificial hand converge towards each other [33]. This contradicts the common notion of perceptual substitution of the real hand by the artificial hand. Rather, they are in line with the view that [34] vision and proprioception are fused into an intermediate percept. This is further evidence that the perception of our body is a flexible multisensory construct that is based on integration principles.

Perception of External Environments. The changes in representation of one's own body also influence the perception of intrinsic properties of objects, in addition to that of their spatial locations because our bodies are implicitly used to calibrate the perception of external objects. In particular, the changes in the size of a body influence the perception of various properties of objects, such as weight [35], size [34], and distance [36].

Body-based scaling is a notion that our body and its action capabilities are used to scale the spatial layout of the environment [34, 37]. In other words, the body acts as a metric that individuals use to scale the apparent sizes of objects in the environment. When body ownership occurs over a smaller body, identical objects at identical distances were perceived as larger and farther away than they were as compared to the larger body [13, 38]. Importantly, even when the size of the object on the retina, binocular disparity when focusing on the object, and demand characteristics were identical, body ownership occurs only in the presence of synchronous multimodal stimuli. Thus, the altered visual perception of size and distance is a consequence of changed body size and it is enhanced by body ownership [34]. Therefore, this is also referred to as the own-body-size effect [39]. In addition, visual distortion of the hand affects both hand shape during object grasping [40] and size perception as measured by a size-matching task [38].

Since we use our body implicitly to judge size and distance as described above, displaying avatars in VR improves distance estimations [41] and perception of size distortion between real and virtual environments [42].

4.2   Cognitive and Behavioral Influences

Body ownership illusions could lead to cognitive changes depending on the appearance of the virtual body.

RHI induces cognitive changes over the target hands such that participants perceived the rubber hand as being more similar morphologically to their own hand [43]. Moreover, multisensory stimulation affects self-face recognition because the face is also a source of rich multisensory experiences. M. Tsakiris showed that synchronous tactile stimulation while watching another person's face was being similarly touched produced a bias in recognizing one's own face, in the direction of the other person included in the representation of one's own face [44].

Body ownership for particular semantic avatars also produces cognitive influences. For example, virtual embodiment of white people in a dark skinned body reduced implicit racial bias [1], virtual alteration of age through embodiment in an elderly person can reduce negative stereotypes toward the elderly [45], and illusory ownership of a virtual child body causes implicit child-like attitude changes [13]. It also produces behavioral influences such that occupying an avatar with the superhero ability to fly increases helping behavior in the real world [2] and embodiment in a casually dressed dark-skinned virtual body increases in their movement patterns for drumming a West-African Djembe hand drum [11].

5   Issues for Future Research in Regard to Influences

Bodily experience brings about the amorphous belief of being a self-sustaining organism and forms the basis of self-identity. In the VR era, it is important to focus on the aspects of the body as an interface between the self and the external world, including both objects and the others in the social context. The latter includes more social aspects. The higher and longer-term cognitive influences on both positive and negative aspects need to be investigated before VR technologies are widely spread into the society in the future. In case of long-term aspects, the influences could change the process of cognition not only in the virtual world but also in the real world. As for the positive aspects, the study mentioned above [2] illustrates the potential of using experiences in virtual reality technology to increase prosocial behavior in the physical world. As for the negative aspects, for example, the sensation of loss or pain of a missing virtual body part may occur as if when we lose a certain body part or something important in the real world.

The effects of obtaining body ownership, for a long duration, over the virtual bodies that are actually different from one's own perpetual bodies need to be examined.

6   Future Prospects for Body Augmentation

We humans have invented tools that are fit for our bodies, and have evolved ourselves by tool-use. However, in virtual environments, we can obtain a surrogate new body without evolution. Body-augmentation technologies can free our bodies from real world constraints such as a physical, fixed, and unchangeable nature. Now VR can be used to create a novel human-tool coevolution. The augmented virtual body can be used to test new uses of existing tools and it produces new tools that are fit for our augmented bodies. These new tools will then help us evolve, and another new way of viewing our body will originate.

During the co-evolution, new combinations of a body and a tool will originate, and unprecedented creations, such as music, art, fashion, sport, and entertainment will be developed. In fact, approaches to human augmentation sports have already developed, such as the superhuman sports society [46]. Superhuman sports aims to augment human abilities and to develop new sports in real environments, but to use VR is an effective approach for the basic examination of body augmentation.

7 Conclusion

In this paper, we surveyed the existing literature on body ownership and categorized factors into bottom-up and top-down processes. We also identified the perceptual, cognitive, and behavioral aspects of body ownership.

We then discussed some promising areas for future research in the VR field. As for factors, it is promising to consider the interaction between the body and the external world, and to develop a unified evaluation standard and theoretical framework for research in this field. As for influences, it is promising to consider the higher, longer-term cognitive influences in the social context, and to apply them in the context of body augmentation in the real world.

Acknowledgments. This work was supported by JSPS Kakenhi Grant-in-aid for Challenging Exploratory Research Number 16K12470.

References

1. Peck, T.C., Seinfeld, S., Aglioti, S.M., Slater, M.: Putting yourself in the skin of a black avatar reduces implicit racial bias. Conscious. Cogn. **22**, 779–787 (2013)
2. Rosenberg, R.S., Baughman, S.L., Bailenson, J.N.: Virtual superheroes: using superpowers in virtual reality to encourage prosocial behavior. PLoS ONE **8**, e55003 (2013)
3. Botvinick, M., Cohen, J.: Rubber hands 'feel' touch that eyes see. Nature **391**, 756 (1998)
4. Tsakiris, M., Haggard, P.: The rubber hand illusion revisited: visuotactile integration and self-attribution. J. Exp. Psychol. Hum. Percept. Perform. **31**, 80–91 (2005)
5. Tsakiris, M.: The sense of body ownership. In: The Oxford Handbook of the Self. Oxford University Press, Oxford (2011)
6. Kilteni, K., Maselli, A., Kording, K.P., Slater, M.: Over my fake body: body ownership illusions for studying the multisensory basis of own-body perception. Front. Hum. Neurosci. **9**, 141 (2015)
7. Riemer, M., Fuchs, X., Bublatzky, F., Kleinböhl, D., Hölzl, R., Trojan, J.: The rubber hand illusion depends on a congruent mapping between real and artificial fingers. Acta Psychol. (Amst) **152**, 34–41 (2014)
8. Sanchez-Vives, M.V., Spanlang, B., Frisoli, A., Bergamasco, M., Slater, M.: Virtual hand illusion induced by visuomotor correlations. PLoS ONE **5**, e10381 (2010)

9. Tsakiris, M., Longo, M.R., Haggard, P.: Having a body versus moving your body: neural signatures of agency and body-ownership. Neuropsychologia **48**, 2740–2749 (2010)

10. Kilteni, K.: Extending body space in immersive virtual reality: a very long arm illusion. PLoS ONE **7**, e40867 (2012)

11. Kilteni, K., Bergstrom, I., Slater, M.: Drumming in immersive virtual reality: the body shapes the way we play. IEEE Trans. Vis. Comput. Graph. **19**, 597–605 (2013)

12. Kokkinara, E., Slater, M.: Measuring the effects through time of the influence of visuomotor and visuotactile synchronous stimulation on a virtual body ownership illusion. Perception **43**, 43–58 (2014)

13. Banakou, D., Groten, R., Slater, M.: Illusory ownership of a virtual child body causes overestimation of object sizes and implicit attitude changes. Proc. Natl. Acad. Sci. USA **110**, 12846–12851 (2013)

14. Franck, N., Farrer, C., Georgieff, N., Marie-Cardine, M., Daléry, J., D'Amato, T., Jeannerod, M.: Defective recognition of one's own actions in patients with schizophrenia. Am. J. Psychiatry **158**, 454–459 (2001)

15. Shimada, S., Fukuda, K., Hiraki, K.: Rubber hand illusion under delayed visual feedback. PLoS ONE **4**, 1–5 (2009)

16. Alais, D., Cass, J.: Multisensory perceptual learning of temporal order: audiovisual learning transfers to vision but not audition. PLoS ONE **5**, 3–38 (2010)

17. Alais, D., Newell, F.N., Mamassian, P.: Multisensory processing in review: from physiology to behaviour. Seeing Perceiving **23**, 3–38 (2010)

18. Hoyet, L., Argelaguet, F., Nicole, C., Lécuyer, A.: "Wow! I have six fingers!": would you accept structural changes of your hand in VR? Front. Robot. AI. **3**, 1–12 (2016)

19. Ogawa, N., Ban, Y., Sakurai, S., Narumi, T.: Metamorphosis hand: dynamically transforming hands. In: Proceedings of the 7th Augmented Human International Conference 2016, pp. 5–6 (2016)

20. Ma, K., Hommel, B.: The role of agency for perceived ownership in the virtual hand illusion. Conscious. Cogn. **36**, 277–288 (2015)

21. Argelaguet, F., Hoyet, L., Trico, M., Lécuyer, A.: The role of interaction in virtual embodiment: Effects of the virtual hand representation. In: Proceedings - IEEE Virtual Reality, pp. 3–10, July 2016

22. Armel, K.C., Ramachandran, V.S.: Projecting sensations to external objects: evidence from skin conductance response. Proc. Biol. Sci. **270**, 1499–1506 (2003)

23. Longo, M.R., Schüür, F., Kammers, M.P.M., Tsakiris, M., Haggard, P.: What is embodiment? A psychometric approach. Cognition **107**, 978–998 (2008)

24. Rao, R.P.N., Ballard, D.H.: Predictive coding in the visual cortex: a functional interpretationof some extra-classical receptive-field effects. Nat. Neurosci. **2**, 79–87 (1999)

25. Körding, K.P., Beierholm, U., Ma, W.J., Quartz, S., Tenenbaum, J.B., Shams, L.: Causal inference in multisensory perception. PLoS ONE **2**, e943 (2007)

26. Cuppini, C., Magosso, E., Ursino, M.: Organization, maturation, and plasticity of multisensory integration: insights from computational modeling studies. Front. Psychol. **2**, 77 (2011)

27. Normand, J.M., Giannopoulos, E., Spanlang, B., Slater, M.: Multisensory stimulation can induce an illusion of larger belly size in immersive virtual reality. PLoS ONE **6**, e16128 (2011)

28. Petkova, V.I., Ehrsson, H.H.: If I were you: perceptual illusion of body swapping. PLoS ONE **3**, e3832 (2008)

29. Ernst, M.O., Banks, M.S.: Humans integrate visual and haptic information in a statistically optimal fashion. Nature **415**, 429–433 (2002)

30. Ehrsson, H.: The concept of body ownership and its relation to multisensory integration. In: Stein, B.E. (ed.) The New Handbook Multisensory Process, pp. 775–792 (2012)

31. Longo, M.R., Mancini, F., Haggard, P.: Implicit body representations and tactile spatial remapping. Acta Psychol. (Amst) **160**, 77–87 (2015)

32. Heed, T., Buchholz, V.N., Engel, A.K., Röder, B.: Tactile remapping: from coordinate transformation to integration in sensorimotor processing. Trends Cogn. Sci. **19**, 251–258 (2015)

33. Fuchs, X., Riemer, M., Diers, M., Flor, H., Trojan, J.: Perceptual drifts of real and artificial limbs in the rubber hand illusion. Sci. Rep. **6**, 24362 (2016)

34. Linkenauger, S.A., Leyrer, M., Bülthoff, H.H., Mohler, B.J.: Welcome to wonderland: the influence of the size and shape of a virtual hand on the perceived size and shape of virtual objects. PLoS ONE **8**, e68594 (2013)

35. Haggard, P., Jundi, S.: Rubber hand illusions and size-weight illusions: self-representation modulates representation of external objects. Perception **38**, 1796–1803 (2009)

36. van der Hoort, B., Guterstam, A., Ehrsson, H.H.: Being barbie: the size of one's own body determines the perceived size of the world. PLoS ONE **6**, e20195 (2011)

37. Proffitt, D.R., Linkenauger, S.A.: Perception viewed as a phenotypic expression. In: Prinz, W., Beisert, M., Herwig, A. (eds.) Action science: Foundations of an Emerging Discipline, pp. 171–198. MIT, Cambridge

38. Linkenauger, S.A., Ramenzoni, V., Proffitt, D.R.: Illusory shrinkage and growth: body-based rescaling affects the perception of size. Psychol. Sci. **21**, 1318–1325 (2010)

39. van der Hoort, B., Ehrsson, H.H.: Body ownership affects visual perception of object size by rescaling the visual representation of external space. Atten. Percept. Psychophys. **76**, 1414–1428 (2014)

40. Marino, B.F.M., Stucchi, N., Nava, E., Haggard, P., Maravita, A.: Distorting the visual size of the hand affects hand pre-shaping during grasping. Exp. Brain Res. **202**, 499–505 (2010)

41. Mohler, B.J., Creem-Regehr, S.H., Thompson, W.B., Bülthoff, H.H.: The effect of viewing a self-avatar on distance judgments in an HMD-based virtual environment. Presence Teleoperators Virtual Environ. **19**, 230–242 (2010)

42. Ogawa, N., Narumi, T., Hirose, M.: Distortion in perceived size and body-based scaling in virtual environments. In: Proceedings of the 8th Augmented Human International Conference on - AH 2017, pp. 1–5. ACM Press, New York (2017)

43. Longo, M.R., Schuur, F., Kammers, M.P.M., Tsakiris, M., Haggard, P.: Self awareness and the body image. Acta Psychol. (Amst) **132**, 166–172 (2009)

44. Tsakiris, M.: Looking for myself: current multisensory input alters self-face recognition. PLoS ONE **3**, e4040 (2008)

45. Yee, N., Bailenson, J.: The proteus effect: the effect of transformed self-representation on behavior. Hum. Commun. Res. **33**, 271–290 (2007)

46. Superhuman Sports Academy: Superhuman Sports Academy Official Website. http://superhuman-sports.org/academy/eindex.html

Considerations for Using Fitness Trackers in Psychophysiology Research

Lauren Reinerman-Jones[✉], Jonathan Harris, and Andrew Watson

University of Central Florida Institute for Simulation and Training Prodigy Laboratory,
3100 Technology Parkway, Orlando, FL 32826, USA
lreinerm@ist.ucf.edu

Abstract. Wrist worn fitness trackers have become ubiquitous in recent years. Economies of scale have drastically reduced the cost of these devices while concurrent advances in technology have expanded their physiological recording capabilities. These devices now contain numerous sensors capable of monitoring and collecting various physiological attributes. Additionally, some of these devices provide access to the application programming interface (API), allowing researchers direct access to the data. The use of these devices offers a wide-ranging benefit to the scientific research community. However, there are several factors to consider when selecting a fitness tracker for use in research. Data rights, data protection, and data quality are all important considerations that must be addressed. In addition, other factors, such as sensor types, capabilities, and sampling rates, can directly affect the utility of a wearable device for use in research. In this paper, the Microsoft Band 2 fitness tracker was selected to evaluate participant mental workload during task performance in a simulated nuclear nower plant (NPP) Main Control Room (MCR) as well as training effectiveness in UH-60A/L simulated environments. The Microsoft Band 2 fitness tracker was selected specifically for its optical hear rate sensor, API access to RR intervals (interval between two continuous heartbeats), and direct access to real-time streaming data from the device. To validate the utility of using the Microsoft Band 2 fitness trackers in scientific research, the RR interval and heart rate sensor readings need to be directly compared to FDA medical approved sensor readings. This paper discusses considerations when using a fitness tracker for psychophysiology research and compares data collected from the Microsoft Band 2 to two different FDA approved medical grade ECG devices.

Keywords: Fitness tracker · Wearables · Psychophysiology · Sensors · Optical heart rate · Photoplethysmography · Microsoft band

1 Introduction

Since the early 1990s on-body computer sensors have been used in research [1]. Early on-body devices used in research were constructed of standard computer components [2]. Recent improvements in sensor technology and manufacturing processes has enabled these devices to shrink in size and weight. This has allowed wearable devices to enter the consumer market. The consumer market for wearable devices has exploded

© Springer International Publishing AG 2017
S. Yamamoto (Ed.): HIMI 2017, Part I, LNCS 10273, pp. 598–606, 2017.
DOI: 10.1007/978-3-319-58521-5_47

in recent years and is expected to reach 245 million units sold by 2019 [3]. The term wearable is a widely used term with various definitions. This paper adopts the simple definition that a wearable device is a computer or electronic technology that can be incorporated into clothing or accessories, and be worn comfortably on the body [4]. This definition differentiates wearables from dedicated sensor devices that are worn on-body since a dedicated device is not incorporated into clothes or used as an accessory. Sarah Wilson from CCS Insight estimates that the wearables market will be $25 billion by 2019 [3]. Fitness trackers are a subset of wearables and account for a substantial share of the wearable market. PC Magazine defines fitness trackers as a wrist-worn device that detects some combination of steps, run distances, heart rate, and/or sleep patterns [5]. By the end of 2015 nearly 33 million fitness trackers had been sold [6]. Fitness trackers come packed with various sensors that monitor the health of the human wearing the device. While mainly developed for health monitoring, fitness trackers are ideal for performing psychophysiology research. However, as with any technology, before incorporating fitness trackers into scientific research, it is important to understand their capabilities and limitations. This paper covers the process that was followed for selecting the most suitable fitness tracker for two field research studies conducted by the Prodigy laboratory at the Institute for Simulation and Training, University of Central Florida. The first study investigated participants' mental workload demands when performing operating procedure tasks in a simulated nuclear power plant main control room environment. The second study conducted a training effectiveness evaluation with UH-60A/L pilots in virtual environments by looking at task engagement.

2 Fitness Tracker Sensors

Fitness trackers provide a low cost and minimally invasive way of sampling certain physiological responses to stimuli [1]. Psychophysiology research is classified as any research where the dependent variable is a physiological measure, and independent variables are behavioral or mental [7]. While sensors in fitness trackers are an ideal psychophysiological instrument for measuring responses to experimental stimuli, the kind of data and its quality depend on the wearable's capabilities. Most commercial fitness trackers such as the Jawbone 4, Fitbit Surge, Garmin vívoactive, and Microsoft Band 2 have accelerometers and gyroscopes to track physical activity, motion, and sleep. The inertial sensors in these devices typically have variable or user configurable sampling rates. In the case of the Microsoft Band, the data stream has three supported sampling frequencies (8/31/62 Hz) for its Accelerometer and Gyroscope [8]. The Microsoft Band 2 also includes digital GPS, barometer, and UVI (ultra violet index) sensors [9]. The data provided by these additional sensors are useful for outdoor operations where environmental conditions have significant impact on the user's vitals.

There are several other common wearable sensors available on consumer fitness trackers. These can monitor temperature (skin and ambient) as well heartbeat. The Microsoft Band 2 uses a more commonly found optical hear-rate sensor. The sensor shines an LED through the skin and measures the light that is reflected back to the sensor. The more blood in a vessel, the more the light gets absorbed. A process called photoplethysmography is used to translate fluctuations in light to heart beats [10]. Another commonly found physiological sensor is the Galvanic Skin Response (GSR) sensor. This instrument measures electrodermal activity or skin conductance. GSR sensors are commonly implemented as a set of conductive probes that measure the resistance across an area of the user's skin [11].

Wearables like the Myo Band contain more exotic sensors found outside of the consumer fitness market. These devices can measure blood pressure, respiratory rate, and even muscle activity (Electromyography).

3   Data Considerations

It is important to consider the legal aspects of data rights when using wearables. When considering a device, it is important to review the legal documents, such as the end user license agreement (EULA) and product safety guides. The EULA will explain data rights and ownership for the wearable. This is particularly important for a study because the organization executing data collection and/or the agency funding the data collection will want to own all of the data for analyses and reporting.

Related, is data storage and retrieval. Reviewing the product website for other relevant information on the wearable that may affect its utility for a study and FAQs pages are good sources to learn about a wearable's capabilities, data formats, and methods for accessing sensor data. There are two approaches for acquiring the sensor data: 1. access through a web interface or 2. access directly from the device.

Most wearable devices provide cloud based services for synchronizing sensor data to the web. For cloud-based storage, an internet connection is required; this is most often done through a tethered phone or PC connected to the internet. Sensor data stored on the web increases the risk of unauthorized persons accessing sensitive data and anonymizing data becomes important. Another issue to consider when accessing data from the web is how much of a delay uploading adds to the data collection process, which potentially affects the data's value as it pertains to direct connection of the physiological response to the stimulus. Cloud based access is not suitable for real-time closed loop research.

A few wearable devices provide local access to sensor data. These wearable devices provide access to sensor data without requiring an internet connection. This is accomplished by synchronizing a computer with the device's local storage and/or real time sensor streaming over a wireless protocol such as Bluetooth. Whichever method used for acquiring data, it is important to understand data formats, sample rates, and sensor reporting units since there are no industry standards for wearables [12].

4   Selecting a Fitness Tracker

4.1   Considerations

Reading online product reviews and consumer ratings provides a wealth of information on a fitness tracker. When reading the reviews, also look to see if the tracker supports

3rd party app development through an API. Most major fitness trackers provide software libraries to allow software developers to get access to sensor data. Some manufactures allow access to sensor data through a real-time stream while others only allow access to aggregated data post hoc through a web portal and often, that aggregated data is from the entire day. Depending on the nature of the research, real-time sensor streaming may be a requirement. However, if accessing data post hoc, be sure to keep accurate time records for when a participant wore the tracker in order to tie the sensor data to the proper stimuli events of the experiment.

Often physiological recording devices are complex and require specialized training for the researcher to use the equipment properly. Fitness trackers on the other hand are simple to use and can be as easy as putting on a watch. This ease of use can be deceptive though, be cautious with placing fitness trackers on participants to be consistent with both sensor orientation and placement on the wrist. Also, optical heart rate sensors are susceptible 60 Hz light sources, so be sure the tracker is worn with the correct tautness and does not shift throughout the experiment. Field studies, and to some degree laboratory studies, benefit from the mobility that fitness trackers provide. However, some trackers require Bluetooth or Wi-Fi connectivity to record data. When testing, look at wireless signal strengths with paired devices and make sure to stay within range throughout the study.

4.2   Selection of Microsoft Band 2

As mentioned previously, determining the appropriate device was important for two studies. The criteria for both studies were to choose a fitness tracker that provided local access to heart beat data. The fitness tracker ideally needed to provide raw photoplethysmogram data. This would allow for post hoc analysis on algorithms for heart beat detection. At a minimum, the tracker needed to provide an R-peak detection. This would allow the tracker to support heart rate (HR) and heart rate variability (HRV) analysis to assess mental workload or task engagement for the Nuclear Power Plant and UH60A/L studies, respectively. Several fitness trackers provided API access to beats per minute data, but the Microsoft Band 2 was the only commercially available fitness tracker that provided RR intervals. Both of the studies chose to use the Microsoft Band 2 as the fitness tracker because the RR interval supports HR and HRV analysis. However, both studies used additional sensors to augment and verify HR and HRV analysis. GSR and skin temperature were collected for both studies due to their correlates with both mental workload and task engagement.

4.3   Lessons Learned

Most fitness trackers have enough battery life to last several days on a single charge for normal daily use. However, when using a fitness tracker for research, it typically will be streaming and recording multiple sensor feeds for the duration of the study. If the study is several hours, battery life could be of concern. During pre-experiment testing, the Microsoft Band 2 lasted well over four hours with all sensors continuously streaming.

However, as a precautionary measure, the fitness trackers were fully charged before each experimental run. Battery life was never an issue for either of the studies.

Psychophysiology studies often require participants to be connected to multiple sensors. Most of these sensors are only mildly invasive; however, there is not much risk of participants forgetting to remove them before concluding the study. This is not the case with fitness trackers. Since fitness trackers are so natural to wear and non-invasive, it is important to have explicit procedures reminding researchers to remove the trackers from participant's wrists before dismissing them. During the two studies no fitness trackers were lost, but even with a checklist, a few occasions required participants to be tracked down in the parking lot to return a fitness tracker.

The default settings on fitness trackers are setup for the consumer and some of the settings need to be changed before conducting research. It is important to go through each setting and make sure the fitness tracker is in a mode that will not interfere with the study. Between piloting and data collection for training effectiveness evaluation with UH-60A/L pilots, the Microsoft Band 2 had a software update. The update changed all the settings back to defaults (including the activity reminder). During experimentation, two of the UH60A/L pilots had a vibration reminder to get up and move due to inactivity. After that experiment, a checklist item was added to visually verify the fitness tracker was in "do not disturb" mode before each experimental session.

It is critical to understand how to retrieve the data from the fitness tracker. Doron Katz of Programmable Web has a great web page that aggregates the popular APIs for fitness trackers along with links to developer pages for each API [13]. The Microsoft Band 2 API provided direct access to the sensor readings from a paired Bluetooth phone or windows PC. Windows PC development requires c# RT metro libraries. The metro app requirement limits the APIs capability of integrating the sensor data with a native windows application. As a workaround, a custom streaming UDP client/server app was developed for data collection. This allowed the metro app to communicate with a native windows app.

Be careful when purchasing a newly released fitness tracker model because technology changes so fast that manufactures often do not have adequate time to perform sufficient product testing. Be sure to adequately put the technology through its paces before using in an experiment. Several of the Microsoft Band 2 that were purchased for experimentation had to be returned due to a charging issue after less than a month of use. Waiting a few months before ordering a newly released fitness tracker can avoid having to return it because of a minor design flaws. On the flip side, do not order fitness trackers that are near the end of life for production. If the fitness tracker breaks in the middle of a study, replacement availability for the specific model may become impossible. Also, select fitness trackers from manufactures that have a history of making quality fitness trackers. While Microsoft is a large company with a proven track record of quality hardware, their line of fitness trackers was discontinued following completion of these two studies due to lack of consumer interest in their high-end fitness tracker.

5   Data Quality Comparisons

5.1   Nuclear Power Plant Study

The nuclear power plant (NPP) main control room (MCR) study used both the Microsoft band 2 fitness tracker and the B-Alert X10 [14] system to collect psychophysiological responses of participants. The B-Alert system was used to sample the participant's electrocardiography signal at 256 Hz. Post hoc analysis was run on the B-Alert sampled signal using a bio signal processing toolkit written in Python called BioSPPy [15]. The Hamilton ECG R-peak segmentation algorithm was used to calculate R-peaks [16]. From the R-peaks, three measures were derived: interbeat interval (IBI), beats per minute (BPM) and HRV. The Microsoft Band 2's R-peaks collected during the same time period allows for a comparison between the fitness tracker and the Hamilton ECG R-peak segmentation algorithm on the B-Alert sampled ECG signal. The table below shows metrics for five participants' data collected during a 25-minute change detection task (Table 1).

Table 1. *Comparison* of Microsoft band 2 and Hamilton ECG algorithm using B-Alert sampled ECG signal. The Microsoft band 2 data is in columns with MB headers and the Hamilton data is in columns with the H headers. IBI values are in milliseconds.

Participant	Min IBI		Max IBI		Mean IBI		Median IBI		BPM		HRV	
	MB	H	MB	H	MB	H	MB	H	MB	H	MB	H
1	3	417	7641	1343	836	631	682	625	71.77	94.95	715.17	58.91
2	3	531	5084	757	690	614	649	609	86.91	97.69	385.96	34.66
3	1	351	11297	1355	731	581	655	574	82.00	103.13	607.91	46.21
4	32	289	2626	1070	801	814	827	832	74.87	73.70	225.14	116.72
5	16	578	2928	2359	803	809	792	757	74.68	74.14	252.01	202.06

A visual inspection of the Microsoft Band 2's R-Peak detection accuracy was done by plotting each participants' data for both the Hamilton and Microsoft band 2's R-peak algorithms overlaid on the B-Alert sampled ECG signal. The graph below shows the ECG signal for the first 5 s from the first participant. The vertical dashed lines represent Microsoft Band 2's detected R-peaks and the solid light gray lines represent the Hamilton detected R-peaks (Fig. 1).

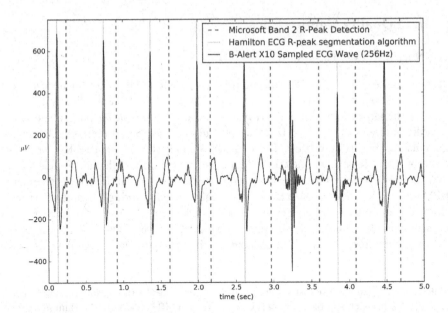

Fig. 1. First 5 s of a former reactor operator performing tasks in an EOP. ECG was collected using B-Alert.

5.2 UH-60A/L Training Effectiveness Study

The UH-60A/L study performed similar analyses, but used a different ECG sensor. The Thought Technologies ProComp Infiniti device [17] was used to sample the electrocardiography signal at 2048 Hz. In the same manner as the NPP study, post hoc analysis was run on the ProComp Infiniti sampled signal using BioSPPy [15]. The Hamilton ECG R-peak segmentation algorithm was also used to calculate R-peaks [16]. Three measures were derived from the R-peaks: IBI, BPM and HRV. In the same manner as the NPP MCR study, the Microsoft Band 2's R-peaks were compared to the Hamilton ECG R-peak segmentation algorithm on the ProComp Infiniti ECG signal. The table below shows metrics for five UH60A/L pilots's data collected during a 60-minute simulated CASEVAC scenario. The scenario was conducted in the Operational Flight Trainer [18] (Table 2).

Table 2. *Comparison* of Microsoft band 2 and Hamilton ECG algorithm using ProComp Infinity sampled ECG signal. The Microsoft band 2 data is in columns with MB headers and the Hamilton data is in columns with the H headers. IBI values are in milliseconds.

Participant	Min IBI		Max IBI		Mean IBI		Median IBI		BPM		HRV	
	MB	H	MB	H	MB	H	MB	H	MB	H	MB	H
1	16	387	2172	1006	753	725	766	716	79.61	82.76	170.88	85.64
2	16	321	2516	907	787	670	812	669	76.25	89.46	235.31	64.25
3	31	287	1797	1045	810	811	828	812	74.03	73.99	159.24	65.38
4	31	277	2016	850	513	432	453	431	116.98	139	187.36	18.15
5	31	550	1828	1238	808	783	828	786	74.24	76.59	199.58	95.42

A visual inspection of the Microsoft Band 2's R-Peak detection accuracy was done by plotting each participants' data for the Microsoft band 2's R-peak algorithms overlaid on the ProComp Infinity sampled ECG signal. The graph below shows the ECG signal for the first 5 s from the first UH-60 pilot. The Vertical dashed lines represent Microsoft Band 2's detected R-peaks and the solid light gray lines represents the Hamilton detected R-peaks (Fig. 2).

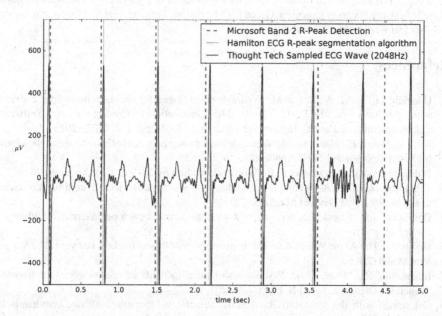

Fig. 2. First 5 s of a pilots ECG during a simulated CASEVAC Mission. ECG was collected using ProComp infinity.

It is clear that the optical heart rate sensor in the Microsoft Band 2 fitness tracker does not provide equivalent R-peak data to electrical sensors designed to provide highly accurate ECG signals. While optical heart rate sensors found in wrist worn fitness trackers provide useful estimates for monitoring health, more work is needed to ensure accurate data is provided for performing certain types psychophysiology research. An incorrect estimate of the R-peak by 100 ms can increase HRV by 100% [19]. While HRV analysis using the band is not practical given the magnitude of error associated with the optical sensors on the wrist, BPM analysis may be accurate enough for some types of analysis. Visual inspection of the Microsoft Band 2 plotted over the raw ECG signal shows roughly one R-peak detected per QRS wave seen in the ECG signal. Also, BPM analysis is more robust to false positives/negatives because one or two missed beats only slightly affects BMP.

Acknowledgments. This report was prepared as an account of work sponsored by (CA# W911NF-14-2-001 and in part (NRC-HQ-12-C-04-0058/NRC-HQ-60-14-T-0001) by an agency of the U.S. Government. Neither the U.S. Government nor any agency thereof, nor any of their employees, makes any warranty, expressed or implied, or assumes any legal liability or responsibility for any third party's use, or the results of such use, of any information, apparatus, product, or process disclosed in this report, or represents that its use by such third party would not infringe privately owned rights. The views expressed in this paper are not necessarily those of the U.S. Army Program Executive Office for Simulation, Training, and Instrumentation or the U.S. Nuclear Regulatory Commission.

References

1. Udovičić, G., Topić, A., Russo, M.: Wearable technologies for smart environments: a review with emphasis on BCI. In: 2016 24th International Conference on Software, Telecommunications and Computer Networks (SoftCOM), pp. 1–9. IEEE (2016)
2. Kim, Y., Wang, H., Mahmud, M.: Wearable body sensor network for health care applications. In: Smart Textiles and Their Applications, p. 161 (2016)
3. Wilson, S.: Wearables Market to Be Worth $25 Billion by 2019 (2015). Accessed 2017
4. Tehrani, K., Michael, A.: Wearable Technology and Wearable Devices: Everything You Need to Know. Wearable Devices Magazine (2014)
5. Definition of: fitness tracker. http://www.pcmag.com/encyclopedia/term/67469/fitness-tracker
6. Goode, L.: The Apple Watch didn't slow down sales of fitness trackers last year. The Verge, Vox Media (2016)
7. Infantolino, Z., Miller, G.A.: Psychophysiological methods in neuroscience. In: Biswas-Diener, R., Diener, E. (eds.) Noba Project (2017)
8. Get started with the Microsoft Band SDK. https://developer.microsoftband.com/bandsdk. Accessed 2017
9. Wetherow, O.: Microsoft Band II Teardown (2016). http://www.chipworks.com/about-chipworks/overview/blog/microsoft-band-ii-teardown
10. Hayes, T.: What's Inside a Fitness Tracker, Anyway? (2014). http://www.digitaltrends.com/wearables/whats-inside-fitness-tracker-anyway/. Accessed 2017
11. bin Syed Noh, S.A.: Galvanic Skin Response (2015)
12. Rhodes, H.B.: Accessing and using data from wearable fitness devices. J. AHIMA **85**(9), 48–50 (2014)
13. Katz, D.: Top 10 Fitness APIs: Apple Health, Fitbit and Nike (2015). https://www.programmableweb.com/news/top-10-fitness-apis-apple-health-fitbit-and-nike/analysis/2015/04/17. Accessed 2017
14. B-Alert X10 EEG Headset System (2015). http://www.advancedbrainmonitoring.com/xseries/x10/. Accessed 2017
15. BioSPPy - Biosignal Processing in Python (2017). https://github.com/PIA-Group/BioSPPy
16. Hamilton, P.: Open Source ECG Analysis Software Documentation (2002)
17. ProComp Infiniti System (2016). http://thoughttechnology.com/index.php/hardware/procomp-infiniti-170.html. Accessed 2017
18. Training, L.S.: UH-60 M Operational Flight Trainer (2010)
19. Mulder, L.: Measurement and analysis methods of heart rate and respiration for use in applied environments. Biol. Psychol. **34**(2), 205–236 (1992)

A Speech-Driven Embodied Communication System Based on an Eye Gaze Model in Interaction-Activated Communication

Yoshihiro Sejima[1(✉)], Koki Ono[2], and Tomio Watanabe[1]

[1] Faculty of Computer Science and System Engineering, Okayama Prefectural University,
Kuboki 111, Soja-shi, Okayama, Japan
sejima@ss.oka-pu.ac.jp
[2] Benesse InfoShell Co., Ltd., Takayanagihigashimachi 10-1, Kita-ku, Okayama, Japan

Abstract. Line-of-sight such as gaze and eye-contract plays an important role to enhance the embodied interaction and communication through avatars. In addition, many gaze models and communication systems with the line-of-sight using avatars have been proposed and developed. However, the gaze behaviors by generating the above-mentioned models are not considered to enhance the embodied interaction such as activated communication, because the models stochastically generate the eyeball movements based on the human gaze behavior. Therefore, we analyzed the interaction between the human gaze behavior and the activated communication by using line-of-sight measurement devices. Then, we proposed an eye gaze model based on the above-mentioned analysis. In this study, we develop an advanced avatar-mediated communication system in which the proposed eye gaze model is applied to speech-driven embodied entrainment characters called "InterActor." This system generates the avatar's eyeball movements such as gaze and looking away based on the activated communication, and provides a communication environment wherein the embodied interaction is promoted. The effectiveness of the system is demonstrated by means of sensory evaluations of 24 pairs of subjects involved in avatar-mediated communication.

Keywords: Human interaction · Nonverbal communication · Activated communication · Eye gaze model

1 Introduction

With the advancements in the field of information technology, it is now becoming possible for humans to use CG characters called avatars to communicate in a 3D virtual space over a network. Furthermore, many researches that support remote communication using CG characters such as avatars and agent are performed [1]. However, current systems do not simulate embodied sharing using synchrony of embodied rhythms, such as the nodding and body movements in human face-to-face communication, because the CG characters express nonverbal behavior based on the key commands. In human face-to-face communication, not only verbal messages but also nonverbal behavior such as nodding, body movement, line-of-sight and facial expression are rhythmically related

© Springer International Publishing AG 2017
S. Yamamoto (Ed.): HIMI 2017, Part I, LNCS 10273, pp. 607–616, 2017.
DOI: 10.1007/978-3-319-58521-5_48

and mutually synchronized between talkers [2]. This synchrony of embodied rhythms in communication is called entrainment, and it enhances the sharing of embodiment and empathy unconsciously in human interaction and accelerates the activated communication in which nonverbal behaviors such as body movements and speech activity increase, and the embodied interaction is activated [3].

In our previous work, we analyzed the entrainment between a speaker's speech and a listener's nodding motion in face-to-face communication, and developed iRT (Inter-Robot Technology), which generates a variety of communicative actions and movements such as nodding and blinking and movements of the head, arms, and waist that are coherently related to voice input [4]. In addition, we developed an interactive CG character called "InterActor" which has functions of both speaker and listener, and demonstrated that InterActor can effectively support human interaction and communication [4]. Moreover, we developed an estimation model of interaction-activated communication based on the heat conduction equation and demonstrated the effectiveness of the model by the evaluation experiment [5].

On the other hand, body movements as well as line-of-sight such as eye contact and gaze duration play an important role in smooth human face-to-face communication [6]. Moreover, it is reported that smooth communication via avatars is realized by expressing the avatar's gaze. For example, Ishii et al. developed a communication system that controls an avatar's gaze based on an estimated line-of-sight model and demonstrated that utterance is facilitated between talkers using this model in an avatar-mediated communication [7]. Also, we analyzed human eyeball movement through avatars by using an embodied virtual communication system with a line-of-sight measurement device, and proposed an eyeball movement model, consisting of an eyeball delay movement model and a gaze withdrawal model [8]. In addition, we developed an advanced avatar-mediated communication system by applying our proposed eyeball movement model to InterActors, and demonstrated that the developed system is effective for supporting the embodied interaction and communication. These systems generate the avatar's eyeball movement by a statistical model based on face-to-face communication characteristics. However, from the viewpoint of promoting the line-of-sight interaction, it is difficult for these systems to enhance the line-of-sight interaction, because the dynamic characteristics of human line-of-sight in the activated communication have not yet been designed. Therefore, in our previous research, we analyzed the interaction between activated communication and human gaze behavior by using a line-of-sight measurement device [8]. On the basis of this analysis, we proposed an eye gaze model, consisting of an eyeball delay movement model and a look away model.

In this paper, we develop an advanced avatar-mediated communication system by applying the proposed eye gaze model to InterActors. This system generates the avatar's eyeball movements such as gaze and looking away based on the proposed model by using only speech input, and provides a communication environment wherein the embodied interaction is promoted. The effectiveness of the proposed and communication system is demonstrated by means of sensory evaluations in an avatar-mediated communication system.

2   A Speech-Driven Embodied Communication System Based on an Eye Gaze Model

2.1   InterActor

In order to support human interaction and communication, we developed a speech-driven embodied entrainment character called InterActor, which has the functions of both speaker and listener [4]. The configuration of InterActor is shown in Fig. 1. Inter-Actor has a virtual skeleton structure such as head, eyes, mouth, neck, shoulders, elbows, hands (Fig. 1(a)). The texture puts on the 3D surface model including the virtual skeleton structure (Fig. 1(b)). In addition, the various facial expressions are realized by applying the smile model in which the previous research was developed (Fig. 1(c)) [9, 10].

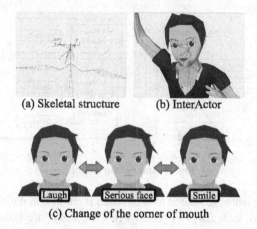

(a) Skeletal structure   (b) InterActor

(c) Change of the corner of mouth

Fig. 1. InterActor: speech-driven embodied entrainment character.

The listener's interaction model includes a nodding reaction model which estimates the nodding timing from a speech ON-OFF pattern and a body reaction model linked to the nodding reaction model [4]. The timing of nodding is predicted using a hierarchy model consisting of two stages; macro and micro (Fig. 2). The macro stage estimates whether a nodding response exists or not in a duration unit which consists of a talkspurt episode $T(i)$ and the following silence episode $S(i)$ with a hangover value of 4/30 s. The estimator $M_u(i)$ is a moving-average (MA) model, expressed as the weighted sum of unit speech activity $R(i)$ in Eqs. (1) and (2). When $M_u(i)$ exceeds a threshold value, nodding $M(i)$ is also a MA model, estimated as the weighted sum of the binary speech signal $V(i)$ in Eq. (3).

$$M_u(i) = \sum_{j=1}^{J} a(j)R(i-j) + u(i) \tag{1}$$

$$R(i) = \frac{T(i)}{T(i) + S(i)} \tag{2}$$

$a(j)$: linear prediction coefficient
$T(i)$: talkspurt duration in the i th duration unit
$S(i)$: silence duration in the i th duration unit
$u(i)$: noise
i: number of frame

$$M(i) = \sum_{j=1}^{K} b(j)V(i-j) + w(i) \qquad (3)$$

$b(j)$: linear prediction coefficient
$V(i)$: voice
$w(i)$: noise

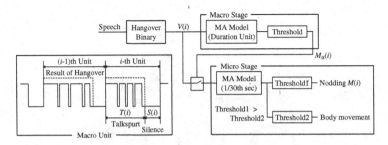

Fig. 2. Interaction model.

The body movements are related to the speech input in that the neck and one of the wrists, elbows, arms, or waist is operated when the body threshold is exceeded. The threshold is set lower than that of the nodding prediction of the MA model, which is expressed as the weighted sum of the binary speech signal to nodding. In other words, when InterActor functions as a listener for generating body movements, the relationship between nodding and other movements is dependent on the threshold values of the nodding estimation.

2.2 Eye Gaze Model

We proposed an eye gaze model that generates a gaze movement and looking away movement for enhancing embodied communication based on the characteristics of the analysis of human eyeball movement. The proposed model consists of the previous eyeball delay movement model [8] and look away model. The outline of the proposed model is indicated as follows:

(1) Eyeball Delay Movement Model
The eyeball delay movement model consists of a delay of 0.13 s with respect to the avatar's head movement. First, the angle of the avatar's gaze direction for the viewpoint in virtual space is calculated using Eq. 4 (Fig. 3(a)). Then, the avatar's gaze is generated by adding the angle of the avatar's head movement to the angle of the avatar's gaze

direction in the fourth previous frame at a frame rate of 30 fps (Eq. 5). Figure 3(b) shows an example of the eyeball delay movement model in an avatar. If the avatar's head moves, the eyeball moves with a delay of 0.13 s with respect to the head movement in the opposite direction.

$$\theta_{AG} = \tan^{-1} \frac{A_{Ex} - P_x}{A_{Ey} - P_y}$$

(4)

θ_{AG}: Rotation angle of gaze direction
A_{Ex}, A_{Ey}: eyeball postion of InterActor
P_x, P_y: position of view point in virtual space

$$\theta_G(i) = \theta_{AH}(i) + \theta_{AG}(i - 4)$$

(5)

$\theta_G(i)$: Rotation angle of eyeball movement
$\theta_{AH}(i)$: Rotation angle of InterActor's head movement
i: number of frame

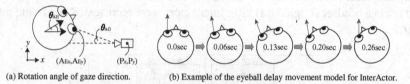

(a) Rotation angle of gaze direction.   (b) Example of the eyeball delay movement model for InterActor.

Fig. 3. Eyeball delay movement model.

(2) Look Away Model

The previous analysis of the human eyeball indicates that direct gaze is limited to about 80% of total conversation time [8]. Therefore, the look away model in this study generates eyeball movement for other gazes such as gaze withdrawal and blinking based on the previous analysis. The avatar's eyeball of looking away is moved at the horizontal direction greatly (Fig. 4), and the effectiveness of this movement was confirmed in a preliminary experiment. When a value which is estimated the degree of interaction-activated communication falls below a threshold value, the looking away movement is generated by the proposed model (Fig. 5). The avatar's gaze would be modulated such that staring is prevented and impressions of the conversation such as unification and vividness are enhanced.

Fig. 4. Looking away movement.

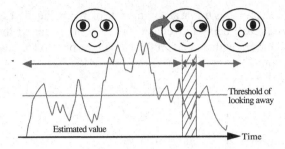

Fig. 5. Look away model.

2.3   Developed System

We developed an advanced communication system in which the proposed model was used with InterActors (Fig. 6). The virtual space was generated by Microsoft DirectX 9.0 SDK (June 2010) and a Windows 7 workstation (CPU: Corei7 2.93 GHz, Memory: 8 GB, Graphics: NVIDIA Geforce GTS250). The voice was sampled using 16 bits at 11 kHz via a headset (Logicool H330). InterActors were represented at a frame rate of 30 fps.

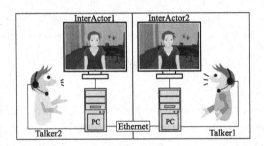

Fig. 6. System setup.

When Talker1 speaks to Talker2, InterActor2 responds to Talker1's utterance with appropriate timing through body movements, including nodding, blinking, and actions, in a manner similar to the body motions of a listener. A nodding movement is defined as the falling-rising movement in the front-back direction at a speed of 0.15 rad/frame. In addition, InterActor2 generates an eyeball movement based on the proposed model. Here, a looking away movement is defined as the left-right motion of eyeballs at a speed of 0.15 rad/frame based on the preliminary experiment. Also, InterActor1 generates communicative actions and movements and avatar's eyeball movements as a speaker by using the MA model and eye gaze model. In this manner, two remote talkers can enjoy a conversation via InterActors within a communication environment in which the sense of unity is shared by embodied entrainment.

3 Communication Experiment

In order to evaluate the developed system, a communication experiment was carried out using the developed system.

3.1 Experimental Method

The experiment was performed on talkers engaged in a free conversation. In this experiment, the following three modes were compared: mode (A) with neither eyeball movement nor facial expression, mode (B) with smile model only, and mode (C) with combined smile model and eye gaze model. We recorded the communication experiment scene using two video cameras and screens as shown in Fig. 7. The subjects were 12 pairs of talkers (12 males and 12 females).

Fig. 7. Example of a communication scene using the system.

The experimental procedure is described as follows. First, the subjects used the system for around 3 min. Next, they were instructed to perform a paired comparison of modes in which, based on their preferences, they selected the better mode. Finally, they were urged to talk in a free conversation for 3 min in each mode. The questionnaire used a seven-point bipolar rating scale from −3 (not at all) to 3 (extremely), where a score of 0 denotes "moderately." The conversational topics were not specified in both experiments. Each pair of talkers was presented with the two modes in a random order.

3.2 Result

The results of the paired comparison are summarized in Table 1. In this table, the number of winner is shown. For example, the number of mode (A)'s winner is six for mode (B), and the number of total winner is nine. Figure 8 shows the calculated results of the evaluation provided in Table 1 based on the Bradley-Terry model given in Eqs. (6) and (7) [11].

$$p_{ij} = \frac{\pi_i}{\pi_i + \pi_j} \tag{6}$$

$$\sum_i \pi_i = const.(= 100) \tag{7}$$

Table 1. Result of paired comparison.

	(A)	(B)	(C)	Total
(A)		6	3	9
(B)	18		5	23
(C)	21	19		40

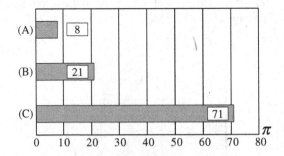

Fig. 8. Comparison of the preference π based on the Bradley-Terry model.

π_i: Intensity of i
p_{ij}: probability of judgment that i is better than j

The consistency of mode matching was confirmed by performing a goodness of fit test $(x^2(1, 0.05) = 3.84 > x_0^2 = 0.28)$ and   a   likelihood   ratio   test $(x^2(1, 0.05) = 3.84 > x_0^2 = 0.27)$. The proposed mode (C), with both smile model and eye gaze model, was evaluated as the best; followed by mode (B), smile model only; and mode (A), no movement.

The questionnaire results are shown in Fig. 9. From the results of the Friedman signed-rank test and the Wilcoxon signed rank test, all categories showed a significance level of 1% among modes (A), (B), and (C). In addition, "Enjoyment," "Interaction-activated communication," "Vividness," and "Natural line-of-sight" had a significance level of 5% between modes (B) and (C).

In both experiments, mode (C) of the proposed eye gaze model was evaluated as the best for avatar-mediated communication. These results indicate the effectiveness of the proposed eye gaze model. These results demonstrate that the combined model is effective.

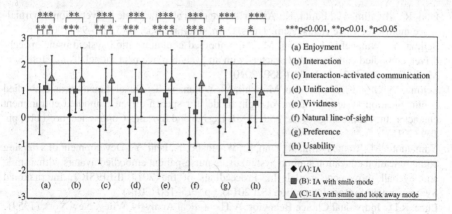

Fig. 9. Seven-points bipolar rating.

4   Conclusion

In this paper, we developed an advanced avatar-mediated communication system in which our proposed eye gaze model is used by speech-driven embodied entrainment characters called InterActors. The proposed model consists of an eyeball delay movement model and a look away model. The communication system generates eyeball movement based on this model by generating the entrained head and body motions of InterActors using only speech input. Sensory evaluations in an avatar-mediated communication system showed the effectiveness of the proposed eye gaze model and communication system.

Acknowledgments. This work was supported by JSPS KAKENHI Grant Numbers JP16K01560, JP26280077.

References

1. Ishii, K., Taniguchi, Y., Osawa, H., Nakadai, K., Imai, M.: Merging viewpoints of user and avatar in telecommunication using image and sound projector. Trans. Inf. Process. Soc. Jpn. **54**(4), 1413–1421 (2013)
2. Condon, W.S., Sander, L.W.: Neonate movement is synchronized with adult speech. Science **183**, 99–101 (1974)
3. Watanabe, T.: Human-entrained embodied interaction and communication technology. In: Fukuda, S. (ed.) Emotional Engineering, pp. 161–177. Springer, Heidelberg (2011)
4. Watanabe, T., Okubo, M., Nakashige, M., Danbara, R.: InterActor: speech-driven embodied interactive actor. Int. J. Hum.-Comput. Interact. **17**(1), 43–60 (2004)
5. Sejima, Y., Watanabe, T., Jindai, M.: Development of an interaction-activated communication model based on a heat conduction equation in voice communication. In: Proceedings of the 23rd IEEE International Symposium on Robot and Human Interactive Communication (RO-MAN 2014), pp. 832–837 (2014)
6. Argyle, M., Dean, J.: Eye contact, distance and affiliation. Sociometry **41**(3), 289–304 (1965)

7. Ishii, R., Miyajima, T., Fujita, K.: Avatar's gaze control to facilitate conversation in virtual-space multi-user voice chat system. Trans. Hum. Interface Soc. **10**(3), 87–94 (2007)
8. Sejima, Y., Watanabe, T., Jindai, M.: An embodied communication system using speech-driven embodied entrainment characters with an eyeball movement model. Trans. Jpn. Soc. Mech. Eng. Ser. C **76**(762), 340–350 (2010)
9. Sejima, Y., Ono, K., Yamamoto, M., Ishii, Y., Watanabe, T.: Development of an embodied communication system with line-of-sight model for speech-driven embodied entrainment character. In: Proceedings of the 25th JSME Design and Systems Conference, no. 1110, pp. 1–9 (2015)
10. Yamamoto, M., Takabayashi, N., Ono, K., Watanabe, T., Ishii, Y.: Development of a nursing communication education support system using nurse-patient embodied avatars with a smile and eyeball movement model. In: Proceedings of the 2014 IEEE/SICE International Symposium on System Integration (SII 2014), pp. 175–180 (2014)
11. Luce, R.D.: Individual Choice Behavior: A Theoretical Analysis. Wiley, New York (1959)

Sharing Indirect Biofeedback Information for Mutual Acceptance

Madoka Takahara$^{(\boxtimes)}$, Fangwei Huang, Ivan Tanev,
and Katsunori Shimohara

Graduate School of Science and Engineering, Doshisha University, Kyoto, Japan
{takahara2012,fhuang2014,itanev,
kshimoha}@sil.doshisha.ac.jp

Abstract. This paper proposes a model of mutual acceptance between a patient, his/her family members and medical staff by sharing information through indirect biofeedback. For upcoming a so-called super aging society, it has been becoming a serious problem how effective and high-quality care support for aged persons could be achieved in Japan. Here we focus on psychological aspect of this problem. That is, it would be a possible way to tackle the problem if an aged patient, his/her family members and medical staff could deepen their mutual understanding and mutual acceptance by sharing indirect biofeedback information of the patient. This paper describes and discusses two mechanisms; indirect biofeedback of a user's sleep state based on analysis and measurement of his/her sleep data, and sharing information of his/her indirect biofeedback with a plant-type indicator through experiments. We conducted an experiment using the elderly people in the facility and healthy people. The participants see the virtual plants which is visualized their own sleep state and the participants try to do mutual understanding and mutual acceptance. We evaluated the measured data as well as the answers to a questionnaire filled out before and after the experiment. The results indicated that the study participants could properly promote mutual understanding and mutual acceptance by using proposed system.

Keywords: Mutual acceptance · Sharing information · Indirect biofeedback · Quality of sleep · Plant-type indicator

1 Introduction

The number of people with stress and mental health problems suffering also from sleep disorder has been gradually increasing in Japan. However, their situation is often not improved only by consulting with specialists in psychiatry or psychosomatic medicine [1].

There is a view postulating that a patient with schizophrenia and the doctor play the "language game," a philosophical concept advocated by L. J. J. Wittgenstein, where the doctor "plays" the role of a doctor rather than understanding the patient, and the patient "plays" the role of patient rather than revealing their true nature to the doctor [2]. In the current state of psychiatric care, a patient might believe that it is sufficient to visit the hospital to get some instructions and prescriptions to alleviate the symptoms, and that

© Springer International Publishing AG 2017
S. Yamamoto (Ed.): HIMI 2017, Part I, LNCS 10273, pp. 617–630, 2017.
DOI: 10.1007/978-3-319-58521-5_49

the situation can be improved by using the remedy given for the disease. On the other hand, the goal of the doctor might be to just ease the symptoms and pain from which the patient is suffering and not remove the cause of the disease.

A consultation with such a specialist could not be very effective if it is a passive experience for the patient. However, if the patient is asked to approach the symptoms of his/her disease in a voluntary and proactive way, the treatment is more likely to succeed. To elicit proactive behavior, the patient with sleep disorder must be made aware of their current sleep state so they can then act appropriately to maintain self-control [3]. A device or mechanism is needed to externalize the sleep state of the patient, while the patient establishes a sense of unity with the external device.

Here we propose an indirect biofeedback mechanism that can help the patient be aware of his/her sleep quality and condition by monitoring a device with visual features that vary according to their sleep data [4]. We also propose a mechanism through which the patient, his/her family members, and doctors and medical staff can share the information of the indirect biofeedback.

2 Information Sharing Through Indirect Biofeedback

2.1 Concept

Figure 1 shows our proposed model of information sharing through indirect biofeedback.

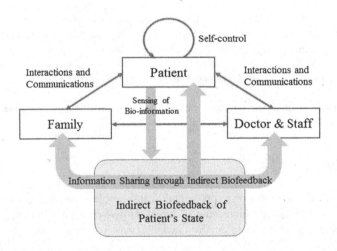

Fig. 1. Model of information sharing through indirect biofeedback

A patient's biological data, such as information related to sleep, heart rate, and respiration, are collected by a mat-type sensor, and sent to and stored in a server every day. Some indicators representing the sleep state and quality are generated by analyzing the data in the server. These indicators, which constitute direct information, are changed and transformed into indirect information. The indirect information is designed to be displayed in a way that anybody can understand and feel [5–7]. Therefore, this indirect information is not only fed back to the patient but also shared with his/her family members, doctors, and medical staff. The indirect biofeedback information can be used by the patient to be easily aware of his/her sleep state and quality, and to control his/her own self. In addition, since his/her family members, doctors, and medical staff can also easily learn about the patient's sleep state and quality, the patient will be able to experience other people understanding and accepting his/her biological state. Therefore, sharing some information about the patient's sleep state and quality influences other people's attitude towards the patient as well as the interactions and/or communications with him/her. Medical staff can change their care plan for the patient, and the patient can be more relaxed and sleep more effectively [8].

2.2   Mutual Awareness by Sharing Information

Information sharing between people is useful for mutual awareness in general, as shown in Fig. 2.

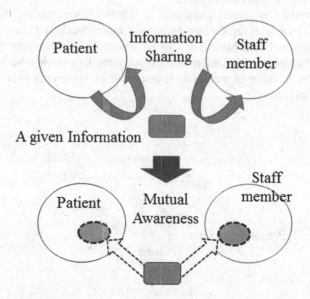

Fig. 2. Image of mutual awareness by sharing information

For example, a patient's friend comes to see the patient, a staff member gets to know the fact, and the patient knows that the staff member knows the fact. That is, mutual awareness denotes that both of them know that they share a given information each other.

The case which we focus on, however, should be different from usual cases, and we have to make some consideration. While medical staff might be in strong position, a patient might be in weak one in a sense that the patient depends on medical care given by the staff. On the other hand, the patient pays to the medical care and services given by the staff. Moreover, information that should be shared by others, such as medical staff and family members is the patient's personal information.

Information sharing between a patient and medical staff, thus, should be carefully designed considering the points mentioned above. It might be quite significant, on the other hand, that a patient would be aware of being understood and accepted by others through information sharing.

2.3   From Mutual Awareness to Mutual Acceptance

Information sharing between a patient and medical staff should be carefully designed, especially, in the sense that information shared by others is a patient's extremely personal information that cannot be usually seen and known by others. In general, the patient does not want others to know his/her extremely personal information, because such information should be too direct and close to his/herself. In addition, direct numerical feedback might give a user a negative feeling by perceiving unfamiliar data which display drastic numerical changes.

Here we could find some significance in indirect representation, that is, indirect biofeedback. Information represented as indirect biofeedback and shared by others is the patient's personal one, but not too direct and close to the patient so that he/she could accept that the personal information is seen and known by others.

Figure 3 shows image of mutual acceptance that we are aiming to create between a patient and others.

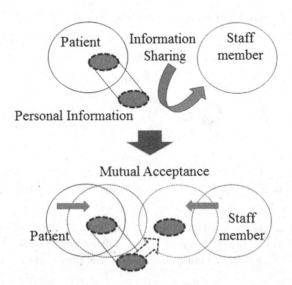

Fig. 3. Image of mutual acceptance by sharing information

Once the personal information that is too direct but close to the patient could be shared, the resulting situation should be expected to be beyond mere mutual awareness, i.e., mutual acceptance.

2.4   Indirect Biofeedback

It is crucial that information sharing is designed attentively, as the information to be shared between a patient and medical staff can be extremely personal and usually should not be seen or known by others. In general, the patient does not want others to know this extremely personal information as it could be too direct and close to him/herself. In addition, direct numerical feedback might give the user a negative feeling due to perceiving unfamiliar data that display drastic numerical changes.

In this case, indirect representation, that is, indirect biofeedback can be useful. The information represented as indirect biofeedback and shared by others is the patient's personal information, but not too direct or close to the patient that he/she feels that their personal information exposed to others.

In this research, we employ virtual plants and their changes as a representation of indirect biofeedback, as shown in Fig. 4. We expect that such a representation will enable not only the externalization and objectification of a patient's physiological information, but also the patient's control of their inner state by being aware of it [9].

Fig. 4. Plant-type avatars

3   Related Works

Biofeedback has been used by psychologists to help treat a variety of issues including post-traumatic stress disorder, attention deficit hyperactivity disorder, headache, and hypertension [9, 10].

Nishino and his team suggested that we spend a significant part of our lives sleeping, which is essential for our physical and psychological well-being. However, sleep can be easily impaired by psychological and physical disease [11, 12]. Professor Shimamoto and his team suggested that a decline in the quality and total duration of sleep decreases physical activity levels and increases daytime sleepiness as well as the risk of lifestyle-related disease and depression [13].

In recent years, Japan has developed a "super-aging" society and care support for elderly people is essential. Takadama and his team focused on this problem and proposed a concierge-based care support system to provide a comfortable and healthy life for elderly people. The system estimates a user's daily sleep stage, and stores this personal data as big data. By doing so, care workers and doctors can design personal care plans for specific users more effectively. The system has the following characteristics:

(1) Estimating sleep stage without connecting any devices to the human body.
(2) Designing home care support that supports elderly people living in their home, facility, or hospital.

Exploring the lifestyle improvement technology [13–16].

4 Information Sharing System Through Indirect Biofeedback

Figure 5 shows the configuration of the proposed information sharing system through indirect biofeedback.

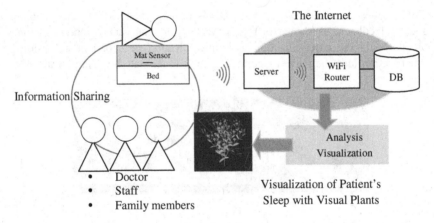

Fig. 5. Information sharing through indirect biofeedback

We use the mat sensor developed by TANITA to get a patient's sleep data, and an i-Pad as a device for display. The data are sent to a server through Wi-Fi, stored in a database, and analyzed into quality of sleep. The result is transformed and visualized as a virtual plant, which is not only provided as feedback to the patient but also shared by medical staff and family members.

4.1 Data on Quality of Sleep

Sleep disorder increases the risk of lifestyle-related diseases and depression. This decline has been observed in Japanese owing to changes in lifestyle. Moreover, the quality and duration of sleep vary greatly with age. Previous studies have shown that sleep disorder commonly occurs in the elderly. The quality and duration of sleep are determined by numerous factors. This time we employ sleep score that is calculated by the server at TANITA based on data which we get with a mattress sensor [11, 12].

A patient's sleep state and/or quality of sleep are evaluated based on the data above. Also, we use these data as objective indicators to judge some effect by indirect biofeedback and information sharing with other people.

In addition, we record a patient's daily events, such as taking a walk and/or bath, having a visitor, singing songs, playing a game, and so on, as well as data on his/her sleep state. Such accumulated data will allow the system to show daily, weekly, monthly, and/or yearly changes of a patient's sleep state as morphing images of virtual plants. Additionally, we can conduct correlation analyses between the above-mentioned events and quality of sleep, and identify an indicator of a causal relationship between a specific event and sleep.

4.2 Representation as Indirect Biofeedback

Based on the data on quality of sleep acquired by the mat sensor, the proposed system calculates the daily average sleep score and compares its change day by day. We can know a patient's quality of sleep directly by observing the changes as well as the daily average score of the sleep factors.

As mentioned above, however, we do not employ direct feedback but indirect biofeedback with virtual plants. Thus, depending on the changes and the daily average sleep score and sleep efficiency, we employ a representation mimicking the growth of the plants, for example, using the number of flowers and leaves, as shown in Fig. 6.

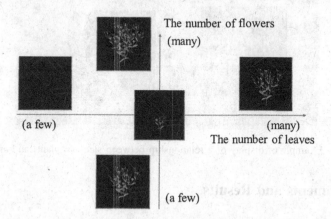

Fig. 6. Mapping of sleep score into virtual plant

4.3 Design of Information Sharing

Since we can obtain sleep patterns by evaluating overall factors of sleep, we can prepare four types of virtual plants according to the sleep patterns; thus, the type of plant displayed would change depending on the sleep patterns. These patterns change daily according to a patient's state of sleep. We will explain the types to a patient, medical staff, and family members in advance, so they can recognize the patient's sleep state by looking at the types of virtual plants. We think this information will be useful for the staff and family members to be able to talk to the patient more effectively. Additionally, by having this information, the patient might be able to change his/her own inner state and actions.

Figure 7 shows an example of a display of the system and Fig. 8 an example of a display showing a relationship between sleep and an event.

Fig. 7. Example of system display

Fig. 8. Example of display of a relationship between sleep (= plant) and an even

5   Experiments and Results

5.1   Experiments

To test the efficacy of our proposed system of indirect biofeedback, we conducted an experiment for 7 weeks (including pre-experiment) with 5 patients (2 males and 3 females, between 67 and 90 years of age) in a senior care home. Afterward, we got the sleep score of a patient with a mattress sensor individually and visualized it to his/her own virtual plant. For the experiment, the patient and his/her support members saw the patient's virtual plant every day and tried to talk to him/her more effectively. It means that the visual plant system seemed to work as a good indicator to trigger communications among them.

5.2 Experimental Results

Before and after the experiment, the patients and their support members were asked to complete questionnaires.

5.2.1 Subjective Evaluation (Questionnaire *Before* the Experiment)

By analyzing the answers provided by study participants to the questionnaires, we evaluated patients' degree of sleep satisfaction which the patients and the support members reported, as shown in Fig. 9.

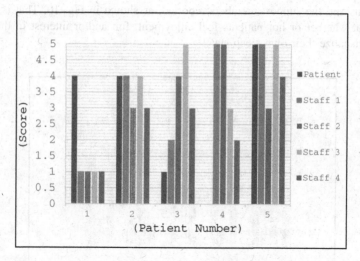

Fig. 9. The degree of sleep satisfaction of the participants (Color figure online)

The black bar shows a patient's degree of sleep satisfaction, and the other color bars show the patient's degree of sleep satisfaction that the support members estimated. Patient 4 is an elderly person with dementia and she could not answer the questionnaire.

Some of patients' opinions to the questionnaires are presented below:

- **How do you think about your sleep?**
    ✓ I think I can sleep well. Because I am not tired.
    ✓ I think I cannot sleep well. Sometimes I wake up and go to washroom.
    ✓ I feel I can sleep well.

Some opinions of the support members to the questionnaires are presented below:

- **Whether do you think the patient's sleep is well?**
    ✓ Yes, the patient does not have any nocturnal awaking.
    ✓ Yes, in the morning, the patient get up easily.
    ✓ No, the person in the same room with the patient sometimes makes some strange sounds.
    ✓ No, the patient gets up and comes to the nurse station in midnight.

Figure 9 and the above answers show that there was some difference on recognition of a patient's sleep state between the patient and the support members *before* the experiment.

5.2.2   Subjective Evaluation (Questionnaire *After* the Experiment)

By analyzing the answers provided by study participants to the questionnaires, we evaluated patients' degree of enjoyment, fun and/or interest to the virtual plant which the patients and the support members reported, as shown in Fig. 10. That is, Fig. 10 shows that whether or not patients feel enjoyment, fun and/or interest in the virtual plant to visualize their own sleep state.

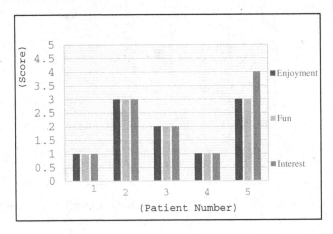

Fig. 10. The degree of enjoyment, fun and/or interest in seeing the virtual plant

Patients who have dementia had no interest in seeing the virtual plant.

Next, we evaluated patients' degree of the understanding and awareness of the virtual plant and its changes, and the degree of acceptance that they felt through this system. Figure 11 shows the results.

As shown in Fig. 11, some patients could understand, and be aware of that the virtual plant and its changes reflected their sleep state, and could feel accepted by others through the virtual plants. Some patients, however, who have Dementia had no interest in it.

Moreover, we evaluated the patients' and staff member's degree of recognition of sleep state through the virtual plants. Figure 12 shows the results.

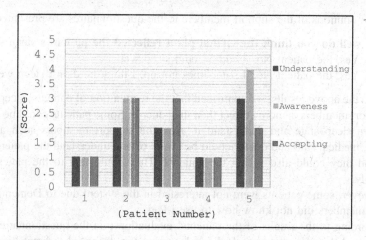

Fig. 11. The degree of understanding, awareness and acceptance

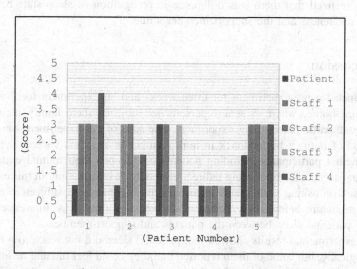

Fig. 12. The degree of recognition of sleep state through virtual plants

As shown in Fig. 12, there are difference in recognition of their sleep state between the patients themselves and a staff member. Some of patients' opinions to the questionnaires are presented below:

- **How well do you think your virtual plant reflected your sleep state?**
  - ✓ I don't know.
  - ✓ Yes, I think the virtual plant was good when I felt good.
  - ✓ No, I could sleep well, but the plant was not good.

Some opinions of the support members to the questionnaires are presented below:

- **How well do you think the virtual plant reflected the patient's sleep state?**
  - ✓ Yes, the patient No. 3 and 5 could sleep well.
  - ✓ Yes, the patient No. 4 sometimes got up, I think he didn't sleep well.

From the above results, we confirmed that the recognition of patients' sleep state by the support members is more correct than the patients. Some patients could be aware of their own sleep state and understand it. And the support members such as family member, medical staff and doctor could be aware of and understand the patients' sleep state, and they could also accept the patients. They could talk to the patients more effectively.

However, some patients were not interested in the system due to Dementia. Some support members did not know how to use i-Pad.

According to the results of the patients' evaluation (via the questionnaires), some patients said they were able to feel fun by using the proposed indirect biofeedback system. The results of the support members' evaluation show that some support members realized that there was difference in recognition of sleep state between the patient's awareness and the support member's one.

6 Discussion

We conducted a pre-experiment for three weeks and an experiment for 2 weeks in a senior care home, where 5 senior persons as subjects, their family members and medical staff participated in this experiment. The aims of this experiment were to verify usefulness of indirect biofeedback in improvement of a patient's sleep and to investigate whether participants including patients can deepen their mutual understanding and mutual acceptance by sharing indirect biofeedback information. In this experiment, we focused on asking participants to answer questionnaires as subjective evaluation. The questionnaire before the experiment showed that there was difference in recognition of patients' sleep between the patients and support members.

The experimental results showed that patients' sleep did not reach to a better state physiologically, but some of them reported that they could feel fun and be interested in the proposed system and that they have started to promote mutual understanding, mutual awareness and mutual acceptance gradually. This experiment confirmed that the averages of patients' sleep score in a senior care home are lower than the average of healthy participants' one. In addition, we confirmed that there should be mutual relationships between their sleep state and events which they had during the experiment. In order to investigate those issues more, we would like to continue to conduct this experiment for the much longer term.

7 Conclusion

We have proposed an indirect biofeedback mechanism that helps a patient be aware of his/her sleep quality and condition by monitoring a device with virtual plants that vary according to their sleep data of the patient. We have also proposed a mechanism through which the patient, his/her family members and doctors and medical staff can share the information of the indirect biofeedback.

We conducted an experiment in a senior care home where 5 elderly people as subjects, their family members and medical staff participate in this experiment. Through the experiment, we tried to clarify usefulness of indirect biofeedback in improvement of a patient's sleep, and to confirm that patients, their family members, and medical staff can deepen their mutual understanding and mutual acceptance by sharing indirect biofeedback information. As the result, we could verify such effect to some extent from the subjective and objective evaluations.

Acknowledgement. I would like to thank all members who support me much when I study. Especially I want to say thank you very much to Kotaro Ishiguro who taught me not only professional knowledge in research. Thank you for taking such care of me.

References

1. Hoshikawa, K.: Religions and Others—Study on Language and Reality—. Shunjusha, Tokyo (2011)
2. Tanaka, M.: PORM Theory and Practice - Trauma Deletion and Process of Self-Expression-. Shunjusha, Tokyo (2003)
3. Matumoto, Y., Mori, N.: Study of mental stress evaluation based on analysis of heart rate variability. Life-Support 22(3), 106–113 (2010)
4. Aoyama, T., Osuga, M.: Breath inducing system for relaxation. Jpn. Soc. Biofeedback Res. 33, 61–62 (2006)
5. Tanaka, H., Matushita, M., Furutani, M.: Cognitive-behavioral intervention to improve the sleep health in the elderly. Jpn. Soc. Physiol. Psychol. Psychophysiol. 25(1), 61–71 (2007)
6. Tanaka, H., Tira, K., Arakawa, M., et al.: Sleep disorder of elderly people. Jpn. Psychogeriatr. Soc. 11(10), 1139–1147 (2000)
7. Shirota, A., Tamaki, H., Hayashi, M., Shirakawa, S., Hort, T.: Volitional life style and activity-rest rhythm of elders. Jpn. J. Physiol. Psychol. Psychophysiol. 15(2), 53–60 (1997)
8. Time to relax: The biofeedback tech fighting a stress epidemic (unpublished)
9. Yucha, C., Gilbert, C.: Evidence-Baced Practice in Biofeedback and Neurobiofeedback. Association for Applied Psychophysiology and Biofeedback, Wheat Ridge (2008)
10. Sasaba, I., Sakuma, H.: Effectiveness of biofeedback on breathing exercise as part of mental support for elite athletes. Jpn. Soc. Biofeedback Res. 41(1), 27–36 (2014)
11. Nishino, S., Taheri, S., Black, J., Nofzinger, E.: The Neurology of Sleep in Relation to Mental Illness. Neurobiology of Mental Illness, pp. 1160–1179. Oxford University Press, New York (2004, in press)
12. Mignot, E., Taheri, S., Nishino, S.: Sleeping with hypothalamus: emerging therapeutic targets for sleep disorders. Nat. Neurosci. 5, 1071–1075 (2002)

13. Shimamoto, H., Shibata, M.: The relationship between physical activity and sleep: a literature review. Center Educ. Liberal Arts Sci. (2), 75–82 (2014)
14. Takadama, K.: Concierge-based care support system for designing your own lifestyle. In: AAAI Spring Symposium, pp. 69–74 (2014)
15. Harada, T., Ueno, F., Komine, T., Tajima, Y., Kawashima, T., Morishima, M., Takadama, K.: Real-time sleep stage estimation from biological data with trigonometric function regression model. In: 2016 AAAI Spring Symposium Series, pp. 348–353 (2016)
16. Takadama, K., Tajima, Y.: Sleep monitoring agent for care support and its perspective. IEICE ESS Fundam. Rev. **8**(2), 96–101 (2014)
17. Takahara, M., Huang, J., Tanev, I., Shimohara, K.: Self-identification of mental state and self-control through indirect biofeedback. IEEJ Transl. Jpn. **3**(1), 50–54 (2016)

Design of Hand Contact Improvisation Interface Supporting Co-creative Embodied Expression

Takuto Takahashi[1(✉)], Takumi Soma[1], Yoshiyuki Miwa[2], and Hiroko Nishi[3]

[1] Graduate School of Creative Science and Engineering, Waseda University, Tokyo, Japan
{chobby75,soma-liverpoolfc}@akane.waseda.jp
[2] Faculty of Science and Engineering, Waseda University, Tokyo, Japan
miwa@waseda.jp
[3] Faculty of Human Science, Toyo Eiwa University, Kanagawa, Japan
hiroko@toyoeiwa.ac.jp

Abstract. This research goal is to establish a new design theory of co-creative expression interface for promoting interpersonal relationship with others, from the conviction that Hand contact improvisation, which is to touch their hands and create embodied improvisational expression together, is useful for deepening relationship with heavily developmentally disabled children who are handicapped about symbolical and oral communication skills. In this paper, inspired by co-creation with movement and touching interaction in music basically, we developed sound-expression Hand contact improvisation interface to motivate children toward bodily expression. This interface is cylindrical device that has contact parts on its both ends that have an ability to measure internal load of each hand, and it present sound from inner device. Sounds are generated by the system using multi phases that represent melodic lines. Interactions of these phases are manipulated by hand load data that are emerged among bodily expressers. When we conducted experiments of bodily expression with this interface, we observed increase tendency of interactions about hand load. Additionally, once we bring the interface to the practical field, we found people including autistic children can interact and bodily express using this interface. We discuss with these results about usefulness of our design method for making inclusive interface that supporting awareness toward bodily expression and induce diverse co-creative expression.

Keywords: Co-creation · Hand contact improvisation · Autistic spectrum disorder · Embodiment · Bodily expression · Interface

1 Background

Co-creation refers to creative activity that people who have different background and value share their dream and thought and achieve them together with allowing diversity of people [1]. This means that inclusive sense and cognition of togetherness are associated with embodied expression together called co-creative expression [2]. To explore the dynamics of co-creation, we have been focusing on practical method called "Hand contact improvisation" which is to contact others hands and embodied express

S. Yamamoto (Ed.): HIMI 2017, Part I, LNCS 10273, pp. 631–639, 2017.
DOI: 10.1007/978-3-319-58521-5_50

impromptu together to achieve co-creation. Nishi, one of Authors of this paper, reported that hand contact improvisation have a facilitation function that deepens interpersonal relationship from individual state to togetherness state according to embodied expression changes shown in Fig. 1 [3, 4].

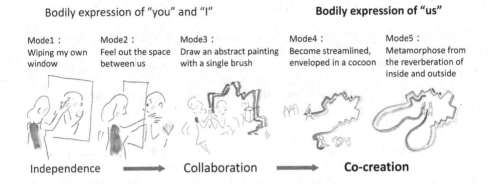

Fig. 1. Deepening process of interpersonal relationship in hand contact improvisation

Furthermore, we have held workshops that various people regardless of developmentally disabled are attending in Ishinomaki and Higashimatsushima Miyagi prefecture, which are East Japanese great earthquake stricken cities. We found that hand contact improvisation is also useful for promote relationship with children who are developmentally disabled including autism spectrum disorder (ASD) which is characterized by tending to avoid interpersonal interaction. In our previous works, we developed interfaces to bring out embodied expression from developmentally disabled children for deepen interpersonal relationship with unpredictable others. This interface is cylindrical device that are used by holding both ends with others and embodied express

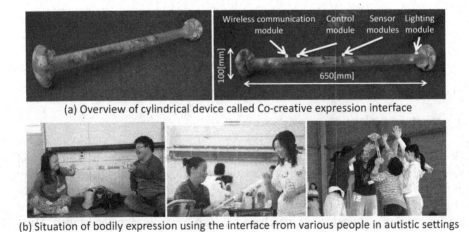

(a) Overview of cylindrical device called Co-creative expression interface

(b) Situation of bodily expression using the interface from various people in autistic settings

Fig. 2. Co-creative expression interface at embodied expression

together three dimensionally like hand contact improvisation [6]. Once we bring this interface to workshop, we observed that children who are developmentally disabled including ASD express hand contact improvisation using this interface shown in Fig. 2. However, it is difficult to find quantitative evaluation method about subjective interpersonal relationship from embodied expression yet [5]. In this research, we develop measurement interface toward establish quantitative evaluation method about subjective interpersonal relationship in hand contact improvisation from physical measurement data. In the beginning, we developed device for measuring load and orientation of interface in hand contact improvisation based on our previous works about single axis hand contact improvisation system [7, 8]. Also, we designed new sound media system with this interface toward deepening interpersonal relationship with unpredictable others by generating music from measurement data and present music from inner device.

2   Measurement Interface

2.1   Design Requirements

For evaluating interpersonal relationship through hand contact improvisation in three-dimensional movement, our interface needs to be able to measure load data of each hand and relationship of hand positions without interrupting embodied expression. We set design requirements of this interface below based on our previous work of single axis hand contact improvisation system.

1. The interface must have ability to measure load and orientation of hands.
2. The interface must be suitable size and weight for holding by two person's hands.
3. The interface must not interrupt embodied expression by structure or mechanism of interface.

To meet these design requirements, new measurement interface needs to have measurement ability range from −20 to 20 kgf that is sufficient for measure hand contact improvisation hand load. Wireless communication system is also needed to prevent interruption to embodied expression and area of movement. Thus, we developed cylindrical measurement interface installing load cells and orientation sensor based on our previous interface design.

2.2   Overview of Measurement System

This interface is composed by three parts: frame part, sensor part, and record part. In a frame part, duralumin (A2017) is used as a fitting structure element due to the advantage for withstanding compression/tension loading and bending/torsional moment. In a sensor part, load cells (Minebea, CB17-3 K-11) are mounted to both ends of a frame part, and orientation sensor (Arduino nine axis motion) is installed to the center of a frame part. In addition to this, contact grip which is made by ABS are attached to load cell for holding them. In a record part, measurement data from a sensor part are recorded with 50 Hz sampling frequency by using wireless communication modules (Digi International, XBee S2B). In this way, we developed interface with 1146 g weight and

430 mm length and 110 mm width and range of load measurement from −20 to 20 kgf shown in Fig. 3.

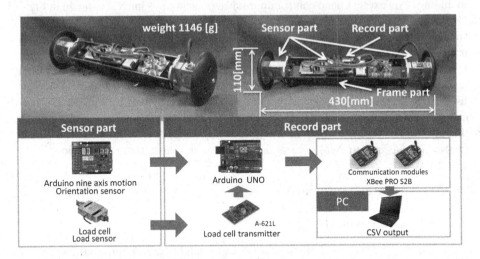

Fig. 3. System overview of the measurement interface

2.3 Performance Test

We measure three-dimensional position and load and orientation simultaneously using the measurement interface as a performance test. Test subject press and rotate the measurement interface alternately with 60 bpm metronome sounds. Results of the test performance are shown in Fig. 4(c). This figure shows three-dimensional position, load, and orientation defined by Fig. 4(b) of the interface. We can see that pressing and rotation are detected by interface based on the order in Fig. 4(a) from the measurement results.

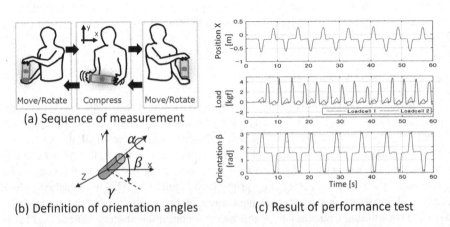

(a) Sequence of measurement

(b) Definition of orientation angles

(c) Result of performance test

Fig. 4. Performance test of the measurement interface

This result suggests that the interface have ability to measure load and orientation of itself simultaneously.

3 Sound Media System

3.1 Design of Sound Media System

To bring out diverse embodied expression and deepen interpersonal relationship, we designed new sound media system using this interface shown in Fig. 5. This media system is composed by three parts: measurement part, sound media generation part, sound presentation part. Measurement part achieves load and orientation data using same system as measurement interface. Sound media generation part produce sound media with sound processing software (Max/MSP) in real-time by using achieved data from measurement part. Sound media presenting part have Bluetooth wireless speaker installed in the center of interface and the speaker presents sound media. This structure make music sound source position move according to embodied expression movement. Method of generating sound media is shown below.

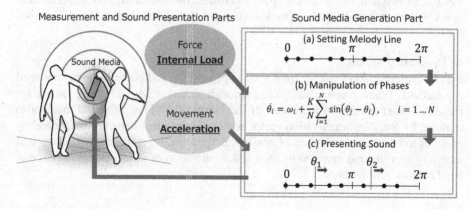

Fig. 5. System overview of sound media system for hand contact improvisation

3.2 Method of Sound Media

Music of sound media system needs to be changed by body movement and load of hands in hand contact improvisation. Music of sound media also need to be diverse and having unpredictability. This time, we focused on phase music that is famous for Minimal music of Steve Reich works. Phase music uses repetitive melody lines and phase difference for generating diverse music from simple rules. We designed phase music system using load and acceleration data for manipulating volume of sound and phase difference. This sound media is mainly generated by three processes: setting melody line, manipulation of phases, presenting sound. Sound generation processes are shown below.

(a) Setting Melody Line

Melody line in this media system is data for setting sounds tone and timing. Timing of sounds is described by set of numbers from 0 to 2π. For simplification of system, we constrain sound tone and used set of numbers which are randomly chosen from 2π divided by 12 as sounds timing.

(b) Manipulation of Phases

To play sound using melody line set by process (a), we used parameters called phases that have ranges from 0 to 2π. To make change in music from phase music, phases are needed to be manipulated toward both synchronous state which has small difference of phase difference and asynchronous state which has large phase difference. For making these states, we manipulated phases using phase oscillator model described below [9].

$$\dot{\theta}_i = \omega_i + \frac{K}{N} \sum_{j=1}^{N} \sin\left(\theta_j - \theta_i\right), \ i = 1 \ldots N \tag{1}$$

where θ is phase. Change rate of θ is defined by natural oscillation frequency ω and member of distance between phases and a coefficient K that decides effect of entrainment. In this system, two phases are used and natural oscillation frequency ω is set near to π. Coefficient K is manipulated by load data to make synchronous and asynchronous states.

(c) Presenting Sound

System present sound by using timing set in process (a) and phase value manipulated (b) method. When phase value passes through timing value, arbitrary sounds are presented from speaker in the center of the interface. Volume of sound media also changed by length of acceleration vector achieved from measurement data for adding effect of movement in embodied expression. In this way, we achieved to design sound media system that has changed by load and acceleration of measurement interface in hand contact improvisation.

4   Results and Discussion

Measurement interface are used for hand contact improvisation in a range of 2.0 m width and 2.0 m depth and 2.5 m height with 90 s experiment time by two subjects. We measured three-dimensional position and load and orientation of the measurement interface and hip position of subjects simultaneously. Results are classified by an expert of embodied expression to condition of co-creation and condition of not co-creation. Figure 6(a) shows three-dimensional position and orientation data form measurement data. To evaluate movement of interface, we plot return map of local maximum value and local minimum value about back and forth position and vertical position of the measurement interface in Fig. 6(b). We can observe that distribution of return map in co-creative condition is larger than not co-creative one. Figure 7 shows load data and average value and difference value. From a perspective of fluctuation range, we can find differences between co-creative condition and not co-creative condition in both load average and difference. These results suggest that this new measurement interface have an ability to evaluate interpersonal relationship through hand contact improvisation.

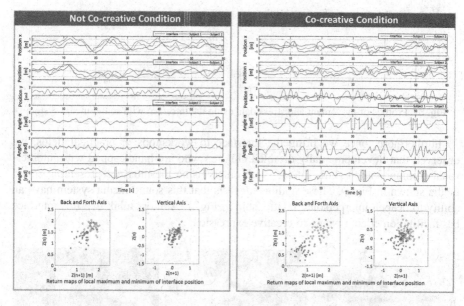

Fig. 6. Profiles of movement data in hand contact improvisation

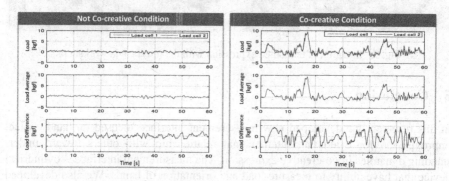

Fig. 7. Profiles of stress data achieved from the measurement interface

We also conducted experiments about sound media with the interface. The interface is used with 90 s embodied expression comparing situation of using sound media and situation of not using sound media. Results of experiments are shown in Fig. 8. We can see increase tendency in peak number more than 3.0 kgf of load data by using sound media.

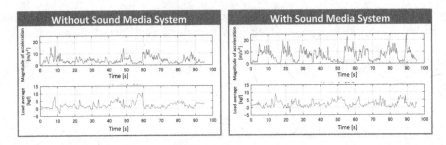

Fig. 8. Profiles of movement and stress data using the interface with sound media system

Furthermore, once we bring the interface to workshops or practical fields, we observed that developmentally disabled children who are handicapped with interpersonal communication skills interact with others using the interface presenting sound media shown in Fig. 9. These finding suggests that this sound media system have an ability to deepen interpersonal relationship in Fig. 1. Authors think that this interface has facilitation effect toward co-creative expression.

Fig. 9. Situation of embodied expression with the interface in workshops

5   Conclusion

In this research, we developed new measurement interface focused on hand contact improvisation for evaluating interpersonal relationship with others toward understanding dynamics of co-creative expression. The measurement interface is cylindrical device that have ability to measure load and orientation of hands. We also developed sound media system which represents hand contact improvisation for deepening interpersonal relationship with others. We conducted experiments about hand contact improvisation using the measurement interface and results showed that differences between co-creative state and not co-creative state in load data. In addition to this, we observed that sound media system with the measurement interface is used for embodied expression by children who are developmentally disabled including ASD children. These results suggest that our new design method of interface is not only useful for evaluating interpersonal relationship through hand contact improvisation but also have function of facilitation that brings out diverse embodied expression toward co-creative expression.

Acknowledgements. This study received support from the research project "Principle of emergence for empathetic 'Ba' and its applicability to communication technology" conducted at the Waseda University Research Institute for Science and Engineering, as well as from the JSPS Grant-in-Aid for Scientific Research (grant number: 25282187). Our deepest appreciation goes to the day care service facility Mirai for supporting execution of the demonstration. We also would like to express our gratitude to our graduate students: Masanori Tsuruta, and Yusuke Ono about development of the system.

In order to maintain our participants' personal privacy, we got permission upon review from the Waseda University Ethical Review Committee for all information collected of this study.

References

1. Shimizu, H., Kume, T., Miwa, Y., Miyake, Y.: Ba and Co-creation. NTT Publishing, Tokyo (2000)
2. Miwa, Y.: Co-creative expression and support for communicability. J. Soc. Instrum. Control Eng. **51**(11), 1016–1022 (2012)
3. Nishi, H., Miwa, T.: Deepening sympathetic awareness and co-creative expression in disaster affected areas. J. Art Meet Care (AMC) **7**, 01–18 (2016)
4. Nishi, H.: Sympathetic body awareness: from a joint harmony of body movement to a creative state of join being. Ann. Inst. Thanatology, 87–108 (2012)
5. Boucenna, S., Narzisi, A., Tilmont, E., Muratori, F., Pioggia, G., Cohen, D., Chetouani, M.: Interactive technologies for autistic children: a review. Cogn. Comput. **6**(4), 722–740 (2014)
6. Takahashi, T., Hayashi, R., Miwa, Y., Nishi, H.: Co-creative expression interface: aiming to support embodied communication for developmentally disabled children. In: Yamamoto, S. (ed.) HIMI 2016. LNCS, vol. 9735, pp. 346–356. Springer, Cham (2016). doi: 10.1007/978-3-319-40397-7_33
7. Miwa, Y., Itai, S., Watanabe, T., Nishi, H.: Generation dynamics of sympathetic embodied awareness in hand contact improvisation. In: Proceedings of IASDR 2013 - 5th International Congress of International Association of Societies of Design Research, Tokyo (2013)
8. Watanabe, T., Miwa, Y.: Duality of embodiment and support for co-creation in hand contact improvisation. J. Adv. Mech. Des. Syst. Manuf. **6**(7), 1307–1318 (2012)
9. Kuramoto, Y.: Chemical Oscillations, Waves, and Turbulence, vol. 19. Springer Science & Business Media, Heidelberg (2012)

Development of a Communication Robot for Forwarding a User's Presence to a Partner During Video Communication

Michiya Yamamoto[1(✉)], Saizo Aoyagi[1], Satoshi Fukumori[1],
and Tomio Watanabe[2]

[1] School of Science and Technologies,
Kwansei Gakuin University, Sanda, Japan
michiya.yamamoto@kwansei.ac.jp
[2] Faculty of Computer and Systems Engineering,
Okayama Prefectural University, Soja, Japan

Abstract. In recent years, the need for remote communication that can provide a greater sense of presence to the communicating parties has been felt. In this study, we propose a framework for forwarding a user's presence via a robot to a partner during video communication. We developed a prototype of a oneself robot, which is a robot personalized to resemble a user and can be easily assembled by the communication partner. We conducted a public demonstration and an evaluation experiment; the results of which demonstrate the effectiveness of the robot. The participants enjoyed remote communication by using the prototype of oneself robot.

Keywords: Remote communication support · Embodied interaction · Presence forwarding

1 Introduction

Recently, various remote communication systems have appeared in accordance with the increasing variety of people's lifestyles. For example, many families are living independently and many friends are separated after graduation. In these circumstances, people need to feel connected and enjoy sharing emotions even in remote communication.

Messenger and LINE on smartphones and Skype on PCs are widespread. Only audio and video are communicated in these applications. On the other hand, we focus on the importance of users' presence. When we reviewed related studies, physical media is thought to be necessary to make users feel the presence of those with whom they are communicating. For example, there are some commercial telepresence robots that combine video communication and movable hardware, such as the Double telepresence robot by Double Robotics [1], and Kubi by Revolve Robotics [2]. In other studies, presence is generated only by hardware. For example, realistic human size and appearance is reproduced in the Geminoid HI-1 [3]. Telenoid by ATR [4] and OriHime by OryLab [5] are other examples that are as small as PCs or tablets and bring a

© Springer International Publishing AG 2017
S. Yamamoto (Ed.): HIMI 2017, Part I, LNCS 10273, pp. 640–649, 2017.
DOI: 10.1007/978-3-319-58521-5_51

moderate sense of presence. These robots can be used practically in some situations, but are not suitable for daily communication support.

In this study, we propose a concept of robot calling, which introduces the personality of a user and an appropriate sense of presence by using a robot during video communication. For this purpose, we developed a prototype of a oneself robot [6], which can forward a user's presence to a partner. We performed experiments to evaluate the effectiveness of the system.

2   Concept

2.1   Robot Calling

In this study, we propose a concept of robot calling, which introduces the personality of a user and an appropriate sense of presence by using a robot during video communication as shown in Fig. 1. Here, a user's sense of presence is generated at another user's side by using both video and a oneself robot. To forward a sense of presence, we characterized the personality of a user and introduced it to a small size physical robot as shown in Fig. 1. Another user's robot is located at a user. Both of the robots generate communicative motions and actions automatically. They also follow the movement of the users. In this way, we realize another communication channel by using robots.

Fig. 1. Concept of robot calling.

2.2   D. I. Y. of Oneself Robot

To realize robot calling, we also focused on the importance of do-it-yourself (D. I. Y.) of the oneself robot as shown in Fig. 2. We prepared a frame of a oneself robot by using a 3D printer. We characterized the personality of a user, such as face, hair, and clothes, such that they can be printed using 2D or 3D printers. In this way, if one user receives another user's information, they can easily assemble the other user's oneself robot. This process may lead to creation of a oneself robot printer in the near future.

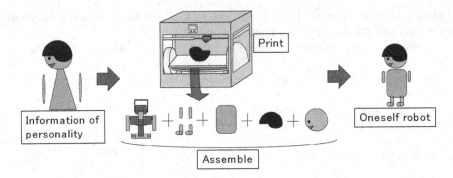

Fig. 2. D. I. Y. of a oneself robot.

3 Prototype of a Oneself Robot

3.1 System Configuration

Figure 3 shows the system configuration of the prototype of a oneself robot. We used a Windows 7 PC (Microsoft Surface Pro 3) for video calling, and two Windows 7 PCs (HP Zbook 15s) for video calling and robot control. Two hands-free headsets (Audio-Technica AT 810Fs), an audio mixer (TEAC DR-680), and audio interface (Creative Technology SB-DM-PXV) were used to input the voice of both users. A speaker (BOSE SoundLink mini) was used for voice output. We integrated Microsoft Kinect to detect the face of a user. Voice calling was done using Skype, Microsoft and the Internet.

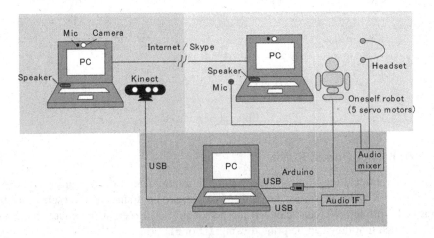

Fig. 3. System configuration.

We integrated four servo motors (JR PROPO RBS582s) in the robot's body and one servo motor (Tower Pro MG90S) in the robot's head. All the servo motors were controlled by an Arduino Duemilanove platform via serial communication from a robot control PC. These servos generated the motions of head, mouth, arms, and waist.

Robot calling is done by a user via Skype on a PC. Then the user arranges Kinect to detect his face direction. The information of direction is applied to the oneself robot via an Arduino control PC, and a servo motor for waist rotation. By using other servo motors, communicative motions and actions are generated automatically by using iRT [7] only from voice input. Details are described in Sect. 3.2.

3.2 Appearance of the Robot

Based on the proposed concept, we developed a frame of the robot as shown in Fig. 4 (left). We also developed face, shoulders, and body as shown in Fig. 4 (right). All the frames were created using 3D printers. To avoid the uncanny valley effect, we used a deformed design with round curves. All the parts are easily assembled by snapping them together.

Fig. 4. Frame of the robot.

Figure 5 (left) shows the template of clothes. A user takes a picture, and arranges it in the template. Then the user prints it and cuts off the cloth parts. After that, the user puts them on the shoulders, body, and bottom of the frame as shown in Fig. 5 (right).

Figure 6 shows a prototype of a oneself robot. The face of the robot was based on Mii by Nintendo. We created a Mii character of a user, and made the face color flat, printed it, and put it on the face parts. The size of the robot was 200 mm in height. The weight was about 370 g.

3.3 Motions and Actions of the Robot

The motions and actions of the robot were achieved by using a control PC and generated by five servo motors in the robot via an Arduino platform. We generated two

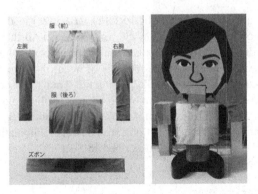

Fig. 5. Template of clothes.

Fig. 6. A prototype of a oneself robot.

kinds of motions and actions automatically – communicative motions and actions, and synchronized motions. Communicative motions and actions were generated using iRT [7], which can generate them by only speech input. Nodding was generated by a servo motor in head. Embodied motions and actions were generated by using servo motors for the arms. Lip movement was generated by a servo motor in the mouth. The synchronized motions are measured using Kinect, and applied to the motion of a servo motor in the waist. In this way, users can use a oneself robot and enjoy communication without any effort.

4 Evaluation Experiment

4.1 Preliminary Experiment on Arrangement

Before performing an experimental evaluation, we performed a preliminary experiment on the arrangement of a oneself robot. It was performed at The Lab. in Grand Front Osaka as a public experiment as shown in Fig. 7. In the experiment, we asked visitors to answer three questions:

Fig. 7. Experimental scene at Grand Front Osaka.

- Q1: Which communication do you like?
- Q2: Which has more sense of presence?
- Q3: By which do you easily recognize expressions?

They were asked to choose one of three modes: only a oneself robot, only Skype, or both oneself robot and Skype. 55 visitors answered the questions.

As a result, 67% of the visitors selected both a oneself robot and Skype for Q1. Oneself robot only and Skype only were 17% and 16%, respectively. Figure 8 shows the results for Q2 and Q3. Both results show the effectiveness of using both physical and video media.

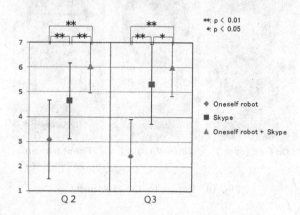

Fig. 8. Result of preliminary experiment

4.2 Experimental Setup

Based on the results of the preliminary experiment, we performed an evaluation experiment by assuming remote communication. It was performed by two subjects, one as a user and another as a partner, who were acquainted with each other. They sat in different rooms as shown in Fig. 9 and used prototypes of oneself robots.

Fig. 9. Experimental scene.

For the experiment, we prepared oneself robots for two users' side subjects and a robot without personality as shown in Fig. 10. In the experiment, we evaluated three modes: oneself robot, robot without personality, and no robot. First, we asked subjects to make short conversations by way of a compliment, using Skype as a test. Then we selected one of the modes, and asked subjects to enjoy their daily communications. We prepared three topics and selected one: what you enjoyed recently, why you felt most unhappy recently, and what surprised you recently. The communication was for three minutes. Then, we asked a partner side subject to answer 8 items of 7 grades bipolar rating as shown in Table 1.

Oneself robot 1   Oneself robot 2   Robot without personality

Fig. 10. Robots for the experiment.

Table 1. 8 items for questionaire.

(1) Enjoyment	(5) Lively communication
(2) Easy communication	(6) Sense of unity with a partner
(3) Lively atmosphere	(7) Resemblance with a partner
(4) Presence of a partner	(8) Want to use again

Then, we changed the mode and topic and performed two other communications. The combinations of modes and topics were randomly selected. After the experiment, we analyzed how they laughed during the experiment. The subjects were two males on the user's side and 32 (16 males and 16 females) on the partner's side.

4.3 Results

Figure 11 shows the results of the questionnaire. We performed a Friedman test and Bonferroni correction. As a result, there were significant differences in items (1), (3), (4), (5), and (6) at 5% and item (8) at 1% between oneself robot and robot without personality. There were significant differences in items (1), (4), and (6) at 1% and in items (3) and (5) at 5% between oneself robot and no robot. In addition, there were significant differences in items (4) and (8) at 5% between robot without personality and no robot. Item (7) was rated high enough.

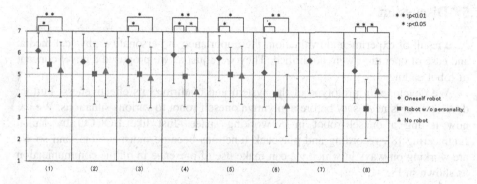

Fig. 11. Results of questionnaires.

Figure 12 shows the result of communication analysis. Time of laughter was long in only the oneself robot. As a result of the Bonferroni correction, there was a significant difference of 1%.

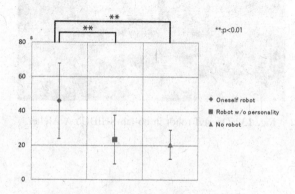

Fig. 12. Time of laughter in each modes.

4.4   Discussion

Significant differences in items (1), (3), and (5) between the oneself robot and robot without personality show the importance of personality in communication support. Especially because face and clothes were the only difference between the two modes, they turned out to be important in daily communication support.

Significant differences in items (4) and (6) show the importance of physical media in presence. However, these results show that personality also plays an important role.

There were no significant differences in item (2). This shows that robot calling was as easy as conventional video calling. This shows the effectiveness of a oneself robot on different sides.

As a result of item (8), subjects rated the oneself robot, no robot and robot without personality in this order. It was surprising that robot without personality was rated the lowest. However, this also shows the importance of personality in a oneself robot.

5   Discussion

As a result of experimental evaluation, the importance of personality, physical media, and ease of operation were confirmed. They were just as we proposed a novel concept of robot calling.

We developed a prototype of the system and confirmed its effectiveness. Further development is necessary before applying a oneself robot to various situations. We are now testing a oneself-robot in co-working space. Just like BOCCO by Yukai Engineering [8], recording and playback functions become indispensable, and so we are working on ways in which we can make use of presence in offline communication as shown in Fig. 13.

Fig. 13. Oneself robot in co-lab SHIBUYA Alelier.

6 Conclusions

In this study, we proposed the concept of robot calling and the oneself robot. We developed a prototype of a oneself robot, which is a robot personalized to resemble a user and can be easily assembled by the communication partner. It was done by preparing a robot frame and template for easy assembly. We also developed software to generate communicative motions and actions, and we synchronized actions so that users can use a oneself robot without any effort. We conducted an evaluation experiment assuming remote communication; the results of which demonstrate the effectiveness of the robot. The participants felt a sense of presence and enjoyed remote communication by using the prototype of a oneself robot.

Acknowledgement. This research was partially supported by JST A-STEP FS AS262Z02496H, JSPS KAKENHI 16H03225, etc.

References

1. Double Robotics: Telepresence Robot for Telecommuters. https://www.doublerobotics.com/. Accessed 10 Feb 2017
2. Relolve Robotics: Kubi Telepresence. https://www.revolverobotics.com/. Accessed 10 Feb 2017
3. Sakamoto, D., Ishiguro, H.: Geminoid: remote-controlled android system for studying human presence. Kansei Eng. Int. **8**(1), 3–9 (2009)
4. Sorbello, R., Chella, A., Calí, C., Giardina, M., Nishio, S., Ishiguro, H.: Telenoid android robot as an embodied perceptual social regulation medium engaging natural human-humanoid interaction. Robot. Auton. Syst. J. **62**(9), 1329–1341 (2014)
5. OryLab: OriHime. http://orihime.orylab.com/. Accessed 10 Feb 2017
6. Tatsumi, T., Fukumori, S., Aoyagi, S., Yamamoto, M., Watanabe, T.: Oneself-robot: a framework for forwarding a user's presence via a robot to a partner during video communication. In: Proceedings of the 24th IEEE International Symposium on Robot and Human Interactive Communication, IS11 (2015)
7. Watanabe, T., Okubo, M., Nakashige, M., Danbara, R.: Inter actor: speech-driven embodied interactive actor. Int. J. Hum.-Comput. Interact. **17**(1), 43–60 (2004)
8. Yukai Engineering: BOCCO. http://www.bocco.me/. Accessed 10 Feb 2017

Author Index

Author Index

Printed in the United States
By Bookmasters